Microsoft Certified Professional Guide

WINDOWS® 95

Microsoft Certified Professional Guide

WINDOWS® 95

Written by James M. Blakely, MCSE, MCT, MSMVP
with Carmen M. Rodero, MCSE, MCT, MSMVP

Windows® 95 Microsoft Certified Professional Guide

Copyright© 1996 by Que® Corporation.

Library of Congress Catalog No.: 96-67561

ISBN: 0-7897-0744-6

98 97   6 5 4 3 2

Interpretation of the printing code: the rightmost double-digit number is the year of the book's printing; the rightmost single-digit number, the number of the book's printing. For example, a printing code of 96-1 shows that the first printing of the book occurred in 1996.

Screen reproductions in this book were created using Collage Plus from Inner Media, Inc., Hollis, NH.

Credits

President
Roland Elgey

Vice President and Publisher
Marie Butler-Knight

Publishing Director
Brad R. Koch

Editorial Services Director
Elizabeth Keaffaber

Managing Editor
Michael Cunningham

Acquisitions Manager
Elizabeth A. South

Product Director
Lisa D. Wagner

Product Development Specialist
Teri Guendling

Production Editor
Thomas F. Hayes

Technical Editors
Robert Bogue
Greg Dew

Editors
Charlie Bowles
Lisa Gebken
Tim Huddleston

Technical Specialist
Nadeem Muhammed

Acquisitions Coordinator
Carmen Krikorian

Operations Coordinator
Patty Brooks

Book Designer
Ruth Harvey

Cover Designer
Ruth Harvey

Production Team
Stephen Adams
Marcia Brizendine
Erin M. Danielson
Jenny Earhart
Daniel Harris
Daryl Kessler
Clint Lahnen
Bob LaRoche
Michelle Lee
Ryan Oldfather
Kaylene Riemen
Laura Robbins
Bobbi Satterfield
Julie Searls
Kelly Warner
Donna Wright

Indexer
Tim Tate

Composed in **Bembo** and **Avenir** by Que Corporation.

Dedication

To my parents, Thomas J. and Betty J. Scardelis, who have always been there for me.

Acknowledgements

The author would like to thank the following people and companies for their support during this project:

Elizabeth South, Lisa Wagner, Brad Koch, and Thomas Hayes at Que, who made this book possible.

Scott Miller, Cyndy Thomas Fitzgerald, Sandy Anderson, Elizabeth Fox, and Charles Earnest at Microsoft Corporation for their on-going assistance.

David Warren at MMC Software, developer extraordinaire of network utilities and applications.

Valda Hilley, MCPS, at Convergent Press Ltd., agent to the stars of the computer industry.

David Mutterer, who always comes through.

Linda Briggs, editor at *Microsoft Certified Professional Magazine*, for her understanding when book and magazine deadlines conflict.

About the Authors

James M. Blakely, MCSE, MCT, MSMVP, is a partner with RS Consulting, a Microsoft Solution Provider in Naples, Florida. He is co-author of *Windows 3.1 Configuration Secrets*, and a contributor to several other books. He can be reached on CompuServe at **75665, 436**, through the MSEDCERT Forum, on the Internet at **frodo@rscon.com**, or at 888-477-6273.

Carmen M. Rodero, MCSE, MCT, CNE, CNI, is a partner with RS Consulting. She is originally from Puerto Rico, where she holds the distinction as the first woman CNI, MCT, and MCSE, and hosted a live call-in radio show on computers. She can be reached on CompuServe at **76453, 1506**, on the Internet at **cmyriam@rscon.com**, or at 888-477-6273.

Jerry Honeycutt is a business-oriented technical manager with broad experience in software development. He has served companies such as The Travelers, IBM, Nielsen North America, and, most recently, Information Retrieval Methods as Director of Windows Application Development. Jerry has participated in the industry since before the days of Microsoft Windows 1.0, and is completely hooked on Windows 95.

Jerry is the author of *Using Microsoft Plus!*, *Using the Internet with Windows 95*, and *Windows 95 Registry & Customization Handbook* published by Que. He is also a contributing author on *Special Edition Using Windows 95*, *Special Edition Using Netscape*, *Platinum Edition Using Windows 95*, and *Visual Basic for Applications Database Solutions* published by Que. He has been published in *Computer Language* magazine and is a regular speaker at the Windows World and Comdex trade shows on topics related to software development and corporate solutions for Windows 95.

Jerry graduated from the University of Texas at Dallas in 1992 with a B.S. degree in Computer Science. He currently lives in the Dallas suburb of Frisco, Texas with Becky, two Westies, Corky and Turbo, and a cat called Scratches. Please feel free to contact Jerry on the Internet at **jerry@honeycutt.com**, on CompuServe at **76477,2751**, or on the Microsoft Network at **Honeycutt**.

Rob Tidrow has been using computers for the past six years and has used Windows for the past four years. Tidrow is a technical writer and recently was the Manager of Product Development for New Riders Publishing, a division of Macmillan Computer Publishing. Rob is co-author of the best-selling *Windows for Non-Nerds*, and has co-authored several other books, including *Inside the World Wide Web, New Riders' Official CompuServe Yellow Pages, Inside Microsoft Office Professional, Inside WordPerfect 6 for Windows, Riding the Internet Highway, Deluxe Edition*, and the *AutoCAD Student Workbook*. In the past, Tidrow created technical documentation and instructional programs for use in a variety of industrial settings. He has a degree in English from Indiana University. He resides in Indianapolis with his wife, Tammy, and their two boys, Adam and Wesley. You can reach him on the Internet at **rtidrow@iquest.net**.

Judith Harper has been writing and talking about technology for longer than she cares to admit—first as a chemist, then as a chemical engineer, and, most recently, as a low-level guru for technophobic business people. She is (of course) a full-time freelance science and technology writer and part-time trainer based in Cincinnati, Ohio.

We'd Like to Hear from You!

As part of our continuing effort to produce books of the highest possible quality, Que would like to hear your comments. To stay competitive, we *really* want you, as a computer book reader and user, to let us know what you like or dislike most about this book or other Que products.

You can mail comments, ideas, or suggestions for improving future editions to the address below, or send us a fax at 317-581-4663. For the online inclined, Macmillan Computer Publishing has a forum on CompuServe (type **GO QUEBOOKS** at any prompt) through which our staff and authors are available for questions and comments. The address of our World Wide Web site is **http://www.mcp.com/que**.

In addition to exploring our forum, please feel free to contact me personally to discuss your opinions of this book: I'm **74404,3307** on CompuServe, and I'm **lwagner@que.mcp.com** on the Internet.

Thanks in advance—your comments will help us to continue publishing the best books available on computer topics in today's market.

Lisa Wagner
Product Director
Que Corporation
201 W. 103rd Street
Indianapolis, Indiana 46290
USA

> **Note** Although we cannot provide general technical support, we're happy to help you resolve problems you encounter related to our books, disks, or other products. If you need such assistance, please contact our Tech Support department at 800-545-5914 ext. 3833.

For your convenience author Jim Blakeley maintains an update and corrections list for this book on his Website. Please check **http://www.rscon.com/win95exup.htm** before contacting Tech Support.

Contents at a Glance

Table of Contents

7 File I/O and Disks   121

10 ╎ **Understanding Windows 95 Video Display   157**

11 ╎ **Understanding Printing   167**

12 • Using Windows 95's Disk Utilities   187

15 • Windows 95 Networking Introduction   231

21 · Mobile Computing   329

Lab Exercises   423

Introduction

This book was written by Microsoft Certified Professionals, for Microsoft Certified Professionals, and MCP Candidates. It is designed, in combination with your real-world experience, to prepare you to pass the **Windows 95 Exam (70-63)**, as well as give you a background in general networking, both Microsoft and Novell NetWare.

The exams cost $100 each. Each one consists of 50 to 100 questions and takes up to two hours to complete. Depending on the certification level, you may have to take as many as six exams, covering Microsoft operating systems, application programs, networking, and software development. Each test involves preparation, study, and, for some of us, heavy doses of test anxiety. Is certification worth the trouble?

Microsoft has cosponsored research that provides some answers.

Benefits for Your Organization

At companies participating in a 1994 Dataquest survey, a majority of corporate managers stated that certification is an *important factor* to the overall success of their companies because:

+ Certification increases customer satisfaction. Customers look for indications that their suppliers understand the industry and have the ability to respond to their technical problems. Having Microsoft Certified Professionals on staff reassures customers; it tells them that your employees have used and mastered Microsoft products.

+ Certification maximizes training investment. The certification process specifically identifies skills that an employee is lacking or areas where additional training is needed. By so doing, it validates training and eliminates the costs and loss of productivity associated with unnecessary training. In addition, certification records enable a company to verify an employee's technical knowledge and track retention of skills over time.

A study released by International Data Corporation (IDC) in October, 1995, found that companies supporting employee certification experience:

+ *Reduced downtime.* IDC categorized survey respondents as advocates (companies requiring certification when hiring information technology employees) and nonbelievers (companies that do not require certification). Nonbelievers experienced an average of 5.3 hours of unscheduled downtime, with a per-incident cost per server of $1,102. Advocates, on the other hand, reported an average of 3.5 hours of unscheduled downtime with a per-incident cost per server of $669. On a monthly basis, advocates lost $866 less per server than did nonbelievers.

+ *Higher productivity.* On the average, advocate companies support roughly the same number of PCs as do nonbeliever companies, but the PCs at advocate companies are distributed across almost twice as many sites. And the advocate companies support these PCs across more distributed environments with roughly the same number of employees (144 employees for advocate companies, and 146 employees for nonbelievers).

+ *An ROI payback of less than nine months.* The IDC research found that a certified employee costs about $9,500 more per year than an uncertified employee (based on an average cost of $3.728 to certify added to a pay difference of 11.7%). IDC then weighed this against a monthly support cost difference for advocates of $285 less per month, and the monthly server downtime costs of $866 less per month. The result? A total annual saving of $13,812 for the advocates and an under–nine-month payback.

Benefits Up Close and Personal

Microsoft also cites a number of benefits that accrue to the certified individual:

+ Industry recognition of expertise, enhanced by Microsoft's promotion of the Certified Professional community to the industry and potential clients.

+ Access to technical information directly from Microsoft

+ Dedicated CompuServe and Microsoft Network forums that enable Microsoft Certified Professionals to communicate directly with Microsoft and with one another.

+ A complimentary one-year subscription to *Microsoft Certified Professional Magazine.*

+ Microsoft Certified Professional logos and other materials to publicize MCP status to colleagues and clients.

+ An MCP newsletter to provide regular information on changes and advances in the program and exams.

+ Invitations to Microsoft conferences, technical training sessions, and special events program newsletters from the MCP program.

Additional benefits, depending upon the certification, include:

+ Microsoft TechNet or Microsoft Developer Network membership or discounts.

+ Free product support incidents with the Microsoft Support Network 7 days a week, 24 hours a day.

+ One-year subscription to the Microsoft Beta Evaluation program, providing up to 12 monthly CD-ROMs containing beta software for upcoming Microsoft software products.

+ Eligibility to join the Network Professional Association, a worldwide independent association of computer professionals.

Some intangible benefits of certification are:

+ Enhanced marketability with current or potential employers and customers, along with an increase in earnings potential.

+ Methodology for objectively assessing current skills, individual strengths, and specific areas where training is required.

How does this Book Fit In?

One of the challenges that has always faced the would-be Microsoft Certified Professional is to decide how to best prepare for an examination. In doing so, there are always conflicting goals, such as how to prepare for the exam as quickly as possible, and still actually learn how to do the work that passing the exam qualifies you to do.

Our goal for this book was to make your studying job easier by filtering through the reams of Windows 95 technical material, and presenting in the chapters and lab exercises only the information that you actually need to *know* when installing and supporting Microsoft Windows 95 as a Microsoft Certified Professional. Other information that we think is important for you to have available while you're working has been relegated to the appendixes.

How to Study with this Book

This book is designed to be used in a variety of ways. Rather than lock you into one particular method of studying, force you to read through sections you're already intimately familiar with, or tie you to your computer, we've made it possible for you to read the chapters at one time, and do the labs at another. We've also made it easy for you to decide whether you need to read a chapter by giving you a list of the prerequisite topics and skills at the beginning of each chapter.

Labs are arranged topically, not chapter-by-chapter, so that you can use them to explore the areas and concepts of Windows 95 that are new to you, or that you need reinforcement in. We've also decided not to intermix them with the text of the chapter, since nothing is more frustrating than not being able to continue reading a chapter because your child is doing his homework on the computer, and you can't use it until the weekend.

The chapters are, however, intended to be read in sequential order. This is particularly true of the chapters that cover networking (chapters 14 through 20). Don't have any practical networking experience? You will when you finish reading through the Networking Basics and Novell NetWare Basics chapters, and working through the networking labs.

Don't skip the lab exercises, either. Some of the knowledge and skills you need to pass the Windows 95 MCP exam can only be acquired by working with Windows 95, and the lab exercises help you acquire these skills.

How this Book is Organized

The book is broken up into 27 chapters, each focusing on a particular topic that is an important piece of the overall picture.

+ Chapter 1, "Microsoft Certified Professional Program," gives you an overview of the Microsoft Certified Professional program, what certifications are available to you, and where Windows 95 and this book fit in.

+ Chapter 2, "Introduction to Windows 95," is an overview of Windows 95 itself, including Microsoft's design goals for it, and a guide to how you decide between Windows 95 and Windows NT.

+ Chapter 3, "Windows 95 Setup," covers all aspects of installing Windows 95 on a stand-alone workstation. Details include planning and hardware and software requirements, such as what version of MS-DOS is required in order to upgrade to Windows 95. The various Windows 95 Setup options, hardware detection and Safe Recovery are all covered in this chapter.

+ Chapter 4, "Configuring Windows 95," is about configuring Windows 95 by using the Windows 95 Control Panel and viewing the configuration by using Registry Editor. The structure of the registry is covered here as well.

+ Chapter 5, "Windows 95 Architecture Overview," describes the Windows 95 architecture, from basic topics like the memory protection features of the Intel x86 series of processors through the internals of Windows 95 and how various types of applications (16-bit Windows applications, 32-bit Windows applications, and MS-DOS applications) are supported under Windows 95.

+ Chapter 6, "Plug and Play," is about Plug and Play, the seemingly magical mechanism that Windows 95 uses to automatically detect and configure hardware components. Another key topic in Chapter 6 is support for docking and un-docking portable computers.

+ Chapter 7, "File I/O and Disks," covers File and Disk I/O topics, such as the Installable File System Manager, VFAT, Long Filenames, and CDROM support.

+ Chapter 8, "Threads and Processes," is about threads and processes, including the difference between a thread and a process. Other topics include preemptive and cooperative multitasking, and how threads are scheduled to run. The legendary Win16Mutex is explained here.

+ Chapter 9, "Understanding Memory," is all about memory, including the various types of memory that are available to applications under Windows 95, what virtual memory is, and how its used, and how the virtual address space is mapped.

+ Chapter 10, "Understanding Windows 95 Video Display," covers the display adapter support in Windows 95, including display drivers, the DIB engine, and how applications interact with the video subsystem.

+ Chapter 11, "Understanding Printing," covers printing to local printers. Details include printer drivers, enhanced metafile support, and installing and configuring a printer.

+ Chapter 12, "Using Windows 95's Disk Utilities," is about the disk utilities included with Windows 95 and how to use them. Details include ScanDisk, Windows 95, Backup, and the Disk Defragmenter.

+ Chapter 13, "Understanding the Windows 95 Boot Sequence," details the Windows 95 boot process from the BIOS power-on self test to the moment the Windows 95 login screen appears.

+ Chapter 14, "Networking Basics," is designed to give you a firm background in networking, or refresh the one you already have.

+ Chapter 15, "Windows 95 Networking Introduction," is the actual introduction to Windows 95 Networking; the foundation on which support for both Novell and Microsoft network interoperability rides.

+ Chapter 16, "TCP/IP and Windows 95," covers the native support in Windows 95 for TCP/IP, the all important networking protocol used on the worldwide Internet.

+ Chapter 17, "Using Windows 95 with Microsoft Networks," details the support in Windows 95 for interoperating with Microsoft Networks, such as other Windows 95 computers, Windows NT servers, and LAN Manager servers. Security issues, such as user-level security using a Windows NT domain, and browsing issues, such as designating a Master Browser, are included.

+ Chapter 18, "Novell NetWare Basics." If you've never administered a Novell NetWare-based network, this chapter will help you obtain the basic knowledge needed to understand the support that Windows 95 has for interoperating with Novell NetWare servers and clients.

+ Chapter 19, "Using Windows 95 with Novell NetWare," details the support in Windows 95 for interoperating with Novell NetWare-based networks, including the Microsoft Client for NetWare Networks and File and Printer Sharing for NetWare NetWorks.

+ Chapter 20, "Network Printing," wraps up the networking chapters by describing Windows 95's support for network printing. All aspects of network printing are covered in this chapter, including Point and Print, printing to printers attached to both Windows NT and Novell NetWare servers, and two network-attached printers, the HP JetDirect and Digital PrintServer printers.

+ Chapter 21, "Mobile Computing," is about Windows 95 support for mobile computing, including file synchronization via the Briefcase and Dial-up Networking.

+ Chapter 22, "Windows 95 Administration," covers all aspects of Windows 95 administration, including both user profiles and system policies. The administrative tools, including Net Watcher and Registry Editor, are detailed here as well.

+ Chapter 23, "Server-Based Setup of Windows 95," is about Server-Based Setup, the support for installing Windows 95 onto a network server, both to provide a central installation point and for setting up shared installations of Windows 95.

+ Chapter 24, "Windows 95 Communications," covers Windows 95 support for communications—serial ports and modems, including the telephony support (TAPI).

+ Chapter 25, "Using Microsoft Exchange," details Microsoft Exchange, including installing and configuring Exchange, including support for Microsoft Mail, CompuServe mail, Internet mail, and Microsoft Fax.

+ Chapter 26, "Troubleshooting Windows 95," is about Windows 95 troubleshooting and solving a wide range of problems, ranging from what happens when you choose the wrong type of display adapter to what you should do if Windows 95 won't boot.

+ Chapter 27, "Additional Resources," covers those additional Microsoft technical resources and support that every MCP needs to know about.

Following these chapters are the Lab Exercises. As mentioned earlier, you can do these exercises at your own pace, when you want to—you're not tied down to the computer for every chapter.

All of the Windows 95 exam objectives are covered in the material contained in the text of the chapters and the lab exercises. Information contained in sidebars is provided to give history, or other details, but is not actual exam material.

Finally, the many appendixes in this book provide you with additional advice, resources, and information that can be helpful to you as you prepare and take the Windows 95 Certified Professional exam, and onwards, as you work as a Windows 95 Certified Professional:

+ Appendix A, "Glossary," provides you with definitions of terms that you need to be familiar with as a Windows 95 MCP.

+ Appendix B, "Certification Checklist," provides an overview of the certification process in the form of a to-do list, with milestones you can check off on your journey to certification.

+ Appendix C, "How do I Get There from Here," provides step-by-step guidelines for successfully navigating the wilderness between initial interest and final certification.

+ Appendix D, "Testing Tips," gives you tips and pointers for maximizing your performance when you take the certification exam.

+ Appendix E, "Contacting Microsoft," lists contact information for certification exam resources at Microsoft and at Sylvan Prometric testing centers.

+ Appendix F, "Suggested Reading," presents a list of reading resources that can help you prepare for the certification exam.

+ Appendix G, "File Listing of the Windows 95 CD," is a complete list of the locations and names of all the files that ship with Windows 95.

+ Appendix H, "Internet Resources for Windows 95," is a list of places to visit on the Internet related to Windows 95.

+ Appendix I, "Using the CD-ROM," gives you the basics of how to install and use the CD-ROM included with this book, which includes skill self-assessment tests and simulated versions of the Microsoft exam.

+ Appendix J, "Sample Tests."

Special Features of this Book

The following features are used in this book:

Chapter prerequisites

Chapter prerequisites help you determine what you need to know before you read a chapter. You meet the prerequisites either by reading other chapters in this book, or through your prior work experiences.

Notes

Notes present interesting or useful information that isn't necessarily essential to the discussion. This secondary track of information enhances your understanding of Windows, but you can safely skip notes and not be in danger of missing crucial information. Notes look like this:

Note Microsoft posts beta exam notices on the Internet (**http://www.microsoft.com**), and mails notices to certification development volunteers, past certification candidates, and product beta participants. ▪

Tips

Tips present short advice on quick or often overlooked procedures. These include shortcuts that save you time. A tip looks like this:

Tip

A larger CD-ROM cache is not necessarily better than a smaller CD-ROM cache. You should experiment with several sizes of the applications that you use to find the optimal cache setting for your computer.

Key Concept

A Key Concept points out those concepts that are vital to your success as a Windows 95 MCP. Pay close attention to these, and make sure you understand all of the Key Elements.

Key Concept

You should be able to look at a description of a typical company's hardware and software, and determine the best operating system choice for it.

In addition to these special features, there are several conventions used in this book to make it easier to read and understand. These conventions include the following:

Underlined Hot Keys, or Mnemonics

Hot keys in this book appear underlined, as they appear on-screen. In Windows, many menus, commands, buttons, and other options have these hot keys. To use a hot-key shortcut, press Alt and the key for the underlined character. For instance, to choose the Properties button, press Alt and then R. You should not study for the MCP exam by using the hot keys, however. Windows 95 is a mouse-centric environment, and you will be expected to know how to navigate it using the mouse – clicking, right-clicking, and using drag and drop.

Shortcut Key Combinations

In this book, shortcut key combinations are joined with plus signs (+). For example, Ctrl+V means hold down the Ctrl key while you press the V key.

Menu Commands

Instructions for choosing menu commands have this form:

Choose File, New.

This example means open the File menu and select New, which in this case opens a new file.

Instructions involving the new Windows 95 Start menu are an exception. When you are to choose something through this menu, the form is

Open the Start menu and choose Programs, Accessories, WordPad.

In this case, you open the WordPad word processing accessory. Notice that in the Start menu you simply drag the mouse pointer and point at the option or command you want to choose (even through a whole series of submenus); you don't need to click anything.

This book also has the following typeface enhancements to indicate special text, as indicated in the following table.

Typeface	Description
Italic	Italics are used to indicate terms and variables in commands or addresses.
Boldface	Bold is used to indicate text you type, and Internet addresses and other locators in the online world.
`Computer type`	This command is used for on-screen messages and commands (such as DOS copy or UNIX commands).
My Filename.doc	File names and folders are set in a mixture of upper- and lowercase characters, just as they appear in Windows 95.

Chapter Prerequisite

This chapter has no prerequisites, only a desire to become a Microsoft Certified Professional.

1

Microsoft Certified Professional Program

As Microsoft products take an increasing share of the marketplace, the demand for trained personnel grows, and the number of certifications follows suit. As of August, 1996, the team of Microsoft Certified Professionals had grown to 69,000 product specialists, 10,000 engineers, and 2,000 solution developers. And there were 30,000 *Microsoft Certified Systems Engineer (MCSE)* candidates working on their certification requirements, waiting to move up from the farm team to the big leagues.

This chapter covers the Microsoft Certified Professional Program. Terms and concepts covered include:

+ **Microsoft Certified Professional**
+ **Microsoft Certified Systems Engineer (MCSE)**
+ **Microsoft Certified Product Specialist (MCPS)**
+ **Microsoft Certified Solutions Developer (MCSD)**
+ **Microsoft Certified Trainer (MCT)**

Exploring Available Certifications

When Microsoft started certifying people to install and support their products, there was only one certification available, the Microsoft Certified Professional (MCP). As time went on, demand by employers and prospective customers of consulting firms for more specialized certifications grew.

There are now four available certifications in the MCP program, as described in the following sections.

Microsoft Certified Systems Engineers (MCSE)

Microsoft Certified Systems Engineers are qualified to plan, implement, maintain, and support information systems based on Microsoft Windows NT and the BackOffice family of client-server software. The MCSE is a widely respected certification because it does not focus on a single aspect of computing, such as networking. Instead, the MCSE has demonstrated skills and abilities on the full range of software, from client operating systems to server operating systems to client-server applications.

Microsoft Certified Solution Developers (MCSD)

Microsoft Certified Solution Developers are qualified to design and develop custom business solutions with Microsoft development tools, platforms, and technologies, such as Microsoft BackOffice and Microsoft Office.

Microsoft Certified Product Specialists (MCPS)

Microsoft Certified Product Specialists have demonstrated in-depth knowledge of at least one Microsoft operating system or programming techniques and tools. Candidates may pass additional Microsoft certification exams to further qualify their skills with Microsoft BackOffice products, development tools, or desktop applications.

The Microsoft Certified Product Specialist Areas of Specialization (AOS) that lead to the MCSE certification include:

- *Networking.* This AOS requires the candidate to pass the Windows NT Server exam, one desktop operating system exam, such as the Windows 95 exam, and one networking exam, such as the Networking Essentials for BackOffice exam.
- *TCP/IP.* This AOS requires the candidate to pass the Windows NT Server exam and the Internetworking TCP/IP on Windows NT exam.
- *Mail.* This AOS requires the candidate to pass the Windows NT Server exam and the Microsoft Mail (Enterprise) exam.
- *SQL Server.* This AOS requires the candidate to pass the Windows NT Server exam and both SQL Server exams.
- *Systems Management Server.* This AOS requires the candidate to pass the Windows NT Server exam and the SMS exam.
- *SNA Server.* This AOS requires the candidate to pass the Windows NT Server exam and the SNA Server exam.

The Microsoft Certified Product Specialist product-specific exams are your first steps into the world of Microsoft certification. After establishing a specialty, you can work toward additional certification goals at the MCSE or MCSD level.

Microsoft Certified Trainers (MCT)

Microsoft Certified Trainers are instructionally and technically qualified to deliver Microsoft Official Curriculum through Microsoft-authorized education sites.

Understanding the Exam Requirements

The exams are computer-administered tests that measure your ability to implement and administer Microsoft products or systems, troubleshoot problems with installation, operation, or customization, and provide technical support to users. The exams do more than test your ability to define terminology and/or recite facts. Product *knowledge* is an important foundation for superior job performance, but definitions and feature lists are just the beginning. In the real world, you need hands-on skills and the ability to apply your knowledge—to understand confusing situations, solve thorny problems, and optimize solutions to minimize downtime and maximize current and future productivity.

To develop exams that test for the right competence factors, Microsoft follows an eight-phase exam development process:

- In the first phase, experts analyze the tasks that make up the job being tested. This job analysis phase identifies the knowledge, skills, and abilities relating specifically to the performance area to be certified.

- The next phase develops objectives by building on the framework provided by the job analysis. That means translating the job function tasks into specific and measurable units of knowledge, skills, and abilities. The resulting list of objectives (the *objective domain*, in educational theory-speak) is the basis for developing certification exams and training materials.

- Selected contributors rate the objectives developed in the previous phase. The reviewers are technology professionals who are currently performing the applicable job function. After prioritization and weighting based on the contributors' input, the objectives become the blueprint for the exam items.

- During the fourth phase, exam items are reviewed and revised to ensure that they are technically accurate, clear, unambiguous, plausible, free of cultural bias, and not misleading or tricky. Items also are evaluated to confirm that they test for high-level, useful knowledge, rather than obscure or trivial facts.

- During alpha review, technical and job function experts review each item for technical accuracy, reach consensus on all technical issues, and edit the reviewed items for clarity of expression.

The next step is the beta exam. Beta exam participants take the test to gauge its effectiveness. Microsoft performs a statistical analysis, based on the responses of the beta participants, including information about difficulty and relevance, to verify the validity of the exam items and to determine which will be used in the final certification exam. When the statistical analysis is complete, the items are distributed into multiple parallel forms, or versions, of the final certification exam.

Note   Microsoft posts beta exam notices on the Internet (**http://www.microsoft.com**), and mails notices to certification development volunteers, past certification candidates, and product beta participants.

TIP

If you participate in a beta exam, you may take it at a cost that is lower than the cost of the final certification exam, but it should not be taken lightly. Beta exams actually contain the entire pool of possible questions, of which about 30 percent are dropped after the beta. The remaining questions are divided into the different forms of the final exam. If you decide to take a beta exam, you should review and study as seriously as you would for a final certification exam. Passing a beta exam counts as passing the final exam—you receive full credit for passing a beta exam.

Also, since you will be taking *all* of the questions that will be used for the exam, expect a beta to take 2-3 times longer than the final exam. For example, the final version of the Windows 95 exam has a time limit of an hour. The beta version had a time limit of over three hours, and more than three times as many questions as the final versions of the exams!

Also during this phase, a group of job function experts determines the cut, or minimum passing score for the exam. (The cut score differs from exam to exam because it is based on an item-by-item determination of the percentage of candidates who answered the item correctly.)

The final phase—Exam Live!—is administered by Sylvan Prometric™, an independent testing company. The exams are always available at Sylvan Prometric testing centers worldwide.

Note If you're interested in participating in any of the exam development phases (including the beta exam), contact the Microsoft
Certification Development Team by sending a fax to (206) 936-1311.
Include the following information about yourself: name, complete address, company, job title, phone number, fax number, e-mail or Internet
address, and product areas of interest or expertise.

Microsoft Certified Systems Engineer Core Exams

In order to achieve the Microsoft Certified Systems Engineer certification, a candidate must pass four required ("core") exams, plus two elective exams. There are two possible paths, or "tracks" that lead to an
MCSE certification—the Windows NT 4.0 track, and the Windows
NT 3.51 track.

Microsoft Windows NT 4.0 Track to an MCSE

The Microsoft Windows NT 4.0 track to an MCSE is significantly
different from the earlier Windows NT 3.51 track, although there are
still four core exams. The first two, the Windows NT 4.0 exams, are
required:

+ Implementing and Supporting Microsoft Windows NT 4.0
  (70-67). This exam covers installing and supporting Windows
  NT 4.0 in a single-domain environment. This exam will also
  qualify candidates as an MCPS.

+ Implementing and Supporting Microsoft Windows NT 4.0 in
  the Enterprise (70-68). This exam covers installing and supporting Windows NT 4.0 in an enterprise computing environment
  with mission-critical applications and tasks. This exam does *not*
  qualify a candidate as an MCPS.

The third required core exam can be fulfilled by one of four different
exams:

+ Microsoft Windows 3.1 (70-30). Legacy support.

+ Microsoft Windows for Workgroups 3.11 (70-48). Legacy
  support.

+ Implementing and Supporting Microsoft Windows 95 (70–63). Tests a candidate's ability to implement and support Microsoft Windows 95 in a variety of environments, including as a network client on Novell NetWare. This exam qualifies a candidate as an MCPS.

+ Implementing and Supporting Microsoft Windows NT Workstation 4.0 (70-73). Tests a candidate's ability to implement and support Microsoft Windows NT Workstation 4.0. This exam qualifies a candidate as an MCPS.

The fourth core exam can be fulfilled by one of the following:

Note This exam is waived for those candidates who also are Novell Certified NetWare Engineers (CNE) or Banyan Certified Banyan Engineers (CBE). ■

+ Networking with Windows for Workgroups 3.11 (70–46). Legacy support.

+ Networking with Windows 3.1 (70–47). Legacy support.

+ Networking Essentials (70–58). Tests the candidate's networking skills required for implementing, administering, and troubleshooting systems that incorporate Windows 95 and BackOffice.

Windows NT 3.51 Track to the MCSE Certification

Most current Microsoft Certified Systems Engineers followed, or are following, this track, which will continue to be a valid track.

There are four core exams. The first two, the Windows NT 3.51 exams, are required:

+ Implementing and Supporting Microsoft Windows NT Server 3.51 (70-43). This exam covers installing and supporting Windows NT Server 3.51 in a variety of environments. This exam will also qualify a candidate as an MCPS.

+ Implementing and Supporting Microsoft Windows NT Workstation 3.51 (70-42). This exam covers installing and supporting Windows NT Workstation 3.51. This exam qualifies a candidate as an MCPS.

The third required core exam can be fulfilled by one of three different exams:

+ Microsoft Windows 3.1 (70-30). Legacy support.
+ Microsoft Windows for Workgroups 3.11 (70-48). Legacy support.
+ Implementing and Supporting Microsoft Windows 95 (70-63). Tests a candidate's ability to implement and support Microsoft Windows 95 in a variety of environments, including as a network client on Novell NetWare. This exam qualifies a candidate as an MCPS.

The fourth core exam can be fulfilled by one of the following:

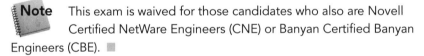

Note This exam is waived for those candidates who also are Novell Certified NetWare Engineers (CNE) or Banyan Certified Banyan Engineers (CBE). ▓

+ Networking with Windows for Workgroups 3.11 (70-46). Legacy support.
+ Networking with Windows 3.1 (70-47). Legacy support.
+ Networking Essentials (70-58). Tests the candidate's networking skills required for implementing, administering, and trouble-shooting systems that incorporate Windows 95 and BackOffice.

Electives for the Microsoft Certified Systems Engineers

In addition to the core exam requirements, in order to complete a Microsoft Certified Systems Engineer certification, you must pass two elective exams. The list in table 1.1 was current as of March 1996.

Table 1.1   Microsoft Certified Systems Engineer Electives

Exam	Number
Microsoft SNA Server	70–12
Implementing and Supporting Microsoft Systems Management Server 1.0	70–14
System Administration of Microsoft SQL Server 6.0	70–26
Implementing a Database Design on Microsoft SQL Server 6.0	70–27
Microsoft Mail for PC Networks— Enterprise	70–37
Internetworking Microsoft TCP/IP on Microsoft Windows NT 3.5	70–53

Continuing Certification Requirements

Once you attain an MCP certification, such as the Microsoft Certified Systems Engineer certification, your work isn't over. Microsoft requires you to maintain your certification by updating your exam credits as new products are released and old ones are withdrawn.

A Microsoft Certified Trainer is required to pass the exam for a new product within three months of the exam's release. For example, the Windows 95 exam (70-63) was released on October 9, 1995. All MCTs, including the authors of this book, were required to pass exam 70-63 by January 9, 1996 or lose certification to teach the course.

Holders of the other MCP certifications (MCPS, MCSD, MCSE), are required to replace an exam that is giving them qualifying credit within six months of the withdrawal of that exam. For example, the Windows for Workgroups 3.10 exam was one of the original electives for the MCSE certification. When it was withdrawn, MCSEs had six months to replace it with another elective exam, such as the TCP/IP exam.

Chapter Prerequisite

Before reading this chapter, you should have a basic understanding of the Microsoft Windows product family, computer hardware specifications, and applications.

Introduction to Windows 95

This chapter is a basic introduction to Windows 95—why it exists, what you can do with it, and how to choose between Windows 95 and Windows NT Workstation for a given environment.

Terms and concepts you learn in this chapter include:

+ **Design goals**
+ **Application compatibility**
+ **Security**

Windows 95 is the successor to Microsoft MS-DOS, Windows 3.1, and Windows for Workgroups. It is rich in features, offering improvements in virtually every area, while retaining compatibility with applications written for the operating systems it replaces.

Understanding the Design Goals of Windows 95

As Microsoft engineers began to design what was to become Windows 95, a number of design goals emerged:

- *Compatibility with applications designed for previous versions of MS-DOS and Windows.* Windows 95 supports virtually all applications written for MS-DOS and Windows 3.x. In fact, this is the overriding goal in Windows 95. Whenever a choice had to be made between compatibility and something else, such as speed or security, compatibility always won.

- *Performance.* Windows 95 is designed to run 16-bit Windows applications at least as fast as Windows 3.1 did, on a minimum configuration of a 386DX processor with 4M of RAM.

- *Hardware compatibility.* Windows 95 supports all existing hardware and device drivers (even MS-DOS device drivers) while simultaneously supporting the next generation of hardware through Plug and Play.

- *System stability.* Windows 95 is designed to be more stable than Windows 3.x. Most Windows 95 users will not experience system crashes, whereas most Windows 3.x users experienced crashes.

- *Improving the computing experience.* Novice computer users have traditionally found the computer to be intimidating, filled with obscure commands that they have to learn. Windows 95 makes the PC environment more friendly and less intimidating than it previously was. Power users find themselves more empowered—able to do more in less time, and with fewer steps than before.

Exploring Features New to Windows 95

Windows 95 introduces a wide variety of new features. Some of the more significant ones include the following:

- *The new user interface.* Windows 95 includes a markedly different interface than previous versions of Windows. Novice users and expert users can now use their PC's power to the fullest. A key part of the new user interface, the Windows Explorer, provides a consistent, object-oriented mechanism to browse the file system of their local computer and network resources.

- *Plug and Play.* Plug and Play makes it easier to expand the capabilities of your PC with new hardware devices. Previous operating systems required users to have detailed knowledge of their hardware's configuration options, install software, flip switches, and the like. With a Plug and Play computer with Plug and Play components, you install a hardware device, and it works.

- *Long file names.* Windows 95 supports long file names, enabling you to give informational names to files, such as My Budget for March 1996, instead of cryptic 8.3 file names (for example, MAR95BUD.XLS).

- *System performance improvements.* Much of Windows 95 is implemented in fast 32-bit code, resulting in improved performance for all types of applications.

- *Preemptive multitasking.* 32-bit Windows applications are preemptively multitasked so that performance is smooth and efficient.

  See "Multitasking," **p. 134**

- *Built-in messaging and fax.* Windows 95 provides fax and electronic messaging, enabling users to communicate with others.

- *Internet access.* Windows 95 makes it easy to access the Internet with support for electronic mail, newsgroups, World Wide Web servers, and other Internet resources through dial-up or hardwired service providers.

Ch
2

+ *32-bit applications.* Windows 95 supports 32-bit applications that comply with the Win32 API, the same application programming interface supported by Windows NT.

+ *Mobile computing support.* Windows 95 includes features for mobile computer users, including remote networking and file synchronization.

+ *Networking support.* Windows 95 is the first version of Windows designed for use on large networks. It supports multiple network clients, multiple network transports, and even multiple driver standards simultaneously (Windows 95 supports NDIS and ODI drivers simultaneously on the same computer).

+ *Remote administration tools.* Windows 95 includes tools for network administrators to remotely monitor and configure the Windows 95 environment over a LAN or WAN.

+ *System management application support.* Windows 95 can be incorporated into existing system management consoles, such as HP OpenView, through its built-in agents, including the SNMP agent.

+ *Safe booting.* Windows 95 includes a safe booting mode that enables you to recover from configuration problems or errors.

+ *Local or server-based installations.* Windows 95 can be configured to run either from the local hard disk of a computer or from a network server. In addition, administrators can control the options that are available to the user.

+ *Diskless workstation/remote boot.* Windows 95 can be installed on computers that do not have a hard drive, and boot from floppy. In environments where computers do not even have floppy drives (for security reasons), it can be configured for a *Remote Initial Program Load (RIPL)* boot off of a network server.

+ *System policies.* Windows 95 enables network administrators to control what the user can configure, hide functionalities of the user interface, lock a user into the user interface, and allow them to only run a given set of applications.

+ *User profiles.* Multiple users can share a single computer and still use their own custom settings and configurations.

+ *Roving user support.* A single user can use multiple computers on the network, and receive his own desktop and configuration on all of the computers automatically.

+ *User-level security.* When Windows 95 is on a network with a server running either Windows NT or Novell NetWare, it can provide user-level security. With user-level security, you can protect a shared resource by designating which users have access to the resource. Windows 95 reads the user list from these networks, and passes authentication requests to servers on these networks.

Ch
2

Comparing Windows 95 to Windows NT

Both Windows 95 and Windows NT Workstation are designed to provide great application support, ease of use, a wide variety of connectivity options, and manageability. Both products provide a platform for running 32-bit Windows-based applications.

Key Concept

You should be able to look at a description of a typical company's hardware and software, and determine the best operating system choice for them.

In order to choose the right operating system, you should first consider the needs of the users:

+ Developers, engineers, and other technical computer users should generally choose Windows NT.

+ Mobile computer users should use Windows 95 because of its support for power management, PC Cards, Plug and Play, and the Windows 95 Briefcase feature.

If your hardware supports Windows NT, and all of your applications and hardware devices are supported by Windows NT, install Windows NT Workstation. If you have older hardware, older applications, or older devices, install Windows 95.

Developers, engineers, and other technical users usually run processing-intensive applications in addition to general business software. They often have multiple computers on their desks: one, a PC to run their general business applications, and the other a UNIX-based workstation to run technical applications.

With the power of Windows NT, these users can combine both types of applications on a single Windows NT Workstation, receiving the same efficiency of a high-performance workstation at a fraction of the cost.

On the other hand, mobile computer users typically need features such as electronic mail, fax, and remote network support to ease access to information from wherever they happen to be. They need a high level of compatibility with their existing hardware and applications, and an operating system that places moderate demands on the system. Plug and Play device configuration services are important as the user docks and undocks the computer. These users should use Windows 95.

On a business desktop, analyze the business problem that you're trying to solve with your computers. Ask yourself the following three questions to determine if Windows NT Workstation is compatible with your existing hardware and applications.

- Do your existing computers have the resources to run Windows NT Workstation, or do you have the budget to upgrade those systems? (Windows NT Workstation requires a minimum of 12M, preferably 16M, and 90M of free hard disk space.)

- Are there Windows NT drivers for the hardware you have in place? Refer to the Windows NT Hardware Compatibility List to determine if your hardware is supported.

- Are your applications compatible with Windows NT Workstation?

If you can answer each question "yes," then you should use Windows NT Workstation.

Another consideration is whether you need the additional protections offered by Windows NT Workstation. In particular, Windows NT Workstation can run 16-bit Windows applications in their own virtual machines, providing an extra level of protection for the system if a 16-bit Windows application goes awry. In addition, Windows NT Workstation can be configured to automatically restart in the event of a system crash.

Data security is another area you can examine. While both Windows 95 and Windows NT can help prevent naive users from damaging their configuration, Windows NT supports a secure file system, NTFS. The use of NTFS can prevent loss of system data from malicious users. Windows NT is also C2 security certifiable, meaning that it can be included in a secure government installation.

In general, however, Windows 95 is the best choice when trying to preserve a business's investment in existing hardware and software by using existing resources while making a gradual transition to 32-bit Windows applications and better hardware.

Table 2.1 shows a comparison of Windows 95 and Windows NT features.

Ch

2

Table 2.1   Comparing Windows 95 and Windows NT

Feature	Windows 95	Windows NT
Protection between 16-bit applications through separate address spaces	No	Yes
C2 certifiable user-level security over access to local resources	No	Yes
Secure workgroup member profiles to control access to desktop, programs, and system configuration	Partial	Yes

continues

Table 2.1 Continued

Feature	Windows 95	Windows NT
Data protection via transacted file system	No	Yes
Automatic recovery from system failure	No	Yes
Runs MS-DOS applications	Yes	Most
Supports file systems other than FAT	No	Yes
Runs OS/2 1.x and POSIX applications	No	Yes
Runs MS-DOS device drivers	Yes	No
Runs 16-bit Windows device drivers	Yes	No
Supports FAT volume disk compression	Yes	No
Runs on multiple hardware platforms	No	Yes
Supports multiprocessor configurations	No	Yes
Win32 API	Yes	Yes
OLE for data sharing across applications	Yes	Yes
Preemptive multitasking of Win32 applications	Yes	Yes
Runs most 16-bit Windows applications	Yes	Yes
Advanced multimedia APIs (DibEngine, DirectDraw, Direct Sound, and so on.)	Yes	Future Release

Feature	Windows 95	Windows NT
OpenGL graphic libraries for 3D graphics	Future Release	Yes
Automatic detection and configuration of hardware during installation	Yes	Yes
Next-generation (Windows Explorer) interface	Yes	Future Release
Plug and Play	Yes	Future Release
Support for inserting and removing PC Cards while the system is running	Yes	No
LAN Connectivity (Client)	Yes	Yes
Peer-to-peer networking	Yes	Yes
Remote Access	Yes	Yes
Microsoft Exchange Client	Yes	Future Release
The Microsoft Network client access software	Yes	Future Release
Open system management architecture	Yes	Yes
DMI and SNMP support	Yes	Yes
System Policies	Yes	Future Release
User profiles to provide support for roving users or multiple users of one computer	Yes	Yes
Remote monitoring of system performance	Yes	Yes
Takes full advantage of 386DX, 486, and Pentium hardware	Yes	Yes

Ch
2

Taking the Disc Test

 If you have read and understood the material in the chapter, you are ready to test your knowledge. Insert the CD-ROM that comes with this book and run the self-test software as described in Appendix I, "Using the CD-ROM."

Chapter Prerequisite

You should be familiar with MS-DOS version 6.0 or later, be able to navigate directories, copy files, edit files, and optimize MS-DOS. You should also understand the basics of the *BIOS*, memory, hard disks, CPU types (in particular, the Intel x86 series), serial and parallel ports, video adapters, and mice.

Windows 95 Setup

Setting up Windows 95 is considerably easier than setting up previous versions of Windows thanks to the many improvements in Windows 95 Setup, including automatic detection of hardware components. The Microsoft Certified Professional, however, needs a complete understanding of all aspects of Setup, including what happens at each stage, to be able to recover from any problems with Setup that may occur.

Note You also should be aware of the technical details of PC hardware configuration, including *IRQs* (interrupt requests), *DMA* (direct memory access), and I/O Addresses.

You should be experienced in supporting Microsoft Windows 3.x or Windows for Workgroups 3.x, and have the ability to install and configure Windows 3.x. ▪

Terms you learn in this chapter include:

- **CD key**
- **Compatible component**
- **Compact setup**
- **Custom setup**
- **Invasive-detection**
- **Logo component**
- **Minimal Windows**
- **Portable setup**
- **Safe-detection**
- **Safe recovery**
- **Typical setup**

Preparing to Install

Preparation is perhaps the single most important aspect of any software installation, and yet, for some unknown reason, it also seems to be the aspect that people devote the least amount of time to. Windows 95 Setup does require a certain degree of preparation—making sure that you have the correct hardware and software before you start the actual setup. But for most installations other than network server-based installations (see Chapter 23), you will not need to do a lot of planning.

What You Need to Know Before You Start

Before you start Windows 95 Setup, you need to make sure that you have a computer that meets the basic hardware requirements, that you have an appropriate version of Windows 95 (either floppy-based or CD-ROM), and that the software already installed on the computer meets the Windows 95 requirements.

The information in this chapter applies to installing Windows 95 on a local hard disk. Network-based installations will be covered in Chapter 23, "Server-Based Setup of Windows 95." In addition, this section assumes that you are installing Windows 95 from a CD-ROM.

Hardware Requirements

Microsoft, like other software companies, lists hardware requirements for its products on the product's packaging, in sales material, and in the product's technical documentation. As anyone who has tried to work with an application installed on a computer that meets the application's requirements knows, the requirements are the absolute minimum that the developers could come up with. About the only thing you can be sure of when running on the minimum hardware is that the program will load and run—it might take an hour for the first user prompt to come up, but it will come up.

Key Concept

Keeping this in mind, the minimum hardware requirements for Windows 95 are

- Intel 80386DX, 20MHz processor or higher (*cannot be a B-step processor*)
- A high-density 3.5-inch floppy drive and a hard disk
- 4M of RAM
- VGA video adapter and display
- Mouse or equivalent pointing device
- 20M free hard disk space for Windows 95
- Enough free disk space for a swap file, so that the amount of RAM, plus the size of the swap file, equals 14M.

Intel 386DX or Better Processor

The B-step 80386 processors were early versions of the 386 that had a defect in them that made a number of 32-bit instructions unusable. These processors were recalled by Intel, and should bear a label reading "16-bit only." 386 processors made after the defect was discovered were stamped with two Greek Sigma letters ($\Sigma\Sigma$), giving them the nickname *double-sigma processors*.

The required processor specification mentions 80386DX processors. While Windows 95 will run on 80386SX processors, the design of the SX series results in 32-bit software generally running slower on them than 16-bit software did. The reason for this is that while the 80386SX series are true 32-bit processors on the inside of the chip, they are 16-bit chips on the outside because there are only 16 data lines going to the chip. This means that for every 32-bit instruction, the 386SX chip must make two read requests to RAM, once for each 16-bit chunk, resulting in a significant performance hit.

486SX processors do not suffer from this same problem, because they are 32-bit both inside and out.

Key Concept: How Much RAM did You Say?

While the minimum requirement is 4M, Microsoft strongly recommends a minimum of 8M of RAM. In fact, in order to use Microsoft Exchange or The Microsoft Network online service, or run more than one 32-bit application at a time, you *must* have 8M.

Other Recommended Hardware

Microsoft also recommends a Super VGA adapter capable of at least 256 colors and 800×600 resolution, a printer, an MPC2-compatible CD-ROM drive, a network adapter, and a sound card. A modem is a must if you want to access The Microsoft Network online service.

Software Requirements

Windows 95 can be installed either as an upgrade to an existing operating system (with or without a previous version of Microsoft Windows) or as the first operating system on a new computer. You must make sure that you purchase the correct version of Windows 95, whether the upgrade version or the "full" version.

MS-DOS Version

In order to install the upgrade version of Windows 95, your computer must have MS-DOS version 3.2 or later, or an equivalent OEM version that supports hard disk partitions larger than 32MB. Because there are many OEM versions of MS-DOS 3.2, however, Microsoft recommends that your computer be running MS-DOS version 5.0 or later. The full version comes with startup disks so you don't need any operating system on the computer when you start installation.

Note   You must make sure that your computer's hard disk is partitioned properly. For example, if you are running MS-DOS 3.2, and have an 80M hard disk, but have it partitioned into 32M partitions, you might not be able to install Windows 95 if you have any other software installed on the partition. In this instance, you would have to delete the partitions, and reformat the disk with larger partitions. ■

Upgrade Requirements

In addition to requiring the appropriate version of MS-DOS, the upgrade version of Windows 95 will not install onto a computer that does not have a "qualifying" previous operating system installed on it. Qualifying previous operating systems are

- Microsoft Windows 3.0 or higher
- Microsoft Windows for Workgroups 3.1 or higher
- Microsoft Windows NT 3.1 or higher
- Microsoft Windows 95
- IBM OS/2 2.0 or higher

If Setup does not find one of the qualifying operating systems installed on the computer, it will prompt the user to insert the original disk #1 from the previous operating system into drive A:. After verifying the disk, Setup will proceed.

Ch
3

The Hardware Compatibility List

As with other Microsoft operating systems, Microsoft maintains a list of hardware components that Windows 95 has been tested on by the hardware manufacturer. These components are either designated as *compatible*, or as *Logo*. Logo components have undergone more in-depth testing, and meet requirements set forth by Microsoft. Compatible components have been tested and work with Windows 95, but do not meet the requirements of the Logo program.

Microsoft recommends choosing Logo components. You can identify Logo components when shopping because they bear the "Designed for Windows 95" logo.

On the Web

A list of Logo components can be acquired from the Microsoft World Wide Web Site at

http://www.microsoft.com/windows

Understanding Installation Issues

When installing Windows 95 onto a computer that has a previous operating system on it, there are some issues that could arise, depending on whether you want to still be able to use the previous operating system, or overwrite it.

Another issue is migration of information from the previous operating system that you want to be able to use when running Windows 95, such as the contents of program groups.

Installing over Windows 3.x

The most common method of upgrade installation is onto a computer already running Windows 3.0 or higher. The default (and recommended) method is to install Windows 95 into the existing Windows 3.x directory, overwriting the previous version. This directory is normally C:\Windows.

Key Concept

If you install over the previous version of Windows, you will not be able to run the previous version any more. However, all of the program group items and most user preferences will be migrated automatically, and application software that was installed under the previous version of Windows should function normally.

Optionally, you can save the previous version of Windows in case you want to uninstall Windows 95. To save the previous version, simply choose to back up the previous version of Windows when prompted during Windows 95 Setup. Choosing this option will save the previous version of Windows in a hidden, compressed file on the computer's hard disk. To actually uninstall Windows 95, you use the Control Panel's Add/Remove Software utility.

Dual-Booting with Windows 3.x

If you do not want to install over the previous version of Windows, you must install Windows 95 into a different directory than the one the previous version is installed in. Any application programs that were installed under the previous version of Windows will need to be reinstalled under Windows 95.

Incompatible utilities that were included with the previous version of MS-DOS will automatically be deleted. Versions of some of them that can be used with Windows 95 can be found on the Windows 95 CD-ROM.

> **Caution**
>
> Running the previous version of Windows is not recommended because using versions of Windows or MS-DOS other than Windows 95 can cause loss of long file names.

You can set up to dual-boot between Windows 95 and the previous version of MS-DOS and Windows by pressing the F4 key during the Windows 95 boot sequence. Dual-boot to the previous version of MS-DOS is only available if MS-DOS version 5.0 or later was installed on the computer, and if the line BootMulti=1 is present in Msdos.sys.

 Note Dual-boot is *not* available with any version of DR-DOS. ▪

Installing over OS/2

Installation of Windows 95 to a computer that was previously running IBM OS/2 is supported. You cannot install Windows 95 into the same directory that OS/2 is installed in, and no migration of program and application information is available. Dual boot with OS/2 is supported only through the OS/2 Boot Manager. If your OS/2 computer is not

Ch
3

already configured to dual-boot with MS-DOS, you must install MS-DOS first, and then run Windows 95 Setup from MS-DOS.

Windows 95 Setup disables the OS/2 Boot Manager (a warning appears as a reminder). To re-enable Boot Manager, run Windows 95 FDISK, and set the Boot Manager partition as the active partition.

Because Windows 95 does not support HPFS, any partitions formatted with the HPFS file system will not be visible from Windows 95.

Dual-Booting with Windows NT

Before installing Windows 95 on a computer running Microsoft Windows NT, make sure that you have a Windows NT Emergency Repair Disk. To create a Windows NT Emergency Repair disk, log in as an Administrator under Windows NT and run the RDISK utility.

Dual-booting with Windows NT depends upon the Windows NT Flex Boot Loader. If the Windows NT Flex Boot Loader does not appear after installing Windows 95, boot from the Windows NT Setup disk, and choose Repair. A dialog box with four options on it will appear. Clear all options except for Inspect Boot Sector and select Continue. When prompted, insert the Windows NT Emergency Repair disk.

When the Windows NT Flex Boot Loader appears after rebooting the computer, you can choose Windows or MS-DOS (whichever appears) to start Windows 95.

Program group and software migration is not available when installing Windows 95 onto a Windows NT computer. In addition, you should not install Windows 95 into the same directory that Windows NT is installed, due to conflicts between the two operating systems' 32-bit components.

Because Windows 95 does not support NTFS or HPFS, partitions that are formatted with these file systems will not be visible from Windows 95.

Installing Windows 95

There are several decisions you must make before beginning to install Windows 95. The first decision is whether to run Windows 95 Setup from the MS-DOS command line or from within a previous version of Windows.

When to Run Setup from a Previous Version of Windows

Windows 95 Setup is a Microsoft Windows 3.1 application, and should be run from within Windows if possible. If you run Setup from the MS-DOS command line, Setup will check to see if the computer has Windows 3.1 or later installed on it; if it does, Setup will recommend that you run Setup from Windows instead.

The reason for this check is the fact that a version of Windows that is already successfully running on a computer is probably optimized for that system, and will be able to run Setup faster than the Minimal Windows installed if you run Setup from the MS-DOS prompt.

When to Run Setup from the MS-DOS Prompt

If you do not have Windows 3.1 or higher installed, you will need to run Setup from the MS-DOS prompt. After verifying that Windows is not installed, Setup will install a version of Windows called *Minimal Windows*.

Minimal Windows contains just enough functionality to run Setup.

Key Concept: Setup Options

Windows 95 Setup provides several different installation options: Typical, Compact, Portable, and Custom. Choosing an option determines what Windows components will be installed. Table 3.1 shows which components are installed by default for each option.

Ch
3

Table 3.1 Components Installed by the Windows 95 Setup Options

Component	Typical	Compact	Portable	Custom
Accessories	yes	no	no	yes
Audio Codecs	yes	no	yes	yes
Backup	Yes	no	no	yes
Briefcase	no	no	yes	no
Desktop Wallpaper	yes	no	yes	yes
Direct Cable Connection	yes	no	yes	yes
Disk Compression	yes	yes	yes	yes
Disk Tools	yes	yes	yes	yes
Document Templates	yes	no	no	yes
Games	yes	no	no	yes
HyperTerminal	yes	no	yes	yes
Multimedia Applications	yes	no	yes	yes
Multimedia Clips	yes	no	yes	yes
Musica Sound Scheme	yes	no	yes	yes
Paint	yes	no	no	yes
Quick Viewers	yes	no	yes	yes
Screen Savers	yes	no	yes	yes
Video Codecs	yes	no	yes	yes
Windows 95 Tour	yes	no	no	yes
WordPad	yes	no	no	yes

Typical Setup

Typical Setup is the easiest way to install Windows 95. As shown in table 3.1, the same components are installed by default for both Typical and Custom Setup options.

Typical Setup is considerably safer than Custom Setup because it limits the information that is requested from the user. When using the Typical option, Setup will automatically detect the computer's hardware, and then configure it optimally.

When installing Windows 95 with the Typical option, you only need to specify the directory where Windows 95 will be installed, provide the user and computer name, and choose to create a startup disk.

Compact Setup

The compact installation installs the minimum set of files required to run Windows 95. This option is intended for those users who have very limited disk space.

Portable Setup

Users with portable computers should choose this option. Components that are useful to mobile users are installed, including Briefcase and Direct Cable Connection. (See Chapter 21 for details.)

Custom Setup

Custom Setup is for those users who want control over the application and hardware settings that Windows 95 Setup configures and which network components will be installed. The files that are installed depend on which choices you make, although the default set of files is the same as those installed by the Typical option.

The Anatomy of a Windows 95 Installation

The Windows 95 installation process was designed in a modular fashion. Setup is broken up into a series of modules that treat the computer as a collection of individual devices rather than as a single entity.

From the user's perspective, Windows 95 Setup proceeds in three phases:

- Information gathering
- File copying
- Restart/Final install

Ch
3

Each of these phases actually involves several different steps from the computer's perspective. As a Microsoft Certified Professional supporting Windows 95, it is important that you understand the installation process from both the user's and the computer's point of view.

Windows 95 Setup from the User's Perspective

The user's view of Windows 95 Setup begins with the user running Setup either from the MS-DOS command line or from Windows 3.1. If necessary, Setup will load Minimal Windows. Regardless of which way Setup was started, the user's view begins with the Welcome Dialog box (see fig. 3.1).

FIG. 3.1 ⟹

Welcome to Windows 95 Setup!

The user chooses to Continue, and Windows 95 Setup loads the Windows 95 Setup Wizard components. While the Setup Wizard is loading, Setup displays a progress indicator (see fig. 3.2).

FIG. 3.2 ⟹

Setup informs the user by displaying a progress indicator.

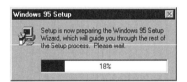

Microsoft software is licensed to the user, not sold. You are required to agree to the terms of the Microsoft License Agreement applicable to your copy of Windows 95. Notice in figure 3.3 that neither Yes nor No is highlighted—the person installing this copy of Windows 95 must make the choice of whether or not he or she agrees to the license. You cannot skip over the dialog box.

If you choose Yes, Setup continues. If you choose No, Setup will exit.

FIG. 3.3 ⇒

You cannot install Windows 95 without explicitly agreeing to the license.

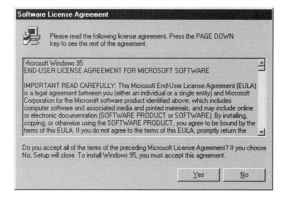

Next, Setup checks to see if Windows 95 has been installed on this computer already. A dialog box (see fig. 3.4) is displayed asking if you really intended to run Setup again.

FIG. 3.4 ⇒

Are you sure you want to run Windows 95 Setup again?

Note   In previous versions of Windows, you had to run Setup in order to add or change certain system components, such as your video display driver. In Windows 95, those kinds of changes are made through the Windows Control Panel, and the dialog box serves to remind you. If you need to use Control Panel, you can just click Cancel, and Windows 95 Setup will exit.

If you really do intend to run Setup again, you need to choose one of two options. The first, Restore Windows files that are changed or corrupted, is the more commonly used of the two. Choosing this option causes Setup to test each of the Windows 95 files installed on the computer, and to replace any that have changed or became corrupted since Windows 95 was first installed.

This enables you to easily repair installations where critical files have, for example, been accidentally deleted by a user.

The second option, Copy all windows files again, does exactly what it suggests. It causes Setup to treat this installation in the same manner as it would treat a brand-new installation. All Windows 95 files will be copied over, even if they are unchanged.

 Note If you have installed a later version of a file, Windows 95 Setup will prompt you before overwriting a newer file with an older one. ▨

Once the pre-installation procedures are completed, the Windows 95 Setup Wizard displays its welcome dialog box (see fig. 3.5). The Setup Wizard informs the user about the three parts of Setup, and highlights the phase that it is about to begin.

The Setup Wizard returns to this dialog box at the beginning of each of the remaining two phases.

As with other Microsoft wizards, you can click the Next button to proceed to the next dialog box. Clicking the Back button will take you to the previous dialog box.

FIG 3.5 ⇒

The Setup Wizard guides you through Setup.

Figure 3.6 shows the Choose Directory dialog box. The Setup Wizard
will recommend a directory (by default, C:\WIN95) to install Windows
95 into. If a previous version of Microsoft Windows 3.x or Windows for
Workgroups 3.x is present on the computer, the Setup Wizard will recommend that you install into the directory that the previous Windows
version is installed into.

FIG. 3.6 ⇒

The Setup Wizard
recommends an
installation
directory.

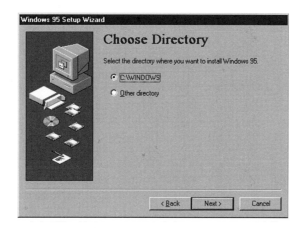

Key Concept

You *must* install Windows 95 into the same directory that your previous
Windows 3.x or Windows for Workgroups 3.x installation was in if you
want to migrate group and application settings (.ini files). You cannot
migrate these settings by copying the .grp and .ini files after installation,
because they must be migrated into the Windows 95 Registry (see
Chapter 4, "Configuring Windows 95").

The Setup Wizard then verifies that the computer has enough disk
space to install Windows 95, and checks to see if any Windows 95 components are already installed. During this time, the Setup Wizard displays a progress indicator (see fig. 3.7).

FIG. 3.7 ⇒

The Setup Wizard checks for disk space and installed components.

Table 3.2 shows the disk space requirements for various types of installations with the Typical and Compact setup options.

Table 3.2   Disk Space Requirements for Windows 95 Setup

Installation Type	Typical	Compact
New installation	40M	30M
Upgrade from Windows 3.1	20M	30M
Upgrade from Windows for Workgroups 3.11	10M	20M

After checking for disk space, the Setup Wizard displays the Setup Options dialog box (see fig. 3.8). Here you must choose the Setup Option discussed earlier that you wish to use. Typical is the default.

After choosing a setup option, the Setup Wizard asks for User Information (your name and company), and your product ID number. If you are installing Windows 95 from CD-ROM, the product ID number is the *CD key*, a serial number that is found on a yellow sticker on the Windows 95 CD-ROM version package. If installing from disk, you will find the number on your Certificate of Authenticity.

The user name and product ID are required. If you are installing from a network server (see Chapter 23, "Server-Based Setup of Windows 95") or reinstalling Windows 95, you may not need to enter a Product ID.

FIG. 3.8 ⇒

You must choose one of the four setup options.

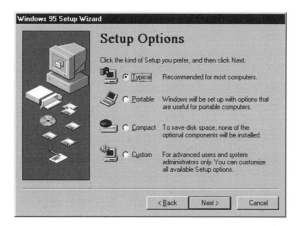

At this point, Setup enters the hardware detection phase. Depending on the chosen setup option, Windows 95 can detect some or all of the hardware present in the computer.

The Typical setup option enables you to skip detection of hardware that Setup did not find during its safe-detection examination. If you know that a device exists that Setup is suggesting you skip, you can override the suggestion and force Setup to detect the device.

The Custom setup option gives you full control over the hardware detection phase. You can choose to enable Setup to detect all of the hardware, or select exactly which devices Setup can look for. You can use this option if you know that performing the detection for a particular device will cause your computer to lock up.

Hardware detection proceeds in two phases: safe-detection and invasive detection.

Safe-Detection

Safe-detection is so named because it consists of actions that are completely safe, such as reading from existing configuration files, ROM signatures, and currently running drivers. These detections will not cause the system to crash.

Windows 95 safe-detection begins by looking for hints by reading Config.sys. Then Setup loads detection modules based on information found in the Msdet.inf file. Msdet.inf lists different device classes and the class-specific INF file that contains device information.

Ch

3

Windows 95 performs the safe detections shown in table 3.3.

Table 3.3 Safe Detections Performed by Windows 95 Setup

Device Type	Detection	Action if Detected
Network Adapter	Look for Lsl.com in memory	Inquire for network adapter settings
	Look for Ipx.com in memory	Inquire for network adapter settings
	Look for Protocol.ini in the Windows, Windows for Workgroups, and LAN Manager	Obtain network adapter settings by reading the file directories
SCSI Controllers	Check for device drivers in Config.sys	If no device drivers found, check adapter ROM for manufacturer names
		Use detection module for each class of SCSI controller that matches driver or ROM string
Proprietary CD-ROM adapters	Check Config.sys for device drivers	Use detection module for each device that matches driver
Sound cards	Look in Config.sys and System.ini for hints	If hint found, load detection module. Windows 95 Setup will not scan I/O ports for sound cards as this will always cause the computer to hang

If Windows 95 Setup does not find drivers for a CD-ROM drive or a multimedia adapter through safe-detection, the dialog shown in figure 3.9 appears. If you check any of the device classes listed on this dialog, Windows 95 Setup loads the appropriate detection modules.

FIG. 3.9 ⇒

When Windows 95 Setup doesn't see one of these devices through safe-detection, this dialog prompts you.

Invasive Hardware Detection

Windows 95 performs invasive hardware detection based on the information found during safe-detection, as well as for device classes (types of devices) that do not have safe-detection routines. While performing invasive hardware detection, Windows 95 Setup displays the dialog box shown in figure 3.10.

FIG. 3.10 ⇒

Windows 95 is trying invasive methods of hardware detection.

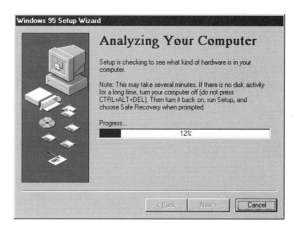

The progress indicator in the Analyzing Your Computer dialog box is extremely important because it serves as your indicator of setup failure. Should the progress bar stop, and there is no disk activity "for a long time," you must turn off the computer. Then you must turn it back on and restart Windows 95 setup.

Key Concept

This is probably the most misunderstood part of Windows 95 Setup, and causes the most support calls. The dialog box specifies "a long time," and it means just that. The progress indicator has, on certain hardware configurations, taken as much as ten minutes or longer before resuming, so be sure to allow enough time before turning the computer off.

Also, make sure that you turn the computer off, and wait a minute or two before turning it back on. This enables the hardware to recover from whatever detection caused the lock up.

When you restart Setup, you will be asked if you want to use Safe Recovery. Always select Yes. Safe Recovery will cause Windows 95 Setup to skip the detection that caused the lock up. (See "Detection Log Files" later in this chapter for technical details.)

If Setup locks up again during invasive detection, turn the computer off and restart Setup with Safe Recovery again. *Repeat this procedure as many times as is necessary until Setup completes the detection phase without locking up.* Eventually, the computer will make it all the way through because every iteration causes a detection that caused a lock up to be skipped.

Deciding Which Components Get Installed

After completing hardware detection, Windows 95 Setup displays the dialog box shown in figure 3.11. The components listed in this dialog box provide connectivity via e-mail and online services, and all are dependent upon Microsoft Exchange as their e-mail client.

FIG. 3.11 ⟹

Windows 95 Setup
prompts you to
install e-mail and
online services.

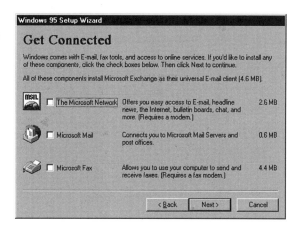

The Microsoft Network is Microsoft's online service. You should become familiar with it, since it is a valuable support tool. You must have a
modem to use The Microsoft Network. You can install the software
necessary to use The Microsoft Network by checking the checkbox.

If you are using Microsoft Mail Servers, you can install the Microsoft
Mail Information Service for Microsoft Exchange by checking the
Microsoft Mail check box. For details on connecting Windows 95
and Microsoft Exchange to Microsoft Mail, see Chapter 25.

If your computer has a fax modem, you can install Microsoft Fax by
checking the Microsoft Fax check box. For details on configuring and
using Microsoft Fax, see Chapter 25.

Windows 95 Setup displays the Get Connected dialog box shown in
figure 3.12 if you chose the Typical setup option. If you choose the
default, Install the most common components, only those components
listed in table 3.1 will be installed.

If you choose Show me the list of components so I can choose, or if
you are installing Windows 95 with the Custom setup option, the dialog box shown in figure 3.13 opens.

Ch

3

FIG. 3.12 ⟹
You can decide to install optional components with the Typical setup option.

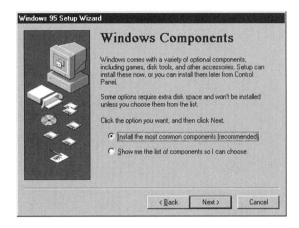

FIG. 3.13 ⟹
Selecting the components to install.

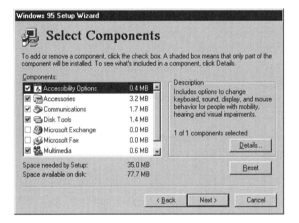

Notice that some of the listed components, such as Communications, have a check mark in the check box; some, such as Accessories, have a check mark in a filled-in check box; and some, such as Microsoft Fax, have an empty check box. The state of the check box is used to indicate how many of the listed component's sub-components are selected for installation.

The plain check mark indicates that all of the component's sub-components will be installed. The check mark in a filled-in check box indicates that only some of the sub-components will be installed. The empty check box indicates that none of the sub-components will be installed.

By highlighting one of the components, as Accessories is in figure 3.14, you can see a description of the component in the right-hand pane. The description includes the total number of sub-components available in this component, and a count of how many are selected. Clicking the <u>D</u>etails button opens up the dialog box in figure 3.15, which enables you to select or deselect individual sub-components. As each sub-component is highlighted, its description appears in the right-hand pane.

FIG. 3.14 ⇒

By highlighting a component, you can see its description.

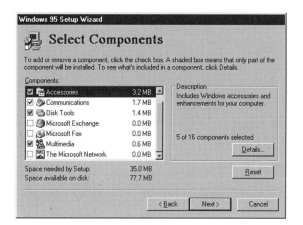

FIG. 3.15 ⇒

Each individual sub-component can be selected or deselected.

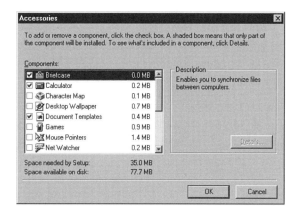

The last step of the information gathering phase is to gather the information that will be used to identify the computer on the network. You must supply a unique name for the computer, the appropriate workgroup name (see "Workgroups" in Chapter 17, "Using Windows

95 with Microsoft Networks," for more information on workgroups), and, optionally, a description of the computer, which will be visible to other network users (see fig. 3.16).

FIG. 3.16 ⟹

You must give your computer a name on the network.

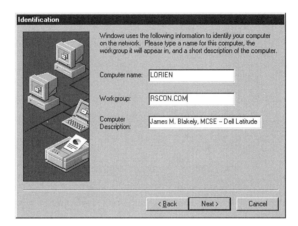

The copying files phase begins with creating a startup disk. The dialog box shown in figure 3.17 opens. You should always select the default option, Yes, particularly if you are performing an upgrade over a previous version of Windows.

Note If you do not create a startup disk, and Setup fails during the Copying Files phase while you are upgrading from Windows 3.x, you might not be able to restart Setup without re-installing your previous version of Windows.

The Windows 95 Upgrade Check requires the previous version of Windows to be intact. However, once files have started to be copied, the previous installation will no longer be usable. When you boot the computer from the startup disk, Windows 95 will be partially running, which will satisfy the Upgrade Check. ▓

FIG. 3.17 ⇒

Always choose to
create a startup
disk.

As shown in figure 3.18, all files present on the disk used for the startup
disk will be deleted, and a startup disk can only be created in drive A:.

Ch

3

FIG. 3.18 ⇒

The startup disk is
created in drive A:

To create the startup disk, Windows 95 Setup formats the disk, and copies the following files to the disk:

File	Description
Attrib.exe	used to change file attributes
Command.com	command processor
Drvspace.bin	drivespace compression utility
Ebd.sys	startup disk utility
Edit.com	editor
Fdisk.exe	used to partition hard disks
Format.com	used to format disks

continues

continued

File	Description
Io.sys	Windows 95 boot file
Msdos.sys	Windows 95 boot file
Regedit.exe	Registry Editor (real mode)
Scandisk.exe	used to test and repair disks
Scandisk.ini	configuration file
Sys.com	used to transfer system files

The Windows 95 Startup Disk does not contain system recovery information like the Windows NT Emergency Disks. In order to recover a working Windows 95 system, you should copy System.dat, Config.sys, Autoexec.bat, Win.ini, System.ini, and any device drivers, such as your system's real-mode CD-ROM drivers, into a subdirectory on the startup disk.

The next step in Setup can take a couple of minutes while Windows 95 Setup determines which files it needs to copy, based on the information it has gathered. During this time, an animated icon indicates that Setup is still running. You can abort the installation before file copying begins by clicking the Exit button (see fig. 3.19).

FIG. 3.19 ⇒

You can abort setup by clicking the Exit button before file copying begins.

As Windows 95 Setup copies files to the disk, a progress indicator is continuously updated. Setup displays informative messages, such as the Welcome to Windows 95 message shown in figure 3.20 as copying continues. The message changes as each new group of files are copied.

FIG. 3.20 ⇒
Windows 95 displays informative messages as files are being copied.

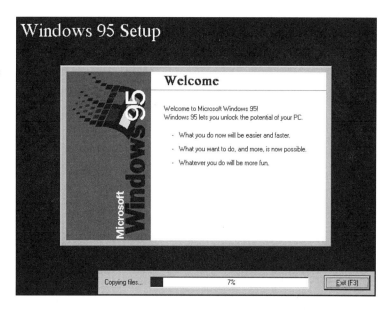

When file copying is complete, Windows 95 Setup prompts you to remove all disks from the computer. Then click Finish (see fig. 3.21) to restart the computer.

FIG. 3.21 ⇒
Windows 95 Setup is ready to restart the computer.

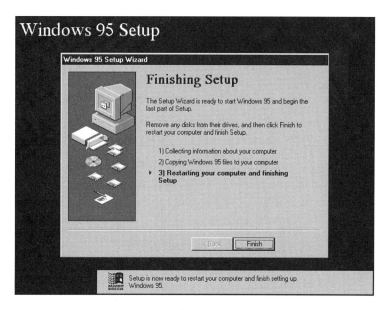

Key Concept

Before the computer restarts and boots from Windows 95 for the first time, Windows 95 Setup modifies the boot sector on the boot drive, and adds a new system file called Io.sys, which takes the place of the Msdos.sys and Io.sys files used by MS-DOS. The old MS-DOS files are renamed to Msdos.dos and Io.dos.

After the computer restarts, you will be guided through the configuration of peripheral devices by wizards, and may be prompted to restart the computer another time. After this final restart, Windows 95 Setup is complete.

Setup from the Computer's Perspective

From the computer's perspective, Windows 95 Setup performs a number of steps:

1. The user starts Setup from the MS–DOS command prompt.

2. Setup runs Scandisk to check for hard disk problems.

3. Setup searches for Windows 3.1 or later. If found, Setup prompts the user to restart Setup under that version of Windows.

4. Setup verifies that the computer's hardware meets the minimum hardware requirements.

5. Setup verifies that an XMS provider, such as Himem.sys, is loaded. If one is not loaded, Setup loads a special XMS provider for the duration of the session.

6. Setup verifies that a disk cache is loaded, and loads SmartDrive if one is not already loaded.

7. Setup checks for TSR programs that are known to cause problems with Setup. If they are present, Setup either unloads them or halts and instructs the user to restart without them.

8. If Setup was not started from Windows, Minimal Windows is loaded.

9. Setup switches the processor into protected mode. Prior to this point, the system was running in real mode.

10. Setup creates the system registry, and performs hardware detection.

11. Setup prompts the user for required information.

12. Setup copies the necessary files to the computer.

13. Setup modifies the boot files.

14. The workstation is rebooted.

15. Final configuration phase starts.

> **Note** If the system fails after the final configuration phase has begun, simply restart the system. You do not need to restart Setup. ■

16. Wininit.exe combines all virtual device drivers (VxDs) into Vmm32.vxd.

17. System.dat is renamed to System.dao, and System.new is renamed to System.dat.

18. A flag is set in the Registry that this is the first time Windows 95 has been run.

19. A module runs that completes the initial configuration of PCMCIA and MIDI devices, and sets up printers and runs any custom hardware setup programs.

20. The program group conversion utility, GRPCONV, converts existing Windows 3.x .grp files.

Key Concept: Detection Log Files

Windows 95 Safe Recovery depends upon several log files generated by Windows 95 Setup. In addition, you can use these files for troubleshooting.

A computer might lock up at any of three possible points during Windows 95 Setup: before, after, or during hardware detection.

If the computer fails before hardware detection, Windows 95 Setup will look in the Setuplog.txt file to determine what point the failure occurred at, and what needs to be skipped.

If the computer fails after hardware detection, Windows 95 Setup will recognize that detection has already taken place, and completely skip detection.

continues

Ch
3

continued

If the computer fails during hardware detection, Windows 95 Setup creates a file called Detcrash.log, which details exactly what detection module was running, and what it was trying to do. If Setup finds this file, it verifies all of the devices it had already written to the Registry, and then skips detection up to the point of failure. Once detection successfully completes, the Detcrash.log file is deleted. Detcrash.log is readable only by Setup. Windows 95 Setup creates an equivalent text file, Setuplog.txt, for you to read and use.

In addition to the Setup log files, Windows 95 creates Detcrash.log when hardware detection is run as part of the Add New Hardware Wizard in Control Panel (see Chapter 4, "Configuring Windows 95"). The equivalent text file that is created when the detection process is run this way is Detlog.txt.

Finally, detected network component information is logged in Netlog.txt.

Taking the Disc Test

 If you have read and understood the material in the chapter, you are ready to test your knowledge. Insert the CD-ROM that comes with this book and run the self-test software as described in Appendix I, "Using the CD-ROM."

Configuring Windows 95

Windows 95 was designed with ease of configuration in mind. Virtually every aspect of the Windows 95 environment can be tailored by the user to suit his or her preferences.

Concepts and skills covered in this chapter include:

✛ Understanding the **Registry** and **Control Panel**, and how to use them to configure Windows 95.

✛ Adding and removing Windows 95 components and applications, by using the **Add/Remove Software Wizard.**

Understanding the Registry

The concept of a *registry* was introduced with Windows 3.1 as a database of information used by OLE to store information about OLE servers, such as what file types are associated with what OLE server. Other information included what operations the server supported (i.e., Print or Open), and the commands necessary to invoke the server. This concept was extended into a system registry with the release of Windows NT.

The registry is a hierarchical database contained in several binary files. The registry replaces the collection of .ini files that held configuration information in previous Windows versions.

Not all .ini files are gone, however. Many 16-bit Windows applications expect to be able to directly access their private .ini files, and even directly edit the .ini files used by Windows itself. Windows 95 still supports .ini files for backwards compatibility. In particular, Windows 95 still supports both the Win.ini and System.ini files, and even creates a couple of its own, such as Telephon.ini, which is used by the telephony-support components.

Windows 95 does not trap and interpret the API calls that edit .ini files into registry changes (as Windows NT does). Instead, Windows 95 will read both the registry files and the System.ini file to determine what drivers to load. In the event of a conflict, the registry takes precedence.

The use of a system registry provides several benefits over the use of .ini files:

+ The registry is a binary file, optimized for rapid access.
+ The registry is a single source for configuration information, rather than dozens of individual files. It is easily backed up and restored in the event of system failure.
+ The registry can be edited remotely using the Windows 95 administration tools (see Chapter 22, "Windows 95 Administration").

+ The registry is designed to facilitate *roving users* on a network, making it possible for users to have their own preferences and desktop, no matter what computer on a network they log into.

+ Registry entries can contain more information than .ini file entries can contain. This is particularly true of entries that contain string variables. An .ini file's entries could only contain a single string, while registry entries can contain multiple strings.

+ Registry entries can contain binary data. An .ini file can only contain text values.

Understanding the Registry Tree

Key Concept

The registry is logically a hierarchical tree. Physically, the branches of the registry are divided between two files: one containing settings that are specific to the computer (System.dat), and one containing settings that are specific to the user (User.dat).

Ch

4

The registry contains six top-level *subtrees*:

+ HKEY_CLASSES_ROOT: Contains information about OLE servers and file associations. It is essentially the same information the OLE registry contained in the Reg.dat file under Windows 3.1, with the addition of Windows 95 information, such as information about shortcuts.

+ HKEY_CURRENT_USER: Contains the currently logged-in user's desktop preferences and network connection settings. This key is copied from the user's subtree in HKEY_USERS at login.

+ HKEY_LOCAL_MACHINE: Contains the configuration settings for all of the hardware devices *that were ever installed on this computer*. Because devices can be present during one session, and not during another (such as when a laptop is docked and undocked), this key is used to speed access to the data for each possible device.

+ HKEY_USERS: Contains the desktop preferences and network connection settings for *every user that ever logged onto this computer.* Each user has a subtree, which is created and updated from HKEY_CURRENT_USER.

+ HKEY_CURRENT_CONFIG: Contains the configuration settings for all of the hardware devices that are currently installed and attached to this computer, and which are not included in the hardware tree in HKEY_DYN_DATA. This key maps to the Config subtree in HKEY_LOCAL_MACHINE.

+ HKEY_DYN_DATA: Contains performance-monitoring data for various system devices. This key is not stored in the disk files. Instead, it is created dynamically. In addition, it contains a subtree, HKEY_DYN_DATA\Configuration Manager, also known as the *hardware tree*, which contains the current hardware configuration.

Each subtree contains keys and values.

Tip

Think of keys in the same way you think of directories. Think of values in the same way you think of files.

Anatomy of a Registry Entry

Registry entries are discussed using notation that is similar to that used for directories and files. When discussing a particular entry, you separate the keys from each other and from the value by backslashes, starting at the top of the registry. For example, the name of the registered owner of the copy of Windows 95 that is installed on a computer is found in:

`HKEY_LOCAL_MACHINE\SOFTWARE\Microsoft\Windows\CurrentVersion\RegisteredOwner`

Registry values have three properties in Windows 95:

+ *Name.* Every registry value has a name, which programs use to access it.

+ *Data type.* Can be Binary, String, or DWORD. A *Binary* value can represent anything. It is simply a collection of bits. A *String* value consists of readable characters (the registry value just mentioned is a String value). A *DWORD* is similar to a binary value, except that a DWORD is limited to 4 bytes in size.

⊥ *Value.* This is the actual numeric or string value this setting has. For example, "c:\Program Files\The Microsoft Network" could be a string value, 00 00 00 11 could be a binary value, and F34A could be a DWORD value.

Using the Registry Editor

You use the Registry Editor to view registry entries. Because the improper use of the Registry Editor can result in a corrupted registry, Windows 95 Setup does not add the Registry Editor into the Programs folder. In other words, you have to know it's location and purpose in order to use it.

Windows 95 Setup copies the Registry Editor (Regedit.exe) into the Windows directory *if setup is run from the Windows 95 CD.* The Registry Editor is not available if you have the floppy disk version of Windows 95. To run the Registry Editor, either double-click Regedit.exe from Windows Explorer, or click the Start button, choose Run, and type **regedit**.

Ch

4

> **Caution**
>
> Microsoft does not support or encourage editing of the registry by users. You should only edit the registry to modify the registry settings used by an application if directed to by the vendor of that application. You should only use the Registry Editor to *view* registry entries, and make all configuration changes through the supplied interfaces in Control Panel and other system tools. Network administrators can prevent users from editing the registry by setting the DisableRegistryEditingTools system policy (see "Policies" in Chapter 22).

The Registry Editor interface, seen in figure 4.1, consists of two panes. The left pane displays the registry tree, in the same format that Explorer uses to display directories. The right pane displays the values contained within the currently selected key (indicated by the open folder icon).

FIG. 4.1 ⇒

Use the Registry
Editor to view the
registry.

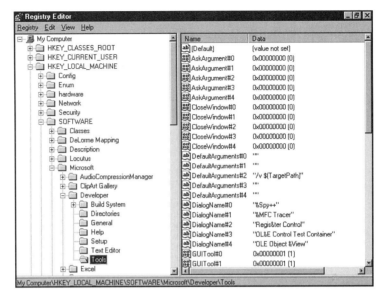

The name of the currently selected key is displayed in the status line, as
in figure 4.1.

Values are displayed in alphabetical order, starting with the (Default)
value, which is present for all keys. The data type of the values is indicated by an icon.

Editing Registry Entries

Double-clicking a string value opens the dialog box in figure 4.2. To
change the value, simply type the new value data in the Value data box.

FIG. 4.2 ⇒

Editing a string
value is as simple as
typing it in the
Value data box.

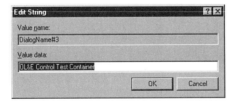

When you double-click on a DWORD value, the dialog box in figure
4.3 opens. You can enter value data into a DWORD value using either
decimal or hexadecimal notation. You make the appropriate selection
using the radio buttons in the Base area in the Edit DWORD Value
dialog box (see fig. 4.3).

FIG. 4.3 ⇒

You choose <u>H</u>exa-decimal or <u>D</u>eci-mal when editing a DWORD value.

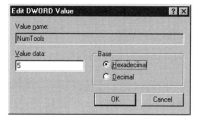

To edit a binary value, the Registry Editor uses an interface similar to that used by other binary editors. The entry area is divided into three columns. The first is a four-digit number that is used to indicate what numeric position in the data the first number in the second column is. For example, the 3D in figure 4.4 is the ninth entry in the data.

FIG. 4.4 ⇒

Editing a binary value.

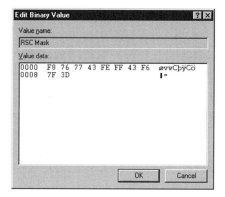

The second column is the data itself, represented as hexadecimal numbers. By clicking in this area, you can move the insertion point into the hexadecimal data. You can then edit or add data by typing hexadecimal numbers.

The third column is an ASCII representation of the data. If you position the insertion point in this column, you can change the data by typing ASCII characters.

Regardless of which column you use to enter data, both columns update simultaneously.

Adding New Entries

Sometimes, you will need to add a registry key or value. To add a key or value, right-click the key that you want to create the key or value

Ch

4

under, and choose <u>N</u>ew from the context menu. Choose the appropriate type (<u>K</u>ey, <u>S</u>tring Value, <u>B</u>inary Value, or <u>D</u>WORD Value) for the entry you wish to add (see fig. 4.5).

FIG. 4.5 ⇒

Adding a new key or value is just a right-click away.

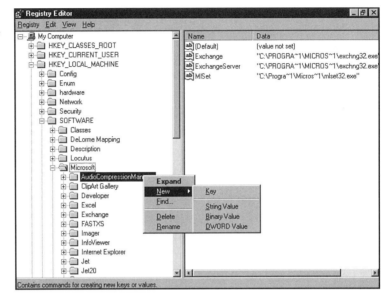

Working with the Control Panel

To configure Windows 95 or a Windows 95 component, you should use the Control Panel. The Windows 95 Control Panel is accessed by clicking the Start button and choosing Settings, Control Panel or by opening My Computer and then opening the Control Panel folder contained within My Computer.

Similar in overall structure to the Control Panel in previous versions of Windows, the Windows 95 Control Panel contains a number of icons, called *options*. By double-clicking one of these options, you can access the property page for the option.

The Control Panel on your computer may include all or some of the following options, depending on the type of computer you have and the setup options you chose:

- *Accessibility Options.* Controls the Accessibility features for the handicapped: StickyKeys, FilterKeys, ToggleKeys, SoundSentry, ShowSounds, High Contrast, MouseKeys, and SerialKeys.

- *Add New Hardware.* Opens the Add New Hardware Wizard, used to add new legacy (non-Plug and Play) hardware after Windows 95 has been set up. See Chapters 3 and 6 for more details.

- *Add/Remove Programs.* Enables you to add and remove Windows 95 components, as well as third-party programs that support the Windows 95 uninstall specification. See "Adding/Removing Windows 95 Components," later in this chapter.

- *Date/Time.* Enables you to change the date and time on the system, as well as select the time zone that you are currently in.

- *Desktop Themes.* Enables you to select a "theme" for your computer, including alternative wallpaper, sounds, cursors, and so on. Available only if Microsoft Plus! is installed on this computer.

- *Display.* Controls display-related settings, such as the background, screen saver, display adapter, and monitor settings (see Chapter 10, "Understanding Windows 95 Video Display").

- *Find Fast.* This option may be added by Microsoft Office for Windows 95. It configures the Office Find Fast indexer, which creates an index to the contents of files on your disk, helping Office to find files that contain particular text faster.

- *Fonts.* The Fonts option is the most markedly changed option from previous versions of Windows. It is now implemented as a folder, and you can drag-and-drop fonts in and out of it.

- *Internet.* If you have installed the Microsoft Internet Jumpstart kit, this option enables you to choose how you want to connect to the Internet. The Internet Jumpstart Kit is part of Microsoft Plus!, but can be obtained through other sources as well.

 Note Using this option may cause TCP/IP configuration problems, see Chapter 16, "TCP/IP and Windows 95."

Ch
4

- *Keyboard*. This option enables you to select the keyboard layout you are using, and what language your keyboard supports.

- *Mail and Fax*. Controls options related to Microsoft Exchange. (See Chapter 25, "Using Microsoft Exchange," for details.)

- *Microsoft Mail Postoffice*. Like Windows for Workgroups and Windows NT, Windows 95 includes the capability to create a "workgroup" version of Microsoft Mail (see Chapter 25).

- *Modems*. Windows 95 supports modems directly. By using this option to add, remove, and configure your modem, you are freed from having to set it up in communications applications (see Chapter 24, "Windows 95 Communications"). This option also controls TAPI configuration, including dialing locations.

- *Mouse*. Controls mouse properties, such as cursors, double-click speed, button configuration, speed, and so on.

- *Multimedia*. Controls multimedia devices, volume settings, MIDI configuration, and so on.

- *Network*. Configures networking settings, such as network client, network adapter, transport protocols, and network services (as discussed in Chapters 15, 16, 17, 19, 20).

- *ODBC and 32-bit ODBC*. Controls Open Database Connectivity components, usually installed by an application. ODBC provides an application program interface that allows applications to access databases using a standard, database-independent set of functions.

- *Passwords*. Controls passwords, remote administration, and user profiles (see Chapter 22, "Windows 95 Administration").

- *PC Card (PCMCIA)*. If 32-bit support for PC Cards is installed, you can stop PC Cards and configure the PCMCIA socket support through this option (see Chapter 6, "Plug and Play").

- *Power*. Advanced Power Management options are configured through this option. Most often used with portable computers, APM includes options like how long to wait after the computer becomes inactive to go into power-saving mode.

- ✝ *Printers.* Like the Fonts option, the Printers option is set up as a folder. (See Chapters 11 and 20 for details on printer support.)

- ✝ *Regional Settings.* In Windows 3.x, this was called the International option. This option controls locally defined settings, such as the currency symbol and what format the date is printed in.

- ✝ *Sounds.* Just like the Windows 3.1 version, this option is used to assign sounds to system events.

- ✝ *System.* The General property page in this option displays the serial number of the copy of Windows 95 (and Microsoft Plus!) installed on the computer, the registered owner, and the total amount of RAM in the system. Other pages include Device Manager, Performance, and Troubleshooting (see Chapters 6, 7, and 26).

Adding and Removing Windows 95 Components and Applications

Ch
4

With previous versions of Windows, if you wanted to add a component after installing Windows, you ran Windows Setup. If you wanted to install an application, you had to figure out what command the application uses to install itself, and then run the install program. If you wanted to uninstall a program, you often had to figure out what files the program used, and manually remove them—hoping that you didn't remove a file that another installed program needed.

In Windows 95, most of these problems have been alleviated with the Add/Remove Software option in Control Panel (see fig. 4.6). With Windows 95, all a user has to do to install software is to click the Install button to start up a wizard that does most of the work. In addition, applications that support the Windows 95 uninstall specification can be uninstalled by highlighting the application and choosing the Add/Remove button.

FIG. 4.6 ⇒

You can install and uninstall applications with the Add/Remove Programs option.

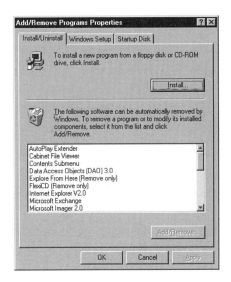

Adding or removing Windows 95 components is just as easy. (You do, of course, have to have access to the Windows 95 installation media, whether on the network, CD-ROM, or floppy disk.) In the same dialog box, click the Windows Setup tab shown in figure 4.7, and check or uncheck the check box next to the component you want to install or remove.

FIG. 4.7 ⇒

Adding or removing Windows 95 components.

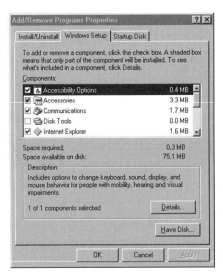

Notice that in figure 4.7, some of the listed components, such as Communications, have simple check marks in the check boxes; others, such as Accessories, show check marks in shaded check boxes; and still others, such as Microsoft Fax, have empty check boxes. The state of the check box is used to indicate how many of the listed component's subcomponents are currently installed:

- The plain check mark indicates that all of the component's subcomponents are installed.
- The check mark in a shaded check box indicates that only some of the subcomponents are installed.
- The empty check box indicates that none of the subcomponents is installed.

By highlighting one of the components, you can see a description of the component, as shown in figure 4.7. The description includes the total number of subcomponents available in this component and a count of how many are selected. Clicking the Details button opens a dialog box that enables you to select or deselect individual subcomponents. As each subcomponent is highlighted, its description appears.

You also can install Windows 95 components that are not listed in the dialog box, such as the administration tools, by clicking the Have Disk button. You then enter the path to the directory containing the component files in the dialog box that opens (see fig. 4.8).

After the component's files have been read, the component will be added as a choice in the Windows Setup tab.

Ch

4

FIG. 4.8 ⇒

Installing a new component with the Install From Disk dialog box.

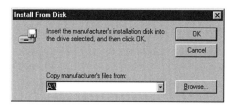

Creating a Startup Disk

The final tab in the Add/Remove Software option is the Startup Disk tab. To create a Startup Disk, click the Create Disk button. To create the Startup Disk, Windows 95 Setup will format the disk, and copy the following files to the disk:

File	Description
Attrib.exe	Used to change file attributes
Command.com	Command processor
Drvspace.bin	Drivespace compression utility
Ebd.sys	Startup disk utility
Edit.com	Text Editor
Fdisk.exe	Used to partition hard disks
Format.com	Used to format disks
Io.sys	Windows 95 boot file
Msdos.sys	Windows 95 boot file
Regedit.exe	Registry editor (real mode) – allows you to implement registry repairs in real mode
Scandisk.exe	Used to test and repair disks
Scandisk.ini	Configuration file
Sys.com	Used to transfer system files

The Windows 95 Startup Disk does not contain system recovery information like the Windows NT Emergency Disks. In order to recover a working Windows 95 system, you should copy System.dat, Config.sys, Autoexec.bat, Win.ini, System.ini, and any device drivers, such as your system's real-mode CD-ROM drivers, into a subdirectory on the Startup disk.

You should have created a startup disk during Setup (see Chapter 3, "Windows 95 Setup"). The Startup Disk tab in the Add/Remove Software option is provided to give you a method of creating a replacement disk in the event the one created during Setup is lost or damaged.

For detailed information on understanding and working with the Windows 95 Registry, see Que's *Special Edition Using the Windows 95 Registry*. For additional information on configuring Windows 95, see Que's *Windows 95 Installation and Configuration Handbook*.

Taking the Disc Test

 If you have read and understood the material in the chapter, you are ready to test your knowledge. Insert the CD-ROM that comes with this book and run the self-test software as described in Appendix I, "Using the CD-ROM."

Ch

4

Chapter Prerequisite

You should have a basic understanding of the Windows 95
design (see Chapter 2, "Introduction to Windows 95") and
the difference between 16-bit
and 32-bit applications. You also
should have a basic understanding of memory management
and application support under
MS-DOS, Windows 3.1, and
Windows for Workgroups 3.11.

Windows 95 Architecture Overview

An operating system's *architecture* describes the basic design and functions supported by the operating system. This chapter describes the
architecture of Windows 95.

Terms and concepts you learn in this chapter include:

+ **DLL**
+ **Driver**
+ **GDI**
+ **General protection fault (GPF)**
+ **Kernel**
+ **Local restart**
+ **Memory management**
+ **Memory protection**

+ **Message**
+ **Message queue**
+ **OLE**
+ **Privilege level**
+ **Program information file (.pif file)**
+ **Thunking**
+ **User mode**
+ **Virtual device (VxD)**
+ **Virtualize**
+ **Virtual machine (VM)**
+ **WinNet**

Intel Memory Protection Architecture

Windows 95 runs on Intel 386 and higher microprocessors only, and depends on the memory management and memory protection capabilities of the microprocessor chip.

Memory management and memory protection are related. *Memory management* refers to the methods used by Windows 95 and the microprocessor to assign various parts of memory to the system and applications. Memory management is discussed in detail in Chapter 9, "Understanding Memory."

Memory protection is the mechanism used by Windows 95 and the microprocessor to ensure that an application cannot access—or damage—memory that has been assigned to another running application, or Windows 95 itself.

Ring "0" and Ring "3"

The Intel 386 microprocessor architecture defines four *privilege levels*. These levels are designed to protect code and data from being damaged either intentionally or inadvertently by less privileged code. Privilege level 0 (zero) is the highest level; privilege level 3 is the least privileged. Another term used to refer to privilege level 3 is *user mode*.

The best way to visualize the privilege levels is shown in figure 5.1. Each "ring" represents a privilege level. Imagine a laboratory that has some very critical experiments, stored in the center of the building in Ring 0. In the outermost ring of the building, Ring 3, are the waiting rooms and publicly accessible areas of the lab. All of the doors in the laboratory are computer-controlled. In order for someone to access the experiments located in Ring 0, he or she must have a key with level 0 privilege, which opens all of the doors. Someone with a level 3 privilege would only be able to access his own area in Ring 3.

FIG. 5.1 ⇒

The protection rings of the Intel 386 Processor range from 3 (least trusted) to 0 (most trusted).

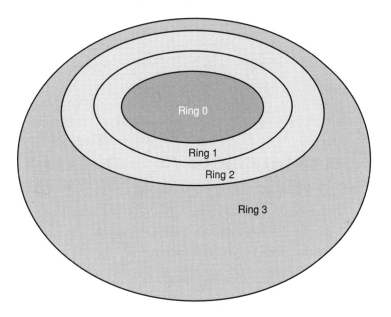

Although the microprocessor supports four rings, Windows 95 is designed to use only Ring 0 and Ring 3. Windows 95 runs its core components in Ring 0. All user application programs and noncritical system components are run in Ring 3.

In addition to protecting code that is running in Ring 0 from damage by code running in Ring 3, the microprocessor also places restrictions on the operations that can be executed by code running outside of Ring 0. For example, all of the operations involving memory management, and direct access to hardware, are privileged operations that can only be executed by Ring 0 code. This also means that a Ring 3 program that fails cannot cripple the entire system.

Ch

5

Ring 0 components are also protected from each other by the microprocessor. Ring 3 components depend upon the protection provided by the operating system and memory manager to protect their code and data from other Ring 3 components.

Virtual Machines

A *virtual machine (VM),* is an illusional environment created by the operating system in memory. To an application program running in a virtual machine, the VM acts like a complete computer that has all of the resources that the application needs to run.

By using virtual machines, the application developer can write programs that behave as though they own the entire computer, not sharing resources. This leaves the job of sorting out, for example, which application is receiving keyboard input at the moment, to Windows 95.

Virtual Machines in Windows 95

MS-DOS applications were designed to run on Intel 8086 or higher microprocessors. Because MS-DOS was a single-user, single-tasking operating system, many MS-DOS programs were designed to access the system hardware directly.

This need for direct hardware access made it impossible to run more than one MS-DOS application on the 286 processor, even though that processor supported a memory protection mechanism similar to the 386. This problem was so significant that Intel added the capability to create virtual 8086 machines to the 386 processor.

Figure 5.2 shows the virtual machines used by Windows 95. All virtual machines run in Ring 3.

MS-DOS Virtual Machines

Each MS-DOS application runs in its own virtual machine, and is isolated from all other applications. Using the virtual 8086 machine support of the 386 processor, any attempts by the MS-DOS application to directly access hardware are redirected to Windows 95, which simulates the results of the hardware access.

FIG. 5.2 ⇒
Windows 95's use of virtual machines.

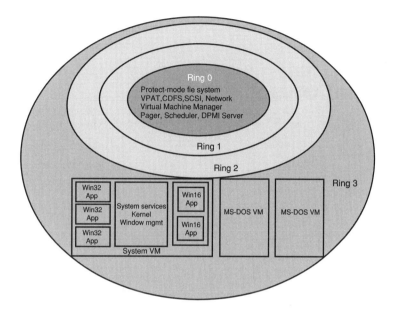

System Virtual Machine

Key Concept

All non-MS-DOS applications, including both 16-bit and 32-bit Windows applications, run in the System Virtual Machine. In addition, all system processes (other than the Ring 0 core components) run in the System VM.

16-bit Windows applications share a single address space within the System VM. This means that it is possible for one 16-bit Windows application to access another 16-bit application's memory. Windows 95 supports 16-bit Windows applications in this way for compatibility with applications that expect to be able to share information with other 16-bit Windows applications by accessing each other's memory.

Ch
5

A 32-bit Windows application receives its own address space within the System VM. 32-bit Windows applications cannot access each other's memory.

For more details on address spaces, see Chapter 9, "Understanding Memory."

Windows 95 Internals

Windows 95 is implemented in several components, each of which communicates with the others. The key functionalities are implemented in the core components and device drivers, with many secondary Windows functions implemented in other various system components, such as multimedia, OLE, and WinNet.

Windows 95 Core Components

Windows 95, like its predecessor, Windows 3.x, has three core components. These components are Kernel, User, and GDI. Under Windows 3.x, each component resides in a single *dynamic link library (.DLL)*. Windows 95 differs from its predecessor by adding a 32-bit DLL for each of the components in addition to a 16-bit DLL.

Windows 95 maintains the 16-bit DLLs for backwards compatibility. In addition, some 16-bit code was retained where using 32-bit code would significantly increase memory requirements without a corresponding increase in performance. (Contrary to the popular view, 32-bit code is not always faster than 16-bit code, and can often be significantly slower.)

Although both 16-bit and 32-bit DLLs exist, each operating system function is implemented in only one of the DLLs (which one depends on the particular function). The other DLL contains entry points for the function, and code that calls the other version of the function. All 16-bit applications call the 16-bit DLL, and 32-bit applications call the 32-bit DLL, regardless of where the function is actually implemented.

For example, the Windows 95 Kernel is completely 32-bit. When a 16-bit application needs to use a function provided by the Kernel, it makes a 16-bit function call into the 16-bit version of the Kernel DLL. The 16-bit version of that function uses a process called *thunking* to call the 32-bit version in the 32-bit DLL to implement the function call.

Windows 95 applications and system components use thunking to communicate with both 16-bit and 32-bit processes. Thunking is a mechanism to convert 16-bit function calls to 32-bit, and 32-bit calls to 16-bit. Thunking is implemented by a layer in the VM.

Kernel Functions

The Windows 95 Kernel is responsible for the basic operating system functionality in Windows 95. This functionality includes managing virtual memory (see Chapter 9, "Understanding Memory"), task scheduling (see Chapter 8, "Threads and Procedures") and File I/O services (see Chapter 7, "File I/O and Disks").

The Kernel is completely 32-bit, and its implementation is in Kernel32.dll.

User Functions

The User component manages the user interface, such as windows, icons, menus, and so on. User also manages input from devices such as the keyboard and pointing devices, and interactions with sound drivers, communication ports, and timers.

Most of the User functions are implemented as 16-bit functions for compatibility with Windows 3.1. Others are implemented as 32-bit functions. The User functions are implemented in User32.dll and User.exe.

GDI

The Graphical Device Interface (GDI) draws graphic primitives, manipulates bitmaps, and interacts with device-independent graphic drivers. When a pixel on the video display is turned on, GDI is responsible for instructing the video display device driver to turn the pixel on. When a circle needs to be drawn on a printer, GDI turns the graphics primitive, the circle, into the pattern of dots that will make up the circle on the printed page. This process is called *rasterization*.

The Windows 95 GDI also supports Image Color Matching, using technology licensed to Microsoft by Kodak. Image Color Matching helps ensure that the color seen on the screen or detected by a scanner matches the color printed on a color printer.

Many of the GDI functions, including the TrueType rasterizer, print subsystem, print spooler, and the new Device Independent Bitmap engine (DIBengine), are implemented as 32-bit functions in Gdi32.dll. Functions that were implemented as 16-bit functions include the existing Windows 3.1 graphics management functions, and some new graphics functions, including Bezier curve handling, and enhanced metafiles.

The existing Windows 3.1 graphics management functions were retained for compatibility with Windows 3.1 applications that expect to be able to use undocumented functions and data structures that were present in Windows 3.1. The other 16-bit functions were implemented because the 16-bit code performs faster than equivalent 32-bit code for these functions.

Other System DLLs

Other important system DLLs include:

- *Multimedia.* Implements the interface for multimedia device drivers and I/O functions, including audio and video compression/decompression and synchronization.
- *OLE.* Originally known as Object Linking and Embedding version 2, OLE implements Windows Objects, including object manipulation, compound storage, and data sharing.
- *WinNet.* The WinNet DLLs implement network access in a device-independent way.

  See "Examining Network Architecture," **p. 239**

Drivers

A *driver* is a piece of software that translates requests from one form into another. Most commonly, drivers are used to provide a device-independent way to access hardware. For example, there are many different video adapters on the market, and each one requires a different method of accessing the adapter to put a pixel on the display. Instead of writing different versions of the GDI for each video adapter (a virtually impossible task), there is only one version of the GDI, which makes a function call to a video display driver. There are different video display drivers for each type of video display adapter, but they all have the same functions available for GDI to call in the same way for each. The driver translates the request that GDI makes into the appropriate adapter-specific actions, and communicates them to the adapter.

Using drivers instead of accessing hardware directly also means that Windows 95 and Windows applications can work with new hardware versions as they become available, rather than requiring operating system updates to support the new hardware, as was necessary in the mainframe world.

In fact, one of the reasons for the popularity of Windows is the fact that all Windows applications depend upon the Windows printer drivers to print graphics on a wide variety of printers. Prior to Windows, each application had to know how to draw on every type of printer, requiring massive support on the part of application developers. Windows applications, however, do not have to know anything about the printer that they are printing on and, more important, a printer manufacturer only has to write a Windows driver; the printer is fully supported by all Windows applications.

Windows 95 uses drivers for virtually all devices, including:

+ Computer systems
+ Pointing devices
+ Video display adapters
+ Sound and other multimedia devices
+ Printers
+ Network adapters
+ Modems

Ch
5

↓ SCSI adapters

↓ Disk drives

Windows 95, unlike Windows NT, supports Windows 3.1 and MS-DOS device drivers for compatibility reasons. However, a Windows 95 driver will almost always be faster than the Windows 3.1 driver for the same device. In addition, a protected-mode device driver, also known as a *virtual device driver (VxD)*, takes advantage of the processor's architecture to provide faster access to the device.

Virtual device drivers *virtualize* the device. Virtualizing permits the use of a single device by multiple applications by controlling shared access to the device. Each application believes that it has sole control of the device, much in the same way that a virtual machine looks like a complete computer to the application.

Key Concept

Windows 95 supports three different types of device drivers:

↓ *Real-mode MS-DOS device drivers*. These are loaded from the Config.sys file, and have the .sys extension. Windows 95 Setup will remove real-mode device drivers if Windows 95 supports the device with Windows 95 drivers.

↓ *Real-mode Windows drivers*. These are usually loaded from the System.ini file, have a .drv extension, and are located in the \Windows\System folder. These drivers are 16-bit, intended for earlier versions of Windows.

↓ *Protected-mode Windows drivers*. These usually have a .vxd or .386 extension and are found in the \Windows\System folder, these drivers are 32-bit.

New Windows 95 drivers are added to the \Windows\System\vmm32 folder. The next time that Windows 95 Setup is run, the drivers are combined with the other Windows 95 drivers in use in that particular Windows 95 installation into the Vmm32.vxd file (see Chapter 3, "Windows 95 Setup," for details on Windows 95 Setup). Until the next time Windows 95 Setup is run, the drivers will be loaded from the \Windows\System\Vmm32 folder.

Windows 95 uses a *minidriver* approach to most of the common device drivers. In this approach, a portion of the device driver is common code, written by Microsoft, and another, device-specific part, the minidriver, is written by the hardware device's manufacturer.

The use of minidrivers, especially in the printer and display drivers, minimizes the possibility that a driver will fail.

Messaging

Unlike older operating systems, such as MS-DOS, Windows uses a "message-passing" model to control applications. Instead of a program executing from one point and proceeding along to its end, prompting the user for information and outputting whatever is appropriate, Windows programs sit in a loop, waiting for *messages*. This means that Windows applications don't have a specific beginning and ending point, nor a predictable path of execution—they sit and respond to external events, much as we humans do.

Every event that happens in the system generates a message. For example, moving the mouse generates "mouse move" messages. Pressing a key on a keyboard generates "key pressed," "key released," and "character typed" messages. A Windows program also can generate messages to request that the operating system do something, or just to pass information.

Every message that is generated is placed in a queue to await processing. Windows applications read the queue to obtain their messages.

Every task (called a *thread*) in a 32-bit Windows application has its own message queue, while 16-bit Windows applications all share a single message queue. This means that if a 32-bit Windows application stops processing messages, it will not have an effect on any other running application. (See Chapter 8 for more information on threads.)

On the other hand, because 16-bit Windows applications share a single queue, if a 16-bit Windows application stops processing, all other Windows applications will stop processing. Their messages will be blocked until the stopped program is forcibly terminated by the user. Notice that this behavior is strictly dependent on the single message queue, and not how the 16-bit Windows applications are multitasked.

See "Multitasking," **p. 134**

Windows 95 and Applications

Because Windows 95 replaces both MS-DOS and Windows 3.x, it must be able to run virtually all applications that ran under these previous operating systems. In addition, one of the Windows 95 design goals was to run 16-bit Windows applications at least as well as they ran under Windows 3.1.

Windows 95 supports interoperability between different kinds of applications, including OLE and cut-and-paste. For example, a 16-bit OLE server can communicate with a 32-bit OLE client, and data can be cut from a 32-bit Windows application and pasted into a running MS-DOS application.

Support for 32-Bit Windows Applications

Windows 95 supports each type of application differently. For example, 32-bit Windows applications are run in their own address spaces within the System VM. Each thread in a 32-bit Windows application has its own message queue, and if a 32-bit Windows application fails, it will not affect other running applications. 32-bit Windows applications are preemptively multitasked.

Support for 16-Bit Windows Applications

Programs designed for previous versions of Windows run in the System VM. All 16-bit Windows applications are cooperatively multitasked within a common address space and share a common message queue.

A poorly written 16-bit Windows application might be able to damage or interfere with other 16-bit Windows applications, and even monopolize the system. Windows 95 support for 16-bit Windows applications was designed this way to ensure compatibility with applications written for Windows 3.1.

If a Program Fails

There are only two basic ways that a computer program can fail. The first way is when the program stops responding or "hangs." The second is when the program attempts to access memory that does not belong to it.

Windows 95 handles failing programs differently depending on what type of application caused the failure, and what type of failure occurred.

Applications Stop Responding to the System

A still-running application is said to have "hung" when it no longer responds to the operating system. The result of a hung application is different for each type of application, although there are some potential problems that are common to all types of hung applications.

Hung 32-Bit Windows Applications

A hung 32-bit Windows application does not affect other applications because of the separate message queues. You can terminate a hung 32-bit Windows application by performing a *local restart*.

To perform a local restart, simply press Ctrl+Alt+Del. The dialog box shown in figure 5.3 opens. The hung application is indicated by the words "(not responding)." There are three options:

+ *End Task*. Clicking this button immediately terminates the application.

+ *Shut Down*. Clicking this button causes Windows 95 to wait a few seconds to see if the application responds. If it does not respond within the allotted time, the application terminates.

+ *Cancel*. Clicking this button closes the dialog box without taking any action.

Ch
5

Hung 16-Bit Windows Applications

If a 16-bit Windows application stops responding to the system, all other 16-bit Windows applications will eventually stop running. Because they all share a single message queue, a message intended for the hung application will block the other application's messages at the top of the queue.

FIG. 5.3 ⇒

The Close Program dialog box is displayed after pressing Ctrl+Alt+Del.

After performing a local restart to terminate the hung application, the blocked applications should resume. Notice that 32-bit Windows applications and MS-DOS applications continue to run even if a 16-bit Windows application is hung.

Hung MS-DOS Applications

If an MS-DOS application running in the Windows 95 graphical environment hangs, simply perform a local restart and terminate the application. No other applications are affected.

Potential Problems Caused by Hung Applications

If an application hangs while using a resource that is needed by another application, the other application will be stopped. Both applications will appear to have hung.

If you perform a local restart, the Close Program dialog box will indicate what application actually stopped responding to the system. Terminating it will enable the other application to resume.

Another possible source of problems, such as not being able to open more windows, are the system resources that are used by programs that need to be terminated. This is primarily of concern with 16-bit Windows applications because they may use resources without the knowledge of Windows 95. In addition, because 16-bit Windows applications run in a shared address space, they might also share resources. However, resources used by both MS-DOS and 32-bit Windows applications are tracked and returned to the system when the applications are terminated.

Windows 95 does not recover resources used by 16-bit Windows applications to the system until the last 16-bit Windows application terminates. Then, it returns all of the resources to the system, including any
that may have been orphaned by hung 16-bit Windows applications.

General Protection Faults

Windows 95 displays a *General Protection Fault (GPF)* dialog box when a
program attempts to access protected memory or performs some other
illegal operation. A GPF is usually the result of an improperly written
application. What happens when a GPF occurs depends on what type
of application caused the GPF:

- If a 32-bit Windows application causes a GPF, it does not affect
  any other running applications. The application is terminated
  when you click the Close button in the GPF dialog.

- If a 16-bit Windows application causes a GPF, the system traps
  the error and displays a GPF dialog box. All other 16-bit
  Windows applications will stop running until you close the
  dialog box.

- If an MS-DOS based application fails, only that application is
  affected because MS-DOS applications run in separate virtual
  machines. When the user closes the GPF dialog box, the MS-
  DOS program and its virtual machine are terminated.

MS-DOS Based Applications

Windows 95 supports running MS-DOS applications. However, like
previous versions of Windows, not all MS-DOS applications can be run
within the Windows 95 graphical environment.

MS-DOS Mode

Key Concept

Some MS-DOS applications expect to have control over the full resources of the computer. Windows 95 provides *MS-DOS mode*, which
enables you to run these applications.

Ch
5

If Windows 95 detects that an MS-DOS application requires full access to the computer, it suggests that you run the application in MS-DOS mode. You can force an MS-DOS application to run in MS-DOS mode through a property page.

> **Note**   When entering MS-DOS mode, all currently running applications will be terminated. MS-DOS mode is identical to running a previous version of MS-DOS; the processor enters real mode, and any devices that require protected-mode drivers will not be available. ▥

MS-DOS Application Properties

In order to run MS-DOS applications under previous versions of Windows, you had to create a *program information file (.pif file)* using a utility called the PIF Editor. The .pif file associated with an MS-DOS application contained settings that told Windows how to configure the virtual machine for the application.

Windows 95 still uses .pif files, but the PIF Editor is not used. Instead, the .pif file settings are controlled through the property pages of the application. To access the property pages, right-click the application's executable (.exe) file in Windows Explorer, and choose Properties from the context menu.

Figure 5.4 shows the General property page. Like the General property page of Windows applications, it contains information about the file, including items such as the file size, the MS-DOS shortname of the file (see Chapter 7, "File I/O and Disks,"), and the file dates and attributes.

In addition to the MS-DOS application's name, the Program property tab (see fig. 5.5) contains:

- *Cmd Line*. This shows the command line that is executed to run the application (including any necessary parameters).
- *Working*. This shows the working directory for the program. Windows sets the current directory for the VM to this directory before executing the command line.
- *Batch File*. Because each MS-DOS application runs in its own virtual machine, there might be other applications or commands that must run in the VM before this application is started.

You can create a batch file containing these commands, and then enter the batch file's name in this box.

FIG. 5.4 ⇒

Information about the file is displayed by the General property page.

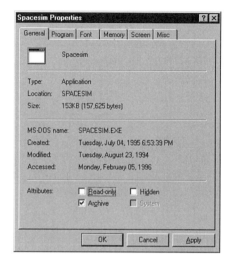

Spacesim Properties

General | Program | Font | Memory | Screen | Misc

Spacesim

Type: Application
Location: SPACESIM
Size: 153KB (157,625 bytes)

MS-DOS name: SPACESIM.EXE
Created: Tuesday, July 04, 1995 6:53:39 PM
Modified: Tuesday, August 23, 1994
Accessed: Monday, February 05, 1996

Attributes: ☐ Read-only   ☐ Hidden
                    ☑ Archive   ☐ System

OK   Cancel   Apply

+ *Shortcut Key.* If you want this application to be started whenever a certain key combination is pressed, enter that combination here.

+ *Run.* MS-DOS applications can be run inside of a window. This drop-down box provides three choices controlling how the window is displayed: Normal Window, Minimized, and Maximized.

+ *Close on Exit.* If this box is checked, the window will be closed when the application terminates.

To change the icon displayed for the application in Explorer, click the Change Icon button.

Clicking the Advanced button opens the Advanced Program Settings dialog box (see fig. 5.6).

Prevent MS-DOS-Based Programs from Detecting Windows can be selected for applications that require you to exit from Windows 3.x in order to run them. Because Windows 95 is much more compatible with MS-DOS applications than previous versions of Windows 3.x, this option is available to bypass the checking for the presence of Windows that these applications perform.

Ch
5

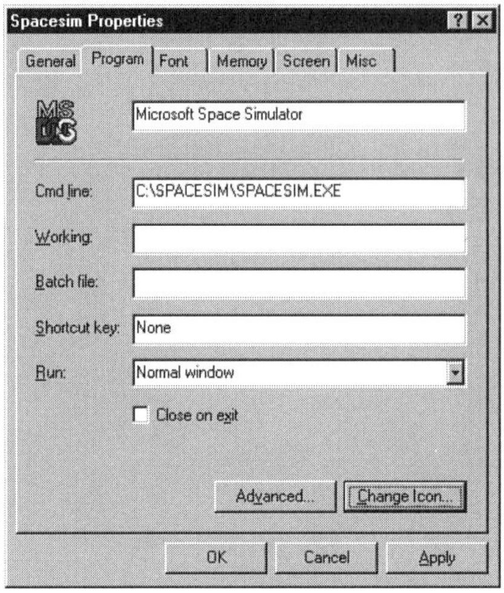

FIG. 5.5 ⇒

The Program property page controls what file is actually executed.

FIG. 5.6 ⇒

The Advanced Program Settings dialog box.

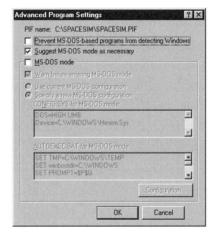

If the Suggest MS-DOS Mode as necessary box is selected (the default), Windows 95 automatically detects MS-DOS behavior that requires MS-DOS mode, such as a program attempting to directly access the hardware.

Selecting the MS-DOS mode box changes the dialog box to that shown in figure 5.7. When this box is selected, the application will always run in MS-DOS mode. Because MS-DOS mode terminates all other applications, you should leave the Warn before entering MS-DOS mode option selected.

FIG. 5.7 ⇒

MS-DOS mode properties dialog.

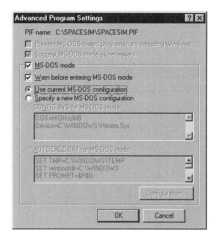

Because different applications might need different MS-DOS configurations (for example, an application that needs as much conventional memory as possible or one that needs a particular MS-DOS device driver loaded), you can specify the MS-DOS configuration used by this application's VM. To do so, choose the Specify a new MS-DOS configuration option, which changes the dialog box to that shown in figure 5.8. You can specify both a custom Config.sys and Autoexec.bat file.

FIG. 5.8 ⇒

You can specify a new MS-DOS configuration for this application's VM.

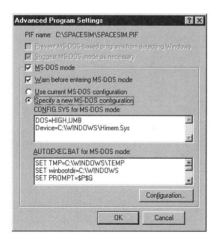

Ch

5

The Font property page (see fig. 5.9) enables you to control the font that is used to display the MS-DOS application's text when running in

a window. If you set a particular font size, the window size will be
adjusted accordingly.

FIG. 5.9 ⇒

You can control
the font size used
to display an
MS-DOS appli-
cation.

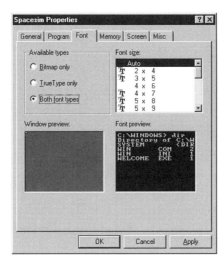

The Memory property page (see fig. 5.10) enables you to control the
memory configuration of the VM. When set to Auto, Windows 95 assigns the maximum amount of memory available to the VM.

FIG. 5.10 ⇒

You can control
the memory con-
figuration of the
virtual machine.

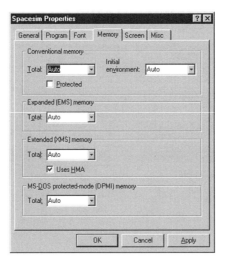

The Screen property page (see fig. 5.11) controls the appearance of the
MS-DOS application. If an MS-DOS-based application has trouble
running in a window, try running it full-screen before resorting to
MS-DOS mode.

FIG. 5.11 ⇒
Choose the <u>F</u>ull-
screen option
button when an
MS-DOS applica-
tion has trouble
running in a
window.

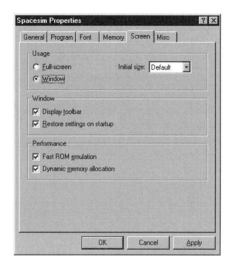

The Misc tab includes the following groups of options:

+ *Foreground.* The only option in this group controls whether the
  Windows 95 screen saver can run when this MS-DOS application is active in the foreground.

+ *Background.* Checking the Always <u>s</u>uspend box will cause the
  MS-DOS application to be suspended whenever it is not in the
  foreground.

+ *Idle Sensiti<u>v</u>ity.* Windows 95 suspends inactive MS-DOS applications after waiting a certain amount of time. This slider controls
  how long that time is. Certain applications, such as some 3270
  emulators, may appear to be inactive when they actually are not.
  Setting this slider to its lowest level avoids problems with these
  programs.

+ *Mouse.* When QuickEdit is selected, the mouse will select text
  within an MS-DOS window without having to select the Edit
  mode. Do not use QuickEdit if the application uses the mouse.

Ch
5

You can restrict the mouse to the MS-DOS application's window by selecting the E<u>x</u>clusive mode box.

↓ *Windows shortcut <u>k</u>eys.* MS-DOS applications may need to use keystrokes, such as PrintScrn, that are normally used by Windows for some other purpose. Deselecting a shortcut key's checkbox here, disables the normal meaning of the key when running this application in the foreground.

FIG. 5.12 ⇒

Miscellaneous properties page.

Taking the Disc Test

If you have read and understood the material in the chapter, you are ready to test your knowledge. Insert the CD-ROM that comes with this book and run the self-test software as described in Appendix I, "Using the CD-ROM."

Chapter Prerequisite

Before reading this chapter,
you should be familiar with the
Windows 95 Setup process
(see Chapter 3, "Windows 95
Setup"), know how to configure Windows 95 (see Chapter
4, "Configuring Windows 95"),
and understand the Windows
95 System Architecture (see
Chapter 5, "Windows 95 Architecture Overview").

Plug and Play

Personal computers have touched just about every aspect of how people
live and work. No longer the exclusive tool of the scientist or math-
ematician, today's personal computers are found in virtually every business and many homes. In early 1996, more than 25 percent of American
homes had a PC, and many had more than one.

With the advent of Windows 95, a new concept in making computers
easier to use was introduced—Plug and Play. This chapter covers Plug
and Play, including the following concepts:

- **Bus**
- **Bus enumerator**
- **Configuration Manager**
- **Device Manager**
- **Device Node**
- **Docking**

- **PC Card**
- **PCMCIA**
- **Plug and Play**
- **Resource arbitrator**

The types of tasks that are accomplished with the help of a computer have changed, too. While they certainly still help perform the traditional productivity types of applications, the modern PC now serves to facilitate information exchange, education, and entertainment.

Of course, the addition of these genres could not be achieved without the advances in hardware technology that have occurred since the PC was introduced. These advances have not only made the PC more powerful and less expensive, but they have also introduced millions of PC users to the problems associated with trying to configure many pieces of hardware so that they will work together.

Added to these problems is the increasing use of portable computers, which must be reconfigured when they detach from their office networks, and again when they are docked back in.

Defining Plug and Play

Plug and Play is actually both an overall design philosophy and a set of specifications that help achieve the Plug and Play goal—making the computer, add-in devices, drivers, and operating system work together automatically without requiring intervention from the user. A system that is made of components that are all Plug and Play-compatible will achieve this goal.

A completely Plug and Play system consists of the following:

- A Plug and Play operating system, such as Windows 95
- A Plug and Play BIOS
- Plug and Play hardware and the associated drivers

History of Plug and Play

The Plug and Play specification was the result of the work by an industry committee made up of both hardware and software vendors. The committee was formally introduced at the Windows Hardware Engineering Conference in March 1993 by Microsoft, Intel, and Compaq.

Less than a year later, at COMDEX (fall 1993), the first 18 Plug and Play devices were demonstrated to the show's attendees. By late 1995, hundreds of Plug and Play devices from dozens of vendors throughout the computer industry were available.

Plug and Play specifications cover the full range of hardware, including BIOS, Advanced Power Management (APM), Industry Standard Architecture (ISA) bus, Small Computer Systems Interface (SCSI) bus, printer ports, communication ports, PCI bus, VL bus, PCMCIA sockets and cards (also known as *PC cards*), and the VESA DDC specification for Plug and Play monitors.

Most manufacturers of personal computers and add-on hardware are delivering many—if not all—of their product lines with Plug and Play configurations. For more information on Plug and Play support, a forum is available on CompuServe (**GO PLUGPLAY**).

Understanding Docking

Docking refers to the process by which a mobile computer reestablishes its link to a docking station. Docking usually connects additional hardware resources, such as network cards, hard drives, monitors—any device that is not required for booting the computer—to the mobile computer.

Prior to the advent of Plug and Play, mobile computer users often found the use of docking stations to be a challenge, because there was no easy way to reconfigure Windows 3.x for different hardware. This often resulted in users settling for the least common denominator in hardware, rather than hardware configurations that took full advantage of the hardware available in the docking stations.

Ch
6

A good example of this is the video monitor. Most notebooks supported only 640 × 480 × 256 colors, while the docking station was connected to a monitor that could support 1,024 × 768 × 16 million colors. Because Windows 3.1 display drivers each only supported one resolution, users had to manually reload drivers each time they docked or undocked the notebook.

With Windows 95 and Plug and Play, the notebook can automatically and dynamically reconfigure itself based on the currently available devices, and whether it is docked.

Docking Types

Three types of docking are supported by Windows 95:

+ Hot

+ Warm

+ Cold

The type of docking that is supported depends upon the design of the docking station or port replicator.

Docking stations usually hold the entire PC within them, while a *port replicator* usually just provides a means of rapid connect/disconnect for all of the ports on the back of a notebook computer. An *advanced port replicator* adds some port or ports that would not be available without the replicator. Typical additional ports are SCSI and network adapters.

Hot Docking

Hot docking means that the computer can be running at full power when it is docked or undocked. Microsoft has designed hot docking support into Windows 95 in partnership with portable computer manufacturers such as Toshiba and Compaq, and BIOS vendors such as Phoenix Technologies.

On the hardware side, manufacturers design the PC and docking station to enable docking operations when power is applied to the computer.

On the software side, Windows 95, when possible, anticipates the effect on the system of the hardware change (such as files that need to be closed) and will load and unload the appropriate drivers, as well as manage conflicts caused by the hardware change.

There are two types of hot docking available:

- Auto-eject
- Manual, also known as "surprise" docking

Auto-Eject

A portable computer and docking station equipped with an auto-eject docking system resembles a videocassette and a VCR. The user places the computer in the appropriate place, and a motor draws the computer into the docking station and automatically makes the right connections.

When the user clicks the Start button and chooses Eject PC, Windows 95 checks to see if any problems will be caused by ejecting the PC. If there are any (such as a file open on a drive in the docking station), the user is prompted to take appropriate action. Then, the computer automatically reconfigures itself to match the new configuration, including changing the video characteristics to match those of the new system configuration.

Manual

The key difference between the manual and auto-eject system lies in the fact that a manual system is just that—manual. No hardware interlock exists, which also means that extra care must be taken during docking to make sure that no damage occurs to either hardware or software.

Warm

A computer that can be warm-docked must be placed into a lower-power (also known as *sleep*) mode when it is docked or undocked.

Cold

A computer that must be turned off before docking takes place is said to only support *cold* docking. Most laptops support cold docking.

Ch
6

Understanding Critical Resources

Personal computer add-on devices communicate with the rest of the system using one or more methods. These methods are known as *critical resources* because they cannot be shared, and so must be managed by Plug and Play. The critical resources are:

- I/O addresses
- Interrupt Requests (IRQs)
- Direct Memory Access channels (DMA)

I/O Addresses

Intel processors support a concept known as *I/O Addresses*, which are similar to memory, but are implemented as a separate memory area from system RAM. The I/O Address space allows for 65,535 I/O addresses, which are usually expressed in hexadecimal from 0 through FFFF. Each I/O address used is referred to as an *I/O port*.

Memory

Some devices, such as display adapters, make use of system memory addresses. These addresses normally fall in the upper 384K of the first megabyte of RAM (see Chapter 9, "Understanding Memory").

Interrupts

When a peripheral device wants to notify a program that an event has occurred, it triggers an *interrupt request* using one of the lines built into the CPU. When the first IBM PC was designed, IBM added a *programmable interrupt controller (PIC)* to manage interrupts—it expanded the number of interrupts the system could recognize to eight distinct levels, ranging from 0–7.

When the 80286-based IBM PC/AT was released in 1984, IBM added a second PIC to the computer, connecting the output of the second PIC to the interrupt 2 input on the first, or master, PIC. This added interrupts numbered 8–15, with the connection being called a *cascade*. In order to allow devices that had been designed to access *interrupt request line (IRQ)* 2 to still function, IBM wired the bus so that the IRQ 2 line on the bus is connected to IRQ 9 on the second PIC.

Most devices use an interrupt. In fact, because there are only 16 possible interrupts—and some of them must be used by motherboard devices—the IRQ is the most precious of the critical resources. To help manage this resource, a number of IRQs have preassigned uses (see table 6.1).

Table 6.1   Personal Computer Interrupt Assignments

IRQ	Used By
0	System Timer
1	Keyboard
2	Cascade to second controller
3	Communication Port 2
4	Communication Port 1
5	Parallel Port 2 (usually free)
6	Floppy disk drive
7	Parallel Port 1 (usually shareable)
8	Real-Time Clock
9	Available
10	Available
11	Available
12	Available
13	Math Coprocessor
14	IDE disk controller (primary)
15	IDE disk controller (secondary)

Ch

6

DMA

Another scarce system resource is *direct memory access* (*DMA*) channels. DMA allows peripheral devices to access memory without involving the CPU, which can greatly improve the transfer rate to and from the peripheral.

DMA channels are numbered from 0–7, with channel 4 reserved for the DMA controller, and channel 2 used by the floppy disk controller.

Examining the Plug and Play Hierarchy

Plug and Play views the computer as a number of devices arranged in a hierarchical structure called the *system tree*. Each branch of the tree is called a *device node*. If a device node has child nodes connected to it, it is called a *bus*.

Every device node requires several items of configuration information:

+ *Unique identifier.* A string of data that identifies the object to Plug and Play.

+ *Resource requirements.* Includes resource type, such as IRQ or memory address, and any constraints.

+ *Resources allocated.* Some devices require specific resources, such as COM2 requiring IRQ 3.

+ Whether the device is a bus.

The operating system must identify every device node in the computer system and its resource requirements. It then stores the information in a system Registry and loads the appropriate device drivers.

Understanding the Plug and Play Process

Windows 95 implements Plug and Play both at system startup and while the system is running. At startup, it polls the hardware for its identification and configuration information. If a device is added to the system while it is running, Windows 95 receives the device's identification from the device dynamically. Plug and Play then completes the configuration of the device automatically.

The Plug and Play specification defines the mechanism used by Windows 95 to configure ISA Plug and Play adapters. There are several steps to the process:

- Configuration mode
- Isolate cards
- Read specifications
- Allocate resources
- Activate cards

Configuration Mode

First, the Windows 95 Plug and Play software uses three 8-bit I/O ports to send commands to any present Plug and Play adapters. A series of commands, called the *initiation key*, is sent that causes the adapters to activate their Plug and Play logic circuitry.

Isolate Cards

All Plug and Play adapters listen to the same I/O ports. In order to address just one card at a time, the software uses the unique identification number on the card to isolate the card so that it can assign the card a handle. *Assigning a handle* removes the necessity for performing the complicated isolation process to select a card after this phase completes.

Read Specifications

The Plug and Play software then reads the resource data structure from the card to discover what resources are supported (and requested) by the functions implemented on the card. A given card can support more than one function—such as a sound card that supports wave, MIDI, joysticks, and a CD-ROM—all on one adapter card. Each implemented function is referred to as a *logical device*.

Ch

6

Each logical device has separate configuration information, and each logical device is configured separately.

Allocate Resources

After the Plug and Play system determines all the capabilities and demands of the adapters in the system, it then figures out how to allocate resources to each of the cards. The Plug and Play system attempts to allocate resources in a conflict-free manner.

Activate Cards

Once the cards are configured, Plug and Play removes them from configuration mode. Once out of Configuration mode, only by reissuing the initiation key can you cause the cards to reenter configuration mode. This prevents accidental changing of the configuration when the cards are operating.

Handling Legacy Cards

If the system contains only Plug and Play cards, fully automatic configuration is possible. However, many systems contain adapters that were designed before Plug and Play existed. These adapters are called *legacy cards*, and must be configured through other means.

Windows 95 uses both safe and invasive detection methods to discover the configuration of legacy cards. Legacy devices are always assigned resources before Plug and Play cards, because they are usually less flexible.

See "Safe Detection," **p. 49**
See "Invasive Hardware Detection," **p. 51**

Exploring Plug and Play Components

Plug and Play changes all the components of a computer system. The remainder of this chapter describes the components that make up Plug and Play:

- Bus enumerators

꜀ Plug and Play BIOS

꜀ Hardware tree and registry

꜀ Operating system

꜀ Devices and device drivers

Bus Enumerators

The *hardware tree* (the in-RAM record of devices on the system) is enumerated (built) by the bus enumerators. A *bus enumerator* is a type of driver based on a specific bus architecture. Each bus enumerator understands the details of its bus type, and can identify devices on its bus, read its resource requirements, and configure them as directed by the Configuration Manager.

The bus enumerator assigns a unique and consistent identification code to each device on its bus. This allows Windows 95 to maintain a database of hardware settings.

Windows 95 includes enumerators for several types of bus:

꜀ PCI (Pci.vxd)

꜀ EISA (Eisa.vxd)

꜀ ISA (Isapnp.vxd)

꜀ SCSI (the SCSI driver is the bus enumerator)

꜀ PC Card (the Card Services driver is the bus enumerator)

Bus enumerators are responsible for building (enumerating) the hardware tree on a Plug and Play system. The bus enumerators are a new type of driver. *Enumerators* are based on specific bus architectures and understand the implementation details of their bus types. Therefore, an ISA enumerator can identify the devices on an ISA bus, read its resource requirements, and configure them as instructed by the Configuration Manager. Other enumerators include those for VLB, PCI, SCSI, PCMCIA, serial ports, and parallel ports. During installation, Windows automatically determines which bus enumerators are applicable to a given computer.

Ch

6

BIOS

The Plug and Play BIOS provides boot device configuration and dynamic event notification to Windows 95. It configures the system board devices such as the PIC, DMA controller, Video controller, and so on, before it hands the configuration process to the operating system.

Following the Power On Self Test, the BIOS supplies the system board configuration information to the operating system. It is also responsible for notifying the operating system of events such as the hot docking of a portable computer, which require dynamic reconfiguration of the system.

Hardware Tree and the Registry

The *hardware tree* is a record in RAM of the current system configuration. The information is taken from the record in the registry of configuration information for all devices ever installed on this computer, whether they are currently installed or not.

A new hardware tree is created every time the system boots, and is automatically updated when dynamic configuration changes occur. The user can view the information in the hardware tree by using Device Manager.

See "Device Manager," **p. 117**

Storage Location (HKEY_LOCAL_MACHINE)

HKEY_LOCAL_MACHINE contains the computer's configuration data (hardware tree). The information stored here is used by Windows 95, device drivers, and applications to determine the system's configuration data, without regard to which user is logged in or what software is being used.

Hardware devices place information in HKEY_LOCAL_MACHINE automatically through Plug and Play. Device drivers place information here using the Win32 API, and users place information here using Control Panel or Device Manager.

There are several subkeys in HKEY_LOCAL_MACHINE:

- *Config*. Contains a collection of possible configurations for this computer, also known as *hardware profiles*. (Hardware profiles are used to support different configurations for a computer, such as docked and undocked).

- *Enum*. Contains information about the hardware on the system.
- *Hardware*. Contains information about serial ports and modems.
- *Network*. Contains information about the network, including network provider, server validation, and other information related to operating this computer on a network.
- *Security*. Contains information about network security and remote administration.
- *Software*. Contains information about software installed on this computer.
- *System*. The database of system startup, device driver loading, and operating system behavior information.

Operating System

In order for a computer system to be considered a Plug and Play system, it must have three major components:

- Plug and Play BIOS
- Plug and Play hardware
- Plug and Play operating system

A Plug and Play operating system, such as Windows 95, needs several components:

- *Configuration Manager*. Software that controls the configuration process and communicates with all of the components involved in the configuration process.
- *Hardware tree*. The database of configuration information stored in RAM.
- *Bus enumerators*. The drivers that identify the device nodes and their resource requirements.
- *Resource arbitrators*. Drivers that allocate resources to the devices.

Ch
6

Devices and Device Drivers

Plug and Play builds on the existing device driver technology to add programming interfaces for Plug and Play functions. In addition, the devices themselves must support software configuration.

Device Drivers

Plug and Play device drivers not only provide a device-independent method for the system to operate and access the device, but they also communicate with other parts of the Plug and Play system to provide the configuration of the device.

Plug and Play device drivers must:

+ Register with the Configuration Manager when they are loaded.

+ Wait to be assigned resources before becoming active.

+ Respond to dynamic configuration changes and communicate them to applications. For example, an application program may want to save and close files before a removable disk is ejected from the system.

Devices

The level of support that Plug and Play offers depends on the types of devices.

Microchannel and EISA

Microchannel is an IBM proprietary bus specification used in IBM's PS/2 line of computers, as well as in a handful of other vendors' computers. *EISA* (*Extended ISA*) is a bus design that was specified by an industry consortium in response to IBM's Microchannel. Unlike the Microchannel, EISA cards are upwardly compatible from ISA, and ISA cards can be used in an EISA bus-based computer.

Both Microchannel and EISA use software-based configuration, requiring only a bus enumerator to incorporate that information into the hardware tree.

Windows 95 ships with an EISA bus enumerator, but does not supply a Microchannel enumerator. The manufacturer of a Microchannel computer is responsible for supplying a bus enumerator for it.

Windows 95 will not reconfigure EISA cards—it only reads the pre-configured data from the card and incorporates it in the hardware tree.

SCSI

The Small Computer Standard Interface (SCSI)—pronounced "scuzzy"—standard permits the connection of a chain of multiple devices such as hard disks and CD-ROM drives to a single adapter card. Plug and Play SCSI devices support dynamic changes to the configuration and automatic configuration of SCSI device IDs and bus termination.

There are two distinct processes in the configuration of a SCSI device:

+ First, the SCSI bus must be configured, ensuring that both ends of the SCSI bus are terminated, and device IDs are set.

+ Second, the SCSI adapter must be configured, including the critical resources—such as IRQ—used by it.

Configuring a SCSI bus involves a number of issues that can make it challenging for many users. The bus must be terminated at both ends. Every device on the bus must have a unique device ID, usually set by jumpers or a dial. All devices must be set to handle certain SCSI features, such as parity, in the same way.

PC Card

PC Cards are credit-card sized adapters that are typically used with portable notebook computers. They were formerly known as *PCMCIA* cards.

PC Card support requires two drivers—one for the card, and one for the socket on the computer that the card plugs into.

VL and PCI

PCI and VL are specifications that allow connection of high-speed peripherals, such as video or network adapters, to the system.

Ch
6

The PCI bus is Plug and Play-compatible, but it cannot make another bus Plug and Play-compatible. Because most computers use the PCI bus as the secondary bus, if the primary bus is not Plug and Play-compatible, the PCI bus loses its Plug and Play functions.

Windows 95 includes bus enumerators for both VL and PCI bus—the VL enumerator is handled by the ISA PNP enumerator.

IDE

IDE is not currently Plug and Play-compatible, because it does not offer a way to identify devices or allocate resources.

New Technologies

As new technologies become available, the Windows 95 Plug and Play implementation can be extended to support whatever technologies become available.

Resource Arbitrators

The *resource arbitrators* are responsible for allocating specific types of resources, and resolving conflicts between devices that request identical resource assignments.

The resource arbitrators interact with the Configuration Manager to perform the resource assignment process at two times:

+ During system startup
+ In response to dynamic allocation requests

Configuration Manager

The Configuration Manager handles all phases of the configuration process. It is responsible for controlling the entire flow of configuration operations performed by the other Plug and Play components, as well as responding to communications from the BIOS and hardware devices.

The Configuration Manager calls the bus enumerators to identify the devices on the buses attached to the system, and calls the resource arbitrators to allocate the resources the devices need. Configuration Manager loads the device drivers, tells them to wait for resource allocation, and then gives them their allocations.

Device Manager

Device Manager is the primary tool used to modify configurations. It is accessed from the System option in Control Panel. Device Manager has two available views—by type (see fig. 6.1), or by connection (see fig. 6.2).

FIG. 6.1 ⇒

Viewing devices by type.

FIG. 6.2 ⇒

Viewing devices by connection.

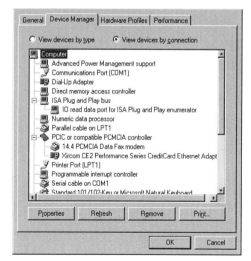

Ch

6

You can view the configuration of a device by selecting it and clicking the Properties button. Most property dialog boxes have two pages: General (see fig. 6.3) and Resources (see fig. 6.4). Device-specific information may be configured through a Settings page.

FIG. 6.3 ⇒

The General property page tells you if the device is working correctly.

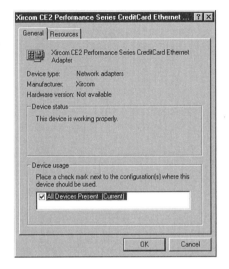

FIG. 6.4 ⇒

The Resources property page lets you manually configure the resources used by a device.

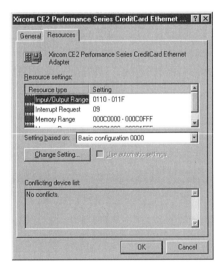

If any devices are conflicting, the conflicting device is listed in the dialog box.

Taking the Disc Test

 If you have read and understood the material in the chapter, you are ready to test your knowledge. Insert the CD-ROM that comes with this book and run the self-test software as described in Appendix I, "Using the CD-ROM."

Ch

6

Chapter Prerequisite

Before reading this chapter, you should be familiar with the Windows 95 Setup process (see Chapter 3, "Windows 95 Setup"), know how to configure Windows 95 (see Chapter 4, "Configuring Windows 95"), and understand the Windows 95 System Architecture (see Chapter 5, "Windows 95 Architecture Overview").

File I/O and Disks

The Windows 95 file system support has many improvements over Windows 3.1, both in functionality and performance, while keeping full compatibility with MS-DOS and prior versions of Windows. Windows 95 supports 32-bit *FAT (File Allocation Table)*, CD, and network file systems as well as 32-bit disk drivers.

This chapter covers File and Disk I/O. Terms and concepts covered include:

+ **8.3 file names**
+ **ASPI**
+ **CDFS**
+ **Installable File System**
+ **IFS Manager**
+ **Long File Names**
+ **SCSI**
+ **VFAT**

Exploring the Installable File System Manager (IFSMGR)

Any discussion of file systems under Microsoft's 32-bit operating systems must start with networking because of the integration of networking into the file system.

Windows 95 uses an *Installable File System* (*IFS*) architecture that allows multiple file systems to coexist on the same computer. Network redirectors, such as the Microsoft Client for NetWare Networks or Client for Microsoft Networks, are implemented as file system drivers. Other file system drivers are the VFAT and CDFS file systems, which provide access to files on hard drive and CD-ROM.

At the core of the Installable File System architecture is the *Installable File System Manager* (*IFSMGR*). It is responsible for managing the interoperability of the various file systems with each other, and with applications. IFSMGR consists of the following component:

    ✢ Ifshlp.sys. A real mode stub for the IFS Manager that hooks the INT21h chain and hands the calls to the protected mode IFS Manager.

All the file system drivers support long file names and, with the exception of the CDFS system, support using the protected mode VCACHE for reads. The CDFS system uses its own cache, discussed later in the chapter. VFAT also supports using VCACHE for a lazy-write cache, so that applications do not have to wait for information to be written to the disk.

File system drivers (*FSDs*) are responsible for managing the high-level I/O requests made by applications. The IFS Manager receives all file I/O calls and arbitrates which file system driver should receive a particular call and process it.

Windows 95 supports a real mode MS-DOS installable file system for compatibility with MS-DOS applications, and to enable the use of MS-DOS block device drivers, including real mode compression drivers loaded from Config.sys.

The installable file system approach also makes it possible for third parties to add file system support to Windows 95. For example, a file system driver could be written by a third party to support UNIX-format disks, and have the files indistinguishable under Windows 95 from files on a VFAT volume.

Virtual FAT (VFAT)

The primary file system in Windows 95 is the *virtual File Allocation Table file system*, or *VFAT*. VFAT is a 32-bit virtualized MS-DOS FAT file system, controlled by VFAT.VxD. VFAT is implemented entirely in 32-bit code, and cannot be disabled.

VFAT is only used for hard disk volumes that use the 32-bit disk access components. Other types of volumes use other installable file systems, such as the CDFS installable file system used for CD-ROM drives, and the real mode MS-DOS file system used for devices that require real mode MS-DOS device drivers.

In Windows 95, the 32-bit VFAT file system is the primary file system and cannot be disabled. VFAT can use 32-bit protected mode drivers or 16-bit real mode drivers. Actual allocation on disk is still 12-bit or 16-bit (depending on the size of the volume), so FAT on the disk uses the same structure as previous versions of this file system. VFAT handles all hard disk drive requests, using 32-bit code for all file access for hard-disk volumes. VFAT was first introduced in Windows for Workgroups version 3.11 as an optional FAT file system that processed file I/O in protected mode.

FAT versus VFAT

The disk volume format used by VFAT is identical to the format used by the MS-DOS FAT file system. It supports both the 12-bit and 16-bit file allocation table formats. (A volume's FAT uses either 12-bit or 16-bit quantities, depending on volume size.)

The distinction between "FAT" and "VFAT" lies in the operating system code (in MS-DOS, 16-bit; in Windows 95, 32-bit) that accesses the volume, not the data structure format of the volume as it is stored on the disk.

Ch

7

I/O Supervisor

The VFAT communicates with the lower layers of the Block I/O subsystem through the I/O supervisor. The Windows 95 *I/O supervisor* provides the services to older 32-bit disk drivers (FastDisk) drivers that the *BLOCKDEV driver in Windows 3.1 provided. In addition, the I/O supervisor registers drivers, routes and queues I/O requests, notifies drivers as necessary, and provides memory allocation and I/O services to drivers.

Volume Tracker

Windows 95 tracks removable media (such as floppy disks, or removable hard disk volumes, such as Syquest cartridges) to make sure that the correct media is in the drive, and warns the user before accessing the incorrect media. There are two ways that the volume tracker tracks removable media:

+ *On writable disks.* The volume tracker adds a unique ID in the disk's FAT header, which is different than the volume serial number.

+ *On write-protected disks.* The volume tracker caches the disk's label, serial number, and BIOS parameter block.

Windows 95 supports MS-DOS-compatible removable media. You can use Windows 95 Fdisk to create partitions on INT 13-based removable media. (*INT 13* is the BIOS interrupt used to access hard disks.)

Windows 95 does not rely on volume serial numbers for volume tracking because the volume serial number is guaranteed to be neither present nor unique. The file system driver assigns unique serial numbers to removable media the first time it mounts the media. Once a serial number has been recorded on the disk, future mounts will result in the driver reading the number from the disk.

If a floppy disk drive supports change line detection, Windows 95 uses it to detect media changes.

Type Specific Drivers

A *type specific driver* (*TSD*) works with a particular type of disk. Windows 95 includes two TSD VxDs:

+ Disktsd.vxd, which supports disks.

+ Cdtsd.vxd, which supports CD-ROM drives.

A TSD handles most of the drive calls for its device type, and then calls the specific port driver to communicate with the device.

Port Drivers

Port drivers are 32-bit protected mode drivers that communicate with a specific disk device, such as a hard disk controller. Port drivers are similar to the FastDisk driver used in Windows 3.1. Windows 95 provides port drivers for IDE/ESDI/RLL/MFM and floppy disk drives.

SCSI

Unlike MS-DOS and Windows 3.x, Windows 95 provides direct support for SCSI disk drives. The process is similar to the situation described earlier for IDE and other types of disk drives, except that SCSI devices do not use a monolithic port driver like other disk drives do.

Instead, in the place of the port driver, there are several layers of software:

+ *SCSI translator driver.* Responsible for constructing the SCSI command blocks for the specific device class and carrying out error recovery and logging. There are two translator drivers, one for each type of device: hard disk (Diskvsd.vxd) and CD-ROM (Cdvsd.vxd).

+ *SCSI Port Manager (Scsiport.pdr).* Manages the interaction between the translator driver and miniport driver.

+ *SCSI miniport drivers.* Like other minidrivers, responsible for detecting, initializing, and communicating with a specific set of SCSI adapters. Miniport drivers have an MPD extension.

ASPI/CAM Support

Windows 95 comes with 32-bit disk device drivers for most of the popular SCSI controllers, including those from Adaptec, Future Domain, and other manufacturers. Windows 95 also supports the *Advanced SCSI Programming Interface (ASPI)*, which is Adaptec's standard for applications designed to access SCSI devices, and *Common Access Method*

Ch

7

(*CAM*), which is Future Domain's standard. This support allows existing MS-DOS and both 16- and 32-bit Windows applications and drivers that use one of these specifications to run under Windows 95.

CDFS

CDFS (*Compact Disk FileSystem*) is to CD-ROM drives as VFAT is to hard disks. The CDFS driver loads dynamically following the detection of a CD-ROM device. The CDFS driver is essentially a protected mode version of MSCDEX, forming the interface between the CD-ROM device and the operating system.

Device Controller Types

Windows 95 supports four different ways of connecting a CD-ROM drive to the computer:

- IDE
- SCSI
- Proprietary (found in ADAPTER.INF)
- Real mode drivers

IDE

Most personal computers today use an IDE hard disk controller. Adding a CD-ROM often required adding another controller card (either a SCSI or proprietary card). To address this problem, Windows 95 supports low-cost IDE CD-ROM drives.

SCSI

The most common way to connect a CD-ROM drive is via a supported SCSI adapter.

Proprietary—Adapter.inf

Controllers from Sony, Panasonic, and Mitsumi are supported using protected mode drivers that are listed in the Adapter.inf file.

Real Mode Drivers

If protected mode drivers are not available for a particular CD-ROM and controller combination, then you can use the same drivers that you would have used with MS-DOS. Windows 95 supports real mode

CD-ROM drivers using the MS-DOS FAT file system and MSCDEX as the CD-ROM extensions. When the real mode drivers are being used, there is no protected mode caching of the CD-ROM.

CD-ROM Caching

The CDFS file system maintains its own cache separate from the Vcache used by VFAT. The CDFS cache is *swappable*, meaning that it can be paged out to the swap file. Paging does not significantly change the effectiveness of the cache, because reading a record that's been paged to disk is still much faster than accessing the compact disc.

 Note The primary reason for having separate disk and CD-ROM caches is to avoid having the hard disk cache fill up with a single CD-ROM data stream.

 Tip

A larger CD-ROM cache is not necessarily better than a smaller CD-ROM cache. You should experiment with several sizes of the applications that you use to find the optimal cache setting for your computer.

To set the CDFS cache size, open the System option in Control Panel, and click Performance, File System; the File System Properties dialog box opens. Choose the CD-ROM tab (see fig. 7.1). Drag the slider to set the size of the cache.

You also should set the value in the Optimize access pattern for drop-down list to the appropriate value for your CD-ROM drive.

The default value of the Optimize access pattern for drop-down list box is related to the size of your system RAM:

+ *8M or less.* The optimize setting is set to single-speed drives, which creates a 64K cache.

+ *8M-12M.* The optimize setting is set to double-speed drives, which creates a 626K cache

+ *12M or more.* The optimize setting is set to quad-speed or higher, which creates a 1,238K cache.

Ch
7

FIG. 7.1 ⇒

Set the cache size used with the CD-ROM by moving the slider.

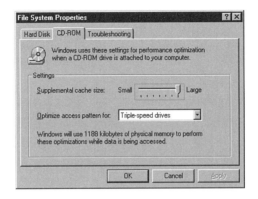

If you must rely on real mode drivers and MSCDEX, you can use the real mode SmartDrive to cache the CD-ROM. There are some drawbacks to using SmartDrive, however:

+ SmartDrive reserves the cache memory out of the conventional memory space.

+ You lose the benefits of the protected mode cache, such as being able to be swapped.

VCACHE

VFAT uses a 32-bit protected mode cache driver called *VCACHE*, which replaces the real mode SmartDrive disk cache that was provided with MS-DOS. VCACHE uses a greatly improved algorithm that results in markedly improved performance versus SmartDrive.

VCACHE allocates its memory dynamically, basing the size of the cache on the amount of available RAM instead of requiring a set amount of RAM be set aside, as was the case with SmartDrive. VCACHE memory is not pageable because paging disk cache contents would be counterproductive.

Understanding Long File Name Support

In MS-DOS, file names could not exceed eight characters, plus a single three-character file extension. The file name is separated from the extension by a period (.), giving rise to the name "8.3 names" for this form of file name.

Windows 95 breaks free of the limitations of the 8.3 names, and allows you to create files with names that are up to 255 characters in length, and that can contain more than one period or even spaces.

Where Long File Names are Supported

Long file names are the native format for Windows 95, and they are supported in all 32-bit applications. Some 16-bit applications that use Windows Common Dialogs also can support long file names.

Shortname Algorithm

Because Windows 95 supports applications that expect 8.3 format names, Windows 95 automatically generates an 8.3 alias name, or *shortname*, for every long file name.

Generating a Shortname

The shortname is generated using a simple algorithm:

1. Any special characters \ : * ? " < > | and spaces are removed.
2. The first six remaining characters are taken, a ~ is added, and a number (1–9) is added. If all of these exist, the first five letters are taken, and a ~ and number starting from 10-99 is added.
3. The extension is the first three legal characters following the last period. If there is no period, there is no extension.

Key Concept

Long file names are not case-sensitive, although they do preserve the case of characters.

8.3 shortnames are neither case-sensitive nor do they preserve the case of characters.

Long file names are preserved on floppy disks.

Ch

7

Traps and Pitfalls

MS-DOS applications, or 16-bit Windows applications running under Windows 3.x, that are not long file name–aware can lose the long file name if they are used to changing the name of the file.

Other traps and pitfalls include:

+ Automatic adding of extension by application
+ Backup tools designed prior to Windows 95

Automatic Adding of Extension by Applications

Most Windows 95 applications add an extension to file names to indicate the type of the file. You should not assume that any particular extension is available for your use. In addition, you should not attempt to use the file extension for other purposes; use long file names instead.

> **Caution**
> Using the wrong extension may prevent a Windows 95 application from being able to open a file, or may result in the wrong application being associated with the file.

Backup Tools

Most backup tools designed prior to Windows 95 do not preserve long file names. If you must use one of these tools, you can back up the long file names to a file with the Lfnbk.exe utility found on the Windows 95 CD-ROM.

Disk Utilities

Do not use disk utilities that were not designed for use with Windows 95 on a disk with long file names on it. The method used to store long file names confuses the disk utility, causing the names to be lost. (Long file names look like extra disk volume labels to these utilities.)

Tuning the File System

Figure 7.2 shows the Hard Disk page of the File System Properties dialog box. You can select the Typical role of this computer. There are three possible roles:

- *Desktop computer.* Smaller disk cache, more RAM for programs.
- *Mobile or docking system.* Larger cache size to reduce power needed to access the hard drive.
- *Network server.* Largest cache size, less RAM for programs.

FIG. 7.2 ⇒
Configuring the
Hard Disk cache.

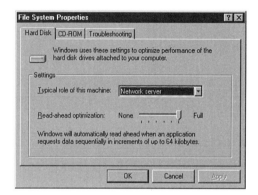

Tip

On a computer with 16M or more RAM, choose Network server even if it is a client workstation.

The Read-ahead optimization setting should be left on Full unless you need to conserve RAM, or the machine is specialized to a purpose where sequential reads do not normally occur.

Using Disk Compression

Disk compression can be used to decrease the amount of space that data takes up on a disk. There are two types of disk compression—real-time and delayed. *Delayed disk compression,* such as that available with the

Ch
7

PKZIP utility, compresses and decompresses files when the user requests. In order to use a file that has been delayed compressed, you must manually decompress it.

Real-time disk compression, such as the DriveSpace compression that is included in Windows 95, allows you to compress all of the files on a disk in a way that is transparent to the user and to application programs.

There are several different disk compression algorithms. Two of the most significant ones replace redundant data with a smaller "token," and consolidate disk free space by storing files on a sector basis, rather than the larger granularity of the normal cluster basis.

A *compressed drive* appears to be a larger drive to the operating system. In reality, it is a large file on the uncompressed disk (called the *host drive*) that contains the compressed files. This large file is called a *Compressed Volume File (CVF)*.

Using DriveSpace

Windows 95 supports both Microsoft and third-party compression software. Microsoft DriveSpace is included with Windows 95, and is implemented as a 32-bit protected mode layer contained within two VxDs: Mrci2.vxd and Drvspacx.vxd.

You can use the DriveSpace utility contained in the System Tools folder to create and manage compressed drives.

Taking the Disc Test

 If you have read and understood the material in the chapter, you are ready to test your knowledge. Insert the CD-ROM that comes with this book and run the self-test software as described in Appendix I, "Using the CD-ROM."

Chapter Prerequisite

Before reading this chapter, you should understand the Windows 95 System Architecture (see Chapter 5, "Windows 95 Architecture Overview"), including the Windows 95 internal messaging model, and how Windows 95 supports applications.

Threads and Processes

This chapter covers processes, threads, and scheduling. Terms and concepts covered include:

- **Cooperative multitasking**
- **Critical section**
- **Mutex**
- **Preemptive multitasking**
- **Priority**
- **Process**
- **Scheduler**
- **Semaphore**
- **Synchronization object**
- **Thread**
- **Win16Mutex**

Understanding Process versus Thread

A *process* is the virtual address space, code, data, and other operating system resources, such as files, pipes, and synchronization objects that make up an executing application. In addition to resources, a process contains at least one thread that executes the process's code.

A *thread* is the basic entity to which the operating system allocates CPU time. A thread can execute any part of the application's code, including a part currently being executed by another thread (reentrancy). Threads cannot own resources; instead, they use the resources of the process they belong to.

Tip

You must understand the difference between a process and a thread in order to understand how Windows looks at and supports running applications.

Multitasking

Multitasking refers to the ability of a computer to run more than one program simultaneously. Windows is a multitasking environment, while MS-DOS is called a single-tasking environment because it can support only one running program at a time.

Windows 95 is designed to run on a computer that has a single processor. In order to create the illusion that multiple applications are running simultaneously, Windows 95 switches the processor among the active tasks so quickly that it appears to the user that all of the tasks are executing simultaneously.

Multitasking also results in a more efficient use of the computer, because the time that a single-tasking system wastes waiting for slow I/O devices and user input can be used instead to run another task that doesn't need input or output (I/O) at that particular moment.

Preemptive

One of the most significant advantages of using a 32-bit Windows application is that Windows 95 uses *preemptive multitasking* for Win32-based applications. With preemptive multitasking, the operating system divides time up into slices (in Windows 95, each slice is about 20 milli-seconds) and proportions the time slices among the running applications. The operating system can actually interrupt a running application when its time slice is up.

Because of preemptive multitasking, 32-bit Windows applications do not have to explicitly yield time to other running applications in order for multitasking to work properly. In addition, 32-bit Windows applications can take advantage of a mechanism called *multithreading*, which allows an application to have multiple simultaneous paths of execution (called *threads*).

By breaking up the processing associated with an application into multiple threads, throughput and responsiveness are enhanced. For example, Microsoft Word for Windows 95 is a multithreaded application. In addition to threads that handle tasks like reading the user's input, Word has a thread that looks at the words the user has typed, in the background, and performs automatic spell-checking, without impacting the user's perception of a smoothly operating word processor.

Cooperative

Previous versions of Windows used a mechanism known as *cooperative multitasking*. With cooperative multitasking, applications are required to relinquish control to the operating system either by explicitly yielding control, or when the application checks the message queue.

In a cooperative multitasking system, an application can "hog" CPU time by not yielding control, and not checking the message queue periodically.

Windows 95 cooperatively multitasks 16-bit Windows applications for compatibility reasons by assigning a single thread to each 16-bit application, and then allowing only one 16-bit thread to become eligible to run (see "Win16Mutex" later in the chapter). The net effect is that the 16-bit Windows applications cooperatively multitask between each other, and the group of running 16-bit Windows applications is preemptively multitasked with the rest of the currently active threads.

Thread Priorities

Every thread in a Windows 95 system has a priority associated with it. The thread priority is used by the schedulers to determine what thread to allow to run next. Thread priority levels can range between 0 and 31 (lowest priority to highest).

The *base priority* for the threads in a process is set by the application's developer. Threads start out with their priority set to the base priority, and can receive priority boosts from the schedulers.

Thread Scheduling

In the Windows 95 environment, each thread is in one of several states at any given point in time. The state that a thread is in changes throughout the lifetime of the thread. The most important states that a thread can be in are

+ *Ready.* A thread in the Ready state may be scheduled for execution the next time the scheduler decides what threads should be executed. Which thread actually gets executed first depends on the thread's priority.

+ *Waiting.* A waiting thread cannot execute at this time because it is waiting for some event to occur, such as I/O, a message, or if the thread is blocked waiting for a synchronization object to become unlocked.

+ *Running.* Only one thread can be running at any one time.

The Virtual Memory Manager (VMM) schedules threads based on a 32-level priority mechanism. Priority values range between 0 and 31 for compatibility with Windows NT. At any given time, the thread that is ready and has the highest priority is running. A thread with the priority of 31 will be run before any other thread; a thread with the priority of zero will run only if no other threads are ready.

The priority value range is divided into two sections: 0–15 are reserved for variable-priority threads, and 16–31 are for so-called *realtime* threads, which have a fixed priority.

Within the VMM are two schedulers: the Primary scheduler and the Secondary (or time-slice) scheduler.

Primary Scheduler

The Primary scheduler is responsible for making sure that the highest-priority thread is running. Notice that the highest-priority thread does not necessarily (or usually) have a value of 31. If there is a thread with a priority of 10 and there are no other threads with a higher value, then 10 is the highest priority, and it will be the running thread until the next time priorities are evaluated.

Secondary Scheduler

The Secondary scheduler is responsible for dynamically adjusting thread priorities so that multitasking happens in a fair manner, ensuring that no thread hogs the CPU.

Dynamic Priority Adjustment

The Primary scheduler always selects the highest-priority thread to run after examining all threads in the system. If two threads have the same priority level, the one in the foreground or associated with the window that has focus gets a priority boost.

Any thread with a priority lower than the highest value is not even considered for execution. The primary scheduler ignores the lower priority threads during the current time slice.

To prevent higher-priority threads from hogging the CPU, the secondary (or time-slice) scheduler periodically raises the priority of ready threads that have not run recently, ensuring that all threads eventually get a chance to run.

The System VM supports multiple threads. If the System VM contains multiple ready threads with equal priorities, it schedules among them in a round-robin fashion to ensure fairness. If a thread fails to consume all of its time slice, the scheduler will give the remainder of the time slice to the next equal-priority thread.

Synchronization

Windows 95 uses *synchronization objects* to synchronize operations between multiple threads, whether in the same process or multiple processes. Synchronization objects are used to:

+ Protect a resource, such as a section of non-reentrant code, from being used by more than one thread at time.

+ Signal another thread that some event, such as the completion of a calculation, has occurred.

The Win32 API (the application programming interface used by 32-bit Windows applications and the Windows 95 system) defines four types of synchronization objects:

+ *Event.* An event object provides notification to one or more waiting threads that an event has occurred.

+ *Semaphore.* A semaphore, like the device used on railroads to protect sections of track from being used by more than one train, is designed to limit how many threads can access a resource. Windows 95 semaphores actually maintain a count between 0 (unused) and a maximum value set by the program that owns the semaphore.

+ *Mutex.* A mutex is similar to a semaphore, but can be owned by only one thread at a time. It provides exclusive access to a shared resource. The word *mutex* is derived from the words *MUTually EXclusive*.

+ *Critical Section.* A critical section is similar to a mutex, except that the object protected by a critical section can only be used by the threads of a single process.

Programs can make two types of requests involving a resource that is protected by synchronization objects:

+ *Synchronous.* A program making a synchronous request will be blocked from further execution until the request completes.

+ *Asynchronous.* A program making an asynchronous request will be allowed to continue executing even though that request has not completed.

Priority Inheritance Boosting

Priority inheritance boosting is a process used to resolve the problem that occurs when a lower-priority thread is using a critical system resource that is needed by a higher-priority thread.

Initially, the higher-priority thread will block while waiting for the resource. The lower-priority thread will be passed over by the scheduler, resulting in a stalemate.

The secondary scheduler will increase the priority of the lower priority thread until it is equal to or greater than that of the blocked thread. This enables the lower-priority thread to run so that it can finish using the resource.

Win16Mutex

As seen in Chapter 5, large parts of the GDI and User system core components are made up of 16-bit code. This 16-bit code is non-reentrant (it is designed to be executed by only one thread at a time).

The Win16Mutex is a special synchronization object in Windows 95 that protects these non-reentrant sections of 16-bit system code. A mutex, as mentioned above, is an exclusive semaphore, which means that only one program can control the Win16Mutex at a time.

Either a 32-bit or 16-bit program can control the Win16Mutex, because both types of programs make calls to system functions that are implemented as 16-bit code, such as the GDI code.

32-Bit Windows Process and the Win16Mutex

If the system only has 32-bit Windows processes running on it, then the Win16Mutex is not a significant issue. The 16-bit APIs all execute very rapidly—so fast, in fact, that the user will see no impact of the mutex at all. When a 32-bit application is executing its own 32-bit code or 32-bit system code, the mutex is not used.

16-Bit Windows Processes and the Win16Mutex

In order for a 16-bit Windows program to run, it must control the Win16Mutex. This means that while a 16-bit Windows application is running, no other 16-bit program can run, and any 32-bit program that needs access to the Win16Mutex will be blocked.

Imagine a railroad that has one track. Obviously, two trains cannot share the same track, and so the railroad uses a signal device to tell oncoming trains that the track section is in use. When an oncoming train sees the signal, it is moved to another track, where it sits and waits for the train that's using the main track to cross.

Once the train finishes using the track, the signal is cleared and the second train is permitted to run over the track. Of course, the signal is set when the second train is using the track, too.

Windows 95 automatically releases the Win16Mutex when the 16-bit Windows application performs a `GetMessage()`, `PeekMessage()`, or `Yield()` system function call. The net result is that if only 16-bit

Windows applications are running on the system, then the system's apparent multitasking behavior will be identical to Windows 3.1.

Both 16-Bit and 32-Bit Windows Processes and the Win16Mutex

If a combination of 32-bit and 16-bit Windows applications are running on the system simultaneously, problems can arise when a 16-bit application does not check its message queue often enough. Since the Win16Mutex is released when the application performs a GetMessage or PeekMessage call (or yields), an application that does not check for messages also does not release the Win16Mutex.

When this occurs, all 32-bit Windows applications are blocked from calling APIs that are implemented in the 16-bit portions of User or GDI. Other 32-bit Windows applications that do not normally make calls into User or GDI—for example, the networking server and print spooler—continue to run, while threads that depend upon these portions of the system block. Typically, this means that system elements such as screen redraws do not update.

When the user performs a local restart (by pressing Ctrl+Alt+Delete) and terminates the hung application, the mutex is released by the system and behavior returns to normal. If Windows 95 detects a problem, such as the crash of a 16-bit Windows application, it displays an error message. When the user closes the error box, the mutex is released.

Taking the Disc Test

If you have read and understood the material in the chapter, you are ready to test your knowledge. Insert the CD-ROM that comes with this book and run the self-test software as described in Appendix I, "Using the CD-ROM."

Chapter Prerequisite

Before reading this chapter, you should understand the Windows 95 System Architecture (see Chapter 5, "Windows 95 Architecture Overview"), including the Intel memory protection architecture.

Understanding Memory

This chapter covers memory. Terms and concepts covered include:

- Conventional memory
- Expanded memory (EMS)
- Extended memory (XMS)
- Linear addressing
- Page
- Physical memory
- Segment
- Swap file
- Virtual memory

Understanding Memory Configuration

Computer memory falls into several classifications, including *conventional*, *extended*, and *expanded* memory. While you can avoid the problems and configuration challenges traditionally associated with memory by using only 32-bit Windows applications, the Microsoft Certified Professional must be able to troubleshoot and configure all types of applications under Windows 95 and thus must understand the nuances of memory configuration.

The reasons for the various types of memory are largely historical. Back in the early 1980s when IBM introduced its first microcomputer—the IBM PC—most microcomputers had 64K or less of RAM. The first IBM PCs were delivered with only 16K of RAM, with sockets on the motherboard that could support only a maximum of 64K.

There was an expansion card available from IBM that would allow you to increase the computer's memory up to a maximum of 512K, and IBM engineers allowed for (and third-party companies supplied) RAM capacity of up to an amazing 640K.

Of course, as we know today, software drives hardware development, and pretty soon software developers were finding 640K of RAM quite limiting. In fact, this limit soon became known as the *640K Barrier*.

The 640K barrier was partly due to IBM's decision to reserve 384K of RAM in case add-in I/O adapters required space to map their ROM memory into, and partly due to Intel's design of the 8086 and 8088 CPUs. The 8086 and 8088 CPUs differed in the way that they talked to memory—both were identical inside the chip, but the 8086 talked 16 bits to the memory bus while the 8088 was an 8-bit chip on the outside, and had to make two 8-bit accesses every time it wanted to do something.

The 8086 CPU was designed with a 1,024K (1 megabyte, or 1M) limit, due to the design of its addressing bus, which could handle up to 20 bits (1M) of addressing information. The number of bits that a bus can handle, which physically relates to the number of connections that make up the bus, is referred to as the *bus width*.

A 20-bit-wide address bus allows for addresses ranging between 00000H and FFFFFH (0 and 1,048,575 decimal, or 1M). IBM reserved the upper 384K of addresses for ROM memory on expansion adapters, leaving addresses 0 to 640K available.

Intel's next processor, the 80186, was not used in PCs.

The next processor to be used in PCs was the Intel 80286. The 286, as it is generally known, had a 24-bit wide address bus, which allowed for as much as 16M of RAM. Later processors—including the 80386, 80486, and Pentium processors—can access up to four gigabytes (4G) of addresses with their 32-bit address buses.

When running MS-DOS, however, all of these advanced processors must use a mode that emulates the original 8086 processor, called *real mode*. When the processor is running in a mode that allows it to access all available memory, it must run in *protected mode*.

The 8086 and 286 processors divide addressable memory into *segments*. Segments are treated differently in protected mode and real mode. The following discussion applies only to real mode and to the 386 and 486 processors' virtual 8086 mode.

Since the 8086 and 286 processors were 16-bit processors with 16-bit registers, all addressing had to fit into 16-bit quantities. The processors used two registers to hold the address of the memory item being used: one to hold the segment address, and the other to hold the offset in the segment that the particular address occupied.

Addresses in this form are usually expressed in notation as follows, with the segment address listed first, separated from the offset by a colon, for example, CFFF:A3F1. Each segment, by definition, begins on a boundary whose address is evenly divisible by 16 (called a *paragraph boundary*).

The segmented form of an address can be converted to a physical address by shifting the segment address to the left by four bits, and then adding in the offset. A side effect of this process is the fact that several segmented addresses could actually refer to the same place in physical memory.

Ch
9

The use of this particular fact by a leading spreadsheet application for the original IBM PC is one of the major reasons that MS-DOS 3.0 could not run in protected mode. Figure 9.1 shows the PC memory space.

For example:

CFFF:A3F1	**CF23:B1B1**
CFFF0	CF230
+0A3F1	+0B1B1
DA3E1	DA3E1

FIG. 9.1 ⇒

The PC Memory Space.

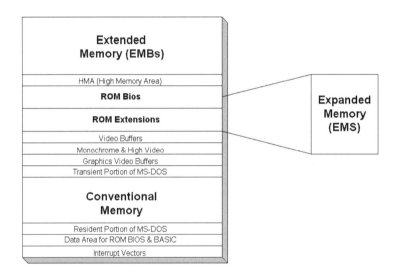

Conventional memory refers to memory that is located below A0000H, and is used for MS-DOS applications. The bottom portion (lowest numbered addresses) is used for MS-DOS, as a data area for ROM BIOS routines, and hardware interrupt vectors. MS-DOS device drivers also occupy part of the conventional memory space, reducing the amount of memory available for other applications.

Upper memory is memory located in the Upper Memory Area, the 384K region located between A0000H (640K) and the 1M line. As previously mentioned, originally this area was reserved by IBM for use by I/O adapters and, in fact, a large chunk of it is mapped to video card video frame buffers.

Unused regions within this area are called *Upper Memory Blocks (UMBs)*, and can be used by programs on computers with 386 or higher processors. UMBs can be used to store MS-DOS device drivers to increase the space available for MS-DOS applications.

The *high memory area (HMA)* is a region between the 1M mark and 1088K. It occupies 16 bytes less than 64K of memory, and is generally reserved for use by a single application or utility. The existence of the HMA is due to a side effect of the 286 or higher processor running in real mode—using FFFF as a segment register generates an address in this area. On an 8086, the result is to "wrap around" to the beginning of memory. This trick of accessing the HMA depends upon the A20 address line being available on the processor, and the software that makes the HMA available is often referred to as an "A20 handler."

Extended memory is the region above the HMA, through the end of physical memory. MS-DOS was not able to directly access extended memory, so a specification called the *eXtended Memory Specification (XMS)* was created to define a way for MS-DOS applications to access this memory, along with the Upper Memory Area, and the HMA.

Expanded memory (EMS) is outside of the normal address range. It was originally designed as a solution to fitting large spreadsheets into memory when the 640K barrier was unbreakable. Expanded memory is defined by the Lotus/Intel/Microsoft Expanded Memory Specification, and originally used a combination of software and hardware. On 386 and higher processors, EMS is created using virtual memory.

EMS depends upon a technique called *bank-switching*, in which regions of physical memory are made available by swapping it in and out of an area of address space, called the *page frame*. This technique allows the use of large amounts of memory (up to 32M) one 64K piece at a time.

Ch

9

Upper Memory

The upper memory area is often used for UMBs. In addition, the upper memory area addresses are one of the critical system resources that are managed by Plug and Play (see Chapter 6, "Plug and Play").

Memory between A0000H and C0000H is usually used for video memory, and some video adapters may require more. Following the video buffer area is the ROM Extension area, where adapter cards can load their ROM memory. This area may also be used to provide an EMS page frame, if one is required.

At the top of the Upper Memory Area is the System ROM, also known as the ROM BIOS. The System ROM is usually 64K in length, occupying segments F000-FFFF, although some systems use 128K, starting at E000.

Memory Drivers

A driver called Himem.sys is responsible for managing extended memory. It converts the first 64K of extended memory into the HMA, and makes the rest of memory available via the XMS specification.

If you do not explicitly load Himem.sys in your computer's Config.sys file, Windows 95 automatically loads it.

A driver called Emm386.exe is used to create Upper Memory Blocks and Expanded Memory from XMS memory. If you do not explicitly load it in your computer's Config.sys file, Windows 95 automatically loads it.

Pages versus Segments

Like Windows NT, Windows 95 uses a demand-paged virtual memory system. It creates a flat, linear address space that programs can access with 32-bit addresses.

Key Concept

Every 32-bit Windows application is allocated its own virtual address space of 2G. In addition to this private 2G space, a shared address space of 2G is allocated to the process as the upper half of the process's address space.

The virtual address space is divided into 4K pieces called *pages*. The term *demand-paged* refers to a method that allows applications' code and data to be larger than physical memory. In a demand-paged system, a process's code and data will be moved between physical memory and a temporary file on disk. When the information in a page is needed by the process, the page is moved, or *swapped*, back into physical memory.

The Windows 95 Memory Manager is responsible for mapping the virtual addresses from the process's address space to pages in the computer's physical memory. This enables the efficient use of memory because the physical organization of memory does not have to match any process's view of it. It also ensures that any running thread can only access its process's memory by hiding other processes' memory from it (see fig. 9.2).

FIG. 9.2 ⇒
Virtual memory is mapped into physical memory pages.

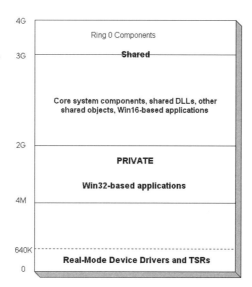

Ch
9

As mentioned earlier, the 80286 and 8086 processors divided memory into 64K segments. In the 80286's protected mode (and in the 386 and higher processors' 16-bit protected mode), the Intel processor memory manager uses segments differently than in real mode. In protected mode, a segment is actually a pointer to a data structure that tells the processor where in physical memory the segment is located. In effect, this breaks physical memory up into 64K segments, which incur a performance penalty when swapping, versus the smaller 4K pages used in the 32-bit protected mode that Windows 95 runs in.

In addition, 16-bit protected mode programs still must access memory using the segmented address forms, meaning that a further performance penalty exists if the application or operating system (such as Windows 3.1) must use information that spans segments.

By using the 32-bit capability of the 386 and higher processors, Windows 95 supports a flat, linear memory model for 32-bit Windows applications and its own operating system functions. This *linear addressing* method removes the performance penalties associated with segments (by reducing the overhead a program incurs while performing segment arithmetic), while simultaneously simplifying application development.

In the linear addressing model, Windows 95 permits use of the full 4G of addressable memory space by 32-bit operating system components and 32-bit Windows applications. In addition, each 32-bit Windows application can access up to 2G of private, addressable memory space, which should be enough to support any conceivable desktop application.

Virtual Memory

Virtual memory refers to the illusion created by an operating system that simplifies an application's view of memory. Applications access virtual memory as though it was physical memory; they are unaware of how the operating system is actually ordering physical memory, or even whether one of their segments is residing in the swap file or in physical memory.

In a virtual memory system design, applications use *virtual addresses* to access memory, not physical addresses. Whenever an application attempts to access memory, the hardware memory manager and operating system transparently translate the virtual address into the actual physical address where the data resides.

The operating system translates virtual addresses to physical addresses so it has control over where code and data are stored. This means that not only can the operating system place code and data in physical memory wherever it wants to, but it also means that it can store code and data outside of the physical memory.

While a computer's processor can only access code and data that is actually present in physical memory, few computers have large amounts of physical memory (RAM) because of the relatively high cost of RAM. Most modern multitasking operating systems compensate for this by extending their virtual memory systems to include a method that allows the operating system to use disk space to store code and data when the processor does not need to access them.

The process of moving pages to and from a swap file is called *swapping* or *paging*, and is done to increase the amount of virtual memory available to applications. Swapping occurs without the knowledge of applications. To the application, it appears as though the computer has more physical memory than is installed.

Thanks to the design of the Intel processor, if an application attempts to access a page of code or data that has been swapped to disk, the Windows 95 virtual memory manager (VMM) receives control. The VMM locates the page in the disk file, and loads it into a free page in physical memory. If a free page in physical memory is not available, the VMM first swaps a page out to disk, and then loads the required page into the now-free page in RAM.

The application is never aware that its code or data was ever swapped to disk.

Virtual Memory Manager

The Windows 95 Virtual Memory Manager is a Ring 0 service provided by the Windows 95 Kernel. It handles memory allocation, paging, and manages virtual memory.

Virtual Address Spaces

Every Windows 95 process is allocated a unique virtual address space, which is a set of addresses available for the process's threads to use. In Windows 95, the virtual address space appears to be 4G in size, with the bottom 2G available to the process for its storage, and the upper 2G a shared space containing operating system components (see fig. 9.3).

FIG. 9.3 ⇒
Every process has a 4G virtual address space.

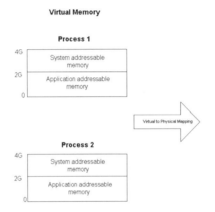

0–4M MS-DOS Compatibility Arena

The bottom 4M, from the base of memory to 4M, is reserved for real-mode device drivers, MS-DOS Terminate-and-Stay-Resident (TSR) components, and 16-bit applications.

The currently active Virtual Machine is mapped into the first megabyte. The remaining 3M is usually empty, but can contain MS-DOS device drivers.

32-bit Windows applications cannot access this arena for any purpose.

4M–2G 32-Bit Windows Applications (Private Arena)

Above the 4M line to the 2G line is the private address space for each 32-bit Windows application. Every 32-bit Widows application process receives its own address space, separate from all other processes' memory.

The process's code, data, and any dynamically allocated memory all exist in its private address space. In addition, all dynamic link libraries (DLLs) loaded by the process, with the exception of the three system shared DLLs (User32.dll, Gdi32.dll and Kernel32.dll) are loaded into the process's private address space.

> **Note** Other DLLs that are part of Windows 95, such as Shell32.dll and Comdlg32.dll, are not system shared DLLs and thus are mapped into the process's private address space. ■

2–3G DLLs and Shared Objects (Shared Arena)

Between 2G and 3G, Windows 95 maps core system components, shared dynamic link libraries (DLLs), and 16-bit Windows applications. These components are mapped identically into every process's address space.

16-bit Windows applications and 16-bit DLLs (both system and application DLLs) all occupy memory allocated from the 16-bit global heap, which resides in this arena. The three 32-bit shared system DLLs (User32.dll, Gdi32.dll, and Kernel32.dll) all occupy memory in this arena.

Both 32-bit and 16-bit Windows applications can read and write to addresses in this arena. They cannot, however, take memory from this address space freely. 16-bit applications and DLLs allocate memory from the 16-bit global heap. When it needs to grow, Krnl386.exe will get memory from the shared arena to add to it.

32-bit Windows applications are not permitted to allocate memory directly from the shared arena. They do, however, always use it for mapping views of file mappings—unlike Windows NT, which maps views of file mappings in the private address space.

Ch
9

The DOS Protected Mode Interface (DPMI) is a specification used by some MS-DOS applications to access more memory than is available in a VM. The DPMI server's memory pool is located in the shared arena.

32-bit Windows applications can pass a buffer to a VxD in the shared arena. This technique is sometimes used for communication between applications and device drivers.

3–4G Reserved System Arena

The Ring 0 components are mapped into the address space greater than 3G. The Ring 0 components include the code and data of the virtual machine manager, DOS extender, DPMI server, and virtual device drivers.

This arena is not addressable by Ring 3 code, such as 32-bit, 16-bit, and MS-DOS applications and DLLs.

Swap Files

Windows 3.1 also provided virtual memory to applications, and used a swap file. However, Windows 3.x required users to choose from an often confusing variety of configuration options and choices for setting up a swap file. For example, they had to choose between a temporary or a permanent swap file, how much disk space to allocate to the swap file, and whether 32-bit disk access should be used to access the swap file.

Windows 3.1 temporary swap files did not need to occupy contiguous disk space, and Windows 3.1 would allocate hard disk space dynamically when Windows was started, and free up the disk space when it terminated. On the other hand, a permanent swap file provided the best performance, but it had to be pre-allocated from contiguous disk space on an uncompressed disk volume.

The Windows 95 swap file implementation greatly simplifies the user's configuration task and, because of improved access and algorithms, combines the best features of both a temporary and permanent swap file. It is dynamic, and shrinks or grows according to the needs of the system. In addition, it can occupy fragmented regions of the hard disk, and can even be located on a compressed disk volume.

In most cases, the Windows 95 default for virtual memory settings of Let Windows Manage my virtual memory settings will result in an optimal swap file configuration (see fig. 9.4). However, if the computer has more than one hard disk, or disk space is at a premium, you can specify your own settings.

FIG. 9.4 ⇒

Virtual memory settings.

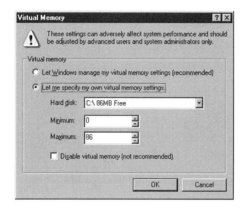

Tip

If your computer has more than one hard disk, and one is faster than the other, place the swap file on the faster disk.

The best way to ensure good swap file performance is to make sure that the disk that contains the swap file has plenty of free disk space.

Windows 95 can use a Windows 3.1 permanent swap file if one is present on the disk. If it does, the file cannot shrink below the size set for it in Windows 3.1.

If your disk is compressed, and the compressed drive is controlled by a protected mode driver, such as Drvspace.vxd, then the swap file can reside on the compressed drive. DriveSpace will mark the swap file as uncompressable and place it as the last file in the volume.

If the computer is running a shared version of Windows 95 from a file server (see Chapter 23, "Server-Based Setup of Windows 95"), the swap file will be placed in the computer's machine directory. If the computer boots from a floppy disk, or via remote booting, the machine directory is on the network. If the computer is started from a local hard disk, the swap file can be stored in the machine directory on the local hard disk.

> **Caution**
>
> Do not completely disable virtual memory unless instructed to do so by a Microsoft technical support representative. Completely disabling virtual memory can cause the computer to stop operating.

To adjust the virtual memory swap file:

1. From the System option in Control Panel, click the Performance tab.

2. Click the Virtual Memory button. The dialog box shown in figure 9.4 opens.

3. To choose a different hard disk or set a maximum or minimum size, click the Let me specify my own virtual memory settings option.

Setting the maximum swap file size to the amount of free space on a drive causes Windows 95 to assume that it can always use any disk space that becomes free. This means that if more disk space becomes available, the swap file could expand to use up that disk space. To impose a limit on the swap file size, you must choose a limit that is less than the current maximum.

Taking the Disc Test

 If you have read and understood the material in the chapter, you are ready to test your knowledge. Insert the CD-ROM that comes with this book and run the self-test software as described in Appendix I, "Using the CD-ROM."

Chapter Prerequisite

Before reading this chapter, you should understand the Windows 95 System Architecture (see Chapter 5, "Windows 95 Architecture Overview"), and be familiar with the configuration of display hardware under previous versions of Windows.

Understanding Windows 95 Video Display

Windows 95 applications communicate with the computer's user through graphics and text placed in windows on the computer's video display monitor. Nothing has as strong an impact on the user's impressions of the system as a whole as the display subsystem.

Terms and concepts covered in this chapter include:

- **Color depth**
- **Device independent bitmap (DIB)**
- **Display**
- **Display driver**
- **Monitor**
- **Resolution**
- **VESA**
- **VGA fallback**

Display Drivers

Windows 95 resolves many of the problems that were caused by the design and implementation of Windows 3.1 display drivers, such as GPF errors caused by buggy manufacturer-written drivers. At the same time, it provides greatly enhanced display functionality while simplifying configuration for the user.

The Windows 95 display driver architecture is based on a minidriver approach, similar to the approach used with printer drivers starting with Windows 3.1. With this approach, more common code is used for the display drivers, with the result of better support for more types of display adapters, with stable and reliable drivers.

Windows 95 Setup automatically detects the computer's display adapter, and installs the appropriate display driver.

The minidriver for the display adapter uses the Windows 95 universal display driver, called the *device-independent bitmap (DIB) engine*. A *bitmap* is the collection of pixel information that makes up an image—for example, a BMP file. In the past, bitmaps were tied to a particular device's characteristics; for example, a bitmap intended for a 256-color display could not be displayed on a 16-color display. A device-independent bitmap contains information that allows it to be displayed on any supported display adapter. The Windows 95 DIB engine handles all in-memory graphics operations (such as copying a bitmap from one section of memory to another) and on-screen operations that are not handled by accelerator hardware on the video adapter. The DIB engine itself consists of high-performance 32-bit code that provides fast drawing on high-resolution and frame-buffer-based display adapters.

By moving the DIB code into a universal driver, the hardware developer only has to write drivers for the hardware-specific functions, and it makes it possible to add hardware acceleration features in an incremental fashion.

Microsoft worked in cooperation with the major manufactures of display adapters and controllers when developing the display drivers included with Windows 95. This high level of support by the hardware manufacturers resulted in highly optimized drivers that take advantage of display adapters' acceleration functions to improve performance.

If you made the wrong display driver choice when configuring Windows 3.x, the result was usually a locked-up computer. Otherwise, it may have been a display screen that was unreadable, requiring you to cold boot the computer, with the accompanying possible loss of information.

Key Concept

Windows 95 includes a mechanism called *VGA fallback* that ensures that an incompatible display driver cannot prevent you from accessing the system. When a Windows 95 display driver fails to load or initialize, Windows 95 uses the generic VGA display driver automatically.

Note   You must have a line reading

```
*DisplayFallback=0
```

in the [boot] section of your computer's System.ini file in order for automatic use of the generic VGA display driver to occur. ▧

Ch
10

Display Resolutions and Color Depth

Display resolution is expressed in terms of the number of displayable pixels horizontally by vertically; for example, 1,024 × 768 means that the display mode supports 1,024 pixels horizontally and 768 pixels vertically.

The number of colors that can be displayed simultaneously, called the *color depth,* depends upon the number of bits that are used to represent the color of each pixel in video memory. This measurement is called *bits per pixel*, abbreviated *bpp*. Table 10.1 shows the relationship between bits per pixel and color depth.

Table 10.1 Relationship between Bits Per Pixel and Color Depth

Color Depth	Bits Per Pixel
Monochrome (not supported by Windows 95)	1
16 colors	4
256 colors	8
32,767 colors (32K)	15
65,535 colors (64K)	16
16.7 million colors	24
16.7 million colors	32

Display Subsystem Architecture

The Windows 95 display subsystem is modular, consisting of these major components: display minidriver, DIB Engine, Vflatd.vxd, and VDD.

Display Minidriver

The minidriver is a hardware-specific dynamic link library (DLL) written by the hardware manufacturer. The minidriver uses the DIB engine for drawing functions, contains only hardware-specific code that accesses the display adapter, and redirects GDI calls to the DIB engine.

DIB Engine

The DIB engine is a generic display driver implemented as a dynamic link library (Dibeng.dll), which contains most of the functions that translate GDI commands into drawings.

Vflatd.vxd

Vflatd.vxd virtualizes display frame buffers larger than 64K. The *frame buffer* is the area of RAM that represents the display image on the adapter card. By virtualizing the buffer, Windows 95 handles all the memory management needed to access the buffer RAM on the adapter card.

A display driver can handle access to video memory in one of two ways—the flat memory model and the flat frame buffer model. Windows drivers use the *flat frame buffer model*, in which an area of RAM is used as a buffer to hold a representation of what is displayed on the monitor. The size of this buffer depends on the particular display adapter's requirement and the resolution/color depth being used. The buffer is used to compensate for the fact that, while display adapters can use several megabytes of onboard memory to represent the display, they are only assigned a small window in the computer's address space to access that memory. 16-bit versions of Windows provided a 64K frame buffer to drivers that needed one, but as video resolutions and color depths increased, the 64K limit required the display driver to map bytes from the larger buffer needed by the driver into the buffer supplied by the system.

The Windows 95 virtual flat frame buffer device driver enables video drivers to access a large logical flat frame buffer. The size of the buffer is specified by the display minidriver and can be up to 4M in size.

Vflatd.vxd handles all memory management issues, enabling the hardware developer to write the minidriver without having to handle video memory management.

VDD

VDD is used by the mini-VDD to virtualize the video hardware. It is called by the grabber whenever an MS-DOS virtual machine needs to access the video display. (The *grabber* is the driver that intercepts video accesses made by MS-DOS applications).

Mini-VDD

The mini-VDD is a hardware-specific VxD supplied by the hardware developer that virtualizes the video hardware, enabling more than one virtual machine to share the same display. The mini-VDD helps to manage the display hardware for the VDD. Virtualization of ports, display modes, and text and graphics output is handled by the VDD, with the mini-VDD handling interactions with the hardware that the VDD cannot perform.

The mini-VDD does not have an API, meaning that applications cannot call the mini-VDD directly. Applications must call the VDD, ensuring that programs and display drivers cannot directly access the video hardware, corrupting the display by writing to it without Windows' knowledge.

Examining Subsystem Interactions

The various components of the video subsystem interact differently depending on what type of application is accessing the display, and what mode (full-screen or windowed) the screen is in.

Full-Screen MS-DOS Application

Full-screen MS-DOS applications interact with the video system in the following way:

1. Program output is trapped by the VDD.
2. The VDD calls the mini-VDD to implement any hardware-specific features.
3. The appropriate commands are passed to the display adapter.

Windowed MS-DOS Application

Windowed MS-DOS applications interact with the video system in the following way:

1. Program output is trapped by the VDD.
2. The VDD calls the mini-VDD to implement any hardware-specific features.
3. Output from the VDD is sent to the grabber.

4. The grabber formats the output into GDI commands.

5. The GDI displays the output using the Windows display system, just as though a Windows-based program was being used.

Windows Application

Windows applications (both 16-bit and 32-bit) interact with the video system in the following way:

1. Windows applications make GDI calls when they want to output to the display.

2. GDI sends commands to the display minidriver.

3. The minidriver reroutes the commands to the DIB engine, and possibly writes the image using the virtual flat frame buffer device.

4. The image is placed on the display adapter by the VDD.

Ch
10

Configuring the Display

The Windows 95 display adapter is configured with the Display option in Control Panel. Unlike Windows 3.1, where a different video driver has to be used for each resolution and color depth combination, Windows 95 drivers support all possible combinations for the hardware.

Display Adapter

Figure 10.1 shows the Settings tab of the Display Properties dialog box. At the top of the dialog box is a simulation of what the desktop would look like with the current settings.

The Color palette drop-down list enables you to choose from among all of the color depth choices available for the video card, regardless of resolution. The choices include:

‡ *16 Color.* The base-level support, at 4bpp (bits per pixel).

‡ *256 Color.* The most commonly selected color depth, 8bpp.

FIG. 10.1 ⇒

You configure the display settings with the Display Properties dialog box.

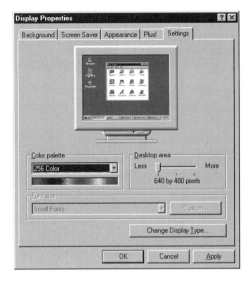

+ *High Color.* Depending on the adapter, High color is either 15bpp or 16bpp.

+ *True Color.* Again, depending on the adapter, True Color is either 24bpp or 32bpp.

The Desktop area slider bar enables you to select the resolution used for the display. The resolution can be changed dynamically under Windows 95 unless a change of driver or color depth is required. In that case, the computer must be restarted.

Clicking the Change Display Type button opens the Change Display Type dialog box (see fig. 10.2).

FIG. 10.2 ⇒

Changing the Display Type.

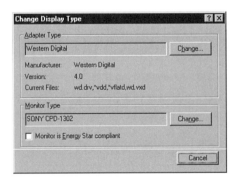

This dialog box shows which drivers are being used, and their version. For example, if *vdd is listed, then a Windows 95 driver is being used.

Monitor Type

In addition to setting the display adapter type, Windows 95 recognizes a monitor type. You should set the monitor type to match your monitor. Windows 95 uses this information to determine which display resolutions to make available to you.

> **Note** Windows 95 does *not* use the monitor type to set the refresh rates for the monitor. You must continue to use the refresh rate utility supplied by the adapter manufacturer. If you do not know the maximum refresh rate for a monitor, always underestimate it to avoid damaging the monitor. ▇

The monitor is usually the single largest consumer of electricity in a computer system. If your monitor supports the Energy-Star specification, Windows 95 can use the energy-saving features of the monitor.

Plug and Play monitors conform to a specification called the VESA Display Data Channel (DDC) specification. A combination of DDC monitor and adapter will enable the display drivers to set refresh rates, and other information automatically, including Image Color Matching (see "Image Color Matching" in Chapter 11).

Taking the Disc Test

If you have read and understood the material in the chapter, you are ready to test your knowledge. Insert the CD-ROM that comes with this book and run the self-test software as described in Appendix I, "Using the CD-ROM."

Ch
10

Understanding Printing

Windows 95 support for printing is an extension of the support provided in Windows 3.1. Improvements include faster spooling of print
jobs, print job handling, and support for Plug and Play printers.

Terms and concepts covered include:

- **Enhanced metafiles (EMF)**
- **Spooler**
- **PostScript**
- **Image Color Matching**
- **Friendly names**
- **Printer configuration**
- **Bidirectional parallel port**
- **Extended Capability Port (ECP)**

Printing Overview

One of the reasons why people started choosing Windows applications in the first place was the device-independent way that Windows 3.x approached printers. Windows 95 printing support builds on this foundation by adding improvements in response to requests from customers and software and hardware vendors:

+ *32-bit architecture.* Many of the printing components in Windows 95 (in particular, the spooler) are fully 32-bit and take advantage of the preemptive multitasking available in Windows 95 to improve performance.

+ *Enhanced metafile (EMF) spooling.* The user gets control of applications back quicker than under Windows 3.1, giving an impression of increased performance.

+ *Support for more printers.* Windows 95 supports over 800 printers out-of-the-box, and can take full advantage of PostScript Level II printers.

+ *MS-DOS application support.* Unlike Windows 3.x, where an MS-DOS application could cause a conflict with the printer, Windows 95 can spool printer output from MS-DOS applications along with the output from Windows applications.

+ *Image Color Matching.* Provides closer matches between color generated on a printer and color displayed on the screen.

+ *Plug and Play.* Installing a new printer is easier, thanks to Plug and Play and user interface improvements.

+ *Deferred printing.* By allowing mobile computer users to "work off line," print jobs can be generated while the computer is undocked, and automatically started when the computer is docked.

+ *Integrated network printing.* Network printing is an extension of the local printing architecture.

This chapter discusses local printing, as well as those areas that are common to local and network printing. For more details on network printing, see Chapter 20, "Network Printing."

Bidirectional Communications

Windows 95 fully supports bidirectional printers. A bidirectional printer can be queried by programs directly, and supplies enhanced status information to Windows 95.

In order to use bidirectional communications with your printer, you must:

- Have a bidirectional printer
- Use an IEEE 1284-compliant printer cable (look for the number 1284 printed or stamped on the cable)
- Configure the computer's port (typically through the BIOS setup routine) to work in a bidirectional (also called *PS/2*) mode. When configured for bidirectional operation, the port can be set (by the driver) into *Nibble mode*, where the 8-bit channel provided by the cabling is split into two 4-bit wide channels: one for data going to the printer, and one for data coming from the printer. (Four bits is called a *nibble*). The normal, or compatibility, mode sends data to the printer along all 8 bits of the cable, a mode also known as *Byte mode*.
- Use a Windows 95 printer driver (such as those listed in table 11.1) that supports bidirectional printing.

Ch
11

Table 11.1 Bidirectional Printers Supported in Windows 95

Non-Postscript Printers	PostScript Printers
HP LaserJet 4	Apple LaserWriter Pro 810 with Fax card
HP LaserJet 4M	Apple LaserWriter Pro 810
HP LaserJet 4M	PlusDigital DEClaser 5100
HP LaserJet 4MLHP	DesignJet 650C
HP LaserJet 4MPHP	DeskJet 1200C/PS
HP LaserJet 4MVHP	LaserJet 4
HP LaserJet 4Si MXHP	LaserJet 4ML

continues

Table 11.1 Continued	
Non-Postscript Printers	PostScript Printers
HP LaserJet 5MPHP	LaserJet 4MP
HP LaserJet 4VHP	LaserJet 4Si/4SiMX PS 300dpi
HP LaserJet 4PHP	LaserJet 4Si/4SiMX PS 600dpi
HP LaserJet 4SiHP	PaintJet XL300
HP LaserJet 4 Plus	TI MicroLaser Pro 600 2013 PS23
HP LaserJet 5P	TI MicroLaser Pro 600 2013 PS65
HP LaserJet 4L	
IBM 4039 LaserPrinter Plus	

Plug and Play Support

Windows 95 Plug and Play support extends to printers as well as plug-in adapters. With Plug and Play printers, you simply plug the printer into a bidirectional parallel port, and Windows 95 detects the printer. Windows 95 selects the appropriate driver based on the Plug and Play device ID returned by the printer, and the dialog box shown in figure 11.1 opens.

FIG. 11.1 ⇒

When a Plug and Play printer is detected, the New Device Found dialog box opens.

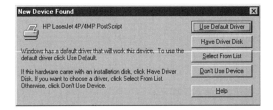

Windows 95 checks for a Plug and Play printer at each of three times: during Setup, during the Windows 95 Boot Sequence, and when the user requests that a detection be made (using the Add New Hardware item in Control Panel).

Extended Capabilities Ports

Extended Capabilities Ports provide high-speed communications to printers and other devices through a parallel port connection. ECP ports can have both standard parallel and ECP devices connected to them, although only ECP devices will show the full I/O performance gain.

Note ECP ports are not the same thing as the earlier EPP ports, which were used on some IBM computers. Windows 95 does not support EPP ports, except as standard bidirectional ports. ▪

Image Color Matching

The *Image Color Matching (ICM)* support in Windows 95 uses technology that Microsoft licensed from Kodak. ICM can be used by applications to increase the consistency between the color of images that are displayed on-screen and the color of the same images printed on an output device.

ICM support is available for the display, printers, and image scanners. When applications take advantage of ICM, color information is portable across applications, users, and platforms. This means that an image that is scanned on a scanner attached to a Macintosh can be displayed with predictable colors on a display attached to a UNIX computer, and printed with accurate color rendition on a color laser printer attached to a Windows 95 computer.

Graphics applications written for Windows 3.1 did not provide ICM support. Instead, the application provided its own color support, and it was up to the application's developers to properly map the colors generated to the display device onto the colors generated by a printer device. Different developers interpreted color information differently, making consistent and predictable results difficult at best.

Windows 95 ICM support simplifies the work for application developers because it removes the burden of mapping colors from them. Windows 95 ICM performs color matching in a device-independent manner, using international (CIE-based) colorimetric standards instead of basing color on any particular device.

Ch
11

Each device's color properties are stored in a profile, whose format was determined by InterColor 3.0, a consortium made up of industry hardware vendors, including Kodak, Microsoft, Apple Computer, Sun Microsystems, and Silicon Graphics, and the industry standards–setting bodies. The operating system uses the device color properties information to transform the internal device–independent color representations into the appropriate color for the actual device.

Understanding Printer Drivers

Windows printer drivers generally depend on the services of the GDI to render device-specific bitmaps. Windows 3.x printer drivers call the GDI, which in turn calls on the display driver for help rendering the picture. This dependence of GDI on the display driver means that the printer driver is only as good as the display driver and, most important, a buggy display driver could affect printing.

The Windows 95 GDI, as mentioned in "Windows 95 Internals" in Chapter 5, does not depend on the display driver to render device-independent bitmaps. Instead, the Windows 95 GDI, and hence, Windows 95 printer drivers, depend on the DIB engine. The only exception is when the display driver does not use the DIB engine and Windows 95 is printing to a monochrome printer. Then, the Unidriver (the driver used for all non-PostScript printing) will check to see if the display driver is the Windows 95 VGA driver. If it is, it uses the monochrome functions of the VGA driver, which are coded identically to the monochrome functions in the DIB engine, to conserve memory.

Windows 95 also supports the use of Windows 3.1 printer drivers. If you are using a Windows 3.1 printer driver, it might make calls into the display driver. If you are using a Windows 95 display driver, the DIB engine will still be used. If you are using a Windows 3.1 display driver as well as a Windows 3.1 printer driver, you can change to the Windows 95 VGA driver as a troubleshooting step if you are having problems.

If printing to a color printer, the Windows 95 printer drivers use Dmcolor.dll rather than the monochrome DIB engine.

Windows 95 Printer Driver Enhancements

Windows 95 printing is based on one of two drivers: either the PostScript driver, which is used to print to PostScript printers, or the Universal Driver (Unidrv.dll), which is used to print to virtually all non-PostScript printers.

Windows 95 printer drivers offer several enhancements over Windows 3.x printer drivers:

+ *Friendly names.* Friendly names enable users to refer to their printers by human-readable names, which can be up to 32 characters in length. You can even refer to your printer as "My cool laser printer" or "Laser in the hall by office 3" instead of "HP4 on LPT3."

+ *EMF Spooling.* This increases the perceived performance of the drivers

+ *Beziers.* The Windows 95 printer drivers directly handle Bezier curves themselves, rather than requiring an application to handle them. *Bezier curves* are a mathematical representation of a curved line segment.

Ch
11

The Universal Printer driver (Unidrv.dll) works with the manufacturer-supplied minidriver. Both Unidriver and the minidriver are 16-bit to retain compatibility with Windows NT 3.5, which also can use the 16-bit minidrivers, allowing a printer manufacturer to write a single minidriver for both platforms.

Unidriver also supports virtually all of the mainstream printer description languages, including HP PCL, Canon CaPSL, Lexmark PPDS, HP HPGL/2, and dot-matrix specifications. It supports device-resident Intellifont and TrueType fonts.

Unidriver now supports up to 600dpi.

The PostScript driver also is significantly enhanced. It supports PostScript level 2, with its support for color imaging and data compression. In fact, the PostScript driver supports Image Color Matching on the printer's processor rather than the computer's processor.

The PostScript driver now supports both the WPD (*Windows Printer Definition*) printer description file format used in Windows 3.x, and the industry-standard PPD (*PostScript Printer Definition*) files that ship with PostScript printers.

Printing a File

To print a file to a Windows 95 printer, simply drag the files to a printer icon. Of course, you also can use the same methods supported by Windows 3.x, such as printing from an application's File menu.

Understanding Spooling

When Windows 95 applications print to a non-PostScript printer, they spool to an Enhanced Metafile spool file.

Enhanced Metafiles (EMF)

Using EMF spooling results in the application returning control to the user faster than with the RAW spool files, which contain the printer commands and binary data that make up the image to be printed on the page, after a print job has been started in either a 16-bit or 32-bit Windows application (see fig. 11.2).

In Windows 3.x, all of the processing of print API calls was handled by the Windows printer driver before the information was spooled (see fig. 11.2) to the Print Manager. This processing is the most time-consuming operation in the print process, as the graphic commands in the API calls are turned into the *raster image* (the collection of pixels that make up the page) to be sent to the printer. Control would not return to the application until after the processing had completed, and Print Manager had started spooling the file.

Users of PostScript printers were not affected by this processing because the processor in the printer performs the rasterizing process. The PostScript driver sends high-level page description language commands to the printer rather than the raw image of the page.

FIG. 11.2 ⇒
A comparison of the Windows 3.x and Windows 95 print processes.

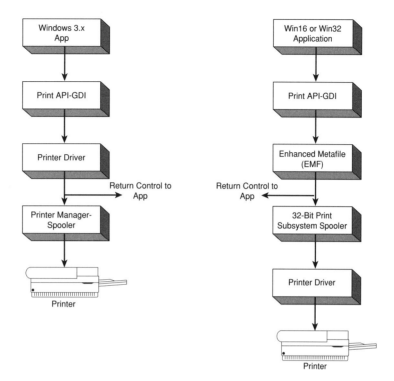

In Windows 95, the time to return to the application from spooling is greatly improved because instead of spooling the raw image file after processing, the high-level GDI commands generated by the print API (called an *enhanced metafile*) are spooled. For example, if a document contains a solid red circle, the EMF contains a command to draw a circle of the given dimensions and color it red.

MS-DOS Application Support

Windows 95 enables MS-DOS applications to spool their print jobs to the 32-bit print subsystem spooler. This is a significant improvement over the situation in Windows 3.x, where users printing from MS-DOS-based applications could not take advantage of the spooler, and, more important, would encounter device contention issues when printing from MS-DOS applications at the same time as printing from Windows applications, often resulting in output that consisted of mixed data—some from the MS-DOS application, and some from the Windows application.

This problem was exasperated in Windows for Workgroups 3.11, which enabled MS-DOS applications to spool to a network printer, but not to a local printer, even on the network server.

Windows 95 solves these problems by enabling an MS-DOS application to print to the 32-bit spooler. The print spooler virtual device handles this support, and takes the output destined for a printer port and places it in the print spooler. This action is automatically installed and configured and is transparent to the user and applications.

RAW

The PostScript driver in Windows 95 does not use Enhanced Metafile spooling because the RAW file consists of page description language commands, and no benefit would be realized from the EMF files.

Installing and Managing Printers

There are two ways a printer is installed under Windows 95—the user explicitly chooses to install a printer, or the printer is detected by Plug and Play.

Local Printers

To add a local printer, follow these steps:

1. Open the Printers folder from within Control Panel (see fig. 11.3).

FIG. 11.3 ⇒

The Printers folder.

2. Double-click the Add Printer icon to start the Add Printer Wizard (see fig. 11.4).

FIG. 11.4 ⇒

The Add Printer Wizard opens.

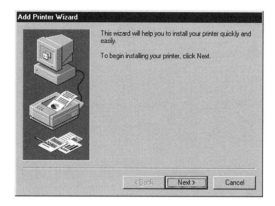

3. Click Next. You are asked whether you are adding a local or network printer (see fig. 11.5). Answer according to your need.

FIG. 11.5 ⇒

Choosing to install a local printer.

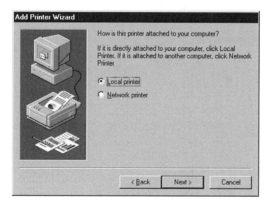

Ch

11

4. Click Next to advance to the next page of the wizard. Choose the manufacturer and model of the printer you're installing (see fig. 11.6).

5. Click Next. On the next page of the wizard, choose the port that the printer is attached to (see fig. 11.7). Notice the FILE: port—if you select FILE:, you are prompted for a file name that the printed output will be placed in.

FIG. 11.6 ⇒

Choosing the type of printer.

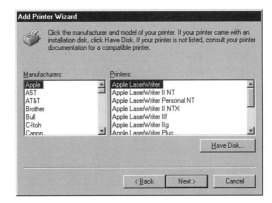

FIG. 11.7 ⇒

Choosing a port.

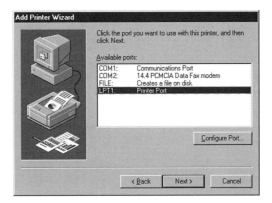

6. Click the Configure Port button to open the dialog box shown in figure 11.8. The default state of the check boxes is to Spool MS-DOS print jobs, and to Check port state before printing.

FIG. 11.8 ⇒

Configuring the port.

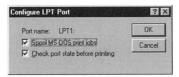

7. Click Next to assign a friendly name to the printer and select the printer as the default printer, which is optional (see fig. 11.9.)

FIG. 11.9 ⇒

Assigning a
friendly name.

8. Click Next to go to the next page of the wizard, so that you can print a test page showing the capabilities of the printer (see fig. 11.10).

9. Click Finish to cause the actual process of installing the printer to begin and to accept the changes you've designated.

FIG. 11.10 ⇒

You can print a test
page.

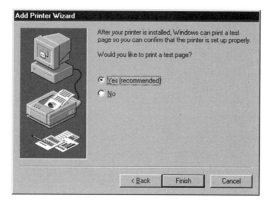

Ch
11

Location of Printing Components

Windows 95 printing components are stored in two places: the registry and on disk.

In the registry, Windows 95 components are stored under the HKEY_LOCAL_MACHINE tree.

On the hard disk, printing components are stored in two folders:

+ \WINDOWS\SYSTEM holds the printer drivers themselves.

+ \WINDOWS\SPOOL\PRINTERS holds spooled print jobs.

Working with the Printers Folder

Printer management is done through the Printers folder (see fig. 11.11). To access it, click the Start, Settings, Printers.

FIG. 11.11 ⇒

The Printers folder.

Every installed printer is shown with visual cues as to the printer's status:

+ Local printers that are shared are displayed with a hand icon.

+ Local printers that are not shared are shown simply as a printer icon.

+ Network printers are shown attached to an image of a cable.

+ Printers that are set to print to the FILE: port are displayed with an image of a disk.

Right-click a printer to open the menu shown in figure 11.12. It enables you to pause printing, purge all of the jobs in the print queue, and work offline.

If a printer is configured to work offline, any print jobs sent to it are saved until it is again configured to work online. This enables mobile computer users to generate print jobs while the computer is undocked.

FIG. 11.12 ⇒
You can pause printing, purge all print jobs, or set a printer to work offline by right-clicking the printer icon.

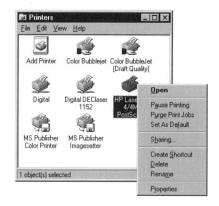

Opening the printer displays the print queue, where you can pause, resume, or cancel a print job.

Configuration Options

Every printer has property pages where you can set various configuration parameters. Not all pages are available with all printers.

General

The General page (see fig. 11.13) displays the printer's friendly name. You can add a comment, specify a page to be printed between jobs (separator page), or print a test page.

Details

The Details page (see fig. 11.14) enables you to change the port the printer is attached to, which driver is used, and spooler settings. Other printer-specific information may also be displayed.

Click the Spool Settings button to set spooler settings (see fig. 11.15). You can select to use EMF or RAW spooling, and whether Windows 95 waits for all pages to be spooled before printing starts. Waiting for all pages to be spooled returns control to the user faster.

Ch
11

FIG. 11.13 ⇒
The General
Printer property
page.

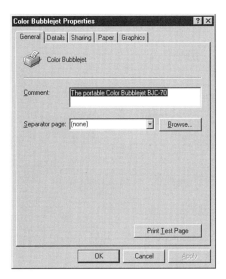

FIG. 11.14 ⇒
The Details Printer
property page.

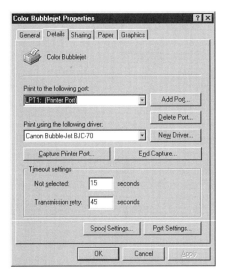

Paper

Information configured with the Paper page (see fig. 11.16) can include the size, orientation, layout, and paper source of the paper being printed on.

FIG. 11.15 ⇒
Changing spool
file type.

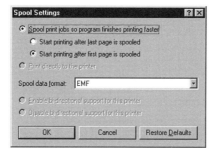

FIG. 11.16 ⇒
Choosing the
paper.

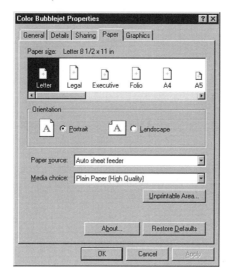

Ch
11

Graphics

The contents of the Graphics page (see fig. 11.17) varies widely by
printer, but typically contains resolution settings. Clicking the Color
button, if present, brings up the Image Color Matching dialog box
(see fig. 11.18).

There are three color rendering intents, which control how ICM
matches colors:

- Saturation will not dither primary or secondary colors, so that
  colors in charts are solid (but not necessarily accurate).

- Contrast preserves the image's contrast, which is best for
  photographs.

⊥ Colorimetric makes the colors match as much as possible, even dithering primary colors if necessary. (*Dithering* is the process of simulating colors by using multiple different color dots. Dithering reduces the resolution of a displayed or printed graphic because it uses multiple pixels to represent a single pixel.)

FIG. 11.17 ⇒

The Graphics page.

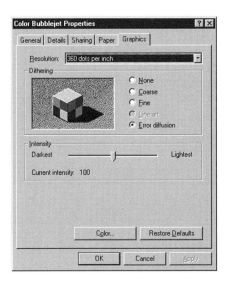

FIG. 11.18 ⇒

Controlling color matching.

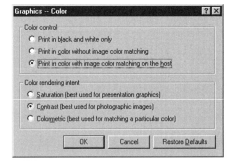

Fonts

PostScript printers print faster when the fonts in the print job match those in the printer. A Fonts page, if present, enables you to configure whether to use the fonts in a printer or to download substitutes or the TrueType font.

Device Options

Device options are printer-specific, and can include things such as memory options, sheet feeders, and the like.

PostScript Issues

PostScript printers may have a tab for configuring the format of the PostScript output sent to the printer. Options can include whether to use PostScript level 2, to download the PostScript header with every print job, use bitmap compression, and so on.

Taking the Disc Test

 If you have read and understood the material in the chapter, you are ready to test your knowledge. Insert the CD-ROM that comes with this book and run the self-test software as described in Appendix I, "Using the CD-ROM."

Ch
11

Chapter Prerequisite

Before reading this chapter, you should be familiar with file systems and disk I/O under Windows 95 (see Chapter 7, "File I/O and Disks"). You also should be familiar with disk utilities used under MS-DOS.

Using Windows 95's Disk Utilities

Disk utilities have several purposes, ranging from protecting against disk failure to repairing and recovering from disk problems to performance optimization to squeezing as much data onto a disk as possible. Windows 95 includes several disk utilities, all of which are compatible with the new disk-related features in Windows 95, such as long file names and support for drives located on secondary IDE controllers.

This chapter covers the disk utilities provided with Windows 95. Terms and concepts covered include:

+ **Disk fragmentation**
+ **ScanDisk**
+ **Backup**

> **Caution**
>
> *Never* use a disk utility that was designed for MS-DOS, or that was available prior to the release of Windows 95. Using an old disk utility may result in loss of data due to the utility not knowing how to handle long file names.

Using ScanDisk

Microsoft first introduced ScanDisk as part of MS-DOS 6.2, as the first major improvement to the original MS-DOS disk repair utility, CHKDSK. The Windows 95 version is a 32-bit application, and can run in the Windows 95 GUI while you're using the computer for something else. The Windows 95 version of ScanDisk also supports the new disk-related features in Windows 95, such as long file names.

ScanDisk is a disk repair utility. Its job is to resolve any disk corruption, such as lost clusters, bad sectors, cross-linked files, and the like, so that the disk can be used without causing further corruption. Refer to Chapter 7, "File I/O and Disks," for information on types of disk corruption.

> **Caution**
>
> Preservation of your data is not the first priority for ScanDisk. Its primary concern is to fix the structure on the disk. If it has to delete your data to do so, it will (after asking permission first). You should protect your data by relying on regularly scheduled backups, rather than trusting ScanDisk to recover lost data.

To start ScanDisk, click the Start button, then choose Programs, Accessories, System Tools, and ScanDisk. (You also can access ScanDisk from the Tools property page for a disk drive.) The dialog in figure 12.1 opens.

FIG. 12.1 ⇒

After choosing ScanDisk, the main dialog opens.

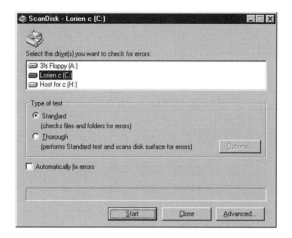

Each disk drive on the computer, including floppy drives, is listed in the box at the top of the screen. Select the drive or drives you want to check.

The next option to configure is what type of test ScanDisk should perform. There are two options:

+ *Standard.* This option checks the logical structure of the disk, verifying that the FAT, directory structure, long file names, and date and time information are all correct.

+ *Thorough.* This option performs a Standard test, and then performs a sector-by-sector scan of the disk's surface to verify the physical integrity of the recording media.

Choosing the Thorough test enables the Options button. Clicking the Options button opens the Surface Scan Options dialog (see fig. 12.2). You can select what sections of the disk you want to scan, as well as whether you want either of two additional options:

+ *Do not perform write-testing.* If this checkbox is checked, ScanDisk will read every sector in the area being scanned. If this checkbox is cleared, ScanDisk will read every sector, and then write the contents back to the sector.

+ *Do not repair bad sectors in hidden and system files.* If this checkbox is checked, ScanDisk ignores errors it finds in hidden and

Ch
12

system files. You should check this checkbox if the computer has old software, such as some MS-DOS-based versions of Lotus 1-2-3, that expect certain files to be in certain physical places on the disk (as a form of copy-protection). Because repairing sectors consists of moving the data in them to another location, repairing one of these files could cause the application to stop functioning.

FIG. 12.2 ⇒

Configuring the options used during Thorough testing.

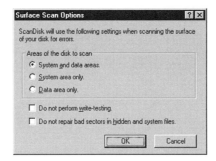

Click OK to close the Surface Scan Options dialog box.

If you want to be informed and prompted for the type of action you want to take when an error is found (see fig. 12.3), leave the Automatically Fix Errors checkbox cleared. If the checkbox is checked, ScanDisk automatically repairs any errors found.

FIG. 12.3 ⇒

ScanDisk can prompt you for the action to take when an error is found.

In the main ScanDisk dialog box, click the Advanced button to open the final configuration option for ScanDisk. The ScanDisk Advanced Options dialog box (see fig. 12.4) allows you to configure several groups of options:

FIG. 12.4 ⇒
Configuring
ScanDisk Ad-
vanced Options.

+ *Display summary.* This option controls the display of a summary
  (see fig. 12.5) of the results of the ScanDisk session. You can
  choose to have a summary display Always, Never, or Only if
  errors are found.

FIG. 12.5 ⇒
A summary of the
results of the
ScanDisk session
can be displayed.

Ch
12

+ *Log file.* This option controls the ScanDisk log. You can choose
  to have the log replaced every time ScanDisk runs, to append
  each session's log to the end of the log, or not to generate a log.
+ *Cross-linked files.* This option controls the action that ScanDisk
  takes by default when it finds cross-linked files. Possible actions
  are to delete both files, copy the contents of the files to new
  files, or just ignore the whole matter.

Tip
The option with the best chance of data recovery is Make copies.

↓ *Lost file fragments.* This option controls the action that ScanDisk takes by default when it finds fragments of lost files on the disk. The Free option will free up the space used by these lost fragments, Convert to Files will give the fragments names, and make them available as files. The files appear in the root directory of the affected disk, with numerically assigned names starting with File0000.chk

↓ *Check files for.* Controls whether ScanDisk checks for files with Invalid Names and/or Invalid Dates and Times. If a file name is invalid, you might not be able to open it. If a file has an invalid date or time, it might not sort correctly, or might not be backed up when selecting files to back up by modification date.

↓ *Check host drive.* If this option is checked, and the selected drive is compressed, ScanDisk tests the host drive first, since corruption on the host drive can affect the structure of the Compressed Volume File.

Using Backup

The primary defense against loss of data due to disk problems is making a *backup*. You access the Windows 95 backup utility called Microsoft Backup from the System Tools folder.

The first time you run Microsoft Backup, a scan of your system is performed. The scan detects any backup hardware, such as a QIC 80 tape drive, that your system might have. After detecting hardware, Microsoft Backup creates a backup file set called Full System Backup (see fig. 12.6).

FIG. 12.6 ⇒

A Full System Backup set is automatically created for you.

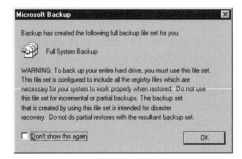

This backup file set is designed to back up all files on all hard disks, and the system registries, in the event of disaster. Notice the warning: `Do not use this backup file set for any other purpose, including partial backups or restores.`

Microsoft Backup can be used to back up to a tape drive, or to a disk volume (including a network disk).

Figure 12.7 shows the main dialog of Microsoft Backup. There are three tabs, each controlling a possible action.

FIG. 12.7 ⇒

Microsoft Backup main dialog.

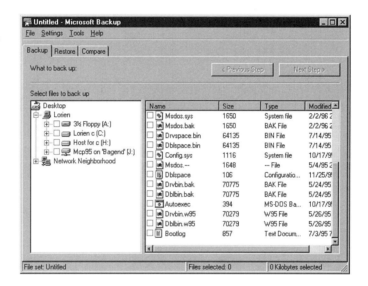

Ch

12

Backing Up

To back up the contents of a disk, check the box next to the disk's icon. To back up just any particular folder, open the tree in the left hand pane until you reach the folder, and then check the box next to the folder.

Similar to the behavior of Windows Explorer, the contents of the currently open folder are displayed in the right hand pane. You can select any particular file to back up by checking the box next to the file in the right hand pane. If you select some of the files, but not all of the files, the checkbox next to the containing folders is filled in (see fig. 12.8).

FIG. 12.8 ⇒

Selecting the files in the directory that you want to back up.

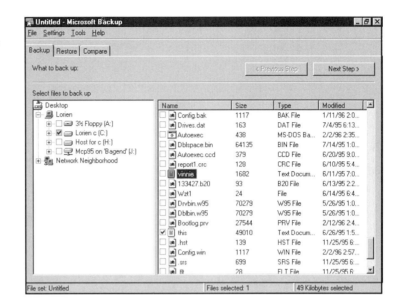

When you are ready to start the backup, click Next Step. The dialog changes (see fig. 12.9) to allow you to choose where to back up to. Clicking Start Backup opens the Backup Set Label dialog (see fig. 12.10). You can keep unauthorized persons from restoring the backup by clicking Password Protect. Choose OK to begin backing up the selected files.

FIG. 12.9 ⇒

Choosing a backup destination.

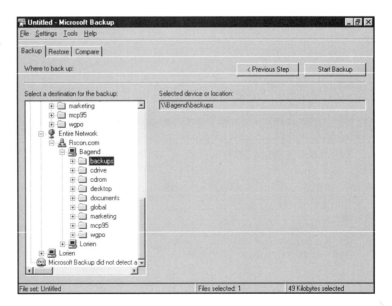

FIG. 12.10 ⇒
Every Backup File
Set has a name.

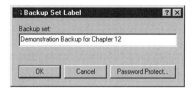

Restoring Files

The opposite of backing up is restoring. To begin a restore, choose the
Restore tab from the Backup main dialog. Locate the backup file set
you want to restore using the tree, and highlight it (see fig. 12.11).
Clicking Next Step opens up the Files to restore: dialog.

In the event that you are recovering from a complete system failure,
after reinstalling Windows 95, you can select the full system backup set
to restore all of the files that were on the computer, and the registry.
You cannot restore a Windows 95 computer without reinstalling a copy
of Windows 95.

FIG. 12.11 ⇒
Choosing files to
restore.

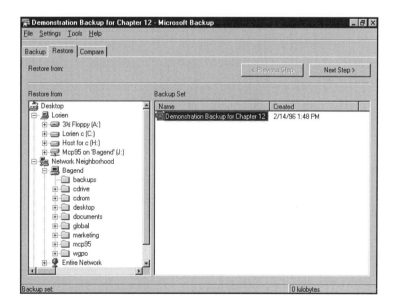

Ch
12

You can select the files you want to restore, and then click Start Restore
to restore them.

Comparisons

Comparing files is identical to restoring files, except that instead of actually restoring the files, Microsoft Backup compares the files on the disk with the backed-up version.

Backup Settings

There are three sets of settings you can configure by choosing the Settings option from the menu bar. These settings are explained in the following sections.

File Filtering

The File Filtering dialog (see fig. 12.12) allows you to choose categories of files you do not want included in backups. You can exclude files based on their Last Modified Date, or by file type.

FIG. 12.12 ⇒
Filtering files lets you exclude some of the files.

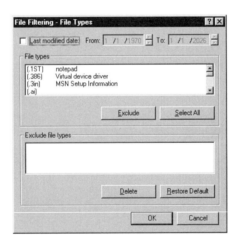

Drag and Drop

The Drag and Drop dialog (see fig. 12.13) allows you to choose the action that is taken when you drop a file set onto the Backup icon. There are three options, each controlling how Backup will respond:

+ *Run Backup minimized.* When this is chosen, Microsoft Backup will be minimized while backing up using a file set that you dropped onto the Backup icon.

+ *Confirm operation before beginning.* If checked, you will be prompted before the backup begins.

+ *Quit Backup after operation is finished.* If checked, Backup automatically terminates after completing the backup.

FIG. 12.13 ⇒

Configuring what happens when you drag and drop a file to Backup.

Options

There are four tabs in the options dialog, one with General options (see fig. 12.14), and one for each possible operation.

FIG. 12.14 ⇒

General options.

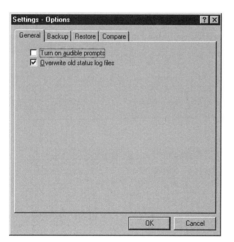

Ch

12

General Options

The General options allow you to choose to have audible prompts, and whether to overwrite the backup log every time an operation is started. Overwriting the backup log will reduce the disk space used, but you will not be able to review the error logs from prior backup sessions.

Backup Options

The available Backup options (see fig. 12.15) are

+ *Type of backup.* A full backup backs up all of the selected files. An Incremental backup only backs up those that have changed since the last full backup. Incremental backups can save backup time, but require you to restore both the last full backup and the incremental backup in order to have an accurate restore of a full system.

+ *Verify backup data by automatically comparing files after backup is finished.* If checked, a compare is automatically run after a backup.

+ *Use data compression.* This squeezes more data onto the backup media by compressing the data.

+ *Format when needed on tape backups.* If an unformatted tape is detected, backup automatically formats it.

+ *Always erase on tape backups.* If this box is checked, the tape is erased before backups are written to it. If it is cleared, the backup appends to the tape.

+ *Always erase on floppy disk backups.* If this box is checked, the disk is erased before backups are written to it. If it is cleared, the backup appends to the disk.

FIG. 12.15 ⇒

Options used when backing up.

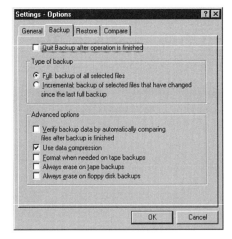

Restore Options

The available Restore options (see fig. 12.16) are

- *Restore backed up files to.* You can restore the files to the location they originally came from, to an alternative location (for example, to verify that a valid restore can take place), or to a specific single folder.

- *Verify restored data by automatically comparing files after the restore has finished.* If checked, a compare is automatically run after a backup.

- *Overwrite files.* If a file already exists, this option controls the action that takes place. You can choose to Never overwrite a file, Overwrite only files that are older than the one being restored, or always overwrite files (with an optional prompt).

FIG. 12.16 ⇒
The Restore options help you save deleting files.

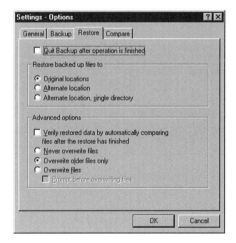

Compare Options

If the files you want to compare with the files on the backup set are in a different location than they were originally backed up from, you can modify the Location of Compare option (see fig. 12.17).

Ch

12

FIG. 12.17 ⇒

The comparison options give you choices on how to compare files.

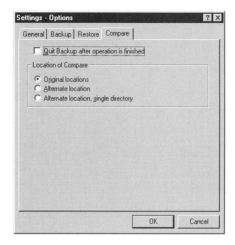

Using Disk Defragmenter

As a disk is used over time, files on it may become *fragmented*. When a file is fragmented, it is broken up into two or more different non-contiguous fragments, located in different parts of the disk. Fragmentation causes performance problems, because the disk heads have to travel in order to access the fragments.

To defragment a drive, start the Disk Defragmenter from the System Tools folder. After choosing the drive you want to defragment, the drive is scanned to determine how fragmented it currently is, and the Disk Defragmenter dialog box opens (see fig. 12.18).

FIG. 12.18 ⇒

The Disk Defragmenter dialog box.

To defragment the drive, choose Start. To change options, click Advanced, which opens the Advanced options dialog (see fig. 12.19). The options are

♣ *Defragmentation method.* Normally, you fully defragment a drive. However, if you only desire to improve file access, you can choose to Defragment files only. If you are installing a large new application, Consolidating free space will ensure that it is not fragmented.

♣ *Check drive for errors.* If this checkbox is checked, ScanDisk will be run before defragmenting starts.

FIG. 12.19 ⇒
The advanced options allow you to check disks for errors.

Taking the Disc Test

If you have read and understood the material in the chapter, you are ready to test your knowledge. Insert the CD-ROM that comes with this book and run the self-test software as described in Appendix I, "Using the CD-ROM. "

Chapter Prerequisite

Before reading this chapter, you should be familiar with Windows 95 Setup (see Chapter 3, "Windows 95 Setup"), configuration (see Chapter 4, "Configuring Windows 95"), System Architecture (see Chapter 5, "Windows 95 Architecture Overview"), and Plug and Play (see Chapter 6, "Plug and Play").

13

Understanding the Windows 95 Boot Sequence

One of the challenges faced by Microsoft in keeping Windows 95 compatible with earlier versions of both MS-DOS and Windows was designing a method to boot the computer that would load the new, protected mode operating system, yet still be able to use MS-DOS and Windows 3.x drivers.

Complicating the task was the fact that many necessary driver functions in MS-DOS were implemented as terminate-and-stay resident (TSR) programs that expected the system to be in a certain state when they load. Most expected to be able to talk to the real mode MS-DOS, and some even expected system data structures to be in certain places in memory and in the same states as when the user typed "WIN" to start Windows 3.x.

This chapter covers the Windows 95 boot sequence. Terms and concepts covered include:

+ **Msdos.sys**
+ **Io.sys**
+ **Real-mode boot components**
+ **Power on self test (POST)**
+ **Master boot record (MBR)**

The Windows 95 boot sequence includes four phases:

+ Bootstrapping phase, starting with the system's BIOS
+ Real mode compatibility phase, where MS-DOS drivers are loaded
+ Initializing static VxDs
+ Loading the protected mode operating system and the rest of the VxDs

Bootstrap Phase

When an Intel x86 processor is first initialized, it executes the instruction that it find at address FFFF0H, which is the starting address of the ROM BIOS. This first instruction is a JMP instruction to the start of the actual BIOS code.

The first action the bootstrap code takes is to perform a *Power On Self Test (POST)*. Following the POST, the BIOS checks for the boot device. Originally, it first checked to see if there was a floppy disk in drive A:, and if it did not find one, then it checked for a hard disk. Most modern computers can be configured via their built-in setup procedures to check the hard disk first.

If it finds a hard disk, the ROM routines then transfer control to the operating system loader code, which loads the disk's *Master Boot Record (MBR)* and executes it. (The master boot record is always the first sector on the disk, and contains the bootstrap code for the operating system.)

On computers with a Plug and Play BIOS (see Chapter 6, "Plug and Play"), the BIOS performs a few steps between the POST and looking for the boot device:

1. The Plug and Play BIOS looks for configuration settings in non-volatile RAM on the computer's motherboard.

2. All Plug and Play devices found are disabled.

3. A resource map is created, which maps the devices to the resources (DMA, I/O Addresses, and Interrupt) that the devices can use.

4. Each Plug and Play device, in turn, is configured and enabled.

If Plug and Play devices are in a computer that does not have a Plug and Play BIOS, they will configure themselves with power-on defaults, and can be reconfigured dynamically once Windows 95 starts.

Real Mode Operating System Compatibility Phase

The Real mode operating system compatibility phase has several parts:

+ Loading the master boot record and boot sector

+ Loading Io.sys

+ Interpreting the Msdos.sys file

+ Real mode configuration

Master Boot Record and Boot Sector

The master boot record code reads the partition table to find out the location of the boot sector in the active partition (the partition containing the bootable operating system). Then, it loads the boot sector, which contains the disk boot program and a disk parameter table.

The disk boot program reads the BIOS parameter block to determine the location of the root directory, and then reads Io.sys from the root directory into memory. (The BIOS parameter block, found on sector 0

Ch
13

of every physical disk, contains information about the disk's geometry, including a media type code, and the sector size used on the disk.)

Io.sys

Io.sys begins by loading a minimal file system, which is capable only of reading Msdos.sys and the opening graphic logo.

It then reads Msdos.sys, which contains configuration values. Unlike previous versions of MS-DOS, Msdos.sys is not an executable file. The Msdos.sys file can contain two sections: [Paths] and [Options]. The Msdos.sys file is required, and must be larger than 1024 bytes (for compatibility reasons).

Msdos.sys [Paths] Section

The entries in the [Paths] section of the Msdos.sys file may include the following:

- `HostWinBootDrv=`—The location of the boot drive's root directory
- `WinBootDir=`—The location of the startup files
- `WinDir=`—The location of the Windows 95 directory

Msdos.sys [Options] Section

The entries in the [Options] section of the Msdos.sys file may include the following:

- `BootDelay=`—The initial startup delay in seconds
- `BootFailSafe=`—If set to 1, safe mode is enabled
- `BootGUI=`—If set to 1, Windows 95 will boot into the graphical mode
- `BootKeys=`—If set to 1, the startup option keys (F5, F6, and F8) can be used
- `BootMenu=`—If set to 1, the Windows 95 Startup menu will always be presented
- `BootMenuDefault=`—Sets the default menu item on the Windows 95 Startup menu
- `BootMenuDelay=`—The number of seconds that will elapse before the default menu item is run automatically

- `BootMulti=`—If set to 1, you can start the previously installed operating system by pressing F4 or F8
- `BootWin=`—If set to 1, Windows 95 is the default operating system
- `DblSpace=`—If set to 1, Dblspace.bin will be automatically loaded
- `DoubleBuffer=`—If set to 1, the double-buffering driver (for SCSI disks) will be automatically loaded
- `DrvSpace=`—If set to 1, Drvspace.bin will be automatically loaded
- `LoadTop=`—If set to 1, Command.com or Drvspace.bin can be loaded at the top of conventional memory
- `Logo=`—If set to 1, the animated logo will be displayed

> **Note** Setting this value to 0 will sometimes resolve incompatibilities with some third-party memory managers. ▪

- `Network=`—If set to 1, Safe Mode with Networking will be a Startup Menu option

Io.sys Continues to Load

After reading Msdos.sys, the Io.sys code will load and display Logo.sys, if it exists. Otherwise, an internal logo file is displayed.

Tip

You can have a bitmap of your own choosing displayed instead of the default Windows 95 logo by creating a 320 x 400 256-color bitmap in Windows Paint. After saving it, copy it to the root directory of your C: drive, and rename it to "Logo.sys" from a Windows 95 command prompt. (You have to open a Windows 95 command prompt because Explorer and Paint won't let you change the file type from .bmp to .sys.)

Next, if a Drvspace.ini or Dblspace.ini file is found in the root directory, the appropriate compression driver (Drvspace.bin or Dblspace.bin) loads.

Ch
13

Note Windows 95 comes with Microsoft's second-generation disk compression software, DriveSpace, which was introduced with MS-DOS 6.22. The first-generation disk compression software, DoubleSpace, was introduced with MS-DOS 6.0, but was discontinued as a result of legal action taken by Stac Corporation. The two companies eventually settled their differences.

If Windows 95 is installed on a disk that was compressed with DoubleSpace, the existing DoubleSpace driver (placed on the disk by MS-DOS 6.0) will be used to access the disk (and a Dblspace.ini file will exist). If the disk was compressed by Windows 95, or by MS-DOS 6.22, the DriveSpace driver built-in to Windows 95 will be used to access the disk (and a Drvspace.ini file will exist).

Io.sys then performs an integrity check on the registry and opens the registry file, System.dat. If System.dat is missing, then System.da0 is loaded, and later copied to System.dat.

If Windows 95 detects that double-buffering is necessary, Dblbuff.sys loads. *Double-buffering* is a technique needed with some SCSI adapters that are not capable of performing DMA transfers to addresses above the 1M mark. When double-buffering is used, a buffer below 1M is created that is used for DMA transfers from the adapter card. After the data is placed in the buffer, it is then moved by the Dblbuff.sys driver to the actual Windows 95 buffer that it is destined for.

The last step before reading Config.sys is to choose a hardware profile from those listed in the registry (see Chapter 6).

Real Mode Configuration

For backwards compatibility, the real mode configuration phase enables loading applications and utilities from the Config.sys and Autoexe.bat files. In addition, a number of drivers and settings are loaded by default, including Himem.sys, Ifshlp.sys, and Setver.exe.

Config.sys defaults include:

```
LastDrive=Z
Files=30
Buffers=22
Stacks=9,256
FCBS=4
DOS=High
DOS=UMB
Shell=C:\Windows\Command.com
```

Autoexec.bat defaults include:

```
PATH=<windows directory>;<windows directory>\COMMAND
```

If there is a Win.com command in Autoexec.bat, Win.com is loaded, and it then calls Vmm32.vxd. If not, the Vmm32.vxd is called directly.

Static VxD Initialization

Vmm32.vxd consists of the real mode loader, the actual Virtual Machine Manager, and compressed VxDs. VMM32 loads any devices specified in System.ini first (for compatibility reasons). Then, for every device in the hardware tree, it attempts to find a .vxd driver for it, which, if found, is automatically loaded.

All known drivers are loaded into Vmm32.vxd at setup time. If you rerun Setup later, any new drivers will be merged from the \\windows\system\vmm32 folder. Typical VxDs that are added into Vmm32.vxd (and which used to be specified in System.ini) include:

*biosxlat	*reboot	*vkd
*configmg	*vcache	*vmcpd
*dynapage	*vcomm	*vmouse
*ebios	*vcond	*vmpoll
*ifsmgr	*vdd	*vsd
*int13	*vdef	*vtdapi
*ios	*vfat	*vwin32
*parity	*vfbackup	*vxdldr

Ch
13

After VMM32 completes loading the static VxDs, it switches the processor to protected mode, and the last phase of the boot process begins.

Loading Protected Mode VxDs at Startup

First, the protected mode Configuration Manager (implemented as part of the virtual memory manager) initializes, and if necessary, loads the dynamically loadable VxDs.

If the computer has a Plug and Play BIOS, the hardware tree is obtained from the BIOS. Otherwise, information provided by the bus enumerators and the hardware detection routines in the registry is used to create the hardware tree.

Then, resource conflicts are resolved and devices are initialized.

Loading the Windows 95 Operating System

The remaining components, making up the Windows 95 operating system proper, load in the following order:

1. Kernel32.dll, which contains the main operating system code, is loaded.

2. Gdi.exe and Gdi32.dll, load next; they contain the graphics engine.

3. User.exe and User32.dll—User interface management.

4. Any resources, such as fonts, load next.

5. Win.ini is read, and used to load or configure applications.

6. The Windows shell (normally Explorer.exe) loads, and policies are enforced.

7. The Desktop loads next.

8. The Logon dialog box is presented, and the user logs in. Logon can consist of loading the user's profile, as well as authenticating on the network, and running any network logon scripts.

9. The Startup group is processed. In addition, anything listed on the RunOnce Registry key is run. Once a program is successfully started, it is removed from the RunOnce Registry key.

Taking the Disc Test

 If you have read and understood the material in the chapter, you are ready to test your knowledge. Insert the CD-ROM that comes with this book and run the self-test software as described in Appendix I, "Using the CD-ROM."

Ch
13

Chapter Prerequisite

This chapter is provided to give you background information for the more advanced networking chapters.

14

Networking Basics

This chapter covers networking basics. Concepts and skills covered include:

+ An understanding of networking in general, including **protocols**, **layers**, **topologies**, **architectures**, and **interface specifications**.

Understanding Networking

Networks provide a method for computers to communicate with each other to share resources. In the early days of computing, prior to the availability of networks, when someone wanted to share the information stored in a file with someone else, he or she had to copy the file to some form of media, such as a disk or tape, and physically carry that media to the other person. This process eventually became known as a *Sneaker-Net*.

Sneaker-Net worked for awhile, but eventually people were spending more of their day walking around than actually working.

The next development was the use of asynchronous communication equipment to transfer files from one computer to another directly. This had several drawbacks, the most significant being speed, and the fact that a communication utility had to be running, to the exclusion of any actual work-related application, while the file was being transferred. (See Chapter 24 for more information on communications with Windows 95.)

The first true networks were proprietary networks connecting mini-computers and mainframes.

Examining the ISO OSI Model

In 1983, the International Standards Organization (ISO) defined a model for networking called the *Open Systems Interconnection (OSI) reference model*. The model describes the flow of information between the physical network and applications.

Networking vendors use the OSI model as a guideline to develop real world systems.

The OSI reference model defines the communication between the computers in a network as a series of *layers* (see fig. 14.1). Each layer implements a particular functionality, such as routing (Network layer) or frame construction (Data Link layer). Layers logically communicate with their counterpart on other computers, but in actuality, each layer provides services to the layer above it and uses the services of the layer below it. The lower layer shields the layers above it from having to know, or deal with, the details handled by the lower layers.

FIG. 14.1 ⇒

The layers of the OSI reference model.

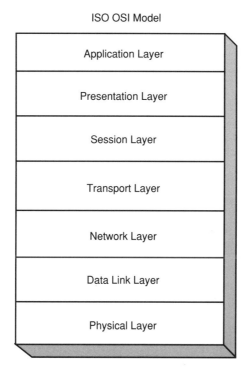

ISO OSI Model

Application Layer

Presentation Layer

Session Layer

Transport Layer

Network Layer

Data Link Layer

Physical Layer

The OSI reference model, like other models, is a set of abstract guidelines only. Actual network implementations may implement a single functional layer in several software layers, or implement many functional layers in a single software component.

The OSI reference model defines seven layers. The layers are usually pictured as shown in figure 14.1, with the Physical layer at the bottom, and the Application layer at the top.

The Seven ISO OSI Layers

Each of the layers communicates with its adjacent layers through an *interface*. The sets of rules that the layers use to communicate logically

Ch

14

with their counterpart on the other computer in a conversation are called *protocols*.

As data passes through each of the layers, from the Application layer down to the Physical layer, it is wrapped with layer-specific information, and passed to the next lower layer, which wraps its own information around the outside of the data, and so on.

On the recipient computer, each layer removes its layer-specific information before passing the data up to the next layer.

There are seven layers, from bottom to top, as discussed in the following sections:

+ Physical
+ Data Link
+ Network
+ Transport
+ Session
+ Presentation
+ Application

Physical Layer

The Physical layer defines the methods used to transfer the bitstream that makes up the data across a physical network. It defines the interfaces (electrical, optical, etc.) to the network cable. The Physical layer carries the signals generated by all of the higher layers directly to its counterpart on the remote computer.

The Physical layer defines the complete configuration of all of the physical parts of the network, including cabling type, pin configurations, signal encoding, etc. It deals with bits only, and does not impose any meaning on the bit stream, although it does ensure that a 1 bit is received as a 1 bit, and not a zero bit. Transmission speed, modulation, and encoding are all defined by this layer.

Data Link Layer

The Data Link layer converts the bit stream received from the Physical layer into data *frames*, or *packets*. A packet is an organized structure that can contain data. The packet contains error correction information in the form of a CRC to ensure that the frame is received properly. The upper layers are guaranteed error-free transmission through this layer.

Usually, the Data Link layer relies on acknowledgments from its counterpart to ensure that a frame was received. If a frame is not acknowledged, the Data Link layer normally retransmits the frame.

The frame also contains the sender ID and destination ID for the frame.

The Data Link layer establishes the logical link between two network nodes, and handles frame sequencing and frame traffic control.

Network Layer

The Network layer addresses messages and translates logical addresses and names into physical addresses. It is also responsible for routing packets from the source computer to the destination computer. It determines the route based on a number of criteria, including network conditions and service priorities.

The Network layer is also responsible for dealing with problems on the network, including network congestion. If the destination computers cannot handle packets as large as the sending computer, the Network layer on the sending computer will break the packets up into smaller packets. The packets will be reassembled by the Network layer on the receiving computer.

Transport Layer

The primary function of the Transport layer is to ensure that messages are delivered to the higher layers without errors, and in the proper sequence, with no losses. This layer also packages messages for efficient transfer; short messages will be combined into larger ones, and large messages may be split into smaller messages. The Transport layer on the receiving computer unpacks the messages into their original form.

The Transport layer also provides session multiplexing; it can multiplex several message streams into a single logical link, and separate them on the receiving node. (Multiplexing refers to any technique that allows multiple message streams to share a logical link.)

Ch
14

Session Layer

The Session layer allows applications on two computers to talk to each other by establishing a conversation, called a *session*. This layer handles name recognition and other functions that permit two applications to communicate with each other over the network.

The Session layer places checkpoints in the data stream. Checkpoints provide a means of synchronizing the data stream on both computers. In the event of a network failure, only the data after the last received checkpoint will need to be resent. This layer also controls which side of a conversation is permitted to transmit and for how long.

Presentation Layer

The primary responsibility of the Presentation layer is to translate applications data into a commonly recognized intermediate format for transmission across the network. On the receiving side, the Presentation layer translates the intermediate format back into the original format.

The network redirector operates at this layer. A *redirector* redirects reads and writes to a server on the network.

Other services of the Presentation layer can include data compression, data encryption, character set translation, and other conversions.

Application Layer

The Application layer allows application processes to access network services. Application layer services directly support user applications such as file transfer, messaging, or database access.

Tip

You can remember the order of the OSI layers by using the mnemonic device: **P**lease **D**o **N**ot **T**rust **S**ales **P**eople **A**lways.

IEEE 802 Model

The Institute of Electrical and Electronic Engineers developed another network model to address the proliferation of LAN products that was beginning to take place in early 1980. This project, named 802, was in development at roughly the same time that the ISO was working on the OSI reference model, resulting in a compatible model.

One key difference between the IEEE committee and the ISO committee is that the IEEE committee was made up of networking vendor representatives from companies who had products to sell. In some instances, the IEEE standard was driven by *products* rather than the other way around.

Most of today's networks comply with the IEEE 802 standards. The IEEE 802 standards, including 802.2 (LLC), 802.3 (Ethernet), and 802.5 (Token Ring) are standards that can actually be implemented, whereas the OSI reference model is a more general abstract set of guidelines.

The key difference between the OSI reference model and the IEEE 802 standard lies in the Data Link layer. The IEEE felt that more detail was needed at this layer, and decided to further divide the layer into two sublayers, the *Media Access Control (MAC)* layer and the *Logical Link Control (LLC)* layer (see fig. 14.2).

FIG. 14.2 ⇒
The IEEE 802 standard divides the Data Link layer into two sublayers.

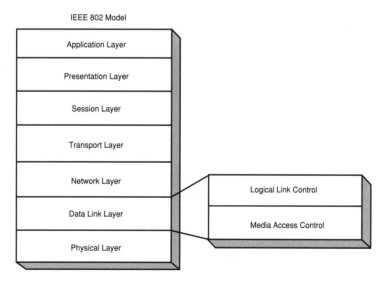

Media Access Control (MAC) Sublayer

The MAC sublayer is the lower of the two sublayers defined by the IEEE. It provides shared access to the computer's network adapter cards. It talks to the network adapter card directly, and is responsible for error-free delivery of packets across the network.

Logical Link Control (LLC) Sublayer

The upper sublayer of the Data Link layer is the Logical Link Control layer. It is responsible for link establishment and control, frame sequencing and acknowledgment, and provides Service Access Points (SAPs) that are used to transfer information to higher layers.

Understanding Network Topologies

The *topology* of a LAN describes the way it is arranged. There are three topologies in current use: ring, bus, and star. Topology is usually used to refer to the logical arrangement, rather than a physical one. For example, the IBM Token Ring network is logically and electrically a ring, but wired physically in a star shape. It's also common for large networks to be hybrids of two or more topologies.

Ring

Nodes in a ring topology (see fig. 14.3) are connected, one to the other, in a closed loop. Although usually physically wired in a star shape, the ring is electrically a complete circuit. Messages may pass though one or more other computers before reaching their destination.

A token-passing access method is used with ring topologies. The only example of an IEEE 802-compliant ring topology is a token-ring network.

Bus

Nodes in a bus topology (see fig. 14.4) are connected to a central cable, known as a *trunk*, or *bus*. The ends of the cable are each connected to a terminator, which is a resistor that typically matches the characteristic impedance of the cable.

FIG. 14.3 ⇒
Ring topology.

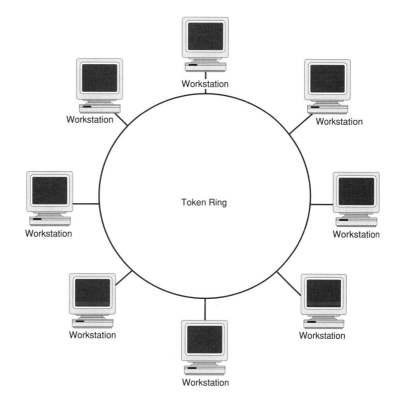

FIG. 14.4 ⇒
Bus topology.

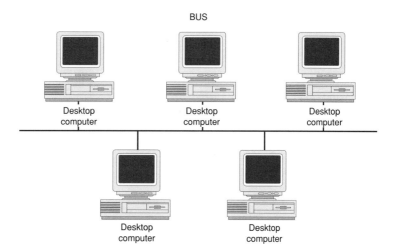

Ch
14

There are two methods commonly used to connect the nodes to the bus. The first, used more often with Thin Ethernet networks, uses T-shaped BNC connectors. One side of the T is connected to the node's network adapter card, and the other two are connected to two cables (or one cable and a terminator) that make up the bus.

The second method, more common with Thick Ethernet networks, places a transceiver on the trunk cable, which is connected to the AUI port on the node's network adapter card with a drop-down cable.

Examples of networks with a bus topology are 10Base2, 10Base5, and Arcnet.

Star

Nodes in a star topology (see fig. 14.5) are connected to a central wiring concentrator, or *hub*. A hub usually acts as an electrical *repeater*,

FIG. 14.5 ⇒

Star topology.

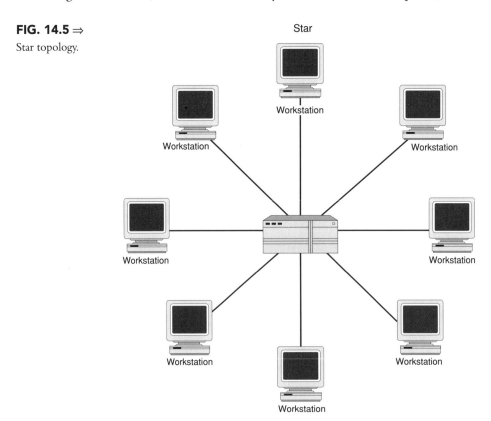

regenerating the signals received from transmitting nodes and sending them to all of the other nodes.

10BaseT is the best example of a star topology network.

Understanding Architectures

The architecture of a network is determined by its topology, media access method, and transmission media.

Token Ring

IEEE standard 802.5 defines the token-ring network access method. It uses the ring topology, although it is physically shaped like a star.

Token-ring networks use a token-passing access method. A *token* is a special bit pattern that is passed around the ring from computer to computer. When a computer possesses the token, it has the right to transmit on the network. After it transmits its data, the computer places the token back on the ring so that the next computer has a chance to transmit.

The token-ring access method is non-competitive, meaning that computers do not have to compete for access to the cable; they merely have to wait their turn. The token-ring standard does impose a maximum limit on how much data a computer may transmit at one time, to ensure that the token is passed on fairly. In fact, a computer that holds the token for too long will be partitioned out of the network by the central Multistation Access Unit (MAU).

The first token-ring network was designed by E. E. Newhall in 1969. The first commercial support for a token-ring network began with an IBM presentation to the IEEE 802 project in March, 1982.

IBM announced the IBM Token Ring Network in 1984, and its design was approved as ANSI/IEEE 802.5 in 1985. Key to the design was the IBM Cabling System, which was based on shielded twisted-pair (a later design allowed the use of unshielded twisted-pair) cable that connected

Ch

14

from the network adapter card to a wall socket, with a centralized hub, a Multistation Access Unit (MAU) located in a centralized location.

The token-ring network cabling is distinguished by a unique genderless connector. (A genderless connector can connect to any replica of itself, rather than having a corresponding part, as a plug and socket do.) The self-shorting design of the connector, coupled with the redundant data path available in the cable, ensure that the ring can remain electrically complete, even if a wire breaks or a computer is turned off. In the former case, the redundant path is automatically switched in by the MAU; in the latter, the cabling to the computer is removed from the ring by the MAU, and reinserted when the computer is turned on. You can recognize a token-ring connector because it is the largest of the connectors used in networking, a roughly cubical shape, about 1.25" on a side.

The original token-ring network used a transmission speed of 4Mbps; it was later adapted to 16Mbps. All network cards on the ring must be configured at the same speed.

Each computer can be up to 100 meters from the MAU when using shielded twisted-pair cable, or 45 meters when using unshielded cable. Cables must be at least 2.5 meters in length.

There can be up to 33 MAUs on a ring, each supporting a maximum of 260 computers with shielded twisted-pair cable.

Token rings are most efficient on heavily loaded networks that have a lot of traffic.

Ethernet

The precursor of the Ethernet network was a wide area network called ALOHA that was developed at the University of Hawaii in the late 1960s. It was the first network to use the Carrier-Sense Multiple Access with Collision Detection (CSMA/CD) access method.

Unlike the token-passing method, which is non-competitive, computers using the CSMA/CD access method compete for a chance to transmit on the cable. A computer that wants to transmit follows several steps:

1. The computer checks the cable to see if a carrier (a transmission signal) is already present. If one is, it waits a random amount of time and tries again. (Carrier-Sense)

2. If there is no carrier present, the computer assumes that the cable is available to it. *Other computers may be accessing the cable at the same time.* (Multiple Access)

3. The computer transmits its data, and listens for a double carrier. If a double carrier is found, then a collision has occurred. A collision is caused by another computer starting to transmit at the same time. (Collision Detection)

4. If a collision is detected, both computers will wait a random amount of time, and begin with step 1 again.

Xerox Corporation started experimenting with CSMA/CD networks in 1972, and by 1975, introduced its first Ethernet product, a 2.94Mbps system that could connect more than 100 computers on a one kilometer-long cable.

The success of the first Ethernet led to Xerox, Intel Corporation, and Digital Equipment Corporation drawing up a standard for the 10Mbps Ethernet, which was used as the basis of the IEEE 802.3 specification. The product complies with most, but not all, of the 802.3 specification.

There are three different types of cable supported by Ethernet networks: thick coaxial cable (ThickNet, or 10base5), thin coaxial cable (ThinNet or 10base2), and unshielded twisted-pair (10baseT).

The 10base5 specification is for baseband communications over thick cabling. The maximum physical segment length is 500 meters. *Baseband communications* refers to communications where the cable is dedicated to a particular type of signal. The alternative, *broadband*, refers to communications where multiple signals are multiplexed over a single cable. An example of broadband communications is cable television.

Ch
14

The 10base2 specification is for baseband communications over thin (RG-58) coaxial cabling. The maximum physical segment length is 185 meters.

The 10baseT specification uses baseband communications over unshielded twisted-pair cable. The maximum physical segment length is 100 meters between the workstation and a wiring concentrator, or hub.

Thicknet (10Base5)

Thick (or Standard) Ethernet uses a thick cable. The IEEE designation is 10Base5 because it is a 10Mbps, baseband network with a maximum segment length of 500 meters.

10Base5 uses a bus topology to support up to 100 nodes per trunk segment. A *node* is a workstation, repeater, or bridge. (A *bridge* is a device that connects two different network segments, passing only traffic destined for another segment. A repeater electrically connects two or more segments, regenerating the signals to each of them.)

Each trunk segment is terminated by resistors at each end. Transceivers are placed along the trunk, and a drop cable attaches to the AUI port on the workstation network adapter cards. Drop cable length is not considered in calculating the length of the trunk cable. As many as five backbone segments can be connected using repeaters.

Thicknet requires a minimum of 2.5 meters between connections on the trunk segment. Drop cables are usually made from shielded-pair cable, and have a maximum length of 50 meters.

Thicknet is typically used to support the network backbone for a building because of its greater resistance to electrical interference and longer segment length.

Thinnet (10Base2)

The 10Base2 network runs over thin, relatively inexpensive coaxial cable (RG-58). The IEEE designation is 10Base2 because it transmits at 10Mbps over a baseband cable for a maximum distance of approximately 200 meters (actually 185 meters).

10Base2 uses a bus topology to support up to 30 nodes per segment.

Each segment is terminated by resistors at each end. Instead of using external transceivers, 10Base2 transceivers are contained on the network adapter card and a T connector is used to connect the cable to the card. There must be at least 0.5 meters of cable between adapters.

As many as five cable segments can be combined using repeaters, giving 10Base2 a maximum of 150 computers per logical segment.

10Base2 was designed to be economical and easy to set up. Many small networks use 10Base2; in fact, Microsoft used to bundle Windows for Workgroups with 10Base2 adapters and cable.

Twisted-Pair (10BaseT)

The most popular form of Ethernet in use today is best known by its IEEE designation, 10BaseT.

10BaseT runs over unshielded twisted-pair cable, similar to that used by ordinary telephone systems. It is designated 10BaseT by the IEEE because it transmits at 10Mbps over a baseband cable for a maximum distance of 100 meters from the wiring hub. Cables must be at least 2.5 meters in length.

10BaseT is wired in a star topology, but it uses a bus system between the adapter card and the hub, which acts as a repeater.

ArcNet

ArcNet (Attached Resource Computer Network) is a proprietary token-passing bus network developed by Datapoint Corporation. It transmits at 2.5Mbs, although later versions support rates up to 20Mbps.

ArcNet is a proprietary network, predating the IEEE 802 project. It bears some resemblance to 802.4, but 802.4 describes a broadband network, while ArcNet is a baseband network. ArcNet can use either a bus or star technology over coaxial cable. Star configurations use active or passive hubs. Active hubs regenerate the signals, while passive hubs simply divide the signals up.

Ch
14

Understanding Transport Protocols

Transport protocols enable you to route information and network requests over LANs and WANs. (A LAN is a Local Area Network, intended to interconnect nodes in the same building or campus, while a WAN, or Wide Area Network, can be world-wide.)

NetBEUI

The *NetBEUI* protocol stack (a *stack* is a particular implementation of a protocol) was designed by Microsoft and IBM for use with IBM's PC Network product which was introduced in 1985. At that time, most people expected LANs to consist of small departmental workgroups that would be connected to mainframes via gateways. In fact, the PC Network hardware could only support a maximum of 72 workstations.

NetBEUI was optimized for use in this environment. One consequence of this optimization is the fact that NetBEUI is not routable.

NetBEUI uses the NetBIOS interface at the top, and NDIS at the bottom (see fig. 14.6).

FIG. 14.6 ⇒
How NetBEUI fits into the OSI/IEEE networking models.

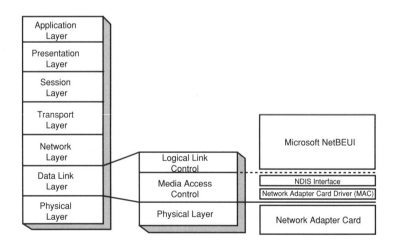

IPX/SPX

IPX was designed by Novell as a routable transport protocol, based on Xerox XNS.

The Microsoft version, *IPX/SPX*-compatible protocol, is completely compatible with Novell's version, but is a fully 32-bit implementation. The Microsoft implementation includes an optional NetBIOS interface, which is required to utilize resource sharing with Microsoft networks.

TCP/IP

The *Transmission Control Protocol/Internet Protocol (TCP/IP)* is a suite of protocols designed specifically for wide-area networks. It was first developed in 1969 as part of an experiment called the ARPANET, whose purpose was to interconnect the networks that were used by the contractors and universities doing research for the U.S. Department of Defense.

For more information on TCP/IP, see Chapter 16, "TCP/IP and Windows 95."

XNS

XNS was the original transport protocol developed by Xerox for use with Ethernet. It is an ancestor of the Novell IPX protocol.

Understanding MAC Drivers

A *MAC driver* is a driver located at the MAC sublayer. It provides support for data transmission to and from the network adapter, as well as managing the adapter itself. MAC drivers are also known as network adapter card drivers.

Understanding Interface Specifications

Device drivers at the MAC and LLC sublayers move data received by the Physical layer up to the other OSI layers.

Until the development of the NDIS standard in 1989, most transport protocol implementations were tied to a proprietary MAC-level interface. Supporting these proprietary interfaces meant that network adapter card manufacturers had to write drivers for each proprietary interface in order to support a variety of network operating systems.

Ch
14

NDIS

In 1989, Microsoft and 3Com developed a joint standard that defined an interface for communicating between the MAC sublayer and transport protocol drivers on layers 3 and 4 of the OSI model. This standard, the *Network Device Interface Specification (NDIS)*, is designed to create an environment where any transport protocol can talk to any network adapter card driver without either one knowing anything about the other.

The initial communication channel between the protocol driver and the MAC driver is established through a process called *binding*, in which the *Protocol Manager* establishes the connection between the MAC and transport protocol drivers.

NDIS also permits a single network adapter to support multiple protocol drivers, as well as supporting multiple network adapters. The Protocol Manager is responsible for routing network requests to the appropriate driver.

ODI

Novell's version of an architecture that allows the use of multiple LAN drivers and protocols is called the *Open Data-Link Interface (ODI)* specification.

There are two parts to an ODI stack. The first, the *Multiple Link Interface Driver (MLID)*, is a network adapter specific driver. The second, the *Link Support Layer (LSL),* provides the interface to the transport protocols.

Taking the Disc Test

If you have read and understood the material in the chapter, you are ready to test your knowledge. Insert the CD-ROM that comes with this book and run the self-test software as described in Appendix I, "Using the CD-ROM."

Chapter Prerequisite

Before reading this chapter, you should be familiar with file systems and disk I/O under Windows 95 (see Chapter 7, "File I/O and Disks"), and networking basics (see Chapter 14, "Networking Basics").

15

Windows 95 Networking Introduction

Windows 95 was designed for networking from the ground up, as a client and a server in both peer-to-peer networks and in server-based networks, including Novell NetWare, Microsoft Windows NT Server, and other third-party proprietary networks.

This chapter introduces Windows 95 networking. Terms and concepts covered include:

- **Application Interfaces**
- **Device drivers**
- **Named pipes**
- **Network Providers**
- **Remote procedure calls (RPC)**
- **Transport Device Interface (TDI)**

- **Transport Protocols**
- **Universal Naming Convention (UNC)**
- **Windows Sockets (WinSock)**

Understanding Integrated Networking

When personal computers first started being attached together in networks, you had to choose a single company's networking software because there were no standards in place. The lack of standards meant that there was no way to allow a single computer to connect to and use resources on servers running a variety of network operating systems.

It wasn't until the release of Windows 95's immediate predecessor, Windows for Workgroups version 3.11, that accessing resources on just two different vendors' networks simultaneously (Windows NT and NetWare) became possible.

As time goes on, networks are becoming larger and larger. Networks are being interconnected with each other, and with the global Internet. As the networks become larger, more and more diverse types of computers are getting connected to them, requiring support from the desktop operating system for a wide variety of network clients and protocols simultaneously.

Windows 95 delivers that support through its integrated networking design. In addition, Windows 95 was designed from the ground up with support of multiple networks a key design goal.

Thanks to this design, installing and managing a network—or even several networks simultaneously with Windows 95—is much easier than with previous desktop operating systems. Windows 95 can support up to ten 32-bit, protected mode network clients through its Network Provider Interface—a series of Application Program Interfaces that Windows 95 uses to access the network for networking tasks, such as logging on and off of a server, and browsing for servers.

Installing network provider support is done through the Network option in the Control Panel, or as part of Windows 95 Setup. A single

Windows 95 computer can run clients for NetWare, Windows NT Server, Banyan Vines, Digital PathWorks, and Sun NFS simultaneously, while still acting as a peer server.

The only exception is if your network includes Apple Macintosh computers. Due to the marked difference between the way the Macintosh handles files and the way that virtually every other operating system handles them, a Windows NT server or Novell NetWare server must be used as a common file server to both the Windows 95 computers and Macintosh computers.

Windows 95 long file name support simplifies the process, however, since the Macintosh users can use long file names, and they can be used without translation by the Windows 95 users to refer to the same files.

Exploring Peer Server and Universal Client

Key Concept

Because Windows 95 computers can support clients for virtually any type of network, it can be referred to as a *universal network client*. In addition to the built-in protected mode clients for Microsoft networks and for Novell NetWare, Windows 95 supports the existing real mode clients for NetWare with NDS (VLMs), Banyan VINES, and other networks. If you need to use these real mode clients, you must have the real mode clients installed under MS-DOS, and running at the time that you run Windows 95 Setup.

However, Windows 95 network support is not limited to functioning as a client. Windows 95 also functions as a network file and print server.

Windows 95 file and print services give other computers access to the resources on your computer. The only difference between the file and print services supplied by Windows 95 and those supplied by traditional network file servers, such as Novell NetWare, is that Windows 95 does not maintain its own network user security, and depends upon some other security provider to authenticate users trying to access shared resources—if you want access to be controlled according to users.

Windows 95 file and print services, default security mode is share-level security. In this mode, you must supply a password when attempting to access a resource.

Windows 95 network services support sharing between any workstation and any other workstation running Windows 95, Windows NT, Windows NT Server, Windows for Workgroups, or even MS-DOS running either the Microsoft network client for DOS or the Novell client software (see Chapters 17 and 19 for details). Because of this support for networking between peers, rather than just between a client computer and some central server, Windows 95's server is sometimes called a *peer server.*

Examining Networking Interfaces

Networking interfaces provide Session-layer APIs for accessing network services. Windows 95 supports several networking interfaces.

Windows Sockets (WinSock)

The *de facto* standard for accessing datagram and session services over the TCP/IP transport protocol is the U.C. Berkeley Sockets API, used widely in the UNIX world. Windows 95 includes a Windows implementation of the sockets API called Windows Sockets. Most of the applications used to access Internet resources that run under Windows 95 use the Windows Sockets API, including Telnet, FTP, and the Internet Explorer.

Key Concept

Windows Sockets is a protocol-independent networking API. It is the result of the work of a committee made up of representatives from some 40 networking vendors that began with a suggestion posed at a discussion session at a trade conference. Windows 95 supports Windows Sockets over both the IPX/SPX and the TCP/IP transport protocols.

The Windows Sockets specification has several design goals:

+ Provide a familiar and interoperable networking API to programmers using either Windows or UNIX.

+ Provide a transport stack–independent interface, so that application and utility vendors could write applications that would run over any vendor's TCP/IP stack. (This was a significant concern in the pre-Windows 95 and pre-Windows NT days when TCP/IP networking was not included as a part of the operating system, and many vendors created proprietary protocol stacks.)

+ Provide an API that supports both connection-oriented and connectionless protocols.

Windows Sockets has a lower overhead than NetBIOS because it does not add a mapping layer (adds additional processing time) and a header (adds additional data to be sent over the network).

Windows Sockets applications provide services through a given "port" or socket number. For example, the Telnet application talks to a Telnet server using port 23. A complete list of port and services assignments can be found in the Services file in your Windows directory.

NetBIOS

NetBIOS is the Session-layer interface most often associated with Microsoft networking, and is used in Windows 95 by the upper-layer networking services—such as the redirector and server—to communicate with the lower layers.

The NetBIOS interface can be used with the TCP/IP, NetBEUI, and IPX/SPX-compatible transport protocols in Windows 95. The Windows 95 NetBIOS interface provides compatibility with NetBIOS applications, and the additional NetBIOS driver (Vnetbios.386) and DLL (Netbios.dll) are used only for those purposes.

NetBIOS was originally defined as part of the same set of specifications that defined the NetBEUI transport protocol, a result of work jointly performed by Microsoft and IBM.

DCE-Compliant RPC

The Microsoft RPC facility is compatible with the industry standard for remote procedure calls, the Open Software Foundation (OSF) Data Communication Exchange (DCE) specification. The Microsoft facility is completely *interoperable* with other DCE-based systems. It is not, however, *compliant* with the OSF specification, because it is not based on the OSF source code.

Remote Procedure Calls

RPC uses other methods of interprocess communication, such as NetBIOS, Windows Sockets, or named pipes, to establish communication between the client and server. RPC facilitates distributed computing by allowing program logic and other procedures to exist on different computers.

RPC uses other IPC mechanisms, such as named pipes, NetBIOS, or Windows Sockets, to establish communications between the client and the server. With the RPC facility, essential program logic and related procedure code can exist on different computers, which is important for distributed applications.

Windows 95 provides client support over NetBIOS, named pipes, and Windows Sockets interfaces. RPC server support is only available over the Windows Sockets interface, however.

This means that if you need to use a named-pipes RPC application, you can run the client portion on a Windows 95 computer, but you must run the named-pipes server portion on a Windows NT computer.

Distributed Computing

Distributed computing means that a computing task is divided into multiple parts. There can be two parts, as in traditional client-server computing, where one part runs on a client computer and requires minimal resources. The second part runs on a server, using large amounts of data, processing power, or specialized hardware.

Another view takes complex tasks and spreads the work among many, coordinated computers, enabling an array of 50 computers to solve in a day what might take a single computer more than a month.

In either case, a connection between the computers at the interprocess level allows data to flow in both directions. Windows 95 supports several interprocess communication (IPC) methods that support distributed computing: Windows Sockets, Remote Procedure Calls, NetBIOS, named-pipes, and mailslots.

Client-Side Named Pipes

Windows 95 includes support for client-side named pipes for compatibility with existing applications written for Microsoft LAN Manager. Windows 95 does not support the server-side of named pipes, meaning that any named-pipe server application would have to be run on a LAN Manager or Windows NT server computer.

Windows 95 named pipe support is limited to the Client for Microsoft Networks, which does not support other networks such as Novell NetWare and Banyan VINES. If support for named pipes on these networks is required, you must use the real mode networking components provided by Novell or Banyan.

Named pipes are easy for an application to use because they can be treated in much the same way that files are. Named pipes are created by the server process, which also manages access to it. The actual resources that make up named pipes are owned by, and actually exist on, the computer where the server process is running.

The named pipe client uses the underlying network protocol services to access the named pipe resources on the remote computer. Communication can be bi-directional, or allow communication in only one direction.

Named pipes are commonly used by Microsoft SQL server-based client-server applications. The named pipe server application runs on Windows NT, while the client portion can run on Windows 95.

Mailslots

Windows 95 supports mailslots for backward compatibility with LAN Manager and Windows for Workgroups applications that use them for interprocess communication.

Both Windows NT and Windows 95 support a subset of the mailslot APIs that were available in the Microsoft OS/2 LAN Manager product. The mailslot APIs are made available in Windows 95 by the Client for Microsoft Networks.

Unlike named pipes, which are limited to one-to-one communication, mailslots can be used for either one-to-one or one-to-many communications.

The full mailslot API includes both first-class and second-class mailslots delivery. First-class delivery is session-oriented, and data transfer is guaranteed. Messages that are set for first-class delivery can only be sent to a mailslot created on a LAN Manager server. For this reason, Windows 95 does not use first-class messaging.

On the other hand, second-class delivery uses datagrams to provide unguaranteed data transfer. Second-class messages can be sent to a mailslot that was created on any computer, or even multiple computers when the message is 400 bytes or smaller.

Second-class mailslots are most useful for identifying other computers or services on a network, and for wide-scale identification of a service. Windows 95 uses second-class mailslots for WinPopup messages and browsing.

Understanding the Universal Naming Convention

When using networking software under previous operating systems, such as MS-DOS, you had to use a network utility, such as the Novell MAP command, or MS-DOS NET USE command, to associate a network drive letter with a network resource in order to use it.

Windows 95 allows you to use *Universal Naming Convention (UNC)* pathnames. A UNC name includes the server name and network share name of the resource in the pathname. For example, a network

directory located on the server "MYSERVER," that has been shared as
"MYDIR," has the UNC name of:

    \\MYSERVER\MYDIR

Subdirectories and file names below the shared directory can be added
onto the end of the pathname:

    \\MYSERVER\MYDIR\SUBDIR\Filename.ext

UNC pathnames can be used everywhere that Windows 95 takes
a file name. You do not have to connect a drive letter to a share in
order to access network resources. This means you can type
\\Accting\Data\Microsoft Excel\Budgets\Fiscal 1995\March
in the File Open box of Microsoft Excel instead of having to first connect a drive letter.

Examining Network Architecture

The Windows 95 network architecture is a marked improvement over
the level of integration and support that was present in previous versions of Windows and MS-DOS.

Windows 95 networking components are implemented as 32-bit virtual
device drivers. They use no conventional memory, and are dynamically
loaded as needed by the system. Performance also benefits because there
is no mode-switching overhead and virtualization between real mode
and protected mode components (as required in Windows 3.1). As a
result, network performance increases the range up to 200 percent.

Windows 95 protected mode networking components are more reliable
than the real mode network components used in Windows 3.1 and
MS-DOS. The use of real mode components can result in memory or
interrupt conflicts that lead to system hangs and errors. This doesn't
happen with Windows 95 protected mode components because Windows 95 arbitrates hardware resource allocation.

The Windows 95 network architecture is modular, including the
Installable File System (IFS) interface, the Network Provider Interface

(NPI) and a new version of the Network Driver Interface Specification (NDIS) version 3.1, which has been enhanced to support Plug and Play network adapters.

Windows 95 supports multiple network providers and redirectors, which allow you to run client support for both Microsoft networks and Novell NetWare at the same time. Windows 95 can support multiple 32-bit protected mode network clients and one real mode network client concurrently. For example, you could have the Microsoft Client for Microsoft Networks, Microsoft Client for NetWare Networks, and the real mode Banyan Vines client all loaded concurrently.

The Windows 95 Protocol Manager (part of the NDIS components) allows you to load multiple transport protocols. Windows 95 includes built-in support for IPX/SPX, TCP/IP, and NetBEUI.

Figure 15.1 shows the layered network architecture in Windows 95. The rest of this chapter discusses each of these layers in detail.

FIG. 15.1 ⇒
The layered net–
work architecture
of Windows 95.

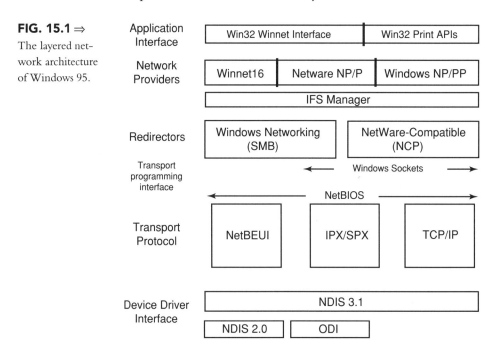

Application Interface

32-bit Windows applications access file and print services through the 32-bit Windows Networking interfaces, Win32 WinNet, and Win32 Print.

Win32 WinNet Interface

Microsoft first included a Windows networking API set in Windows 3.0. This API was subsequently enhanced in Windows 3.1, and provided network platform-independent APIs.

With the release of LAN Manager 2.1, the multi-network DLL, routing requests from the interface to either the NetWare or LAN Manager networks was introduced. Windows for Workgroups 3.1 extended that API and added common network dialog boxes that used the WinNet interface.

Windows NT formalized the multi-net layer as the Multi-Protocol Router and added network browsing to the API, as well as allowing for differing naming conventions and security models.

Windows 95 supports the Win32 WinNet APIs that are defined by Windows NT, while providing backward compatibility with Windows for Workgroups 3.11.

Windows 95 further expands the API. According to Microsoft, the goals of the Windows 95 WinNet interface are

+ Support for the Win32 WinNet APIs as defined in Windows NT.
+ An interface that allows seamless browsing of network resources (network directories and printers, for example). This includes consistent handling of authentication requirements across multiple networks.
+ Backward compatibility with Windows for Workgroups 3.11.

The supported WinNet API calls are divided into groups:

+ *Connection API.* Allows applications to create, manage, and destroy connections to network resources.

+ *Enumeration API.* Allows applications to browse the network and examine details of available resources.

+ *Error Reporting API.* Allows for getting and setting error codes (used by network providers).

+ *Local Device Name API.* Helps standardize device naming (used by network providers).

+ *UNC API.* Processes UNC paths

+ *Password Cache API.* Allows a network provider to use, or prevent the use of, the Windows 95 password cache.

+ *Authentication Dialog API.* Allows a network provider to provide a consistent login (or authentication) interface.

Win32 Print APIs

The Win32 Print APIs handle network printing.

Network Providers

The Windows 95 Network Provider Interface allows anyone to integrate network services seamlessly into Windows 95. The NPI consists of two parts: the network provider API and the network providers themselves.

The network provider API is a single set of APIs used by Windows 95 to request network services, such as connecting to a server, queuing a print job, and disconnecting from a server. The requests are then passed on to the network providers.

One service provided by the NPI is the Windows 95 system logon. Each network provider can provide a logon dialog box that suits the needs of the network server's security model. For example, figure 15.2 shows the dialog box used to logon to a Windows NT Server domain, while figure 15.3 shows the corresponding dialog box to log onto a Novell NetWare server.

After the logon information typed into the dialog box has been validated against the requested server, the password is passed back to Windows 95, which can then use the password to unlock any linked system or network resource. This allows Windows 95 to accommodate the various ways that network servers provide services, while making the interface the user sees consistent.

FIG. 15.2 ⇒

The Windows 95 logon box for Windows NT Server domains.

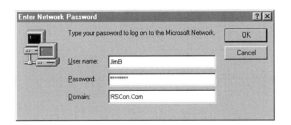

FIG. 15.3 ⇒

The Windows 95 logon box for Novell NetWare.

WinNet 16

As previously mentioned, Windows 95 does support a single 16-bit WinNet driver in addition to up to ten 32-bit network providers. A network product that does not offer a 32-bit network provider is supported in this way. Figure 15.4 shows the architecture of the 16-bit WinNet support.

The components that support the 16-bit WinNet drivers are:

+ *Winnet16.dll.* Provides the 32-bit to 16-bit thunk and translation between the 16-bit WinNet API and the 32-bit NPI.

+ *Winnet16.drv.* The 16-bit Windows 3.x network driver. It provides the basic Map Network Drive dialog box.

+ *Network.vxd.* A Windows 3.x virtual device driver that virtualizes access to the real-mode software.

+ *Real-mode network software.* Whatever proprietary drivers, clients, and utilities are used by the network.

FIG. 15.4 ⇒
Windows 95 sup-
port for 16-bit
WinNet drivers.

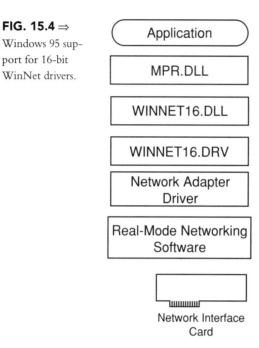

NetWare NP/PP

The Windows 95 NetWare Network Provider and Print Provider is a
32-bit protected mode provider that supports Novell Networks. It allows access to Novell resources, logging on and off of NetWare servers,
and queuing of print jobs on NetWare servers. It can be used by both
16- and 32-bit Windows programs.

Windows NP/PP

The Windows Network Provider and Print Provider is a 32-bit protected mode network provider that supports all networking products
that use SMB (Server Message Block) file sharing. It allows access to
SMB network resources, logging on and off of SMB networks, and
queuing print jobs on SMB print servers. It can be used by both 16-
and 32-bit Windows programs. Most networks, with the notable exception of Novell NetWare, use SMB file sharing.

File System Interface and the IFS Manager

Windows 95 uses an Installable File System architecture that allows multiple file systems to coexist on the same computer. Network redirectors, such as the Microsoft Client for NetWare Networks or Client for Microsoft Networks, are implemented as file system drivers. Other file system drivers are the VFAT and CDFS file systems, which provide access to files on hard disk and CD-ROM.

At the core of the Installable File System architecture is the Installable File System Manager (IFSMGR). It is responsible for managing the interoperability of the various file systems with each other and with applications. IFSMGR consists of two components: Ifshlp.sys, which is a real mode stub for the IFS Manager that hooks the INT21h chain and hands the calls to the protected mode IFS Manager.

All of the file system drivers support long file names and, with the exception of the CDFS system, support using the protected mode VCACHE for reads, including the network redirectors.

File system drivers (FSDs) are responsible for managing the high-level I/O requests made by applications. The IFS Manager receives all file I/O calls and arbitrates which file system driver should receive a particular call and process it.

Redirectors and Services

Network file and print sharing mechanisms are made possible by the redirectors and services.

Redirectors

Both Microsoft-supplied redirectors—the Client for Microsoft Networks and the Client for NetWare—are implemented as IFS File system drivers.

A network *redirector* is responsible for locating, opening, reading, writing, and deleting files, as well as submitting print jobs. It is also responsible for making application services, such as named pipes and mailslots, available.

The network redirector provides the functionality of the OSI application and presentation layers. Windows 95 provides two redirectors:

+ *Client for Microsoft Networks.* Supports all networks based on Microsoft networking and the SMB file sharing protocols. Implemented in Vredir.vxd.

+ *Microsoft Client for NetWare Networks.* Supports the NetWare networking products, which are based on the NCP file sharing protocol.

In addition, other network vendors can supply FSDs for their own networks.

Redirectors are managed by the Installable File System Manager, which decides whether a particular file is on a local file system or needs to be accessed through a network redirector.

Services

A *service* is a DLL or VxD that loads when Windows 95 starts up. The services then become available to applications on the computer, or on remote computers. Services are available even if no one has logged into the computer.

Windows 95 includes the following services:

+ *Arcada Backup Exec Agent.* A network backup.

+ *Cheyenne ARCserve Agent.* A network backup.

+ *HP JetAdmin (NetWare).* Remote administration of HP network attached printers on a NetWare Network.

+ *HP JetAdmin.* Remote administration of HP network attached printers on a Microsoft network.

+ *Microsoft File and Print Sharing for Microsoft Networks.* Shares files and printers on a Microsoft Network

+ *Microsoft File and Print Sharing for NetWare Networks.* Shares files and printers on a Novell NetWare Network.

+ *Microsoft Network Monitor.* Permits remote network monitoring.

+ *Microsoft Remote Registry.* Permits editing of the registry by remote administrators.

Note While multiple clients can be used with Windows 95, only one file and print sharing service may be installed and used at one time.

Transport Device Interface (TDI)

The redirector makes its calls to transport protocols through one of the Transport Device Interfaces. There are two interfaces—Windows Sockets and NetBIOS—as mentioned earlier in the chapter.

Transport Protocols

Windows 95 includes three transport protocols: NetBEUI, IPX/SPX-compatible, and TCP/IP. See Chapters 14 and 16 for details on transport protocols.

Device Driver Interface

Transport protocols talk to the network adapter drivers through the Device Driver interface. Windows 95 supports two DDIs: NDIS and ODI.

NDIS

In 1989, Microsoft and 3Com developed a joint standard that defined an interface for communicating between the MAC sublayer and transport protocol drivers on layers 3 and 4 of the OSI model. This standard, the *Network Device Interface Specification (NDIS)*, is designed to create an environment where any transport protocol can talk to any network adapter card driver without either one knowing anything about the other.

The initial communication channel between the protocol driver and the MAC driver is established through a process called *binding*, in which the *Protocol Manager* binds the MAC and transport protocol drivers.

NDIS also permits a single network adapter to support multiple protocol drivers, as well as supporting multiple network adapters. The Protocol Manager is responsible for routing network requests to the appropriate driver.

Windows 95 supports NDIS-2 and NDIS-3 drivers, but prefers NDIS 3.1 drivers, which have been enhanced to support Plug and Play, as well as support concurrent ODI drivers.

ODI

Novell's version of an architecture that allows the use of multiple LAN drivers and protocols is called the *Open Data-Link Interface (ODI)* specification.

ODI is similar to NDIS-2 drivers. There are two parts to an ODI stack. The first, the *Multiple Link Interface Driver (MLID)*, is a network adapter specific driver. The second, the *Link Support Layer (LSL),* provides the interface to the transport protocols.

Taking the Disc Test

 If you have read and understood the material in the chapter, you are ready to test your knowledge. Insert the CD-ROM that comes with this book and run the self-test software as described in Appendix I, "Using the CD-ROM."

Chapter Prerequisite

Before reading this chapter, you should be familiar with the ISO OSI networking model, transport protocols, network and host addresses (see Chapter 14, "Networking Basics"), and the Windows 95 Networking Architecture (see Chapter 15, "Windows 95 Networking Introduction").

TCP/IP and Windows 95

Transmission Control Protocol/Internet Protocol (TCP/IP) is the most significant network transport protocol. There are two primary reasons for this: its use on the worldwide Internet, and the complexity you may encounter when configuring it.

This chapter covers TCP/IP and Windows 95. Terms you learn include:

+ **ARP**
+ **Default gateway**
+ **DHCP**
+ **DNS**
+ **DNS domain**
+ **FQDN**
+ **ICMP**
+ **NetBIOS**
+ **Octet**

+ **Routable protocol**
+ **SNMP**
+ **Subnet mask**
+ **TCP**
+ **TCP/IP**
+ **UDP**
+ **WINS**

TCP/IP is the protocol used on the worldwide Internet. The Internet, which links millions of computers around the world, has its roots in the network designed by the United States Department of Defense to link research computers in the 1960s.

The result of the phenomenal growth of the Internet is that TCP/IP carries more network traffic than all other protocols combined. In fact, many think it is only a matter of time before all networks run TCP/IP as cable television companies and telephone companies race each other to connect every house and business onto the Internet.

The second reason for TCP/IP's impact on you is the fact that TCP/IP is the most configurable protocol supported by Microsoft. You need to know how to use and configure many utility programs and understand the nuances of the protocol in order to successfully build a TCP/IP-based network.

Configuring TCP/IP

One of the utilities included in the Microsoft Plus! for Windows 95 add-on is an Internet Setup Wizard. Microsoft designed the Wizard to make it easier for end-users to install TCP/IP to access the Internet. Most end-users access the Internet through dial-up connections, and the Wizard allows these users to set up their connection without detailed knowledge of TCP/IP. However, the Internet Setup Wizard is not usable with corporate TCP/IP-based networks. In fact, the Internet Setup Wizard can often break a working local TCP/IP installation by replacing the local configuration values with ones for a dial-up provider.

When this happens, you need to know how to troubleshoot and re-configure TCP/IP back to correct values.

IP Addresses

The first TCP/IP configuration parameter is the IP address. Unlike other transport protocols that use the MAC address burned onto every network card, a network administrator assigns the IP addresses. In addition, every IP address in a network must be unique, and every network adapter has its own IP address. Until recently, probably the most time-consuming portion of an IP network administrator's job was keeping track of IP addresses.

Ch

16

As you'll see in "Dynamically Assigning IP Addresses with DHCP" later in the chapter, Dynamic Host Configuration Protocol (DHCP) makes it possible to automatically assign the IP addresses if a Windows NT Server computer is part of the network.

If you are attaching the computer to the Internet, there is one additional requirement. Your Internet Service Provider (ISP) usually supplies a block of IP addresses that you can use, or you can apply to the InterNIC for your own block. The reason for this is that IP addresses must be unique on the Internet.

An IP address is a 32-bit number, divided into 4 *octets* (an octet is a group of 8 bits). You usually express each octet as a normal decimal number, so that an octet can range between 0 and 255. You separate each octet from the next one by a period. For example, 198.105.232.4 was the IP address for Microsoft's World Wide Web server at the time that this book was written.

Unlike IPX addresses, IP addresses do not have a distinctly separate network and host address. Instead, as you see in "Subnet Masks" later in the chapter, TCP/IP uses an additional configuration parameter, the *subnet mask* to separate the network and host addresses.

If you are not using DHCP on your network, you must manually configure the correct IP address for your computer using the Network configuration dialog. Be careful to select the TCP/IP protocol bound to the network card that you are configuring. In figure 16.1, the highlight is on the TCP/IP protocol bound to the first Xircom network adapter.

FIG. 16.1 ⇒

You must select the TCP/IP protocol bound to the correct network adapter.

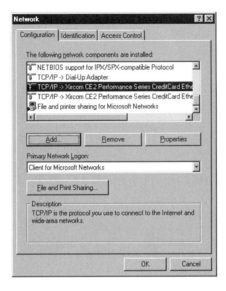

Once you've highlighted the protocol, click the Properties button to open the TCP/IP Properties dialog (see fig. 16.2).

FIG. 16.2 ⇒

The IP address page of the TCP/IP Properties dialog.

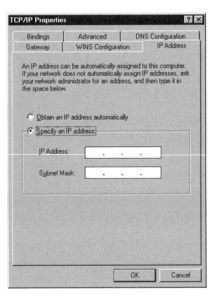

Simply type the IP address into the dialog, making sure to use the period between each of the octets. Using the Tab key causes the cursor to jump to the next item, not the next octet.

Note IP addresses are divided into "classes." The original purpose of classes was to help routers determine where packets should go on the Internet. The early routers did this by looking at the first octet of the IP address. The classes, and the corresponding first octet ranges are:

Class A: 1-126

Class B: 128-191

Class C: 192-223

Being assigned a Class A address gives you 16.7 million IP addresses to use. A Class B gives you 65,535 addresses, and a Class C gives you 256 addresses. The Internet Network Information Center only assigns Class C addresses, because there are no Class A or Class B addresses available anymore, since they have all been used up.

Ch

16

Subnet Masks

As previously mentioned, you use a subnet mask to break an IP address into its component network ID and host ID. The subnet mask is a mask in the programming sense; the subnet mask is binary *AND*ed with the IP address, stripping off the bits that apply to the host ID.

See "How the IP Address and Subnet Mask Interact," **p. 255**

Typically, you choose the subnet mask according to the class of which the IP address is a member. Because the InterNIC is running out of Class C addresses, it is becoming more common to use a subnet mask to further divide a Class C address into smaller networks. The correspondences are:

Class A: 255.0.0.0

Class B: 255.255.0.0

Class C: 255.255.255.0

Tip

To determine the network address when the subnet mask has only 255s and 0s in it, take the IP address octets that correspond with the 255s; those make up the network ID. The octets that correspond with the 0s in the subnet mask are the host ID.

continues

continued

For example, the Microsoft World Wide Web site, 198.105.232.4, has a subnet mask of 255.255.255.0 (see fig. 16.3). This means that this computer is on a subnet with the network ID of 198.105.232.0 (notice the use of the zero as a place holder). The host ID of the computer is 4.

FIG. 16.3 ⇒

You enter the subnet mask in the TCP/IP Properties dialog in the same way you enter the IP address.

Default Gateway

One of the key advantages of TCP/IP is that it is a routable protocol. A *routable protocol* is a protocol that allows the use of routers to interconnect different subnets. However, TCP/IP packets do not contain any routing information in them; they only carry the source and destination address, which means that a router must have a route to the packet's destination already configured.

Obviously, it would be inconvenient for every computer on the Internet to maintain a route to every other computer or network on the Internet. To address this, TCP/IP uses a *default gateway*. Simply put, the default gateway is the TCP/IP host that your computer sends packets destined for remote networks that it doesn't have a route to in its routing tables.

Every host and router on the Internet, except for the routers at the top of the hierarchy (called *backbone routers*), has a default gateway. Your computer forwards packets destined for a remote computer to its default gateway. This computer routes the packet if it has an entry in its routing table, or forwards it to its default gateway if it doesn't. This process continues until the packet reaches a backbone router. Packets do not keep routing information, requiring the backbone routers to have a route to every network on the Internet.

To set the default gateway, use the Gateway tab of the TCP/IP Properties dialog (see fig. 16.4). Windows 95 allows you to add one or more additional gateways. If the first listed gateway is not available, Windows 95 uses one of the additional gateways.

The correct default gateway is supplied by your network administrator or Internet Service Provider.

FIG. 16.4 ⇒
Add default gateways using the Gateway tab of the TCP/IP Properties dialog.

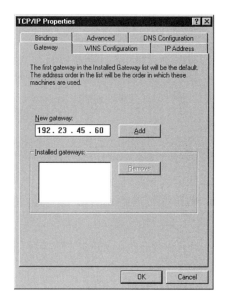

How the IP Address and Subnet Mask Interact

As previously mentioned, the IP address and subnet mask are binary ANDed together to produce the host ID and network ID.

For example, the Microsoft World Wide Web site, IP address **198.105.232.4**, when changed into binary becomes:

> 11000110.01101001.11101000.00000100

Its subnet mask, 255.255.255.0 becomes:

> 11111111.11111111.11111111.00000000

A binary AND consists of comparing each bit with its counterpart. If they are both 1s, the resulting bit is a 1. Otherwise, it's a 0. In the example:

11000110.01101001.11101000.00000100

11111111.11111111.11111111.00000000

yields 11000110.01101001.11101000.00000000

which, when turned back into decimal, gives us **198.105.232.0** as the network ID.

Dynamically Assigning IP Addresses with DHCP

Internet standard RFC 1541 defines the Dynamic Host Configuration Protocol (DHCP). DHCP is an industry-standard method of automatically assigning IP addresses and other configuration parameters. Additional parameters that DHCP can assign include subnet masks, default gateways, and DNS servers.

On the Web

You can obtain copies of the RFCs from

http://www.internic.net

In order to use DHCP, your network must have a computer running Windows NT Server version 3.5 or later, and the DHCP Server software that comes with Windows NT Server.

Windows 95 can be a DHCP client, but not a DHCP server. To configure Windows 95 to obtain its IP address via DHCP, simply select Obtain an IP address automatically in the TCP/IP Properties dialog as shown in figure 16.5.

FIG. 16.5 ⇒

Choosing to use DHCP to automatically assign an IP address.

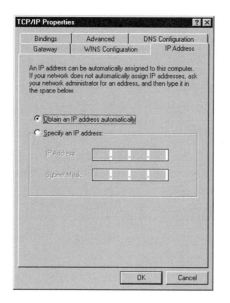

Resolving Network Names

Computers understand numbers like IP addresses. Humans, on the other hand, tend to want to refer to things by name, including network resources.

As you'll learn in Chapter 17, Microsoft networking uses NetBIOS names for a variety of purposes, including computer names and user names. On the other hand, Internet utilities, and therefore TCP/IP utilities, normally use Domain Name Service (DNS) names. This use of NetBIOS names instead of DNS names means that Microsoft had to create methods for resolving NetBIOS names to IP addresses on a TCP/IP network.

Resolving IP Addresses to NetBIOS Names

There are three different methods used by Windows 95 to resolve NetBIOS names to IP addresses, *broadcasts*, *LMHOSTS*, and the *Windows Internet Naming Service (WINS)*. Of the three, WINS is the preferred method, because it generates the least amount of network traffic, and is dynamic.

Ch

16

Name resolution using broadcasts consists of computers simply announcing their names using IP level broadcasts when they attach to the network. If Windows 95 relies on broadcasts, your computer can only resolve names on the local subnet. The limitation is due to the fact that routers do not pass broadcast messages.

You can create an LMHOSTS file in the Windows folder with a text editor such as Notepad. If you do not have a WINS server on your subnet, you must use an LMHOSTS file if you need to resolve names to computers that are on other subnets.

LMHOSTS entries consist of a host's IP address, followed by the host's NetBIOS name, and the keyword #PRE, which tells Windows 95 to pre-load the entry into its name cache. Following are two sample LMHOSTS entries, one for the computer *popular*, with an IP address of 102.54.94.123, and another for the computer *localsrv*, IP address, 102.54.94.117:

```
102.54.94.123    popular              #PRE
localsrv                              #PRE
```

LMHOSTS has two major drawbacks. First, there the management overhead of placing LMHOSTS files on every TCP/IP network client. Second, LMHOSTS is static by nature. If you are using DHCP to assign IP addresses to the Windows 95 computers, and the computers are sharing resources with remote computers, LMHOSTS is unusable.

The solution is to include a WINS Server, which, like a DHCP server, is a Windows NT Server 3.5 or higher computer, on the subnet. WINS then automatically registers and resolves NetBIOS names to IP addresses.

Windows 95 supports up to two WINS Servers to provide a backup server in case the primary server is not available. To automatically assign WINS servers via DHCP, choose Use DHCP for WINS Resolution from the WINS Configuration tab in TCP/IP Properties dialog (see fig. 16.6).

FIG. 16.6 ⇒

Configuring Windows Internet Naming Service resolution.

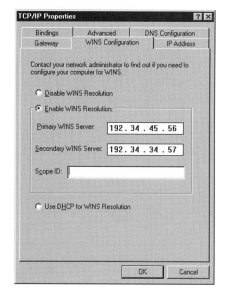

To configure WINS resolution manually, select <u>E</u>nable WINS Resolution in the TCP/IP Properties dialog (refer to fig. 16.6), and enter the IP addresses of the primary and secondary WINS servers. If the primary WINS server is not available, Windows 95 uses the secondary WINS server.

In addition, you can specify a NetBIOS *scope*. You can use a NetBIOS scope to restrict computers from seeing computers in other NetBIOS scopes. You can still talk to computers without using their names by entering their IP address, for example, NET USE F: \\10.10.10.10\C . Normally, you just leave the scope entry blank.

Resolving Internet Names

The Domain Name Service name of a host is the name that most people recognize as an *Internet name*. DNS names are hierarchical, with the largest group in the hierarchy appearing to the right, and the levels separated by periods, such as RSCON.COM. Table 16.1 shows the top level names and their members.

Ch

16

Table 16.1 Top-Level DNS Domain Names

Domain Name	Membership
com	Commercial organizations
edu	Education institutions
gov	Government agencies
mil	Military groups
net	Large ISPs
org	Other organizations, usually non-profit
int	International organization
\<country name\>	Countries, using a geographic, rather than organizational scheme (such as .uk, .aus, .ger)

In Windows 95, there are two ways to resolve DNS names to IP addresses. The first is to create a file called HOSTS in your Windows directory. The HOSTS file has a similar structure to LMHOSTS, except the HOSTS file does not use keywords. A typical line from a HOSTS file might be

```
198.105.232.4          www.microsoft.com
```

By using DNS Server, you eliminate the need to use a HOSTS file. If you are connecting to the Internet, your ISP supplies the address of at least two DNS servers. If configuring a local internetwork, obtain the address of the DNS servers from your network administrator.

DNS servers are often UNIX-based computers, but can be Windows NT-based computers using the DNS software provided with the Windows NT Resource Kit.

To configure the DNS servers used by Windows 95, select the DNS Configuration tab in the TCP/IP Properties dialog (see fig. 16.7). Enter your local computer name, and the DNS domain name for the local computer. Then enter the DNS server addresses, making sure to Add each one.

FIG. 16.7 ⇒

Configuring the
DNS parameters.

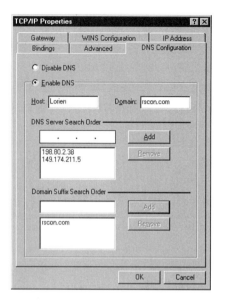

Adding domain suffixes to the Domain Suffix Search Order list enables
you to type a computer name, rather than the entire Fully Qualified
Domain Name (FQDN). Windows 95 normally tries to resolve a name
by adding the local domain suffix. If using the local domain suffix does
not resolve the name, then Windows 95 tries to add the domain suffixes
in this list, one by one in order.

Using TCP/IP Utilities

Several TCP/IP utilities come with Windows 95. In addition to the
provided utilities, Windows 95 also supports any Windows Socket application, including World Wide Web (WWW) browsers, such as Microsoft
Internet Explorer.

The provided utilities fall into two groups: connectivity utilities and
diagnostic utilities.

Connectivity Utilities

The TCP/IP connectivity utilities included with Windows 95 are *Telnet*
and *FTP* clients. Both are accessed via the Start menu's <u>R</u>un option.

Terminal Emulation: Telnet

Telnet emulates a video display terminal. You use telnet to connect to character-based computers, such as an online service over a TCP/IP network. You can specify the computer to connect by either IP address or DNS name. You can use telnet as a diagnostic tool by connecting to either the *chargen* or *echo* ports. Connecting to the chargen (*character generator)* port prints a stream of ASCII characters to your screen. Connecting to the echo port simply results in whatever you type being echoed back to your screen.

Other ports you can connect to include the *qotd* port and the *daytime* port. The qotd port echoes a "quote of the day" back to your screen, and the daytime port sends a string telling you the time of day to your screen.

To connect to an alternative port, use the Port drop-down list from the Connect dialog box (see fig. 16.8).

FIG. 16.8 ⇒

Selecting a port to connect to with Telnet.

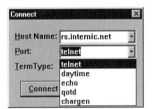

Transferring Files: FTP

You can use the File Transfer Protocol (FTP) utility to transfer files between unlike computers. It is a character-based utility. Table 16.2 lists some common commands used with FTP.

Table 16.2   FTP Commands

Command	Purpose
open <server>	Connects to an FTP server. <server> can be the IP address or DNS name of the computer you wish to connect to
close	Ends the connection

Command	Purpose
quit	Quits FTP
binary	Sets FTP to binary mode, so that binary files can be transferred without alteration
ascii	Sets FTP to ascii mode, so that text files can be transferred with end-of-line character translation
ls	Lists the directory on the remote computer
cd	Changes the current directory on the remote computer
lcd	Changes the current directory on the local computer
get	Transfers a specified file from the remote computer to the local computer
put	Transfers a specified file from the local computer to the remote computer

On the Web

A common FTP site on the Internet that contains updates and patches to Microsoft products is

ftp.microsoft.com

Diagnostic Utilities

Diagnostic utilities include *ping, netstat, route,* and *tracert,* which are command-line utilities, and *winipcfg* (use Start, <u>R</u>un to access winipcfg).

Ping

Ping, the Packet InterNet Groper, is the most commonly used diagnostic utility. Ping is very simple to use; just type *ping* followed by the IP address or DNS name of the remote computer you want to test connectivity to. If ping successfully contacts the computer, a report like the following appears:

```
Pinging 198.105.232.4 with 32 bytes of data:

Reply from 198.105.232.4: bytes=32 time=1ms TTL=32
Reply from 198.105.232.4: bytes=32 time=1ms TTL=32
Reply from 198.105.232.4: bytes=32 time=2ms TTL=32
Reply from 198.105.232.4: bytes=32 time=1ms TTL=32
```

If any of the packets did not successfully make it to the remote computer, or back to your computer (remember the routing must exist in both directions!), you receive a *Request timed out* message instead of a reply.

If you receive a *Request timed out* message, you can try using ping with the address of your computer's default gateway. If that fails, try using ping with the IP address of your computer. If that fails, you can use the special "loopback" address, 127.0.0.1. You can use *tracert* to narrow down the location of the failure.

Netstat

Netstat reports on TCP/IP connections made from your computer. A typical Netstat report looks like:

```
Active Connections

   Proto  Local Address        Foreign Address
State
   TCP    bagend:1030          gateway.moswest.msn.net:569
ESTABLISHED
```

The report shows the ports in use, the state (Established or Idle) of the connection, and which protocol (TCP or UDP) is in use.

Route

To display the routes in your computer's routing table, type *route print* at a command prompt. The resulting report resembles the following:

```
Active Routes:

Network Address          Netmask  Gateway Address     Interface  Metric
       0.0.0.0           0.0.0.0     153.36.48.1    153.36.48.11       1
     127.0.0.0         255.0.0.0      127.0.0.1      127.0.0.1         1
    153.36.0.0       255.255.0.0    153.36.48.11   153.36.48.11       1
   153.36.48.11   255.255.255.255    127.0.0.1      127.0.0.1         1
 153.36.255.255   255.255.255.255  153.36.48.11   153.36.48.11       1
     224.0.0.0         224.0.0.0    153.36.48.11   153.36.48.11
 255.255.255.255     153.36.48.11      0.0.0.0                        1
```

The Network Address and Netmask columns show IP addresses and their subnet mask. Windows 95 forwards packets destined for the Network Address to the host whose IP address is the Gateway address. Windows 95 uses the network adapter whose IP address is under the Interface column to forward the packets.

Notice the use of the loopback address in the line starting with 153.36.48.11—in this example, 153.36.48.11 is the IP address of the local computer. The presence of the loopback address in the Gateway column indicates, that correctly, packets destined for the local computer go to the local computer.

Ch

16

WinIPCfg

WinIPCfg is a graphical tool that displays the current TCP/IP configuration, and optionally, allows you to request the renewal of, or release, a DHCP-assigned IP address.

WinIPCfg presents all of the TCP/IP configuration settings in a single place (see fig. 16.9). Notice that you can change the network adapter's settings you're viewing with the highlighted drop-down box.

FIG. 16.9 ⇒

The fully expanded WinIPCfg dialog.

WinIPCfg is the easiest way to determine what IP address DHCP has assigned to your computer.

The TCP/IP Family of Protocols

TCP/IP is actually a family of related protocols (see Chapter 14, "Networking Basics," for more details on protocols). In addition to IP, which performs the routing function, the Windows 95 TCP/IP implementation includes support for *ARP, SNMP, ICMP*, and both *TCP* and *UDP*.

ARP

Windows 95 resolves the IP addresses for outgoing packets to Media Access Control (MAC) addresses using the Address Resolution Protocol (ARP).

SNMP

Network management systems, such as HP Openview, use the Simple Network Management Protocol (SNMP) to administrate network components.

UDP and TCP

Application programs use the User Datagram Protocol to send network datagrams without establishing a connection. Network datagrams which need the reliability of a connection use the TCP protocol.

ICMP

TCP/IP nodes use the Internet Control Message to share status and error information. For example, the Ping utility uses the ICMP protocol.

Taking the Disc Test

 If you have read and understood the material in the chapter, you are ready to test your knowledge. Insert the CD-ROM that comes with this book and run the self-test software as described in Appendix I, "Using the CD-ROM."

Chapter Prerequisite

You should be familiar with Windows 95 setup (see Chapter 3, "Windows 95 Setup"), configuration (see Chapter 4, "Configuring Windows 95"), networking basics (see Chapter 14, "Networking Basics" and Chapter 15, "Windows 95 Networking Introduction"), and TCP/IP (see Chapter 16, "TCP/IP and Windows 95").

Using Windows 95 with Microsoft Networks

Windows 95 computers can communicate and share resources with computers that run Windows 95, Windows for Workgroups, Windows NT Workstation, Windows NT Server, and Microsoft LAN Manager.

This chapter covers the interaction between Windows 95 and Microsoft networks. Terms and concepts covered include:

- Browse master
- Domain
- Groups
- Home directories
- Logon scripts
- Server Message Block (SMB)
- Share-level security

⊹ **User-level security**

⊹ **Workgroup**

Support for networking with Microsoft and Microsoft-compatible networks is provided by the 32-bit protected mode Client for Microsoft Networks. Other Server Message Block (SMB)-based servers supported by the client include IBM LAN Server, Digital PathWorks, AT&T StarLAN, and the various LAN Manager on UNIX products. Novell NetWare does not use the SMB server protocol; it uses Novell's proprietary NetWare Core Protocol (NCP) instead. For more information on Novell NetWare, see Chapter 18, "Novell NetWare Basics," and Chapter 19, "Using Windows 95 with Novell NetWare."

The Client for Microsoft Networks can be the only network client on the computer, or it can coexist with other networking clients, such as the Client for NetWare networks (see Chapter 19). It supports the complete set of Windows 95 networking features including automatic setup, user profiles, system policies, dial-up networking, both user- and share-level security, and the unified network login.

Understanding Domains and Workgroups

Microsoft networks use two different methods of grouping users for administrative ease, called domains and workgroups. A Windows NT Server computer is required to act as the controller of a domain.

Domains

A *domain* is a collection of computers that share a common security database. This allows for centralized administration of users, groups, and other security policies.

A key feature of a domain is the concept of a domain logon. By logging onto a domain, the user is automatically granted access to any resources on the domain for which she/he has permissions without having to supply additional logon names or passwords.

Domains work well with large networks. Domains with Windows NT Server controllers can even be configured to allow users from other domains (called *trusted* domains) to log on and use resources, making it possible for a user to have one single logon account and password that gives her/him access to every resource in the enterprise that she/he has been given permission for.

> **Note** Every domain must have a unique name.

Workgroups

A *workgroup* is a logical collection of computers that are grouped together for some purpose, such as identifying computers in a department. Workgroups do not involve security issues; they are merely a grouping method.

Workgroups are primarily used to organize the list of computers and resources displayed when the user is browsing the network (*browse list*). Windows NT computers participating in a workgroup maintain their own security databases.

See "Browse Master," **p. 284**

Comparing User-Level and Share-Level Security

Security refers to the method used by the operating system to control access to resources on the network. Windows 95 provides two methods of controlling access to network resources, called share-level and user-level security.

Share-level security controls access to shared network resources by allowing you to assign a password to the resource when sharing it. In order to access the resource from another computer, the user of that computer must type in the matching password. To make a resource available to all users, simply do not assign a password. Share-level

Ch
17

security is only available to control access on computers that have File and Printer Sharing for Microsoft Networks running.

User-level security controls access to shared network resources by allowing you to assign permissions to the resource on a per-user basis. Windows 95 does not, however, maintain a security database of its own. Instead, Windows 95 uses a technique called *pass-through security* to authenticate requests to access resources.

With pass-through security, another computer called a *security provider* authenticates the request by verifying that the user name and password supplied by the user match those in the database on the security provider.

If the Windows 95 computer is running File and Printer Sharing for Microsoft Networks, the security provider must be a Windows NT Workstation computer or a Windows NT Server domain.

When planning and implementing the type of security you choose for your Windows 95 computers, you should:

- Define user accounts on a network server or domain controller if you are going to use user-level security.
- Install File and Printer Sharing for Microsoft Networks, and enable the appropriate type of security.
- Define permissions for resources that are protected by user-level security.
- Use system policies to control access available to the local user of a computer (see Chapter 22, "Windows 95 Administration").

Share-Level Security

As previously mentioned, share-level security is only supported with File and Printer Sharing for Microsoft Networks. Share-level security is similar to the security provided by Windows for Workgroups. Share-level security is usable both in a peer-to-peer network consisting only of Windows 95 computers, and in a network server-based network such as a Windows NT domain-based network. Share-level security is used by default.

Share-level security can even be used in a Novell NetWare-based network, as long as File and Printer Sharing for Microsoft Networks is used.

There are two types of access that you can allow when using share-level security: read-only and full access. You can decide to allow only read-only access, or to provide separate passwords—one for read-only and one for full access—which can be the same, or even blank.

To share a folder, right-click the folder in Explorer, and choose Sharing (see fig. 17.1). The properties dialog for the folder opens, with the Sharing tab automatically selected (see fig. 17.2).

FIG. 17.1 ⇒

Right-click and choose Sharing to open the Sharing tab of the properties dialog.

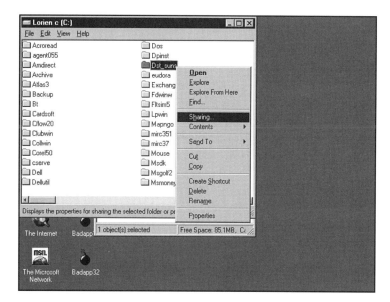

If the chosen folder is contained within another folder that has already been shared, a note appears at the top of the dialog.

To share the folder, change the radio button from Not Shared to Shared As:. After doing so, the rest of the dialog becomes available (see fig. 17.3). There are number of configurable options:

+ *Share Name.* This is the name that network users will use to try to attach to the resource. Although you can make a share name that includes spaces, you should avoid using spaces for compatibility with other network clients. The share name is required.

FIG. 17.2 ⇒
The Sharing tab of
the properties
dialog is opened
automatically.

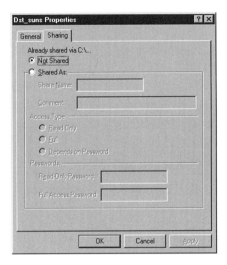

Tip

If you place a dollar sign ($) at the end of a share name, (for example, MYSHARE$), the share name will not appear in browsing lists. A share named in this fashion is called a *hidden share* and is often used for administrative purposes.

⊥ *Comment.* You can add a comment that appears with this share in the browsing dialogs. The comment is optional.

FIG. 17.3 ⇒
Choosing to share
the folder activates
the rest of the
dialog.

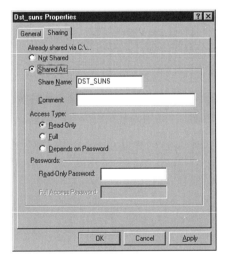

+ Access Types:

- *Read-Only.* If you choose Read-Only access, someone connecting to this share (and supplying the password) will only be able to read from the files in the folder.

- *Full.* If you choose Full access, someone connecting to this share (and supplying the password) will be able to perform any operation on the folder and its files (create, read, write, delete, and so on).

- *Depends on Password.* If you choose this option, the dialog changes to that in figure 17.4, and the share has two different passwords: one that allows read-only access, and the other that allows full access.

FIG. 17.4 ⇒

The three access types.

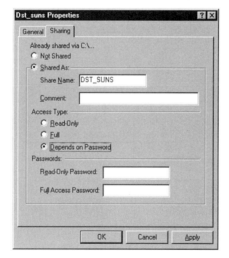

Ch

17

Tip

You can share a directory but hide it from the Network Neighborhood browsing list by adding a dollar-sign character ($) to the end of its share name (for example, PRIVATE$).

User-Level Security

User-level security is available when Windows 95 is running on a network that contains a Windows NT Workstation computer or a Windows NT Server domain that can perform security authentication on behalf of the Windows 95 computer. This process is called *pass-through* security.

Figure 17.5 shows how user-level security works on Microsoft Networks.

FIG. 17.5 ⇒

How user-level security works.

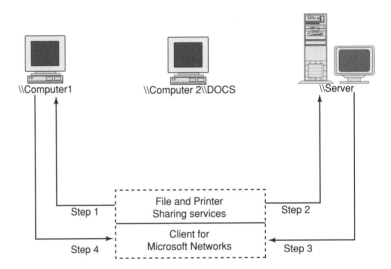

In step 1 of figure 17.5, the user on COMPUTER1, a Windows 95 computer, wants to access the shared DOCS directory on COMPUTER2, another Windows 95 computer configured for user-level security. The security provider on COMPUTER2 is set to \\SERVER.

In step 2, COMPUTER2 asks the security provider, \\SERVER, to verify the user's identity. The security provider checks the supplied user name and password against its database and determines that the user is valid.

In step 3, \\SERVER informs COMPUTER2 that the user is valid.

Finally, in step 4, COMPUTER2 gives access to the requested resource.
The rights assigned to the user are actually stored on the Windows 95
computer with the resources. It just doesn't have the ability to authenticate the users itself.

To activate user-level security on a Windows 95 computer, open the
Network option in Control Panel and select the Access Control tab. By
default, Share-level access control is chosen (see fig. 17.6).

FIG. 17.6 ⇒

The Access Con-
trol tab showing
share-level access
control.

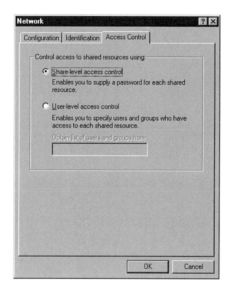

Ch

17

Changing the radio button to User-level access control makes the rest
of the dialog available. Typing the name of the Windows NT Workstation or Windows NT Server in the Obtain list of users and groups
from: box designates the security provider (see fig. 17.7).

If you had any shared folders on the computer, they will be lost as part
of the switch from share-level to user-level security, and you will have
to re-create them (see fig. 17.8).

FIG. 17.7 ⇒
Enter the name
of the security
provider.

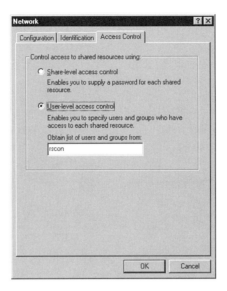

FIG. 17.8 ⇒
Shared folders will
be lost when you
change access
control types.

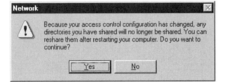

Using Group Accounts

Windows NT has two types of groups: local and global. The distinction
between the two focuses on where they can be used. Windows 95 user-
level security is only aware of global groups.

Global Groups

The primary purpose of Windows NT global groups is to make users
visible from outside the Windows NT domain. For example, if a user
had an account in the GRAPE domain, and he needed to access resources in the ORANGE domain, the administrators of the domains
could establish a trust relationship between the two domains in which
the ORANGE domain trusts the GRAPE domain.

Using a pass–through authentication method, domain controllers in the ORANGE domain would then be able to authenticate users accessing computers in the ORANGE domain with accounts from the GRAPE domain.

Because Windows 95 uses a similar pass–through authentication method, global groups are usable in Windows 95 as well.

Default Groups

Windows NT Server provides several default global groups, which can be used from Windows 95. They include the following:

- *Domain Admins.* The administrators of the domain.
- *Domain Users.* Any authenticated user on the domain.
- *Domain Guests.* Any guest account, usually disabled on Windows NT Server networks.

In addition to the Windows NT default groups, Windows 95 user-level security also has a "World" group, which includes everyone, even if they don't have a valid account.

Ch
17

Implementing Windows 95 User-Level Security with Windows NT

When user-level security is enabled on a Windows 95 computer attached to a Windows NT network, the Sharing tab of a folder's property dialog changes to look like that in figure 17.9.

Changing the radio button to Shared As (see fig. 17.10) allows you to set the share name and control access, similar to when share-level security is in place, except that access control is changed.

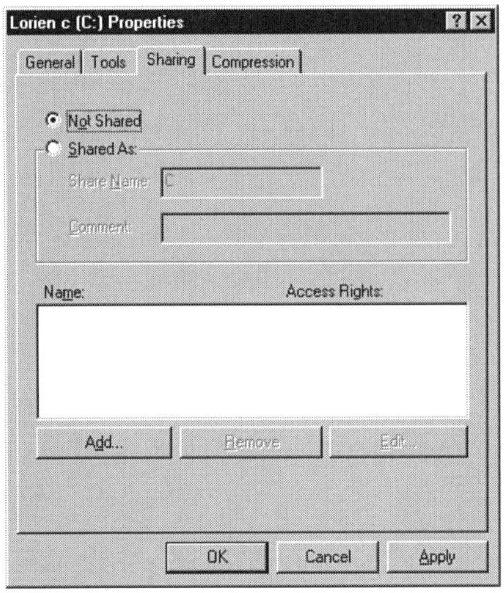

FIG. 17.9 ⇒
The Sharing tab
when user-
level security is
activated.

FIG. 17.10 ⇒
Sharing the
directory.

Available Types of Access

Instead of forcing you to choose separate passwords for full and read-
only access, user-level security allows you to assign access rights to individual users or groups. Clicking Add opens the Add Users dialog (see
fig. 17.11).

To give a person or group read-only or full access, simply highlight the
user or group and click Read Only or Full Access.

FIG. 17.11 ⇒

Adding users to a share.

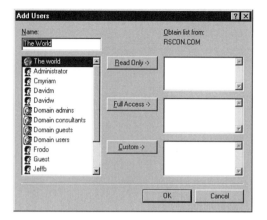

Custom Access

With user-level security, you are not just limited to read-only or full access. You can configure each individual right a user has to the objects in the shared folder by assigning the user custom access by highlighting the user (or group) name and clicking Custom. Figure 17.12 shows the Add users dialog after adding several users. Clicking OK closes the dialog, and opens the Change Access Rights dialog for each user that has been assigned custom access rights (see fig. 17.13). There are seven custom access rights:

+ *Read Files.* The user can read from existing files.

+ *Write to Files.* The user can write to existing files.

+ *Create Files.* The user can create new files and folders.

+ *Delete.* The user can delete existing files and folders.

+ *Change File Attributes.* The user can change attributes, such as Read-Only and Hidden.

+ *List Files.* The user can view a directory listing.

+ *Change Access Control.* The user can change the rights users have to the share.

FIG. 17.12 ⇒
Adding custom
access users.

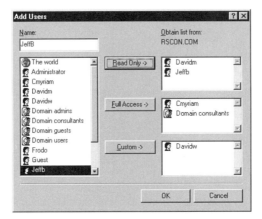

FIG. 17.13 ⇒
You can configure
access rights indi-
vidually for a
custom user.

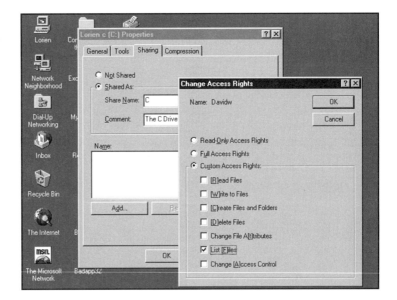

After editing the custom access rights for each user, the Sharing tab is
updated to include a list of users and their access rights (see fig. 17.14).

FIG. 17.14 ⇒
The Sharing tab displays users and their access rights.

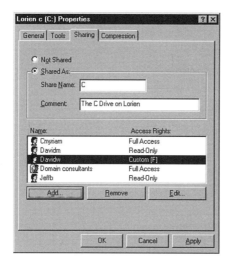

Understanding the Logon Process

When a user logs on to Windows 95 on a Microsoft network, there are several things that can occur automatically, in addition to the possible authentication by a security provider.

Home Directories

On a Windows NT network, users can be assigned a home directory on the network server to store their personal files. You should make sure that you create home directories for all Windows 95 users, since the Client for Microsoft Networks will store each user's profile in their home directories.

Logon Scripts

A *logon script* is a batch file that runs automatically when a user logs on. A logon script is always downloaded from the server that authenticates the user's logon, so you must make sure that all Windows NT domain controllers have all of the login scripts for users in the domain. This is normally accomplished by using the Windows NT Replicator service.

Ch
17

The Logon Process

The logon script implements several steps during the logon process. Most of them occur automatically based on the user's profile and access rights.

Step 1: Profile Determined

If user profiles are enabled (see Chapter 22), then the user will always be prompted to logon even if the user's password is blank, in order to determine which profile to load.

Step 2: Primary Network Logon

If user profiles are not enabled, then the logon dialog box for the network client specified in the Primary Network Logon dialog box in the Network option of Control Panel appears if the network is active (see fig. 17.15).

FIG. 17.15 ⇒

The Primary Network Logon dialog box.

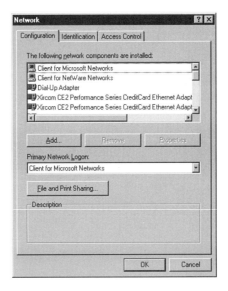

When the network is not active (such as when a notebook computer is undocked) or the Primary Network Logon is set to Windows Logon, then the Windows Logon dialog box will appear first, followed by any network provider logon dialog boxes. If all of the passwords are blank, then Windows 95 can attempt to logon by attempting to open the user's password file with a blank password.

Step 3: Authentication

To ensure that the Client for Microsoft Networks logs into a Windows NT domain, highlight it in the Network option of Control Panel and click the Properties button (see fig. 17.16).

FIG. 17.16 ⇒

Choosing to connect to a Windows NT domain.

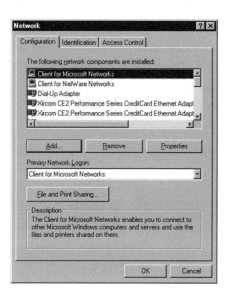

In the Client for Microsoft Networks Properties dialog box, checking the Log on to Windows NT domain option will cause your logon to be validated by the domain. Specify the domain to use in the Windows NT domain box.

The options at the bottom of this dialog box control whether Windows 95 verifies the accessibility of persistent network connections by restoring them at logon, or whether it waits until you actually try to access the resources before making the connections (Quick Logon).

Tip

If you select Quick Logon, you will be able to log on without error messages when you have persistent connections defined even if your computer is not currently connected to the network.

Browsing the Network

Windows 95, like other Microsoft networking systems, provides a method of locating shared resources on the network called *browsing*. The browsing methods used by Windows 95 are based on those used by Windows for Workgroups and Windows NT, and are designed to minimize network traffic generated by browsing.

Browse Master

Browsing depends on the *Browse Master*, a computer on the network which is designated as the maintainer of a list of all active servers in a workgroup. (On a Windows NT domain, the primary domain controller handles this function.)

Servers send a Browser announcement when they join the network, and periodically thereafter.

When a program needs a list of available resources, it obtains a copy of the list of active servers from the Browse Master. The use of a Browse Master reduces the need for every workstation to maintain its own list.

When the workgroup's Browse Master is shut down, the first workstation to request a list and not receive a reply sends out a request for a new Browse Master. The remaining servers in the network perform an election to determine which one will be the new Browse Master.

During the election, and until the new Browse Master has had a chance to update its list, some network resources may not appear on a browse list, although they may be available for use.

While there is only one master browse server for each protocol in any given Windows 95 workgroup, there can be any number of backup browse servers that function to off-load some of the requests. Normally, there will be one backup browser for each protocol for every 15 computers in a workgroup.

You can control whether a given computer can become a browse server through the Advanced property dialog for the File and Printer Sharing for Microsoft Networks service in the Network option of Control Panel (see fig.17.17). There are three possible options:

- *Disabled.* This computer *cannot* be a browse server.
- *Automatic.* This computer *can become* a browse server, if necessary.
- *Enabled.* This computer *will be* a browse server.

FIG. 17.17 ⇒
Configuring a Windows 95 computer as a browse server.

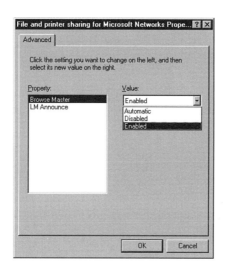

The other option in this property dialog controls whether the resources on this computer will be visible to clients running the old LAN Manager client for MS-DOS.

Building the Browser List

The Windows 95 browse service maintains a list of domains, workgroups and computers, and provides the list to programs when it is requested. The user sees the browse list by selecting Network Neighborhood.

When a Windows 95 computer joins the network, it announces itself to the master browse server for its workgroup, and the master browser adds it to the list, and notifies the backup browsers that a change is available. The backup browsers then request the changes to the list from the master browser. It may take up to 15 minutes for all backup browsers to get

Ch
17

their lists updated, which means that a computer might not appear in a browse list for up to 15 minutes after it starts.

When a computer is properly shut down, it sends a message to the master browser that it is being shut down. The master browser removes the computer from the list, and informs the backup browsers that changes are available. The backup browsers then request the changes, as before.

If the user turns off a computer without shutting it down, the computer may not have a chance to send the shutdown announcement. The master browser will keep a computer in the list until a time out occurs, which can take up to 45 minutes.

On a TCP/IP internetwork, you must use WINS or add #DOM entries to LMHOSTS in order for browsing to work across subnets.

Windows 95 automatically configures itself not to use a computer connected over a slow network connection—such as a Dial-Up Network connection—as a browse server.

Configuring Windows 95 for a Microsoft Network

If you did not configure Windows 95 to support Microsoft Networking during Setup, you can use the Network option in Control Panel to add support (see fig. 17.18).

Client Support

To add client support, click the Add button. The Select Network Component Type dialog box (see fig. 17.19) opens. Highlight Client and click Add.

The Select Network Client dialog box opens. Highlight Microsoft in the Manufacturers pane, and Client for Microsoft Networks in the Network Clients pane, and choose OK.

FIG. 17.18 ⇒

The Network option of Control Panel.

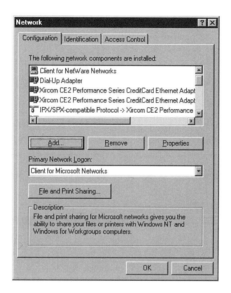

FIG. 17.19 ⇒

Select a network component.

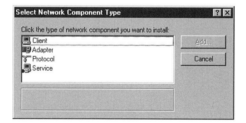

Microsoft Network Services

To add support for sharing files and printers on Microsoft Networks, click the <u>A</u>dd button. The Select Network Component Type dialog box (see fig. 17.20) opens. Highlight Service and click on the <u>A</u>dd button.

FIG. 17.20 ⇒

Select a network
component type.

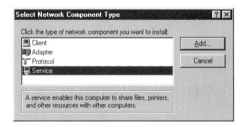

The Select Network Service dialog box opens (see fig. 17.21). Highlight Microsoft in the <u>M</u>anufacturers pane, and File and printer sharing
for Microsoft Networks in the Network Services pane.

FIG. 17.21 ⇒

Selecting a file and
printer sharing
service.

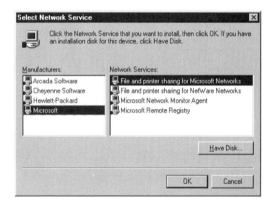

Understanding Protocol Support

Both the Microsoft Client for Microsoft Networks and File and Printer
Sharing for Microsoft Networks support file sharing using the Server
Message Block protocol. Describing the actual protocol is beyond the
scope of this book.

Taking the Disc Test

 If you have read and understood the material in the chapter, you are ready to test your knowledge. Insert the CD-ROM that comes with this book and run the self-test software as described in Appendix I, "Using the CD-ROM."

Ch
17

Chapter Prerequisite

This chapter is intended to provide a foundation for understanding the Windows 95 support for running on NetWare networks.

18

Novell NetWare Basics

This chapter covers Novell NetWare. Terms and concepts covered include:

+ **NetWare**
+ **Capture**
+ **MAP**

Novell, Inc. is one of the world's leading network software providers. Founded in 1983 from the remains of a dying hardware manufacturer, Novell was largely responsible for the inception and growth of the local area network industry.

A testament to the work done by Novell to popularize LANs can still be seen today; Some 60 percent of corporate networks are still based on Novell's network operating system, NetWare.

Types of NetWare Servers

NetWare is a file server-based networking system. Unlike Microsoft operating systems, the NetWare file server is a dedicated server and cannot be used for other tasks, such as running applications. In fact, NetWare servers cannot even be used for administration.

Over the years, Novell released several versions of NetWare, each differing markedly from its predecessor. The original several versions of NetWare were not compatible with Windows 95 (or anything else); I won't discuss them further, beyond mentioning their names: NetWare/68 (designed for a proprietary 68000-based file server), NetWare/86 (designed to run on 8088-based IBM PC/XTs), and Advanced NetWare.

NetWare 2.x

NetWare 2.x is designed to run on 286 or higher processors and provides file and print service. To reconfigure NetWare 2.x for various hardware configurations, a long and involved re-linking of the NetWare operating system is required.

NetWare 2.x security information, consisting of the list of users and their security settings, is stored in a system database called the *bindery* (see "Bindery" later in this chapter for more details). The last version of NetWare 2.x was NetWare 2.2.

NetWare 3.x

Most current NetWare networks use servers running NetWare 3.x. This version of NetWare requires a 386 or higher processor, and uses runtime loadable and unloadable modules called *NetWare Loadable Modules (NLMs)*.

NetWare 3.x uses a bindery. Its latest version is NetWare 3.12, and is still available.

NetWare 4.x

In 1994, Novell released NetWare 4.0. Unlike prior versions of NetWare, NetWare 4.0 uses a hierarchical security and name system called *NetWare Directory Services* (*NDS*). Due to the complexity of this system, and numerous problems, NetWare 4.x has not gained wide acceptance.

For compatibility with software written for earlier versions of NetWare, NetWare 4.x supports *bindery emulation mode,* which makes the server appear as though it uses a bindery. The effect is to make a NetWare 4.x server respond to security inquiries and authentication requests in the same manner that a Neware 3.x server does. The current version of NetWare 4, as of this writing, is 4.1. NetWare 4.1 is significantly more stable than 4.0 was.

Tip

Although Microsoft has released an update to Windows 95 that supports NDS, the out-of-the-box Windows 95 only supports NetWare servers that are in bindery emulation mode.

Ch
18

Defining NetWare Terms

In order to configure Windows 95 on a NetWare network, you must be familiar with the terminology that Novell has defined.

Clients

NetWare was primarily designed to communicate with client computers running MS-DOS; as a result, most of the Novell-supplied client software is MS-DOS-based, running in real mode. Windows 95 supports running over the NetWare real mode client software in addition to the built-in Client for NetWare.

See "Configuring the Microsoft Client for NetWare," **p. 308**

NETX (NetWare Shell)

The original NetWare client software, called the *NetWare shell*, was designed for versions of MS-DOS that did not have networking support. Novell designed the shell to hook into the particular version of MS-DOS that it was being run under. The shell intercepted file I/O and, when necessary, redirected it to the file server.

Even though MS-DOS itself supported networking starting with MS-DOS 3.0, Novell still used the shell approach up through MS-DOS 5.0.

Versions of the shell specific to the MS-DOS version were released for MS-DOS versions 2, 3, and 4. Each version was named NET*x* where the *x* stood for the version of MS-DOS that it worked with (for example, NET3 and NET4). When MS-DOS 5.0 was released, Novell modified the shell so that it would work with any subsequent version of MS-DOS, and named the file Netx.exe.

NetWare DOS Requester

The NetWare DOS Requester replaced the NetWare shell as the MS-DOS client software with the release of NetWare 3.12. Requester is backward compatible with software written for the NetWare shell, however.

Unlike the NetWare shell, which consisted of a single monolithic file, the NetWare DOS Requester is modular in design. It consists of a number of modules called *Virtual Loadable Modules (VLMs)*. The VLMs implement a three-layer design:

- *DOS Redirection Layer.* Unlike the NetWare shell, the Requester includes a true redirector, which is called by MS-DOS when needed.
- *Service Protocol Layer.* Various network services run in this layer, including the NDS support.

Tip
The NetWare DOS Requester is the only way to get support for NetWare Directory Services using the out-of-the-box Windows 95.

- *Transport Protocol Layer.* Some transport protocols, such as TCP/IP, require VLMs at this layer for support.

IPXODI

IPXODI is the module that implements the IPX protocol for workstations using the NetWare DOS Requester. It interfaces with the Requester module and the Link Support Layer of the ODI interface.

See "ODI," **p. 230**

Servers

NetWare is primarily a file and print server system. All NetWare servers are file servers. NetWare servers are *dedicated*, meaning that they cannot be used for other tasks.

NetWare file servers must be a 386 or higher processor, have a network card, and a hard disk. The amount of required RAM varies according to the features and options that are being used, and the size of the hard disks. NetWare does not support virtual memory, so all modules that are in use—plus system tables and caches—must fit into the available RAM, or the server will crash with an "ABEND" (Abnormal END).

NetWare servers first boot MS-DOS. Then, the SERVER command is executed from the Autoexec.bat file, and NetWare is running. Once the basic NetWare server system is running, you have to load disk drivers and NLMs to support the network adapters. The Startup.ncf file loads the disk drivers.

Normally, these modules are loaded from the Autoexec.ncf and Startup.ncf, which are created as part of the installation process and stored on the file server's DOS partition.

The Autoexec.ncf file performs the following tasks:

- Stores the file server's name and internal network number (used by the IPX protocol).
- Loads the drivers, configures the settings for the network adapters, and binds transport protocols to the network adapter drivers.
- May contain any other command that could be typed on the file server's keyboard.

Ch
18

NetWare Loadable Module (NLM)

A NetWare Loadable Module (NLM) is a program that you can load (and unload) from the server while the server is running. Most of NetWare is implemented as NLMs.

NLMs run in ring 0, meaning that a poorly written NLM can cause a server crash.

NetWare allocates memory to the module when it is loaded. The module returns the memory to NetWare when it is unloaded.

There are four types of NLMs:

- *Disk drivers*. Form the interface between NetWare and hard disks. Disk drivers have a DSK extension. They can be loaded and unloaded while the server is running and while users are logged in.
- *LAN drivers*. Form the interface between NetWare and network adapter cards. LAN drivers have a LAN extension, and they can be loaded and unloaded while the server is running and while users are logged in.
- *Management utilities*. Used to monitor and change certain configuration options. It is not possible to fully manage a NetWare server from its console. Management utilities have an NLM extension.
- *Name space modules*. Allow the NetWare server to store non-8.3 naming conventions to be stored in the directories and file name systems.

NLMs are normally stored in the SYS:SYSTEM directory on the NetWare server. They are loaded using the LOAD command on the server.

NameSpaces

As previously mentioned, name space modules allow a NetWare server to support file names that do not conform with the 8.3 naming convention that is supported by MS-DOS. For example, in order to use long file names on a NetWare server, you must load the OS/2 name space.

Adding name space support to a particular disk volume is a two-step process. You must complete these steps:

1. Load the name space NLM. For example, "LOAD OS2"
2. Use the ADD NAME SPACE console command to configure the volume. For example, "ADD NAME SPACE OS2 to SYS:"

Each additional name space added to a volume causes NetWare to create another entry in the directory table for a name that complies with the conventions of that name space. You must make sure that you allow enough space on the volume to hold the additional entries. In addition, the file server will require additional RAM to cache the additional entries.

Protocol Support

NetWare was designed to operate over the IPX/SPX protocol, although Novell added support for TCP/IP in NetWare 4.1. Even though earlier versions of NetWare had support for IPX/SPX "tunneling" over TCP/IP, NetWare did not support operating over TCP/IP without IPX/SPX until version 4.1.

Tip

Novell's implementation of TCP/IP is not compatible with Microsoft TCP/IP. All Microsoft software designed for NetWare support assumes that you must run over IPX/SPX.

IPX/SPX

The primary network protocols used by NetWare are IPX and SPX.

IPX

IPX stands for *Internetwork Packet eXchange*, and was developed by Novell to serve as the primary communication protocol for NetWare. IPX is responsible for addressing and routing packets across a network. It was based on Xerox's XNS transport protocol. IPX uses datagrams; reception is not guaranteed.

Ch
18

Each network cable segment used with IPX must have a unique IPX external network number, which is completely arbitrary and is assigned when the IPX protocol is bound to a network board.

For historical reasons, NetWare supports two frame types when communicating via Ethernet (802.3 and 802.2). Each frame type bound to a board must have a different IPX external network number.

External network numbers are used as part of the internetwork address that is used to address packets. The internetwork address consists of the four-byte external network number, plus the six-byte node number, plus the two-byte socket number.

The IPX internal network number is used to identify a particular NetWare server, and must be unique.

SPX

SPX, or *Sequenced Packet eXchange*, is responsible for verifying and acknowledging successful packet delivery by requesting acknowledgments from the destination. If SPX does not receive a successful acknowledgment, it will retransmit the packet. After a reasonable number of retransmissions, SPX will return an error. SPX uses IPX for data transmission.

TCP/IP

Novell's implementation of TCP/IP is designed to allow NetWare servers and clients to communicate through networks that are based on the industry-standard TCP/IP protocol suite. NetWare TCP/IP focuses on IP routing to forward IP traffic from one network to another. In addition to routing support, NetWare TCP/IP supports *IPX/IP tunneling*, which supports communication between NetWare networks across an IP internet that does not support IPX directly.

NetWare TCP/IP cannot be used to support file and print sharing with the Microsoft Client for NetWare.

For more information on Windows 95 support for TCP/IP, see Chapter 16, "TCP/IP and Windows 95."

NetWare Core Protocol (NCP) File Sharing

NetWare servers follow a protocol called the *NetWare Core Protocol (NCP)* to implement file and printer sharing. An NCP protocol exists for every possible service that a client might request from a service, such as opening a file or reading and writing to a file.

Browsing Protocols

Browsing protocols are protocols that enable clients to locate resources on the network. NetWare servers use the SAP protocol for browing information.

Service Advertising Protocol (SAP)

NetWare servers advertise the services they have available for clients using the *Service Advertising Protocol (SAP)*. Routers maintain a database of currently available servers on the internetwork by listening to the SAP broadcasts.

The routers then send SAP broadcasts periodically (by default, every 60 seconds) to keep all the routers on the internetwork in sync. In addition, routers send SAP broadcasts whenever they detect an internetwork configuration change.

Workstations broadcast "Get Nearest Server" SAP requests to find a server on the network to attach to. To prevent workstations from attaching to a particular server, network supervisors can disable the Get Nearest Server SAP option.

When the NetWare 4.0 time synchronization option is selected, Primary time servers and Single reference servers use SAP to advertise their services.

Security

NetWare security consists of six categories of security features:

+ *Login security*. Controls access to the network.
+ *Trustees*. Controls what users have access to files, directories, and other objects.

Ch
18

- *Rights*. Controls what level of access a trustee has to an object.
- *Inheritance*. Controls how rights are passed from higher to lower levels.
- *Attributes*. Controls what you can do to a particular file.
- *Effective rights*. Net calculated rights that a user has to a file or object.

Login Security

You can use the LOGIN command to identify yourself to a NetWare network. You must know the user name and correct password in order to log into the server.

User names and passwords are established by the network supervisor by creating a User object in NetWare Directory Services (for NetWare 4.x) or by adding a user using the NetWare SYSCON utility (for NetWare 2.x or 3.x).

Properties that can be assigned for a User include legal login times, what workstations the user can log in from, password expiration, and other information. While passwords are not required under NetWare, you should require that users use passwords.

To increase security, several available password options are available:

- *Minimum password length*. A minimum length, which defaults to five characters, prevents the use of passwords that are too short to be effective protection.
- *Periodic change in the password*. By setting this option, which defaults to 90 days, users cannot keep the same password indefinitely.
- *Unique password*. This option prevents users from alternating passwords to defeat the periodic change requirement.

Trustee

A *trustee* is a user or group that has been granted access to a directory, file, or object. Trustee assignments can be made with the RIGHTS, NETADMIN, SYSCON, FILER, or NetWare Administrator utility, depending on the version of NetWare being used.

Rights

The type of access a trustee has to a directory, file, or object is determined by the rights granted to the trustee. For example, if a trustee has been granted the Read right to a file, the trustee can read data from the file.

File rights can be inherited from the directory rights. For example, if a user is granted the Read right to a directory, and no file rights are assigned in the directory, and the file's Inherited Rights Filter doesn't block the directory's rights, then the user will have the Read right to the file.

Inheritance

Inheritance simplifies the job of creating trustees. With inheritance, the rights granted to a trustee apply to everything below the point where the trustee assignment is made, unless another trustee assignment is made or the rights have been blocked by an *Inherited Rights Filter (IRF)*.

Inheritance applies both to directories and files on a volume, and to objects in the directory tree.

Directories and files inherit all access rights. Objects can only inherit object and all property rights; they cannot inherit specific object properties.

Trustees with the Supervisor right on a NetWare server are granted the Supervisor right on all volumes attached to the server.

If you create a file in a directory and want to prevent users who have rights in the directory from having rights to your file, you can create an Inherited Rights Filter. An Inherited Rights Filter is similar to a trustee assignment, only it revokes rights instead of granting them.

If you grant a user the Supervisor right to a directory, that trustee will inherit the Supervisor right for all subdirectories and files, and, the rights cannot be blocked by an Inherited Rights Filter.

Attributes (Flags)

Attributes (also known as *flags*) tell NetWare what actions are allowed on a file. Attributes include such information as whether a file can be deleted, and whether it can be compressed.

Ch
18

File attributes are handled separately from rights; they cannot be inherited, and even a supervisor cannot delete a file whose attributes indicate that it can't be deleted without changing the file's attributes. You must be granted the Modify or Supervisor right by the supervisor in order to change a file's attributes.

Effective Rights

Effective rights are the rights that a user actually has to a file, directory, or object after the effects of trustee assignments, inheritance, and the IRF are calculated.

Trustee assignments to groups, however, are added to previous trustee assignments for User objects.

Bindery

The NetWare *bindery* is a database used in NetWare 2.x and 3.x that contains security definitions for users and groups. The network supervisor can use the bindery to design an organized security environment based on a company's individual requirements.

The bindery enables the network supervisor to design an organized and secure operating environment based on the individual requirements of each of these network entities.

The bindery has three components:

- *Objects*. Physical or logical entities, such as users, groups, servers, or anything that can be given a name.
- *Properties*. Characteristics of objects. Bindery properties include passwords, account restrictions, group members, and account balances.
- *Property data sets*. Consist of the actual values assigned to bindery properties.

The bindery is stored in SYS:SYSTEM directory on the server in three files:

- Net$obj.sys (for objects)
- Net$prop.sys (for properties)
- Net$val.sys (for property data sets)

NetWare Directory Service (NDS)

NetWare Directory Service (*NDS*) is a distributed database that is built into NetWare 4.x. It maintains information about, and controls access to, every resource on the network. In NDS, all network resources are objects organized in a hierarchical tree structure.

Users and administrators can access any network service without having to know the physical location of the server that stores the service.

NDS replaces the bindery, which is used in earlier versions of NetWare. Compatibility with previous versions of NetWare is provided through bindery emulation.

NetWare Administration

NetWare administration tools vary according to the version of NetWare you're using.

NetWare 2.x and 3.x

The NetWare 2.x and 3.x administration tools are MS-DOS based, and have a user interface particular to Novell.

SYSCON

SYSCON, or *System Console*, is used to configure accounting, file server, user, and group information. SYSCON must be run on a network workstation, not the file server.

FILER

FILER can be used by both network supervisors and users to configure volume, file, and directory information, including file attributes and trustees. Users who do not have supervisor equivalence receive an error message when attempting to use FILER to accomplish something that requires supervisor equivalence.

PCONSOLE

PCONSOLE is used to manage NetWare print queues.

Ch
18

NetWare 4.x

NetWare 4.x includes a graphical, Windows-based utility called the *NetWare Administrator* (*NWADMIN*). It presents the NDS structure as a hierarchical tree, and enables you to browse for objects and modify their properties.

Taking the Disc Test

If you have read and understood the material in the chapter, you are ready to test your knowledge. Insert the CD-ROM that comes with this book and run the self-test software as described in Appendix I, "Using the CD-ROM."

Chapter Prerequisite

You should be familiar with
Windows 95 Setup (see Chap-
ter 3, "Windows 95 Setup"),
Windows 95 configuration (see
Chapter 4, "Configuring Win-
dows 95"), networking basics
(see Chapter 14, "Networking
Basics"), and Novell NetWare
basics (see Chapter 18, "Novell
NetWare Basics.").

Using Windows 95 with Novell NetWare

Few companies have had as great an effect on business computing as Novell, whose NetWare product was for many years the driving force in the transition from single-user, isolated computers into the inter-connected local area and wide area networks that business today depends on.

This chapter covers Windows 95 support for Novell NetWare networks. Terms and concepts covered include:

- ↓ **NetWare Core Protocol (NCP)**
- ↓ **ODI driver**
- ↓ **Preferred server**
- ↓ **Login script**

↓ **SAP Advertising**

↓ **User-level security**

Even today, Novell NetWare is the primary network operating system on some 60 percent of corporate networks, making it very likely that the Microsoft Certified Professional will not only encounter it, but also have to configure computers to interoperate with NetWare.

Understanding NetWare and Windows 95 Architecture

Windows 95 contains built-in support for Novell NetWare 2.x, 3.x, and 4.x (in bindery emulation mode) networks. A Windows 95 computer can be both a NetWare client and a server, sharing its own resources with other NetWare clients on the network.

Network Providers

As discussed in Chapter 15, "Windows 95 Networking Introduction," Windows 95 allows multiple, concurrently active network and print providers. Through the included NetWare Network provider, Windows 95 can support Novell NetWare as well as Microsoft networks.

The NetWare Network provider is usable by MS-DOS, 16-bit Windows applications, and 32-bit Windows applications. It is part of the standard Windows 95 networking architecture.

Redirector

The redirector used on NetWare networks is the Microsoft Client for NetWare Networks. The Microsoft Client for NetWare uses the NetWare Core Protocol (NCP), which is NetWare's native protocol for file sharing. NCP is similar in function to the SMB protocol used by Microsoft networks. The NCP redirector uses the IPX/SPX-compatible transport protocol to communicate with the NetWare server.

Services

In addition to acting as a client on a NetWare network, Windows 95 also can provide network file and print services to client computers running NetWare client software. However, although Windows 95 allows multiple redirectors on a computer, it does not allow multiple file and printer sharing services. If you select to use File and Printer Sharing for NetWare Networks, you cannot share files and printers with computers running the File and Printer Sharing for Microsoft Networks.

Transport Protocols

Novell designed the IPX/SPX protocol for use in NetWare. Although later versions of NetWare support a form of TCP/IP, this form of TCP/IP is not compatible with the Microsoft Client for NetWare and cannot be used.

Windows 95 requires the IPX/SPX–compatible transport protocol in order to communicate with NetWare servers. One of the key parameters that can be configured is the frame type. The *frame type* describes the actual format that is used to encapsulate a packet of data when it is being transmitted over the network. For historical reasons, NetWare networks support three basic types of frames:

+ IEEE 802.2
+ IEEE 802.3
+ Ethernet II standards

In order for two computers to communicate using IPX/SPX, they must use a common frame type. While NetWare and Windows NT servers can be configured to use multiple frame types on the same computer, Windows 95 (like most of the NetWare clients) only supports one frame type, although Windows 95 can be set to automatically detect the dominant frame type on the network and configure itself to use it.

Device Driver Interface

Windows 95 supports both ODI and NDIS network device drivers. Although ODI was defined by Novell, NDIS 3 drivers are greatly

Ch
19

preferred under Windows 95 because they are 32-bit protected mode drivers, whereas ODI drivers run in real mode. ODI drivers are supported under Windows 95 for backwards compatibility with network adapters whose manufacturer only supplies ODI drivers for the card.

Configuring the Microsoft Client for NetWare

Configuring the Microsoft Client for NetWare is a straightforward process, similar to installing the Client for Microsoft Networks that you read about in Chapter 17, "Using Windows 95 with Microsoft Networks."

Installing the Client

To install the Microsoft Client for NetWare, choose Add from the Network option in Control Panel. In the Select Network Component Type dialog box, choose Client.

In the Select Network Client dialog box, choose Microsoft as the Manufacturer, and Client for NetWare Networks as the Network Client, and click OK.

When you're returned to the Network Option of Control Panel, double-click the Client for NetWare Networks. The Properties dialog box opens (see fig. 19.1.) Here you have three options you can configure:

+ *Preferred server.* The server used to authenticate your logins and provide login scripts.

+ *First network drive.* The letter of the first drive that is assigned to the NetWare network. Most sites choose F: as the first NetWare drive.

+ *Enable login script processing.* If checked, *and* a Preferred server is set, the NetWare login script is processed.

FIG. 19.1.⇒
Configuring the
Client for NetWare
Networks' proper-
ties.

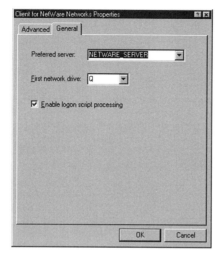

Using Real Mode NetWare Clients

You can use the real mode NetWare clients whenever necessary, such as
to support NDS or an application that depends upon undocumented
functionality of the older shells. However, using the real mode NetWare
clients incurs a significant performance penalty because of the overhead
of context switching necessary to support the real mode components.

There are two possible real mode clients, VLM and NETX. To choose
to install a real mode client, open the Network option of Control Panel
and click <u>A</u>dd. Choose to add a client, and then choose Novell as the
manufacturer. Choices to install either the 3.x shell (NETX) or the 4.x
shell (VLM) will be available.

Configuring File and Printer Sharing
Services for NetWare

You can use the File and Printer Sharing Services for NetWare rather
than the File and Printer Sharing Services for Microsoft Networks if
you want to make resources on your computer available for use by users
of NetWare clients, such as MS-DOS users.

Ch
19

You can only have one file and printer sharing service installed at any one time. You must remove any preexisting sharing service before trying to install a new one.

Installing the Service

To install the File and Printer Sharing Services for NetWare, first make sure that the Microsoft Client for NetWare Networks is installed. Then, from the Network control panel, click <u>A</u>dd, choose to install a Service, and choose Microsoft as the manufacturer. Then choose File and Printer Sharing Service for NetWare, and click OK.

Upon returning to the Network control panel, double-click File and Printer Sharing service for NetWare to open the property dialog. You now have two options:

- ⊥ *SAP* (*Service Advertising Protocol*) Advertising. If you enable this option, other NetWare clients (including MS-DOS clients) see this computer and are able to attach to it, and access files and printers.

- ⊥ *Workgroup Advertising*. Similar to the Browsing architecture on Microsoft Networks. You have four possible settings:

    Disabled. If this option is chosen, this station does not even receive lists of resources.

    Enabled, May Be Master. If this option is chosen, this station can receive browse lists, and can be the browse master.

    Enabled, Preferred Master. If this option is chosen, then this computer should be, and usually is, a master browser.

    Enabled, Will Not Be Master. This station can receive browse lists, but cannot be the master.

Always be sure to have at least one computer that can be the browse master; otherwise, browsing cannot take place.

See "Browsing the Network," **p. 284**

Configuring User-Level Security

File and printer sharing for NetWare Networks requires user-level security. Similar to user-level security with Microsoft Networks, security with the File and Printer Sharing for NetWare Networks is a *pass-through security method*, in which security authentication requests are passed through to a NetWare server for authentication.

Sharing Printers

A *shared printer* on a computer running File and Printer sharing for NetWare Networks appears as a NetWare print queue in browse lists.

Taking the Disc Test

 If you have read and understood the material in the chapter, you are ready to test your knowledge. Insert the CD-ROM that comes with this book and run the self-test software as described in Appendix I, "Using the CD-ROM."

Ch
19

Chapter Prerequisite

Before reading this chapter, you should be familiar with Windows 95 Setup (see Chapter 3, "Windows 95 Setup"), Windows 95 configuration (see Chapter 4, "Configuring Windows 95"), printing (see Chapter 11, "Understanding Printing"), and Windows 95 networking (see Chapters 14–19).

Network Printing

This chapter covers Windows 95 support for network printing. Terms and concepts covered include:

- Point and Print
- JetAdmin
- Print Provider

Examining the Network Printing Architecture

Windows 95 uses a layered approach to network printing, which is much the same as its approach to networking.

Win32 and Win16 Print APIs

Windows 32-bit applications use the functions defined by the Win32 Print API, and Windows 16-bit applications use the functions defined by the Win16 Print API to access printing functionalities. These functions include such capabilities as opening, writing, and closing print jobs, as well as print queue management.

Print Router

Similar to the way that the Multi-Protocol Router directs file requests to the appropriate installable file system, the Print Router—which is implemented as part of Spoolss.dll—routes printing requests to a driver that can complete the request. If the request is for a local printer, the router sends it to the local print provider (again, part of Spoolss.dll); otherwise, if the request is for a network printer, the router sends it to one of the installed network print providers.

Print Providers

The Print Router uses the APIs provided by the Print Provider Interface (PPI) to communicate with the Print Providers. The PPI is modular, and allows any number of 32-bit print providers to be installed simultaneously. For example, you can have both the network and local print providers installed.

A print provider is implemented as a 32-bit DLL. Print providers are responsible for providing functions to handle functionalities such as opening and closing printers, submitting print jobs, and print queue management. Three different kinds of print providers are available:

+ *Local.* Part of Spoolss.dll, which handles printing to local printers.

+ *Network.* Handles print requests for a particular type of network. Network print providers translate the 32-bit PPI call into an appropriate network call.

+ *WinNet16.* Provides backwards compatibility with 16-bit Windows 3.x WinNet16 network drivers. It converts the 32-bit PPI call into a 16-bit WinNet16 API call so that the WinNet16 driver can service the request.

Microsoft Networks

Printing to network printers that are attached to Microsoft network servers is handled by the Microsoft Network Print Provider, which is implemented in Mspp32.dll. It interacts with both the *Installable File System Manager (IFSMGR)* and the network redirector.

Determining which one is used depends on the type of print function being called. If the function is a printing function (open print job, write to print job, close print job), the call is submitted to the IFSMGR, because those functions are the same as file I/O operations in the Win32 API. The IFSMGR then hands the request to the redirector, Vredir.vxd.

On the other hand, if a function is a queue management call, such as view the network queue, it is submitted directly to Vredir.vxd.

NetWare Networks

Windows 95 provides two different methods of supporting network printers that are on Novell NetWare servers: one used with the Microsoft Client for NetWare Networks, and the other used with a real mode NetWare client (NETX or VLM).

Printing with the Microsoft Client for NetWare Networks

Similar to the way printing is implemented with the Microsoft Client for Microsoft Networks, the NetWare Print Provider handles calls made by the print router through the Print Provider Interface.

The NetWare Print Provider is implemented in Nwpp32.dll and Nwnet32.dll. The Print Provider calls IFSMGR, which in turn calls the

Ch
20

redirector, in this case Nwredir.vxd, for functions involving submitting print jobs.

The NetWare Print Provider calls the redirector Nwredir.vxd directly to handle print queue management.

Printing with a Real Mode NetWare Client (NETX or VLM)

When a real mode NetWare client—such as NETX or VLM—must be used (to support NDS), the 32-bit redirector Nwredir.vxd is not used. Instead, a thunking layer, Nw16.dll, is used to translate the calls into a 16-bit call into Vnetware.386, which passes the call to the real mode NetWare client.

WinNet 16

If a network client does not have 32-bit print providers, then network printing uses the Windows 3.1 WinNet16 driver. The WinNet16 Print Provider, implemented in Wnpp32.dll, takes the 32-bit call from the Print Router and thunks it to a 16-bit WinNet16 call, which it passes to the 16-bit Windows 3.x driver.

The 16-bit driver then calls the real mode network client through a VxD, as it would when running under Windows 3.1. If the driver makes Open file calls, the calls are then trapped by IFSMGR, which passes them on to the real mode network client through the VxD.

Print queue management is limited to that level of functionality that is provided by the WinNet16 driver, if any.

Third-Party Providers

The Windows 95 network printing architecture is completely open. Third-party software developers can write additional print providers to submit network requests to a third-party network file system driver. As long as the third-party print provider implements the PPI, it can be added to the computer using the Network option in Control Panel.

Installing Network Printers

Installing a network printer actually involves two separate steps: installing the driver for the printer so that applications can print to it, and telling Windows 95 where the printer is on the network so that the spooler can deliver the print jobs to the printer.

There are two different ways to add a network printer to Windows 95: manually, and through Point and Print.

Manual

The manual process for installing a network printer is very similar to the manual process for installing a local printer.

1. Double-click the Add Printer icon in the Printers folder. The Add Printer Wizard opens (see fig. 20.1.)

2. Click Next to open the dialog box shown in figure 20.2.

3. Choose the Network Printer radio button to add a network printer.

4. Click Next to open the next dialog box (see fig. 20.3), where you enter the network path to the printer. If you do not know the path, you can browse the network for it by clicking the Browse button, which opens the Browse for Printer dialog box (see fig. 20.4).

FIG. 20.1 ⇒

The Add Printer Wizard.

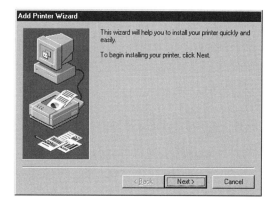

Ch
20

FIG. 20.2 ⇒

Choosing to install a network printer.

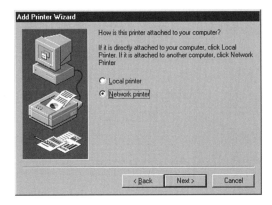

FIG. 20.3 ⇒

Entering the net-work path to the printer.

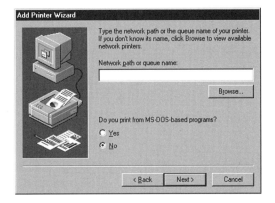

FIG. 20.4 ⇒

Browsing for a printer.

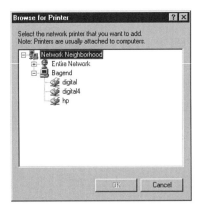

Objects displayed in the Browse dialog box that have a + next to them contain other objects within them. Click the + to expand the view, as you can see in figure 20.4.

Highlight the printer and click OK to enter the UNC path name to the printer in the Network path or queue name box (see fig. 20.5).

FIG. 20.5 ⇒

The printer that you chose in the Browse dialog box is entered in the Network Path box.

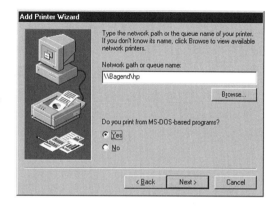

The question in the second half of the dialog box, Do you print from MS-DOS-based programs?, controls whether the Add Printer Wizard will capture a printer port for use by MS-DOS programs. (Windows applications do not need to use a captured port to access a printer.)

Choosing Yes opens the dialog box shown in figure 20.6. Clicking the Capture Printer Port button opens the Capture Printer Port dialog box (see fig. 20.7), which allows you to associate a logical port name with the printer. MS-DOS applications can use this port to print to the network printer.

FIG. 20.6 ⇒

You can choose to capture a printer port.

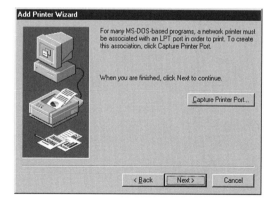

Ch
20

FIG. 20.7 ⇒

You can choose a
port to capture.

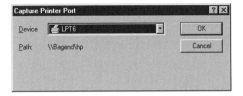

The next dialog box in the wizard (see fig. 20.8) allows you to assign a
friendly name for the printer (just like a local printer), and whether
you want this printer to be the default printer. The last dialog box (see
fig. 20.9) allows you to decide whether you want to print a test page or
not.

FIG. 20.8 ⇒

You can assign a
friendly name for
the printer.

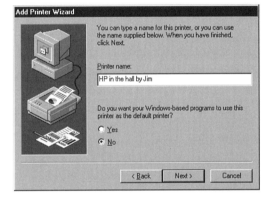

FIG. 20.9 ⇒

You can choose to
print a test page.

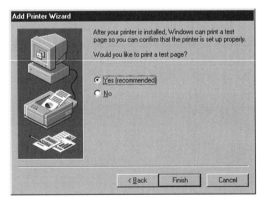

In the last step, after you click Finish, Windows 95 copies the printer
drivers and completes the install.

Point and Print

Point and Print makes installation of network printers much easier because it automates virtually the entire process. There are two forms of Point and Print:

- You can install the driver files for a network printer simply by dragging the network printer icon from Network Neighborhood to the PRINTERS folder. You also can right-click the printer in Network Neighborhood and choose Install from the context menu, or just double-click the printer's icon.

- You can print to a network printer by simply dragging and dropping a document on the network printer's icon in Network Neighborhood. Windows 95 automatically loads drivers, configures the printer, and loads the program associated with the document and prints it.

In order for Point and Print to function, the printer must be Point and Print-enabled. Unfortunately, there is no way to tell if a printer is Point and Print-enabled from its icon or properties. There are different ways to make a printer Point and Print-enabled, depending on what type of network server the printer is attached to.

Point and Print with Windows 95 Server-Attached Printers

Printers attached to Windows 95 servers are automatically Point and Print enabled. Windows 95 supplies the printer drivers through a hidden share on the server called PRINTER$, which is set up automatically with no password and shares the System folder as a read-only share. The work of determining which files need to be copied and copying them is accomplished via a negotiation between VREDIR on the client machine and VSERVER on the server.

Point and Print with Windows NT Server-Attached Printers

Because Windows NT uses different printer drivers than Windows 95, printers attached to Windows NT servers cannot support Point and Print directly. Instead, whenever a user attempts a Point and Print installation of a printer that is attached to a Windows NT Server, Point and Print attempts to copy the driver files from the folder in which Windows 95 was installed.

Ch
20

Tip

This is a great argument for setting up a network installation point for Windows 95 with Server-Based Setup (see Chapter 23, "Server-Based Setup of Windows 95").

If the Windows 95 and Windows NT drivers have the same name and use the same name .inf file, the user will not be prompted for the printer model name.

Point and Print with Novell NetWare Servers (Bindery-Based)

Novell NetWare servers have no concept of Point and Print. However, Windows 95 can write some configuration information into the NetWare server's bindery to inform Windows 95 clients of the location of drivers and the model of the printer on a NetWare print queue.

To add this information to a NetWare server, you must first log into the NetWare server as the Supervisor (or a Supervisor-equivalent user). Then, in Network Neighborhood, right-click the NetWare print queue on the NetWare server, and choose Point and Print Setup from the context menu.

There are two options in Point and Print Setup:

+ *Set Printer Model.* Choosing this option opens the standard Print Setup dialog box. Choose the appropriate printer model from the list.

+ *Set Driver Path.* Choosing this option opens a dialog box prompting you for the UNC path name to the network location where the driver files are stored. Enter the location, and make sure the drivers are stored there, and that *everyone* has at least Read and File Scan rights to that directory.

Managing Remote Print Queues

Remote print queue management capabilities are a function of the capabilities of the network operating system, Windows 95 networking components, and the user's level of access as defined by the network (and set by the network administrator).

At maximum, the user will have the same capabilities as if the printer were a local printer. Any management options not supported by the network are grayed out.

Using Microsoft Print Agent for NetWare (MSPSRV)

Mspsrv.exe is a print agent for Windows 95 that allows a Windows 95 computer to despool print jobs from a NetWare print queue to a local printer. It replaces the NetWare RPRINTER utility.

The Microsoft Print Agent for NetWare is a 32-bit Windows application that can be enabled from the property sheet of any local printer once it has been installed onto your computer.

To install the Microsoft Print Agent for NetWare Networks:

1. Open the Network option in Control Panel and click Add.
2. Choose Service from the Select Component dialog box.
3. Click Add.
4. Click Have Disk. The installation files are found in the \Admin\Nettools\Prtagent folder on the Windows 95 CD-ROM.

Supporting HP Jet Direct

The Hewlett-Packard JetDirect is a network interface adapter that can be installed into HP LaserJet printers to allow them to be attached to a network directly.

Ch
20

Architecture

The HP JetDirect support files provide both a network provider and print provider to support accesses to the JetDirect. They fit into the Windows 95 network printing architecture by providing an SPI interface to handle browsing functions, and a PPI interface to handle the actual printing function calls.

The network and print providers hand their calls to the HP JetDirect DLLs, which call the Hpnw432.dll component, which in turn makes IPX/SPX sockets calls to the 32-bit Windows Sockets interface, which connects to the JetDirect via the IPX/SPX-compatible transport protocol.

HP JetAdmin

Unlike Windows for Workgroups and Windows NT, which require the Microsoft DLC protocol to support HP JetDirect print devices, Windows 95 only supports the JetDirect via the IPX/SPX-compatible transport. You use the HP JetAdmin program to administer the JetDirect.

There are two versions of the HP JetAdmin program: one that supports real mode NetWare clients, such as NETX and VLM, and the other that works with either of the Microsoft-supplied network clients.

To install the JetAdmin program, open the Network option in Control Panel, and click <u>A</u>dd. Choose to add a Service, and then choose the appropriate version of HP JetAdmin from the list.

After it is installed, JetAdmin is accessible as a Control Panel option.

Supporting Digital PrintServer

A Digital PrintServer is a bi-directional, high-speed, network-attached printer. Windows 95 includes drivers and support files that enable Windows 95 to print directly to a PrintServer without needing an intermediary server or host.

Architecture

The Digital PrintServer support is implemented as a Port Monitor. The regular Windows 95 PostScript driver processes the printer stream into a RAW file, which is handed off to the Digital PrintServer port monitor (Decpsmw4.dll), which makes Windows Sockets calls to stream the print job to the PrintServer via TCP/IP.

Installing and Configuring

To install the Digital PrintServer, you must have TCP/IP installed and working.

Install the PrintServer printer as though it was a local printer. Make sure that you choose the correct model number PrintServer (and one with a /Net after its name).

In the Add Printer Wizard dialog box (see fig. 20.10), click Add Port. The Add Port dialog box (see fig. 20.11) opens. Choose the appropriate PrintServer in the Port Type drop-down list. Choose the TCP/IP radio button (DECNet is not supported), enter a name for the port in the Name box, and the IP address of the printer in the Address box.

FIG. 20.10 ⇒
Click the Add Port button.

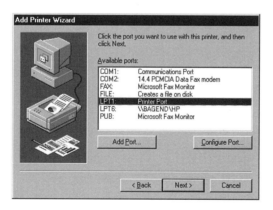

Ch
20

After clicking OK, the port you just created should appear in the Available Ports list (see fig. 20.12). Click Next, give the printer a friendly name, and choose whether to make this printer the default printer (see fig. 20.13).

FIG 20.11 ⇒
Choose the appro-
priate PrintServer.

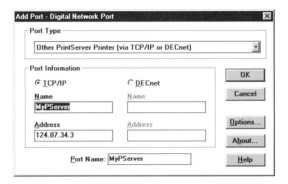

FIG. 20.12 ⇒
The newly created
port appears in the
Available ports list.

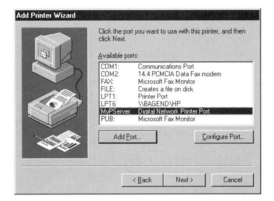

FIG. 20.13 ⇒
You can give the
printer a friendly
name.

The last dialog box enables you to print a test page. You should print a test page to verify that you can use the printer.

Taking the Disc Test

 If you have read and understood the material in the chapter, you are ready to test your knowledge. Insert the CD-ROM that comes with this book and run the self-test software as described in Appendix I, "Using the CD-ROM."

Ch
20

Chapter Prerequisite

Before reading this chapter, you should be familiar with Windows 95 setup (see Chapter 3, "Windows 95 Setup"), Windows 95 configuration (see Chapter 4, "Configuring Windows 95"), all aspects of Windows 95 Networking (Chapters 15-19), and Windows 95 communications (see Chapter 24, "Windows 95 Communications").

Mobile Computing

With the explosion in the portable computer market, more and more people are replacing their office desktop computer systems with portable notebook computers and docking stations. As mentioned in Chapter 6, "Plug and Play," Windows 95 includes several hardware-related features to facilitate the use of a portable computer with a docking station, such as Plug and Play support for hot, cold, and warm docking.

In addition to this hardware support, Windows 95 provides two software features that help you maximize the use of your computer when away from the office.

This chapter covers mobile computing with Windows 95. Terms and concepts covered include:

+ **Briefcase**
+ **Dial-Up Networking (DUN)**
+ **Direct cable connection**
+ **File synchronization**

Using Briefcase

Briefcase is a file synchronization tool. It is designed to ensure that files that are stored in two different places (for example, on a portable computer and a network server) stay identical even though they are being edited separately.

You should think of a Windows 95 Briefcase in much the same way that you think of the briefcase in which you're probably carrying this book to and from the office. It is a holding place for the files, and lets you "take some files home," "work on them at home," and "put them back" when you get back to the office.

There are two ways to use Briefcase. You can place a Briefcase on a disk and use it to store copies of files that are hosted on your computer, or you can place the Briefcase on your computer and use it to store copies of files that are located on a network server.

Tip
You could even place a Briefcase on a removable hard disk volume, such as a Syquest drive attached to your computer, and use it to store copies of files on a network server for safekeeping. In fact, when writing this book we did just that, carrying the removable hard disk with us whenever we left home—just in case.

Creating and Using a Briefcase

To create a Briefcase, simply open the folder that you want to contain the Briefcase (or just use the desktop). Then right click and choose New, Briefcase.

To use a Briefcase, just open it and drag files into it.

After you've edited either the original files or the copy of the files in the Briefcase, you can choose Update All from the Briefcase's File menu to update the files. Briefcase compares the files, using the file's access date and time as the gauge of which file is the updated copy. It then copies the updated file over the older file.

Some programs, such as Microsoft Access for Windows 95, support merging files.

Briefcase Files

A Briefcase is actually a special kind of folder. It holds copies of the files that are placed into it.

In addition to the files placed in the Briefcase, the folder also contains two hidden files:

+ Desktop.ini holds the OLE registration information for Briefcase and some settings.

+ Briefcase database holds the information about the files in the Briefcase, such as the date, time, status, original location, and size when last synchronized.

These two files are always hidden, even if you've set Explorer options to allow the viewing of hidden files.

Using Dial-Up Networking

Dial-Up Networking, like its predecessor, Remote Access Service (RAS), is designed to let your computer act as a node on a network. Instead of being attached by a high-speed network cable, however, you're attached using some kind of dial-up connection, such as an ordinary modem.

There are two parts to Dial-Up Networking: the server and the client. Out of the box, Windows 95 is designed only to be a Dial-Up Networking client. This enables you to use a Windows 95 computer to connect to any of the supported servers:

+ Microsoft Windows NT

+ Microsoft LAN Manager

+ Microsoft Windows for Workgroups

+ LAN Manager for UNIX

Ch
21

+ IBM LAN Server

+ Shiva LanRover (and other dial-up routers that support Microsoft RAS, Novell NRN, SLIP or PPP protocols)

With the addition of Microsoft Plus! for Windows 95, a Windows 95 computer can become a Dial-Up Networking server as well. A Dial-Up Networking server acts as a gateway between the remote computer and the network.

Architecture

The Dial-Up Networking architecture is similar to the normal networking architecture (see Chapter 15, "Windows 95 Networking Introduction"), except that the LLC and physical layers are replaced with the line protocol and modem.

Protocols

There are two types of protocols that you can configure for a Dial-Up Networking connection: the transport protocols and the line protocols.

Transport Protocols

Windows 95 Dial-Up Networking supports all of the transport protocols supported by Windows 95 networking for communication with other Windows 95 computers, including NetBEUI, IPX/SPX-compatible transport, and TCP/IP, although not all line protocols can be used with all transport protocols. The only other requirement is that the computer must be using a protected mode network client.

The transport protocols used by Dial-Up Networking are the same transport protocols used by regular networking. They simply hand off their packets to the line protocol.

Line Protocols

The line protocol takes the packets from the transport protocol and converts them into a form suitable for traveling over the dial-up connection.

Point to Point Protocol (PPP)

The Point to Point Protocol is an industry-standard communication protocol that was originally designed with the TCP/IP world in mind. PPP is the most flexible line protocol available with Dial-Up Networking because it supports all three transport protocols (NetBEUI, IPX/SPX-compatible and TCP/IP) simultaneously. PPP also supports the dynamic assignment of IP addresses to clients, allowing IP addresses to be assigned to a particular dial-up line, rather than by computer.

The Microsoft Windows 95 Dial-Up Networking PPP driver is a subset of the Link Control Protocol and Network Control Protocols defined by the Internet Engineering Task Force.

Serial Line Internet Protocol (SLIP)

SLIP is an older line protocol that was designed to support TCP/IP over serial connections. It is still used by some Internet Service Providers, although it is being phased out in favor of PPP.

Windows 95 supports SLIP, but you must install the support for it from the Windows 95 CD-ROM, where it can be found in the Admin\Apptools\Dscript folder. Installing SLIP also installs Dial-Up Scripting support, which lets you automate the login process to an Internet Service Provider that uses older UNIX systems and requires a cleartext logon sequence.

SLIP only supports TCP/IP as a transport protocol. It does not support NetBEUI or IPX/SPX.

Windows NT RAS

Earlier Microsoft dial-up networking products, such as Windows NT 3.1, used a protocol called AsyBEUI (a special version of NetBEUI designed for asynchronous connections) to support network connections. Windows 95 supports the NetBEUI protocol when dialing into these servers.

NetWare Connect (NRN)

NetWare Connect is a proprietary line protocol that can be used to dial into a Novell NetWare server. You must be running a

Ch
21

NetWare-compatible network client. The only supported protocol is the IPX/SPX transport protocol.

Modem Support

Dial-Up Networking supports all of the modems supported by Windows 95 and TAPI (see Chapter 24, "Windows 95 Communications").

Network Interfaces

Windows 95 supports all of the networking interfaces supported by Windows 95 networking including NetBIOS, Remote Procedure Calls (RPCs), mailslots, named pipes, and Windows Sockets.

Installing and Configuring Dial-Up Networking

If you did not install Dial-Up Networking as part of Windows 95 Setup, you can install it using the Add/Remove Software option in Control Panel. The Dial-Up Networking Option is under the Communications options in Windows Components.

The Dial-Up Networking Server is included with Microsoft Plus! for Windows 95.

Connecting with Dial-Up Networking

In order to connect to a remote workstation with Dial-Up Networking, you must create a *connection*. You can create as many connections as you need; all of the settings, including the phone numbers and network settings, are unique for each connection. Then, you simply double-click the connection when you want to use it.

Creating a Connection

To create a Dial-Up Networking connection, open the Dial-Up Networking folder. You can open the folder by double-clicking My Computer, which opens a window similar to the one in figure 21.1.

Double-clicking the Dial-Up Networking folder opens it. All of your Dial-Up Networking connections will be found inside the folder (see fig. 21.2), along with a special icon, Make New Connection.

FIG. 21.1 ⇒
Dial-Up Network-
ing Folder is found
inside My Com-
puter.

FIG. 21.2 ⇒
The Dial-Up
Networking
Folder.

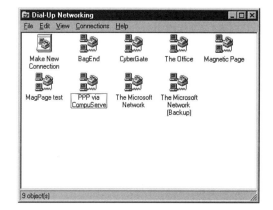

Opening the Make New Connection starts the Make New Connection
Wizard. The first dialog in the Wizard (see fig. 21.3) prompts you for
the name of the new connection, and which modem you want to connect with. (The Configure button opens the properties dialog for the
modem.)

The next dialog configures the telephone number of the computer you
are dialing into (see fig. 21.4). After clicking Next, the dialog in figure
21.5 opens. Click Finish to confirm the creation of the connection.

By default, a PPP connection with all protocols enabled has been created. To change the connection's settings, right-click it and choose
Properties to open the property dialog (see fig. 21.6) for the
connection.

Ch
21

FIG. 21.3 ⇒

The Make New
Connection
wizard.

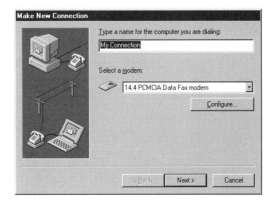

FIG. 21.4 ⇒

Configure the
telephone number
of the connection.

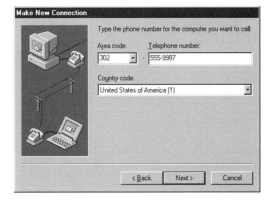

FIG. 21.5 ⇒

Confirm creating
the connection.

FIG. 21.6 ⇒
Change the
properties for
the connection.

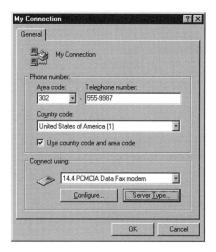

In the properties dialog, you can change the telephone number used by
the connection, choose a different modem (and Configure it with the
Configure button), and change the server type.

Clicking Server Type opens the Server Types dialog box (see fig. 21.7).
The Type of Dial-Up Server drop-down list allows you to choose:

+ PPP: Windows 95, Windows NT 3.5, Internet
+ NRN: NetWare Connect
+ Windows for Workgroups and Windows NT 3.1

The Advanced options let you choose:

+ *Log on to network.* When checked, Windows 95 will attempt to
  log into the network you're dialing into using the current
  username and password supplied when logging into
  Windows 95.

+ *Enable software compression.* When checked, the Windows 95
  Dial-Up Networking software will attempt to compress the
  data going over the connection. Both sides must support
  software compression in order for it to be usable.

+ *Require encrypted password.* When checked, only encrypted
  passwords can be sent by your computer. This provides additional security for the connection, although both sides must
  support it.

Ch

21

FIG. 21.7 ⇒

The Server Types dialog.

The checkboxes at the bottom of the dialog let you configure which protocols you want to use.

Clicking the TCP/IP Settings button opens the dialog box in figure 21.8, which allows you to set the TCP/IP settings used for this connection.

FIG. 21.8 ⇒

TCP/IP settings.

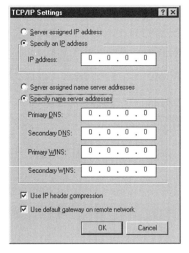

The settings are

- *Server assigned IP address* or *Specify an IP address.* Select whether the computer you're dialing into will supply the IP address or, if not, what IP address should be used.

+ *Server assigned name server addresses* or *Specify name server address.* Configures both DNS and WINS.

+ *Use IP header compression.* IP header compression makes connections more efficient, if supported by the computer you're dialing into.

+ *Use default gateway on remote network.* Should normally be checked, and means that Dial-Up Networking will use the default gateway specified by the server you're dialing into.

Connecting

To connect to a Dial-Up Networking server, simply double-click the connection.

Security

When configuring Dial-Up Networking, there are some security issues you should consider:

+ If running the Dial-Up Networking server, you should use user-level security to control who can access your network.

+ You may want to consider using additional security that can be provided by third-party security tools vendors, such as encryption devices.

+ You can restrict certain users from accessing Dial-Up Networking through user policies

> See "Using Policies," **p. 346**

+ You should use and require encrypted passwords to prevent users of network "sniffers" from capturing the passwords.

+ On the Internet, you should disable file and print sharing to prevent unauthorized access to your computer by Internet users.

+ On the Internet, consider using a firewall. (A firewall is a method of controlling access into a company's network, while still allowing company users to access the Internet.)

Ch
21

Direct Cable Connection

Related to Dial-Up Networking is the Direct Cable Connection support. You must explicitly choose to install Direct Cable Connection from the Add/Remove Software control panel option.

You must run the Direct Cable Connection program on both computers, one which will be the Host and the other, the Guest. The Host is the computer that has the resources you want to access.

You can connect the computers by either a serial (null-modem) cable or a parallel cable. Direct Cable Connection is not compatible with the Interlink utility provided with some versions of MS-DOS.

Taking the Disc Test

If you have read and understood the material in the chapter, you are ready to test your knowledge. Insert the CD-ROM that comes with this book and run the self-test software as described in Appendix I, "Using the CD-ROM."

Chapter Prerequisite

Before reading this chapter, you should be familiar with Windows 95 setup (see Chapter 3, "Windows 95 Setup"), Windows 95 configuration (see Chapter 4, "Configuring Windows 95"), and all aspects of Windows 95 networking (Chapters 15–19).

22

Windows 95 Administration

As any network administrator can attest, Windows 3.x was not easy to administer on a network. There was no mechanism for such basic needs of network users as the ability to use any computer on a network and still receive their own desktop settings and preferences (a feature known as *roving users*). Also missing was an allowance for a given computer to have multiple users—and to keep each user's settings and preferences separate from other users' settings and preferences on the same machine.

This chapter covers how you administer a Windows 95 installation. Terms and concepts covered include:

- ⊥ **Computer policies**
- ⊥ **Group policies**
- ⊥ **Net Watcher**
- ⊥ **Remote administration**
- ⊥ **System Policy Editor**

✢ **User policies**

✢ **User profiles**

Network administrators had to rely on third-party products to address these needs. Many of these third-party products relied upon copying and merging .ini files to control things such as what options were available to users, and copying users' personal settings as they moved around the network.

Windows 95 integrates these features into the operating system. Profiles allow users' preferences and settings to be stored independently of other users' settings on a single computer and, on a server-based network, on a network server to accommodate roving users.

Understanding User Profiles

User profiles can be configured on or off each individual computer. If you want all computers to automatically use them, you can configure the option to be on using a setup batch script.

See "Running Server-Based Setup," **p. 361**

User profiles contain configuration preferences and options for an individual user, including everything in the HKEY_CURRENT_USER section of that user's registry:

✢ Windows 95 user preference settings such as the desktop layout, wallpaper, font choices, and color choices.

✢ Network settings including network connections that are automatically restored at logon for this user.

✢ Application settings that are written to the HKEY_CURRENT_USER registry key. Windows 95 applications use this registry key to store per-user information, such as menu and toolbar configurations, fonts, window sizes, and user name. Only those applications that write configuration settings to this key can follow the user to other network computers. If the application stores its settings in .ini files, or some other application-specific manner, including other places in the registry, they will be computer-specific, rather than user-specific.

User profiles also can include several items that are not stored in the registry, including:

+ Shortcuts on the user's desktop

+ Shortcuts to servers listed in the Network Neighborhood

+ Items appearing on the Start menu and Programs folder

Some items cannot be included in a profile for a network user (for example, one stored on the network server):

+ Desktop folders (only shortcuts can be stored)

+ Programs and files stored on the desktop

+ Network protocols and drivers (they are computer-specific)

Using User Profiles

User profiles, when enabled, are automatic. When you log on to Windows 95, it checks to see if there is a user profile for your user name. If it finds one, it loads the appropriate configuration information into the registry and desktop. If it does not find one, it offers to create one.

Caution

One important thing to keep in mind about user profiles is that while settings are part of a profile, actual program and data files are not. This means that if you set up your profile on a computer that has a particular desktop wallpaper, for example, and then go to another computer that does not have the bitmap file for that wallpaper installed on it, the computer will not be able to display it.

Similarly, if you have a spreadsheet program installed locally on your computer, and create a shortcut on the desktop to it, you will not be able to run the spreadsheet on another computer, even though the shortcut is displayed, unless the spreadsheet program also is installed on that computer.

Finally, Windows 95 user profiles apply to Windows 95 computers only. They are not supported when a roving user moves to a Windows NT computer. A Windows 95 profile is not the same thing as a Windows NT profile.

When logged on to a Novell NetWare or Windows NT network, Windows 95 looks in a particular place on the authenticating network server for a user profile, after looking on the computer for a profile that matches the user name. Windows 95 uses the profile that bears the latest time stamp, so make sure that the clocks on all of your computers are synchronized! You can synchronize the time on your computer with the time on another computer by using the NET TIME command. For example, typing:

NET TIME \\BAGEND /S /Y

will set the time on your computer to the same time as the time on the computer named BAGEND.

On a Windows NT Server domain, the network copy of the user profile is stored in the user's home directory. Make sure that you create home directories.

On a Novell NetWare server, user profiles are stored in the SYS:MAIL/<UserID> directory. Every user account on a NetWare server has a mail directory associated with it, which is named after the eight-digit hexadecimal UserID number that Novell uses to identify the user account. You should ensure that long file name support is installed on the SYS: volume on the server so that all of the user profile settings can be used.

The NetWare system administration tools automatically create the SYS:MAIL/<UserID> directory for every user account, even if there are no NetWare e-mail programs installed. This subdirectory is also used by NetWare to hold the personal login script used for the account.

Network user profile support requires a 32-bit network provider, and requires that the Primary Network Logon (in the Network control panel option) be set to the appropriate network. If you have multiple types of servers on your network, you should make sure that all of them use the same Primary Network Logon so that the same network profile is being used.

Enabling User Profiles

In order to use user profiles on a computer, open the Passwords option in Control Panel. The Passwords properties dialog opens (see fig. 22.1).

FIG. 22.1 ⇒

The Passwords Properties dialog from Control Panel.

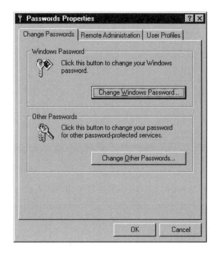

Select the User Profiles tab (see fig. 22.2). To enable user profiles, select the Users can customize their preferences and desktop settings radio button, as shown.

FIG. 22.2 ⇒

Enabling user profiles.

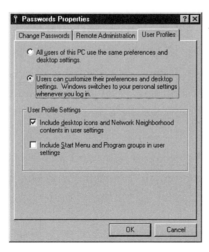

Once user profiles are enabled, the User Profile Settings options are available. These options allow you to control what items are included in a user profile. In other words, you can control what items will be different for each user. There are two options:

+ Include desktop icons and Network Neighborhood contents in user settings. If this item is checked, the user's desktop will be included in the profile.

+ Include Start menu and Program groups in user settings. If this item is checked, the Start menu and Programs menu will be different for each user.

Using Policies

Policies give a network administrator control over what a user can do on the computer. Policies can be set for a particular computer, for particular users, and for groups. In addition, a default user and computer policy can be set to control behaviors when users or computers that are not explicitly named in the policy file log on.

To implement system policies, you need to follow several steps:

1. *Create profiles.* In order for user policies to be used on a computer, you must also enable user profiles.

2. *Create policies.* You must create the policies and store them in a file. You can either create a file on each computer or store them in a network location (determined by the type of network) and have them enforced as part of the network logon process.

3. *Distribute policies.* A central policy file is placed in an access point where it can be accessed by all logged-on users, for example, on a NetWare network the access point is the SYS:PUBLIC directory.

If you want group policy support, you must add the Group Policy item through Add/Remove programs on each client. Group policy support is *not* installed by default.

System Policy Editor

System policies are created and edited using the System Policy Editor. The System Policy Editor is not automatically installed, however. You must add it from the Add/Remove software option in Control Panel by using the Have Disk button and specifying the \Admin\Apptools\Poledit directory on the Windows 95 CD-ROM.

After you have installed it, you can access the System Policy Editor by choosing it from the System Tools group in the Accessories group in the Programs Folder.

The System Policy Editor operates in two different modes: File mode and Registry mode. You place it in File mode by opening a policy file or creating a new policy file (via File, New). The title bar will show the name of the policy file (or Untitled if you haven't saved the file yet). A newly created policy file will contain two entries: Default User and Default Computer (see fig. 22.3).

FIG. 22.3 ⇒

Policy files contain at least the Default User and Default Computer policies.

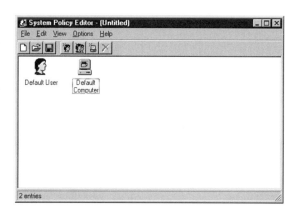

To place the System Policy Editor in Registry mode, open a registry, either by choosing Open Registry or Connect from the File menu. When in Registry mode on the local computer, the title bar shows Local Registry, and contains two entries: Local User and Local Computer (see fig. 22.4).

FIG. 22.4 ⇒

In Registry mode, use the Local User and Local Computer policies.

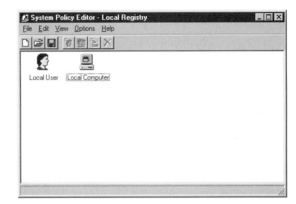

When using the System Policy Editor in Registry mode, changes are made immediately to the System.dat and User.dat files on the local or remote computer. It is not necessary to restart or log on and off.

Note When using the System Policy Editor in File mode, users are not affected until the .pol files have been distributed to the appropriate network location. Then they will be implemented as part of the user's logon process the next time the user logs on. ▨

Policy Templates

The System Policy Editor uses template files to control what items appear in its user interface. The template file controls the available options, how they're organized, and what values, checkboxes, and input fields are available.

The default policy template is Admin.adm, and is stored in the Inf folder within the System folder. You can modify Admin.adm to add additional registry options (such as those used by an application), or even create another template file. To change the template that the System Policy Editor users, choose Template from the Options menu. This opens the dialog shown in figure 22.5. Clicking the Open template button allows you to choose another template file.

FIG. 22.5 ⇒

Choosing a different policy template.

Modifying Policies

The System Policy Editor is somewhat unusual because there are three states each checkbox represents (see fig. 22.6):

- *Checked.* The Remove 'Run' command checkbox in figure 22.6 is checked. This means that this policy will be implemented, and the appropriate settings will be added to the registry. (If the policy shown is implemented, the user will not have access to the Run… command on the Start menu.)

- *Cleared.* The Remove folders from 'Settings' on Start Menu checkbox is cleared. This means that this policy is not implemented, and the appropriate settings will be removed (or turned off) in the registry. (If the policy shown is not implemented, the user will have access to the Control Panel folder.)

- *Grayed.* The Remove Taskbar from 'Settings' on Start Menu checkbox is grayed. This means that the registry key will not be modified from whatever it is set to.

FIG. 22.6 ⇒

There are three possible states for each checkbox in System Policy Editor.

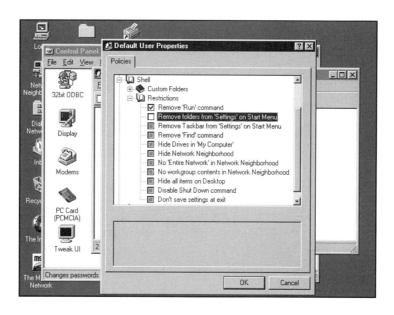

User Policies

When a user logs on, the policy file is checked to see if there is a policy for that user's logon name. If there is, then the policies for that user are applied. If not, the policies for the Default User are applied.

Group Policies

Next, if the user did not have a policy for his/her logon name, Windows 95 determines whether the user is a member of any specified groups. If the user is a member of a group, then the group policies are applied according to their priority order. To specify the group priority, select Group priority from the Option menu.

Computer Policies

After user and group policies are applied, Windows 95 checks to see if there is a policy for this computer's name. If there is, the policies for this computer's name are applied; if not, the Default Computer policies are applied.

Policy Files

Policy files must be placed in the appropriate place on the network in order for automatic updating to occur. If the policy file is named Config.pol, Windows 95 automatically loads it across the network when the user logs in.

Server-Based Policies

On a Windows NT network, place the Config.pol file in the NETLOGON share on the Primary Domain Controller. Unless you enable load balancing, Windows 95 always loads the Config.pol file from the Primary Domain Controller, regardless of which domain controller authenticated the user.

If you enable load balancing, the policy file will be downloaded from the NETLOGON share on the domain controller that authenticated the user. Load balancing spreads the work of providing the policy files among the domain controllers, rather than relying on the PDC.

In order for load balancing to work, you must enable replication on the Windows NT servers.

To enable load balancing, select the Default Computer, then check the Remote Update policy and check the Load-balance box (see fig. 22.7).

FIG. 22.7 ⇒
Enabling load balancing.

On a NetWare network, with the Primary Network Logon set to the Microsoft Client for Novell Networks, place the Config.pol file in the \\<Preferred Server>\SYS\PUBLIC directory.

Using the Administrative Tools

In addition to the System Policy Editor, Windows 95 includes several other administrative tools:

- Net Watcher
- Registry Editor
- Remote Administration

Net Watcher

Net Watcher is installed only if you select it during Custom setup, or by using the Add/Remove software option in Control Panel.

Net Watcher does not require user-level security, but if you are using user-level security, both computers must be running the same type of server (SMB or NCP) and using the same security provider if you want to use Net Watcher to administer a remote computer.

Figure 22.8 shows Net Watcher being used to monitor a remote computer. There are three views in Net Watcher: View by Connections, View by Open Files, and View by Shared Folders. Figure 22.8 shows the View by Connections view.

FIG. 22.8 ⇒

Viewing connections to a remote server.

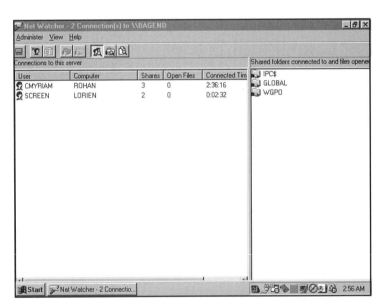

In the View by Connections view, the left pane shows connections to the computer being monitored, listing the User and Computer making the connection, how many shares they are connected to, how many files they have open, and how long they've been connected.

The right pane shows the shares the highlighted user is connected to.

In the View by Shared Folders view (see fig. 22.9), the left pane lists all of the shared folders on the monitored computer. The right pane shows what computers are connected to the highlighted share and what files, if any, are open.

The View by Open Files view (see fig. 22.10) lists the currently open files, what share they are being opened through, what computer has them open, and what mode (Read/Write or Read Only) the file is opened for.

FIG. 22.9 ⇒

Viewing the shared folders on a remote computer.

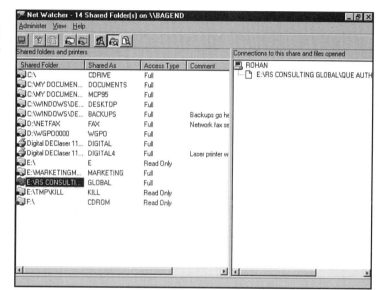

Registry Editor

The Registry Editor is used to view, and optionally modify, the system registry. For details on using the Registry Editor, see Chapter 4, "Configuring Windows 95."

You can use the Registry Editor to edit the registry on remote computers if:

- Both computers are using user-level security and the same security provider.
- You have installed the Remote Registry service from the \Admin\Nettools\Remotereg directory on the Windows 95 CD-ROM on both computers.

FIG. 22.10 ⇒
Viewing the files
open on a remote
computer.

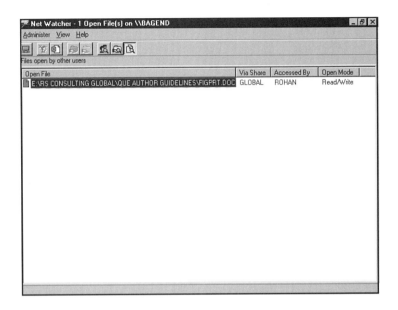

When the Remote Registry service is installed, you can use the Connect Network Registry option from the Registry menu in the Registry Editor.

Remote Administration Tools

The final administration tool allows you to administer the file system.

Granting Remote Administration Permissions

To administer a remote computer, you must first allow Remote Administration through the Password option of Control Panel. Select the Remote Administration tab (see fig. 22.11), check the Enable Remote Administration of this server checkbox, and supply a password to control access to this function.

Administering the File System

To administer the file system on a remote computer, open the property dialog for the computer you want to administer in Network Neighborhood and choose the Tools tab (see fig. 22.12). Click the Administer button and you will be prompted for the password for the ADMIN$ share (see fig. 22.13). The ADMIN$ share is a hidden share (all shares that end with a $ are hidden from browse lists) created by granting remote administration permissions.

FIG. 22.11 ⇒
Enabling remote administration.

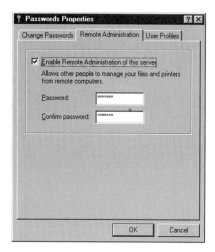

FIG. 22.12 ⇒
Choose the Tools tab to administer this computer.

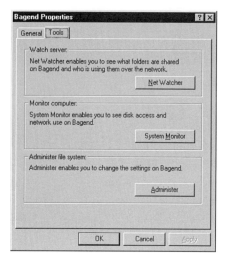

Supplying the password causes an Explorer window to open like that in figure 22.14. In addition to all of the normal shares on the computer, a special share is created by the system for every hard disk volume on the computer, allowing you full access to the computer's file system.

The special shares appear with an icon of a disk drive. Each is named after the drive's letter, plus a $, such as c$, d$, and e$ in figure 22.14.

FIG. 22.13 ⇒
Supply the Admin-
istration password.

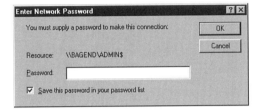

FIG. 22.14 ⇒
The hidden special
shares give access
to the entire file
system of the
computer.

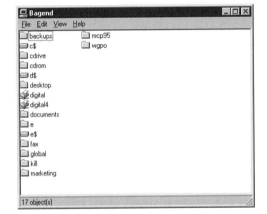

Taking the Disc Test

If you have read and understood the material in the chapter, you are ready to test your knowledge. Insert the CD-ROM that comes with this book and run the self-test software as described in Appendix I, "Using the CD-ROM."

Chapter Prerequisite

Before reading this chapter, you should be familiar with Windows 95 setup (see Chapter 3, "Windows 95 Setup"), configuring Windows 95 (see Chapter 4, "Configuring Windows 95"), Windows 95 networking (see Chapters 15-19), and administrating Windows 95 (see Chapter 22, "Windows 95 Administration").

23

Server-Based Setup of Windows 95

Previous versions of Windows let you install Windows onto a server's hard drive to provide a central point from which you could install Windows on client computers. In addition, you could create a *shared installation*, where the client computers ran Windows from the file server instead of having local copies.

This chapter covers setting up Windows 95 so that users can install (and optionally run) Windows 95 from a network server. Terms and concepts covered include:

- Machine directory
- Batch script
- Shared installation

Windows 95 includes a separate program, Netsetup.exe, which gives an administrator significantly improved control over all aspects of the server-based setup process.

Comparing Server-Based Setup and Administrative Setup

Windows 95 Server–Based Setup is significantly different than the Administrative Setup that was available in previous versions of Windows.

In Windows 3.x, you could run Setup/a to create a central installation point on the network. Setup would decompress all of the installation files on the setup diskettes, and copy them to the specified directory. An administrator could then go through the various .inf files that made up the setup program's configuration, and edit them to change options, such as whether or not games were installed.

Then, if you were going to use a shared installation, you would have to manually create directories on the network for individual machine's configuration settings, possibly create startup disks, and then finally run Setup/n on each workstation.

Windows 95 uses a special Server–Based Setup program called Netsetup. Netsetup is found on the Windows 95 CD–ROM in the \Admin\Nettools\NetSetup directory.

Creating a Shared Installation

There are three steps to creating a shared Windows 95 installation:

1. Run Server-Based Setup under Windows 95.
2. Create a setup script in Msbatch.inf format.
3. Run Windows 95 Setup with the setup script. (For example, setup Msbatch.inf)

All of the other steps, such as creating the network directories for individual machine's configuration settings, etc., are handled automatically.

Understanding Server-Based Setup Issues

Server-Based Setup with Netsetup is only available if you have the CD-ROM version of Windows 95. It is not available with the floppy disk version of Windows 95. In addition, you must have at least one computer already set up and attached to the network server, running a local installation of Windows 95, on which to run Netsetup.

When you decide whether to use shared installations or to install Windows 95 onto the local hard drive of the computers, you should consider the benefits of each approach.

The benefits of installing Windows 95 on the local hard disk include:

+ Better performance.
+ Less network traffic.
+ Computers are available if the network server is down or not available.
+ Depending on system policies, the user has more freedom to customize his/her computer.

The benefits of a shared Windows 95 installation include:

+ Little or no hard disk space is required on the local computer. In fact, the local computer can boot from floppies, or even have no disk drives at all if Remote Initial Program Load (RIPL) is supported.
+ Updating drivers is easier because you can simply upgrade the shared installation.
+ The workstation is considerably more secure, and safer for novice users because a network logon is required in order to access the system files. You also can protect the system files from the users (make them read-only).

Machine Directories

The machine directory is another important consideration when deciding to use a shared installation of Windows 95. Any computer that does not have a hard disk drive on which to store Windows 95 components must have its own directory on the network server called a *machine directory*.

The machine directory is used to store configuration files in much the same way that the Windows directory is used in a local installation. In fact, many of the same files are stored in the machine directory, including Win.com, the full registry (both System.dat and User.dat), and .ini files.

Notice that the machine directories are computer-specific settings, not user-specific settings. Users still have their own home directories on the network server, regardless of which computer they have logged into. If user profiles are also enabled, users will have their own sets of user-specific settings separately stored from the computer, so that no matter what computer they log into, their individual settings are always available—up to the capacity of the computer!

Machine directories (and therefore, the Windows 95 setup contained within them) can actually be shared among all of the computers on a network of a given configuration. This greatly simplifies the task of installing the operating system on many different computers because you can just copy a startup disk for any computer of a given type.

Machine directories do not need to be on the same computer as the shared installation directory. In fact, it is usually best if you put them on different servers to balance the load.

Shared Installation Files

A shared Windows 95 installation stores system files in three locations:

+ *Startup disk.* The startup disk contains the real mode software needed to start up the computer and connect to the shared Windows directory on the network server. It includes the mini-registry that is used to start the computer. The startup disk can be the local hard disk of a computer, a floppy disk, or a remote-boot disk image on a server.

+ *Machine directory.* As mentioned earlier, the machine directory contains the configuration information for the computer on a computer-by-computer basis. It contains the full registry; the default User.dat will be updated with the user's User.dat if user profiles are enabled.

+ *Shared installation directory.* This contains all of the Windows 95 files and is automatically flagged as read-only during the installation of the files.

Using Setup Scripts

Setup scripts are used to control how Windows 95 installs on individual computers. Server-Based Setup enables you to create the default batch script automatically by specifying options when installing the source files on the server.

After Server-Based Setup has completed, you can create additional batch setup scripts by running the Batch.exe utility that is in the same directory (Admin\Nettools\NetSetup) on the Windows 95 CD-ROM as Netsetup.exe.

Running Server-Based Setup

Server-Based Setup is a very procedural program. You must go through it step by step.

First, before starting Server-Based Setup, you must create a shared directory on the network server that will be used as the root of the installation. You must also log into Windows 95 and attach to the network using an account that has full access to this directory.

For historical reasons, the shared installation directory and machine directories must never appear as the root directory of a disk. This means that the directory you created will be used as the root of the directory hierarchy when the installation proceeds, and you must be sure to specify a subdirectory for the installation directory and machine directory paths.

In this example, a directory called NetSetup has already been created (and shared as NETSETUP) on a server named \\Bagend.

When you start Server-Based Setup by running it from the \Admin\Nettools\NetSetup directory on the Windows 95 CD-ROM, the dialog box shown in figure 23.1 opens. The first step you must take is to specify the directory on the server that you will be installing the files to (and users will be running Setup from) on the file server. Click the Set Path button to open the dialog box in figure 23.2.

FIG. 23.1 ⇒

The main dialog box of Server-Based Setup.

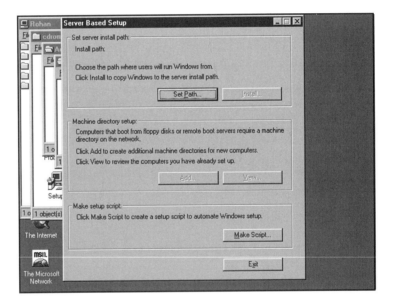

Be sure to specify the subdirectory to use. If the directory does not exist, Server-Based Setup will prompt you to ask if you want it to create the subdirectory automatically. In this example, \\Bagend\Netsetup\Win has been specified.

After the path has been set, you are returned to the main dialog box of Server-Based Setup. The dialog box has changed to indicate the install path, and the Install button is now available (see fig. 23.3).

FIG. 23.2 ⇒

Specify the subdirectory on the server to copy the files to.

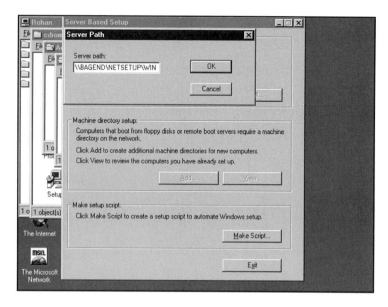

FIG. 23.3 ⇒

The Install path has been set.

Clicking the Install button opens the Source Path dialog box (see fig. 23.4). There are three options to set here:

> ✦ *Install Policy.* If you choose Server, then this is a shared installation of Windows 95. If you choose Local Hard Drive, then

users cannot set up their computers as a shared installation of Windows 95. If you choose Ｕser's Choice, it's up to the user.

⊥ *Path to Install From.* This is the UNC pathname to the location of the Windows 95 files. Normally, this is set to the location of the WIN95 directory on the Windows 95 CD-ROM.

⊥ *Path to Install To.* This is set automatically to the path specified earlier.

FIG. 23.4 ⇒

You must decide whether users will use and store Windows 95 on their local disks, the server, or possibly both.

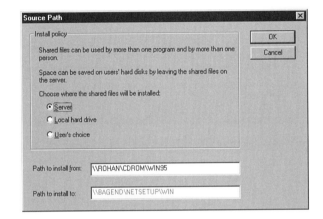

After choosing your install policy and clicking OK, the dialog box shown in figure 23.5 opens. If you press the Ｄon't Create Default button, Msbatch.inf will not be created, and the users will be asked all of the installation questions, as though they were installing from the CD-ROM (see "Step by Step Install," in Chapter 3). If you click Ｃreate Default, the Server-Based Setup Default Properties dialog box opens (see fig. 23.6).

FIG. 23.5 ⇒

Do you want to create a default setup script?

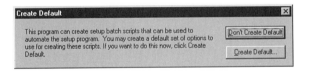

The Server-Based Setup Default Properties dialog box is based on the System Policy Editor, although it creates a setup script instead of a policy file. See Chapter 22, "Windows 95 Administration," for information on using the Policy Editor interface.

FIG. 23.6 ⇒

Setting the properties for the default setup script.

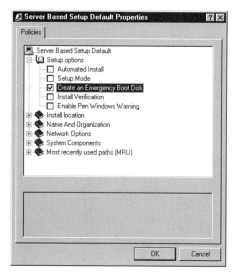

After selecting the installation options you want, the next dialog box asks you for the Product Identification Number (see fig. 23.7). This is the CD Key—the number on the yellow sticker on your Windows 95 CD case.

FIG. 23.7 ⇒

Enter your CD Key.

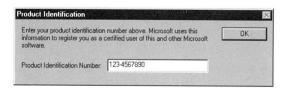

Make sure you enter a valid CD Key, as Server-Based Setup will fail if you don't.

In the next step, Server-Based Setup copies the files to the server (see fig. 23.8). After copying all of the files, it sets each one to read-only (see fig. 23.9).

Server-Based Setup is completed when the message box in figure 23.10 is displayed.

Ch

23

FIG. 23.8 ⇒
Server-Based Setup
copies the files...

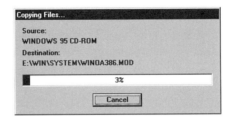

FIG. 23.9 ⇒
...and then marks
them read-only.

FIG. 23.10 ⇒
Server-Based Setup
is complete.

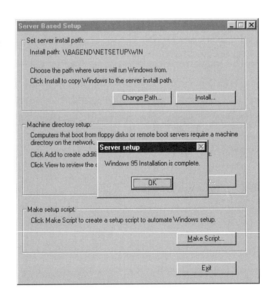

Once Server-Based Setup completes, the main dialog box changes again (see fig. 23.11) to make the Add and View buttons available for creating new machine directories, and looking at the ones that have already been created.

FIG. 23.11 ⇒
You're ready to create any machine directories that are needed.

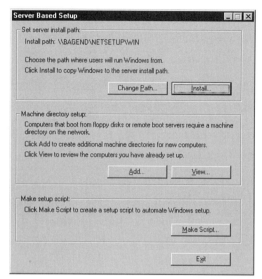

To create a new machine directory, click <u>A</u>dd. The dialog box in figure 23.12 opens.

FIG. 23.12 ⇒
Adding a new machine directory.

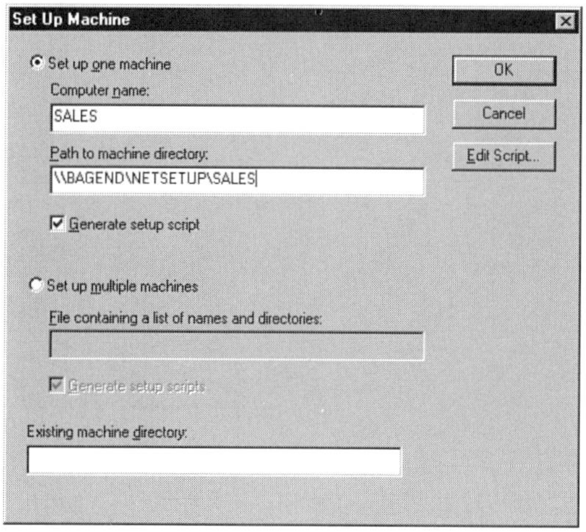

If you only want to create a single machine directory, simply type the computer's name and the directory you want to be that computer's machine director in the appropriate boxes. Check the <u>G</u>enerate Setup Script check box to generate a setup script (based on the default setup script) that will properly install this computer to the machine directory.

Ch

23

You also can create multiple machine directories by selecting the Set up Multiple Machines radio button. If you choose to do so, you must prepare a text file with entries (one per line) in the following format:

```
computer1,\\server\share\path\path\machine_directory
```

Provide the path to the text file in the box.

The final option in the dialog box lets you generate an installation based on an existing machine directory.

The last option in the Server-Based Setup main dialog (see fig. 23.13) lets you create additional scripts using the batch utility. Simply click the Make Script button and you will be in the same Policy Editor-based script editor that you used to create the default script.

FIG. 23.13 ⇒

Choose the Make Script button to make more setup scripts.

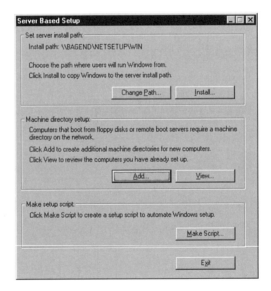

Taking the Disc Test

 If you have read and understood the material in the chapter, you are ready to test your knowledge. Insert the CD-ROM that comes with this book and run the self-test software as described in Appendix I, "Using the CD-ROM."

Chapter Prerequisite

Before reading this chapter, you should have a basic understanding of modems and Windows 95 configuration (see Chapter 4, "Configuring Windows 95").

Windows 95 Communications

Communications refers to the exchange of information between two computers using a point-to-point asynchronous single-channel connection. Communications usually involves either a hardwired serial or parallel port connection, or an intermediary device called a modem.

This chapter covers Windows 95 communications. Concepts and skills covered include:

- The difference between **communications** and **networking**
- How to configure a **modem** for use with Windows 95
- The **Windows 95 Telephony API (TAPI)**
- The **Windows 95 Communication Architecture**

Working with Modems

Modem stands for modulation/demodulation, and refers to the process that the modem uses to make digital communications possible over analog telephone lines. Modems usually understand a set of commands known as *AT commands*, because they all begin with the letters AT (short for Attention). Each modem uses its own interpretation of the AT commands, which, prior to the introduction of the *Telephony API (TAPI)*, required every application that used a modem to be familiar with that particular modem's commands. Most modems support about 90 percent of the standard AT command set; many programs in the past did not allow for the remaining 10 percent of the command set that differed from modem to modem, resulting in compatibility problems.

Installing and Configuring a Modem

Windows 95 enables you to install a modem once, and have those settings available for use in all communications applications. This is a marked improvement over modem support in previous operating systems, where every application that accessed a modem needed to know the full details of how to operate the modem.

To install support for a modem, open Control Panel, and double-click the Modems option. The dialog box shown in figure 24.1 opens.

Click <u>A</u>dd to open the Install New Modem dialog box (see fig. 24.2). The default action will cause Windows 95 to query each of your serial ports, looking for a modem. If it finds one, it interrogates it to determine what brand and model modem it is. If it cannot find a modem that it recognizes, a dialog box offers to let you pick from a list (see fig. 24.3).

When you choose to pick from a list, the dialog box in figure 24.4 opens. The left-hand pane lists modem manufacturers, and the right-hand pane lists modem models. If your modem is not on the list, you can choose one of the standard types or, preferably, obtain an installation disk from the modem's manufacturer.

FIG. 24.1 ⇒
Modems
properties.

FIG. 24.2 ⇒
The Install New
Modem dialog
box.

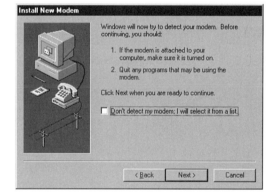

FIG. 24.3 ⇒
If Windows 95
can't find a mo-
dem, you can pick
one.

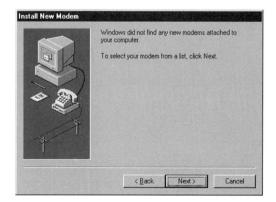

FIG. 24.4 ⇒

Manufacturers on
the left, modems
on the right.

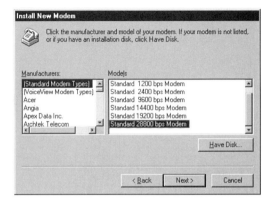

If you have an installation disk, clicking <u>H</u>ave Disk will read the disk.

After choosing your modem from the list and clicking the Next button,
the dialog box in figure 24.5 opens. You must select the port to which
your modem is connected.

FIG. 24.5 ⇒

You must choose
the port your
modem is con-
nected to.

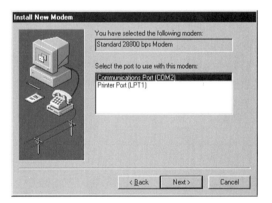

After you choose the port and click the Next button, Windows 95
completes the installation of the modem and makes it available for you
to use.

TAPI Services

The modem support in Windows 95 depends upon the *Telephony API
(TAPI)* to enable application programs to work with modems and other
communication devices in a device-independent way.

Through the use of TAPI, which provides functions for communications features such as call initiation, connection monitoring, and call termination, applications are freed from having to know the specific AT command strings that operate modems. In addition, support for other types of communication devices, such as digital PBX and ISDN systems become automatically available to an application.

In the past, if you used multiple communication applications, you would be forced to install support for your modem into each and every application. If the application didn't support your modem, you often had to manually determine and enter command strings into the application. Now, with a TAPI-compliant application, once you've installed your modem (see the instructions in the previous section), all that you have to do in an application is select which installed modem you want to use. TAPI takes care of the rest.

Ch

24

Locations

One powerful feature TAPI provides is support for dialing locations. This feature is particularly useful with notebook computers because it takes care of what is probably the most annoying drawback to portable computers—the fact that required dialing information usually changes as you move from one place to another.

A *dialing location* is a collection of settings that pertain to a particular place. Each location includes:

+ Area code
+ Country
+ Dialing prefixes for both local and long distance dialing
+ Credit card information
+ Prefix to disable call-waiting
+ Dialing type (pulse or touch-tone)

Most communication applications include a telephone book of some kind. When you travel to a different location, all that you have to do is create a new dialing location, and all of the telephone book entries will automatically be dialed correctly—even if you've traveled to a new country or area code.

To create a new dialing location, follow these steps:

1. Double-click Modems from the Control Panel. This will open the dialog box shown in figure 24.6.

FIG. 24.6 ⇒

To create a dialing location, you must use Modems Properties.

2. Click the Dialing Properties button to open the Dialing Properties dialog box (see fig. 24.7).

FIG. 24.7 ⇒

You can access dialing locations through the Dialing Properties dialog box.

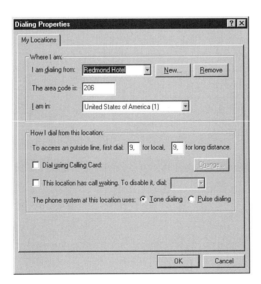

3. Click the <u>N</u>ew button to bring up the Create New Location dialog box (see fig. 24.8).

4. Type the name of the new location and click OK to return to the Dialing Properties dialog box, where you can change the entries as appropriate for the new location.

FIG. 24.8 ⇒

Every dialing location has a name.

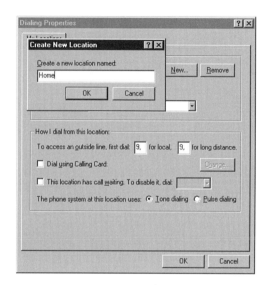

5. Check the Dial <u>u</u>sing Calling Card checkbox to open the Change Calling Card Dialog box. Select the type of calling card you are using, and enter your calling card number.

If the type of calling card you have is not listed, clicking the Ad<u>v</u>anced button enables you to specify your card's requirements.

Phone Dialer

Windows 95 includes a Phone Dialer application that lets you use the computer to dial voice telephone calls. You can access it by choosing <u>P</u>rograms, Accessories from the Start menu.

One of the advantages of using the Phone Dialer is the phone call log that it keeps. Another is the fact that the Phone Dialer, being a TAPI

Ch

24

application, automatically knows from what location you are dialing, and dials prefixes, area codes, and calling card numbers as appropriate. It also supports several "Speed Dial" numbers, so that you can dial frequently called numbers by clicking a button.

Phone Dialer only dials the phone for you—you still have to have a telephone attached to the line to talk with.

Windows 95 Communications Architecture

The communication subsystem in Windows 95 was implemented using a modular architecture. This offers many improvements over the monolithic communications driver approach used in Windows 3.1.

The modular approach makes it easy for hardware and software vendors to write device drivers and communications applications. The communications subsystem has been written from the ground up as 32-bit, to take advantage of the preemptive multitasking nature of Windows 95. This provides vastly improved reliability with high-speed communications.

Plug and Play modems and communication devices are fully supported.

TAPI arbitrates among applications that want to use a given communication port and device. For example, if Microsoft Fax is listening on a modem port for an incoming fax and you want to dial out to The Microsoft Network, you do not have to disable Microsoft Fax. TAPI detects that no communication is actually going on at the moment, and give possession of the port to the appropriate process.

There are several parts to the Windows 95 Communications Architecture:

- *Win32 TAPI and Win32 Comm API.* 32-bit Windows applications use the TAPI and Communications API to control and communicate with communication ports and devices.

- *Unimodem*. Unimodem is the "Universal Modem" driver. Part device driver and part TAPI Service Provider, Unimodem provides the services required so that users do not have to know the details of modem commands. Unimodem works with mini-drivers provided by the modem manufacturers. Microsoft updated Unimodem shortly after the release of Windows 95 with a version, called Unimodem V, that supports voice/data/fax modems.

- *VCOMM*. VCOMM provides the protected-mode services that interface between the Unimodem driver and port drivers to enable Windows applications to access modem and port services. In addition, VCOMM interfaces with the Windows 95 Comm.drv that provides communication support to 16-bit Windows applications.

- *Port Drivers*. Port drivers are responsible for actually accessing the hardware. Windows 95 includes port drivers for both serial and parallel ports, and manufacturers can add port drivers for other types of devices.

Thanks to the layered approach, communication device manufacturers only need to develop a port driver or modem mini-driver, as appropriate. This is a significant improvement over Windows 3.1, which required a complete subsystem replacement if a device manufacturer needed to add a new type of device.

Ch
24

Taking the Disc Test

 If you have read and understood the material in the chapter, you are ready to test your knowledge. Insert the CD-ROM that comes with this book and run the self-test software as described in Appendix I, "Using the CD-ROM."

Chapter Prerequisite

Before reading this chapter, you should be familiar with Windows 95 setup (see Chapter 3, "Windows 95 Setup") and Windows 95 configuration (see Chapter 4, "Configuring Windows 95").

Using Microsoft Exchange

Microsoft began including messaging services in its operating systems when the first workgroup version of Microsoft Mail was included in Windows for Workgroups 3.10. Since that time, every Microsoft operating system has included both a mail client and a workgroup postoffice, which allows users on a small LAN to communicate with each other using electronic mail. The workgroup versions support only one postoffice, while the full version of MS Mail supports many postoffices.

This chapter covers the Microsoft Exchange client included in Windows 95. Terms and concepts covered include:

- **Information service**
- **Microsoft fax**
- **POP3**
- **Profile**

With the release of Windows for Workgroups 3.11, Microsoft began to include Microsoft Fax (originally called At Work Fax), which allowed users on a LAN to share a single fax modem for incoming and outgoing faxes.

Installing Microsoft Exchange

There are two ways to install Microsoft Exchange—during Windows 95 Setup by selecting the checkbox shown in figure 25.1, or from the Add/Remove Software option of Control Panel (see fig. 25.2). Installing Exchange will result in the software being copied to your computer, but configuration does not take place until you first try to use it.

FIG. 25.1 ⇒

You can install Microsoft Exchange during Windows 95 Setup…

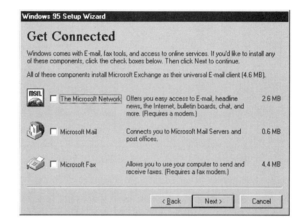

FIG. 25.2 ⇒

…or by using the Add/Remove Software option in Control Panel.

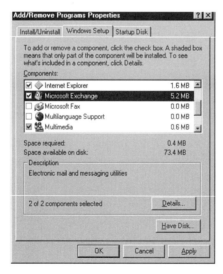

Creating Profiles and Information Services

The first time that you access Microsoft Exchange, the Inbox Setup Wizard starts up automatically (see fig. 25.3). The first screen of the Wizard allows you to select the *information services* you want to include in the default *profile*. Each of the possible information services that can be the profile presents its own set of configuration screens after you click Next. (Each service's configuration screens will be covered later in the chapter.)

FIG. 25.3 ⇒

The Inbox Setup Wizard lets you configure your Microsoft Exchange installation.

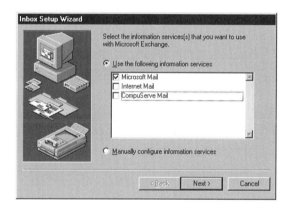

Ch
25

An Exchange profile is a collection of information services that are being used at any one time. Exchange allows you to set up multiple profiles for a variety of reasons:

  ┼ Different users of a Windows 95 computer can have their own Exchange profiles, so that they can have their own separate personal folders.

  ┼ Some information services only allow you to work with one instance of them at a time. By using different profiles, you can configure the service differently in each of the profiles. You can even include the same personal address book and personal folders so that all of your messages go to the same place.

An Exchange *information service* is a service that can send and receive messages, such as an e-mail system, fax system, or online service.

Configuring Personal Address Book and Folders

The two information services that are included in every profile are the Personal Address Book service and the Personal Folders service.

The Personal Address Book allows you to maintain your own address list of people that you send messages to. It is normally stored in C:\Exchange\mailbox.pab. If multiple users use the computer, you should change the name of the file during configuration to match the user's login name.

Similarly, Personal Folders are normally stored in C:\Exchange\Mailbox.pst. If multiple users use the computer, you should change the name of the file to match the user's login name. You also can assign a password to the file so that it is encrypted and only the owner can read from it.

Using Microsoft Fax

Microsoft Fax allows you to send and receive faxes through Microsoft Exchange if your computer, or a computer on the network, has a fax modem attached to it.

Configuring Microsoft Fax

The first configuration screen for Microsoft Fax is shown in figure 25.4. If you have already added a modem to Windows 95, and the modem supports faxing, it may already be listed here. If not, clicking Add opens the dialog box shown in figure 25.5.

If the fax modem you're adding is attached to this computer, highlight Fax modem and click OK. If the fax modem is attached to and shared from a network fax server (another computer), highlight Network fax server and click OK.

FIG. 25.4 ⇒

If a fax modem is already installed, it may appear in the first configuration screen.

FIG. 25.5 ⇒

Choosing whether the fax modem is located on this computer or a network fax server.

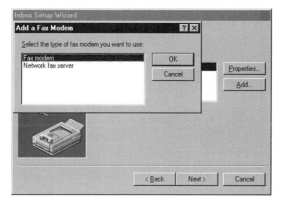

Ch

25

If you chose to install a fax modem, the Install New Modem dialog box opens (see fig. 25.6). If you want Windows 95 to try to detect the fax modem, clear the checkbox in figure 25.6. If you check the checkbox, the dialog box shown in figure 25.7 opens and allows you to pick your modem from a list.

After choosing the fax modem, the dialog box in figure 25.8 opens, letting you choose the port that the fax modem is attached to. Be sure to select the correct ports, because Windows 95 completes the installation as soon as you click Next.

After adding the fax modem, or selecting an existing fax modem, the dialog box in figure 25.9 opens. You can configure whether Microsoft Fax answers incoming calls or not, and which ring to answer them on if it does.

FIG. 25.6 ⇒
Windows 95 can
automatically
detect the modem.

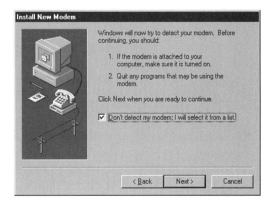

FIG. 25.7 ⇒
You can choose
your fax modem
from the list.

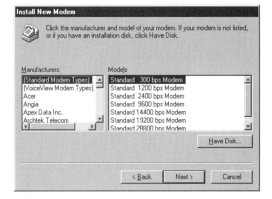

FIG. 25.8 ⇒
Choose the port
your fax modem is
connected to.

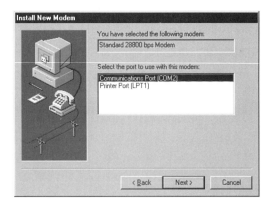

FIG. 25.9 ⇒
Configuring whether Microsoft Fax answers incoming calls.

After configuring the modem properties, Microsoft Fax asks you for some information about the user. The information in the dialog box in figure 25.10 is used by the fax cover pages and to set up TAPI dialing information.

FIG. 25.10 ⇒
Entering your name and fax number.

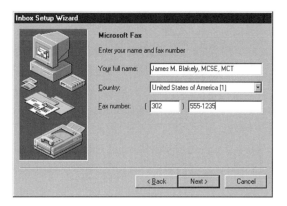

Ch
25

Microsoft Fax Properties

Once Microsoft Fax is installed, there is a number of options that you can configure from within the Inbox. Start Exchange by double-clicking the Inbox icon on your desktop, and select Options from the Microsoft Fax Tools option on the Tools menu.

The Message property page (see fig. 25.11) allows you to set the default options used when sending faxes. There are several options available:

+ *Time to send.* The options in this section set when a fax will be sent. You can choose a specific time, the time when phone rates are discounted (click Set to choose the time range), or as soon as possible.

+ *Message format.* Microsoft Fax can actually send an editable copy of the actual document being sent to another computer using Microsoft Fax. If set to Editable if possible, Microsoft Fax will attempt once to send as an editable document. If it fails, it will try again to send as a regular (not editable) fax document. Editable only will not send to a regular fax machine, and Not editable will send in regular Group III fax format. You can choose the paper size used by a not editable format message by clicking Paper.

+ *Default cover page.* If the Send cover page checkbox is checked, the highlighted cover page will be used by default. All of the cover page files in the Windows directory are listed. You can Browse to find a cover page located elsewhere on the computer or the network. Choosing Open opens the highlighted cover page in the cover page editor, and choosing New allows you to create a cover page.

+ *Let me change the subject line of new faxes I receive.* If this checkbox is checked, you can change the subject line of received faxes. This is particularly valuable when receiving a fax sent from a fax machine, since fax machines don't transmit subject lines.

The Dialing property page (see fig. 25.12) is used to configure how fax numbers are dialed. There are two sections:

+ *I'm dialing from.* Contains two buttons, Dialing Properties., which allows you to set your TAPI location, and Toll Prefixes... which is a list of what numbers in your local area code must be dialed as long distance.

+ *Retries.* Number of retries is the number of times Microsoft Fax will try to call a busy number. It will wait the Time between retries minutes before trying again.

FIG. 25.11 ⇒
The Message
property page.

FIG. 25.12 ⇒
Use the Dialing
properties to con-
figure how fax
numbers are dialed.

Ch
25

The information on the User property page (see fig. 25.13) is used on
cover pages to identify the person sending the fax. The information
includes:

+ Your full name
+ Country

- Fax Number

- Mailbox (optional)

- Company name

- Address

- Title

- Department

- Office Location

- Home telephone number

- Office telephone number

FIG. 25.13 ⇒

The information on the User property page is used on cover pages.

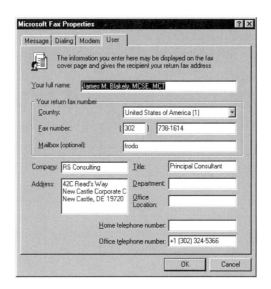

The final property page is the Modem property page (see fig. 25.14). The top portion, Active fax modem allows you to choose the active fax modem. You can choose an existing fax modem, or add a new one. You also can remove a modem from the system. Clicking Properties allows you to set the properties of the modem.

FIG. 25.14 ⇒
Choose a fax
modem from the
Modem property
dialog.

Sharing a Fax Modem

The second half of the Modem property dialog allows you to share
your fax modem with other network users. To share your fax modem,
check <u>L</u>et other people on the network use my modem to send faxes.
The dialog box in figure 25.15 opens. Choose a drive to place the fax
spool directory on, and click OK. Then click OK to save the changes.

Ch
25

FIG. 25.15 ⇒
Choose a drive for
the spool directory.

To use a shared fax modem, click the <u>A</u>dd button from the Modem property dialog (or Inbox Setup Wizard). Highlight Network Fax Server, and click OK. Type the UNC pathname to the shared network fax directory in the dialog box shown in figure 25.16.

FIG. 25.16 ⇒

Type the UNC path to the shared fax.

The network fax modem then appears as one of the choices in the Available fax modems list. Highlight it and click the Set as Active <u>F</u>ax Modem button to use the network fax (see fig. 25.17).

FIG. 25.17 ⇒

The network fax modem is now available.

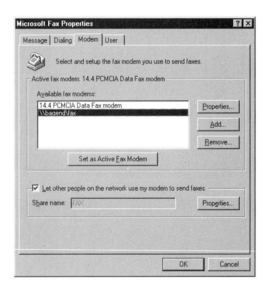

Connecting to the Internet

Microsoft Exchange can connect to an Internet mail server running the *Post Office Protocol 3 (POP3)* if you have Microsoft Plus! installed. You must know the name of the server, and your account name and password.

Connecting to CompuServe

If you have an account on the CompuServe Information Service, you can use Microsoft Exchange to send and receive e-mail. An information service that can access CompuServe is included on the Windows 95 CD-ROM in \Drivers\Other\Exchange\Compuserve.

Connecting to Microsoft Mail

Microsoft Exchange can connect to either a workgroup postoffice (included with Windows 95) or to a full Microsoft Mail Server. You need to know the network path to the postoffice and your user account name on the postoffice in order to configure the MS Mail connection.

Taking the Disc Test

If you have read and understood the material in the chapter, you are ready to test your knowledge. Insert the CD-ROM that comes with this book and run the self-test software as described in Appendix I, "Using the CD-ROM."

Ch
25

26

Troubleshooting Windows 95

Troubleshooting is the art of solving problems. This chapter explores some of the more common problems experienced by users of Windows 95 and the techniques you can use to solve them.

This chapter covers troubleshooting topics. Terms and concepts covered include:

- File system problems
- Long file name problems
- Performance problems
- SCSI problems
- Problems detecting CD-ROMs
- Display problems
- Problems with printing
- Using Win.com startup switches

+ Problems with networking
+ Problems with shared installations of Windows 95
+ Windows 95 log files

Tip

Troubleshooting is one of those skills that really builds with experience; every hour spent practicing will save you lots of hours doing the real thing. You should gain as much experience troubleshooting as you possibly can, but be sure to experiment on your own equipment. Break things and see what messages the computer gives you. Play with the registry settings. Play with System.ini. Choose the wrong hardware drivers. Have fun.

Just remember, don't do any of these things on a production computer—that is, a computer that is actually used for any kind of work. The whole idea of troubleshooting practice is to see how badly you can get the system messed up and still recover from it—at least one of those times, you're going to be recovering from a complete loss of data. Don't forget to make a complete system backup before you begin!

Troubleshooting the File System

Because the Windows 95 file system architecture differs significantly from that of MS-DOS and previous versions of Windows, some programs may not respond correctly when running under it. You can use the File System debugging switches to isolate the problem.

The File System debugging switches are found on the Troubleshooting tab of the File System Properties dialog (see fig. 26.1). To access the File System Properties dialog, click the File System button from the Performance tab of the System icon in Control Panel.

FIG. 26.1⟹

The six file system debugging switches.

Debugging Switches

There are six switches:

- *Disable new file sharing and locking semantics.* Some older programs required the presence of Share.exe under MS-DOS. This switch can be used as a temporary fix until the program is updated by its developer.

- *Disable long name preservation for old programs.* This option disables the Windows 95 feature that attempts to preserve long file names when files are opened and saved by applications that don't recognize long file names. Use it if you're using an MS-DOS or 16-bit Windows application that fails with long file names.

- *Disable protect-mode hard disk interrupt handling.* If this option is set, Windows 95 will not be able to terminate interrupts from the hard disk controller and bypass the ROM routine that normally handles these functions. Checking this option will degrade system performance.

- *Disable synchronous buffer commits.* This option, which should be used only if a program's vendor instructs you to use it, will cause Windows 95 not to wait for a signal from the hard drive when a write has completed writing buffers to the disk.

Ch

26

✛ *Disable all 32-bit protect-mode disk drivers.* This option, which was incorrectly documented in the Windows 95 Resource Kit, disables the 32-bit protect-mode floppy disk driver (hsflop.pdr). Checking this driver causes floppy I/O to be performed as in previous versions of Windows.

✛ *Disable write-behind caching for all drives.* When this option is checked, data is continuously flushed to the hard disk. You should only use this option if you are performing risky operations and need to ensure that data loss is prevented.

Some common file system problems and possible causes are explained in the following sections.

Out of Directory Entries

Long file names are stored as extra directory entries with a special format. This means that every file with a long file name takes up at least two directory entries—one for the short 8.3 alias name, and one for every 12 characters in the long file name.

This problem occurs when you create too many files with long file names in the root directory of a hard disk, where the number of directory entries is fixed, and usually less than 512.

To fix this problem, you'll have to move some files into folders.

Slow Performance

If disks and file systems are performing slowly, a real mode driver is probably being used. Check the Performance tab in System properties. If a real mode driver is in use, the tab will say so.

Sometimes the use of a real mode driver is unavoidable, for example, when a drive has been compressed with a third-party compression program.

Long File Names are Lost

Lost long file names are almost always caused by one of the following causes:

- Renaming a file at the command prompt by using its 8.3 short name instead of the long file name.
- Copying a file at the command prompt by using its 8.3 short name instead of the long file name.
- Using dual-boot to run the previous version of MS-DOS, and performing disk I/O on the files.
- Exchanging a files (on disk) with Windows 3.x or MS-DOS users.
- Using an MS-DOS-based disk utility such as Norton Utilities.
- Using File Manager under Windows 95. (File Manager is a 16-bit application that doesn't understand long file names).

Other Long File Name Problems

Although a long file name can be as long as 256 characters, users will probably encounter problems if they start using names longer than about 50 characters. The reason is the fact that the maximum length of the complete path to the file is limited to 260 characters.

SCSI Problems

Ch
26

Although Windows 95 has SCSI device support built in, due to the inconsistency with which SCSI has been implemented over the years, a number of very unusual SCSI problems are possible. SCSI devices include hard disks, CD-ROM drives and scanners.

SCSI Device Fails to Work

The SCSI bus must be terminated at each end, and only at each end. Check the cables and terminators. Make sure only one device is providing termination power to the bus.

Sometimes, you get a weird collection of devices that don't work together in a particular order on the bus. Try changing the order of devices. For example, the CD-ROM drive and removable hard disk drive I use will not work together if the CD-ROM drive is at the end of the SCSI bus. I had to re-arrange the devices on my SCSI bus so that the removable hard disk drive was at the end of the bus in order for all of my SCSI devices to work together.

SCSI Device Works in MS-DOS but not in Windows 95

Some MS-DOS SCSI drivers require command-line options. You can add these options to the Settings tab in the SCSI controller's property dialog in Device Manager.

Setup does not See the CD-ROM Drive

Certain brands and models of CD-ROM drives must be installed through Add/Remove hardware rather than auto detection.

Troubleshooting Displays

Display drivers have been considerably improved in Windows 95, meaning that the days of driver-caused problems are virtually over. The only exception to this rule is when you have to use a Windows 3.1 driver rather than a Windows 95 driver.

Chipsets

There are actually only a handful of video chip manufacturers who supply the controller chips used on the countless video cards now available. This means that if a driver specific to your video card is not available, then the generic driver for the type of controller chip on the card may work.

If there is not even a generic driver, you can use the generic SVGA driver, which works with any video card that has VESA video mode support in its BIOS. However, the SVGA driver does not use any of the accelerations a card might have, which can have severe performance effects.

As a last resort, you could also use the Windows 3.1 driver for the adapter, if there is one. In addition to performance penalties, using a Windows 3.1 display driver will also disable some features, such as animated cursors and VGA Fallback.

VGA Fallback

If Windows 95 cannot locate a video driver, or the driver that has been configured does not work with the display adapter, Windows 95 will automatically load the VGA driver, providing the user with a usable 640 × 480 display. Once the user logs in to Windows 95, the Display properties dialog box will automatically start, enbling the user to correct the problem.

VGA Fallback only works if a Windows 95 display driver is installed. Windows 3.1 drivers are not capable of supporting VGA Fallback.

In order to support VGA Fallback, the following line is present in System.ini by default:

```
*DisplayFallback=0
```

Graphics Performance Tab

The Advanced Graphics Settings dialog box, which is accessed from the Performance tab of the System option in Control Panel, controls how many of an adapter's accelerator functions are used. The control is a four-position slider bar with the following settings:

Ch
26

- ∔ *Full.* All of the available accelerator functions are used. Use this setting if there are no problems with your display system. (This is the default setting.)

- ∔ *Most.* This setting is useful when using a display adapter based on an S3 or Western Digital controller chip. It attempts to cure mouse pointer problems by disabling the hardware mouse cursor. It adds the following line to the [display] section of System.ini:

```
SWCursor=1
```

⊥ *Basic.* If the system uses a display minidriver (in other words, if it is a Windows 95 driver other than VGA) and it is faulting, or your system is locking up, you should try this setting, which disables nearly all of the hardware accelerations, except for pattern and screen-to-screen *blts* (BLock Transfers). It adds two lines to System.ini:

```
SWCursor=1 (to the [display] section
MMIO=0 (to the [display] section
```

It also adds a line to Win.ini:

```
SafeMode=1 (to the [windows] section
```

⊥ *None.* Moving the slider all the way to the left disables all hardware accelerations. It adds two lines to System.ini:

```
SWCursor=1 (to the [display] section
MMIO=0 (to the [display] section
```

It also adds a line to Win.ini:

```
SafeMode=2 (to the [windows] section
```

Troubleshooting Printing

Windows 95 includes a complete Print Troubleshooter within the Windows 95 help system. It leads you through the steps of determining what your printing problem is from.

In addition to the steps in the Print Troubleshooter, you can use the following troubleshooting steps:

1. Verify that all cables are connected, and that the chosen printer port exists and is functioning.

2. Change the spool file type to Raw. emf spooling is new, and may not be compatible with a given computer or printer.

3. Verify that the printer settings are correct in the printer's properties dialog box.

4. Verify that sufficient hard disk space is available to store the spool files.

5. Check to see if you can print from other programs in Windows 95. For example, if you're having trouble printing from a 16-bit Windows application, try printing from a 32-bit application, and vice versa.

6. Finally, to verify that the driver is emitting the proper RAW file, you can print to a file, and then copy the file to the printer port. If this works, then the problem is in the spool system. If it doesn't, the problem is either driver- or application-related.

Troubleshooting Startup

If you're experiencing startup problems, you can use the Windows 95 startup options to try and troubleshoot the problem.

By pressing the F8 key as soon as the Starting Windows 95 message is displayed, you cause the Windows 95 Startup Menu to open. There are several options:

+ *Normal.* Windows 95 starts normally, as if you had not pressed F8.

+ *Logged.* Windows 95 starts normally, but it also creates a log listing components that load or fail to load. The name of the log file is \Bootlog.txt

+ *Safe Mode.* In safe mode, Windows 95 loads Command.com, but does not process Config.sys or Autoexec.bat if they are present on the system. It also loads only the absolute minimum set of drivers (such as the VGA driver) needed to boot the computer to enable you to recover from an invalid configuration.

+ *Safe Mode with Networking.* Windows 95 loads Command.com and network drivers, but does not process Config.sys or Autoexec.bat if they are present on the system. It also loads only a minimal set of drivers (such as the VGA driver) needed to boot the computer to enable you to recover from an invalid configuration.

Ch
26

+ *Step-by-Step Confirmation.* Prompts you at each stage of boot-up, including loading compression drivers and processing the system registry for a yes or no. You are also asked if you want to execute each individual line of Config.sys and Autoexec.bat.

+ *Command Prompt Only.* Windows 95 stops after loading the real-mode components, and does not load the GUI. This mode is useful for troubleshooting, or repairing problems. You can load the Windows 95 GUI from this mode by typing WIN.

+ *Safe Mode Command Prompt.* Windows 95 stops after loading the real-mode components, and does not load the GUI. In addition, it does not process Config.sys or Autoexec.bat.

+ *Previous Version of MS-DOS.* This option may be available if Windows 95 was installed as an upgrade over a previous version of MS-DOS. You should only use this option as a last resort, as the use of a previous version of MS-DOS could result in loss of long file names.

Startup Switches

There are several switches available for the Win.com file that are included for compatibility reasons. You can use them when starting Windows 95 if you chose the Command prompt only startup menu option.

+ */B.* The /B option causes Bootlog.txt to be created, as when choosing the Logged option from the startup menu.

+ */D:F.* Disables 32-bit disk access.

+ */D:M.* Enables safe mode.

+ */D:N.* Enables safe mode with networking.

+ */D:S.* Disables Windows 95's use of ROM address space between F000 and FFFF for a break point. You might need to use this option with some third-party memory managers.

+ */D:V.* Normally, Windows 95 will intercept interrupts from the hard disk. When this option is enabled, Windows 95 enables the ROM routine to handle them. Use this option to troubleshoot problems accessing your hard disk.

✦ */D:X.* Prevents Windows 95 from using the upper memory area to map memory into. Use this option to troubleshoot a suspected upper-memory conflict with an adapter card.

Troubleshooting Microsoft Networks

Troubleshooting networks starts at figuring out when the problems started to occur. Was any hardware or software changed? Are the network cables still properly connected? Has a protocol been changed?

Domain Issues

When running Windows 95 on a Windows NT Server domain, you should make sure that the network domain is actually validating the user account, and not just allowing guest access to the computer.

Verify that Windows 95 is configured to log into the network by opening the Network option in control panel and opening the properties dialog box for the Client for Microsoft Networks.

Also, check that the network name and password you're using are correct.

Connection Problems

Troubleshooting connection problems should begin with checking the network cables. Is this computer the only one having troubles?

Check the Network Neighborhood. Do the domains, workgroups, and workstations appear? Try to connect to one of them. If you can connect to a server or workstation, then you don't have a generalized networking problem on the computer you're using.

Check to see if you can connect to the server you're trying to connect to from another computer. If others aren't able to connect to it, the problem is probably on the server, or with the cables or routers between you and the server.

Ch
26

Problems connecting to servers via the IPX/SPX protocol are most often caused by using different frame types on the server and client computers.

Sharing Problems

Sharing problems are problems when workstations are trying to connect to shared resources on your computer. Check that File and Printer Sharing are in fact installed on your computer in the Network option of Control Panel.

Missing Components

If a Windows 95 computer locks up when booting, and it is connected to an Ethernet using coaxial cable, make sure the cable is properly terminated. You can troubleshoot this by attaching two terminators to the T connector on the adapter card in the computer.

If a Windows 95 computer can't see other computers, or the network, verify that the appropriate network client and protocols are installed, and that the network adapter is functioning (in Device Manager).

To check the basic network components, you can type **net diag** in an MS-DOS prompt window inside of Windows 95. Net diag is designed to work with a second Windows 95 computer: when you run it on the first one, you will be asked if you want that computer to be a diagnostic server. Answer **yes**, and then start net diag on the second computer. The second will attempt to contact the first.

You also can start the real-mode networking components from MS-DOS mode, or from the Windows 95 command prompt (from the Windows 95 Startup Menu) by typing **net logon**.

Browsing Problems

Browsing problems are usually caused by there not being a browse master on the network. If you have a computer that is always turned on, designate it as a browse master by setting its Browse Master entry to Enabled.

See "Browsing the Network," **p. 284**

Troubleshooting a NetWare Client

There are a few problems that might occur when using the Microsoft Client for NetWare Networks.

No Network Available

If no network is available, you should verify that the Microsoft Client for NetWare Networks is installed by using the Network option in Control Panel.

Logon Scripts don't Run

If NetWare login scripts don't run, be sure the preferred server is set to the server that contains the login scripts, and that the Enable Logon Script Processing check box in the Client for NetWare Networks properties is checked.

Cannot See NetWare Servers

The most common cause of not being able to see NetWare servers is an incorrectly configured frame type in the IPX/SPX compatible protocol. Instead of selecting Auto, select the frame type actually used by the servers you want to connect to. All servers must use the same frame type in order for Windows 95 to access them all because the Auto setting selects only the dominant frame type it sees on the cable.

If your computer is connected to a Novell NetWare 4.x network, the servers must have NetWare 4.x bindery emulation activated in order for the Windows 95 Client for NetWare Networks to see the server.

Tip

Microsoft did release NetWare Directory Services for Windows 95 in early 1996. It adds support for Novell 4.x's native NDS mode (without bindery emulation installed). However, the NDS client is not part of the base Windows 95 packaging, and therefore, an answer of `NetWare 2.x`, `3.x` and `4.x in bindery emulation mode` is the extent of Windows 95 support for NetWare out-of-the-box.

Ch
26

Access is Denied

If you receive an access denied message when trying to access resources on a NetWare server other than the one that authenticated your logon, then you need to synchronize your logon credentials (username and password) between that server and your logon server by using the Novell setpass command.

Troubleshooting Shared Installation

There are several issues that pertain to Shared Installations of Windows 95 that do not apply to local installations:

- MS-DOS mode is not available to a shared installation. This is because Windows 95 networking support is terminated when entering MS-DOS mode. If a user tries to run a program in MS-DOS mode, she/he will receive an error message informing her or him that the mode is not available.

- Docking is not supported.

- Safe mode always runs the Config.sys, Autoexec.bat, and Netstart.bat files to enable the computer to connect to the shared installation files on the network.

Examining the Windows 95 Log Files

Windows 95 is capable of generating a number of log files to help you troubleshoot problems:

- *Bootlog.txt.* This is found in the root directory of the disk and is generated when a Logged startup is chosen from the Windows 95 Startup Menu. It is a record of what happened during the boot-up process, including what drivers were loaded, in what order, which ones didn't load successfully, and so on.

- *Detlog.txt.* Found in the root directory of the disk, this file is generated during setup, and contains information about the devices detected during setup.

+ *Setuplog.txt.* Found in the root directory of the disk, this file contains a list of error messages that were generated by setup.

+ *Ios.log.* Found in the Windows folder, this file contains error messages from the SCSI drivers.

+ *Modem log file.* This file, which you can choose the name of, is enabled in the modem settings Advanced options. It contains a log of the modem use, suitable for finding configuration problems.

+ *Ppplog.txt.* This file, found in the Windows directory, contains information recorded about the operation of the PPP protocol. Useful for diagnosing Dial-Up Networking problems.

Taking the Disc Test

 If you have read and understood the material in the chapter, you are ready to test your knowledge. Insert the CD-ROM that comes with this book and run the self-test software as described in Appendix I, "Using the CD-ROM."

Ch
26

27

Additional Resources

In addition to the somewhat sparse product documentation that is supplied with Windows 95, Microsoft expects that the Microsoft Certified Professional is familiar with, and knows how to use, several additional technical resources.

This chapter covers additional Microsoft technical resources that the MCP should know about. Terms and concepts covered include:

+ **Microsoft Developer Network**
+ **Microsoft on CompuServe**
+ **Microsoft on the Internet**
+ **Microsoft TechNet**
+ **Windows 95 Resource Kit**
+ **The Microsoft Network**

Windows 95 Resource Kit

Microsoft no longer includes printed technical documentation with their products. Instead, all of the technical information has been moved into what Microsoft calls a *resource kit*.

The Windows 95 Resource Kit is supplied with Windows 95 as a Windows Help file on the Windows 95 CD. Unfortunately, Microsoft did not include a way to automatically copy it to your hard disk and add it into your Start menu, so you will have to do so manually, or just load them off of the CD-ROM when you want to use them.

On the Web

Users who do not have the CD-ROM version of Windows 95 can obtain the Windows 95 Resource Kit free of charge on the World Wide Web at

http://www.microsoft.com/windows/software.htm

The Windows 95 Resource Kit files are located on the Windows 95 CD-ROM in the \Admin\Reskit\Helpfile directory. The easiest way to access them is to just insert the Windows 95 CD-ROM into a CD-ROM drive attached to your computer.

The Windows 95 CD-ROM AutoPlay function starts automatically, and the Windows 95 AutoPlay screen will be displayed (see fig. 27.1).

FIG. 27.1 ⇒
The Windows 95 CD-ROM AutoPlay screen starts automatically.

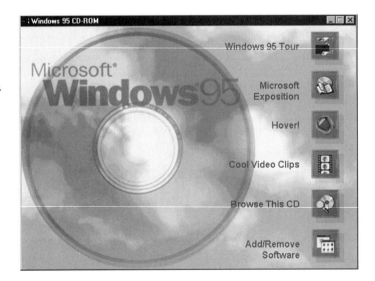

Clicking the Browse This CD icon opens the root directory of the CD-ROM in a window (see fig. 27.2). Opening the Admin\Reskit\Helpfile folders in turn leads you to the helpfiles (see fig. 27.3).

FIG. 27.2 ⇒

Browsing the
Windows 95
CD-ROM.

FIG. 27.3 ⇒

The Windows 95
Resource Kit
Helpfiles.

There are three helpfiles that make up the Windows 95 Resource Kit:

✦ *Win95rk.* This is the main resource kit. It includes the documentation for topics such as Deployment Planning, Installation, Networking, System Management, System Configuration, Communications, a complete Windows 95 reference, and Appendixes filled with every arcane detail about Windows 95.

✦ *Tour4adm.* The Guided Tour for Administrators. This helpfile takes an administrator on a tour of Windows 95 features showing the justifications for deploying Windows 95 in an enterprise.

✦ *Macusers.* This helpfile is aimed at people migrating to Windows 95 who formerly used Apple Macintosh computers. It explains

Ch
27

the answers to questions like, "Why is there another mouse button?"

In addition to the helpfiles, the Windows 95 Resource Kit includes a number of utilities found under the Admin directory on the Windows 95 CD.

Microsoft TechNet

Microsoft TechNet is Microsoft's primary resource for technical support professionals. It provides fast, complete answers to technical questions about installing, configuring and supporting Microsoft Desktop and System products, including Windows 95.

A subscription to Microsoft TechNet includes:

+ Twelve monthly updates of CD 1 containing the complete US Microsoft Knowledge Base, resource kits, evaluation and reviewers guides, training materials, conference session notes, customer solution profiles, strategic information, and third-party integration studies.

+ Twelve monthly updates of CD 2 containing drivers and patches.

+ For international users, the International Version includes the International Supplemental CD.

+ Dedicated MS CompuServe forum and forum map. Members also receive WinCIM, a Windows based front-end for accessing CompuServe.

TechNet is available on an annual subscription basis. The annual subscription fee is $299 ($399 CAN) per user. Additional single user licenses are $40 ($50 CAN) per user. A single-server license for unlimited users license is $699 ($999 CAN).

A subscription to Microsoft TechNet including the new International Supplemental CD costs $329 annually for a single-user license, or $729 annually for a single-server license for unlimited users, which is just $30 more than the price of a regular TechNet subscription.

TechNet will run on any computer that can run Windows 95. In addition, it will run on any computer meeting the following specifications:

- A personal computer with an 80386 or higher processor (80386DX at 20 MHz or higher recommended), 4M of RAM (6-8M recommended), a hard disk with 2M of free disk space (6M or more recommended), and a VGA or higher-resolution graphics adapter and compatible monitor.
- A CD-ROM drive compatible with MPC Level 1 specifications.
- Microsoft Windows version 3.1 or Windows for Workgroups version 3.1, or Windows NT 3.1 or higher.
- Any of the following systems running Windows NT—Intel, MIPS, R4000, or DEC Alpha AXP.
- MS-DOS version 3.1 or later (version 6.2 recommended).
- Microsoft Compact Disc Extensions (MSCDEX) version 2.2 or later and compatible CD-ROM driver (for MS-DOS based systems)
- A mouse or equivalent pointing device compatible with Windows.
- A printer compatible with Windows (optional).

As mentioned above, a TechNet subscription includes two CDs monthly (three in the International Edition). The first CD, the actual TechNet CD 1, contains:

- Microsoft Knowledge Base lets you answer support questions using the same extensive library of technical support information Microsoft Product Support Specialists use every day. Many of the technical details of Windows 95 and other products are found only in the Knowledge Base, which is Microsoft's continually updated body of technical information. Even things like the Windows 95 confirmed bug list (article Q141602) and the error list for the Windows 95 Resource Kit (article Q135849) are included in the Knowledge Base.

Ch
27

- Resource kits packed with technical references, troubleshooting information, utilities and accessories aid in installing and supporting Microsoft products. The Windows 95 Resource Kit is included, making it possible to easily search for and locate information that you need.

- Technical information tells you how you to get the most out of products. Microsoft products are designed to be powerful and easy to use; TechNet gives you the "how to" information you need to increase your productivity.

- Migration information helps you move people in an organization from one product to another or from one environment to another. What issues are involved in migrating from a mainframe-based e-mail system to a LAN-based one? TechNet tells you.

- Product facts and features help you evaluate Microsoft products and compare versions of products to better understand the advantages of upgrading.

- Educational materials such as tutorials, conference session slides with notes, and Windows NT training materials are included.

- Customer solution profiles detail how your colleagues solve real information technology problems.

- Strategic information on technologies keeps you up-to-date on the direction Microsoft and its products are taking now and will take in the future. If you want to know more about such topics as multimedia, ODBC, MAPI, or OLE, TechNet is the place to look.

- The complete Microsoft Software Library, a collection of sample files, patches, and drivers, is included.

- Session notes from key Microsoft conferences provide timely information straight from the technical professionals themselves.

TechNet also includes many articles by third parties, such as Microsoft Certified System Engineers, about topics dealing with interoperability, migration, and other significant support issues involving Microsoft products and other company's products working together.

The second CD, also known as the Drivers and Patches CD, includes printer, video, audio, storage, pen, and network drivers, as well as installs for the Windows NT and other Service Packs. For instance, the Service Pack 1 for Microsoft Windows 95 is on CD 2, beginning with the April 1996 issue.

The optional third CD includes the international versions of the Knowledge Base and other localized information in 15 languages, created by Microsoft subsidiaries.

To obtain a subscription to Microsoft Technet, within the United States and Canada, call 800-344-2121. Outside the US and Canada, contact your local Microsoft subsidiary.

Installing TechNet

Microsoft TechNet is fairly easy to use. When you first place the monthly CD 1 in your CD-ROM drive, Windows 95 AutoPlay will open a dialog that informs you that you need to install the issue, and gives you a button to click on to complete installation (see fig. 27.4).

FIG. 27.4 ⇒
TechNet AutoPlay offers to install TechNet automatically.

The next time you use it, the dialog will be slightly different, and the button will allow you to run TechNet instead of installing it.

Ch
27

Using TechNet

Figure 27.5 shows the TechNet screen when you first run it. There are several different panes.

FIG. 27.5 ⇒

The main TechNet screen.

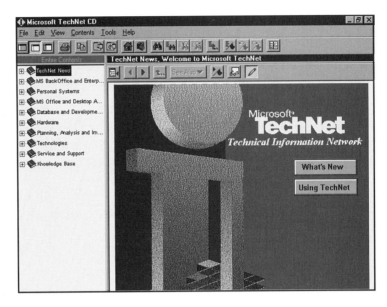

The pane on the left holds a hierarchical representation of the information on the TechNet CD. You can use the tree in this pane to browse the TechNet CD looking for content.

The pane on the right shows the contents of the currently selected item.

TechNet's real power lies in its powerful query engine that lets you specify a search string, and then lets you browse through articles containing that string.

Selecting Query from the Tools menu opens the Query dialog box (see fig. 27.6). From here you can type a query string, even including Boolean operators such as "and" "or" "near". For example, the query displayed in figure 27.6, "win95 and confirmed bug" is asking for all articles that are about Windows 95 (win95 is a special keyword for Windows 95) that also have the phrase "confirmed bug" in them. After clicking on the Run Query button, the Query Results window is displayed (see fig. 27.7).

FIG. 27.6 ⇒

Querying
TechNet.

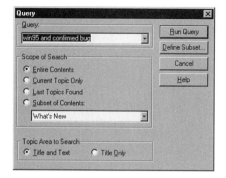

FIG. 27.7 ⇒

Results of a query.

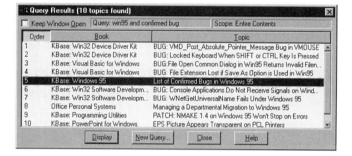

To display one of the resulting articles, simply highlight it and choose
Display. The selected article will be displayed in the right hand pane of
the main TechNet window (see fig. 27.8).

FIG. 27.8 ⇒

Your selected
article is displayed.

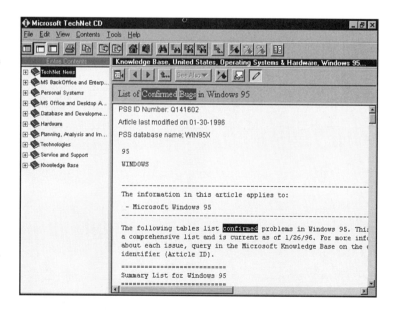

Ch

27

Note   TechNet looks best when displayed on a 800 × 600 or greater resolution display. ▨

The Query dialog also allows you to limit your queries to certain "books" within TechNet, to narrow a query that returned too many items, and to repeat past queries.

Once you've located an article of interest, you can copy and paste it to other applications or print it.

Note   TechNet's license only allows you to redistribute its articles within your company or organization. Be sure to read and comply with the license agreement. ▨

Microsoft Developer Network

The Microsoft Developer Network subscriptions are similar to Microsoft TechNet, except that they are delivered quarterly, and contain information and utilities of interest to those who are developing software to run on Microsoft operating systems.

For more information about the Microsoft Developer Network, call 800-759-5474 within the United States and Canada, or contact your local Microsoft subsidiary.

Microsoft ATEC

Microsoft Authorized Technical Education Centers (ATECs) deliver face-to-face Microsoft Official Curriculum courses. In order to deliver a Microsoft Official Curriculum course, the instructor must first be certified by Microsoft as a Microsoft Certified Trainer for that course.

Table 27.1 lists Microsoft Official Curriculum courses taught at ATECs.

Table 27.1—Microsoft Official Curriculum Courses (as of 3/96)

Course Name	Course Number
Mastering Microsoft Access	627
Microsoft Access for Windows 95	609
Microsoft Access 2.0	435 & 367
Microsoft Excel for Windows 95	560 & 349
Microsoft Exchange Server	630
Microsoft Exchange Development	676
Microsoft Internet Development	377
Microsoft Internet Information Server	673 & 662
Microsoft Mail	341
Microsoft SNA Server	562
Microsoft SQL Server	574 & 576
Microsoft Systems Management Server	646
Microsoft TCP/IP for Windows NT	472
Mastering Visual Basic	626
Microsoft Visual Basic	403 & 404
Mastering Visual C++	629
Mastering Visual FoxPro	625
Microsoft Visual FoxPro	455
Microsoft Windows 95	540 & 546
Microsoft Windows NT	505
Microsoft Windows NT Server	659
Microsoft Windows Programming	483 & 484

Ch
27

For a referral to a Microsoft Authorized Technical Education Center near you, within the United States, call 1–800–SOL–PROV. Outside the United States, contact your local Microsoft subsidiary.

Microsoft OnLine Institute

The Microsoft OnLine Institute (MOLI) is a virtual campus on The Microsoft Network, where you can "attend" classes on Microsoft products.

The concept of MOLI is a cross between traditional instructor-led classes and self-study, giving you Online access to learning materials, instructor expertise, product information, developer articles, user forums, and other resources for Microsoft product and technology information. Users will also find training and support materials on Windows 95 that includes classes, certification information, books, videos, computer-based training titles, white papers, and more. From MSN Central, click the Edit menu, click Other Location, and then type the GO word "moli" in the Go To Service box.

 Note   For information on the availability of Windows 95 courses on MOLI that use this book as their courseware, send e-mail to **frodo@rscon.com**.

Microsoft on the Internet

Microsoft has a very strong presence on the Internet. Some key Internet services of interest to the Windows 95 MCP are:

- Microsoft Windows 95 Home Page at

    http://www.microsoft.com/windows

- Microsoft Network Home Page at

    http://www.msn.com

- Microsoft FTP Server at

    ftp://ftp.microsoft.com

- Microsoft Gopher Server at

    gopher://gopher.microsoft.com

Windows 95 on The Microsoft Network

Use the GO word "Windows" to access the Windows 95 area on The Microsoft Network.

Microsoft on CompuServe

There are several areas on CompuServe that concern Windows 95 and the Microsoft Windows 95 MCP.

- GO MECFORUM. The Microsoft Education and Certification Forum
- GO MSWIN95. Windows 95 support forum
- GO SETUP95. Windows 95 support forum (Setup-related issues only)

Microsoft Most Valuable Professionals (MVPs) and ClubWin Members

Support on the online services is largely limited to user-to-user support. If you have a support need that requires direct one-to-one interaction with Microsoft, you should use one of the support options in your Windows 95 documentation.

The Microsoft Enduser Most Valued Professional (MVP) Program is a program to recognize the people who contribute their technical expertise, enthusiasm, and vitality to member-to-member communities such as this forum. Through their hard work in providing assistance and education to foster and strengthen developer communities, MVPs have helped make these forums an invaluable member-to-member resource.

The Windows 95 MVPs (as of April 1996) are Sue Mosher, Paul Clapman, William Cheek, Bill Sanderson, James M. Blakely, Bill Starbuck, Carmen M. Rodero, and David Warren.

Ch
27

ClubWin members are customers who have been on the technical beta and are very knowledgeable about Windows 95. Because of their long time experience with Windows 95 and technical expertise, they are an invaluable resource on the online forums. Many ClubWin members also support Windows 95 on the Internet, through World Wide Web pages and chats on the Internet Relay Chat (IRC) network.

WinNews Electronic Newsletter

WinNews is a periodically released electronic newsletter available. Subscribers receive this newsletter by mail, eliminating the need for regularly checking the WinNews areas for updates. To subscribe, type an Internet mail message addressed to **enews@microsoft.nwnet.com** with the words **subscribe winnews** as the only text in your message.

Lab Exercises

The lab exercises are an important part of your preparation for the MCP exam. They provide a starting point for your journey to gather the necessary real-world experience that is required to pass the exam.

The labs have been designed to be topic-oriented, rather than chapter-oriented. You can choose to perform all of the labs, or just the ones that cover areas of Windows 95 that you're unfamiliar with. The only lab that is actually required for everyone is Lab 1, "Installing Windows 95," because it is a prerequisite for every other lab.

We recommend that you perform all of the labs, however, since reading all of the chapters and performing all of the labs is the only way to be sure that you've been exposed to all of the required material.

You can do all the labs at once after reading the book, or you can do them as you go along. It's up to you.

Equipment Requirements

To complete the hands-on labs included with this book, you must have *two computers* configured as follows:

- Intel 486/33 or better processor
- 8M RAM
- 250M of free disk space
- Mouse
- A Windows 95-compatible network adapter

Caution

Computers must be test computers that do not contain valuable data. All data on the computers may be lost during the process of working through the labs.

Each computer should have the following software installed:

- Microsoft MS-DOS 5.0 or higher

   In addition, one of the computers should have Microsoft Windows 3.x installed.

If you want to complete the hands-on lab covering interoperability with Microsoft Networks (Lab 13, "Using Windows 95 as a Client of a Microsoft Windows NT Network"), an additional computer is required, running either Windows NT Workstation or Windows NT Server, version 3.5 or higher.

If you want to complete the hands-on labs covering interoperability with Novell NetWare (Lab 15, "Using Windows 95 as a Client on a Novell NetWare Network"), an additional computer is required, running Novell NetWare version 2.x, 3.x, or 4.x in bindery emulation mode.

These exercises have been designed with as little interdependency as possible. Because of this, the labs can be done in any order you desire, with the exception of Lab 1, "Installing Windows 95."

Each lab begins with a list of its objectives and any special requirements needed to complete it.

Lab 1: Installing Windows 95

 Note To complete this lab, you need:

- A copy of Windows 95 on CD-ROM (make sure your computer has a CD-ROM drive)
- A computer that meets the Windows 95 requirements (see Chapter 3)
- Existing operating system MS-DOS 5.0 or higher and Windows 3.1 or higher
- Network adapter compatible with Windows 95
- Blank floppy disk ■

In this lab, you use two computers. The first (Computer A) you use to upgrade from Windows 3.1 or higher. Computer B should only have MS-DOS installed.

Decide what user name, computer names, and workgroup name you are going to use. If you are already on a network, ask your network administrator for this information so that you don't choose a name that is already being used. Each of the names must be unique.

User Name: _____

Computer A Name: _____

Computer B Name: _____

Workgroup Name: _____

Check the Readme and Setup.txt for any information or notes concerning your computer's hardware.

Also, check your Config.sys and Autoexec.bat for any unnecessary TSRs (Terminate and Stay Resident programs) and disable them by placing the word REM at the beginning of the line that they're loaded from. Leave any TSRs and drivers for sound cards, SCSI cards, and CD-ROMs alone.

Upgrading from Windows 3.1 or Windows for Workgroups 3.11

1. Start your computer in the usual way. If Windows is not loaded, type **Win** at the prompt.

2. From Program Manager, select File, Run. In the dialog, type **x:\setup** (where **x** is the letter of your CD-ROM drive). You will see a dialog called the Windows 95 Setup Wizard. Click the Next button.

3. In the Choose Directory dialog, use the default c:\windows (or whatever directory it suggests).

4. In the Setup Options dialog, select Typical.

5. Setup will ask you for your name and company. Fill in the appropriate information.

Note The Analyzing your Computer dialog appears if Setup cannot determine what CD-ROM or sound card you have using safe detection. If this dialog appears, be sure to check the checkbox by the type of device your computer has. ▪

6. Setup now needs to analyze your computer hardware. Click the Next button to begin this process. Be sure to allow enough time, since this might take awhile.

When the analysis finishes, make sure your network adapter was recognized.

7. If Setup fails at this point, *turn off the machine* and go back to step 1. When prompted, choose Safe Recovery and repeat all your choices. (See Chapter 3 for more information on Safe Recovery.)

Note If Setup continues to fail during hardware detection, continue to repeat the shut off, restart Setup, select Safe Recovery procedure until Setup succeeds. *Always select Safe Recovery, no matter how many times you have to do it.* Safe Recovery skips the detection that caused the failure each time, so it will eventually succeed even if it ends up skipping all the detections. ▪

Note If the Get Connected dialog appears, verify that all of the checkboxes are cleared, and click Next. ▪

8. The next dialog is the Windows Components dialog. Select the default, Install the most common components (recommended), and click the Next button.

9. The next step is to configure your protocols. Make sure you don't select TCP/IP as one of your protocols. (If TCP/IP is selected, highlight it and remove it.) Don't make any other changes at this point. Click Next. (TCP/IP is installed in a later lab.)

10. In the next dialog, you need to select a name for your computer. This name must be unique, so make sure that none of the other computers on your network has the same name. Enter the workgroup name and a description of your computer. Make sure that none of the names has spaces, since this can give you problems in the future.

11. In the following dialogs, click the Next button until you get to the dialog asking you if you want to create a Startup Disk. Insert the blank floppy disk in the floppy drive. Select Yes, I want a Startup disk (recommended). Click the Next button to continue.

Labs

12. Setup will be busy for awhile copying files onto the hard disk. Be patient.

13. When the Time Zone dialog opens, select your time zone by pointing to your location on the map with the arrow. Verify that the correct time zone for your location appears in the drop-down box.

14. The next dialog is used to select a printer. Press Cancel. (You learn to install printers in a later lab.)

Installing Windows 95 from MS-DOS

1. Because you are installing from a CD-ROM, make sure your CD-ROM is accessible from the MS-DOS environment (follow the manufacturer's instructions).

2. Put the disc in the CD-ROM drive.

3. Change to the CD-ROM drive and type *x*: (where *x* is the CD-ROM letter), then press Enter.

4. At the command prompt, type **setup**, then press Enter. At this point, follow the instructions on the dialog.

5. If you are using the upgrade version of Windows 95, you may be prompted for a disk from a qualifying product. Be sure to insert it when prompted.

6. When the Windows 95 Setup Wizard appears on your screen, click the Next button. When prompted to choose a directory, use the default c:\windows (or whatever directory it suggests).

7. On the Setup Options dialog, select Typical.

8. Setup asks you for your name and company. Fill in the appropriate information.

9. Setup now needs to analyze your computer hardware. Click the Next button in this dialog. Be sure to allow enough time, since this might take awhile.

   When the analysis finishes, make sure your network adapter was recognized.

10. If Setup fails at this point, *turn off the machine* and go back to step 1. When prompted, choose Safe Recovery and repeat all your choices. (See Chapter 3 for more information on Safe Recovery.)

Note If Setup continues to fail during hardware detection, continue to repeat the shut off, restart Setup, select Safe Recovery procedure until Setup succeeds. *Always select Safe Recovery, no matter how many times you have to do it.* Safe Recovery skips the detection that caused the failure each time, so it will eventually succeed even if it ends up skipping all the detections. ■

11. The next dialog is the Windows Components dialog. Select the default, Install the most common components (recommended), and click the Next button.

12. The next step is to configure your protocols. Make sure you don't select TCP/IP as one of your protocols. (If TCP/IP is selected, highlight it and remove it.) Don't make any other changes at this point. Click Next. (TCP/IP is installed in a later lab.)

13. In the next dialog, you need to select a name for your computer. This name must be unique, so make sure that none of the other computers on your network has the same name. Enter the workgroup name and a description of your computer. Make sure that none of the names has spaces, since this can give you problems in the future.

14. In the following dialogs, click the Next button until you get to the dialog asking if you want to create a Startup Disk. Insert the blank floppy in the floppy drive. Select Yes, I want a Startup disk (recommended). Click the Next button to continue.

15. Setup will be busy for awhile copying files onto the hard disk. Be patient.

16. When the Time Zone dialog opens, select your time zone by pointing to your location on the map with the arrow.

17. The next dialog is used to select a printer. Press Cancel. (You learn to install printers in a later lab.)

Labs

Lab 2: Getting Used to the Explorer Shell

 Note To complete this lab, you must have Windows 95 installed on your computer (see Lab 1). ■

Navigating on Explorer

1. Start your computer in the normal fashion. Notice that the Windows 95 desktop (called the Explorer) is markedly different from the Windows 3.x desktop.

2. Along the bottom edge of your screen you can see the taskbar. The taskbar has a button at its left end, called the Start button.

3. Click this button only once. (Notice that in Windows 95, double-clicking is not required.) You see a menu pop up from it. This menu, called the Start menu, has all the options, like Programs, Settings, and any utilities you might need.

4. Some of the options in the menu have an arrow next to them. This arrow indicates that there is another menu within that

menu. Highlight one of the options with the arrow. Notice that another menu shows up, and that you don't need to click anything to make it appear. Every time you see an arrow, there is another menu within that option, even if that option is contained within yet another option. This behavior is called *cascading menus*.

5. At the right end of the taskbar, in an area called the *tray*, you can see the current time. If you point your cursor to the time (do not click), the date appears.

6. The desktop is the backdrop upon which everything occurs. By default, there are several icons on your desktop. These icons include the following:

- My Computer
- Network Neighborhood (if your computer is part of a network)
- Recycle Bin
- Inbox (if you install Exchange)
- The Microsoft Network or Setup the Microsoft Network (if the Microsoft Network isn't set up).

You should be able to see most of these icons in your current desktop.

Creating an Icon on Your Desktop

On your desktop, you can create a folder or shortcut. A folder is similar to a directory, but can contain objects.

1. Move your mouse pointer into any empty part of your desktop (make sure you are not on top of an icon).

2. Right-click on your desktop. On the context menu that appears, you have several options:

- Arrange Icons
- Line up Icons
- Paste

Labs

- Paste Shortcut
- New
- Properties

3. Select New. From the New menu, select Folder. A folder appears on your desktop (if it doesn't, press F5 to refresh the desktop).

4. The system prompts you to give the folder a new name by highlighting the folder's name. Type **and now, the moment you've all been waiting for** and press Enter. You have just created a folder into which you can place objects and files. Do not place anything into the folder now.

Renaming the Folder

1. To rename a folder on your desktop, select the folder by just clicking once on it.

2. Right-click the folder. Look at all the options you have there. Notice that all of these options are related to the object selected (the new folder just created). This type of menu is called a *context menu.*

3. Select Rename, and type **we proudly present for your viewing pleasure** and press Enter.

4. Just to make sure you did it right, rename the file. Right-click the folder's icon again and select Rename. This time type **The Microsoft Windows 95 Product Team!** and press Enter.

5. Open the folder you just renamed by pressing Enter. If you did all the steps correctly, you should be able to see the names of the team of people involved in the Windows 95 development. If not, try it again later just for fun.

Note You must type each of the lines as shown, including capitalization and punctuation. The trick (called the Easter Egg) won't work if you make any mistakes.

Creating a Shortcut on the Desktop

Next, you learn to create a shortcut on the desktop. There are two ways to do it—by using the context menu or by dragging.

Context Menu

1. Right-click the desktop and select New.

2. Select Shortcut.

3. A wizard opens. If you know the path for the option you want to add onto the desktop, just type it in the command box and go to step 5.

4. Click Browse. From your c: drive, select your Windows folder. Then select the Calc file, and click Open.

5. Click Next.

6. Type the name of the shortcut in the box, and then click Finish. An icon of the Calculator should appear in your desktop.

Now you have a shortcut for the Calculator on your desktop. This means that you don't need to dig down to Start\Programs\Accessories\Calc to open the Calculator.

Tip

You can create shortcuts for any frequently used applications or documents on your desktop. You can even create a shortcut to a folder, or create a folder and fill it with shortcuts to keep your desktop relatively clear.

Via Dragging

1. Open My Computer.

2. Select the drive on which your Windows folder is located. Open the drive by right-clicking and choosing Open.

3. Select the Windows folder and double-click it.

4. Look for the Calculator program and select it.

5. Right-click the Calculator program's icon once and, while holding the right mouse button, drag and drop the icon on to

Labs

the desktop and release the mouse button. From the context menu that appears, select Create Shortcut Here. Now you have a shortcut on your desktop for the Calculator.

Changing the Position of the Taskbar

By default, the Windows 95 taskbar appears at the bottom of your screen, but you can move it around to better suit your personal working habits.

1. Place the mouse pointer on top of the taskbar.
2. While pressing the left button of the mouse, drag the taskbar to another edge of your desktop, such as the top of your screen or the left or right sides, and drop it there.

Explorer View versus Open View

The difference between the two views is how you see them. Open view (the default) displays the files in a single window with large icons. Explorer view, on the other hand, has two panes, with files listed in the right-hand pane, and the folder hierarchy in the left-hand pane.

Explorer View

To open a folder using Explorer, use one of these two methods:

- Click the Start button, choose Programs, then choose Windows Explorer.
- Right-click My Computer and choose Explore.

Open View

Right-click My Computer and choose Open, or just double-click My Computer. A window opens showing all of the drives on your computer, Control panel, Printers, and Dial-Up Networking.

Opening a File Using a Different Application

By default, most files are associated with a particular application or program. When you double-click the file, Windows automatically opens that program and then the selected file. Occasionally, however, you may want to open the file using a different application. In the following example, you use WordPad to open a Readme file, which is normally associated with Notepad.

1. Open My Computer.

2. Select the drive that includes Windows 95.

3. Select the Readme file in the Windows folder.

4. Double-click the Readme file. Notice that by default it opens the application it is associated with—in this case, Notepad. Now close Notepad.

5. Select the Readme file again, and this time, press Shift and right-click the mouse. In the menu, you can see an option that wasn't there when you didn't press the Shift button. This option is Open With, which enables you to open a file with another application.

6. Select Open With. A dialog will open.

7. Select WordPad (scroll down until you find it). Notice that the same file you previously opened with Notepad is now opened with WordPad.

The Taskbar

You can easily customize the appearance of your taskbar. Click Start, choose Settings, and then select Taskbar. The dialog box that opens has several options. Experiment with them until you are comfortable with each:

+ *Always on Top:* This option keeps the taskbar in front of any application you have open.

+ *Auto Hide:* This option makes the taskbar hide every time you are not using it. Just move the arrow to the botton edge of the screen to see how this works.

+ *Show Small icons in the task menu:* This option enables you to reduce the size of the icons and the fonts on the taskbar and the Start menu.

+ *Show Clock:* This option lets you see the time at the right corner of the taskbar.

Labs

Adding Items to the Start Menu

There are two ways to add items to the Start menu—by dragging them to the Start button or using the taskbar settings control.

Via Taskbar Settings

1. Click Start, choose Settings, then choose Taskbar.

2. Select the Start Menu program tab.

3. Select Add. A wizard opens.

4. If you know the path to the file, type it in the command line box; if not, click the Browse button.

5. Select your Windows folder, then select the Calc program and click the open button. Click Next.

6. The wizard prompts you to select the location at which you want to place your shortcut.

7. Select Start Menu, then click Next.

8. Type the name you want to give the shortcut, and click Finish.

9. Click Start again and see the results.

Via Dragging

1. Right-click My Computer and select Explore.

2. Select the drive on which the Windows folder is located, and open the Windows folder.

3. Select the icon for a file called Sol (this is the Solitaire game).

4. Hold down the left mouse button, drag the icon to the Start button, and release the mouse button.

5. When you click the Start button again, you will see that Solitaire now appears on the Start Menu.

Removing Items from the Start Menu

1. Click Start, choose Settings, then choose Taskbar.

2. Select the Start Menu Programs tab.

3. Select the Remove button. A wizard opens.

4. Scroll down to the end. The last items are the ones that are present on the Start menu.

5. Select the Calc or the Solitaire item and click Remove. Select Close. Then select OK.

6. Click Start and make sure the item is no longer in the menu.

Labs

Lab Objective

In this lab, you learn:

⊥ How to configure Win-
dows 95 using Control
Panel

⊥ How to configure Win-
dows 95 using the
Registry

Lab 3: Configuring Windows 95

 Note To complete this lab, you need one computer with Windows 95 installed. ▪

 Note The following lab covers all of the icons in Control Panel that are not used in other labs and defines those that are used in other labs. ▪

To begin experimenting with the Control Panel options, use one of the following methods:

⊥ Click Start, choose Settings, then choose Control Panel.

⊥ Open My Computer and select Control Panel.

Accessibility Options

This option provides enhancements for users with various disabilities so that they can use Windows 95 more easily. There are several options in this area; we will explore them all.

1. Double-click Accessibility options in Control Panel. The Keyboard tab is displayed. Notice that there are four options:

- *StickyKeys:* Use this option if you want to use the Ctrl, Alt, or Shift key by pressing one at a time, rather than holding them down in conjunction with another key.

- *FilterKeys:* Use this option if you want Windows to ignore brief or repeated keystrokes or to slow the repeat rate.

- *ToggleKeys:* Use this option if you want to hear the tones when pressing Caps Lock, Number Lock, or Scroll Lock.

- *Show extra keyboard help in programs:* Use this option if you want programs to show extra help about using the keyboard.

2. Select the Sound tab. There are two options:

   - *Sound Sentry:* This option lets you see visual warnings every time a sound is played.

   - *ShowSounds:* This option tells your applications to display a caption for any speech and/or sounds they make.

3. Select the Display tab. The High Contrast option enables you to use colors and fonts designed for easy reading.

4. Select the Mouse tab. The MouseKeys option enables you to control the pointer with the numeric keypad on the keyboard.

5. Select the General tab. There are three major options:

   - *Automatic Reset:* If selected, this option turns off the accessibility features after being idle for the length of time defined in the provided box.

   - *Notification* has two options:

     - If the first option, Give warning message when turning a feature on, is selected, you receive a warning message when turning a feature on.

     - If the second option, Make a sound when turning a feature on or off, is selected, you receive a sound every time you turn a feature on or off.

   - *SerialKey device:* This option enables you to access the keyboard and mouse features for an alternative keyboard device, such as a blow stick.

Labs

Add New Hardware

When you select Add New Hardware, the Add New Hardware wizard opens. This wizard guides you through the installation of additional hardware that was not present or detected during setup. You'll practice this option in detail in other labs.

Add/Remove Programs

When you select Add/Remove Programs, this option enables you to install and uninstall programs. You can also select or deselect the windows components using the Windows Setup tab. The last tab, Startup Disk, enables you to create a startup disk. You'll practice this option in detail in other labs.

Date/Time

To change the time and date or time zone, use the Date/Time option on your Control Panel. You can also double-click the time display in the taskbar to reach this option.

1. Double-click the Date/Time icon.

2. To change the date, select the number of the date with the pointer and click once.

3. To change the month, click the arrow and select the correct month from the pull-down menu.

4. Use the spin buttons (up and down arrows) to change the time into the correct hour and minutes. You also can highlight the numbers and type the correct ones.

5. To change the time zone, select the tab for Time Zone. You can either point to the correct place on the map or select the correct time zone from the drop-down list. Optionally, you can select Automatically adjust clock for daylight savings to have Windows keep track of Daylight Savings Time changes.

Display

Display enables you to customize your desktop and display environment by changing the wallpaper, adjusting the Screen Saver waiting period, and other options. You work with these options later in Lab 8, "Working with the Display."

Fonts

This option allows you to install new fonts into the system.

1. Open the Fonts folder.
2. Select File, and from the pull-down menu, select Install new font.
3. Select the folder, network location, or floppy disk drive on which the new fonts are located.

Keyboard

This option allows you to set options that affect the operation of your keyboard, including auto repeat speed and language.

1. Open the Keyboard option in Control Panel.
2. By default, you should be on the Speed tab; if not, select it now.
3. The Repeat Delay option causes a delay every time you press a key on the keyboard before repeating the character. Change the Repeat Delay by moving the slider all the way to the left.
4. Now place the cursor on the box provided for testing.
5. Now press the letter **s** and hold it down. What happened?
6. Return the slider to its original position, then go to the testing box and type **s** again, hold it down, and notice how the action has changed. (The delay in starting to repeat the letter should be longer the first time than the second.)
7. The Repeat Rate option increases or decreases the speed of the character being repeated. Change the repeat rate by moving its slider all the way to the left or to the right.

Labs

8. Go to the testing box, press the letter **s** again, and hold it down. Notice the difference in the speed of the letter while it is repeating.

9. Return the slider to its original position.

10. Press and hold down the letter again in the test box. Notice the difference in speed.

11. Cursor Blinking Rate controls the speed at which the cursor blinks. Move the slider all the way to the left. Notice how the cursor example decreases the speed of blinking.

12. Move the slider back into its original position.

13. You can add other languages and keyboard support to your system. If you do so, make sure that you have the Windows 95 installation media available. From the top of the dialog box, select the Language tab.

14. Select the Add option. A dialog box with languages appears.

15. From the pull-down menu, select Spanish (Modern sort), and press OK.

16. Highlight the language for which you want to customize the keyboard.

17. Click the Properties button and select Latin America from the pull-down menu.

Tip

If you want to remove a language, just highlight the language and select Remove.

18. Click OK. Windows prompts you for the original location of the Windows 95 setup files.

19. On your taskbar appears the letters En for English or Es for Español (Spanish).

20. Click once on the letters in your taskbar. Notice the options. Now you can change the keyboard from one language to the other on the fly.

21. Open the Keyboard again.

22. Select the General tab.

23. Click Change. Choose the Show All Devices radio button. *DO NOT MAKE ANY CHANGES!* Click Cancel.

24. Click Cancel.

Mail and Fax

This option allows you to configure the mail options, such as which services will be active (like CompuServe Mail, Microsoft Fax, etc.). You will practice this option in detail in other labs.

Microsoft Mail Postoffice

Microsoft Mail Postoffice allows you to create and administer a postoffice. You will practice this option in detail in other labs.

Modems

The Modems option enables you to add and remove modems on the system and configure them. This option also provides an option to test the modem. You will practice this option in detail in other labs.

Mouse

This option allows you to configure your mouse, including the assignment of the mouse buttons and the cursor speed.

1. Open the Mouse option.

2. Select the Left-Handed option.

3. Click the Apply button. Notice that the changes take place immediately.

Tip

Clicking the Apply button causes changes made in any tab in a tabbed dialog to be accepted. Apply is similar to the OK button, except it does not close the dialog.

Labs

4. Now try clicking with the mouse on top of the right-handed option.

   Notice that nothing happened.

5. Right-click the option; notice that now the option is selected.

6. Click Apply; the changes take effect immediately.

   Notice that the control returns to the side of the mouse that was originally configured.

7. Let's now try the speed of the double-click; let's move the slider all the way to the right.

8. Double-click the Jack-in-the-box. Notice how the box won't open.

9. Move the slider to the left corner. Double-click the box, see how Jack comes out of the box.

10. Double-click again on the box; this causes the box to close.

11. Return the slider to its original position.

12. Select the Pointer tab.

13. Go to the Scheme option and click the down arrow. Select Windows Standard (extra large).

14. Notice the different cursors. If you click Apply, the cursor changes.

15. Go back to Scheme, select None, and click Apply. This returns the cursor to its original position.

16. Select the Motion tab.

17. Move the slider from the Pointer speed to the left. Click apply. Notice the difference of the speed when you move the pointer on the desktop.

18. Click the check box on the pointer trail. Click Apply. Notice the trail every time you move the pointer.

    Change the options back if you want.

19. Select the General tab. Here is where you define what kind of mouse you have. Do not make changes here, it should have the correct mouse defined on the installation.

Multimedia

Multimedia enables you to configure Audio, Video, CD-ROM, and MIDI. You will practice this option in detail in other labs.

Network

The Network option enables you to add/remove protocols, clients, network interfaces cards, drives, and all the networking configuration aspects. You will learn about and practice this in detail in several labs.

Passwords

This option allows you to change your passwords, and enable or disable remote administration and user profiles.

1. Open the Passwords option on Control Panel.
2. Click Change Windows password. A dialog box appears prompting you for the old and new passwords.
3. Other Passwords refers to server passwords on networks, screen saver passwords, or passwords for other applications. At this point, you are not configured for a server-based network.
4. Select the Remote Administrator Tab. This option allows you to administer your printers and files from other locations on the network. Type a password, so only people who know the password can connect to the computer for administration purposes.
5. Select the User Profile tab. The first option turns off profiles; the second turns on profiles. Turning on the profiles enables different users to use the same computer, each with his or her own customized environment.

The last two options enable you to include different options in your desktop as part of your profile.

Printers

This option enables you to add and configure printers. You will learn about this option in detail in other labs.

Labs

Regional Settings

This option allows you to configure regional settings, such as the formats used to display numeric information and currency symbol.

1. The first tab, Regional Settings, enables you to define the country you are in.

2. Select the Number tab. As you can see, this option enables you to define all the numeric formats used to display numeric information in your system.

3. Select the Currency tab. This option enables you to specify the monetary symbols. Use it to display your country's currency.

4. Select the Time tab. This option enables you to define the format you prefer for the time to be displayed.

5. Select the Date tab. This option enables you to define the format in which the date appears.

Sounds

This option lets you assign a sound to a system event. You also can test sounds.

1. Select Critical Stop.

2. Click on the arrow in the preview section. You can listen to the sound of the selected event.

System

The System option has several utilities, like the Device Manager, that let you see and change the options on the devices installed on your computer.

- Performance lets you change settings such as the virtual memory that affect the performance of your computer.

- General shows you the type of computer you have, amount of memory, serial number registration, and other information.

This option of the control panel is discussed in several other labs.

Lab Objective

In this lab, you learn

⊥ How 32-bit and 16-bit
applications run under
Windows 95, and what
happens when they fail

Lab 4: Running Applications on Windows 95

 Note To complete this lab, you need:
- One computer with Windows 95 installed.
- The CD-ROM that accompanies this book. ▪

Running 32-Bit Applications

1. Start your computer.
2. Click Start, choose Programs, Accessories, and then open WordPad.
3. From the CD provided with the book, run the Badapp32.exe application in the Labs folder.
4. Click the GPF button.
5. What happened? What message did you get?
6. Try to switch to the WordPad. What Happened? Were you able to switch to WordPad? Why would this be?

Labs

7. Press Control+Alt+Del once.

8. From the Close programs window, select the Badapp32 program and click End Task.

9. Run Badapp32 again.

10. Click the Stop responding button. What happened? What message did you get?

11. Try to switch to WordPad. What Happened? Were you able to switch? Why would this be?

12. From the Close programs window, select the Badapp32 program and click End Task.

Running 16-Bit Applications

1. Click Start, choose Programs, choose Accessories, and open WordPad.

2. Click Start, choose Programs, and open an MS-DOS session.

3. From the CD provided with the book, run the Badapp16.exe application.

4. Click the GPF button. What happened? What message did you get?

5. Try to switch to WordPad and MS-DOS. What happened? Were you able to switch? Why would this be?

6. Press Control+Alt+Del once.

7. From the Close programs window, select the Badapp16 program and click End Task.

8. Run Badapp16 again.

9. Click the Stop responding button. What happened? What message did you get?

10. Try to switch to the WordPad and MS-DOS. What happened? Were you able to switch? Why would this be?

11. From the Close programs window, select the Badapp32 program and click End Task.

Lab Objective

In this lab, you:

+ Explore the long file
  name support in
  Windows 95.

Lab 5: File System Support in Windows 95

 Note To complete this lab, you need one computer with Windows 95 installed. ▪

Creating a Long File Name

1. Click Start, choose Programs, Accessories, and open WordPad.
2. Type the following: **This is my long file name test file**.
3. Choose File, Exit.
4. Choose Yes when prompted "Save changes to the Document?"
5. Make sure you are in the \Windows\Desktop directory.
6. In the File name box, type the following: **This is my long name file**.
7. Click Save. WordPad will close after saving the file.
8. Click Start, choose Programs, and select MS–DOS prompt.
9. Press Alt+Enter if you have a full screen, so it changes to a window.

Labs

10. Move to the Windows folder (e.g., **cd windows**).

11. Move to the Desktop folder (e.g., **cd desktop**).

12. At the command prompt, type **dir**. You should see something like this:

```
THISIS-1 DOC 4,608 03-06-96 11:50p This is my long name file.doc
```

Notice the 8.3 alias name plus the long file name format at the right.

Multiple Files with Similar Names

1. Click Start, choose Programs, Accessories, and open WordPad.

2. Type the following: **This is my long file name test file 2**.

3. Choose File, Save. A dialog box appears.

4. Make sure you are in the \Windows\Desktop directory.

5. Type in the File name box the following: **This is my long name file 2**.

6. Click Save.

7. Choose File, New.

8. Repeat steps 2 to 7, but increase the number at the end of the file name each time. Repeat 4 times.

9. Click Start, choose Programs, and select MS-DOS prompt.

10. Press Alt+Enter if you have a full screen, so it changes to a window.

11. Move to the Windows folder (e.g., **cd windows**).

12. Move to the Desktop folder (e.g., **cd desktop**).

13. At the command prompt, type **dir**. You should see something like this:

```
THISIS-1 DOC   4,608  03-07-96 12:44a This is my long name file.doc
THISIS-2 DOC   4,608  03-07-96 12:44a This is my long name file 2.doc
THISIS-3 DOC   4,608  03-07-96 12:45a This is my long name file 3.doc
THISIS-4 DOC   4,608  03-07-96 12:45a This is my long name file 4.doc
THISIS-5 DOC   4,608  03-07-96 12:46a This is my long name file 5.doc
```

Notice the 8.3 alias name plus the long file name format at the right.

Lab Objective

In this lab, you:

+ Explore the use of threads by different types of programs under Windows 95.

Lab 6: Exploring Threads and Processes

 Note To complete this lab, you need one computer with Windows 95 installed. ▣

1. Start your computer.
2. Click Start, choose Programs, Accessories, and then choose System Tools.
3. Open System Monitor.
4. At the bottom border of the screen (the status line), look for the Kernel Threads. If you do not see that line in the border of the screen, go to the next step. If you do, go to step 8.
5. On the System Monitor, select Edit, Add.
6. From Categories, select Kernel.
7. From Item, select Threads and click OK.
8. Look at the status line. Now you should see the following line:

   `"Kernel: Threads Last Value:(Number) Peak Value:(Number)`
9. What are the Values of:

   `Kernel: Threads Last Value:_____ Peak Value:____`

10. While System Monitor is open, click Start, choose Programs, Accessories, and then select WordPad.

11. After WordPad is loaded, what are the values of:

    `Kernel: Threads Last Value:_____ Peak Value:_____`

12. What is the difference in values:

    `Kernel: Threads Difference Last Value:_____ Difference Peak Value:_____`

13. Click Start, choose Programs, Accessories, Games, and then open Solitaire.

14. What are the new values for:

    `Kernel: Threads Last Value:_____ Peak Value:_____`

15. What is the difference in values using the totals from step 11:

    `Kernel: Threads Difference Last Value:_____ Difference Peak Value:_____`

16. Click Start, choose Programs, then choose MS-DOS Command.

17. What are the new values for:

    `Kernel: Threads Last Value:_____ Peak Value:_____`

18. What is the difference in values using the totals on step 17:

    `Kernel: Threads Difference Last Value:_____ Difference Peak Value:_____`

19. Click Start, choose Programs, and open another MS-DOS session.

20. What are the new values for:

    `Kernel: Threads Last Value:_____ Peak Value:_____`

21. What is the difference in values using the totals on step 20:

    `Kernel: Threads Difference Last Value:_____ Difference Peak Value:_____`

Lab 7: Creating and Optimizing Virtual Memory

 Note To complete this lab, you need one computer with Windows 95 installed. ▪

1. Open Control Panel, open System Icon, and click the Performance tab.

2. From the Performance tab, click Virtual Memory.

 Tip

The recommended setting is to let Windows 95 manage the virtual memory.

3. Click Let Me specify my own Virtual Memory Settings.

4. In the Hard disk box, select your c: drive.

 Tip

You may select another drive if you are running out of disk space on drive c:, or if you have a faster hard disk than your c: drive.

Labs

5. For the Minimum, type **10** or select it using the spin buttons.

6. For the Maximum, type **50** (make sure you have more than 50M of free disk space) in the box, or select the Using the spin buttons.

Note The Disable Virtual Memory option should appear only if you are having problems with your hard disk and you need to do intense troubleshooting. ▪

7. Click OK. The message shown in figure L.1 appears.

FIG. L.1 ⇒
Windows 95 will warn you when you change virtual memory settings.

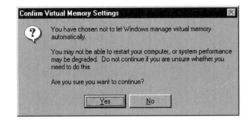

8. Click Yes. The system restarts.

The result of changing these values is that the pagefile will never be smaller than 10M, nor larger than 50M.

In this lab, you learn:

- How to change the display options
- How to configure the display for MS-DOS applications
- How to navigate the Windows 95 display options

Lab 8: Working with the Display

 Note To complete this lab, you need one computer with Windows 95 installed. ■

Caution
The following lab could be very helpful, but also could be very dangerous.

Accessing the Display Properties

One of the Windows 95 design goals was to make configuring the display much easier. You configure the display via its properties dialog.

You can access the Display properties via the Start menu or from the Desktop:

- For Control Panel access, choose Start, Settings, Control Panel, then double-click the Display icon.
- To open the Display properties dialog from the Desktop, right-click your Desktop and select Properties.

Labs

Adjusting Display Settings

1. From the Display properties, select Settings.

2. From Color palette, select 256 color. Notice the changes in the emulation screen.

3. Change the desktop area to 1024 by 768 pixels (if your computer's display is already configured for this setting, select another value). Notice the differences in the emulation screen.

4. You can choose the size of your fonts from either Small or Large.

Caution
Make sure you don't press Apply or OK—some settings may not be suitable for your computer.

The most important part of this control panel is the display driver.

1. From the Settings tab, select Display Type.

2. Click Change in the adapter type section.

3. Select Show all devices.

4. From the list, select (standard display types).

5. From Models, select Super VGA.

6. Because you don't want to make the changes now (this is only a demonstration) click Cancel.

Working with Wallpaper and Screen Savers

1. Select the Background tab.

2. From the Wallpaper option, select Clouds. (If you do not have this option, then select Forest or the Setup wallpaper.)

3. Select Tile and notice the difference on the emulation screen.

4. Select the Center option again. Notice the differences on the screen.

5. Click the Screen Saver tab.

6. From the pull-down menu, select Flying Windows.

7. Click the Settings button. Here you can adjust the settings of that particular screen saver. In this case, you can change the number and velocity of the flying windows. Make any changes you want.

8. Click OK and notice the differences.

9. To increase the security on your computer, you can set up a password by clicking Password. Fill in the appropriate boxes. Windows 95 prompts you for a password before deactivating the screen saver and allowing you to use the computer.

10. Also, you can adjust the amount of idle time the system should wait before activating the screen saver.

11. Click the Appearance tab.

12. Click the pull-down menu of the Scheme window.

13. Choose a scheme and notice the changes.

Labs

Lab 9: Printing

 Note To complete this lab, you need one computer with Windows 95 installed. You should not have a printer attached to your computer. ■

Creating a Printer

1. Choose Start, Settings, Printers.

2. Double-click Add Printer. A Wizard appears.

3. Click Next, then select Local Printer.

4. Click Next. From the manufacturers list, select HP.

5. From the printers list, select HP LaserJet Series II.

6. Click Next. From Available ports, select LPT1.

7. Click Next. Type a name for the printer in the box.

8. Select No when prompted "Do you want your Windows-based Programs to use this printer as a default printer?"

9. Click Next. Select No when prompted "Print a test page?"

10. Click Finish. If the Windows 95 setup files are not already installed, you are prompted to supply them.

11. In the Printers window, right-click the icon of the printer you just installed and select Properties.

12. Click the Paper tab.

13. On Orientation, select Landscape. Notice there are lots of options to customize the way your printer behaves. Feel free to explore this option.

14. Click OK.

Sharing a Printer

1. Click Start, choose Settings, and select Printers.

2. Right-click the printer you just installed.

3. Select Sharing.

4. Select Share as.

5. In the box provided, type the name you want to use to identify the shared printer.

6. If you want to control the access to the printer, set a password.

7. Click OK.

Administering a Printer

1. Click Start, choose Settings, and select Printers.

2. Double-click the printer you just created.

3. Click Start, choose Programs, Accessories, and open WordPad.

4. Type **The meaning of life is**.

5. Choose File, Print.

6. In the Name box, press the down arrow button.

7. Select the new printer you just installed.

8. Click OK.

Labs

9. Click the print job.

10. On the taskbar, select the printer window that is open. Notice that the file is in the print queue.

11. From the Printer menu, select Pause. Notice the job is now paused. It will remain this way until you reset it.

12. Choose Printer and click Pause again.

Note Notice in the Printer menu and in the Document menu that both have the Pause Printing Option. One pauses the printer, the other pauses that particular document, respectively.

13. Select the document by clicking it.

14. Choose Document and select Cancel.

15. Choose Printer and select Purge Print Job.

Lab 10: Using Disk Utilities

 Note To complete this lab, you need one computer with Windows 95
installed. ▨

Using ScanDisk

1. Choose Start, Programs, Accessories, System Tools, and open
   ScanDisk.

2. Select drive c:.

3. Select Thorough.

4. Click Options.

5. Click System and Data.

6. Click OK.

7. Click Advanced.

8. Make sure that the settings are as follows:

Option	Setting
Display Summary	Always
Log File	Replace Log
Cross-Linked Files	Make Copies
Lost File Fragments	Convert to Files
Checks Files for	Invalid file names

9. Make sure Check Host Drive First is selected.

10. Click OK.

11. Click Start and wait. Observe the error messages, if any appear.

12. After ScanDisk is finished, you may repeat the process for other drives on your system.

13. Close ScanDisk.

Using Disk Defragmenter

1. Choose Start, Programs, Accessories, System Tools, and open Disk Defragmenter.

2. Select drive c: and click OK.

3. After a moment, the dialog box indicates whether or not the disk needs to be defragmented.

4. Click Advanced.

5. Make sure your settings are as follows:

   - Defragmentation Method: select Full defragmentation (both files and free space).

   - Check drive for errors should be selected.

   - Save these options and use them every time also should be selected.

6. Click OK.

7. Click Start.

8. Click Details.

9. Close Disk Defragmenter.

Installing and Using Backup

1. First make sure you have the Backup utility installed by clicking on Start, choosing Programs, Accessories, and then choosing System Tools. You should be able to see the Backup utility. If not, go to the next step; if you do, go to step 9.

2. Choose Start, Settings, Control Panel, and select Add\Remove Programs.

3. Click the Windows Setup tab.

4. Double-click Disk Tools.

5. Select Backup and click OK.

6. Click OK again and make sure you have the Windows 95 CD in the drive.

7. Choose Start, Programs, Accessories, System Tools, and select Backup.

8. Click OK after reading the Welcome screen, then read the next message about Full System backup.

9. Choose File, open a file set, and select Full System Backup.

10. The Backup begins making a copy of the Registry and selecting the files. This takes some time, so be patient.

11. After the file selection is finished, notice that there are check marks on the boxes of all files.

12. Click Next Step. Here you need to select the media onto which you want to perform the backup.

13. If this was a real backup, you would need to click Start. (If you have a tape backup or another Hard Disk that is empty, you may do this now.)

14. Select Previous.

15. Close Backup.

Labs

Lab Objective

In this lab, you learn:

+ The files involved in the boot process, and how to boot Windows 95 in Safe Mode.

Lab 11: Understanding the Windows 95 Boot Process

 Note To complete this lab, you need one computer with Windows 95 installed. ■

Exploring the Boot Process

1. Start your Computer. What do you see when your computer is starting?

2. While your computer is starting and you see the Windows 95 screen, press the Esc key. What happened? At this point you can see part of the boot process.

3. After the boot is complete, click Start, select Shut Down, select Restart the computer, and click Yes.

4. This time, when you see "Starting Windows 95," press the F8 key.

Tip

You must press F8 within two seconds after the message appears.

5. Notice all the different options. Select 5. Step by Step Confirmation.

6. Answer Yes to everything except "Process the system registry," to which you should answer No.

7. Note any changes to the system at this point after the boot process finishes.

8. Restart the Computer by clicking Start, choosing Shut Down, and selecting restart.

9. Press the F8 key when Starting Windows 95 appears.

Tip

You must press F8 within two seconds after the message appears.

10. Select 3 for Safe mode.

11. After Windows 95 finishes the boot process, notice the Safe Mode labels on the screen. What else is different?

   This option is the most used for troubleshooting purposes.

12. Restart your computer.

Labs

Lab 12: Using TCP/IP with Windows 95

Note To complete this lab, you need:
- One computer with Windows 95 installed
- A network adapter card
- Another computer, such as a Windows NT Server, with TCP/IP
  installed ■

Installing and Configuring the Protocol

1. Start your computer.

2. From the Start menu, select Settings and choose Control Panel.

3. Double-click Network.

4. Click Add.

5. Double-click Protocols.

6. From the list of Manufacturers, select Microsoft.

7. From the right-hand pane, choose TCP/IP. Make sure you have the Windows 95 CD on hand. When prompted, make sure the CD is in the drive.

8. Click OK.

9. Click OK to close the Network Control Panel.

10. The Properties dialog appears.

11. On the IP address tab, select "Specify an IP address."

12. At IP Address, enter **120.110.10.1**.

13. At Subnet Mask, enter **255.255.255.0**.

14. Select the Gateway tab and type **120.110.10.100**. Click the Add button.

15. Click OK and restart your computer.

16. Make sure that TCP/IP is bound to your network interface card or a dial-up adapter on the Network control panel. Scroll through the list of network components. Look for an arrow pointing to either adapter, as in TCP/IP -> Intel Etherexpress 16.

Testing TCP/IP

1. From the Start menu, choose Run.

2. Type **winipcfg**. Notice the values of the IP Address, Subnet Mask, and the Default Gateway.

3. Choose Start, Programs, MS-DOS Prompt.

4. Type **Ping 127.0.0.1**. This causes the packets to be responded to by your own computer. You should see the following information. If you don't get those results, you need to reconfigure your TCP/IP.

```
C:\>ping 127.0.0.1
Pinging 127.0.0.1 with 32 bytes of data:
Reply from 127.0.0.1: bytes=32 time=1ms TTL=32
Reply from 127.0.0.1: bytes=32 time=1ms TTL=32
Reply from 127.0.0.1: bytes=32 time=1ms TTL=32
Reply from 127.0.0.1: bytes=32 time=1ms TTL=32
```

Lab

5. Type **Ping 120.110.10.1**. Your results should look like this:

```
C:\>ping 120.110.10.1
Pinging 120.110.10.1 with 32 bytes of data:
Reply from 120.110.10.1: bytes=32 time=1ms TTL=32
Reply from 120.110.10.1: bytes=32 time=1ms TTL=32
Reply from 120.110.10.1: bytes=32 time=1ms TTL=32
Reply from 120.110.10.1: bytes=32 time=1ms TTL=32
```

Testing TCP/IP Communication

Note   For this section, you need another computer configured with TCP/IP running either Windows 95 or Windows NT. The TCP/IP settings on the second computer should be:

IP Address 120.110.10.2

Subnet Mask 255.255.255.0

Default Gateway 120.110.10.100

1. On the first computer, open an MS-DOS section.

2. Type **Ping 120.110.10.2**. You should get results like the following:

```
C:\>ping 120.110.10.2
Pinging 120.110.10.2 with 32 bytes of data:
Reply from 120.110.10.2: bytes=32 time=8ms TTL=32
Reply from 120.110.10.2: bytes=32 time=2ms TTL=32
Reply from 120.110.10.2: bytes=32 time=2ms TTL=32
Reply from 120.110.10.2: bytes=32 time=3ms TTL=32
```

3. Close the MS-DOS window.

Lab 13: Using Windows 95 as a Client of a Microsoft Windows NT Network

 Note To complete this lab, you need:

- One computer with Windows 95 installed
- A computer that is a Windows NT Server domain controller ▪

Connecting to a Windows NT Server Domain

1. Start your computer.
2. Right-click Network Neighborhood on your desktop.
3. Select Properties.
4. From the Configuration tab, highlight Client for Microsoft Networks and click Properties.
5. Check the box that says Logon to Windows NT domain.
6. Type the name of your Windows NT domain and click OK.

Lab

7. Make sure the Microsoft Client for Microsoft Networks is selected as the Primary Network Logon.

8. Click OK.

9. At this point, you need to restart your computer. As it restarts, notice that the Logon dialog box appears. It includes three boxes for you to provide your user ID, the domain name, and the password. (Make sure you have an account on the Windows NT domain or that the guest account is active.)

Implementing User-Level Security

1. Open Windows Explorer.

2. Create a new directory by selecting drive c: and choosing File, New, Folder. Name the folder Net_Test.

3. After the folder is created, right-click it and select Sharing.

4. Select Share as. Name the share Net_Test. Leave the folder as read-only and do not assign a password. Notice that logging into Windows NT didn't change the way you share a directory when using Share-level access control.

5. Go to Control Panel and open the Network icon.

6. Click the Access Control tab.

7. Select User-level access control.

8. In the Obtain List Of Users And Groups From dialog box, type the name of your domain and click on the OK button.

9. Restart your computer.

10. Notice the message that your shares are lost. You need to reshare the folders. Open Windows Explorer.

11. Select the Net_Test folder. Right-click it and select Sharing.

12. Share the folder as Net_Test. Notice the new Sharing dialog box. Experiment with the options—notice that the list of users comes from the Windows NT domain controller.

    After you have experimented with the Sharing dialog, click OK. The next step is to restore Share-level access control.

13. Go to Control Panel and open the Network icon.

14. Click the Access Control tab.

15. Select Share-level access control.

16. Restart your computer.

Lab 14: Creating a Peer-to-Peer Network with a Windows 95 Machine

 Note To complete this lab, you need two computers on a network with Windows 95 installed. ▪

Setting Up a Peer-to-Peer Network

1. Start your computer.
2. Open Windows Explorer.
3. Create a directory by selecting drive c:.
4. Choose File, New, Folder. Name the folder Peer_Test.
5. After the folder is created, right-click it and select sharing.
6. Select Share as. Name the share Peer_Test, and choose Full access; do not put a password on it.

7. On the other machine, if you are running Windows 95 on it, click Start, choose Run, and type ***Computer 1*\Peer_Test**, substituting the name of your computer where *Computer 1* is.

   If you are running Windows NT on the second computer, go to File Manager, choose Disk, Connect, and in the provided box type the same path as before. (Use the default drive letter.)

8. Click OK.

9. Go to the first computer and start Net Watcher by clicking Start, choosing Accessories, System Tools, and then selecting Net Watcher. With the By Connections Option selected, you should see the second machine connected to the first. If the connection has any open files, you should be able to see them.

10. Click Start, choose Programs, Accessories, and open WordPad.

11. Create a file and save it in the Peer_Test Folder.

12. On the second computer, open Network Neighborhood.

13. Double-click *Computer 1*.

    You should be able to see all the shared directories on the first computer.

14. Open the Peer_Test folder.

15. Open the file you created before. Is it the same file?

Labs

Lab Objective

In this lab, you see:

↓ How Novell NetWare
security affects Windows
95 clients

↓ How you can integrate a
Windows 95 computer
into a Novell NetWare
network

Lab 15: Using Windows 95 as a Client on a Novell NetWare Network

 Note To complete this lab, you need:

- One computer with Windows 95 installed
- A Novell NetWare 2.x, 3.x, or 4.x (bindery emulation mode)
  server (you must have Supervisor privileges on the server) ▪

Installing the Microsoft Client for NetWare Networks

1. Start your Computer.
2. Right-click Network Neighborhood on your desktop.
3. Select Properties.
4. Click Add.
5. Double-click Client.
6. Click Microsoft.
7. Select Client for NetWare networks.

8. Click OK.

9. Verify that the Primary Network Logon is set to Client for NetWare networks.

10. Click OK.

11. Restart your computer.

12. As you restart your computer, notice that the logon dialog box appears. It has three boxes—fill in your User ID, the NetWare server name, and your password. (Make sure that you have an account on the NetWare server or that the NetWare Guest account is active.)

User-Level Security

1. Open Windows Explorer.

2. Create a directory by selecting drive c:.

3. Choose File, New; choose Folder, and name the folder Nov_Test.

4. After the folder is created, right-click it and select Sharing.

5. Select Share as. Name the share Nov_Test and leave it as Read Only. Do not put a password on it.

6. Go to Control Panel and open the Network icon.

7. Click the Access Control tab.

8. Select User-level access control.

9. Type the name of the NetWare server in the "Obtain list of users and groups from" box.

10. Restart your computer.

11. Note the message that your shares may be lost and you will need to reshare the folders.

12. Open Network Neighborhood.

13. Double-click on Entire Network.

14. Double-click the NetWare server. Notice that all of the NetWare directories are shown as shares.

Labs

Lab 16: Printing over the Network

Note To complete this lab, you need:

- One computer with Windows 95 installed
- A Windows NT or Novell NetWare (bindery based) server ▦

Connecting to a Printer

1. Click Start, choose Settings, and select Printers.

2. Double-click Add Printer. A wizard opens.

3. Click Next.

4. Select Network Printer.

5. Click Next.

6. Click Browse.

7. Select the Computer you already have a printer configured on (refer to Lab 9).

8. Click the printer you want to connect to.

9. Make sure the No is selected for "Do you print from MS-DOS based programs."

10. Click Next.

11. Type the name you want to refer to this printer by.

12. Select No when prompted "Do you want your Windows-based programs to use this Printer as the default printer?"

13. Click Next.

14. Choose No when prompted to print a test page.

15. Click Finish.

Labs

Lab 17: Using the Briefcase

 Note To complete this lab, you need:

- Two computers on a network with Windows 95 installed
- A blank floppy disk ▪

Creating a Briefcase on a Floppy Disk

1. Make sure the floppy disk is formatted.
2. Open My Computer.
3. Put the floppy disk in drive a:.
4. Double-click the Drive A icon.
5. Right-click the Drive A window and select Briefcase. A new briefcase is created here.
6. Name the briefcase "Test Briefcase."
7. Click Start, choose Programs, and open Windows Explorer.
8. Select drive c:.

9. From the toolbar, select File, choose New, and create a new folder. Name it "test."

10. Click Start, choose Programs, Accessories, and open WordPad.

11. Type **There is more to see than can ever be seen, more to do than can ever be done**.

12. Save the file as File1 in the test folder you just created on drive c:, and close it.

13. From the taskbar, select the button for the floppy drive.

14. Double-click the Briefcase.

15. From Windows Explorer, select the file you just created and drag and drop it inside the Briefcase.

16. Notice the Status column on Briefcase that says Up-to-Date for the file you just dragged.

17. Go back to WordPad. Open and edit File1 that you just created by adding "A difference that makes no difference is no difference."

18. Save the file and close it.

19. Go to your Briefcase and notice that the status column should say, "Needs Updating."

20. To update, you can either choose File, Update All or right-click the Briefcase icon and select Update All.

21. While you are updating, you will see several screens:

    The first one is when the files are being selected.

    The second one is to confirm those files. In this screen, you should see both files, with an arrow pointing from the newest version to the oldest.

22. Right-click the top of the arrow. You can select Skip if you don't want to update the file, or if you want to change the direction of the update. Don't change it; leave it as it was.

23. Click OK.

Labs

24. Create a new file on the test directory by going to WordPad and creating and saving another file. Close the file.

25. Update the Briefcase again. What happened? Does the new file get updated?

    No. It wasn't updated because the file is an orphan. To be able to update all the files, including the new ones and the so-called orphans, you could have dragged the whole folder to the Briefcase instead of just the file or files. Any file in a Briefcase that is not linked to an outside file is an orphan.

Lab 18: Working with Profiles

 Note To complete this lab, you need one computer with Windows 95
installed. ■

Creating Multiple User Profiles

1. Start your computer.

2. Click Start, choose Settings, Control Panel, and open the
   Network icon.

3. Double-click Passwords.

4. Select the User Profiles tab.

5. Click "User can customize their preferences."

6. Verify that both check boxes are selected in the User profiles
   settings.

7. Restart your computer.

8. Log on to your computer using USER1 as your username.

9. Change the display settings like colors, wallpaper, and add icons to the desktop.

10. Click Start, choose Shut Down. Select "Close all Programs and log on as a different user."

11. Log on as USER2. Do you have the same settings and color you selected previously?

12. Change the Display settings, the colors, the wallpaper, and add some icons to the desktop.

13. Log off, then log on again as USER1. Have any of your original settings as USER1 changed?

Lab 19: Working with Policies

 Note To complete this lab, you need one computer with Windows 95 installed. ▪

System Policy Editor

1. Click Start, choose Settings, and open Control Panel.

2. Open Add\Remove programs.

3. Click the Windows Setup tab.

4. Click Have Disk.

5. Select your CD-ROM drive.

6. Double-click Admin\Apptools\Poledit.

7. Click OK.

8. Click OK in the path screen.

9. Click OK on the Main Window.

10. Click Start, choose Programs, Accessories, System Tools, and open the System Policy Editor.

11. Choose File, Open Registry.

12. Double-click Local Computer.

13. Choose Network, Check Logon Banner. This activates a message after boot up and before logon with the message you define.

> **Caution**
>
> Be careful. Any changes you make to the policies might affect the performance of your system, possibly even requiring a reinstallation of Windows 95.

14. Close all the open windows.

15. Restart the computer.

16. Can you see the banner with the Security Message? If you can't see it, go back and verify that the Logon Banner is selected.

17. If you don't like the Banner, you may edit the message or clear the box in the Logon Banner policy.

Lab Objective

In this lab, you learn:

+ How to use Net Watcher
  and System Monitor

Lab 20: Using Administrative Tools

 Note To complete this lab, you need:

- One computer with Windows 95 installed
- A second Windows 95 computer or a Windows NT
  computer ■

System Monitor

1. Start your Computer.

2. Click Start, choose Programs, Accessories, System Tools, and open System Monitor.

3. Choose Edit, Add Item.

4. From Category, select Kernel, and from the Item section, select Threads. Make sure you do not select items that are already present on the charts.

5. Also select Memory Manager, and from the Item section, Page Faults. From the Memory Manager section, add the item Swapfile in use.

Labs

Network Watcher

1. Start your Computer.

2. Click Start, choose Programs, Accessories, System Tools, and open Net Watcher.

3. Choose View, Shared Folders. This enables you to see all the Objects shared on your computer. Notice all of the predefined shares on your computer.

4. Choose View, By Connection.

 Note Continue with the following steps only if you have another computer with Windows 95 or Windows NT configured for networking.

5. Open Windows Explorer.

6. Create a directory by selecting drive c:.

7. Choose File, New, and select Folder. Name it Test2.

8. After the folder is created, right-click it and select Sharing.

9. Select Share as. Name the share Test2 and leave it as Read Only. Do not assign a password.

10. From the other machine, if you are running Windows 95 on it click Start, choose Run, and type **Computer 1****Test2** (substitute your computer's name for *Computer 1*).

    If you are running Windows NT on the second computer, go to File Manager, choose Disk, Connect, and in the provided box type the same path as before. Accept whatever disk letter is suggested, and click OK.

11. Click OK.

12. Go to the first computer and look at the Net Watcher. Under the By Connections Option, you should see the second machine connected to the first. If the connection has any open files, you should be able to see them.

13. From the Administer menu, you can either disconnect the user from the computer or select another server on the network to monitor.

Lab Objective

In this lab, you learn:

+ How to set up files for
  network installation and
  shared use

Lab 21: Windows 95 Server-Based Setup

 Note To complete this lab, you need two computers on a network
with Windows 95 installed. ▓

Server-Based Setup

1. Start your computer.

2. Place the Windows 95 CD in the drive.

3. Create a shared directory on the network server that will be
   used as the root of the installation. Name it NETSETUP.

4. Log into Windows 95 and attach to the network using an
   account that has full access to this directory.

5. Create a subdirectory on the server to copy the files to, such as
   WIN95.

6. Start Server Based Setup by running it from the
   \Admin\Nettools\Netsetup directory on the Windows 95
   CD-ROM.

Labs

7. Click the Set Path button to open the dialog box.

8. Type the path to the share on your server, *Server***NETSETUP****Win95**. Be sure to specify the subdirectory to use. If the directory does not exist, Server-Based Setup asks if you want it to create the subdirectory automatically.

   The dialog has changed to indicate the install path, and the Install button is now available.

9. Clicking Install opens the Source Path dialog box.

10. Select Local Hard Drive.

11. Enter the Path to install from (specify your CD-ROM drive).

12. Click OK. The Create Default dialog box appears.

13. Click the Create Default button, the properties for the default batch script appear.

14. Double-click Name and Organization.

15. Check the Organization Box and type the name of your organization.

16. Check the Name Box and type your name.

17. Double-click Network Options.

18. Check the Workgroup Box and type your workgroup name.

19. Click OK.

20. Type your Product Identification Number (the number on the yellow sticker on your Windows 95 CD-ROM packaging).

21. Click OK to start the process of copying files. This may take some time.

22. When the process is finished, click OK.

23. Click Add and create a home directory on the server.

24. Select Setup on Machine.

25. Enter the computer name.

26. Enter the path on the share for the machine specific directory.

27. Click OK.

28. Close the Server-based Setup dialog box.

Lab 22: Working with Modems

 Note To complete this lab, you need one computer with Windows 95 installed. ▪

1. Start your computer.
2. Click Start, choose Settings, and open Control Panel.
3. Double-click the Modem icon.
4. Click Add. A wizard window appears.
5. Make sure the Don't detect modem check box is selected.
6. Click Next.
7. A list of Manufacturers and Models displays. Select yours. If you do not have a modem, select US Robotics, Inc., Sportster External 28800.
8. Click Next.
9. Select the Port the modem will be hooked to—either Com1 or Com2, for example.
10. Click Next.
11. Click Finish.

Labs

Lab Objective

In this lab, you learn how to:

↓ How to install and configure Microsoft Exchange

↓ How to install and configure support to connect to
Microsoft Mail

Lab 23: Working with Mail and Exchange

 Note To complete this lab, you need one computer with Windows 95 installed. ▪

Installing the Exchange Program

1. Start your computer.
2. Click Start and choose Settings, Control Panel.
3. Double-click Add/Remove Programs.
4. Click the Windows Setup tab.
5. Check the Microsoft Exchange box. Make sure you have the Windows 95 CD in the drive.
6. Click Details.
7. Select everything and click OK.
8. Click OK. Be sure to restart your computer after you finish.

Creating and Administering a Postoffice

1. Open Control panel.

2. Double-click the Microsoft Mail Postoffice icon. A wizard appears.

3. Select Create New Workgroup Postoffice. Click Next.

4. On Postoffice location, keep the default. Click Next.

5. Click Next on the confirmation screen for the location of the Postoffice.

6. Type the Full name of the Postoffice Administrator; do not change the password.

7. On Control Panel, double-click the Microsoft Mail Postoffice icon.

8. Select Administer an existing postoffice.

9. Click Next.

10. Select the path of the postoffice to be administered if different from the default.

11. Click Next.

12. Type **password** in the password box and click Next. The postoffice manager window appears.

13. Click Add user.

14. In Name, type **Rose**. In Mailbox, type **RoseD**. Leave the password as is.

15. Add another user named **Conchita**. For the mailbox, type **ConchyM**, leaving the default password.

16. Open Windows Explorer.

17. Select the \wgpo0000 directory. Right-click it and select Sharing.

18. Click Full Access and do not type a password.

19. Close Explorer.

Labs

Connecting Users to the Postoffice

Be sure to log on with the ID you have configured Exchange with.

1. On your desktop, open the Inbox.

2. A wizard starts.

3. The screen shows you the available information services. Select only Microsoft Mail.

4. Click Next.

5. It asks you the profile name. Type your user ID as your profile name.

6. Click Next.

7. When prompted, type the path to the postoffice. (C:\wgpo0000 if you are on the same machine where the postoffice is.) If you are on another machine on the network than the machine that has the postoffice, enter the UNC path to the postoffice, such as \\Server\Wgpo.

8. Click Next.

9. Pick your mail ID from the list.

10. Click Next.

11. Type **password** when prompted for password.

12. Click Next.

13. When prompted for your personal address book, type **ID.pab**.

14. Click Next (substitute any of the mailboxes you created above, either RoseD or ConchyM for *ID*).

15. When prompted for your personal information store PST File, type **ID.pst**.

16. Click Next.

17. Click Finish.

Sending Mail

This section is to verify that mail is configured correctly.

1. Log on with one ID (RoseD, ConchyM, or the administrator you created at the beginning of section 2).

2. Open the Inbox on your desktop.

3. Choose Compose, New Message.

4. Click To.

5. In the Show Names from dialog, select Postoffice.

6. Select another ID different from the one you are using at the moment.

7. Click the To button and make sure the name ends on the Messages Recipients list. Click OK.

8. Type a Subject and a message.

9. When finished, choose File, Send (or click the send button on the toolbar).

10. Log on as the user ID you send the mail to. Make sure that ID profile is configured. If not, repeat the previous section for this user ID.

11. Open the Inbox, choose Tools, Deliver Now Using, and then select Microsoft Mail.

12. Make sure you receive the mail sent with the other ID.

Labs

Lab 24: Faxing

 Note To complete this lab, you need one computer with Windows 95
installed. ▧

Installing the Fax Program

1. Start your computer.

2. Click Start and choose Settings, Control Panel.

3. Double-click Add/Remove Programs.

4. Click the Windows Setup tab.

5. Check the Microsoft Fax box. Make sure you have the
   Windows 95 CD in the drive.

6. Click Details.

7. Select all of the options, and then click OK.

8. Click OK, making sure to restart your computer after you
   finish.

9. Open the Inbox.

10. Choose Tools, Services.

11. From the Services dialog, click Add.

12. Select Microsoft Fax.

13. Click OK.

    If you do not have a modem installed, you will receive a message dialog box asking you to specify the modem configuration.

    If you have a modem, go to step 24.

14. Click Yes.

15. Click the Modem tab.

16. Click Add. A wizard window appears.

17. Make sure the Don't detect modem check box is checked.

18. Click Next.

19. A list of Manufacturers and Models shows; select yours. If you do not have a modem, select US Robotics, Inc., Sportster External 28800.

20. Click Next.

21. Select the Port the modem will be hooked to—either Com1 or Com2.

22. Click Next.

23. Click Finish.

24. Make sure the modem is selected as the active fax device.

25. Click the User tab.

26. Enter your information (you must enter at least your name and fax number).

27. Click OK.

28. Click OK.

29. Click Close.

Labs

Lab 25: Connecting to CompuServe

 Note To complete this lab, you need:

- One computer with Windows 95 installed
- A modem
- A CompuServe account ▪

Installing the CompuServe Mail Driver

1. Start your computer.

2. Make sure your Windows 95 CD is in the drive.

3. Click Start, and choose Run.

   Make sure Exchange is Closed.

4. Type **x:\Drivers\Other\Exchange\Compuserve\Setup** (where x is the letter of your CD-ROM Drive).

5. Answer Yes to "Do you wish to add CompuServe for Microsoft Exchange to your default profile?"

6. Right-click the Inbox icon.

7. Select Properties.

8. Click the Services tab.

9. Click Add.

10. Select CompuServe.

11. Click OK.

12. The CompuServe Mail Settings dialog opens.

13. Type your name.

14. Type your CompuServe account.

15. Type the password for your CompuServe account.

16. Click the Connection.

17. Type the local CompuServe access phone number.

18. Click the Advanced tab.

19. Make sure all three check boxes are checked.

20. Click OK.

21. Click OK.

22. Open Exchange.

23. Choose Tools, Deliver Now Using, and then choose CompuServe.

Labs

Lab 26: Connecting to The Microsoft Network

 Note   To complete this lab, you need:

- One computer with Windows 95 installed
- A modem

1. Start your computer.

2. Click Start, choose Settings, Control Panel.

3. Double-click Add/Remove Programs.

4. Click the Windows Setup tab.

5. Check The Microsoft Network box. Make sure you have the Windows 95 CD in the drive.

6. Click Details.

7. Select everything, and then click OK.

   If you have a modem, go to the next step.

8. Double-click The Microsoft Network icon.

9. Follow the steps to sign on to The Microsoft Network.

    After you install The Microsoft Network, you do not need to make any other changes; Exchange will be automatically configured.

Labs

Lab Objective

In this lab, you learn:

+ How to connect to an
  Internet Mail Provider
  (POP3) using Microsoft
  Exchange

Lab 27: Connecting to the Internet

 Note To complete this lab, you need:

- One computer with Windows 95 installed
- A modem
- Microsoft Plus! for Windows 95
- An Internet account from an Internet Service Provider ▪

Install Internet Mail

1. Install Microsoft Plus! Select all options.
2. Click Start and choose Programs, Accessories, Internet Tools.
3. Open the Setup Wizard.
4. Click Next.
5. Click Using my phone line.
6. If you get a security message about your files services running, click No.

7. Click I already have an account with a different service provider.

8. Click Next.

9. From the Name of Service Provider, select yours.

   If you do not have your service provider in the list, you need to configure it in the Dialup Networking option on Accessories.

10. Click Next.

11. Type your Internet provider's phone number.

12. Click Next.

13. Type your account ID and password in the boxes provided.

14. Click Next.

15. On the IP Address screen select "My Internet Service provider automatically assigns me one."

16. Do not type anything on the DNS screen.

17. Click Next.

18. Type your e-mail address and the name of your Internet mail server.

19. Click Next.

20. On the Exchange profile list, select your profile.

21. Click Next.

22. Click Finish.

Lab

Lab 28: Using Multimedia

 Note To complete this lab, you need:

- One computer with Windows 95 installed
- A sound card

Exploring Sounds

1. Start your computer.

2. Open Control Panel.

3. Double-click the Multimedia icon.

4. Go through all the tabs and look at every option available.

5. Click OK.

6. Double-click the Sounds icon.

7. In the events section, select Maximize Event.

8. In the Sound section, click the pull-down menu and select The Microsoft Sound.

9. In the Preview window, click Play.

10. Click OK.

11. Maximize a window.

12. Did the Microsoft Sound play?

Lab Objective

In this lab, you learn:

↓ How to configure
  Windows Explorer

↓ How to find files on your
  computer

Lab 29: Configuring Windows Explorer

 Note To complete this lab, you need one computer with Windows 95
installed. ▪

Explorer

1. Start your computer.

2. Click Start and choose Programs, Windows Explorer.

3. Choose View, Toolbar.

4. Choose View, Details.

   Notice the difference between the detail information related to
   the file that you can see now, and what was displayed before.
   Also, notice the change in the size of the icon.

5. Select any of the files and right-click them.

   Notice all the options in the context menu.

6. Select Send to. Notice that you can send this file to a floppy disk or another destination. If you have mail installed, you can even send the file to someone else via mail.

7. From the folders displayed at the left side of your Explorer window, select Control Panel. Notice that all the options included in the Control Panel can be seen on the right side of the Explorer window.

Finding a File

1. Open Windows Explorer.

2. Choose Tool, Find.

3. Select Files and Folders.

4. In Name, type **Readme*.***.

   Notice that wild cards are accepted here.

5. In Look in, select My Computer.

6. Click the Date Modified and make sure all files are selected.

7. Click Advanced Tab and make sure that Of Type is set to "All files and Folders."

8. Click Find Now.

9. How many Readme files did you find?

Lab

Lab 30: Understanding the Registries

 Note To complete this lab, you need one computer with Windows 95 installed. ▥

Viewing the Registry

1. Start your computer.
2. Click Start and choose Run.
3. Type **regedit**.
4. Click OK.
5. Double-click HKEY_Local_Machine.
6. Click Software.
7. Click Microsoft.
8. Click Windows.
9. Click Current Version.
10. What is the version number of your Windows 95?

Glossary

A

access time   If a file is executable, the last time it was run, otherwise, the last time the file was read or written to.

access-control entry (ACE)   An entry in an access-control list that defines a set of permissions for a group or user.

access-control list (ACL)   A list containing access-control-entries. An ACL determines the permissions associated with an object, which can be anything in a Win32 environment.

ACE   See *access-control entry*.

ACK   Short for **acknowledgment**. A control character sent to the other computer in a conversation. Usually used to indicate that transmitted information has been received correctly, when using a communications protocol, such as Xmodem.

ACL   See *access-control list.*

active window   The window the user is currently working with. Windows identifies the active window by highlighting its title bar and border.

Advanced Program-to-Program Communications (APPC) A method of interprogram communication, usually used by applications intended for use with IBM SNA-based networks.

Advanced Research Project Agency (ARPA)   The agency responsible for the formation of the forerunner of the Internet. See also *Defense Advanced Research Projects Agency.*

agent   Software that runs on a client computer for use by administrative software running on a server. Agents are typically used to support administrative actions, such as detecting system information or running services.

American National Standards Institute (ANSI)   A standards-making organization based in the United States of America.

American Standard Code for Information Interchange (ASCII)   A scheme that assigns letters, punctuation marks, etc., to specific numeric values. The standardization of ASCII enabled computers and computer programs to exchange data.

ANSI   See *American National Standards Institute.*

ANSI character set   An 8-bit character set used by Microsoft Windows that enables you to represent up to 256 characters (0–255) using your keyboard. The ASCII character set is a subset of the ANSI set. See *American National Standards Institute.*

API   See *application programming interface.*

APPC   See *Advanced Program-to-Program Communications*

application   A computer program that is designed to do some specific type of work. An application is different from a utility which performs some type of maintenance (such as formatting a disk).

application programming interface (API)   An API is a list of supported functions. Windows 95 supports the MS-DOS API, Windows

API, and Win32 API. If a function is a member of the API, it is said to be a supported, or documented function. Functions that make up Windows, but are not part of the API are referred to as *undocumented* functions.

ARPA   See *Advanced Research Project Agency*.

ASCII   See *American Standard Code for Information Interchange*.

ASCII character set   A 7 bit character set widely used to represent letters and symbols found on a standard U.S. keyboard. The ASCII character set is identical to the first 128 characters in the ANSI character set.

association   The process of assigning a filename extension to a particular application. When an extension has been associated with an application, Windows 95 will start the application when you choose to open the file from the Windows Explorer. Associations are critical to the concept of document-centric computing.

Audio Video Interleaved (AVI)   The format of the full-motion video files used by Windows 95.

Autoexec.bat   A file in the root directory of the boot disk that contains a list of MS-DOS commands that are automatically executed when the system is started. Autoexec.bat can be created by either the user or the operating system. Windows 95 Setup examines the Autoexec.bat file looking for hints.

auxiliary audio device   Audio devices whose output is mixed with the Musical Instrument Digital Interface (MIDI) and waveform output devices in a multimedia computer. An example of an auxiliary audio device is the compact disc audio output from a CD-ROM drive.

AVI   See *Audio Video Interleaved*.

B

background window   Any window created by a thread other than the thread running in the foreground.

Basic Input/Output System (BIOS)   The bootstrap code of a PC. The low-level routines that support the transfer of information between the various parts of a computer system, such as memory, disks, and the monitor. Usually built into the machine's read-only memory (ROM). The BIOS can have a significant effect on the performance of the computer system.

batch program   A file that contains one or more commands that are executed when you type the filename at the command prompt. Batch programs have the .BAT extension.

binding   The process that links a protocol driver and a network adapter driver.

BIOS   See *Basic Input/Output System*.

BIOS enumerator   In a Plug and Play system, the BIOS enumerator is responsible for identifying all of the hardware devices on the computer's motherboard.

bit   Short for **binary digit**, the smallest unit of data a computer can store. Bits are expressed as 1 or 0.

bitmap   Originally, an array of bits, but now expanded to include arrays of bytes or even 32 bit quantities that specify the dot pattern and colors that describe an image on the screen or printed paper.

BMP   The extension used for Windows bitmap files.

branch   A segment of the directory tree, representing a directory and any subdirectories it contains.

browse   To look through a list on a computer system. Lists include directories, files, domains, or computers.

buffer   A temporary holding place reserved in memory, where data is held while in transit to or from a storage device or another location in memory.

buffering   The process of using buffers, particularly to or from I/O devices such as disk drives and serial ports.

bus enumerator   A driver, responsible for building the hardware tree on a Plug and Play system.

byte   8 bits.

C

Card Services   A protected-mode VxD, linked with the PCMCIA bus drivers. Card Services passes event notifications from socket services to the PCMCIA bus driver, provides information from the computer's cards to the PCMCIA bus driver, and sets up the configuration for cards in the adapter sockets.

cascading menu   A menu that is a sub menu of a menu item. Also known as a hierarchical menu. The menus accessed via the Windows 95 Start Button are cascading menus.

CCITT   See *International Telephone and Telegraph Consultative Committee.*

CD-DA   See *Compact Disc-Digital Audio.*

CD-ROM   See *Compact Disc Read-Only Memory.*

CD-ROM/XA   See *Compact Disc Read-Only Memory Extended Architecture.*

CD-XA   See *Compact Disc-Extended Architecture.*

CDFS   See *compact disc file system.*

central processing unit (CPU)   The computational and control unit of a computer; the device that interprets and executes instructions. The CPU or microprocessor, in the case of a microcomputer, has the ability to fetch, decode and execute instructions and to transfer information to and from other resources over the computer's main data-transfer path, the bus. The CPU is the chip that functions as the "brain" of a computer.

character   A letter, number, punctuation mark, or a control code. Usually expressed in either the ANSI or ASCII character set.

character mode   A mode of displaying information on the screen, where all information is displayed using text characters (as opposed to graphical symbols). MS-DOS applications run in character mode.

check box   In the Windows 95 interface, a square box that has two or three states, and is used by the user to select an option from a set of options. A standard check box is a toggle, with two states: checked and unchecked. A three-state check box has an additional state: disabled (grayed).

class   For OLE, a data structure and the functions that manipulate that data structure. An object is a member of a class. For hardware, a grouping of devices and buses for the purpose of installing and managing devices and device drivers, and allocating the resources used by them. The Windows 95 hardware tree is organized by device class.

clear-to-send (CTS)   A signal sent from one computer to the other in a communications conversation to indicate readiness to accept data.

client   A computer that accesses shared network resources provided by another computer, called a server. See also *server*.

code names   A name assigned to conceal the identity or existence of something or someone. The code name for Microsoft Windows 95 was "Chicago," which still appears as an identifier in several places in the released product, including hardware setup files.

codec   **Co**mpression/**dec**ompression technology for digital video and stereo audio.

Command.com   The command processor for MS-DOS. Windows 95 loads Command.com to process commands typed in MS-DOS mode, or in an MS-DOS prompt.

communications protocol   The rules that govern a conversation between two computers that are communicating via an asynchronous connection. The use of a communications protocol ensures error-free delivery of the data being communicated.

communications resource   A device that provides a bidirectional, asynchronous data stream. Examples include serial and parallel ports, and modems. Applications access the resource through a service provider.

compact disc file system (CDFS)   Controls access to the contents of CD-ROM drivers.

Compact Disc–Digital Audio (CD-DA)   An optical data-storage format that provides for the storage of up to 73 minutes of high-quality digital-audio data on a compact disc. Also known as Red Book audio or music CD.

Compact Disc–Extended Architecture (CD-XA)   see *Compact Disc-Read-Only Memory Extended Architecture (CD-ROM/XA)*.

Compact Disc–Read-Only Memory (CD-ROM)   A form of storage characterized by high capacity (roughly 600 megabytes) and the use of laser optics rather than magnetic means for reading data.

Compact Disc–Read-Only Memory Extended Architecture (CD-ROM/XA)   An extended CD-ROM format developed by Philips, Sony, and Microsoft. CD-ROM/XA format is consistent with the ISO 9660 (High Sierra) standard, with further specification of ADPCM (adaptive differential pulse code modulation) audio, images, and interleaved data.

computer name   A unique name that identifies a particular computer on the network. Microsoft networking uses NetBIOS names, which can have up to 15 characters, and cannot contain spaces.

Config.sys   An ASCII text file that contains configuration commands. Used by MS-DOS, OS/2 and Windows 95 to load real-mode device drivers.

Configuration Manager   One of three central components of a Plug and Play system (one for each of the three phases of configuration management). The configuration managers drive the process of locating devices, setting up the hardware tree, and allocating resources.

context menu   The menu that is displayed at the location of a set menu that is displayed when you right click. It is called the context menu because the contents of the menu depend upon the context it is invoked in.

Control Panel   The primary Windows 95 configuration tool. Each option that you can change is represented by an icon in the Control Panel window.

Controller   See *Domain Controller.*

conventional memory   The first 640KB of memory in your computer, used to run real-mode MS-DOS applications.

cooperative multitasking   A form of multitasking in which threads cooperate with each other by voluntarily giving up control of the processor. See also *preemptive multitasking.*

CPU   See *central processing unit.*

crash   A serious failure of the software being used.

CTS   See *clear-to-send.*

cursor   A bitmap whose location on the screen is controlled by a pointing device, such as a mouse, pen, or trackball. See also *bitmap.*

D

DARPA   See *Defense Advanced Research Projects Agency.*

data frame   The structured packets into which data is placed by the Data Link layer.

datagram   A packet of information and delivery data that is routed on a network.

DDE   See *Dynamic Data Exchange.*

default   An operation or value that the system assumes, unless the user makes an explicit choice.

Defense Advanced Research Projects Agency (DARPA)   An agency of the U.S. Department of Defense that sponsored the development of the protocols that became the TCP/IP suite. DARPA was previously known as ARPA, the Advanced Research Project Agency, when ARPANET was built.

desktop   The background of your screen, on which windows, icons, and dialog boxes appear.

destination directory   The directory to which you intend to copy or move one or more files.

device   A generic term for a computer component, such as a printer, serial port, or disk drive. A device frequently requires its own controlling software called a device driver.

device contention   The method that Windows 95 uses to allocate access to peripheral devices when multiple applications are attempting to use them.

device driver   A piece of software that translates requests from one form into another. Most commonly, drivers are used to provide a device-independent way to access hardware.

device ID   A unique ASCII string created by enumerators to identify a hardware device and used to cross-reference data about the device stored in the Registry.

device node   One of the data structures that make up the hardware tree, a device node is built by the Configuration Manager into memory at system startup. Device nodes contain information about a given device, such as the resources it is using.

DHCP   See *Dynamic Host Configuration Protocol.*

dialog box   The type of window that is displayed by Windows 95 when user input is needed. Usually contains one or more buttons, edit controls, radio buttons, and drop-down lists.

dial-up networking   Formerly known as **remote access service (RAS)**, it provides remote access to networks. Dial-up networking allows a remote user to access their network. Once connected, it is as if the remote computer is logically on the network—the user can do anything that he or she could do when physically connected to the network.

DIP switch   Short for **Dual In-line Package switch**. Used to configure hardware options, especially on adapter cards.

Direct Memory Access (DMA)   A technique used by hardware adapters to store and retrieve information from the computer's RAM memory without involving the computer's CPU.

directory   Part of a structure for organizing your files on a disk. A directory can contain files and other directories (called subdirectories).

disk caching   A method to improve performance of the file system. A section of memory is used as a temporary holding place for frequently accessed file data. Windows 95 dynamically allocates its disk cache.

disk operating system (DOS)   See *MS-DOS*.

DLL   See *dynamic-link library*.

DMA   See *Direct Memory Access*.

DMA channel   A channel for DMA transfers, those that occur between a device and memory directly, without involving the CPU.

DNS   See *Domain Name Service*.

DNS name servers   The servers that hold the DNS name database, and supply the IP address that matches a DNS name in response to a request from a DNS client. See also *Domain Name Service*.

dock   To insert a portable computer into a base unit. Cold docking means the computer must begin from a power-off state and restart before docking. Hot docking means the computer can be docked while running at full power.

docking station   The base computer unit into which a user can insert a portable computer, to expand it to a desktop equivalent. Docking stations usually include drives, expansion slots, AC power, network and SCSI connections, and communication ports.

document   Whatever you work with in an application.

domain   For DNS, a group of workstations and servers that share a single group name. For Microsoft networking, a collection of computers that share a security context and account database stored on a Windows NT Server domain controllers. Each domain has a unique name. See also *Domain Name Service*.

Domain Controller   The Windows NT Server computer that authenticates domain logons and maintains a copy of the security database for the domain.

Domain Name Service (DNS)   A static, hierarchical name service for TCP/IP hosts. Do not confuse DNS domains with Windows NT domains.

DOS   See *Microsoft Disk Operating System*.

DOS Protected Mode Interface (DPMI)   A technique used to allow MS-DOS based applications to access extended memory.

dpi   Short for **dots per inch**. A measurement of the resolution of a monitor or printer.

DPMI   See *DOS Protected Mode Interface*.

drag and drop   To select one or more files, drag them to an open application, and drop them there.

DRAM   See *Dynamic Random-Access Memory*.

Dynamic Data Exchange (DDE)   A form of interprocess communication (IPC) implemented in the Microsoft Windows family of operating system. DDE uses shared memory to exchange data. Most DDE functions have been superseded by OLE.

Dynamic Host Configuration Protocol (DHCP)   A protocol for automatic TCP/IP configuration that provides static and dynamic address allocation and management.

Dynamic Random-Access Memory (DRAM)   A computer's main memory.

dynamic-link library (DLL)   A file functions compiled, linked, and saved separately from the processes that use them. Functions in DLLs can be used by more than one running process. The operating system maps the DLLs into the process's address space when the process is starting up or while it is running. Dynamic-link libraries are stored in files with the .DLL extension.

E

Eform   See *electronic mail form*.

EISA   See *Extended Industry Standard Architecture*.

electronic mail (e-mail)   A message in a electronic mail system.

electronic mail form (Eform)   A programmed form used to send e-mail in an electronic mail system.

electronic messaging system (EMS)   A system that allows users or applications to correspond using a store-and-forward system.

e-mail   See *electronic mail*.

EMM   See *Expanded Memory Manager*.

EMS   See *Expanded Memory Specification, electronic messaging system*.

Encapsulated PostScript (EPS)   A file format used to represent graphics written in the PostScript page description language.

enhanced metafile   An intermediate file format, consisting of GDI objects and commands, used in the Windows 95 printing system.

enumerator   A Plug and Play device driver that detects devices below its own device node, creates unique devices Ids, and reports to Configuration Manger during startup.

environment variable   A symbolic variable that represents some element of the operating system, such as a path, a filename, or other literal data. Typically used by batch files, environment variables are created with the SET command.

EPROM   See *Erasable Programmable Read-Only Memory.*

EPS   See *Encapsulated PostScript.*

EPS file   A file containing code written in the Encapsulated PostScript printer programming language. Often used to represent graphics for use by desktop publishing applications.

Erasable Programmable Read-Only Memory (EPROM)
A computer chip containing non-volatile memory. It can be erased (for reprogramming) by exposure to an ultraviolet light.

event   An action or occurrence to which an application might respond, such as mouse clicks, key presses, mouse movements, or a system event. System events are any significant occurrence that may require user notification, or some other action by an application.

expanded memory   Memory that complies with the Lotus-Intel-Microsoft Expanded Memory specification. Used by MS-DOS based spreadsheet applications.

Expanded Memory Manager (EMM)   The device driver that controls access to expanded memory. In Windows 95, the EMM is EMM386.exe.

Expanded Memory Specification (EMS)   The specification that controls and defines Expanded Memory. Also known as the Lotus-Intel-Microsoft (LIM) specification, after the three major companies that designed it.

Extended Industry Standard Architecture (EISA)   An enhancement to the bus architecture used on the IBM PC/AT, which allows the use of 32-bit devices in the same type of expansion slot used by an ISA adapter card. EISA slots and adapters were formerly common in server computers, but have been mostly replaced with PCI slots.

extended memory   Memory that occupies physical addresses above the 1 megabyte mark.

Extended Memory Manager (XMM)   The device driver that provides access to XMS memory. In Windows 95, the XMM is Himem.sys.

Extended Memory Specification (XMS) The specification for the application program interfaces that allow an application to access and use extended memory.

F

family name The name of a given font family. Windows employs five family names—*Decorative, Modern, Roman, Script, and Swiss.* A sixth family name, *Dontcare,* specifies the default font. See also *font family.*

FAT See *file allocation table.*

FAT file system A file system based on a file allocation table. Windows 95 uses a 32-bit implementation called VFAT. See also *file allocation table, virtual file allocation table.*

FIFO See *First In, First Out.*

file A collection of information stored on a disk, and accessible using a name.

file allocation table (FAT) A table or list maintained by some operating systems to keep track of the status of various segments of disk space used for file storage. See also *virtual file allocation table.*

file attribute A characteristic of a file that indicates whether the file is read only, hidden, system, archived, a directory, or normal.

file sharing The ability of a network computer to share files or directories on its local disks with remote computers. Windows 95 allows you to share your files if the File and Print Sharing services are enabled on your computer.

file system In an operating system, the overall structure in which files are named, stored, and organized.

file time A 64 bit value representing the number of 100-nanosecond intervals that have elapsed since January 1, 1601.

file transfer program (FTP) A utility defined by the TCP/IP protocol suite, used to transfer files between dissimilar systems.

file transfer protocol (FTP)   The standard method of transferring files using TCP/IP. FTP allows you to transfer files between dissimilar computers, with preservation of binary data, and optional translation of text file formats.

First In, First Out (FIFO)   Used to describe a buffer, where data is retrieved from the buffer in the same order it went in.

floppy disk   A disk that can be inserted in and removed from a disk drive.

focus   The area of a dialog box which receives input. The focus is indicated by highlighted text or a button enclosed in dotted lines.

folder   In Windows Explorer, a container object, that is, an object that can contain other objects. Examples include disk folders, the fonts folder, and the printers folder.

font   A collection of characters, each of which has a similar appearance—for example, the Arial font.

font family   A group of fonts that have similar characteristics.

font mapper   The routine within Windows that maps an application's request for a font with particular characteristics to the available font that best matches those characteristics.

frame   See *data frame*.

free space   Unused space on a hard disk.

friendly name   A human-readable name used to give an alternative to the often cryptic computer, port and sharenames. For example, "Digital 1152 Printer In The Hall" as opposed to "HALLPRT."

FTP   See *file transfer program, file transfer protocol*.

G

gateway   A computer connected to multiple networks, and capable of moving data between networks using different transport protocols.

GDI See *graphics device interface.*

graphical user interface (GUI) A computer system design in which the user interacts with the system using graphical symbols, tools and events, rather than text-based displays and commands, such as the normal Windows 95 user interface.

graphics device interface (GDI) The subsystem that implements graphic drawing functions.

GUI See *graphical user interface.*

H

handle An interface (usually a small black square) added to an object to enable the user to move, size, reshape, or otherwise modify the object.

hardware branch The hardware archive root key in the Registry, which is a superset of the memory-resident hardware tree. The name of this key is Hkey_Local_Machine\Hardware.

hardware tree A record in RAM of the current system configuration, based on the configuration information for all devices in the hardware branch of the Registry. The Hardware tree is created each time the computer is started or whenever a dynamic change occurs to the system configuration.

high memory area (HMA) A 64K memory block located just above the 1 MB address in a Virtual DOS Machine (VDM). Originally made possible by a side-effect of the 80286 processor design, the memory is usable when the A20 address line is turned on.

High-Performance File System (HPFS) File System primarily used with OS/2 operating system Version 1.2 or later. It supports long filenames but does not provide security. Windows 95 will detect HPFS partitions, but cannot use them.

Hive A discrete body of Registry information, usually stored in a single disk file.

HKEY_CLASSES_ROOT   The Registry tree that contains data relating to OLE. This key is a symbolic link to a subkey of HKEY_LOCAL_MACHINE\SOFTWARE.

HKEY_CURRENT_USER   The Registry tree that contains the currently logged in user's preferences, including desktop settings, application settings and network connections. This key maps to a subkey of HKEY_USERS.

HKEY_LOCAL_MACHINE   The Registry tree that contains configuration settings that apply to the hardware and software on the computer.

HKEY_USERS   The Registry tree that contains the preferences for every user that ever logged onto this computer.

HMA   See *high memory area.*

home directory   A directory that is accessible to a particular user and contains that user's files and programs on a network server.

host   Any device that is attached to the internetwork and uses TCP/IP.

host ID   The portion of the IP address that identifies a computer within a particular network ID.

host name   The name of an internet host. It may or may not be the same as the computer name. In order for a client to access resources by host name, it must appear in the client's HOSTS file, or be resolvable by a DNS server.

host table   The HOSTS and LMHOSTS files, which contain mappings of known IP addresses mapped to host names.

HOSTS file   A local text file in the same format as the 4.3 Berkeley Software Distribution (BSD) UNIX /etc/hosts file. This file maps host names to IP addresses. In Windows 95, this file is stored in the \WINDOWS directory.

hot key   Keystrokes used in place of mouse clicks.

HPFS   See *High-Performance File System.*

I

I/O addresses   One of the critical resources used in configuring devices. I/O addresses are used to communicate with devices. Also known as **port**.

I/O bus   The electrical connection between the CPU and the I/O devices. There are several types of I/O buses: ISA, EISA, SCSI, VLB and PCI.

I/O device   Any device in or attached to a computer that is designed to receive information from, or provide information to the computer. For example, a printer is an output-only device, while a mouse is an input-only device. Other devices, such as modems, are both input and output devices, transferring data in both directions. Windows 95 must have a device driver installed in order to be able to use an I/O device.

ICMP   See *Internet control message protocol.*

icon   A small bitmap (usually 16 × 16 pixels or 32 × 32 pixels) that is associated with an application, file type, or a concept.

IEEE   See *Institute of Electrical and Electronic Engineers.*

IETF   See *Internet Engineering Task Force.*

IFS   See *installable file system.*

IHV   See *independent hardware vendor.*

independent hardware vendor (IHV)   A manufacturer of computer hardware. Usually used to describe the makers of add-on devices, rather than makers of computer systems.

Industry Standard Architecture (ISA)   A computer system that is built on the Industry Standard Architecture is one that adheres to the same design rules and constraints that the IBM PC/AT adhered to.

INF file   A file, usually provided by the manufacturer of a device, that provides the information that Windows 95 Setup needs in order to set up a device. INF files usually include a list of valid logical configurations for the device, the names of driver files associated with the device, and other information.

INI files   Initialization files used by Windows-based applications to store configuration information. Windows 95 supports INI files for backwards compatibility. Also known as .ini files (pronounced "dot-I-N-I").

installable file system (IFS)   A file system that can be installed into the operating system as needed, rather than just at startup time. Windows 95 can support multiple installable file systems at one time, including the file allocation table (FAT) file system, network redirectors and the CD-ROM file system (CDFS).

instance   A particular occurrence of an object, such as a window, module, named pipe, or DDE session. Each instance has a unique handle that distinguishes it from other instances of the same type.

Institute of Electrical and Electronic Engineers (IEEE)   An organization that issues standards for electrical and electronic devices.

Integrated Services Digital Network (ISDN)   A digital communications method that permits connections of up to 128Kbps. ISDN requires a special adapter for your computer. An ISDN connection is available in most areas of the United States for a reasonable cost.

internal command   Commands that are built-in to the Command.com file.

International Organization for Standardization (ISO)   The organization that produces many of the world's standards. Open Systems Interconnect (OSI) is only one of many areas standardized by the ISO.

International Telephone and Telegraph Consultative Committee (CCITT)   International organization that creates and publishes telecommunications standards, including X.400. The initials CCITT actually stand for the real name of the organization, which is in French.

Internet   The worldwide interconnected wide-area network, based on the TCP/IP protocol suite.

Internet control message protocol (ICMP)   A required protocol in the TCP/IP protocol suite. It allows two nodes on an IP network to share IP status and error information. ICMP is used by the ping utility.

Internet Engineering Task Force (IETF)   A consortium that introduces procedures for new technology on the Internet. IETF specifications are released in documents called Requests for Comments (RFCs).

Internet group name   A name known by a DNS server that includes a list of the specific addresses of systems that have registered the name.

Internet protocol (IP)   The Network layer protocol of TCP/IP, responsible for addressing and sending TCP packets over the network.

interprocess communications (IPC)   A set of mechanisms used by applications to communicate and share data.

interrupt   An event that disrupts normal processing by the CPU, and results in the transfer of control to an interrupt handler. Both hardware devices and software can issue interrupts—software executes an INT instruction, while hardware devices signal the CPU by using one of the interrupt request (IRQ) lines to the processor.

interrupt request level (IRQL)   Interrupts are ranked by priority. Interrupts that have a priority lower than the processor's interrupt request level setting can be masked (ignored).

interrupt request lines (IRQ)   Hardware lines on the CPU that devices use to send signals to cause an interrupt. Normally, only one device is attached to any particular IRQ line.

IP   See *Internet protocol.*

IP address   Used to identify a node on a network and to specify routing information on an internetwork. Each node on the internetwork must be assigned a unique IP address, which is made up of the network ID, plus a unique host ID assigned by the network administrator. The subnet mask is used to separate an IP address into the host ID and network ID. In Windows 95, you can either assign an IP address manually, or automatically using DHCP.

IP router   A system connected to multiple physical TCP/IP networks that can route or deliver IP packets between the networks. See also *gateway.*

IPC   See *interprocess communications.*

IPX/SPX   Internetworking Packet eXchange / Sequenced Packet eXchange. Transport protocols used in Novell NetWare networks. Windows 95 includes the Microsoft IPX/SPX compatible transport protocol.

IRQ   See *interrupt request level*.

IRQL   See *interrupt request lines*.

ISA   See *Industry Standard Architecture*.

ISDN   See *Integrated Services Digital Network*.

ISO Development Environment (ISODE)   A research tool developed to study the upper-layer of OSI. Academic and some commercial ISO products are based on this framework.

ISO   See *International Organization for Standardization*.

ISODE   See *ISO Development Environment*.

K

K   Standard abbreviation for kilobyte; equals 1024 bytes.

Kbps   Kilobits per second

Kernel   The Windows 95 core component responsible for implementing the basic operating system functions of Windows 95 including virtual memory management, task scheduling and File I/O services. The Kernel is completely 32 bit, and its implementation is in Kernel32.dll.

L

LAN   See *local area network*.

legacy   Hardware and device cards that don't conform to the Plug and Play standard.

link   A connection at the LLC layer that is uniquely defined by the adapter's address and the destination service access point (DSAP). Also, a connection between two objects, or a reference to an object that is linked to another.

list box   In a dialog box, a box that lists available choices. For example, a list of all files in a directory. If all the choices do not fit in the list box, there is a scroll bar.

LLC   See *logical link control.*

LMHOSTS file   A local text file that maps IP addresses to the computer names of Windows networking computers. In Windows 95, LMHOSTS is stored in the WINDOWS directory.

local area network (LAN)   A computer network confined to a single building or campus.

local printer   A printer that is directly connected to one of the ports on your computer, as opposed to a network printer.

localization   The process of adapting software for different countries, languages, or cultures.

logical drive   A division of an extended partition on a hard disk, accessed using a drive letter.

logical link control (LLC)   One of the two sub-layers of the Data Link layer of the OSI reference model, as defined by the IEEE 802 standards. See Logical Link Control (LLC) Sublayer in Chapter 15 for more information.

login   The process by which a user is identified to the computer in a Novell NetWare network.

logon   The process by which a user is identified to the computer in a Microsoft network.

logon script. In Microsoft networking, a batch file that runs automatically when a user logs into a Windows NT Server. Novell networking also uses logon scripts, but they are not batch files.

M

M   Standard abbreviation for megabyte, or 1,024 kilobytes.

MAC   See *media access control.*

MAC address   The address for a device as it is identified at the media access control layer in the network architecture. MAC addresses are usually stored in ROM on the network adapter card, and are unique.

machine directory   The directory that contains required configuration files for a particular computer in a shared Windows 95 installation. The machine directory contains WIN.COM, the Registry, and startup configuration files.

mailslot   A form of interprocess communications used to carry messages from an application on one network node to another. Mailslots are one-way.

mailslot client   A process that writes a message to a mailslot.

mailslot server   A process that creates and owns a mailslot and can read messages from it. See also *process.*

management information base (MIB)   A set of objects used by SNMP to manage devices. MIB objects represent various types of information about a device.

map   To translate one value into another.

MAPI   See *Messaging Application Program Interface.*

mapped I/O, or mapped file I/O   This is the file I/O that is performed by reading and writing to virtual memory that is backed by a file.

MCI   See *Media Control Interface.*

MDI   See *multiple document interface.*

media access control (MAC)   The lower of the two sublayers of the data-link layer in the IEEE 802 network model.

Media Control Interface (MCI)   High-level control software that provides a device-independent interface to multimedia devices and media files. MCI includes a command–message interface and a command-string interface.

memory   A temporary storage area for information and applications.

memory object   A number of bytes allocated from the heap.

message   A structure or set of parameters used for communicating information or a request. Every event that happens in the system causes a message to be sent. Messages can be passed between the operating system and an application, different applications, threads within an application, and windows within an application.

message loop   A program loop that retrieves messages from a thread's message queue and dispatches them.

Messaging Application Program Interface (MAPI)   A set of calls used to add mail-enabled features to other Windows-based applications. One of the WOSA technologies.

metafile   A collection of structures that stores a picture in a device-independent format. (There are two metafile formats—the enhanced format and the Windows format.)

MIB   See *management information base*.

Microsoft Disk Operating System (MS-DOS)   The dominant operating system for personal computers from the introduction of the IBM Personal Computer until the introduction of Windows 95.

MIDI   See *Musical Instrument Digital Interface*.

minidriver   The part of the device driver that is written by the hardware manufacturer, and provides device-specific functionality.

MS-DOS   See *Microsoft Disk Operating System*.

MS-DOS based application   An application designed to run under MS-DOS. Windows 95 supports most MS-DOS based applications.

multiple document interface (MDI)   A specification that defines the standard user interface for Windows-based applications. An MDI application enables the user to work with more than one document at the same time. Microsoft Word is an example of an MDI application. Each of the documents is displayed in a separate window inside the application's main window.

multitasking   The process by which an operating system creates the illusion that many tasks are executing simultaneously on a single processor. See also *cooperative multitasking, preemptive multitasking.*

multithreading   The ability of a process to have multiple, simultaneous paths of execution (*threads*).

Musical Instrument Digital Interface (MIDI)   A standard protocol for communication between musical instruments and computers.

mutex object   An interprocess synchronization object whose state is signaled when it is not owned by any thread, and nonsignaled when it is owned. Only one thread at a time can own a mutex. Windows 95 uses a mutex, called Win16Mutex to protect non-reentrant segments of 16-bit code. Mutex is derived from the term MUTally EXclusive.

N

name registration   The way a computer registers its unique name with a name server on the network, such as a WINS server.

name resolution   The process used on the network to determine the address of a computer by using its name.

named pipe   A one-way or two-way pipe used for communications between a server process and one or more client processes. A server process specifies a name when it creates one or more instances of a named pipe. Each instance of the pipe can be connected to a client. Microsoft SQL Server clients use named pipes to communicate with the SQL Server.

NBF transport protocol   NetBEUI frame protocol. A descendant of the NetBEUI protocol, which is a Transport layer protocol, not the programming interface NetBIOS.

NCB   See *network control block.*

NDIS   See *network device interface specification.*

NetBEUI transport   NetBIOS (Network Basic Input/Output System) Extended User Interface. A transport protocol designed for use on small subnets. It is not routable, but it is fast.

NetBIOS interface   A programming interface that allows I/O requests to be sent to and received from a remote computer. It hides networking hardware from applications.

NetBIOS Over TCP/IP   The networking module that provides the functionality to support NetBIOS name registration and resolution across a TCP/IP network.

network   A group of computers and other devices that can interact by means of a shared communications link.

network adapter driver   Software that implements the lower layers of a network, providing a standard interface to the network card.

network basic input/output system (NetBIOS)   A software interface for network communication. See also *NetBIOS interface.*

network control block (NCB)   A memory structured used to communicate with the NetBIOS interface.

Network DDE DSDM service   The Network DDE DSDM (DDE share database manager) service manages shared DDE conversations. It is used by the Network DDE service.

Network DDE service   The Network DDE (dynamic data exchange) service provides a network transport and security for DDE conversations. Network DDE is supported in Windows 95 for backwards compatibility, as most of its functions are superseded by OLE.

network device driver   Software that coordinates communication between the network adapter card and the computer's hardware and other software, controlling the physical function of the network adapter cards.

network device interface specification (NDIS)   In Windows networking, the interface for network adapter drivers. All transport drivers call the NDIS interface to access network adapter cards.

network directory   See *shared directory*.

Network File System (NFS)   A service for distributed computing systems that provides a distributed file system, eliminating the need for keeping multiple copies of files on separate computers. Usually used in connection with UNIX computers. Windows 95 does not include an NFS client, although it does support third-party NFS clients.

network ID   The portion of the IP address that identifies a group of computers and devices located on the same logical network. Separated from the Host ID using the subnet mask.

Network Information Service (NIS)   A service for distributed computing systems that provides a distributed database system for common configuration files.

network interface card (NIC)   An adapter card that connects a computer to a network.

network operating system (NOS)   The operating system used on network servers, such as Windows NT Server or Novell NetWare.

network provider   The Windows 95 component that allows Windows 95 to communicate with the network. Windows 95 includes providers for Microsoft networks and for Novell NetWare networks. Other network vendors supply providers for their networks.

network transport   This can be either a particular layer of the OSI Reference Model between the network layer and the session layer, or the protocol used between this layer on two different computers on a network.

network-interface printers   Printers with built-in network cards, such as Hewlett-Packard laser printers equipped with Jet Direct cards. The advantage of network-interface printers is that they can be located anywhere on the network.

New Technology file system (NTFS)   The native file system used by Windows NT. Windows 95 can detect, but not use, NTFS partitions.

NFS   See *Network File System*.

NIC   See *network interface card*.

NIS   See *Network Information Service*.

NOS   See *network operating system*.

NTFS   See *Windows NT file system*.

O

object linking and embedding (OLE)   The specification that details the implementation of Windows Objects, and the interprocess communication that supports them.

object   A particular instance of a class. Most of the internal data structures in Windows 95 are objects.

OCR   See *Optical Character Recognition*.

OEM   See *original equipment manufacturer*.

OLE   See *object linking and embedding*.

Open Systems Interconnect (OSI)   The networking architecture reference model created by the ISO.

operating system (OS)   The software that provides an interface between a user or application and the computer hardware. Operating system services usually include memory and resource management, I/O services and file handling. Examples include Windows 95, Windows NT and UNIX.

Optical Character Recognition (OCR)   A technology that is used to generate editable text from a graphic image.

original equipment manufacturer (OEM)   Software that is sold by Microsoft to OEMs only includes the operating system versions that are pre-loaded on computers before they are sold.

OS   See *operating system*.

OSI   See *Open Systems Interconnect*.

P

PAB   See *personal address book.*

packet   A transmission unit of fixed maximum size that consists of binary information representing both data, addressing information and error-correction information, created by the data-link layer.

page   A unit of memory used by the system in managing memory. The size of a page is computer-dependent (the Intel 386 computer, and therefore, Windows 95, uses 4K pages).

page map   An internal data structure used by the system to keep track of the mapping between the pages in a process's virtual address space, and the corresponding pages in physical memory.

paged pool   The portion of system memory that can be paged to disk.

paging file   A storage file the system uses to hold pages of memory swapped out of RAM. Also known as a swap file.

parity   Refers to an error-checking procedure in which the number of 1's must always be the same (either even or odd) for each group of bits transmitted without error. Also used in the main RAM system of a computer to verify the validity of data contained in RAM.

partition   A partition is a portion of a physical disk that functions as though it were a physically separate unit. See also *system partition.*

partition table   The partition table contains entries showing the start and end point of each of the primary partitions on the disk. The partition table can hold four entries.

password   A security measure used to restrict access to computer systems. A password is a unique string of characters that must be provided before a logon or an access is authorized.

path   The location of a file or directory. The path describes the location in relation to either the root directory, or the current directory, for example, C:\Windows\System. Also, a graphic object that represents one or more shapes.

PCI   See *Peripheral Component Interconnect.*

PCMCIA   See *Personal Computer Memory Card International Association.*

performance monitoring   The process of determining the system resources an application uses, such as processor time and memory. Done with the Windows 95 System Monitor.

Peripheral Component Interconnect (PCI)   The local bus being promoted as the successor to VL. This type of device is used in most Intel Pentium computers and in the Apple PowerPC Macintosh.

persistent connection   A network connection that is restored automatically when the user logs on. In Windows 95, persistent connections are created by selecting the Reconnect at Logon checkbox.

personal address book (PAB)   One of the information services provided with the Microsoft Exchange client included with Windows 95. It is used to store the name and e-mail address of people you correspond with.

Personal Computer Memory Card International Association (PCMCIA)   The industry association of manufacturers of credit-card sized adapter cards (PC cards).

PIF   See *program information file.*

pixel   Short for **picture element**, a dot that represents the smallest graphic unit of measurement on a screen. The actual size of a pixel is screen-dependent, and varies according to the size of the screen and the resolution being used. Also known as **pel**.

platform   The hardware and software required for an application to run.

Plug and Play   A computer industry specification, intended to ease the process of configuring hardware.

Plug and Play BIOS   A BIOS with responsibility for configuring Plug and Play cards and system board devices during system power-up, provides run-time configuration services for system board devices after startup.

p-node   A NetBIOS implementation that uses point-to-point communications with a name server to resolve names as IP addresses

Point to Point protocol (PPP)   The industry standard that is implemented in dial-up networking. PPP is a line protocol used to connect to remote networking services, including Internet Service Providers. Prior to the introduction of PPP, another line protocol, SLIP, was used.

pointer   The arrow-shaped cursor on the screen that follows the movement of a mouse (or other pointing device) and indicates which area of the screen will be affected when you press the mouse button. The pointer may change shape during certain tasks.

port   The socket that you connect the cable for a peripheral device to. See also *I/O addresses*.

port ID   The method TCP and UDP use to specify which application running on the system is sending or receiving the data.

Postoffice   The message store used by Microsoft Mail to hold the mail messages. It exists only as a structure of directories on disk, and does not contain any active components.

PostScript   A page-description language, developed by Adobe Systems, Inc., that offers flexible font capability and high-quality graphics. PostScript uses English-like commands to control page layout and to load and scale fonts.

PPP   See *Point to Point protocol*.

preemptive multitasking   A multitasking technique that breaks time up into timeslices, during which the operating system allows a particular program thread to run. The operating system can interrupt any running thread at any time. Preemptive multitasking usually results in the best use of CPU time, and overall better perceived throughput. See also *cooperative multitasking*.

primary partition   A primary partition is a portion of a physical disk that can be marked for use by an operating system. There can be up to four primary partitions (or up to three, if there is an extended partition) per physical disk. A primary partition cannot be subpartitioned.

print device   Refers to the actual hardware device that produces printed output.

print monitor   Keeps track of printers and print devices. Responsible for transferring information from the print driver to the printing device, including any necessary flow control.

print provider   A software component that allows the client to print to a network printer. Windows 95 includes print providers for Microsoft networks and Novell networks.

printer driver   The component that translates GDI objects into printer commands.

printer fonts   Fonts that are built into your printer.

priority class   A process priority category (high, normal, or idle) used to determine the scheduling priorities of a process's threads. Each priority class has five levels. See also *thread*.

private memory   Memory owned by a process, and not accessible by other processes.

privileged instruction   Processor-privileged instructions have access to system memory and the hardware. Privileged instructions can only be executed by Ring 0 components.

process   The virtual address space, code, data, and other operating system resources, such as files, pipes, and synchronization objects that make up a an executing application. In addition to resources, a process contains at least one thread that executes the process's code.

profile   A set of data describing a particular configuration of a computer. This information can describe a user's preferences (user profile) or the hardware configuration. Profiles are usually stored in the Registry, for example, the key HKEY_USERS contains the profiles for the various users of the computer.

program file   A file that starts an application or program. A program file has an .exe, .pif, .com, or .bat filename extension.

program information file (PIF)   Windows 95 stores information about how to configure the VM for running MS-DOS applications in PIF files.

Programmable Read-Only Memory (PROM)   A type of integrated circuit usually used to store a computer's BIOS. PROM chips, once programmed, can only be read from, not written to.

PROM   See *Programmable Read-Only Memory.*

properties   In Windows 95, the dialogs that are used to configure a particular object.

protocol   A set of rules and conventions by which two computers pass messages across a network. Protocols are used between instances of a particular layer on each computer. Windows 95 includes NetBEUI, TCP/IP, and IPX/SPX–compatible protocols. See also *communications protocol.*

provider   The component that allows Windows 95 to communicate with the network. Windows 95 includes providers for Microsoft and Novell networks.

push installation   A method of installing Windows 95 automatically. Push installations are mandatory, and usually implemented using the network logon script.

R

random access memory (RAM)   The RAM memory in a computer is the computer's main memory, where programs and data are stored while the program is running. Information stored in RAM is lost when the computer is turned off.

read-only   A device, document or file is read-only if you are not permitted to make changes to it.

read-write   A device, document or file is read-write if you can make changes to it.

reboot   To restart a computer. To reboot a Windows 95 computer, click the Start Button, choose Shutdown, and then choose Restart Your Computer.

redirector   The networking component that intercepts file I/O requests and translates them into network requests. Redirectors (also called **network clients**) are implemented as installable file system drivers in Windows 95.

REG_BINARY   A data type for Registry value entries that designates binary data.

REG_DWORD   A data type for Registry value entries that designates data represented by a number that is four bytes long.

REG_SZ   A data type for Registry value entries that designates a data string that usually represents human readable text.

Registry   Windows 95's and Windows NT's binary system configuration database.

Registry Editor (Regedit.exe)   A utility supplied with the CD-ROM version of Windows 95 that allows the user to view and edit Registry keys and values.

Registry key   A Registry entry that can contain other Registry entries.

remote access service (RAS)   See *dial-up networking*.

remote administration   The process of administrating one computer from another computer across a network.

remote initiation program load (RIPL)   A technique that allows a workstation to boot by using an image file on a network server instead of a disk.

remote procedure call (RPC)   An industry-standard method of interprocess communication across a network. Used by many administration tools.

Requests for Comments (RFCs)   The official documents of the Internet Engineering Task Force that specify the details for protocols included in the TCP/IP family.

requirements   The conceptual design and functional description of a software product, and any associated materials. Requirements describe the features, user interface, documentation, and other functionalities the product will provide.

resource   Windows resources include icons, cursors, menus, dialog boxes, bitmaps, fonts, keyboard-accelerator tables, message-table entries, string-table entries, version data, and user-defined data. The resources used by an application are either part of the system, or private resources stored in the application's program file. Also, a part of a computer system that can be assigned to a running process, such as a disk drive, or memory segment.

RFCs   See *Requests for Comments*.

RIP   See *routing information protocol*.

RIPL   See *remote initiation program load*.

router   A computer with two or more network adapters, each attached to a different subnet. The router forwards packets on a subnet to the subnet that they are addressed to.

routing   The process of forwarding packets until they reach their destination.

routing information protocol (RIP)   A protocol that supports dynamic routing. Used between routers.

RPC   See *remote procedure call*.

RPC server   The program or computer that processes remote procedure calls from a client.

S

screen buffer   A memory buffer that holds a representation of an MS-DOS VM's logical screen.

screen saver   Pictures or patterns that appear on your screen when your computer has not been used for a certain amount of time. Originally intended to protect the monitor from damage, modern screen savers are used mostly for their entertainment value.

scroll   To move through text or graphics (up, down, left, or right) in order to see parts of the file that cannot fit on the screen.

scroll arrow   An arrow on either end of a scroll bar that you use to scroll through the contents of the window or list box.

scroll bar   A bar that appears at the right and/or bottom edge of a window or list box whose contents are not completely visible. The scroll bar consists of two scroll arrows and a scroll box, which you use to scroll through the contents.

scroll box   In a scroll bar, a small box that shows where the information currently visible is, relative to the contents of the entire window.

SCSI   See *Small Computer System Interface*.

sequence number   Sequence numbers are used by a receiving node to properly order packets.

Serial Line Internet Protocol (SLIP)   The predecessor to PPP, SLIP is a line protocol supporting TCP/IP over a modem connection. SLIP support must be added to Windows 95. See also *Point to Point protocol*.

server message block (SMB)   A block of data that contains a work request from a workstation to a server, or that contains the response from the server to the workstation. SMBs are used for all network communications in a Microsoft network.

server   A computer or application that provides shared resources to clients across a network. Resources include files and directories, printers, fax modems, and network database services. See also *client*.

service   A process that performs a specific system function and often provides an application programming interface (API) for other processes to call. Windows 95 services include File and Print Sharing and the various backup agents.

session   A layer of the OSI reference model that performs name recognition and the functions needed to allow two applications to communicate over the network. Also, a communication channel established by the session layer.

share   In Microsoft networking, the process of making resources, such as directories and printers, available for network users.

share name   The name that a shared resource is accessed by on the network.

shared directory   A directory that has been shared so that network users can connect to.

shared memory   Memory that two or more processes can read from and write to.

shared network directory   See *shared directory*.

shared resource   Any device, data, or program that is used by more than one other device or program. Windows 95 can share directories and printers.

sharepoint   A shared network resource, or the name that one is known by.

shell   The part of an operating system that the user interacts with. The Windows 95 shell is Windows Explorer.

shortcut key   A combination of keys that result in the execution of a program, or selection of an option, without going through a menu.

shut down   The process of properly terminating all running programs, flushing caches, and preparing the system to be powered off.

signaled   One of the possible states of a mutex.

SIMM   See *Single In-Line Memory Module*.

Simple Mail Transfer Protocol (SMTP)   The application layer protocol that supports messaging functions over the Internet.

Simple Network Management Protocol (SNMP)   A standard protocol for the management of network components. Windows 95 includes an SNMP agent.

Single In-Line Memory Module (SIMM)   One of the types of RAM chips.

SLIP See *Serial Line Internet Protocol.*

Small Computer System Interface (SCSI) A standard for connecting multiple devices to a computer system. SCSI devices are connected together in a daisy chain, which can have up to seven devices (plus a controller) on it. (Pronounced "scuzzy.")

SMB See *server message block.*

SMTP See *Simple Mail Transfer Protocol.*

SNMP See *Simple Network Management Protocol.*

socket A channel used for incoming and outgoing data defined by the Windows Sockets API. Usually used with TCP/IP.

socket services The protected-mode VxD that manages PCMCIA sockets adapter hardware. It provides a protected-mode PCMCIA Socket Services 2.x interface for use by Card Services. A socket services driver is required for each socket adapter.

source directory The directory where files in a copy or move operation start out in.

spooler A scheduler for the printing process. It coordinates activity among other components of the print model and schedules all print jobs arriving at the print server.

static VxD A VxD that is loaded at system startup.

string A sequence of characters representing human-readable text.

subdirectory A directory within a directory.

subkey A Registry key contained within another Registry key. All Registry keys are subkeys except for the six top level keys.

subnet On the Internet, any lower network that is part of the logical network identified by the network ID.

subnet mask A 32 bit value that is used to distinguish the network ID portion of the IP address from the host ID.

swap file A special file on your hard disk that is used to hold memory pages that are swapped out of RAM. Also called a **paging file**.

syntax The order in which you must type a command and the elements that follow the command.

system directory The directory that contains the Windows DLLs and drivers. Usually c\windows\system.

system disk A disk that contains the files necessary to start an operating system.

system partition The volume that contains the hardware-specific files needed to load Windows 95.

T

TAPI See *Telephony Application Program Interface.*

TCP/IP transport Transmission Control Protocol / Internet Protocol. The primary wide area network (WAN) transport protocol used on the worldwide Internet, which is a world-wide internetwork of universities, research laboratories, military installations, organizations, and corporations. TCP/IP includes standards for how computers communicate and conventions for connecting networks and routing traffic, as well as specifications for utilities.

TCP See *Transmission Control Protocol.*

TDI See *transport driver interface.*

Telephony Application Program Interface (TAPI) An API that enables applications to control modems and telephony equipment in a device-independent manner. TAPI routes application function calls to the appropriate "Service Provider" DLL for a modem.

telnet The application layer protocol that provides virtual terminal service on TCP/IP networks.

Terminate and Stay-Resident (TSR) A technique, used by MS-DOS applications, that allow more than one program to be loaded at a time.

text file A file containing only ASCII letters, numbers, and symbols, without any formatting information except for carriage return/ linefeeds.

thread   The basic entity to which the operating system allocates CPU time. A thread can execute any part of the application's code, including a part currently being executed by another thread (re-entrancy). Threads cannot own resources, instead, they use the resources of the process they belong to.

thread local storage   A storage method in which an index can be used by multiple threads of the same process to store and retrieve a different value for each thread. See also *thread*.

thunking   The transformation between 16-bit and 32-bit formats, which is carried out by a separate layer in the VDM.

time-out   If a device is not performing a task, the amount of time the computer should wait before detecting it as an error.

toolbar   A frame containing a series of shortcut buttons providing quick access to commands, usually located below the menu bar, although many applications provide "dockable" toolbars which may be moved to different locations on the screen.

Transmission Control Protocol (TCP)   A connection-based protocol, responsible for breaking data into packets, which the IP protocol sends over the network. This protocol provides a reliable, sequenced communication stream for internetwork communication.

Transmission Control Protocol/Internet Protocol (TCP/IP) The primary wide area network used on the world-wide Internet, which is a world-wide internetwork of universities, research laboratories, military installations, organizations, and corporations. TCP/IP includes standards for how computers communicate and conventions for connecting networks and routing traffic, as well as specifications for utilities.

transport driver interface (TDI)   The interface between the session layer and the network layer, used by network redirectors and servers to send network-bound requests to network transport drivers.

transport protocol   Defines how data should be presented to the next receiving layer in the networking model and packages the data accordingly. It passes data to the network adapter card driver through the NDIS Interface, and to the redirector through the Transport Driver Interface.

TrueType fonts   Fonts that are scaleable and sometimes generated as bitmaps or soft fonts, depending on the capabilities of your printer. TrueType fonts can be sized to any height, and they print exactly as they appear on the screen. They are stored as a collection of line and curve commands, together with a collection of hints that are used to adjust the shapes when the font is scaled.

TSR   See *Terminate and Stay-Resident.*

U

UDP   See *user datagram protocol.*

UNC   See *universal naming convention.*

Unimodem   The universal modem driver used by TAPI to communicate with modems. It uses modem description files to control its interaction with VCOMM.

uninterruptible power supply (UPS)   A battery operated power supply connected to a computer to keep the system running during a power failure.

universal naming convention (UNC)   Naming convention, including a server name and share name, used to give a unique name to files on a network. The format is as follows: \\servername\sharename\path\filename

UPS   See *uninterruptible power supply.*

UPS service   A software component that monitors an uninterruptible power supply, and shuts the computer down gracefully when line power has failed, and the UPS battery is running down.

usability   A determination of how well users can accomplish tasks using a software product. Usability considers the characteristics of a product such as software, manuals, tutorials, help, etc.

user account   Refers to all the information that identifies a user to Windows 95, including user name and password, group membership, and rights and permissions.

user datagram protocol (UDP)   The transport protocol offering a connectionless-mode transport service in the Internet suite of protocols. See also *Transmission Control Protocol*.

user name   A unique name identifying a user account in Windows 95. User names must be unique, and cannot be the same as another user name, workgroup or domain name.

V

value entry   A parameter under a key or subkey in the Registry. A value entry has three components: name, type, and value. The value component can be a string, binary data, or a DWORD.

VDM   See *virtual DOS machine*.

VFAT   See *virtual file allocation table*.

virtual DOS machine (VDM)   A virtual machine provides a complete MS-DOS environment and a character-based window in which to run an MS-DOS based application. Every MS-DOS application runs in its own VDM.

virtual file allocation table (VFAT)   See also *file allocation table*.

virtual machine (VM)   An environment created by the operating system in memory. By using virtual machines, the application developer can write programs that behave as though they own the entire computer. This leaves the job of sorting out, for example, which application is receiving keyboard input at the moment, to Windows 95.

virtual memory   The technique by which Windows 95 uses hard disk space to increase the amount of memory available for running programs.

visual editing   The ability to edit an embedded object in place, without opening it into its own window. Implemented by OLE.

VL   Local bus standard for a bus that allows high-speed connections to peripherals, which preceded the PCI specification. Due to limitations in the specification, usually only used to connect video adapters into the system. Also known as **VESA bus**.

VM   See *virtual machine*.

volume   A partition that have been formatted for use by the file system.

VxD   Virtual device driver. The x represents the type of device— for example, a virtual device driver for a display is a VDD and a virtual device driver for a printer is a VPD.

W

wildcard   A character that is used to represent one or more characters, such as in a file specification. The question mark (?) wildcard can be used to represent any single character, and the asterisk (*) wildcard can be used to represent any character or group of characters that might match that position in other filenames.

Win32 API   The 32 bit application programming interface used to write 32 bit Windows based applications. It provides access to operating system and other functions.

window handle   A 32 bit value that uniquely identifies a window to Windows 95.

window name   A text string that identifies a window for the user.

Windows Internet Name Service (WINS)   A name resolution service that resolve Windows networking computernames to IP addresses in a routed environment. A WINS server handles name registrations, queries, and releases.

Windows NT   The portable, secure, 32 bit preemptive-multitasking member of the Microsoft Windows Operating system family. Windows

NT server provides centralized management and security, advanced fault tolerance, and additional connectivity. Windows NT Workstation provides operating system and networking functionality for computers without centralized management.

Windows NT file system (NTFS)   The native file system used by Windows NT. Windows 95 can detect, but not use, NTFS partitions.

WINS   See *Windows Internet Name Service.*

Wizard   A Windows 95 tool that asks you questions and performs a system action according to your answers. For example, you can use the New Hardware Wizard to detect and install drivers for new hardware.

workgroup   A collection of computers that are grouped for viewing purposes, but which do not share security information. Each workgroup is identified by a unique name. See also *domain.*

WYSIWYG   Stands for "What You See Is What You Get."

X

X.121   The addressing format used by X.25 base networks.

X.25   A connection-oriented network facility.

X.400   An international messaging standard, used in electronic mail systems.

x86-based computer   A computer using a microprocessor equivalent to an Intel 80386 or higher chip. Only x86-based computers can run Windows 95.

XMM   See *Extended Memory Manager.*

XModem/CRC   A communications protocol for transmitting binary files that uses a cyclic redundancy check (CRC) to detect any transmission errors. Both computers must be set to transmit and receive eight data bits per character.

XMS   See *Extended Memory Specification.*

Certification Checklist

In addition to a resource like this book, this list of tasks tells you what you need to know to get on with the certification process.

Get Started

Once you have decided to start the certification process, you should use the following list as a guideline for getting you started:

1. Get the Microsoft Roadmap to Education and Certification. (See "The Certification Roadmap" sidebar at the end of this appendix.)

2. Use the Roadmap Planning Wizard to determine *your* certification path.

3. Take the Windows 95 Assessment Exams located on the CD-ROM that accompanies this book to determine *your* competency level. For Microsoft products other than Windows 95, you can use the Assessment Exams located on the Roadmap to get a feel for the type of questions that appear on the exam. (See "Sample Tests," in Appendix J.)

Get Prepared

Getting started is one thing, but getting prepared to take the certification exam is a rather difficult process. The following guidelines will help you prepare for the exam:

1. Use the training materials listed in the Planning Wizard:

   - Microsoft Online Institute (MOLI). (See "The Microsoft Online Training Institute," in Appendix C.)

   - Self-Paced Training. (See "Self-Paced Training," in Appendix C.)

   - Authorized Technical Training Center (ATEC). (See "Training Resources," in Appendix C.)

   - Additional study materials listed in the Roadmap.

2. Review the Exam Study Guide in Appendix C.

3. Review the Exam Prep Guide on the Roadmap.

4. Gain experience with Windows 95.

Get Certified

Call Sylvan Prometric at 1–800–755–EXAM to schedule your exam at a location near you. (See "How Do I Register for the Exam?" in Appendix C; and Appendix D, "Testing Tips.")

Get Benefits

Microsoft will send your certification kit approximately 2–4 weeks after passing the exam. This kit qualifies you to become a Microsoft Certified Professional. (See "Benefits Up Close and Personal," in the Introduction to this book.)

The Certification Roadmap

The Microsoft Roadmap to Education and Certification is an easy-to-use Windows-based application that includes all the information you need to plan a successful training and certification strategy. The roadmap:

- Provides comprehensive information on the requirements for Microsoft Certified Professional certifications, with detailed exam topic outlines and preparation guidelines.

- Includes detailed outlines and prerequisites for Microsoft courses that are related to specific certification exams, helping you determine which courses teach the skills you need to meet your certification goals.

- Includes information on related Microsoft products and services.

- Helps you create a personal training and certification plan and print a to-do list of required certification activities.

You can request the Roadmap from Microsoft. In the US and Canada, call 1-800-636-7544. Outside the US and Canada, contact your local Microsoft office.

Or you can download it at the following online addresses:

- The Internet:

   ftp://ftp.microsoft.com/Services/MSEdCert/E&CMAP.ZIP

continues

continued

- The Microsoft Network (MSN): Go To MOLI, Advising Building, E&C Roadmap.
- Microsoft TechNet: Search for "Roadmap" and install from the built-in setup link.

How do I Get There from Here

Becoming certified requires a certain level of commitment. The information in this appendix will answer some of the questions you may have about the certification process.

What will I be Tested On?

You should be able to apply your knowledge and experience with Windows 95 to perform the following tasks:

- Install software or hardware
- Establish and repair network and communication connections
- Answer "how to" hardware or software questions from users
- Tune and optimize systems
- Customize system and user environments
- Troubleshoot systems and solve user hardware or software problems
- Recommend software products, versions, or upgrades
- Collect requests for additional software features and functions

To successfully complete the Windows 95 exam, you need, according to Microsoft, "a comprehensive understanding of Microsoft Windows 95 concepts and procedures, and you should be able to analyze what you know about Microsoft Windows 95 to synthesize configuration, optimization, and troubleshooting decisions and solutions."

Analysis is Good, but Synthesis is Harder

Microsoft Certified Professional exams test for specific cognitive skills needed for the job functions being tested. Educational theorists postulate a hierarchy of cognitive levels, ranging from the most basic (knowledge) up to the most difficult (evaluation) and a set of skills associated with each level.

- *Knowledge* is the lowest cognitive level at which you can identify, define, locate, recall, state, match, arrange, label, outline, and recognize items, situations, and concepts. Questions that ask for definitions or recitation of lists of characteristics test at this level.

◆ *Comprehension*, the level built immediately upon knowledge, requires that you translate, distinguish between, give examples, discuss, draw conclusions, estimate, explain, indicate, and paraphrase, rather than simply play back answers learned by rote.

◆ *Application* is the level at which hands-on activities come into play. Questions at this level ask you to apply, calculate, solve, plot, choose, demonstrate, design a procedure, change, interpret, or operate.

◆ *Analysis*, one of the top three levels, requires a thorough grounding in the skills required at lower levels. You operate at this level when you analyze, state conclusions, detect logic errors, compare and contrast, break down, make an inference from, map one situation or problem to another, diagnose, diagram, or discriminate.

◆ *Synthesis* (which is harder than analysis) requires some creativity and the ability to rebuild and reintegrate what may have been disassembled during analysis. This level requires you to construct a table or graph, design, formulate, integrate, generalize, predict, arrange, propose, tell in your own words, or show the relationship between.

◆ *Evaluation*, the highest cognitive level, is based on all the skills accumulated at lower levels. At this level, you assess, apply standards, decide, indicate fallacies, weigh, show the relationship between, summarize, decide, look at a situation and tell what is likely to occur, or make a judgment.

App
C

Exam Objectives

The following list of objectives defines the specific skills Microsoft wants the exam to measure. As you review the list, you can see the level at which the Windows 95 exam tests your knowledge and ability to implement, maintain, and troubleshoot the operating system. When an objective or item on the exam includes a verb or verb phrase associated with a given cognitive level (see the preceding section, "Analysis is Good, but Synthesis is Harder"), it is asking you to perform at that cognitive level.

For example, the exam objective "Discriminate between a process and a thread" asks you to perform at the Analysis level because it asks you to "discriminate" between items. It's a good idea to be prepared to be tested at the Analysis level or higher for each objective.

You should review the following objectives and be able to apply the listed skills to the tasks described earlier in "What will I be Tested On?"

Planning and Installation

You will be tested for these specific planning and installation skills:

- Identify appropriate hardware requirements for Windows 95 installation
- Maintain program groups and user preferences when upgrading from Windows 3.1
- Determine when to use Windows 95 and when to use Microsoft Windows NT Workstation
- Configure a Windows 95 computer on a network using the appropriate protocol
- Select the appropriate security to meet various needs
- Determine the appropriate installation method for various situations
- Install the Windows 95 operating system
- Troubleshoot setup and system startup
- Set up files for network installation and for shared use
- Recognize files used in troubleshooting the installation process

Architecture and Memory

You will be tested for your understanding of Windows 95 architecture and memory, specifically how to

- Compare and contrast the memory usage of a Microsoft MS-DOS–based application, a 16-bit Windows–based application, and a 32-bit Windows–based application operating in Windows 95

Customizing and Configuring Windows 95

You will be tested for your ability to perform the following tasks involved in customizing and configuring Windows 95:

◆ Identify and explain the differences between the Windows 3.1 interface and the Windows 95 interface

◆ Set up a dual-boot system for Windows 95

◆ Install new hardware devices on various systems that support Plug and Play

◆ Given a specific bus configuration, identify areas of limitation for full Plug and Play

◆ Configure the taskbar

◆ Configure shortcuts

◆ Add items to the Start menu

◆ Choose an appropriate method to accomplish a specified task, by using the user interface

◆ Customize the desktop for a specified set of criteria

◆ Use the Windows 95 interface to create, print, and store a file

◆ Configure and use Windows Explorer

◆ Access the network through Network Neighborhood

◆ Configure the property sheet for an object

◆ Define the purpose of the Registry

◆ Classify types of information in the Registry

◆ Determine where the Registry is stored

◆ Identify situations in which it is appropriate to modify the Registry

◆ Modify the contents of the Registry

◆ Choose the appropriate course of action when OLE information in the Registry becomes corrupted

App
C

Editing User and System Profiles

You will be tested for your ability to edit user and system profiles for Windows 95, specifically how to

◆ Modify a user workstation to meet specified criteria

◆ Grant remote administration privileges on your computer

◆ Modify user profiles

◆ Set up user profiles

◆ Set up computer policies

◆ Define the System Policy Editor, and describe how it is used

◆ Create, share, and monitor a remote resource

◆ Administer a remote computer

Networking and Interoperability

You will be tested for your understanding of Windows 95 networking and interoperability issues, including how to

◆ Configure a Windows 95 computer to access the Internet

◆ Configure a Windows 95 computer to use NetWare user-level security

◆ Configure a Windows 95 computer as a client or server in a NetWare network

◆ Identify the limitations of a Windows 95 NetWare server

◆ Configure a Windows 95 computer to use Windows NT Server user-level security

◆ Configure a Windows 95 computer as a client in a Windows NT Server domain

◆ Configure a Windows 95 computer as a client in a NetWare network

◆ Recognize how the UNC is used

◆ Configure Browse Master for Microsoft networks

◆ Configure Browse Master for NetWare

◆ Identify advantages and disadvantages of user-level and share-level security

◆ Identify elements of the Windows 95 operating system network architecture

◆ Install and configure TCP/IP for use with Windows 95

Managing Disk Resources and Utilities

You will be tested for your ability to manage disk resources and utilities, specifically how to

◆ Manage long and short file names in a mixed environment

◆ Troubleshoot problems and perform disk compression

◆ Select the appropriate disk-management tool for a given situation

◆ Use Disk Defragmenter to optimize for speed

◆ Use ScanDisk in appropriate situations

◆ Use Backup in appropriate situations

Managing Printers

You will be tested for your ability to manage printers for Windows 95, including how to

◆ Implement printers for Windows 95

◆ Identify situations in which metafile spooling is appropriate

◆ Set up point-and-print printing

◆ Access a printer through a NetWare network

◆ Create, reorder, and delete a Windows 95 print queue

◆ Set up and remove printer drivers in Windows 95

◆ Use Windows 95 to share a printer on the network

App
C

Running Applications

You will be tested for your ability to run various applications under Windows 95, specifically how to

- Configure Windows 95 to run MS-DOS–based applications
- Predict potential problems when configuring 16-bit Windows-based applications
- Distinguish between MS-DOS Mode and the standard method for running MS-DOS–based applications
- Determine when an application should be run in MS-DOS mode
- Resolve general protection faults
- Determine the appropriate course of action when the application stops responding to the system

Mobile Services

You will be tested for your understanding of mobile services as implemented under Windows 95, specifically how to

- Implement the appropriate level of security for use with Dial-Up Networking
- Choose applications that would be appropriate to run over Dial-Up Networking
- Configure Dial-Up Networking to be a client
- Configure Dial-Up Networking on a server
- Configure a modem to meet a specific set of user requirements
- Implement the various telephony options to meet a specific set of user requirements
- Use Briefcase to transfer and synchronize data between two computers

Microsoft Exchange

You will be tested for your understanding of Microsoft Exchange, including how to

- ◆ Share a fax
- ◆ Configure a fax for both stand-alone and shared situations
- ◆ Configure Microsoft Exchange to access the Internet
- ◆ Configure a Windows 95 computer to send and receive mail
- ◆ Configure a Windows 95 computer to access CompuServe mail

Plug and Play

You will be tested for your understanding of Plug and Play issues with Windows 95. You need to know how to

- ◆ Explain how Windows 95 handles components that are not compatible with Plug and Play
- ◆ Explain hot docking and the potential consequences of the dynamic device changes
- ◆ Given a specific configuration, use Device Manager to manually reconfigure a Plug and Play device

Troubleshooting

You will be tested for your ability to monitor and resolve problems with Windows 95 installations, specifically how to

- ◆ Resolve problems using appropriate resources
- ◆ Select appropriate tools for troubleshooting
- ◆ Monitor Windows 95 performance, and resolve performance problems
- ◆ Audit access to a Windows 95 local resource
- ◆ Optimize the system to use the Windows 95 drivers
- ◆ Optimize a computer for desktop performance

- ◆ Optimize a computer for network performance
- ◆ Optimize printing
- ◆ Discriminate between preemptive and cooperative multitasking
- ◆ Explain Windows 95 multitasking of 16-bit Windows-based applications and 32-bit Windows-based applications
- ◆ Discriminate between a process and a thread
- ◆ Discriminate between resource usage in Windows 3.1, Windows 95, and Windows NT
- ◆ Explain how Windows 95 performs memory paging as compared to Windows 3.*x*
- ◆ Choose the appropriate course of action when the installation process fails
- ◆ Use the startup disk to repair a faulty network setup
- ◆ Choose the appropriate course of action when an application fails
- ◆ Choose the appropriate course of action when a print job fails
- ◆ Choose the appropriate course of action when the boot process fails
- ◆ Choose the appropriate course of action when file system problems occur
- ◆ Choose the appropriate course of action when Dial-Up Networking problems occur
- ◆ Predict the consequences to the operating system when MS-DOS–based applications, 16-bit Windows-based applications, and 32-bit Windows-based applications fail to respond to the system while running under Windows 95

What Kinds of Questions can I Expect?

Certification exams include three types of items: multiple-choice, multiple-rating, and enhanced. The way you indicate your answer and the number of points you can score depend on the item type.

Multiple-Choice Item

A multiple-choice item presents a problem and a list of possible answers. You must select the best answer (single response) or the best set of answers (multiple response) to the given question from a list.

Example:

You are configuring a Windows 95 computer to use Microsoft Exchange. What is the minimum amount of RAM required?

    A. 2M

    B. 4M

    C. 8M

    D. 16M

Your response to a multiple-choice item is scored as either correct (1 point) or incorrect (0 points). If the item is a multiple-choice, multiple-response item (for which the correct response consists of more than one answer), your response is scored as being correct only if all the correct answers are selected. No partial credit is given for a response that does not include all the correct answers.

The answer to the above question is (C) 8M.

App
C

Multiple-Rating Item

In a multiple-choice item, you are asked to select the best answer or answers from a selection of several potential answers. A multiple-rating item presents you with a list of proposed solutions to a task and asks you to rate how well each proposed solution would produce the specified results.

Example:

You are developing a plan to improve network support. Your current network configuration is as follows:

    ◆ 12 Networks on a WAN, each located in a different city

    ◆ 25 Servers running Microsoft Windows NT Server

◆ 2,000 client computers

◆ Network protocol: Microsoft TCP/IP

You must establish a central help desk to support all locations. This result is required. You also have several optional, but desired results: 1) You want to implement monitoring of network statistics, and 2) you want to implement a solution to provide hardware inventory.

Proposed solution:

Implement Microsoft Systems Management Server, including all of this product's features.

Set up a parent site at company headquarters and child sites at all other locations.

Set up a centralized help desk at company headquarters to support all locations.

Which results does the proposed solution produce?

A. The proposed solution produces the required result and produces both of the optional desired results.

B. The proposed solution produces the required result and produces only one of the optional desired results.

C. The proposed solution produces the required result but does **not** produce any of the optional desired results.

D. The proposed solution does **not** produce the required result.

Answer: The correct response to this item is A, because the proposed solution produces the required result and produces both of the optional desired results.

Enhanced Item

An enhanced item asks you to select a response from a number of possible responses and indicate your answer in one of three ways:

◆ Type the correct response, such as a command name.

◆ Review an exhibit (such as a screen shot, a network configuration drawing, or a code sample), and then use the mouse to select the area of the exhibit that represents the correct response.

◆ Review an exhibit, and then select the correct response from the list of possible responses.

Your response to an enhanced item is scored as either correct (1 point) or incorrect (0 points).

How Should I Prepare for the Exam?

It's simple: the best way to prepare for the Windows 95 Certified Product Specialist exam, is to study, learn, and master Windows 95. If you'd like a little more guidance, Microsoft recommends these specific steps:

1. Identify the objectives you'll be tested on. (See "Exam Objectives" earlier in this appendix.)

2. Assess your current mastery of those objectives.

3. Practice tasks and study the areas you haven't mastered.

Following are some tools and techniques, in addition to this book, that may offer a little more help.

Assessment Exams

Microsoft provides self-paced practice, or assessment, exams, that you can take at your own computer. Assessment exams let you answer questions that are very much like the items in the actual certification exams. Your assessment exam score doesn't necessarily predict what your score will be on the actual exam, but its immediate feedback lets you determine the areas requiring extra study. And the assessment exams offer an additional advantage; they use the same computer-based testing tool as the certification exams, so you don't have to learn to use the tool on exam day.

An assessment exam exists for almost every certification exam. You can find a complete list of available assessment exams in the Certification Roadmap.

Microsoft Resources

A number of useful resources available from Microsoft are listed below.

1. Microsoft Windows 95. A key component of your exam preparation is your actual use of the product. Gain as much "real world" experience with Windows 95 as possible. As you work with the operating system, study the documentation in the Microsoft Windows 95 Resource Kit, focusing on areas relating to the exam objectives.

2. Microsoft TechNet, an information service for support professionals and system administrators. If you're a TechNet member, you receive a monthly CD full of technical information.

Note To join TechNet, refer to the TechNet section in the Microsoft Education and Certification Roadmap (see "The Certification Roadmap" sidebar in Appendix B.) ▓

4. The Microsoft Developer Network, a technical resource for Microsoft developers. If you're a member of the Developer Network, you can receive information on a regular basis through the Microsoft Developer Network CD, *Microsoft Developer Network News*, or the Developer Network Forum on CompuServe.

Note To join the Microsoft Developer Network, refer to the Microsoft Developer Network section in the Roadmap. ▓

5. The Windows 95 Exam Preparation Guide, a Microsoft publication that provides important specifics about the Windows 95 test. The Exam Preparation Guide is updated regularly to reflect changes and is the source for the most up-to-date information about Exam 70-63.

Note The exam preparation guide can change at any time without prior notice, solely at Microsoft's discretion. Before you register for an exam, make sure that you have the current exam preparation guide by contacting one of the following sources:

- Microsoft Sales Fax Service. Call 800-727-3351 in the United States and Canada. Outside the US and Canada, contact your local Microsoft office.

- CompuServe. **GO MSEDCERT**, Library Number 5.
- Internet. Anonymous ftp to **ftp.microsoft.com**, /Services/ MSEdCert/Certification/ExamPreps
- Sylvan Prometric. Call 800-755-EXAM in the US and Canada. Outside the US and Canada, contact your local Sylvan office. ▪

Microsoft Online Training Institute (MOLI)

The Microsoft Online Training Institute on MSN, The Microsoft Network, is an interactive learning and information resource where Learning Advisors (instructors) pair their expert knowledge, guidance, and motivation with electronic self-study materials.

You enroll in a class, pay a small tuition fee (to cover the cost of materials and the Learning Advisor's time and expertise), and then receive a shortcut to the classroom. As a student, you can participate in class by interacting with a Learning Advisor and fellow students online via Exchange (e-mail), bulletin boards, forums, or other online communication services available through MSN. You control your own time by studying when and where you choose, working at your own speed, and attending the virtual "class" as often or as little as you wish.

Only students enrolled in a class can participate in its online chat sessions and view the contents of the classroom, such as courseware and other materials provided by the Learning Advisor. In addition to MOLI campus resources, you have access to several other resources:

◆ The Assignments BBS gives you access to courseware assignments, test questions that measure subject-matter comprehension, chapter review guides, lab assignments, and information about certification exam topics. You can take advantage of these resources anytime.

◆ One or more chat sessions per week allow you to supplement class courseware, interact with other classmates to solve "real life" situations, and get expert advice.

◆ The Notes BBS lets students download and play files, tips and tools, and resources available through Microsoft.

App
C

For example, *Supporting Windows 95* is a typical online class offering. designed to provide students with the knowledge and skills needed to support Microsoft Windows 95. Topics in such a course include:

◆ Installation and configuration

◆ User interface features

◆ System architecture

◆ Customization and optimization

◆ Network integration

◆ Administration

◆ Troubleshooting

◆ Messaging

◆ Other support issues

At course completion, you will be able to:

◆ Install and configure Windows 95 to meet the needs of various users

◆ Identify and correct problems when running MS-DOS and 16- or 32-bit Windows programs

◆ Discuss the network architecture

◆ Remotely manage a workstation in a network

◆ Implement share-level and user-level security

◆ Manage printing

◆ Implement messaging services

◆ Diagnose and solve problems

Self-Paced Training

If you prefer to learn on your own, you can obtain Microsoft Official Curriculum training (as well as non-Microsoft Official Curriculum courses) in self-paced formats. Self-paced training kits are available through courses offered on the Microsoft Online Training Institute. with materials available in book, computer-based training (CBT), and mixed-media (book and video) formats.

Microsoft Approved Study Guides, such as this book, are self-paced training materials developed by Independent Courseware Vendors (ICVs) to help you prepare for Microsoft Certified Professional exams. The Study Guides include both single self-paced training courses and series of training courses that map to one or more MCP exams.

Self-training kits and study guides are often available through Microsoft authorized training centers; or you can purchase them where books from Microsoft Press are sold.

Other Online Resources

Both The Microsoft Network (MSN) and CompuServe (GO MECFORUM) provide access to technical forums for open discussions and questions about Microsoft products. Microsoft's World Wide Web site (**http:\\www.microsoft.com**) also allows you to access information about certification and education programs.

Training Resources

Microsoft product groups have designed training courses to support the certification process. The Microsoft Official Curriculum is developed by Microsoft course designers, product developers, and support engineers to include course the help you prepare for MCP exams.

Authorized Technical Education Centers (ATECs) are approved by Microsoft to provide training on Microsoft products and related technologies. By enrolling in a course taught by a Microsoft Solution Provider ATEC, you will get high-end technical training on the design, development, implementation, and support of enterprise-wide solutions using Microsoft operating systems, tools, and technologies.

You also may take MOC courses via face-to-face training offered by Microsoft Authorized Academic Training Program (AATP) institutions. AATP schools use authorized materials and curriculum designed for the Microsoft Certified Professional program and deliver Microsoft authorized materials, including the Microsoft Official Curriculum, over an academic term.

Supporting Microsoft Windows 95, Course 540, available from Microsoft authorized training institutions, may help you prepare for the exam. According to the course syllabus, Course No. 540 is five days long. At the end of the course, you should be able to install Windows 95; configure the system to meet the requirements of different users; identify and correct problems when running programs for MS-DOS, 16-bit Windows, or 32-bit Windows; discuss the networking architecture; remotely manage a workstation in a network; implement share-level and user-level security; manage printing; implement messaging services; and diagnose and solve problems.

For a referral to an AATP or ATEC in your area, call 800-SOLPROV.

Suggested Reading

When you're looking for additional study aids, check out the books listed in the bibliography (Appendix F).

How do I Register for the Exam?

Registering for the Windows 95 certification exam is simple:

1. Contact Sylvan Prometric at (800) 755-EXAM, with the examination number (70-63), your social security number, and credit card at the ready.

2. Complete the registration procedure by phone. (Your SSN becomes the ID attached to your private file; the credit card takes care of the $100 test fee.) Request contact information for the testing center closest to you.

3. After you receive the registration and payment confirmation letter from Sylvan Prometric, call the testing center to schedule your exam. When you call to schedule, you'll be provided with instructions regarding the appointment, cancellation procedures, and ID requirements, and information about the testing center location.

You can verify the number of questions and time allotted for your exam at the time of registration. You can schedule exams up to six weeks in advance, or as late as one working day ahead, but you must take the exam within one year of your payment. To cancel or reschedule your exam, contact Sylvan Prometric at least two working days before your scheduled exam date.

 Note   At some locations, same-day registration (at least two hours before test time) is available, subject to space availability. ■

App
C

Testing Tips

You've mastered the required tasks to take the exam. After reviewing and re-reviewing the exam objectives, you're confident that you have the skills specified in the exam objectives. You're ready to perform at the highest cognitive level. And it's time to head for the testing center. This appendix covers some tips and tricks to remember.

Before the Test

◆ Wear comfortable clothing. You want to focus on the exam, not on a tight shirt collar or pinching pair of shoes.

◆ Allow plenty of travel time. Get to the testing center 10 or 15 minutes early; nothing's worse than rushing in at the last minute. Give yourself time to relax.

◆ If you've never been to the testing center before, make a trial run a few days before to make sure that you know the route to the center.

◆ Carry with you at least two forms of identification, including one photo ID (such as a driver's license or company security ID). You will have to show them before you can take the exam.

Remember that the exams are closed-book. The use of laptop computers, notes, or other printed materials is not permitted during the exam session.

At the test center, you'll be asked to sign in. The test administrator will give you a Testing Center Regulations form that explains the rules that govern the examination. You will be asked to sign the form to indicate that you understand and will comply with its stipulations.

When the administrator shows you to your test computer, make sure that:

◆ The testing tool starts up and displays the correct exam. If a tutorial for using the instrument is available, you should be allowed time to take it.

Note If you have any special needs, such as reconfiguring the mouse buttons for a left-handed user, you should inquire about them when you register for the exam with Sylvan Prometric. Special configurations are not possible at all sites, so you should not assume that you will be permitted to make any modifications to the equipment setup and configuration. Site administrators are *not* permitted to make modifications without prior instructions from Sylvan. ■

- You have a supply of scratch paper for use during the exam. (The administrator collects all scratch paper and notes made during the exam before your leave the center.) Some centers are now providing you with a wipe-off board and magic marker to use instead of paper. You are not permitted to make any kind of notes to take with you, due to exam security.

- Some exams may include additional materials, or exhibits. If any exhibits are required for your exam, the test administrator will provide you with them before you begin the exam and collect them from you at the end of the exam.

- The administrator tells you what to do when you complete the exam.

- You get answers to any and all of your questions or concerns before the exam begins.

As a Microsoft Certification examination candidate, you are entitled to the best support and environment possible for your exam. If you experience any problems on the day of the exam, inform the Sylvan Prometric test administrator immediately.

App
D

During the Test

The testing software lets you move forward and backward through the items, so you can implement a strategic approach to the test.

1. Go through all the items, answering the easy questions first. Then go back and spend time on the harder ones. Microsoft guarantees that there are no trick questions. The correct answer is always among the list of choices.

2. Eliminate the obviously incorrect answer first to clear away the clutter and simplify your choices.

3. Answer all the questions. You aren't penalized for guessing, so it can't hurt.

4. Don't rush. Haste makes waste (or substitute the cliché of your choice).

After the Test

When you have completed an exam:

- ◆ The testing tool gives you immediate, online notification of your pass or fail status, except for beta exams. Because of the beta process, your results for a beta exam are mailed to you approximately 6-8 weeks after the exam.

- ◆ The administrator gives you a printed Examination Score Report indicating your pass or fail status and your exam results by section.

- ◆ Test scores are automatically forwarded to Microsoft within five working days after you take the test. If you pass the exam, you receive confirmation from Microsoft within two to four weeks.

If you don't pass a certification exam:

- ◆ Review your individual section scores, noting areas where your score must be improved. The section titles in your exam report generally correspond to specific groups of exam objectives.

- ◆ Review the exam information in this book, then get the latest Exam Preparation Guide and focus on the topic areas that need strengthening.

- ◆ Intensify your effort to get your real-world, hands-on experience and practice with Windows 95.

- ◆ Try taking one or more of the approved training courses.

- ◆ Review the suggested readings listed in Appendix F or in the Exam Preparation Guide.

- ◆ Take (or retake) the Windows 95 Assessment Exam.

- ◆ Call Sylvan Prometric to register for, pay for, and schedule the exam again.

Contacting Microsoft

Microsoft encourages feedback from exam candidates, especially suggestions for improving any of the exams or preparation materials.

To provide program feedback, to find out more about Microsoft Education and Certification materials and programs, to register with Sylvan Prometric, or to get other useful information, check the following resources.

 Note Outside the United States or Canada, contact your local Microsoft office or Sylvan Prometric testing center. ▪

Microsoft Certified Professional Program

(800) 636-7544

For information about the Microsoft Certified Professional program and exams, and to order the Microsoft Roadmap to Education and Certification.

Sylvan Prometric Testing Centers

(800) 755-EXAM

To register to take a Microsoft Certified Professional exam at any of more than 700 Sylvan Prometric testing centers around the world.

Microsoft Sales Fax Service

(800) 727-3351

For Microsoft Certified Professional Exam Preparation Guides and Microsoft Official Curriculum course descriptions and schedules.

Education Program and Course Information

(800) SOLPROV

For information about Microsoft Official Curriculum courses, Microsoft education products, and the Microsoft Solution Provider Authorized Technical Education Center (ATEC) program, where you can attend a Microsoft Official Curriculum course.

Microsoft Certification Development Team

Fax: (206) 936-1311

To volunteer for participation in one or more exam development phases or to report a problem with an exam. Address written correspondence to:

> Certification Development Team
> Microsoft Education and Certification
> One Microsoft Way
> Redmond, WA 98052

Microsoft TechNet Technical Information Network

(800) 344-2121

For support for professionals and system administrators. (Outside the U.S. and Canada, call your local Microsoft subsidiary for information.)

Microsoft Developer Network (MSDN)

(800) 759-5474

The official source for software development kits, device driver kits, operating systems, and information about developing applications for Microsoft Windows and Windows NT.

App
E

Microsoft Technical Support Options

(800) 936-3500

For information about the technical support options available for Microsoft products, including technical support telephone numbers and Premier Support options. (Outside the U.S. and Canada, call your local Microsoft subsidiary for information.)

Microsoft Online Institute (MOLI)

(800) 449-9333

For information about Microsoft's new online training program.

Suggested Reading

Titles from Que

Que Corporation offers a wide variety of technical books for all levels of users. Following are some recommended titles, in alphabetical order, that can provide you with additional information on many of the exam topics and objectives.

Tip

To order any books from Que Corporation or other imprints of Macmillan Computer Publishing (Sams, New Riders Publishing, Ziff-Davis Press, and others), call 800-428-5331, visit Macmillan's Information SuperLibrary on the World Wide Web (**http://www.mcp.com**), or check your local bookseller.

Killer Windows 95

Author: Allen Wyatt, et. al.

ISBN: 0-7897-0001-8

Geared toward the intermediate user, this one-stop resource covers the most popular features of the new Windows 95 and Windows applications. It contains expert tips and troubleshooting information, as well as a CD-ROM to help users get productive quickly.

- ◆ Covers customizing, boosting performance, using applications, printing, and more.
- ◆ CD-ROM contains sounds, animations, sample multimedia programs, screen savers, graphic viewers, and more.
- ◆ Special coverage of the Internet, multimedia, and child-proofing a system.

Platinum Edition Using Windows 95

Author: Ron Person, et. al.

ISBN: 0-7897-0797-7

With two CD-ROMs, this is the most comprehensive collection of techniques and tools anywhere. It features coverage of hot topics like Registry and customization, dial-up networking, and the World Wide Web. A "must have" resource for accomplished and expert users who want information precisely targeted at their needs and delivered in a clear, focused, "content-dense" manner.

- ◆ Complete coverage of all of the new Windows 95 service pack updates.
- ◆ Expert tips on integrating MS Exchange, FAX, and telephony features with the Internet, all major online services as well as company networks.
- ◆ CD #1 contains hundreds of the best connectivity, Internet, customization, performance tuning, backup, security, and training tools available—the best of which are preregistered, full-working copies.

◆ CD #2 contains full working versions of *PC Magazine's* WinBench '96 and Winstone '96—the industry's best system benchmarking and performance evaluation programs.

Special Edition Using Windows 95

Author: Ron Person, et. al.

ISBN: 1-56529-921-3

The latest version of Windows is here, and with it a new era of computing. For the millions who rely on Que for the best information, this special edition contains everything users need to get productive with the new features—including professional tips from a team of experts.

◆ Step-by-step lessons on Windows basics such as managing files, using applications, and printing.

◆ Advanced information on networking, online communications, multimedia, OLE, and more.

◆ Includes special troubleshooting section with hundreds of common problems—and their solutions.

◆ Each section is written by an expert in the field.

Windows 95 Communications Handbook

Authors: Jim Boyce, Robin Hohman, Kate Chase, D. Rorbaugh

ISBN: 0-7897-0675-X

This guide shows readers how to efficiently and effectively communicate with Windows 95, covering the wide array of built-in communication tools. Readers will discover the power of the Internet and learn how to work with the most popular online services.

App

F

◆ CD-ROM contains Internet tools, 32-bit communications software, and utilities, as well as working versions of CompuServe and America Online.

◆ Demystifies the installation and configuration of Windows 95's tremendous communications tools.

◆ Covers the use and integration of Microsoft Exchange, fax and telephony features with the Internet, all major online services, company networks, and more.

Windows 95 Installation & Configuration Handbook

Author: Rob Tidrow, et. al.

ISBN: 0–7897–0580–X

With extensive coverage of installing and configuring the many pieces of hardware and software Windows 95 must interact with, this book presents all the information users will need to get up and running immediately with Windows 95.

◆ CD-ROM contains dozens of tools designed to help you set up Windows 95 and keep it running smoothly.

◆ Provides a wealth of tips and techniques from a team of authors who have been working with Windows 95 since the early beta stages.

◆ Perfect for both the corporate MIS person installing Windows 95 on the company network and the user who is upgrading from Windows 3.1.

Windows 95 Registry & Customization Handbook

Author: Jerry Honeycutt, et. al.

ISBN: 0–7897–0725–X

Covers step-by-step how to accomplish the most commonly requested yet most difficult customizations tasks and performance tips. Also provides additional information on tuning and configuring SYS and INI files, and system management tools like REGEDIT.

Other Titles

Advanced Windows, by Jeffrey Richter (Microsoft Press; ISBN: 1-55615-677-4)

Hardware Design Guide for Microsoft Windows 95 (Microsoft Press; ISBN: 1-55615-642-1)

Inside Windows 95, by Jim Boyce, et. al. (New Riders Publishing; ISBN: 1-56205-375-2)

Introducing Microsoft Windows 95 (Microsoft Press; ISBN: 1-55615-860-2)

Peter Norton's Complete Guide To Windows 95, by Peter Norton (Sams; ISBN: 0-672-30791-X)

Programmer's Guide to Microsoft Windows 95 (Microsoft Press; ISBN: 1-55615-834-3)

Programmer's Guide to Pen Services for Microsoft Windows 95 (Microsoft Press; ISBN: 1-55615-835-1)

Programming Windows 95 Unleashed (Sams; ISBN: 0-672-30602-6)

The Microsoft Windows 95 Developer's Guide, by Stefano Maruzzi (Ziff-Davis Publishing; ISBN: 1-56276-335-0)

The Windows Interface Guidelines for Software Design, by Tandy Trower (Microsoft Press; ISBN: 1-55615-679-0)

Transition to Windows 95 for Windows 3.x Users, by Shelley O'Hara (Que Education and Training; ISBN: 1-57576-251-X)

Upgrading to Windows 95 Step by Step, by Catapult, Inc. (Microsoft Press; ISBN: 1-55615-816-5)

Windows 95 for Network Administrators, by Kevin Stoltz (New Riders Publishing; ISBN: 1-56205-380-9)

Windows 95 Registry Troubleshooting, by Rob Tidrow (New Riders Publishing; ISBN: 1-56205-556-9)

App
F

Windows 95 Step by Step, by Catapult, Inc. (Microsoft Press; ISBN: 1-55615-683-9)

Windows 95 Unleashed, by Ed Tiley, et. al. (Sams; ISBN: 0-672-30474-0)

File Listing of the
Windows 95 CD

One of the most overwhelming aspects of Windows 95 is the volume
of files it relies on. If you purchase Windows 95 on CD-ROM, you'll
find more than 1,600 files that Windows 95 uses. If you're a technician,
help desk supporter, or other IS person, you often might not know
whether a file is a native Windows 95 file, or whether it was copied
from a third-party application.

This appendix lists all of the files found on the release version of Windows 95 (CD-ROM version). You can use it as a reference to help you
find a file you are searching for, find the correct cabinet file that stores
the file, or find the original size of a particular file. (Cabinet files have
the extension of CAB on the Windows 95 CD-ROM or floppy disks.)
Each file includes the following criteria:

+ *Date of File.* Shows the file save date.

+ *Size of File.* Shows the expanded file size after it is installed on your machine.

+ *Installed Name.* Lists the expanded name of the file after it is installed on your machine.

+ *Installed Location.* Shows you where the file is copied to during Windows 95 Setup.

+ *Type of File.* Lists the extension of the specified file.

+ *Location on CD.* Shows the folder in which the specified file is stored on the CD-ROM. If you have Windows 95 on floppy disk, these locations might differ.

Note   Depending on your specific setup and configuration, some of the listed locations might differ from your actual setup. If you are looking for a specific file or file type, use Windows 95 Find, Files or Folders command (located in the Explorer on the Tools menu) and search for a name or file extension.

Date of File	Size of File	Installed Name	Installed Location	Type of File	Location on CD
7/11/95	27,961	VDHCP.386	C:\WINDOWS\SYSTEM	386	\WIN95\CAB_12.CAB
7/11/95	62,614	VIP.386	C:\WINDOWS\SYSTEM	386	\WIN95\CAB_12.CAB
7/11/95	95,969	VNBT.386	C:\WINDOWS\SYSTEM	386	\WIN95\CAB_12.CAB
7/11/95	5,668	VPMTD.386	C:\WINDOWS\SYSTEM	386	\WIN95\CAB_03.CAB
7/11/95	47,377	VTCP.386	C:\WINDOWS\SYSTEM	386	\WIN95\CAB_12.CAB
7/11/95	5,687	VTDI.386	C:\WINDOWS\SYSTEM	386	\WIN95\CAB_12.CAB
7/11/95	98,144	SXCIEXT.DLL	C:\WINDOWS\SYSTEM	3GR	\WIN95\CAB_04.CAB
7/11/95	18,944	IMAADP32.ACM	C:\WINDOWS\SYSTEM	ACM	\WIN95\CAB_08.CAB
7/11/95	17,920	MSADP32.ACM	C:\WINDOWS\SYSTEM	ACM	\WIN95\CAB_08.CAB
7/11/95	10,240	MSG711.ACM	C:\WINDOWS\SYSTEM	ACM	\WIN95\CAB_08.CAB
7/11/95	25,088	MSGSM32.ACM	C:\WINDOWS\SYSTEM	ACM	\WIN95\CAB_08.CAB
7/11/95	8,704	TSSOFT32.ACM	C:\WINDOWS\SYSTEM	ACM	\WIN95\CAB_08.CAB
7/11/95	13,456	WFM0200.ACV	C:\WINDOWS\SYSTEM	ACV	\WIN95\CAB_08.CAB
7/11/95	5,184	WFM0201.ACV	C:\WINDOWS\SYSTEM	ACV	\WIN95\CAB_08.CAB
7/11/95	9,056	WFM0202.ACV	C:\WINDOWS\SYSTEM	ACV	\WIN95\CAB_08.CAB
7/11/95	9,056	WFM0203.ACV	C:\WINDOWS\SYSTEM	ACV	\WIN95\CAB_08.CAB
7/11/95	8,274	APPSTART.ANI	C:\WINDOWS\CURSORS	ANI	\WIN95\CAB_10.CAB
7/11/95	12,144	HOURGLAS.ANI	C:\WINDOWS\CURSORS	ANI	\WIN95\CAB_10.CAB
7/11/95	15,624	GENFAX.APD	C:\WINDOWS\SYSTEM	APD	\WIN95\CAB_05.CAB

Date of File	Size of File	Installed Name	Installed Location	Type of File	Location on CD
7/11/95	410,588	CLOSEWIN.AVI	C:\WINDOWS	AVI	\WIN95\CAB_16.CAB
7/11/95	306,608	DRAGDROP.AVI	C:\WINDOWS	AVI	\WIN95\CAB_16.CAB
7/11/95	872,208	EXPLORER.AVI	C:\WINDOWS	AVI	\WIN95\CAB_16.CAB
7/11/95	488,492	FIND.AVI	C:\WINDOWS	AVI	\WIN95\CAB_16.CAB
7/11/95	754,922	MOVEWIN.AVI	C:\WINDOWS	AVI	\WIN95\CAB_16.CAB
7/11/95	1,011,692	PASTE.AVI	C:\WINDOWS	AVI	\WIN95\CAB_16.CAB
7/11/95	1,510,732	SCROLL.AVI	C:\WINDOWS	AVI	\WIN95\CAB_16.CAB
7/11/95	832,222	SIZEWIN.AVI	C:\WINDOWS	AVI	\WIN95\CAB_16.CAB
7/11/95	425,742	TASKSWCH.AVI	C:\WINDOWS	AVI	\WIN95\CAB_16.CAB
7/11/95	745,920	WHATSON.AVI	C:\WINDOWS	AVI	\WIN95\CAB_16.CAB
7/11/95	576	_PWMOVE.BAT	C:\DOS	BAT	\WIN95\CAB_11.CAB
7/11/95	403	DBLSPACE.BAT	C:\DOS	BAT	\WIN95\PRECOPY2.CAB
7/11/95	339	DEFRAG.BAT	C:\DOS	BAT	\WIN95\PRECOPY2.CAB
7/11/95	329	DRVSPACE.BAT	C:\DOS	BAT	\WIN95\PRECOPY2.CAB
7/11/95	2,456	INSTBE.BAT	C:\PROGRAM FILES\ THE MICROSOFT NETWORK	BAT	\WIN95\CAB_07.CAB
7/11/95	152	SCANDISK.BAT	C:\DOS	BAT	\WIN95\PRECOPY2.CAB
7/11/95	816	SUCHECK.BAT	C:\WINDOWS	BAT	\WIN95\PRECOPY2.CAB
7/11/95	751	SUFAIL.BAT	C:\WINDOWS	BAT	\WIN95\PRECOPY2.CAB
7/11/95	40,742	DCAMAC.BIN	C:\WINDOWS	BIN	\WIN95\CAB_11.CAB
7/11/95	71,287	DRVSPACE.BIN	C:\DOS	BIN	\WIN95\PRECOPY1.CAB
7/11/95	26,880	EAGLECAF.BIN	C:\WINDOWS	BIN	\WIN95\CAB_11.CAB
7/11/95	26,880	EAGLEMAC.BIN	C:\WINDOWS	BIN	\WIN95\CAB_11.CAB
7/11/95	51,350	MDGMPORT.BIN	C:\WINDOWS	BIN	\WIN95\CAB_11.CAB
7/11/95	4,096	NE3200.BIN	C:\WINDOWS	BIN	\WIN95\CAB_11.CAB
7/11/95	110,720	NETFLX.BIN	C:\WINDOWS	BIN	\WIN95\CAB_11.CAB
7/11/95	3,279	UNICODE.BIN	C:\WINDOWS\SYSTEM	BIN	\WIN95\CAB_13.CAB
7/11/95	407	XLAT850.BIN	C:\WINDOWS\SYSTEM	BIN	\WIN95\CAB_03.CAB
7/11/95	2,754	3DBLOCKS.BMP	C:\WINDOWS	BMP	\WIN95\CAB_02.CAB
7/11/95	590	BAMBOO.BMP	C:\WINDOWS	BMP	\WIN95\CAB_03.CAB
7/11/95	2,118	BUBBLES.BMP	C:\WINDOWS	BMP	\WIN95\CAB_03.CAB
7/11/95	190	CIRCLES.BMP	C:\WINDOWS	BMP	\WIN95\CAB_03.CAB
7/11/95	307,514	CLOUDS.BMP	C:\WINDOWS	BMP	\WIN95\CAB_02.CAB
7/11/95	582	EGYPT.BMP	C:\WINDOWS	BMP	\WIN95\CAB_03.CAB
7/11/95	66,146	FOREST.BMP	C:\WINDOWS	BMP	\WIN95\CAB_03.CAB
7/11/95	32,850	GATOR.BMP	C:\WINDOWS	BMP	\WIN95\CAB_03.CAB
7/11/95	190	HALFTONE.BMP	C:\WINDOWS	BMP	\WIN95\CAB_03.CAB
7/11/95	470	HOUNDS.BMP	C:\WINDOWS	BMP	\WIN95\CAB_03.CAB
7/11/95	36,182	MESH.BMP	C:\WINDOWS	BMP	\WIN95\CAB_03.CAB
7/11/95	578	PSTRIPE.BMP	C:\WINDOWS	BMP	\WIN95\CAB_03.CAB
7/11/95	198	PYRAMID2.BMP	C:\WINDOWS	BMP	\WIN95\CAB_03.CAB
7/11/95	578	REDTILE.BMP	C:\WINDOWS	BMP	\WIN95\CAB_03.CAB

App

G

continues

Date of File	Size of File	Installed Name	Installed Location	Type of File	Location on CD
7/11/95	194	RIVETS2.BMP	C:\WINDOWS	BMP	\WIN95\CAB_03.CAB
7/11/95	32,854	SAND.BMP	C:\WINDOWS	BMP	\WIN95\CAB_03.CAB
7/11/95	38,462	SETUP.BMP	C:\WINDOWS	BMP	\WIN95\CAB_10.CAB
7/11/95	182	THATCH2.BMP	C:\WINDOWS	BMP	\WIN95\CAB_03.CAB
7/11/95	4,678	WEAVE2.BMP	C:\WINDOWS	BMP	\WIN95\CAB_03.CAB
7/11/95	1,189	BACKUP.CNT	C:\WINDOWS\HELP	CNT	\WIN95\CAB_04.CAB
7/11/95	797	MAPIF0.CFG	C:\WINDOWS\SYSTEM	CFG	\WIN95\CAB_06.CAB
7/11/95	799	MAPIF1.CFG	C:\WINDOWS\SYSTEM	CFG	\WIN95\CAB_06.CAB
7/11/95	3,989	MAPIF2.CFG	C:\WINDOWS\SYSTEM	CFG	\WIN95\CAB_06.CAB
7/11/95	795	MAPIF3.CFG	C:\WINDOWS\SYSTEM	CFG	\WIN95\CAB_06.CAB
7/11/95	787	MAPIF4.CFG	C:\WINDOWS\SYSTEM	CFG	\WIN95\CAB_06.CAB
7/11/95	826	MAPIF5.CFG	C:\WINDOWS\SYSTEM	CFG	\WIN95\CAB_06.CAB
7/11/95	1	MIDIMAP.CFG	C:\WINDOWS\SYSTEM	CFG	\WIN95\CAB_08.CAB
7/11/95	9,744	IOSCLASS.DLL	C:\WINDOWS\SYSTEM	DLL	\WIN95\CAB_03.CAB
7/11/95	1,912	AWFAX.CNT	C:\WINDOWS\HELP	CNT	\WIN95\CAB_05.CAB
7/11/95	508	CALC.CNT	C:\WINDOWS\HELP	CNT	\WIN95\CAB_05.CAB
7/11/95	643	CDPLAYER.CNT	C:\WINDOWS\HELP	CNT	\WIN95\CAB_13.CAB
7/11/95	16,384	CHIADI.DLL	C:\WINDOWS\HELP	CNT	\WIN95\CAB_04.CAB
7/11/95	440	CLIPBOOK.CNT	C:\WINDOWS\HELP	CNT	\WIN95\CAB_02.CAB
7/11/95	411	CLIPBRD.CNT	C:\WINDOWS\HELP	CNT	\WIN95\CAB_02.CAB
7/11/95	552	DIALER.CNT	C:\WINDOWS\HELP	CNT	\WIN95\CAB_02.CAB
7/11/95	822	DRVSPACE.CNT	C:\WINDOWS\HELP	CNT	\WIN95\CAB_05.CAB
7/11/95	1,639	EXCHNG.CNT	C:\WINDOWS\HELP	CNT	\WIN95\CAB_06.CAB
7/11/95	653	FAXCOVER.CNT	C:\WINDOWS\HELP	CNT	\WIN95\CAB_05.CAB
7/11/95	204	FAXVIEW.CNT	C:\WINDOWS\HELP	CNT	\WIN95\CAB_05.CAB
7/11/95	342	FILEXFER.CNT	C:\WINDOWS\HELP	CNT	\WIN95\CAB_17.CAB
7/11/95	196	FREECELL.CNT	C:\WINDOWS\HELP	CNT	\WIN95\CAB_05.CAB
7/11/95	3,386	HPJAHLP.CNT	C:\WINDOWS\HELP	CNT	\WIN95\CAB_16.CAB
7/11/95	910	HYPERTRM.CNT	C:\WINDOWS\HELP	CNT	\WIN95\CAB_02.CAB
7/11/95	509	MOUSE.CNT	C:\WINDOWS\HELP	CNT	\WIN95\CAB_05.CAB
7/11/95	1,042	MPLAYER.CNT	C:\WINDOWS\HELP	CNT	\WIN95\CAB_08.CAB
7/11/95	1,221	MSFS.CNT	C:\WINDOWS\HELP	CNT	\WIN95\CAB_06.CAB
7/11/95	206	MSHEARTS.CNT	C:\WINDOWS\HELP	CNT	\WIN95\CAB_05.CAB
7/11/95	13,392	MSN.CNT	C:\WINDOWS\HELP	CNT	\WIN95\CAB_07.CAB
7/11/95	246	MSNPSS.CNT	C:\WINDOWS\HELP	CNT	\WIN95\CAB_07.CAB
7/11/95	1,978	MSPAINT.CNT	C:\WINDOWS\HELP	CNT	\WIN95\CAB_02.CAB
7/11/95	391	NETWATCH.CNT	C:\WINDOWS\HELP	CNT	\WIN95\CAB_13.CAB
7/11/95	571	NOTEPAD.CNT	C:\WINDOWS\HELP	CNT	\WIN95\CAB_05.CAB
7/11/95	940	PACKAGER.CNT	C:\WINDOWS\HELP	CNT	\WIN95\CAB_02.CAB
7/11/95	919	PROGMAN.CNT	C:\WINDOWS\HELP	CNT	\WIN95\CAB_10.CAB
7/11/95	544	REGEDIT.CNT	C:\WINDOWS\HELP	CNT	\WIN95\CAB_06.CAB
7/11/95	392	SNDVOL32.CNT	C:\WINDOWS\HELP	CNT	\WIN95\CAB_08.CAB
7/11/95	157	SOL.CNT	C:\WINDOWS\HELP	CNT	\WIN95\CAB_05.CAB

Date of File	Size of File	Installed Name	Installed Location	Type of File	Location on CD
7/11/95	1,023	SOUNDREC.CNT	C:\WINDOWS\HELP	CNT	\WIN95\CAB_08.CAB
7/11/95	263	SYSMON.CNT	C:\WINDOWS\HELP	CNT	\WIN95\CAB_13.CAB
7/11/95	1,722	W_OVER.CNT	C:\WINDOWS\HELP	CNT	\WIN95\CAB_16.CAB
7/11/95	144	W_TOUR.CNT	C:\WINDOWS\HELP	CNT	\WIN95\CAB_17.CAB
7/11/95	13,743	WINDOWS.CNT	C:\WINDOWS\HELP	CNT	\WIN95\CAB_05.CAB
7/11/95	2,169	WINFILE.CNT	C:\WINDOWS\HELP	CNT	\WIN95\CAB_10.CAB
7/11/95	930	WINHLP32.CNT	C:\WINDOWS\HELP	CNT	\WIN95\CAB_05.CAB
7/11/95	168	WINMINE.CNT	C:\WINDOWS\HELP	CNT	\WIN95\CAB_05.CAB
7/11/95	403	WINPOPUP.CNT	C:\WINDOWS\HELP	CNT	\WIN95\CAB_11.CAB
7/11/95	1,920	WORDPAD.CNT	C:\WINDOWS\HELP	CNT	\WIN95\CAB_03.CAB
7/11/95	5,175	CHOICE.COM	C:\WINDOWS\COMMAND	COM	\WIN95\CAB_08.CAB
7/11/95	92,870	COMMAND.COM	C:\WINDOWS	COM	\WIN95\PRECOPY1.CAB
7/11/95	21,959	DISKCOPY.COM	C:\WINDOWS\COMMAND	COM	\WIN95\CAB_08.CAB
7/11/95	15,431	DOSKEY.COM	C:\WINDOWS\COMMAND	COM	\WIN95\CAB_08.CAB
7/11/95	69,886	EDIT.COM	C:\WINDOWS\COMMAND	COM	\WIN95\CAB_02.CAB
7/11/95	40,135	FORMAT.COM	C:\WINDOWS\COMMAND	COM	\WIN95\CAB_02.CAB
7/11/95	19,927	KEYB.COM	C:\WINDOWS\COMMAND	COM	\WIN95\CAB_08.CAB
7/11/95	29,191	MODE.COM	C:\WINDOWS\COMMAND	COM	\WIN95\CAB_08.CAB
7/11/95	10,471	MORE.COM	C:\WINDOWS\COMMAND	COM	\WIN95\CAB_08.CAB
7/11/95	28	NWRPLTRM.COM	C:\WINDOWS	COM	\WIN95\CAB_17.CAB
7/11/95	13,239	SYS.COM	C:\WINDOWS\COMMAND	COM	\WIN95\CAB_02.CAB
7/11/95	4,357	CONFDENT.CPE	C:\WINDOWS	CPE	\WIN95\CAB_05.CAB
7/11/95	4,473	FYI.CPE	C:\WINDOWS	CPE	\WIN95\CAB_05.CAB
7/11/95	5,935	GENERIC.CPE	C:\WINDOWS	CPE	\WIN95\CAB_05.CAB
7/11/95	4,345	URGENT.CPE	C:\WINDOWS	CPE	\WIN95\CAB_05.CAB
7/11/95	58,870	EGA.CPI	C:\WINDOWS\COMMAND	CPI	\WIN95\CAB_13.CAB
7/11/95	49,754	ISO.CPI	C:\WINDOWS\COMMAND	CPI	\WIN95\CAB_13.CAB
7/11/95	57,344	ACCESS.CPL	C:\WINDOWS\SYSTEM	CPL	\WIN95\CAB_02.CAB
7/11/95	63,488	APPWIZ.CPL	C:\WINDOWS\SYSTEM	CPL	\WIN95\CAB_10.CAB
7/11/95	8,704	DESK.CPL	C:\WINDOWS\SYSTEM	CPL	\WIN95\CAB_03.CAB
7/11/95	48,640	INTL.CPL	C:\WINDOWS\SYSTEM	CPL	\WIN95\CAB_03.CAB
7/11/95	7,680	JETADMIN.CPL	C:\WINDOWS\SYSTEM	CPL	\WIN95\CAB_16.CAB
7/11/95	51,200	JOY.CPL	C:\WINDOWS\SYSTEM	CPL	\WIN95\CAB_08.CAB
7/11/95	67,584	MAIN.CPL	C:\WINDOWS\SYSTEM	CPL	\WIN95\CAB_03.CAB
7/11/95	42,768	MLCFG32.CPL	C:\WINDOWS\SYSTEM	CPL	\WIN95\CAB_06.CAB
7/11/95	193,024	MMSYS.CPL	C:\WINDOWS\SYSTEM	CPL	\WIN95\CAB_08.CAB
7/11/95	52,096	MODEM.CPL	C:\WINDOWS\SYSTEM	CPL	\WIN95\CAB_07.CAB
7/11/95	5,312	NETCPL.CPL	C:\WINDOWS\SYSTEM	CPL	\WIN95\CAB_11.CAB
7/11/95	37,376	PASSWORD.CPL	C:\WINDOWS\SYSTEM	CPL	\WIN95\CAB_11.CAB
7/11/95	221,776	SYSDM.CPL	C:\WINDOWS\SYSTEM	CPL	\WIN95\CAB_03.CAB
7/11/95	33,272	TELEPHON.CPL	C:\WINDOWS\SYSTEM	CPL	\WIN95\CAB_11.CAB
7/11/95	49,152	TIMEDATE.CPL	C:\WINDOWS\SYSTEM	CPL	\WIN95\CAB_03.CAB
7/11/95	32,528	WGPOCPL.CPL	C:\WINDOWS\SYSTEM	CPL	\WIN95\CAB_06.CAB

App
G

continues

Date of File	Size of File	Installed Name	Installed Location	Type of File	Location on CD
7/11/95	2,238	WFM0200A.CSP	C:\WINDOWS	CSP	\WIN95\CAB_08.CAB
7/11/95	6,776	WFM0201A.CSP	C:\WINDOWS	CSP	\WIN95\CAB_08.CAB
7/11/95	9,004	WFM0202A.CSP	C:\WINDOWS	CSP	\WIN95\CAB_08.CAB
7/11/95	9,004	WFM0203A.CSP	C:\WINDOWS	CSP	\WIN95\CAB_08.CAB
7/11/95	766	ARROW_1.CUR	C:\WINDOWS\CURSORS	CUR	\WIN95\CAB_17.CAB
7/11/95	766	ARROW_L.CUR	C:\WINDOWS\CURSORS	CUR	\WIN95\CAB_17.CAB
7/11/95	766	ARROW_M.CUR	C:\WINDOWS\CURSORS	CUR	\WIN95\CAB_13.CAB
7/11/95	766	BEAM_1.CUR	C:\WINDOWS\CURSORS	CUR	\WIN95\CAB_13.CAB
7/11/95	766	BEAM_L.CUR	C:\WINDOWS\CURSORS	CUR	\WIN95\CAB_13.CAB
7/11/95	766	BEAM_M.CUR	C:\WINDOWS\CURSORS	CUR	\WIN95\CAB_13.CAB
7/11/95	766	BUSY_1.CUR	C:\WINDOWS\CURSORS	CUR	\WIN95\CAB_13.CAB
7/11/95	766	BUSY_L.CUR	C:\WINDOWS\CURSORS	CUR	\WIN95\CAB_13.CAB
7/11/95	766	BUSY_M.CUR	C:\WINDOWS\CURSORS	CUR	\WIN95\CAB_13.CAB
7/11/95	766	CROSS_1.CUR	C:\WINDOWS\CURSORS	CUR	\WIN95\CAB_13.CAB
7/11/95	766	CROSS_L.CUR	C:\WINDOWS\CURSORS	CUR	\WIN95\CAB_13.CAB
7/11/95	766	CROSS_M.CUR	C:\WINDOWS\CURSORS	CUR	\WIN95\CAB_13.CAB
7/11/95	766	HELP_1.CUR	C:\WINDOWS\CURSORS	CUR	\WIN95\CAB_13.CAB
7/11/95	766	HELP_L.CUR	C:\WINDOWS\CURSORS	CUR	\WIN95\CAB_13.CAB
7/11/95	766	HELP_M.CUR	C:\WINDOWS\CURSORS	CUR	\WIN95\CAB_13.CAB
7/11/95	766	MOVE_1.CUR	C:\WINDOWS\CURSORS	CUR	\WIN95\CAB_13.CAB
7/11/95	766	MOVE_L.CUR	C:\WINDOWS\CURSORS	CUR	\WIN95\CAB_13.CAB
7/11/95	766	MOVE_M.CUR	C:\WINDOWS\CURSORS	CUR	\WIN95\CAB_13.CAB
7/11/95	766	NO_1.CUR	C:\WINDOWS\CURSORS	CUR	\WIN95\CAB_13.CAB
7/11/95	766	NO_L.CUR	C:\WINDOWS\CURSORS	CUR	\WIN95\CAB_13.CAB
7/11/95	766	NO_M.CUR	C:\WINDOWS\CURSORS	CUR	\WIN95\CAB_13.CAB
7/11/95	766	PEN_1.CUR	C:\WINDOWS\CURSORS	CUR	\WIN95\CAB_13.CAB
7/11/95	766	PEN_L.CUR	C:\WINDOWS\CURSORS	CUR	\WIN95\CAB_13.CAB
7/11/95	766	PEN_M.CUR	C:\WINDOWS\CURSORS	CUR	\WIN95\CAB_13.CAB
7/11/95	766	SIZE1_1.CUR	C:\WINDOWS\CURSORS	CUR	\WIN95\CAB_13.CAB
7/11/95	766	SIZE1_L.CUR	C:\WINDOWS\CURSORS	CUR	\WIN95\CAB_13.CAB
7/11/95	766	SIZE1_M.CUR	C:\WINDOWS\CURSORS	CUR	\WIN95\CAB_13.CAB
7/11/95	766	SIZE2_1.CUR	C:\WINDOWS\CURSORS	CUR	\WIN95\CAB_13.CAB
7/11/95	766	SIZE2_L.CUR	C:\WINDOWS\CURSORS	CUR	\WIN95\CAB_13.CAB
7/11/95	766	SIZE2_M.CUR	C:\WINDOWS\CURSORS	CUR	\WIN95\CAB_13.CAB
7/11/95	766	SIZE3_1.CUR	C:\WINDOWS\CURSORS	CUR	\WIN95\CAB_13.CAB
7/11/95	766	SIZE3_L.CUR	C:\WINDOWS\CURSORS	CUR	\WIN95\CAB_13.CAB
7/11/95	766	SIZE3_M.CUR	C:\WINDOWS\CURSORS	CUR	\WIN95\CAB_13.CAB
7/11/95	766	SIZE4_1.CUR	C:\WINDOWS\CURSORS	CUR	\WIN95\CAB_13.CAB
7/11/95	766	SIZE4_L.CUR	C:\WINDOWS\CURSORS	CUR	\WIN95\CAB_13.CAB
7/11/95	766	SIZE4_M.CUR	C:\WINDOWS\CURSORS	CUR	\WIN95\CAB_13.CAB
7/11/95	766	UP_1.CUR	C:\WINDOWS\CURSORS	CUR	\WIN95\CAB_13.CAB
7/11/95	766	UP_L.CUR	C:\WINDOWS\CURSORS	CUR	\WIN95\CAB_13.CAB
7/11/95	766	UP_M.CUR	C:\WINDOWS\CURSORS	CUR	\WIN95\CAB_13.CAB

Date of File	Size of File	Installed Name	Installed Location	Type of File	Location on CD
7/11/95	766	WAIT_1.CUR	C:\WINDOWS\CURSORS	CUR	\WIN95\CAB_13.CAB
7/11/95	766	WAIT_L.CUR	C:\WINDOWS\CURSORS	CUR	\WIN95\CAB_13.CAB
7/11/95	766	WAIT_M.CUR	C:\WINDOWS\CURSORS	CUR	\WIN95\CAB_13.CAB
7/11/95	23,200	ESCP2MS.DRV	C:\WINDOWS\SYSTEM	DRV	\WIN95\CAB_09.CAB
7/11/95	10,098	800950.DAT	C:\PROGRAM FILES\ THE MICROSOFT NETWORK	DAT	\WIN95\CAB_07.CAB
7/11/95	524	850.dat	C:\PROGRAM FILES\ THE MICROSOFT NETWORK	DAT	\WIN95\CAB_05.CAB
7/11/95	13,824	ADVAPI32.DLL	C:\WINDOWS\SYSTEM	DLL	\WIN95\CAB_11.CAB
7/11/95	72,272	AVICAP.DLL	C:\WINDOWS\SYSTEM	DLL	\WIN95\CAB_08.CAB
7/11/95	59,904	AVICAP32.DLL	C:\WINDOWS\SYSTEM	DLL	\WIN95\CAB_08.CAB
7/11/95	88,064	AVIFIL32.DLL	C:\WINDOWS\SYSTEM	DLL	\WIN95\CAB_08.CAB
7/11/95	109,424	AVIFILE.DLL	C:\WINDOWS\SYSTEM	DLL	\WIN95\CAB_08.CAB
7/11/95	41,344	AVWIN.DLL	C:\WINDOWS\SYSTEM	DLL	\WIN95\CAB_13.CAB
7/11/95	10,240	AWBMSC32.DLL	C:\WINDOWS\SYSTEM	DLL	\WIN95\CAB_05.CAB
7/11/95	5,120	AWBTRV32.DLL	C:\WINDOWS\SYSTEM	DLL	\WIN95\CAB_05.CAB
7/11/95	9,216	AWCAPI32.DLL	C:\WINDOWS\SYSTEM	DLL	\WIN95\CAB_05.CAB
7/11/95	22,528	AWCL1_32.DLL	C:\WINDOWS\SYSTEM	DLL	\WIN95\CAB_05.CAB
7/11/95	24,064	AWCL2_32.DLL	C:\WINDOWS\SYSTEM	DLL	\WIN95\CAB_05.CAB
7/11/95	24,576	AWCODC32.DLL	C:\WINDOWS\SYSTEM	DLL	\WIN95\CAB_05.CAB
7/11/95	6,144	AWDCXC32.DLL	C:\WINDOWS\SYSTEM	DLL	\WIN95\CAB_05.CAB
7/11/95	7,248	AWDEVL16.DLL	C:\WINDOWS\SYSTEM	DLL	\WIN95\CAB_05.CAB
7/11/95	6,656	AWDEVL32.DLL	C:\WINDOWS\SYSTEM	DLL	\WIN95\CAB_05.CAB
7/11/95	116,736	AWFAXP32.DLL	C:\WINDOWS\SYSTEM	DLL	\WIN95\CAB_05.CAB
7/11/95	123,392	AWFEXT32.DLL	C:\WINDOWS\SYSTEM	DLL	\WIN95\CAB_05.CAB
7/11/95	15,360	AWFMON32.DLL	C:\WINDOWS\SYSTEM	DLL	\WIN95\CAB_05.CAB
7/11/95	35,840	AWFR32.DLL	C:\WINDOWS\SYSTEM	DLL	\WIN95\CAB_05.CAB
7/11/95	49,152	AWFXAB32.DLL	C:\WINDOWS\SYSTEM	DLL	\WIN95\CAB_05.CAB
7/11/95	116,224	AWFXCG32.DLL	C:\WINDOWS\SYSTEM	DLL	\WIN95\CAB_05.CAB
7/11/95	44,032	AWFXIO32.DLL	C:\WINDOWS\SYSTEM	DLL	\WIN95\CAB_05.CAB
7/11/95	49,152	AWFXRN32.DLL	C:\WINDOWS\SYSTEM	DLL	\WIN95\CAB_05.CAB
7/11/95	27,136	AWKRNL32.DLL	C:\WINDOWS\SYSTEM	DLL	\WIN95\CAB_05.CAB
7/11/95	34,304	AWLFT332.DLL	C:\WINDOWS\SYSTEM	DLL	\WIN95\CAB_05.CAB
7/11/95	13,312	AWLHUT32.DLL	C:\WINDOWS\SYSTEM	DLL	\WIN95\CAB_05.CAB
7/11/95	32,256	AWLINZ32.DLL	C:\WINDOWS\SYSTEM	DLL	\WIN95\CAB_05.CAB
7/11/95	8,192	AWLZRD32.DLL	C:\WINDOWS\SYSTEM	DLL	\WIN95\CAB_05.CAB
7/11/95	34,304	AWNFAX32.DLL	C:\WINDOWS\SYSTEM	DLL	\WIN95\CAB_05.CAB
7/11/95	20,480	AWPWD32.DLL	C:\WINDOWS\SYSTEM	DLL	\WIN95\CAB_05.CAB
7/11/95	11,264	AWRAMB32.DLL	C:\WINDOWS\SYSTEM	DLL	\WIN95\CAB_05.CAB
7/11/95	8,192	AWRBAE32.DLL	C:\WINDOWS\SYSTEM	DLL	\WIN95\CAB_05.CAB
7/11/95	26,624	AWRESX32.DLL	C:\WINDOWS\SYSTEM	DLL	\WIN95\CAB_05.CAB
7/11/95	6,144	AWRNDR32.DLL	C:\WINDOWS\SYSTEM	DLL	\WIN95\CAB_05.CAB

App

G

continues

Date of File	Size of File	Installed Name	Installed Location	Type of File	Location on CD
7/11/95	46,592	AWSCHD32.DLL	C:\WINDOWS\SYSTEM	DLL	\WIN95\CAB_05.CAB
7/11/95	13,824	AWSRVR32.DLL	C:\WINDOWS\SYSTEM	DLL	\WIN95\CAB_05.CAB
7/11/95	33,280	AWT30_32.DLL	C:\WINDOWS\SYSTEM	DLL	\WIN95\CAB_05.CAB
7/11/95	40,448	AWUTIL32.DLL	C:\WINDOWS\SYSTEM	DLL	\WIN95\CAB_05.CAB
7/11/95	11,264	AWVIEW32.DLL	C:\WINDOWS\SYSTEM	DLL	\WIN95\CAB_05.CAB
7/11/95	820,224	BACKUP.EXE	C:\WINDOWS\SYSTEM	DLL	\WIN95\CAB_04.CAB
7/11/95	39,936	BKUPNET.DLL	C:\WINDOWS\SYSTEM	DLL	\WIN95\CAB_17.CAB
7/11/95	40,960	BKUPPROP.DLL	C:\WINDOWS\SYSTEM	DLL	\WIN95\PRECOPY2.CAB
7/11/95	148,528	CARDS.DLL	C:\WINDOWS\SYSTEM	DLL	\WIN95\CAB_05.CAB
7/11/95	29,696	CCAPI.DLL	C:\WINDOWS\SYSTEM	DLL	\WIN95\CAB_07.CAB
7/11/95	13,312	CCEI.DLL	C:\PROGRAM FILES\ THE MICROSOFT NETWORK	DLL	\WIN95\CAB_07.CAB
7/11/95	13,824	CCPSH.DLL	C:\PROGRAM FILES\ THE MICROSOFT NETWORK	DLL	\WIN95\CAB_07.CAB
7/11/95	11,792	CHEYPROP.DLL	C:\WINDOWS\SYSTEM	DLL	\WIN95\PRECOPY2.CAB
7/11/95	15,360	CHIKDI.DLL	C:\WINDOWS\SYSTEM	DLL	\WIN95\CAB_04.CAB
7/11/95	22,016	CHOOSUSR.DLL	C:\WINDOWS\SYSTEM	DLL	\WIN95\CAB_11.CAB
7/11/95	6,304	CMC.DLL	C:\WINDOWS\SYSTEM	DLL	\WIN95\CAB_06.CAB
7/11/95	46,480	COMCTL31.DLL	C:\WINDOWS\SYSTEM	DLL	\WIN95\PRECOPY1.CAB
7/11/95	182,272	COMCTL32.DLL	C:\WINDOWS\SYSTEM	DLL	\WIN95\CAB_10.CAB
7/11/95	92,672	COMDLG32.DLL	C:\WINDOWS\SYSTEM	DLL	\WIN95\CAB_10.CAB
7/11/95	48,112	COMMCTRL.DLL	C:\WINDOWS\SYSTEM	DLL	\WIN95\PRECOPY1.CAB
7/11/95	97,936	COMMDLG.DLL	C:\WINDOWS\SYSTEM	DLL	\WIN95\PRECOPY1.CAB
7/11/95	43,504	COMPLINC.DLL	C:\WINDOWS\SYSTEM	DLL	\WIN95\PRECOPY1.CAB
7/11/95	30,976	COMPOBJ.DLL	C:\WINDOWS\SYSTEM	DLL	\WIN95\CAB_09.CAB
7/11/95	23,552	CONFAPI.DLL	C:\WINDOWS\SYSTEM	DLL	\WIN95\CAB_07.CAB
7/11/95	161,280	CRTDLL.DLL	C:\WINDOWS\SYSTEM	DLL	\WIN95\CAB_03.CAB
7/11/95	17,776	CSPMAN.DLL	C:\WINDOWS\SYSTEM	DLL	\WIN95\CAB_08.CAB
7/11/95	12,800	DATAEDCL.DLL	C:\PROGRAM FILES\ THE MICROSOFT NETWORK	DLL	\WIN95\CAB_07.CAB
7/11/95	6,928	DCIMAN.DLL	C:\WINDOWS\SYSTEM	DLL	\WIN95\CAB_08.CAB
7/11/95	5,632	DCIMAN32.DLL	C:\WINDOWS\SYSTEM	DLL	\WIN95\CAB_08.CAB
7/11/95	32,240	DDEML.DLL	C:\WINDOWS\SYSTEM	DLL	\WIN95\CAB_03.CAB
7/11/95	21,504	DEBMP.DLL	C:\WINDOWS\SYSTEM\ VIEWERS	DLL	\WIN95\CAB_13.CAB
7/11/95	369,664	DECPSMW4.DLL	C:\WINDOWS\SYSTEM	DLL	\WIN95\CAB_16.CAB
7/11/95	241,600	DEFRAG.EXE	C:\WINDOWS	DLL	\WIN95\CAB_04.CAB
7/11/95	8,192	DEHEX.DLL	C:\WINDOWS\SYSTEM\ VIEWERS	DLL	\WIN95\CAB_13.CAB
7/11/95	40,448	DEMET.DLL	C:\WINDOWS\SYSTEM\ VIEWERS	DLL	\WIN95\CAB_13.CAB
7/11/95	83,472	DESKCP16.DLL	C:\WINDOWS\SYSTEM	DLL	\WIN95\CAB_03.CAB

Date of File	Size of File	Installed Name	Installed Location	Type of File	Location on CD
7/11/95	36,352	DESS.DLL	C:\WINDOWS\SYSTEM\ VIEWERS	DLL	\WIN95\CAB_13.CAB
7/11/95	48,128	DEWP.DLL	C:\WINDOWS\SYSTEM\ VIEWERS	DLL	\WIN95\CAB_13.CAB
7/11/95	201,136	DIBENG.DLL	C:\WINDOWS\SYSTEM	DLL	\WIN95\CAB_03.CAB
7/11/95	15,872	DISKCOPY.DLL	C:\WINDOWS\SYSTEM	DLL	\WIN95\CAB_10.CAB
7/11/95	6,992	DISPDIB.DLL	C:\WINDOWS\SYSTEM	DLL	\WIN95\CAB_08.CAB
7/11/95	18,272	DMCOLOR.DLL	C:\WINDOWS\SYSTEM	DLL	\WIN95\CAB_09.CAB
7/11/95	17,408	DOCPROP.DLL	C:\WINDOWS\SYSTEM	DLL	\WIN95\CAB_10.CAB
7/11/95	189,456	DSKMAINT.DLL	C:\WINDOWS\SYSTEM	DLL	\WIN95\PRECOPY2.CAB
7/11/95	94,720	DUNZIPNT.DLL	C:\WINDOWS\SYSTEM	DLL	\WIN95\CAB_07.CAB
7/11/95	6,160	ENABLE3.DLL	C:\WINDOWS\SYSTEM	DLL	\WIN95\CAB_02.CAB
7/11/95	14,336	FAXCODEC.DLL	C:\WINDOWS\SYSTEM	DLL	\WIN95\CAB_05.CAB
7/11/95	5,728	FINDMVI.DLL	C:\WINDOWS\SYSTEM	DLL	\WIN95\CAB_08.CAB
7/11/95	10,752	FINDSTUB.DLL	C:\PROGRAM FILES\ THE MICROSOFT NETWORK	DLL	\WIN95\CAB_07.CAB
7/11/95	188,848	FINSTALL.DLL	C:\WINDOWS\SYSTEM	DLL	\WIN95\CAB_09.CAB
7/11/95	105,984	FONTEXT.DLL	C:\WINDOWS\SYSTEM	DLL	\WIN95\CAB_10.CAB
7/11/95	53,248	FTE.DLL	C:\WINDOWS\SYSTEM	DLL	\WIN95\CAB_17.CAB
7/11/95	66,048	FTMAPI.DLL	C:\WINDOWS\SYSTEM	DLL	\WIN95\CAB_07.CAB
7/11/95	231,936	FTSRCH.DLL	C:\WINDOWS\SYSTEM	DLL	\WIN95\CAB_05.CAB
7/11/95	131,072	GDI32.DLL	C:\WINDOWS\SYSTEM	DLL	\WIN95\CAB_11.CAB
7/11/95	58,368	HOMEBASE.DLL	C:\PROGRAM FILES\ THE MICROSOFT NETWORK	DLL	\WIN95\CAB_07.CAB
7/11/95	21,504	HPALERTS.DLL	C:\WINDOWS\SPOOL	DLL	\WIN95\CAB_16.CAB
7/11/95	45,056	HPARRKUI.DLL	C:\WINDOWS\SPOOL	DLL	\WIN95\CAB_16.CAB
7/11/95	105,984	HPCOLA.DLL	C:\WINDOWS\SPOOL	DLL	\WIN95\CAB_16.CAB
7/11/95	18,496	HPCOLOR.DLL	C:\WINDOWS\SPOOL	DLL	\WIN95\CAB_09.CAB
7/11/95	25,088	HPDMIPX.DLL	C:\WINDOWS\SPOOL	DLL	\WIN95\CAB_16.CAB
7/11/95	5,152	HPJD.DLL	C:\WINDOWS\SPOOL	DLL	\WIN95\CAB_16.CAB
7/11/95	48,640	HPJDCOM.DLL	C:\WINDOWS\SPOOL	DLL	\WIN95\CAB_16.CAB
7/11/95	8,704	HPJDMON.DLL	C:\WINDOWS\SPOOL	DLL	\WIN95\CAB_16.CAB
7/11/95	12,288	HPJDNP.DLL	C:\WINDOWS\SPOOL	DLL	\WIN95\CAB_16.CAB
7/11/95	48,640	HPJDPP.DLL	C:\WINDOWS\SPOOL	DLL	\WIN95\CAB_16.CAB
7/11/95	116,224	HPJDUI.DLL	C:\WINDOWS\SPOOL	DLL	\WIN95\CAB_16.CAB
7/11/95	23,552	HPJDUND.DLL	C:\WINDOWS\SPOOL	DLL	\WIN95\CAB_16.CAB
7/11/95	15,872	HPNETSRV.DLL	C:\WINDOWS\SPOOL	DLL	\WIN95\CAB_16.CAB
7/11/95	1,431	HPNW416.DLL	C:\WINDOWS\SPOOL	DLL	\WIN95\CAB_16.CAB
7/11/95	18,944	HPNW432.DLL	C:\WINDOWS\SPOOL	DLL	\WIN95\CAB_16.CAB
7/11/95	21,504	HPNWPSRV.DLL	C:\WINDOWS\SPOOL	DLL	\WIN95\CAB_16.CAB
7/11/95	27,648	HPNWSHIM.DLL	C:\WINDOWS\SPOOL	DLL	\WIN95\CAB_16.CAB
7/11/95	18,944	HPPJL.DLL	C:\WINDOWS\SPOOL	DLL	\WIN95\CAB_16.CAB

App

G

continues

Date of File	Size of File	Installed Name	Installed Location	Type of File	Location on CD
7/11/95	168,448	HPPJLEXT.DLL	C:\WINDOWS\SPOOL	DLL	\WIN95\CAB_16.CAB
7/11/95	7,680	HPPRARRK.DLL	C:\WINDOWS\SPOOL	DLL	\WIN95\CAB_16.CAB
7/11/95	36,864	HPPRNTR.DLL	C:\WINDOWS\SPOOL	DLL	\WIN95\CAB_16.CAB
7/11/95	7,680	HPPRRUSH.DLL	C:\WINDOWS\SPOOL	DLL	\WIN95\CAB_16.CAB
7/11/95	246,784	HPPRUI.DLL	C:\WINDOWS\SPOOL	DLL	\WIN95\CAB_16.CAB
7/11/95	24,576	HPRUSHUI.DLL	C:\WINDOWS\SPOOL	DLL	\WIN95\CAB_16.CAB
7/11/95	152,064	HPSNMP.DLL	C:\WINDOWS\SPOOL	DLL	\WIN95\CAB_16.CAB
7/11/95	41,472	HPTABS.DLL	C:\WINDOWS\SPOOL	DLL	\WIN95\CAB_16.CAB
7/11/95	5,632	HPTRBIT.DLL	C:\WINDOWS\SPOOL	DLL	\WIN95\CAB_16.CAB
7/11/95	11,264	HPVBIT.DLL	C:\WINDOWS\SPOOL	DLL	\WIN95\CAB_16.CAB
7/11/95	25,216	HPVIOL.DLL	C:\WINDOWS\SPOOL	DLL	\WIN95\CAB_09.CAB
7/11/95	13,280	HPVMON.DLL	C:\WINDOWS\SPOOL	DLL	\WIN95\CAB_09.CAB
7/11/95	21,072	HPVRES.DLL	C:\WINDOWS\SPOOL	DLL	\WIN95\CAB_09.CAB
7/11/95	49,104	HPVUI.DLL	C:\WINDOWS\SPOOL	DLL	\WIN95\CAB_09.CAB
7/11/95	24,576	HPWIZ.DLL	C:\WINDOWS\SPOOL	DLL	\WIN95\CAB_16.CAB
7/11/95	20,480	HTICONS.DLL	C:\PROGRAM FILES\ ACCESSORIES\ HYPERTERMINAL	DLL	\WIN95\CAB_02.CAB
7/11/95	326,144	HYPERTRM.DLL	C:\PROGRAM FILES\ ACCESSORIES\ HYPERTERMINAL	DLL	\WIN95\CAB_02.CAB
7/11/95	77,824	ICCVID.DLL	C:\WINDOWS\SYSTEM	DLL	\WIN95\CAB_08.CAB
7/11/95	140,288	ICM32.DLL	C:\WINDOWS\SYSTEM	DLL	\WIN95\CAB_06.CAB
7/11/95	6,496	ICMP.DLL	C:\WINDOWS\SYSTEM	DLL	\WIN95\CAB_11.CAB
7/11/95	22,016	ICMUI.DLL	C:\WINDOWS\SYSTEM	DLL	\WIN95\CAB_06.CAB
7/11/95	77,712	ICONLIB.DLL	C:\WINDOWS\SYSTEM	DLL	\WIN95\CAB_09.CAB
7/11/95	6,144	IMM32.DLL	C:\WINDOWS\SYSTEM	DLL	\WIN95\CAB_06.CAB
7/11/95	5,120	INDICDLL.DLL	C:\WINDOWS\SYSTEM	DLL	\WIN95\CAB_06.CAB
7/11/95	50,512	INETMIB1.DLL	C:\WINDOWS	DLL	\WIN95\CAB_11.CAB
7/11/95	66,192	INSTL50.DLL	C:\	DLL	\WIN95\CAB_17.CAB
7/11/95	66,192	INSTL51.DLL	C:\	DLL	\WIN95\CAB_17.CAB
7/11/95	193,024	IR32_32.DLL	C:\WINDOWS\SYSTEM	DLL	\WIN95\CAB_08.CAB
7/11/95	411,136	KERNEL32.DLL	C:\WINDOWS\SYSTEM	DLL	\WIN95\CAB_11.CAB
7/11/95	154,880	KOMMCTRL.DLL	C:\WINDOWS\SYSTEM	DLL	\WIN95\PRECOPY1.CAB
7/11/95	13,824	LINKINFO.DLL	C:\WINDOWS\SYSTEM	DLL	\WIN95\CAB_10.CAB
7/11/95	5,632	LZ32.DLL	C:\WINDOWS\SYSTEM	DLL	\WIN95\CAB_11.CAB
7/11/95	9,936	LZEXPAND.DLL	C:\WINDOWS\SYSTEM	DLL	\WIN95\MINI.CAB
7/11/95	23,696	LZEXPAND.DLL	C:\WINDOWS\SYSTEM	DLL	\WIN95\PRECOPY1.CAB
7/11/95	22,096	MAINCP16.DLL	C:\WINDOWS\SYSTEM	DLL	\WIN95\CAB_03.CAB
7/11/95	441,088	MAPI.DLL	C:\WINDOWS\SYSTEM	DLL	\WIN95\CAB_06.CAB
7/11/95	592,896	MAPI32.DLL	C:\WINDOWS\SYSTEM	DLL	\WIN95\CAB_06.CAB
7/11/95	5,440	MAPIU.DLL	C:\WINDOWS\SYSTEM	DLL	\WIN95\CAB_06.CAB
7/11/95	4,384	MAPIU32.DLL	C:\WINDOWS\SYSTEM	DLL	\WIN95\CAB_06.CAB
7/11/95	4,448	MAPIX.DLL	C:\WINDOWS\SYSTEM	DLL	\WIN95\CAB_06.CAB

Date of File	Size of File	Installed Name	Installed Location	Type of File	Location on CD
7/11/95	6,000	MAPIX32.DLL	C:\WINDOWS\SYSTEM	DLL	\WIN95\CAB_06.CAB
7/11/95	5,584	MCIOLE.DLL	C:\WINDOWS\SYSTEM	DLL	\WIN95\CAB_08.CAB
7/11/95	99,840	MCM.DLL	C:\WINDOWS\SYSTEM	DLL	\WIN95\CAB_07.CAB
7/11/95	30,720	MF3216.DLL	C:\WINDOWS\SYSTEM	DLL	\WIN95\CAB_03.CAB
7/11/95	322,832	MFC30.DLL	C:\WINDOWS\SYSTEM	DLL	\WIN95\CAB_02.CAB
7/11/95	133,904	MFCANS32.DLL	C:\WINDOWS\SYSTEM	DLL	\WIN95\CAB_03.CAB
7/11/95	55,808	MFCD30.DLL	C:\WINDOWS\SYSTEM	DLL	\WIN95\CAB_02.CAB
7/11/95	15,872	MFCN30.DLL	C:\WINDOWS\SYSTEM	DLL	\WIN95\CAB_02.CAB
7/11/95	133,392	MFCO30.DLL	C:\WINDOWS\SYSTEM	DLL	\WIN95\CAB_02.CAB
7/11/95	5,632	MFCUIA32.DLL	C:\WINDOWS\SYSTEM	DLL	\WIN95\CAB_09.CAB
7/11/95	4,096	MFCUIW32.DLL	C:\WINDOWS\SYSTEM	DLL	\WIN95\CAB_09.CAB
7/11/95	1,300	MINIKBD.DLL	C:\WINDOWS\SYSTEM	DLL	\WIN95\MINI.CAB
7/11/95	12,048	MLSHEXT.DLL	C:\PROGRAM FILES\ MICROSOFT EXCHANGE	DLL	\WIN95\CAB_06.CAB
7/11/95	13,536	MMCI.DLL	C:\WINDOWS\SYSTEM	DLL	\WIN95\CAB_08.CAB
7/11/95	268,176	MMFMIG32.DLL	C:\WINDOWS\SYSTEM	DLL	\WIN95\CAB_06.CAB
7/11/95	5,152	MMMIXER.DLL	C:\WINDOWS\SYSTEM	DLL	\WIN95\CAB_08.CAB
7/11/95	103,248	MMSYSTEM.DLL	C:\WINDOWS\SYSTEM	DLL	\WIN95\CAB_08.CAB
7/11/95	53,248	MMVDIB12.DLL	C:\PROGRAM FILES\ THE MICROSOFT NETWORK	DLL	\WIN95\CAB_07.CAB
7/11/95	27,504	MODEMUI.DLL	C:\WINDOWS\SYSTEM	DLL	\WIN95\CAB_07.CAB
7/11/95	84,412	MORICONS.DLL	C:\WINDOWS	DLL	\WIN95\CAB_10.CAB
7/11/95	107,520	MOSABP32.DLL	C:\WINDOWS\SYSTEM	DLL	\WIN95\CAB_07.CAB
7/11/95	24,576	MOSAF.DLL	C:\PROGRAM FILES\ THE MICROSOFT NETWORK	DLL	\WIN95\CAB_07.CAB
7/11/95	47,616	MOSCC.DLL	C:\WINDOWS\SYSTEM	DLL	\WIN95\CAB_07.CAB
7/11/95	15,360	MOSCFG32.DLL	C:\WINDOWS\SYSTEM	DLL	\WIN95\CAB_07.CAB
7/11/95	36,864	MOSCL.DLL	C:\WINDOWS\SYSTEM	DLL	\WIN95\CAB_07.CAB
7/11/95	149,504	MOSCOMP.DLL	C:\PROGRAM FILES\ THE MICROSOFT NETWORK	DLL	\WIN95\CAB_07.CAB
7/11/95	21,504	MOSCUDLL.DLL	C:\WINDOWS\SYSTEM	DLL	\WIN95\CAB_07.CAB
7/11/95	25,600	MOSFIND.DLL	C:\PROGRAM FILES\ THE MICROSOFT NETWORK	DLL	\WIN95\CAB_07.CAB
7/11/95	9,216	MOSMISC.DLL	C:\WINDOWS\SYSTEM	DLL	\WIN95\CAB_07.CAB
7/11/95	26,624	MOSMUTIL.DLL	C:\WINDOWS\SYSTEM	DLL	\WIN95\CAB_07.CAB
7/11/95	56,832	MOSRXP32.DLL	C:\WINDOWS\SYSTEM	DLL	\WIN95\CAB_07.CAB
7/11/95	182,784	MOSSHELL.DLL	C:\PROGRAM FILES\ THE MICROSOFT NETWORK	DLL	\WIN95\CAB_07.CAB
7/11/95	7,680	MOSSTUB.DLL	C:\PROGRAM FILES\ THE MICROSOFT NETWORK	DLL	\WIN95\CAB_07.CAB

App
G

continues

Date of File	Size of File	Installed Name	Installed Location	Type of File	Location on CD
7/11/95	87,040	MPCCL.DLL	C:\PROGRAM FILES\ THE MICROSOFT NETWORK	DLL	\WIN95\CAB_07.CAB
7/11/95	40,448	MPR.DLL	C:\WINDOWS\SYSTEM	DLL	\WIN95\CAB_11.CAB
7/11/95	119,296	MPRSERV.DLL	C:\WINDOWS\SYSTEM	DLL	\WIN95\CAB_11.CAB
7/11/95	61,952	MSAB32.DLL	C:\WINDOWS\SYSTEM	DLL	\WIN95\CAB_11.CAB
7/11/95	53,552	MSACM.DLL	C:\WINDOWS\SYSTEM	DLL	\WIN95\CAB_08.CAB
7/11/95	91,648	MSACM32.DLL	C:\WINDOWS\SYSTEM	DLL	\WIN95\CAB_08.CAB
7/11/95	402,944	MSFS32.DLL	C:\WINDOWS\SYSTEM	DLL	\WIN95\CAB_06.CAB
7/11/95	1,264	MSMIXMGR.DLL	C:\WINDOWS\SYSTEM	DLL	\WIN95\CAB_08.CAB
7/11/95	25,600	MSNDUI.DLL	C:\PROGRAM FILES\ THE MICROSOFT NETWORK	DLL	\WIN95\CAB_07.CAB
7/11/95	60,416	MSNET32.DLL	C:\WINDOWS\SYSTEM	DLL	\WIN95\CAB_11.CAB
7/11/95	67,584	MSNP32.DLL	C:\WINDOWS\SYSTEM	DLL	\WIN95\CAB_11.CAB
7/11/95	36,400	MSPCIC.DLL	C:\WINDOWS\SYSTEM	DLL	\WIN95\CAB_09.CAB
7/11/95	32,256	MSPCX32.DLL	C:\PROGRAM FILES\ ACCESSORIES	DLL	\WIN95\CAB_02.CAB
7/11/95	17,920	MSPP32.DLL	C:\WINDOWS\SYSTEM	DLL	\WIN95\CAB_11.CAB
7/11/95	55,872	MSPRINT.DLL	C:\WINDOWS\SYSTEM	DLL	\WIN95\PRECOPY1.CAB
7/11/95	48,128	MSPRINT2.DLL	C:\WINDOWS\SYSTEM	DLL	\WIN95\PRECOPY1.CAB
7/11/95	386,560	MSPST32.DLL	C:\WINDOWS\SYSTEM	DLL	\WIN95\CAB_06.CAB
7/11/95	15,360	MSPWL32.DLL	C:\WINDOWS\SYSTEM	DLL	\WIN95\CAB_11.CAB
7/11/95	11,264	MSRLE32.DLL	C:\WINDOWS\SYSTEM	DLL	\WIN95\CAB_08.CAB
7/11/95	74,752	MSSHRUI.DLL	C:\WINDOWS\SYSTEM	DLL	\WIN95\CAB_11.CAB
7/11/95	26,832	MSTCP.DLL	C:\WINDOWS\SYSTEM	DLL	\WIN95\PRECOPY1.CAB
7/11/95	253,952	MSVCRT20.DLL	C:\WINDOWS\SYSTEM	DLL	\WIN95\CAB_02.CAB
7/11/95	129,536	MSVFW32.DLL	C:\WINDOWS\SYSTEM	DLL	\WIN95\CAB_08.CAB
7/11/95	30,208	MSVIDC32.DLL	C:\WINDOWS\SYSTEM	DLL	\WIN95\CAB_08.CAB
7/11/95	113,664	MSVIDEO.DLL	C:\WINDOWS\SYSTEM	DLL	\WIN95\CAB_08.CAB
7/11/95	147,968	MSVIEWUT.DLL	C:\WINDOWS\SYSTEM\ VIEWERS	DLL	\WIN95\CAB_13.CAB
7/11/95	112,128	MVCL14N.DLL	C:\PROGRAM FILES\ THE MICROSOFT NETWORK	DLL	\WIN95\CAB_07.CAB
7/11/95	51,712	MVPR14N.DLL	C:\PROGRAM FILES\ THE MICROSOFT NETWORK	DLL	\WIN95\CAB_07.CAB
7/11/95	77,312	MVTTL14C.DLL	C:\PROGRAM FILES\ THE MICROSOFT NETWORK	DLL	\WIN95\CAB_07.CAB
7/11/95	10,240	MVUT14N.DLL	C:\PROGRAM FILES\ THE MICROSOFT NETWORK	DLL	\WIN95\CAB_07.CAB
7/11/95	14,032	NDDEAPI.DLL	C:\WINDOWS	DLL	\WIN95\CAB_11.CAB
7/11/95	10,768	NDDENB.DLL	C:\WINDOWS	DLL	\WIN95\CAB_11.CAB
7/11/95	106,960	NETAPI.DLL	C:\WINDOWS\SYSTEM	DLL	\WIN95\PRECOPY1.CAB

Date of File	Size of File	Installed Name	Installed Location	Type of File	Location on CD
7/11/95	4,096	NETAPI32.DLL	C:\WINDOWS\SYSTEM	DLL	\WIN95\CAB_11.CAB
7/11/95	6,656	NETBIOS.DLL	C:\WINDOWS\SYSTEM	DLL	\WIN95\CAB_11.CAB
7/11/95	7,885	NETDET.INI	C:\WINDOWS	DLL	\WIN95\PRECOPY1.CAB
7/11/95	282,832	NETDI.DLL	C:\WINDOWS\SYSTEM	DLL	\WIN95\PRECOPY1.CAB
7/11/95	24,400	NETOS.DLL	C:\WINDOWS\SYSTEM	DLL	\WIN95\PRECOPY1.CAB
7/11/95	5,632	NTDLL.DLL	C:\WINDOWS\SYSTEM	DLL	\WIN95\CAB_03.CAB
7/11/95	6,528	NW16.DLL	C:\WINDOWS\SYSTEM	DLL	\WIN95\CAB_11.CAB
7/11/95	25,600	NWAB32.DLL	C:\WINDOWS\SYSTEM	DLL	\WIN95\CAB_11.CAB
7/11/95	21,504	NWNET32.DLL	C:\WINDOWS\SYSTEM	DLL	\WIN95\CAB_11.CAB
7/11/95	77,312	NWNP32.DLL	C:\WINDOWS\SYSTEM	DLL	\WIN95\CAB_11.CAB
7/11/95	43,008	NWPP32.DLL	C:\WINDOWS\SYSTEM	DLL	\WIN95\CAB_11.CAB
7/11/95	39,744	OLE2.DLL	C:\WINDOWS\SYSTEM	DLL	\WIN95\CAB_09.CAB
7/11/95	57,328	OLE2CONV.DLL	C:\WINDOWS\SYSTEM	DLL	\WIN95\CAB_09.CAB
7/11/95	169,440	OLE2DISP.DLL	C:\WINDOWS\SYSTEM	DLL	\WIN95\CAB_09.CAB
7/11/95	153,040	OLE2NLS.DLL	C:\WINDOWS\SYSTEM	DLL	\WIN95\CAB_09.CAB
7/11/95	557,664	OLE32.DLL	C:\WINDOWS\SYSTEM	DLL	\WIN95\CAB_09.CAB
7/11/95	232,720	OLEAUT32.DLL	C:\WINDOWS\SYSTEM	DLL	\WIN95\CAB_09.CAB
7/11/95	82,944	OLECLI.DLL	C:\WINDOWS\SYSTEM	DLL	\WIN95\CAB_09.CAB
7/11/95	12,288	OLECLI32.DLL	C:\WINDOWS\SYSTEM	DLL	\WIN95\CAB_09.CAB
7/11/95	40,576	OLECNV32.DLL	C:\WINDOWS\SYSTEM	DLL	\WIN95\CAB_09.CAB
7/11/95	112,640	OLEDLG.DLL	C:\WINDOWS\SYSTEM	DLL	\WIN95\CAB_09.CAB
7/11/95	24,064	OLESVR.DLL	C:\WINDOWS\SYSTEM	DLL	\WIN95\CAB_09.CAB
7/11/95	6,144	OLESVR32.DLL	C:\WINDOWS\SYSTEM	DLL	\WIN95\CAB_09.CAB
7/11/95	79,424	OLETHK32.DLL	C:\WINDOWS\SYSTEM	DLL	\WIN95\CAB_09.CAB
7/11/95	20,480	PANMAP.DLL	C:\WINDOWS\SYSTEM	DLL	\WIN95\CAB_10.CAB
7/11/95	82,816	PIFMGR.DLL	C:\WINDOWS\SYSTEM	DLL	\WIN95\CAB_03.CAB
7/11/95	12,288	PJLMON.DLL	C:\WINDOWS\SYSTEM	DLL	\WIN95\CAB_09.CAB
7/11/95	48,880	PKPD.DLL	C:\WINDOWS\SYSTEM	DLL	\WIN95\CAB_03.CAB
7/11/95	11,776	PKPD32.DLL	C:\WINDOWS\SYSTEM	DLL	\WIN95\CAB_03.CAB
7/11/95	26,608	PMSPL.DLL	C:\WINDOWS\SYSTEM	DLL	\WIN95\CAB_11.CAB
7/11/95	55,152	POINTER.DLL	C:\WINDOWS	DLL	\WIN95\CAB_08.CAB
7/11/95	12,800	POWERCFG.DLL	C:\WINDOWS\SYSTEM	DLL	\WIN95\CAB_03.CAB
7/11/95	72,192	PRODINV.DLL	C:\WINDOWS\SYSTEM	DLL	\WIN95\CAB_07.CAB
7/11/95	28,672	PSMON.DLL	C:\WINDOWS\SYSTEM	DLL	\WIN95\CAB_09.CAB
7/11/95	1,632	RASAPI16.DLL	C:\WINDOWS\SYSTEM	DLL	\WIN95\CAB_10.CAB
7/11/95	147,456	RASAPI32.DLL	C:\WINDOWS\SYSTEM	DLL	\WIN95\CAB_10.CAB
7/11/95	178,176	RICHED32.DLL	C:\WINDOWS\SYSTEM	DLL	\WIN95\CAB_04.CAB
7/11/95	11,776	RNANP.DLL	C:\WINDOWS\SYSTEM	DLL	\WIN95\CAB_10.CAB
7/11/95	5,408	RNASETUP.DLL	C:\WINDOWS\SYSTEM	DLL	\WIN95\PRECOPY1.CAB
7/11/95	5,120	RNATHUNK.DLL	C:\WINDOWS\SYSTEM	DLL	\WIN95\CAB_10.CAB
7/11/95	54,272	RNAUI.DLL	C:\WINDOWS\SYSTEM	DLL	\WIN95\CAB_10.CAB
7/11/95	31,232	RNDSRV32.DLL	C:\WINDOWS\SYSTEM	DLL	\WIN95\CAB_05.CAB

App

G

continues

Date of File	Size of File	Installed Name	Installed Location	Type of File	Location on CD
7/11/95	8,192	RPCLTC1.DLL	C:\WINDOWS\SYSTEM	DLL	\WIN95\CAB_11.CAB
7/11/95	7,584	RPCLTC3.DLL	C:\WINDOWS\SYSTEM	DLL	\WIN95\CAB_11.CAB
7/11/95	9,200	RPCLTC5.DLL	C:\WINDOWS\SYSTEM	DLL	\WIN95\CAB_11.CAB
7/11/95	8,128	RPCLTC6.DLL	C:\WINDOWS\SYSTEM	DLL	\WIN95\CAB_11.CAB
7/11/95	9,168	RPCLTS3.DLL	C:\WINDOWS\SYSTEM	DLL	\WIN95\CAB_11.CAB
7/11/95	10,736	RPCLTS5.DLL	C:\WINDOWS\SYSTEM	DLL	\WIN95\CAB_11.CAB
7/11/95	9,696	RPCLTS6.DLL	C:\WINDOWS\SYSTEM	DLL	\WIN95\CAB_11.CAB
7/11/95	30,832	RPCNS4.DLL	C:\WINDOWS\SYSTEM	DLL	\WIN95\CAB_11.CAB
7/11/95	202,240	RPCRT4.DLL	C:\WINDOWS\SYSTEM	DLL	\WIN95\CAB_11.CAB
7/11/95	23,040	RPLIMAGE.DLL	C:\WINDOWS\SYSTEM	DLL	\WIN95\PRECOPY2.CAB
7/11/95	1,312	RSRC16.DLL	C:\WINDOWS\SYSTEM	DLL	\WIN95\CAB_02.CAB
7/11/95	4,608	RSRC32.DLL	C:\WINDOWS\SYSTEM	DLL	\WIN95\CAB_02.CAB
7/11/95	29,184	SACLIENT.DLL	C:\PROGRAM FILES\ THE MICROSOFT NETWORK	DLL	\WIN95\CAB_07.CAB
7/11/95	9,216	SAPNSP.DLL	C:\WINDOWS\SYSTEM	DLL	\WIN95\CAB_11.CAB
7/11/95	32,256	SCCVIEW.DLL	C:\WINDOWS\SYSTEM\ VIEWERS	DLL	\WIN95\CAB_13.CAB
7/11/95	25,088	SECUR32.DLL	C:\WINDOWS\SYSTEM	DLL	\WIN95\CAB_11.CAB
7/11/95	15,360	SECURCL.DLL	C:\PROGRAM FILES\ THE MICROSOFT NETWORK	DLL	\WIN95\CAB_07.CAB
7/11/95	12,032	SERIALUI.DLL	C:\WINDOWS\SYSTEM	DLL	\WIN95\CAB_03.CAB
7/11/95	6,240	SETUP4.DLL	C:\WINDOWS\SYSTEM	DLL	\WIN95\CAB_10.CAB
7/11/95	355,136	SETUPX.DLL	C:\WINDOWS\SYSTEM	DLL	\WIN95\PRECOPY1.CAB
7/11/95	41,600	SHELL.DLL	C:\WINDOWS\SYSTEM	DLL	\WIN95\PRECOPY1.CAB
7/11/95	817,664	SHELL32.DLL	C:\WINDOWS\SYSTEM	DLL	\WIN95\CAB_10.CAB
7/11/95	24,576	SHSCRAP.DLL	C:\WINDOWS\SYSTEM	DLL	\WIN95\CAB_10.CAB
7/11/95	16,512	SLENH.DLL	C:\WINDOWS\SYSTEM	DLL	\WIN95\CAB_07.CAB
7/11/95	91,136	SPOOLSS.DLL	C:\WINDOWS\SYSTEM	DLL	\WIN95\CAB_09.CAB
7/11/95	7,168	STEM0409.DLL	C:\WINDOWS\SYSTEM	DLL	\WIN95\CAB_05.CAB
7/11/95	4,208	STORAGE.DLL	C:\WINDOWS\SYSTEM	DLL	\WIN95\CAB_09.CAB
7/11/95	9,936	SUEXPAND.DLL	C:\WINDOWS\SYSTEM	DLL	\WIN95\PRECOPY1.CAB
7/11/95	11,264	SVCPROP.DLL	C:\WINDOWS\SYSTEM	DLL	\WIN95\CAB_07.CAB
7/11/95	13,312	SVRAPI.DLL	C:\WINDOWS\SYSTEM	DLL	\WIN95\CAB_11.CAB
7/11/95	55,296	SYNCENG.DLL	C:\WINDOWS\SYSTEM	DLL	\WIN95\CAB_05.CAB
7/11/95	151,040	SYNCUI.DLL	C:\WINDOWS\SYSTEM	DLL	\WIN95\CAB_05.CAB
7/11/95	12,880	SYSCLASS.DLL	C:\WINDOWS\SYSTEM	DLL	\WIN95\CAB_09.CAB
7/11/95	318,304	SYSDETMG.DLL	C:\WINDOWS\SYSTEM	DLL	\WIN95\PRECOPY1.CAB
7/11/95	16,432	SYSTHUNK.DLL	C:\WINDOWS\SYSTEM	DLL	\WIN95\CAB_03.CAB
7/11/95	161,712	TAPI.DLL	C:\WINDOWS\SYSTEM	DLL	\WIN95\CAB_11.CAB
7/11/95	11,776	TAPI32.DLL	C:\WINDOWS\SYSTEM	DLL	\WIN95\CAB_11.CAB
7/11/95	20,616	TAPIADDR.DLL	C:\WINDOWS\SYSTEM	DLL	\WIN95\CAB_11.CAB
7/11/95	12,112	TOOLHELP.DLL	C:\WINDOWS\SYSTEM	DLL	\WIN95\CAB_03.CAB
7/11/95	967,104	TOURANI.DLL	C:\WINDOWS\SYSTEM	DLL	\WIN95\CAB_17.CAB

Date of File	Size of File	Installed Name	Installed Location	Type of File	Location on CD
7/11/95	9,568	TOURSTR.DLL	C:\WINDOWS\SYSTEM	DLL	\WIN95\CAB_17.CAB
7/11/95	638,528	TOURUTIL.DLL	C:\WINDOWS\SYSTEM	DLL	\WIN95\CAB_17.CAB
7/11/95	17,408	TREEEDCL.DLL	C:\PROGRAM FILES\ THE MICROSOFT NETWORK	DLL	\WIN95\CAB_07.CAB
7/11/95	16,384	TREENVCL.DLL	C:\WINDOWS\SYSTEM	DLL	\WIN95\CAB_07.CAB
7/11/95	17,408	TSD32.DLL	C:\WINDOWS\SYSTEM	DLL	\WIN95\CAB_08.CAB
7/11/95	177,856	TYPELIB.DLL	C:\WINDOWS\SYSTEM	DLL	\WIN95\CAB_09.CAB
7/11/95	1,952	UMDM16.DLL	C:\WINDOWS\SYSTEM	DLL	\WIN95\CAB_03.CAB
7/11/95	6,144	UMDM32.DLL	C:\WINDOWS\SYSTEM	DLL	\WIN95\CAB_03.CAB
7/11/95	197,024	UNIDRV.DLL	C:\WINDOWS\SYSTEM	DLL	\WIN95\CAB_09.CAB
7/11/95	44,544	USER32.DLL	C:\WINDOWS\SYSTEM	DLL	\WIN95\CAB_11.CAB
7/11/95	398,416	VBRUN300.DLL	C:\WINDOWS\SYSTEM	DLL	\WIN95\CAB_17.CAB
7/11/95	4,096	VDMDBG.DLL	C:\WINDOWS\SYSTEM	DLL	\WIN95\CAB_03.CAB
7/11/95	9,008	VER.DLL	C:\WINDOWS\SYSTEM	DLL	\WIN95\MINI.CAB
7/11/95	9,008	VER.DLL	C:\WINDOWS\SYSTEM	DLL	\WIN95\PRECOPY2.CAB
7/11/95	6,656	VERSION.DLL	C:\WINDOWS\SYSTEM	DLL	\WIN95\CAB_10.CAB
7/11/95	14,768	VERX.DLL	C:\WINDOWS\SYSTEM	DLL	\WIN95\PRECOPY2.CAB
7/11/95	42,496	VLB32.DLL	C:\WINDOWS\SYSTEM	DLL	\WIN95\CAB_06.CAB
7/11/95	48,640	VSAMI.DLL	C:\WINDOWS\SYSTEM\ VIEWERS	DLL	\WIN95\CAB_13.CAB
7/11/95	17,920	VSASC8.DLL	C:\WINDOWS\SYSTEM\ VIEWERS	DLL	\WIN95\CAB_13.CAB
7/11/95	24,064	VSBMP.DLL	C:\WINDOWS\SYSTEM\ VIEWERS	DLL	\WIN95\CAB_13.CAB
7/11/95	29,184	VSDRW.DLL	C:\WINDOWS\SYSTEM\ VIEWERS	DLL	\WIN95\CAB_13.CAB
7/11/95	38,400	VSEXE2.DLL	C:\WINDOWS\SYSTEM\ VIEWERS	DLL	\WIN95\CAB_13.CAB
7/11/95	64,512	VSFLW.DLL	C:\WINDOWS\SYSTEM\ VIEWERS	DLL	\WIN95\CAB_13.CAB
7/11/95	25,088	VSMP.DLL	C:\WINDOWS\SYSTEM\ VIEWERS	DLL	\WIN95\CAB_13.CAB
7/11/95	33,792	VSMSW.DLL	C:\WINDOWS\SYSTEM\ VIEWERS	DLL	\WIN95\CAB_13.CAB
7/11/95	37,376	VSPP.DLL	C:\WINDOWS\SYSTEM\ VIEWERS	DLL	\WIN95\CAB_13.CAB
7/11/95	86,016	VSQPW2.DLL	C:\WINDOWS\SYSTEM\ VIEWERS	DLL	\WIN95\CAB_17.CAB
7/11/95	34,816	VSRTF.DLL	C:\WINDOWS\SYSTEM\ VIEWERS	DLL	\WIN95\CAB_13.CAB
7/11/95	43,520	VSW6.DLL	C:\WINDOWS\SYSTEM\ VIEWERS	DLL	\WIN95\CAB_13.CAB
7/11/95	78,848	VSWK4.DLL	C:\WINDOWS\SYSTEM\ VIEWERS	DLL	\WIN95\CAB_13.CAB
7/11/95	35,328	VSWKS.DLL	C:\WINDOWS\SYSTEM\ VIEWERS	DLL	\WIN95\CAB_13.CAB

App

G

continues

Date of File	Size of File	Installed Name	Installed Location	Type of File	Location on CD
7/11/95	28,160	VSWMF.DLL	C:\WINDOWS\SYSTEM\VIEWERS	DLL	\WIN95\CAB_13.CAB
7/11/95	64,512	VSWORD.DLL	C:\WINDOWS\SYSTEM\VIEWERS	DLL	\WIN95\CAB_13.CAB
7/11/95	28,672	VSWORK.DLL	C:\WINDOWS\SYSTEM\VIEWERS	DLL	\WIN95\CAB_13.CAB
7/11/95	43,008	VSWP5.DLL	C:\WINDOWS\SYSTEM\VIEWERS	DLL	\WIN95\CAB_13.CAB
7/11/95	51,712	VSWP6.DLL	C:\WINDOWS\SYSTEM\VIEWERS	DLL	\WIN95\CAB_13.CAB
7/11/95	27,136	VSWPF.DLL	C:\WINDOWS\SYSTEM\VIEWERS	DLL	\WIN95\CAB_13.CAB
7/11/95	81,408	VSXL5.DLL	C:\WINDOWS\SYSTEM\VIEWERS	DLL	\WIN95\CAB_13.CAB
7/11/95	81,168	WGPOADMN.DLL	C:\WINDOWS\SYSTEM	DLL	\WIN95\CAB_06.CAB
7/11/95	3,888	WHLP16T.DLL	C:\WINDOWS\SYSTEM	DLL	\WIN95\CAB_05.CAB
7/11/95	10,240	WHLP32T.DLL	C:\WINDOWS\SYSTEM	DLL	\WIN95\CAB_05.CAB
7/11/95	3,200	WIN32S16.DLL	C:\WINDOWS\SYSTEM	DLL	\WIN95\CAB_03.CAB
7/11/95	11,904	WIN87EM.DLL	C:\WINDOWS\SYSTEM	DLL	\WIN95\CAB_03.CAB
7/11/95	12,800	WIN87EM.DLL	C:\WINDOWS\SYSTEM	DLL	\WIN95\MINI.CAB
7/11/95	342,640	WIN95BB.DLL	C:\WINDOWS\SYSTEM	DLL	\WIN95\PRECOPY2.CAB
7/11/95	3,536	WINASPI.DLL	C:\WINDOWS\SYSTEM	DLL	\WIN95\CAB_03.CAB
7/11/95	49,152	WINMM.DLL	C:\WINDOWS\SYSTEM	DLL	\WIN95\CAB_08.CAB
7/11/95	2,000	WINNET16.DLL	C:\WINDOWS\SYSTEM	DLL	\WIN95\CAB_11.CAB
7/11/95	42,080	WINSOCK.DLL	C:\WINDOWS	DLL	\WIN95\CAB_11.CAB
7/11/95	211,456	WMSFR32.DLL	C:\WINDOWS\SYSTEM	DLL	\WIN95\CAB_06.CAB
7/11/95	877,568	WMSUI32.DLL	C:\WINDOWS\SYSTEM	DLL	\WIN95\CAB_06.CAB
7/11/95	16,384	WNASPI32.DLL	C:\WINDOWS\SYSTEM	DLL	\WIN95\CAB_03.CAB
7/11/95	13,824	WNPP32.DLL	C:\WINDOWS\SYSTEM	DLL	\WIN95\CAB_11.CAB
7/11/95	4,096	WOW32.DLL	C:\WINDOWS\SYSTEM	DLL	\WIN95\CAB_11.CAB
7/11/95	462,848	WPS_UPDT.DLL	C:\WINDOWS\SYSTEM	DLL	\WIN95\CAB_10.CAB
7/11/95	8,672	WPSAPD.DLL	C:\WINDOWS\SYSTEM	DLL	\WIN95\CAB_05.CAB
7/11/95	13,312	WPSMON.DLL	C:\WINDOWS\SYSTEM	DLL	\WIN95\CAB_10.CAB
7/11/95	8,080	WPSMON16.DLL	C:\WINDOWS\SYSTEM	DLL	\WIN95\CAB_10.CAB
7/11/95	16,896	WPSUNIRE.DLL	C:\WINDOWS\SYSTEM	DLL	\WIN95\CAB_05.CAB
7/11/95	66,560	WSOCK32.DLL	C:\WINDOWS\SYSTEM	DLL	\WIN95\CAB_11.CAB
7/11/95	4,608	WINWORD.DOC	C:\WINDOWS	DOC	\WIN95\CAB_10.CAB
7/11/95	1,769	WINWORD2.DOC	C:\WINDOWS	DOC	\WIN95\CAB_10.CAB
7/11/95	11,105	AM2100.DOS	C:\WINDOWS\COMMAND	DOS	\WIN95\CAB_11.CAB
7/11/95	16,955	CPQNDIS.DOS	C:\WINDOWS\COMMAND	DOS	\WIN95\CAB_11.CAB
7/11/95	46,573	DC21X4.DOS	C:\WINDOWS\COMMAND	DOS	\WIN95\CAB_11.CAB
7/11/95	15,593	DEPCA.DOS	C:\WINDOWS\COMMAND	DOS	\WIN95\CAB_11.CAB
7/11/95	35,647	DNCRWL02.DOS	C:\WINDOWS\COMMAND	DOS	\WIN95\CAB_11.CAB
7/11/95	22,192	E100.DOS	C:\WINDOWS\COMMAND	DOS	\WIN95\CAB_11.CAB
7/11/95	16,332	E20ND.DOS	C:\WINDOWS\COMMAND	DOS	\WIN95\CAB_11.CAB

Date of File	Size of File	Installed Name	Installed Location	Type of File	Location on CD
7/11/95	8,832	E21ND.DOS	C:\WINDOWS\COMMAND	DOS	\WIN95\CAB_11.CAB
7/11/95	10,512	E22ND.DOS	C:\WINDOWS\COMMAND	DOS	\WIN95\CAB_11.CAB
7/11/95	16,002	E30ND.DOS	C:\WINDOWS\COMMAND	DOS	\WIN95\CAB_11.CAB
7/11/95	8,031	E31ND.DOS	C:\WINDOWS\COMMAND	DOS	\WIN95\CAB_11.CAB
7/11/95	17,430	EL59X.DOS	C:\WINDOWS\COMMAND	DOS	\WIN95\CAB_11.CAB
7/11/95	9,792	ELNK16.DOS	C:\WINDOWS\COMMAND	DOS	\WIN95\CAB_11.CAB
7/11/95	15,519	ELNK3.DOS	C:\WINDOWS\COMMAND	DOS	\WIN95\CAB_11.CAB
7/11/95	11,322	ELNKII.DOS	C:\WINDOWS\COMMAND	DOS	\WIN95\CAB_11.CAB
7/11/95	9,542	ELNKMC.DOS	C:\WINDOWS\COMMAND	DOS	\WIN95\CAB_11.CAB
7/11/95	17,116	ELNKPL.DOS	C:\WINDOWS\COMMAND	DOS	\WIN95\CAB_11.CAB
7/11/95	19,230	EPNDIS.DOS	C:\WINDOWS\COMMAND	DOS	\WIN95\CAB_11.CAB
7/11/95	16,995	EPRO.DOS	C:\WINDOWS\COMMAND	DOS	\WIN95\CAB_11.CAB
7/11/95	14,544	ES3210.DOS	C:\WINDOWS\COMMAND	DOS	\WIN95\CAB_11.CAB
7/11/95	11,299	EVX16.DOS	C:\WINDOWS\COMMAND	DOS	\WIN95\CAB_11.CAB
7/11/95	9,509	EWRK3.DOS	C:\WINDOWS\COMMAND	DOS	\WIN95\CAB_08.CAB
7/11/95	10,478	EXP16.DOS	C:\WINDOWS\COMMAND	DOS	\WIN95\CAB_11.CAB
7/11/95	14,299	HPFEND.DOS	C:\WINDOWS\COMMAND	DOS	\WIN95\CAB_11.CAB
7/11/95	15,470	HPLAN.DOS	C:\WINDOWS\COMMAND	DOS	\WIN95\CAB_11.CAB
7/11/95	11,744	HPLANB.DOS	C:\WINDOWS\COMMAND	DOS	\WIN95\CAB_11.CAB
7/11/95	17,936	HPLANE.DOS	C:\WINDOWS\COMMAND	DOS	\WIN95\CAB_11.CAB
7/11/95	12,640	HPLANP.DOS	C:\WINDOWS\COMMAND	DOS	\WIN95\CAB_11.CAB
7/11/95	10,279	I82593.DOS	C:\WINDOWS\COMMAND	DOS	\WIN95\CAB_11.CAB
7/11/95	10,112	IBMTOK.DOS	C:\WINDOWS\COMMAND	DOS	\WIN95\CAB_11.CAB
7/11/95	59,448	IRMATR.DOS	C:\WINDOWS\COMMAND	DOS	\WIN95\CAB_11.CAB
7/11/95	42,802	NCC16.DOS	C:\WINDOWS\COMMAND	DOS	\WIN95\CAB_11.CAB
7/11/95	34,880	NDIS39XR.DOS	C:\WINDOWS\COMMAND	DOS	\WIN95\CAB_11.CAB
7/11/95	35,160	NDIS89XR.DOS	C:\WINDOWS\COMMAND	DOS	\WIN95\CAB_11.CAB
7/11/95	38,251	NDIS99XR.DOS	C:\WINDOWS\COMMAND	DOS	\WIN95\CAB_11.CAB
7/11/95	14,020	NE1000.DOS	C:\WINDOWS	DOS	\WIN95\CAB_11.CAB
7/11/95	13,964	NE2000.DOS	C:\WINDOWS	DOS	\WIN95\CAB_11.CAB
7/11/95	33,582	NE3200.DOS	C:\WINDOWS	DOS	\WIN95\CAB_11.CAB
7/11/95	78,996	NETFLX.DOS	C:\WINDOWS\COMMAND	DOS	\WIN95\CAB_11.CAB
7/11/95	10,472	NI5210.DOS	C:\WINDOWS\COMMAND	DOS	\WIN95\CAB_11.CAB
7/11/95	11,070	NI6510.DOS	C:\WINDOWS\COMMAND	DOS	\WIN95\CAB_11.CAB
7/11/95	55,710	OLITOK16.DOS	C:\WINDOWS\COMMAND	DOS	\WIN95\CAB_11.CAB
7/11/95	50,400	PCNTND.DOS	C:\WINDOWS\COMMAND	DOS	\WIN95\CAB_11.CAB
7/11/95	30,721	PE2NDIS.DOS	C:\WINDOWS\COMMAND	DOS	\WIN95\CAB_11.CAB
7/11/95	22,266	PENDIS.DOS	C:\WINDOWS\COMMAND	DOS	\WIN95\CAB_11.CAB
7/11/95	29,090	PRO4.DOS	C:\WINDOWS\COMMAND	DOS	\WIN95\CAB_11.CAB
7/11/95	33,770	PRO4AT.DOS	C:\WINDOWS\COMMAND	DOS	\WIN95\CAB_11.CAB
7/11/95	22,810	PROTMAN.DOS	C:\WINDOWS	DOS	\WIN95\CAB_12.CAB
7/11/95	13,578	SLAN.DOS	C:\WINDOWS\COMMAND	DOS	\WIN95\CAB_11.CAB

continues

App
G

Date of File	Size of File	Installed Name	Installed Location	Type of File	Location on CD
7/11/95	88,809	SMARTND.DOS	C:\WINDOWS\COMMAND	DOS	\WIN95\CAB_11.CAB
7/11/95	20,327	SMC_ARC.DOS	C:\WINDOWS\COMMAND	DOS	\WIN95\CAB_11.CAB
7/11/95	12,271	SMC3000.DOS	C:\WINDOWS\COMMAND	DOS	\WIN95\CAB_11.CAB
7/11/95	35,584	SMC8000.DOS	C:\WINDOWS\COMMAND	DOS	\WIN95\CAB_11.CAB
7/11/95	62,496	SMC8100.DOS	C:\WINDOWS\COMMAND	DOS	\WIN95\CAB_11.CAB
7/11/95	31,232	SMC8232.DOS	C:\WINDOWS\COMMAND	DOS	\WIN95\CAB_12.CAB
7/11/95	17,184	SMC9000.DOS	C:\WINDOWS\COMMAND	DOS	\WIN95\CAB_12.CAB
7/11/95	41,946	STRN.DOS	C:\WINDOWS\COMMAND	DOS	\WIN95\CAB_12.CAB
7/11/95	37,939	T20ND.DOS	C:\WINDOWS\COMMAND	DOS	\WIN95\CAB_12.CAB
7/11/95	45,388	T30ND.DOS	C:\WINDOWS\COMMAND	DOS	\WIN95\CAB_12.CAB
7/11/95	19,972	TCCARC.DOS	C:\WINDOWS\COMMAND	DOS	\WIN95\CAB_12.CAB
7/11/95	24,954	TCCTOK.DOS	C:\WINDOWS\COMMAND	DOS	\WIN95\CAB_12.CAB
7/11/95	12,426	TLNK.DOS	C:\WINDOWS\COMMAND	DOS	\WIN95\CAB_12.CAB
7/11/95	10,896	TLNK3.DOS	C:\WINDOWS\COMMAND	DOS	\WIN95\CAB_12.CAB
7/11/95	24,930	UBNEI.DOS	C:\WINDOWS\COMMAND	DOS	\WIN95\CAB_12.CAB
7/11/95	20,257	UBNEPS.DOS	C:\WINDOWS\COMMAND	DOS	\WIN95\CAB_12.CAB
7/11/95	94,768	ATIM32.DRV	C:\WINDOWS\SYSTEM	DRV	\WIN95\CAB_04.CAB
7/11/95	66,336	ATIM64.DRV	C:\WINDOWS\SYSTEM	DRV	\WIN95\CAB_04.CAB
7/11/95	128,800	ATIM8.DRV	C:\WINDOWS\SYSTEM	DRV	\WIN95\CAB_04.CAB
7/11/95	24,336	AVCAPT.DRV	C:\WINDOWS\SYSTEM	DRV	\WIN95\CAB_13.CAB
7/11/95	42,080	AZT16C.DRV	C:\WINDOWS\SYSTEM	DRV	\WIN95\CAB_08.CAB
7/11/95	43,664	AZT16W.DRV	C:\WINDOWS\SYSTEM	DRV	\WIN95\CAB_08.CAB
7/11/95	9,962	BIGMEM.DRV	C:\WINDOWS\SYSTEM\IOSUBSYS	DRV	\WIN95\CAB_03.CAB
7/11/95	13,648	BRHJ770.DRV	C:\WINDOWS\SYSTEM	DRV	\WIN95\CAB_10.CAB
7/11/95	16,464	BROTHER9.DRV	C:\WINDOWS\SYSTEM	DRV	\WIN95\CAB_10.CAB
7/11/95	32,528	BROTHR24.DRV	C:\WINDOWS\SYSTEM	DRV	\WIN95\CAB_10.CAB
7/11/95	29,104	CANON330.DRV	C:\WINDOWS\SYSTEM	DRV	\WIN95\CAB_10.CAB
7/11/95	10,000	CANON800.DRV	C:\WINDOWS\SYSTEM	DRV	\WIN95\CAB_10.CAB
7/11/95	80,864	CANONLBP.DRV	C:\WINDOWS\SYSTEM	DRV	\WIN95\CAB_10.CAB
7/11/95	25,328	CHIPS.DRV	C:\WINDOWS\SYSTEM	DRV	\WIN95\CAB_04.CAB
7/11/95	57,632	CIRRUS.DRV	C:\WINDOWS\SYSTEM	DRV	\WIN95\CAB_04.CAB
7/11/95	35,344	CIRRUSMM.DRV	C:\WINDOWS\SYSTEM	DRV	\WIN95\CAB_04.CAB
7/11/95	40,544	CIT24US.DRV	C:\WINDOWS\SYSTEM	DRV	\WIN95\CAB_10.CAB
7/11/95	29,184	CIT9US.DRV	C:\WINDOWS\SYSTEM	DRV	\WIN95\CAB_10.CAB
7/11/95	5,360	CITOH.DRV	C:\WINDOWS\SYSTEM	DRV	\WIN95\CAB_10.CAB
7/11/95	5,856	COMM.DRV	C:\WINDOWS\SYSTEM	DRV	\WIN95\CAB_03.CAB
7/11/95	9,280	COMM.DRV	C:\WINDOWS\SYSTEM	DRV	\WIN95\MINI.CAB
7/11/95	82,080	COMPAQ.DRV	C:\WINDOWS\SYSTEM	DRV	\WIN95\CAB_04.CAB
7/11/95	12,048	DEC24PIN.DRV	C:\WINDOWS\SYSTEM	DRV	\WIN95\CAB_10.CAB
7/11/95	14,192	DEC3200.DRV	C:\WINDOWS\SYSTEM	DRV	\WIN95\CAB_10.CAB
7/11/95	181,840	DESKJETC.DRV	C:\WINDOWS\SYSTEM	DRV	\WIN95\CAB_09.CAB
7/11/95	5,136	DICONIX.DRV	C:\WINDOWS\SYSTEM	DRV	\WIN95\CAB_10.CAB
7/11/95	25,168	EPSON24.DRV	C:\WINDOWS\SYSTEM	DRV	\WIN95\CAB_09.CAB

Date of File	Size of File	Installed Name	Installed Location	Type of File	Location on CD
7/11/95	31,776	EPSON9.DRV	C:\WINDOWS\SYSTEM	DRV	\WIN95\CAB_10.CAB
7/11/95	43,936	ES1488.DRV	C:\WINDOWS\SYSTEM	DRV	\WIN95\CAB_08.CAB
7/11/95	50,128	ES1688.DRV	C:\WINDOWS\SYSTEM	DRV	\WIN95\CAB_08.CAB
7/11/95	36,976	ES488.DRV	C:\WINDOWS\SYSTEM	DRV	\WIN95\CAB_08.CAB
7/11/95	47,008	ES688.DRV	C:\WINDOWS\SYSTEM	DRV	\WIN95\CAB_08.CAB
7/11/95	17,920	ESSFM.DRV	C:\WINDOWS\SYSTEM	DRV	\WIN95\CAB_08.CAB
7/11/95	9,904	ESSMPORT.DRV	C:\WINDOWS\SYSTEM	DRV	\WIN95\CAB_08.CAB
7/11/95	8,240	ESSMPU.DRV	C:\WINDOWS\SYSTEM	DRV	\WIN95\CAB_08.CAB
7/11/95	15,152	EXPRSS24.DRV	C:\WINDOWS\SYSTEM	DRV	\WIN95\CAB_10.CAB
7/11/95	16,752	FRAMEBUF.DRV	C:\WINDOWS\SYSTEM	DRV	\WIN95\CAB_04.CAB
7/11/95	32,176	FUJI24.DRV	C:\WINDOWS\SYSTEM	DRV	\WIN95\CAB_10.CAB
7/11/95	12,224	FUJI9.DRV	C:\WINDOWS\SYSTEM	DRV	\WIN95\CAB_10.CAB
7/11/95	90,560	HPDSKJET.DRV	C:\WINDOWS\SYSTEM	DRV	\WIN95\CAB_09.CAB
7/11/95	202,992	HPPCL.DRV	C:\WINDOWS\SYSTEM	DRV	\WIN95\CAB_09.CAB
7/11/95	525,856	HPPCL5MS.DRV	C:\WINDOWS\SYSTEM	DRV	\WIN95\CAB_09.CAB
7/11/95	66,976	HPPLOT.DRV	C:\WINDOWS\SYSTEM	DRV	\WIN95\CAB_10.CAB
7/11/95	15,024	IBM238X.DRV	C:\WINDOWS\SYSTEM	DRV	\WIN95\CAB_10.CAB
7/11/95	30,560	IBM239X.DRV	C:\WINDOWS\SYSTEM	DRV	\WIN95\CAB_10.CAB
7/11/95	19,216	IBM5204.DRV	C:\WINDOWS\SYSTEM	DRV	\WIN95\CAB_10.CAB
7/11/95	25,920	IBMPPDSL.DRV	C:\WINDOWS\SYSTEM	DRV	\WIN95\CAB_10.CAB
7/11/95	73,440	JP350.DRV	C:\WINDOWS\SYSTEM	DRV	\WIN95\CAB_10.CAB
7/11/95	12,688	KEYBOARD.DRV	C:\WINDOWS\SYSTEM	DRV	\WIN95\CAB_06.CAB
7/11/95	7,568	KEYBOARD.DRV	C:\WINDOWS\SYSTEM	DRV	\WIN95\MINI.CAB
7/11/95	30,608	KYOCERA.DRV	C:\WINDOWS\SYSTEM	DRV	\WIN95\CAB_10.CAB
7/11/95	7,984	LMOUSE.DRV	C:\WINDOWS\SYSTEM	DRV	\WIN95\CAB_08.CAB
7/11/95	12,928	LMOUSE31.DRV	C:\WINDOWS\SYSTEM	DRV	\WIN95\MINI.CAB
7/11/95	34,160	MANTAL24.DRV	C:\WINDOWS\SYSTEM	DRV	\WIN95\CAB_10.CAB
7/11/95	22,992	MANTAL9.DRV	C:\WINDOWS\SYSTEM	DRV	\WIN95\CAB_10.CAB
7/11/95	67,520	MCIAVI.DRV	C:\WINDOWS\SYSTEM	DRV	\WIN95\CAB_08.CAB
7/11/95	12,800	MCICDA.DRV	C:\WINDOWS\SYSTEM	DRV	\WIN95\CAB_08.CAB
7/11/95	13,712	MCIPIONR.DRV	C:\WINDOWS\SYSTEM	DRV	\WIN95\CAB_13.CAB
7/11/95	18,672	MCISEQ.DRV	C:\WINDOWS\SYSTEM	DRV	\WIN95\CAB_08.CAB
7/11/95	95,776	MCIVISCA.DRV	C:\WINDOWS\SYSTEM	DRV	\WIN95\CAB_13.CAB
7/11/95	22,016	MCIWAVE.DRV	C:\WINDOWS\SYSTEM	DRV	\WIN95\CAB_08.CAB
7/11/95	110,528	MGA.DRV	C:\WINDOWS\SYSTEM	DRV	\WIN95\CAB_04.CAB
7/11/95	16,976	MIDIMAP.DRV	C:\WINDOWS\SYSTEM	DRV	\WIN95\CAB_08.CAB
7/11/95	3,104	MMSOUND.DRV	C:\WINDOWS\SYSTEM	DRV	\WIN95\CAB_03.CAB
7/11/95	7,712	MOUSE.DRV	C:\WINDOWS\SYSTEM	DRV	\WIN95\CAB_08.CAB
7/11/95	21,872	MSACM.DRV	C:\WINDOWS\SYSTEM	DRV	\WIN95\CAB_08.CAB
7/11/95	7,744	MSJSTICK.DRV	C:\WINDOWS\SYSTEM	DRV	\WIN95\CAB_08.CAB
7/11/95	10,672	MSMOUS31.DRV	C:\WINDOWS\SYSTEM	DRV	\WIN95\MINI.CAB
7/11/95	8,704	MSMPU401.DRV	C:\WINDOWS\SYSTEM	DRV	\WIN95\CAB_08.CAB

App

G

continues

Date of File	Size of File	Installed Name	Installed Location	Type of File	Location on CD
7/11/95	7,072	MSNET.DRV	C:\WINDOWS\SYSTEM	DRV	\WIN95\CAB_12.CAB
7/11/95	17,952	MSOPL.DRV	C:\WINDOWS\SYSTEM	DRV	\WIN95\CAB_08.CAB
7/11/95	40,848	MSSBLST.DRV	C:\WINDOWS\SYSTEM	DRV	\WIN95\CAB_08.CAB
7/11/95	39,728	MSSNDSYS.DRV	C:\WINDOWS\SYSTEM	DRV	\WIN95\CAB_08.CAB
7/11/95	8,304	MTLITE.DRV	C:\WINDOWS\SYSTEM	DRV	\WIN95\CAB_10.CAB
7/11/95	12,640	MVI401.DRV	C:\WINDOWS\SYSTEM	DRV	\WIN95\CAB_08.CAB
7/11/95	38,432	MVI514MX.DRV	C:\WINDOWS\SYSTEM	DRV	\WIN95\CAB_08.CAB
7/11/95	41,232	MVIFM.DRV	C:\WINDOWS\SYSTEM	DRV	\WIN95\CAB_08.CAB
7/11/95	19,760	MVIWAVE.DRV	C:\WINDOWS\SYSTEM	DRV	\WIN95\CAB_08.CAB
7/11/95	59,568	MVMIXER.DRV	C:\WINDOWS\SYSTEM	DRV	\WIN95\CAB_08.CAB
7/11/95	26,128	MVPROAUD.DRV	C:\WINDOWS\SYSTEM	DRV	\WIN95\CAB_08.CAB
7/11/95	23,424	NEC24PIN.DRV	C:\WINDOWS\SYSTEM	DRV	\WIN95\CAB_10.CAB
7/11/95	416	NOMOUSE.DRV	C:\WINDOWS\SYSTEM	DRV	\WIN95\MINI.CAB
7/11/95	40,848	OKI24.DRV	C:\WINDOWS\SYSTEM	DRV	\WIN95\CAB_10.CAB
7/11/95	18,336	OKI9.DRV	C:\WINDOWS\SYSTEM	DRV	\WIN95\CAB_10.CAB
7/11/95	48,720	OKI9IBM.DRV	C:\WINDOWS\SYSTEM	DRV	\WIN95\CAB_10.CAB
7/11/95	24,176	OLIDM24.DRV	C:\WINDOWS\SYSTEM	DRV	\WIN95\CAB_10.CAB
7/11/95	33,232	OLIDM9.DRV	C:\WINDOWS\SYSTEM	DRV	\WIN95\CAB_10.CAB
7/11/95	19,040	P351SX2.DRV	C:\WINDOWS\SYSTEM	DRV	\WIN95\CAB_10.CAB
7/11/95	53,200	PA3DMXD.DRV	C:\WINDOWS\SYSTEM	DRV	\WIN95\CAB_08.CAB
7/11/95	7,664	PAINTJET.DRV	C:\WINDOWS\SYSTEM	DRV	\WIN95\CAB_10.CAB
7/11/95	31,312	PANSON24.DRV	C:\WINDOWS\SYSTEM	DRV	\WIN95\CAB_10.CAB
7/11/95	28,000	PANSON9.DRV	C:\WINDOWS\SYSTEM	DRV	\WIN95\CAB_10.CAB
7/11/95	1,920	POWER.DRV	C:\WINDOWS\SYSTEM	DRV	\WIN95\CAB_07.CAB
7/11/95	12,192	PROPRINT.DRV	C:\WINDOWS\SYSTEM	DRV	\WIN95\CAB_10.CAB
7/11/95	11,120	PROPRN24.DRV	C:\WINDOWS\SYSTEM	DRV	\WIN95\CAB_10.CAB
7/11/95	13,856	PS1.DRV	C:\WINDOWS\SYSTEM	DRV	\WIN95\CAB_10.CAB
7/11/95	393,200	PSCRIPT.DRV	C:\WINDOWS\SYSTEM	DRV	\WIN95\CAB_09.CAB
7/11/95	5,776	QUIETJET.DRV	C:\WINDOWS\SYSTEM	DRV	\WIN95\CAB_10.CAB
7/11/95	17,648	QWIII.DRV	C:\WINDOWS\SYSTEM	DRV	\WIN95\CAB_10.CAB
7/11/95	57,632	S3.DRV	C:\WINDOWS\SYSTEM	DRV	\WIN95\CAB_04.CAB
7/11/95	46,000	SB16SND.DRV	C:\WINDOWS\SYSTEM	DRV	\WIN95\CAB_08.CAB
7/11/95	23,216	SBAWE32.DRV	C:\WINDOWS\SYSTEM	DRV	\WIN95\CAB_08.CAB
7/11/95	4,128	SBFM.DRV	C:\WINDOWS\SYSTEM	DRV	\WIN95\CAB_08.CAB
7/11/95	31,376	SEIKO24E.DRV	C:\WINDOWS\SYSTEM	DRV	\WIN95\CAB_10.CAB
7/11/95	18,736	SEIKOSH9.DRV	C:\WINDOWS\SYSTEM	DRV	\WIN95\CAB_10.CAB
7/11/95	3,440	SOUND.DRV	C:\WINDOWS\SYSTEM	DRV	\WIN95\MINI.CAB
7/11/95	63,088	STAR24E.DRV	C:\WINDOWS\SYSTEM	DRV	\WIN95\CAB_10.CAB
7/11/95	38,160	STAR9E.DRV	C:\WINDOWS\SYSTEM	DRV	\WIN95\CAB_10.CAB
7/11/95	52,320	SUPERVGA.DRV	C:\WINDOWS\SYSTEM	DRV	\WIN95\CAB_04.CAB
7/11/95	2,288	SYSTEM.DRV	C:\WINDOWS\SYSTEM	DRV	\WIN95\CAB_03.CAB
7/11/95	2,304	SYSTEM.DRV	C:\WINDOWS\SYSTEM	DRV	\WIN95\MINI.CAB
7/11/95	6,752	THINKJET.DRV	C:\WINDOWS\SYSTEM	DRV	\WIN95\CAB_10.CAB

Date of File	Size of File	Installed Name	Installed Location	Type of File	Location on CD
7/11/95	5,056	TI850.DRV	C:\WINDOWS\SYSTEM	DRV	\WIN95\CAB_10.CAB
7/11/95	10,880	TOSHIBA.DRV	C:\WINDOWS\SYSTEM	DRV	\WIN95\CAB_10.CAB
7/11/95	28,864	TSENG.DRV	C:\WINDOWS\SYSTEM	DRV	\WIN95\CAB_04.CAB
7/11/95	31,152	TTY.DRV	C:\WINDOWS\SYSTEM	DRV	\WIN95\CAB_10.CAB
7/11/95	52,064	VGA.DRV	C:\WINDOWS\SYSTEM	DRV	\WIN95\CAB_04.CAB
7/11/95	73,200	VGA.DRV	C:\WINDOWS\SYSTEM	DRV	\WIN95\MINI.CAB
7/11/95	21,680	WD.DRV	C:\WINDOWS\SYSTEM	DRV	\WIN95\CAB_04.CAB
7/11/95	3,552	WINSPL16.DRV	C:\WINDOWS\SYSTEM	DRV	\WIN95\CAB_09.CAB
7/11/95	18,944	WINSPOOL.DRV	C:\WINDOWS\SYSTEM	DRV	\WIN95\CAB_09.CAB
7/11/95	145,456	WPSUNI.DRV	C:\WINDOWS\SYSTEM	DRV	\WIN95\CAB_05.CAB
7/11/95	12,864	XGA.DRV	C:\WINDOWS\SYSTEM	DRV	\WIN95\CAB_04.CAB
7/11/95	24,734	PRORAPM.DWN	C:\WINDOWS\SYSTEM	DWN	\WIN95\CAB_12.CAB
7/11/95	5,378	RCV0000.EFX	C:\WINDOWS\SYSTEM	EFX	\WIN95\CAB_05.CAB
7/11/95	293	ENVOY.EVY	C:\WINDOWS\SHELLNEW	EVY	\WIN95\CAB_10.CAB
7/11/95	24,576	ACCSTAT.EXE	C:\WINDOWS	EXE	\WIN95\CAB_02.CAB
7/11/95	14,336	ADDREG.EXE	C:\WINDOWS\SYSTEM	EXE	\WIN95\CAB_09.CAB
7/11/95	168,448	ARCSRV32.EXE	C:\WINDOWS\SYSTEM	EXE	\WIN95\CAB_17.CAB
7/11/95	19,536	ARP.EXE	C:\WINDOWS	EXE	\WIN95\CAB_12.CAB
7/11/95	15,252	ATTRIB.EXE	C:\WINDOWS\COMMAND	EXE	\WIN95\CAB_02.CAB
7/11/95	9,728	AWADPR32.EXE	C:\WINDOWS\SYSTEM	EXE	\WIN95\CAB_05.CAB
7/11/95	74,240	AWFXEX32.EXE	C:\WINDOWS\SYSTEM	EXE	\WIN95\CAB_05.CAB
7/11/95	35,328	AWSNTO32.EXE	C:\WINDOWS\SYSTEM	EXE	\WIN95\CAB_05.CAB
7/11/95	23,834	BACKUP.CFG	C:\PROGRAM FILES\ ACCESSORIES	EXE	\WIN95\CAB_04.CAB
7/11/95	33,018	BACKUP.HLP	C:\WINDOWS\HELP	EXE	\WIN95\CAB_04.CAB
7/11/95	61,952	BKUPAGNT.EXE	C:\WINDOWS	EXE	\WIN95\CAB_17.CAB
7/11/95	59,392	CALC.EXE	C:\WINDOWS	EXE	\WIN95\CAB_02.CAB
7/11/95	27,296	CARDDRV.EXE	C:\WINDOWS	EXE	\WIN95\CAB_09.CAB
7/11/95	22,016	CCDIALER.EXE	C:\PROGRAM FILES\ THE MICROSOFT NETWORK	EXE	\WIN95\CAB_07.CAB
7/11/95	88,064	CDPLAYER.EXE	C:\WINDOWS	EXE	\WIN95\CAB_13.CAB
7/11/95	14,752	CHARMAP.EXE	C:\WINDOWS	EXE	\WIN95\CAB_13.CAB
7/11/95	27,248	CHKDSK.EXE	C:\WINDOWS\COMMAND	EXE	\WIN95\CAB_02.CAB
7/11/95	57,664	CLIPBOOK.EXE	C:\WINDOWS	EXE	\WIN95\CAB_02.CAB
7/11/95	17,376	CLIPBRD.EXE	C:\WINDOWS	EXE	\WIN95\CAB_02.CAB
7/11/95	16,608	CLIPSRV.EXE	C:\WINDOWS	EXE	\WIN95\CAB_02.CAB
7/11/95	14,596	CONAGENT.EXE	C:\WINDOWS\SYSTEM	EXE	\WIN95\CAB_03.CAB
7/11/95	2,112	CONTROL.EXE	C:\WINDOWS	EXE	\WIN95\CAB_10.CAB
7/11/95	7,954	CPQAE05.EXE	C:\WINDOWS\SYSTEM	EXE	\WIN95\CAB_09.CAB
7/11/95	7,288	CPQAE06.EXE	C:\WINDOWS\SYSTEM	EXE	\WIN95\CAB_09.CAB
7/11/95	20,522	DEBUG.EXE	C:\WINDOWS\COMMAND	EXE	\WIN95\CAB_02.CAB
7/11/95	19,019	DELTREE.EXE	C:\WINDOWS\COMMAND	EXE	\WIN95\CAB_08.CAB

continues

App

G

Date of File	Size of File	Installed Name	Installed Location	Type of File	Location on CD
7/11/95	63,240	DIALER.EXE	C:\WINDOWS	EXE	\WIN95\CAB_02.CAB
7/11/95	60,416	DIRECTCC.EXE	C:\WINDOWS	EXE	\WIN95\CAB_10.CAB
7/11/95	3,584	DNR.EXE	C:\PROGRAM FILES\ THE MICROSOFT NETWORK	EXE	\WIN95\CAB_07.CAB
7/11/95	336,736	DRVSPACE.EXE	C:\WINDOWS	EXE	\WIN95\CAB_08.CAB
7/11/95	125,495	EMM386.EXE	C:\WINDOWS	EXE	\WIN95\CAB_08.CAB
7/11/95	20,240	EXCHNG32.EXE	C:\PROGRAM FILES\ MICROSOFT EXCHANGE	EXE	\WIN95\CAB_06.CAB
7/11/95	204,288	EXPLORER.EXE	C:\WINDOWS	EXE	\WIN95\CAB_10.CAB
7/11/95	33,280	EXPOSTRT.EXE	C:\WINDOWS	EXE	\WIN95\CAB_16.CAB
7/11/95	191,488	FAXCOVER.EXE	C:\WINDOWS	EXE	\WIN95\CAB_05.CAB
7/11/95	166,912	FAXVIEW.EXE	C:\WINDOWS	EXE	\WIN95\CAB_05.CAB
7/11/95	20,494	FC.EXE	C:\WINDOWS\COMMAND	EXE	\WIN95\CAB_08.CAB
7/11/95	59,128	FDISK.EXE	C:\WINDOWS\COMMAND	EXE	\WIN95\CAB_02.CAB
7/11/95	48,128	FILEXFER.EXE	C:\WINDOWS	EXE	\WIN95\CAB_17.CAB
7/11/95	6,658	FIND.EXE	C:\WINDOWS\COMMAND	EXE	\WIN95\CAB_08.CAB
7/11/95	6,656	FONTREG.EXE	C:\WINDOWS\SYSTEM	EXE	\WIN95\CAB_11.CAB
7/11/95	36,352	FONTVIEW.EXE	C:\WINDOWS	EXE	\WIN95\CAB_11.CAB
7/11/95	28,560	FREECELL.EXE	C:\WINDOWS	EXE	\WIN95\CAB_05.CAB
7/11/95	46,592	FTMCL.EXE	C:\PROGRAM FILES\ THE MICROSOFT NETWORK	EXE	\WIN95\CAB_07.CAB
7/11/95	37,520	FTP.EXE	C:\WINDOWS	EXE	\WIN95\CAB_12.CAB
7/11/95	312,208	GDI.EXE	C:\WINDOWS\SYSTEM	EXE	\WIN95\CAB_03.CAB
7/11/95	149,456	GDI.EXE	C:\WINDOWS\SYSTEM	EXE	\WIN95\MINI.CAB
7/11/95	33,280	GRPCONV.EXE	C:\WINDOWS	EXE	\WIN95\CAB_11.CAB
7/11/95	110,080	GUIDE.EXE	C:\PROGRAM FILES\ THE MICROSOFT NETWORK	EXE	\WIN95\CAB_07.CAB
7/11/95	30,720	HPPROPTY.EXE	C:\WINDOWS\SYSTEM	EXE	\WIN95\CAB_16.CAB
7/11/95	6,144	HYPERTRM.EXE	C:\PROGRAM FILES\ ACCESSORIS\ HYPERTERMINAL	EXE	\WIN95\CAB_02.CAB
7/11/95	12,800	INTERNAT.EXE	C:\WINDOWS\SYSTEM	EXE	\WIN95\CAB_06.CAB
7/11/95	693,760	JETADMIN.EXE	C:\WINDOWS\SYSTEM	EXE	\WIN95\CAB_16.CAB
7/11/95	124,416	KRNL386.EXE	C:\WINDOWS\SYSTEM	EXE	\WIN95\CAB_03.CAB
7/11/95	75,490	KRNL386.EXE	C:\WINDOWS\SYSTEM	TYPE	\WIN95\MINI.CAB
7/11/95	9,260	LABEL.EXE	C:\WINDOWS\COMMAND	EXE	\WIN95\CAB_08.CAB
7/11/95	32,768	LIGHTS.EXE	C:\WINDOWS\SYSTEM	EXE	\WIN95\CAB_10.CAB
7/11/95	4,785	LMSCRIPT.EXE	C:\WINDOWS\SYSTEM	EXE	\WIN95\CAB_12.CAB
7/11/95	12,135	LOGIN.EXE	C:\WINDOWS\	EXE	\WIN95\CAB_12.CAB
7/11/95	7,488	MAPISP32.EXE	C:\WINDOWS\SYSTEM	EXE	\WIN95\CAB_07.CAB
7/11/95	24,272	MAPISRVR.EXE	C:\WINDOWS\SYSTEM	EXE	\WIN95\CAB_07.CAB
7/11/95	32,082	MEM.EXE	C:\WINDOWS\COMMAND	EXE	\WIN95\CAB_08.CAB
7/11/95	33,792	MKCOMPAT.EXE	C:\WINDOWS\SYSTEM	EXE	\WIN95\CAB_03.CAB

Date of File	Size of File	Installed Name	Installed Location	Type of File	Location on CD
7/11/95	6,367	ML3XEC16.EXE	C:\WINDOWS\SYSTEM	EXE	\WIN95\CAB_07.CAB
7/11/95	24,336	MLSET32.EXE	C:\PROGRAM FILES\ MICROSOFT EXCHANGE	EXE	\WIN95\CAB_07.CAB
7/11/95	69,632	MOSCP.EXE	C:\PROGRAM FILES\ THE MICROSOFT NETWORK	EXE	\WIN95\CAB_07.CAB
7/11/95	55,296	MOSVIEW.EXE	C:\PROGRAM FILES\ THE MICROSOFT NETWORK	EXE	\WIN95\CAB_07.CAB
7/11/95	27,235	MOVE.EXE	C:\WINDOWS\COMMAND	EXE	\WIN95\CAB_09.CAB
7/11/95	147,968	MPLAYER.EXE	C:\WINDOWS	EXE	\WIN95\CAB_08.CAB
7/11/95	12,800	MPREXE.EXE	C:\WINDOWS\SYSTEM	EXE	\WIN95\CAB_12.CAB
7/11/95	25,473	MSCDEX.EXE	C:\WINDOWS\COMMAND	EXE	\WIN95\CAB_04.CAB
7/11/95	31,284	MSDLC.EXE	C:\WINDOWS\COMMAND	EXE	\WIN95\CAB_12.CAB
7/11/95	10,192	MSGSRV32.EXE	C:\WINDOWS\SYSTEM	EXE	\WIN95\CAB_09.CAB
7/11/95	122,240	MSHEARTS.EXE	C:\WINDOWS	EXE	\WIN95\CAB_05.CAB
7/11/95	17,408	MSNEXCH.EXE	C:\WINDOWS\SYSTEM	EXE	\WIN95\CAB_07.CAB
7/11/95	52,224	MSNFIND.EXE	C:\PROGRAM FILES\ THE MICROSOFT NETWORK	EXE	\WIN95\CAB_07.CAB
7/11/95	311,808	MSPAINT.EXE	C:\PROGRAM FILES\ ACCESSORIES	EXE	\WIN95\CAB_02.CAB
7/11/95	33,371	NBTSTAT.EXE	C:\WINDOWS	EXE	\WIN95\CAB_12.CAB
7/11/95	375,962	NET.EXE	C:\WINDOWS	EXE	\WIN95\CAB_12.CAB
7/11/95	54,992	NETDDE.EXE	C:\WINDOWS	EXE	\WIN95\CAB_12.CAB
7/11/95	23,776	NETSTAT.EXE	C:\WINDOWS	EXE	\WIN95\CAB_12.CAB
7/11/95	63,488	NETWATCH.EXE	C:\WINDOWS	EXE	\WIN95\CAB_17.CAB
7/11/95	6,940	NLSFUNC.EXE	C:\WINDOWS\COMMAND	EXE	\WIN95\CAB_09.CAB
7/11/95	34,304	NOTEPAD.EXE	C:\WINDOWS	EXE	\WIN95\CAB_02.CAB
7/11/95	13,824	NWLSCON.EXE	C:\WINDOWS\SYSTEM	EXE	\WIN95\CAB_12.CAB
7/11/95	71,680	NWLSPROC.EXE	C:\WINDOWS\SYSTEM	EXE	\WIN95\CAB_12.CAB
7/11/95	4,197	ODIHLP.EXE	C:\WINDOWS\HELP	EXE	\WIN95\CAB_12.CAB
7/11/95	74,240	ONLSTMT.EXE	C:\PROGRAM FILES\ THE MICROSOFT NETWORK	EXE	\WIN95\CAB_07.CAB
7/11/95	65,024	PACKAGER.EXE	C:\WINDOWS	EXE	\WIN95\CAB_02.CAB
7/11/95	4,608	PBRUSH.EXE	C:\WINDOWS	EXE	\WIN95\CAB_02.CAB
7/11/95	23,299	PCSA.EXE	C:\WINDOWS	EXE	\WIN95\CAB_17.CAB
7/11/95	23,506	PE3NDIS.EXE	C:\WINDOWS	EXE	\WIN95\CAB_12.CAB
7/11/95	12,128	PING.EXE	C:\WINDOWS	EXE	\WIN95\CAB_12.CAB
7/11/95	37,344	POINTER.EXE	C:\WINDOWS	EXE	\WIN95\CAB_08.CAB
7/11/95	113,456	PROGMAN.EXE	C:\WINDOWS	EXE	\WIN95\CAB_11.CAB
7/11/95	14,952	PROTMAN.EXE	C:\WINDOWS	EXE	\WIN95\CAB_12.CAB
7/11/95	20,992	QUIKVIEW.EXE	C:\WINDOWS	EXE	\WIN95\CAB_13.CAB
7/11/95	13,312	REDIR32.EXE	C:\WINDOWS\SYSTEM	EXE	\WIN95\CAB_03.CAB

continues

App

G

Date of File	Size of File	Installed Name	Installed Location	Type of File	Location on CD
7/11/95	120,320	REGEDIT.EXE	C:\WINDOWS	EXE	\WIN95\CAB_02.CAB
7/11/95	176,640	REGWIZ.EXE	C:\WINDOWS\SYSTEM	EXE	\WIN95\CAB_07.CAB
7/11/95	25,600	RNAAPP.EXE	C:\WINDOWS\SYSTEM	EXE	\WIN95\CAB_10.CAB
7/11/95	23,696	ROUTE.EXE	C:\WINDOWS	EXE	\WIN95\CAB_12.CAB
7/11/95	81,644	RPCSS.EXE	C:\WINDOWS\SYSTEM	EXE	\WIN95\CAB_12.CAB
7/11/95	15,360	RSRCMTR.EXE	C:\WINDOWS	EXE	\WIN95\CAB_02.CAB
7/11/95	4,912	RUNDLL.EXE	C:\WINDOWS	EXE	\WIN95\CAB_11.CAB
7/11/95	8,192	RUNDLL32.EXE	C:\WINDOWS	EXE	\WIN95\CAB_11.CAB
7/11/95	11,264	RUNONCE.EXE	C:\WINDOWS\SYSTEM	EXE	\WIN95\CAB_10.CAB
7/11/95	4,608	SCANDSKW.EXE	C:\WINDOWS\SYSTEM	EXE	\WIN95\CAB_09.CAB
7/11/95	264,384	SCANPST.EXE	C:\PROGRAM FILES\ MICROSOFT EXCHANGE	EXE	\WIN95\CAB_07.CAB
7/11/95	240,322	SELECT.EXE	C:\WINDOWS	EXE	\WIN95\CAB_17.CAB
7/11/95	57,209	SETMDIR.EXE	C:\WINDOWS\COMMAND	EXE	\WIN95\CAB_17.CAB
7/11/95	18,939	SETVER.EXE	C:\WINDOWS\COMMAND	EXE	\WIN95\CAB_09.CAB
7/11/95	108,544	SF4029.EXE	C:\WINDOWS\COMMAND	EXE	\WIN95\CAB_10.CAB
7/11/95	10,304	SHARE.EXE	C:\WINDOWS\COMMAND	EXE	\WIN95\CAB_09.CAB
7/11/95	202,752	SIGNUP.EXE	C:\PROGRAM FILES\ THE MICROSOFT NETWORK	EXE	\WIN95\CAB_07.CAB
7/11/95	6,122	SNAPSHOT.EXE	C:\WINDOWS	EXE	\WIN95\CAB_17.CAB
7/11/95	105,472	SNDREC32.EXE	C:\WINDOWS	EXE	\WIN95\CAB_08.CAB
7/11/95	54,784	SNDVOL32.EXE	C:\WINDOWS	EXE	\WIN95\CAB_08.CAB
7/11/95	171,392	SOL.EXE	C:\WINDOWS	EXE	\WIN95\CAB_05.CAB
7/11/95	25,802	SORT.EXE	C:\WINDOWS\COMMAND	EXE	\WIN95\CAB_03.CAB
7/11/95	20,992	SPOOL32.EXE	C:\WINDOWS\SYSTEM	EXE	\WIN95\CAB_09.CAB
7/11/95	9,216	START.EXE	C:\WINDOWS\COMMAND	EXE	\WIN95\CAB_09.CAB
7/11/95	17,904	SUBST.EXE	C:\WINDOWS\COMMAND	EXE	\WIN95\CAB_09.CAB
7/11/95	352,608	SUWIN.EXE	C:\WINDOWS\SYSTEM	EXE	\WIN95\PRECOPY2.CAB
7/11/95	19,488	SYSEDIT.EXE	C:\WINDOWS\SYSTEM	EXE	\WIN95\CAB_02.CAB
7/11/95	65,024	SYSMON.EXE	C:\WINDOWS	EXE	\WIN95\CAB_17.CAB
7/11/95	26,112	SYSTRAY.EXE	C:\WINDOWS\SYSTEM	EXE	\WIN95\CAB_07.CAB
7/11/95	1,784	TAPIEXE.EXE	C:\WINDOWS\SYSTEM	EXE	\WIN95\CAB_11.CAB
7/11/95	7,632	TAPIINI.EXE	C:\WINDOWS	EXE	\WIN95\CAB_11.CAB
7/11/95	28,672	TASKMAN.EXE	C:\WINDOWS	EXE	\WIN95\CAB_11.CAB
7/11/95	66,672	TELNET.EXE	C:\WINDOWS	EXE	\WIN95\CAB_12.CAB
7/11/95	53,248	TEXTCHAT.EXE	C:\PROGRAM FILES\ THE MICROSOFT NETWORK	EXE	\WIN95\CAB_07.CAB
7/11/95	339,456	TOUR.EXE	C:\WINDOWS	EXE	\WIN95\CAB_17.CAB
7/11/95	9,056	TRACERT.EXE	C:\WINDOWS	EXE	\WIN95\CAB_12.CAB
7/11/95	76,496	UNINSTAL.EXE	C:\WINDOWS	EXE	\WIN95\CAB_02.CAB
7/11/95	462,112	USER.EXE	C:\WINDOWS\SYSTEM	EXE	\WIN95\CAB_03.CAB
7/11/95	264,016	USER.EXE	C:\WINDOWS\SYSTEM	EXE	\WIN95\MINI.CAB
7/11/95	10,240	VVEXE32.EXE	C:\WINDOWS\SYSTEM	EXE	\WIN95\CAB_17.CAB

Date of File	Size of File	Installed Name	Installed Location	Type of File	Location on CD
7/11/95	16,384	WELCOME.EXE	C:\WINDOWS	EXE	\WIN95\CAB_11.CAB
7/11/95	155,408	WINFILE.EXE	C:\WINDOWS	EXE	\WIN95\CAB_11.CAB
7/11/95	2,416	WINHELP.EXE	C:\WINDOWS	EXE	\WIN95\CAB_05.CAB
7/11/95	306,688	WINHLP32.EXE	C:\WINDOWS	EXE	\WIN95\CAB_05.CAB
7/11/95	40,801	WININIT.EXE	C:\WINDOWS	EXE	\WIN95\CAB_10.CAB
7/11/95	38,912	WINIPCFG.EXE	C:\WINDOWS	EXE	\WIN95\CAB_12.CAB
7/11/95	24,176	WINMINE.EXE	C:\WINDOWS	EXE	\WIN95\CAB_05.CAB
7/11/95	27,600	WINPOPUP.EXE	C:\WINDOWS	EXE	\WIN95\CAB_12.CAB
7/11/95	3,632	WINVER.EXE	C:\WINDOWS	EXE	\WIN95\CAB_10.CAB
7/11/95	183,296	WORDPAD.EXE	C:\PROGRAM FILES\ ACCESSORIES	EXE	\WIN95\CAB_03.CAB
7/11/95	5,120	WRITE.EXE	C:\WINDOWS	EXE	\WIN95\CAB_02.CAB
7/11/95	6,960	WSASRV.EXE	C:\WINDOWS\SYSTEM	EXE	\WIN95\CAB_12.CAB
7/11/95	3,878	XCOPY.EXE	C:\WINDOWS\COMMAND	EXE	\WIN95\CAB_09.CAB
7/11/95	40,960	XCOPY32.EXE	C:\WINDOWS\COMMAND	EXE	\WIN95\CAB_09.CAB
7/11/95	26,624	PCXIMP32.FLT	C:\PROGRAM FILES\ ACCESSORIES	FLT	\WIN95\CAB_02.CAB
7/11/95	10,992	8514FIX.FON	C:\WINDOWS\SYSTEM	FON	\WIN95\CAB_05.CAB
7/11/95	12,288	8514OEM.FON	C:\WINDOWS\SYSTEM	FON	\WIN95\CAB_05.CAB
7/11/95	9,600	8514SYS.FON	C:\WINDOWS\SYSTEM	FON	\WIN95\CAB_05.CAB
7/11/95	44,320	APP850.FON	C:\WINDOWS\SYSTEM	FON	\WIN95\CAB_05.CAB
7/11/95	23,424	COURE.FON	C:\WINDOWS\SYSTEM	FON	\WIN95\CAB_05.CAB
7/11/95	31,744	COURF.FON	C:\WINDOWS\SYSTEM	FON	\WIN95\CAB_05.CAB
7/11/95	44,304	DOSAPP.FON	C:\WINDOWS\SYSTEM	FON	\WIN95\CAB_05.CAB
7/11/95	7,968	MODERN.FON	C:\WINDOWS\SYSTEM	FON	\WIN95\CAB_05.CAB
7/11/95	57,952	SERIFE.FON	C:\WINDOWS\SYSTEM	FON	\WIN95\CAB_05.CAB
7/11/95	57,936	SERIFE.FON	C:\WINDOWS\SYSTEM	FON	\WIN95\MINI.CAB
7/11/95	81,744	SERIFF.FON	C:\WINDOWS\SYSTEM	FON	\WIN95\CAB_05.CAB
7/11/95	24,352	SMALLE.FON	C:\WINDOWS\SYSTEM	FON	\WIN95\CAB_05.CAB
7/11/95	19,632	SMALLF.FON	C:\WINDOWS\SYSTEM	FON	\WIN95\CAB_05.CAB
7/11/95	64,544	SSERIFE.FON	C:\WINDOWS\SYSTEM	FON	\WIN95\CAB_05.CAB
7/11/95	64,544	SSERIFE.FON	C:\WINDOWS\SYSTEM	FON	\WIN95\MINI.CAB
7/11/95	89,680	SSERIFF.FON	C:\WINDOWS\SYSTEM	FON	\WIN95\CAB_05.CAB
7/11/95	56,336	SYMBOLE.FON	C:\WINDOWS\SYSTEM	FON	\WIN95\CAB_05.CAB
7/11/95	80,928	SYMBOLF.FON	C:\WINDOWS\SYSTEM	FON	\WIN95\CAB_05.CAB
7/11/95	5,232	VGA850.FON	C:\WINDOWS\SYSTEM	FON	\WIN95\CAB_03.CAB
7/11/95	5,360	VGAFIX.FON	C:\WINDOWS\SYSTEM	FON	\WIN95\CAB_05.CAB
7/11/95	5,360	VGAFIX.FON	C:\WINDOWS\SYSTEM	FON	\WIN95\MINI.CAB
7/11/95	5,168	VGAOEM.FON	C:\WINDOWS\SYSTEM	FON	\WIN95\CAB_05.CAB
7/11/95	5,168	VGAOEM.FON	C:\WINDOWS\SYSTEM	FON	\WIN95\MINI.CAB
7/11/95	7,296	VGASYS.FON	C:\WINDOWS\SYSTEM	FON	\WIN95\CAB_05.CAB
7/11/95	7,280	VGASYS.FON	C:\WINDOWS\SYSTEM	FON	\WIN95\MINI.CAB
7/11/95	47,506	31USERS.HLP	C:\WINDOWS\HELP	HLP	\WIN95\CAB_06.CAB
7/11/95	34,923	ACCESS.HLP	C:\WINDOWS\HELP	HLP	\WIN95\CAB_02.CAB

continues

App
G

Date of File	Size of File	Installed Name	Installed Location	Type of File	Location on CD
7/11/95	58,872	APPS.HLP	C:\WINDOWS\HELP	HLP	\WIN95\CAB_05.CAB
7/11/95	8,651	AUDIOCDC.HLP	C:\WINDOWS\HELP	HLP	\WIN95\CAB_05.CAB
7/11/95	58,931	AWFAX.HLP	C:\WINDOWS\HELP	HLP	\WIN95\CAB_05.CAB
7/11/95	8,679	AWPRT.HLP	C:\WINDOWS\HELP	HLP	\WIN95\CAB_05.CAB
7/11/95	31,886	CALC.HLP	C:\WINDOWS\HELP	HLP	\WIN95\CAB_05.CAB
7/11/95	20,579	CDPLAYER.HLP	C:\WINDOWS\HELP	HLP	\WIN95\CAB_13.CAB
7/11/95	20,029	CLIPBOOK.HLP	C:\WINDOWS\HELP	HLP	\WIN95\CAB_02.CAB
7/11/95	13,015	CLIPBRD.HLP	C:\WINDOWS\HELP	HLP	\WIN95\CAB_02.CAB
7/11/95	22,233	COMMON.HLP	C:\WINDOWS\HELP	HLP	\WIN95\CAB_05.CAB
7/11/95	235,199	DECPSMW4.HLP	C:\WINDOWS\HELP	HLP	\WIN95\CAB_16.CAB
7/11/95	19,193	DIALER.HLP	C:\WINDOWS\HELP	HLP	\WIN95\CAB_02.CAB
7/11/95	23,816	DRVSPACE.HLP	C:\WINDOWS\HELP	HLP	\WIN95\CAB_05.CAB
7/11/95	10,790	EDIT.HLP	C:\WINDOWS\COMMAND	HLP	\WIN95\CAB_05.CAB
7/11/95	100,371	EXCHNG.HLP	C:\WINDOWS\HELP	HLP	\WIN95\CAB_06.CAB
7/11/95	9,079	EXPO.HLP	C:\WINDOWS\HELP	HLP	\WIN95\CAB_17.CAB
7/11/95	15,185	FAXCOVER.HLP	C:\WINDOWS\HELP	HLP	\WIN95\CAB_05.CAB
7/11/95	12,186	FAXVIEW.HLP	C:\WINDOWS\HELP	HLP	\WIN95\CAB_05.CAB
7/11/95	14,007	FILEXFER.HLP	C:\WINDOWS\HELP	HLP	\WIN95\CAB_17.CAB
7/11/95	21,491	FINSTALL.HLP	C:\WINDOWS\SYSTEM	HLP	\WIN95\CAB_09.CAB
7/11/95	11,618	FREECELL.HLP	C:\WINDOWS\HELP	HLP	\WIN95\CAB_05.CAB
7/11/95	57,660	HPJDUND.HLP	C:\WINDOWS\HELP	HLP	\WIN95\CAB_16.CAB
7/11/95	10,119	HPPLOT.HLP	C:\WINDOWS\HELP	HLP	\WIN95\CAB_10.CAB
7/11/95	26,913	HPPRARRK.HLP	C:\WINDOWS\HELP	HLP	\WIN95\CAB_16.CAB
7/11/95	81,937	HPPRNTR.HLP	C:\WINDOWS\HELP	HLP	\WIN95\CAB_16.CAB
7/11/95	17,166	HPVDJC.HLP	C:\WINDOWS\HELP	HLP	\WIN95\CAB_10.CAB
7/11/95	21,473	HYPERTRM.HLP	C:\WINDOWS\HELP	HLP	\WIN95\CAB_02.CAB
7/11/95	285,953	JETADMIN.HLP	C:\WINDOWS\HELP	HLP	\WIN95\CAB_16.CAB
7/11/95	26,905	LICENSE.HLP	C:\WINDOWS\HELP	HLP	\WIN95\CAB_03.CAB
7/11/95	13,101	MFCUIX.HLP	C:\WINDOWS\HELP	HLP	\WIN95\CAB_05.CAB
7/11/95	9,584	MMDRV.HLP	C:\WINDOWS\HELP	HLP	\WIN95\CAB_08.CAB
7/11/95	16,577	MOUSE.HLP	C:\WINDOWS\HELP	HLP	\WIN95\CAB_05.CAB
7/11/95	26,940	MPLAYER.HLP	C:\WINDOWS\HELP	HLP	\WIN95\CAB_08.CAB
7/11/95	34,832	MSFS.HLP	C:\WINDOWS\HELP	HLP	\WIN95\CAB_06.CAB
7/11/95	11,661	MSHEARTS.HLP	C:\WINDOWS\HELP	HLP	\WIN95\CAB_05.CAB
7/11/95	17,780	MSN.HLP	C:\WINDOWS\HELP	HLP	\WIN95\CAB_07.CAB
7/11/95	52,454	MSNBBS.HLP	C:\WINDOWS\HELP	HLP	\WIN95\CAB_07.CAB
7/11/95	28,695	MSNCHAT.HLP	C:\WINDOWS\HELP	HLP	\WIN95\CAB_07.CAB
7/11/95	107,361	MSNFULL.HLP	C:\WINDOWS\HELP	HLP	\WIN95\CAB_06.CAB
7/11/95	32,773	MSNINT.HLP	C:\WINDOWS\HELP	HLP	\WIN95\CAB_06.CAB
7/11/95	48,932	MSNMAIL.HLP	C:\WINDOWS\HELP	HLP	\WIN95\CAB_07.CAB
7/11/95	34,974	MSNPSS.HLP	C:\WINDOWS\HELP	HLP	\WIN95\CAB_07.CAB
7/11/95	43,620	MSPAINT.HLP	C:\WINDOWS\HELP	HLP	\WIN95\CAB_02.CAB
7/11/95	164,352	MSWD6_32.WPC	C:\WINDOWS\HELP	HLP	\WIN95\CAB_03.CAB

Date of File	Size of File	Installed Name	Installed Location	Type of File	Location on CD
7/11/95	12,339	NETWATCH.HLP	C:\WINDOWS\HELP	HLP	\WIN95\CAB_13.CAB
7/11/95	88,385	NETWORK.HLP	C:\WINDOWS\HELP	HLP	\WIN95\CAB_05.CAB
7/11/95	11,708	NOTEPAD.HLP	C:\WINDOWS\HELP	HLP	\WIN95\CAB_05.CAB
7/11/95	255,760	OVERVIEW.HLP	C:\WINDOWS\HELP	HLP	\WIN95\CAB_16.CAB
7/11/95	23,529	PACKAGER.HLP	C:\WINDOWS\HELP	HLP	\WIN95\CAB_02.CAB
7/11/95	24,466	PROGMAN.HLP	C:\WINDOWS\HELP	HLP	\WIN95\CAB_11.CAB
7/11/95	20,439	PSCRIPT.HLP	C:\WINDOWS\HELP	HLP	\WIN95\CAB_09.CAB
7/11/95	57,437	QIC117.VXD	C:\WINDOWS\HELP	HLP	\WIN95\CAB_04.CAB
7/11/95	18,338	REGEDIT.HLP	C:\WINDOWS\HELP	HLP	\WIN95\CAB_06.CAB
7/11/95	14,135	SCANPST.HLP	C:\WINDOWS\HELP	HLP	\WIN95\CAB_07.CAB
7/11/95	22,948	SERVER.HLP	C:\WINDOWS\HELP	HLP	\WIN95\CAB_05.CAB
7/11/95	11,120	SNDVOL32.HLP	C:\WINDOWS\HELP	HLP	\WIN95\CAB_08.CAB
7/11/95	10,145	SOL.HLP	C:\WINDOWS\HELP	HLP	\WIN95\CAB_05.CAB
7/11/95	24,895	SOUNDREC.HLP	C:\WINDOWS\HELP	HLP	\WIN95\CAB_08.CAB
7/11/95	10,558	SYSMON.HLP	C:\WINDOWS\HELP	HLP	\WIN95\CAB_13.CAB
7/11/95	7,315	TELEPHON.HLP	C:\WINDOWS\HELP	HLP	\WIN95\CAB_11.CAB
7/11/95	24,099	TELNET.HLP	C:\WINDOWS\HELP	HLP	\WIN95\CAB_12.CAB
7/11/95	11,606	TTY.HLP	C:\WINDOWS\SYSTEM	HLP	\WIN95\CAB_05.CAB
7/11/95	15,343	UNIDRV.HLP	C:\WINDOWS\SYSTEM	HLP	\WIN95\CAB_09.CAB
7/11/95	519,340	WINDOWS.HLP	C:\WINDOWS\HELP	HLP	\WIN95\CAB_05.CAB
7/11/95	43,833	WINFILE.HLP	C:\WINDOWS\HELP	HLP	\WIN95\CAB_11.CAB
7/11/95	27,507	WINHLP32.HLP	C:\WINDOWS\HELP	HLP	\WIN95\CAB_06.CAB
7/11/95	9,133	WINMINE.HLP	C:\WINDOWS\HELP	HLP	\WIN95\CAB_05.CAB
7/11/95	11,591	WINPOPUP.HLP	C:\WINDOWS\HELP	HLP	\WIN95\CAB_12.CAB
7/11/95	28,422	WORDPAD.HLP	C:\WINDOWS\HELP	HLP	\WIN95\CAB_03.CAB
7/11/95	13,623	HPVCM.HPM	C:\WINDOWS\SYSTEM	HPM	\WIN95\CAB_10.CAB
7/11/95	829	AT&TMA~1.HT	C:\PROGRAM FILES\ ACCESSORIS\ HYPERTERMINAL	HT	\WIN95\CAB_02.CAB
7/11/95	829	COMPUS~1.HT	C:\PROGRAM FILES\ ACCESSORIS\ HYPERTERMINAL	HT	\WIN95\CAB_02.CAB
7/11/95	829	MCIMAI~1.HT	C:\PROGRAM FILES\ ACCESSORIS\ HYPERTERMINAL	HT	\WIN95\CAB_02.CAB
7/11/95	12,504	BJC600.ICM	C:\WINDOWS\SYSTEM\ COLOR	ICM	\WIN95\CAB_10.CAB
7/11/95	12,684	BJC800.ICM	C:\WINDOWS\SYSTEM\ COLOR	ICM	\WIN95\CAB_10.CAB
7/11/95	12,628	EPSONSTY.ICM	C:\WINDOWS\SYSTEM\ COLOR	ICM	\WIN95\CAB_10.CAB
7/11/95	12,716	HP1200C.ICM	C:\WINDOWS\SYSTEM\ COLOR	ICM	\WIN95\CAB_06.CAB
7/11/95	24,600	HP1200PS.ICM	C:\WINDOWS\SYSTEM\ COLOR	ICM	\WIN95\CAB_06.CAB
7/11/95	12,176	HPCLRLSR.ICM	C:\WINDOWS\SYSTEM\	ICM	\WIN95\CAB_10.CAB

continues

App
G

Date of File	Size of File	Installed Name	Installed Location	Type of File	Location on CD
			COLOR		
7/11/95	12,956	HPDESK.ICM	C:\WINDOWS\SYSTEM\ COLOR	ICM	\WIN95\CAB_10.CAB
7/11/95	6,514	HPSJTW.ICM	C:\WINDOWS\SYSTEM\ COLOR	ICM	\WIN95\CAB_06.CAB
7/11/95	12,700	HPXL300.ICM	C:\WINDOWS\SYSTEM\ COLOR	ICM	\WIN95\CAB_10.CAB
7/11/95	24,596	HPXL30PS.ICM	C:\WINDOWS\SYSTEM\ COLOR	ICM	\WIN95\CAB_10.CAB
7/11/95	24,416	KODAKCE.ICM	C:\WINDOWS\SYSTEM\ COLOR	ICM	\WIN95\CAB_06.CAB
7/11/95	59,564	MNB22G15.ICM	C:\WINDOWS\SYSTEM\ COLOR	ICM	\WIN95\CAB_06.CAB
7/11/95	59,564	MNB22G18.ICM	C:\WINDOWS\SYSTEM\ COLOR	ICM	\WIN95\CAB_06.CAB
7/11/95	59,564	MNB22G21.ICM	C:\WINDOWS\SYSTEM\ COLOR	ICM	\WIN95\CAB_06.CAB
7/11/95	59,964	MNEBUG15.ICM	C:\WINDOWS\SYSTEM\ COLOR	ICM	\WIN95\CAB_06.CAB
7/11/95	59,964	MNEBUG18.ICM	C:\WINDOWS\SYSTEM\ COLOR	ICM	\WIN95\CAB_06.CAB
7/11/95	59,964	MNEBUG21.ICM	C:\WINDOWS\SYSTEM\ COLOR	ICM	\WIN95\CAB_06.CAB
7/11/95	59,980	MNP22G15.ICM	C:\WINDOWS\SYSTEM\ COLOR	ICM	\WIN95\CAB_06.CAB
7/11/95	59,980	MNP22G18.ICM	C:\WINDOWS\SYSTEM\ COLOR	ICM	\WIN95\CAB_06.CAB
7/11/95	59,980	MNP22G21.ICM	C:\WINDOWS\SYSTEM\ COLOR	ICM	\WIN95\CAB_06.CAB
7/11/95	24,348	PS4079.ICM	C:\WINDOWS\SYSTEM\ COLOR	ICM	\WIN95\CAB_06.CAB
7/11/95	24,716	QMS10030.ICM	C:\WINDOWS\SYSTEM\ COLOR	ICM	\WIN95\CAB_10.CAB
7/11/95	24,844	TPHA200I.ICM	C:\WINDOWS\SYSTEM\ COLOR	ICM	\WIN95\CAB_06.CAB
7/11/95	24,804	TPHAIII.ICM	C:\WINDOWS\SYSTEM\ COLOR	ICM	\WIN95\CAB_06.CAB
7/11/95	766	MAPIF0L.ICO	C:\WINDOWS\SYSTEM	ICO	\WIN95\CAB_06.CAB
7/11/95	766	MAPIF0S.ICO	C:\WINDOWS\SYSTEM	ICO	\WIN95\CAB_06.CAB
7/11/95	766	MAPIF1L.ICO	C:\WINDOWS\SYSTEM	ICO	\WIN95\CAB_06.CAB
7/11/95	766	MAPIF1S.ICO	C:\WINDOWS\SYSTEM	ICO	\WIN95\CAB_06.CAB
7/11/95	766	MAPIF2L.ICO	C:\WINDOWS\SYSTEM	ICO	\WIN95\CAB_06.CAB
7/11/95	766	MAPIF2S.ICO	C:\WINDOWS\SYSTEM	ICO	\WIN95\CAB_06.CAB
7/11/95	766	MAPIF3L.ICO	C:\WINDOWS\SYSTEM	ICO	\WIN95\CAB_06.CAB
7/11/95	766	MAPIF3S.ICO	C:\WINDOWS\SYSTEM	ICO	\WIN95\CAB_06.CAB
7/11/95	766	MAPIF4L.ICO	C:\WINDOWS\SYSTEM	ICO	\WIN95\CAB_06.CAB
7/11/95	766	MAPIF4S.ICO	C:\WINDOWS\SYSTEM	ICO	\WIN95\CAB_06.CAB
7/11/95	766	MAPIF5L.ICO	C:\WINDOWS\SYSTEM	ICO	\WIN95\CAB_06.CAB

Date of File	Size of File	Installed Name	Installed Location	Type of File	Location on CD
7/11/95	766	MAPIF5S.ICO	C:\WINDOWS\SYSTEM	ICO	\WIN95\CAB_06.CAB
7/11/95	654	GENERAL.IDF	C:\WINDOWS\CONFIG	IDF	\WIN95\CAB_08.CAB
7/11/95	4,788	ADAPTER.INF	C:\WINDOWS\INF	INF	\WIN95\PRECOPY2.CAB
7/11/95	2,578	APM.INF	C:\WINDOWS\INF	INF	\WIN95\PRECOPY2.CAB
7/11/95	22,326	APPLETPP.INF	C:\WINDOWS\INF	INF	\WIN95\PRECOPY2.CAB
7/11/95	45,231	APPLETS.INF	C:\WINDOWS\INF	INF	\WIN95\PRECOPY2.CAB
7/11/95	62,339	APPS.INF	C:\WINDOWS\INF	INF	\WIN95\CAB_06.CAB
7/11/95	19,824	AWFAX.INF	C:\WINDOWS\INF	INF	\WIN95\PRECOPY2.CAB
7/11/95	2,191	AWUPD.INF	C:\WINDOWS\INF	INF	\WIN95\PRECOPY2.CAB
7/11/95	2,893	BKUPAGNT.INF	C:\WINDOWS\INF	INF	\WIN95\PRECOPY2.CAB
7/11/95	35,608	CEMMF.INF	C:\WINDOWS\INF	INF	\WIN95\PRECOPY2.CAB
7/11/95	1,657	CHEYENNE.INF	C:\WINDOWS\INF	INF	\WIN95\PRECOPY2.CAB
7/11/95	2,213	CLIP.INF	C:\WINDOWS\INF	INF	\WIN95\CAB_10.CAB
7/11/95	2,497	CONTROL.INF	C:\WINDOWS\SYSTEM	INF	\WIN95\CAB_11.CAB
7/11/95	33,338	COPY.INF	C:\WINDOWS\INF	INF	\WIN95\PRECOPY2.CAB
7/11/95	2,436	DECPSMW4.INF	C:\WINDOWS\INF	INF	\WIN95\PRECOPY2.CAB
7/11/95	36,793	DEL.INF	C:\WINDOWS\INF	INF	\WIN95\PRECOPY2.CAB
7/11/95	765	DISKDRV.INF	C:\WINDOWS\INF	INF	\WIN95\PRECOPY2.CAB
7/11/95	1,121	DRVSPACE.INF	C:\WINDOWS\INF	INF	\WIN95\CAB_09.CAB
7/11/95	2,971	ENABLE.INF	C:\WINDOWS\INF	INF	\WIN95\PRECOPY2.CAB
7/11/95	24,626	FONTS.INF	C:\WINDOWS\INF	INF	\WIN95\PRECOPY2.CAB
7/11/95	5,297	HPNETPRN.INF	C:\WINDOWS\INF	INF	\WIN95\PRECOPY2.CAB
7/11/95	2,049	ICM.INF	C:\WINDOWS\INF	INF	\WIN95\PRECOPY2.CAB
7/11/95	2,830	JOYSTICK.INF	C:\WINDOWS\INF	INF	\WIN95\PRECOPY2.CAB
7/11/95	6,953	KEYBOARD.INF	C:\WINDOWS\INF	INF	\WIN95\PRECOPY2.CAB
7/11/95	51,173	LAYOUT.INF	C:\WINDOWS\INF	INF	\WIN95\PRECOPY2.CAB
7/11/95	12,922	LICENSE.TXT	C:\WINDOWS\INF	INF	\WIN95\PRECOPY2.CAB
7/11/95	40,671	LOCALE.INF	C:\WINDOWS\INF	INF	\WIN95\PRECOPY2.CAB
7/11/95	30,827	MACHINE.INF	C:\WINDOWS\INF	INF	\WIN95\PRECOPY2.CAB
7/11/95	4,993	MAPISVC.INF	C:\WINDOWS\INF	INF	\WIN95\CAB_07.CAB
7/11/95	12,865	MDMATI.INF	C:\WINDOWS\INF	INF	\WIN95\CAB_07.CAB
7/11/95	29,686	MDMATT.INF	C:\WINDOWS\INF	INF	\WIN95\CAB_07.CAB
7/11/95	35,436	MDMAUS.INF	C:\WINDOWS\INF	INF	\WIN95\CAB_07.CAB
7/11/95	23,455	MDMBOCA.INF	C:\WINDOWS\INF	INF	\WIN95\CAB_07.CAB
7/11/95	25,304	MDMCOMMU.INF	C:\WINDOWS\INF	INF	\WIN95\CAB_07.CAB
7/11/95	33,941	MDMCPI.INF	C:\WINDOWS\INF	INF	\WIN95\CAB_07.CAB
7/11/95	40,135	MDMCPQ.INF	C:\WINDOWS\INF	INF	\WIN95\CAB_07.CAB
7/11/95	37,416	MDMDSI.INF	C:\WINDOWS\INF	INF	\WIN95\CAB_07.CAB
7/11/95	37,676	MDMEXP.INF	C:\WINDOWS\INF	INF	\WIN95\CAB_07.CAB
7/11/95	23,617	MDMGATEW.INF	C:\WINDOWS\INF	INF	\WIN95\CAB_07.CAB
7/11/95	33,192	MDMGEN.INF	C:\WINDOWS\INF	INF	\WIN95\CAB_07.CAB
7/11/95	47,472	MDMGVC.INF	C:\WINDOWS\INF	INF	\WIN95\CAB_07.CAB
7/11/95	42,229	MDMHAYES.INF	C:\WINDOWS\INF	INF	\WIN95\CAB_07.CAB

App
G

continues

Date of File	Size of File	Installed Name	Installed Location	Type of File	Location on CD
7/11/95	28,232	MDMINFOT.INF	C:\WINDOWS\INF	INF	\WIN95\CAB_07.CAB
7/11/95	17,067	MDMINTEL.INF	C:\WINDOWS\INF	INF	\WIN95\CAB_07.CAB
7/11/95	26,967	MDMINTPC.INF	C:\WINDOWS\INF	INF	\WIN95\CAB_07.CAB
7/11/95	23,124	MDMMCOM.INF	C:\WINDOWS\INF	INF	\WIN95\CAB_07.CAB
7/11/95	4,576	MDMMETRI.INF	C:\WINDOWS\INF	INF	\WIN95\CAB_07.CAB
7/11/95	30,549	MDMMHRTZ.INF	C:\WINDOWS\INF	INF	\WIN95\CAB_07.CAB
7/11/95	36,008	MDMMOTO.INF	C:\WINDOWS\INF	INF	\WIN95\CAB_07.CAB
7/11/95	22,953	MDMMTS.INF	C:\WINDOWS\INF	INF	\WIN95\CAB_07.CAB
7/11/95	2,972	MDMNOKIA.INF	C:\WINDOWS\INF	INF	\WIN95\CAB_07.CAB
7/11/95	12,342	MDMNOVA.INF	C:\WINDOWS\INF	INF	\WIN95\CAB_07.CAB
7/11/95	9,964	MDMOSI.INF	C:\WINDOWS\INF	INF	\WIN95\CAB_07.CAB
7/11/95	26,351	MDMPACE.INF	C:\WINDOWS\INF	INF	\WIN95\CAB_07.CAB
7/11/95	33,251	MDMPNB.INF	C:\WINDOWS\INF	INF	\WIN95\CAB_07.CAB
7/11/95	25,055	MDMPP.INF	C:\WINDOWS\INF	INF	\WIN95\CAB_07.CAB
7/11/95	25,804	MDMRACAL.INF	C:\WINDOWS\INF	INF	\WIN95\CAB_08.CAB
7/11/95	62,394	MDMROCK.INF	C:\WINDOWS\INF	INF	\WIN95\CAB_08.CAB
7/11/95	50,109	MDMROCK2.INF	C:\WINDOWS\INF	INF	\WIN95\CAB_08.CAB
7/11/95	9,208	MDMSIER.INF	C:\WINDOWS\INF	INF	\WIN95\CAB_08.CAB
7/11/95	23,370	MDMSONIX.INF	C:\WINDOWS\INF	INF	\WIN95\CAB_08.CAB
7/11/95	11,458	MDMSPEC.INF	C:\WINDOWS\INF	INF	\WIN95\CAB_08.CAB
7/11/95	15,275	MDMSUPRA.INF	C:\WINDOWS\INF	INF	\WIN95\CAB_08.CAB
7/11/95	5,864	MDMTDK.INF	C:\WINDOWS\INF	INF	\WIN95\CAB_08.CAB
7/11/95	31,377	MDMTELBT.INF	C:\WINDOWS\INF	INF	\WIN95\CAB_08.CAB
7/11/95	5,861	MDMTI.INF	C:\WINDOWS\INF	INF	\WIN95\CAB_08.CAB
7/11/95	45,577	MDMTOSH.INF	C:\WINDOWS\INF	INF	\WIN95\CAB_08.CAB
7/11/95	50,070	MDMUSRCR.INF	C:\WINDOWS\INF	INF	\WIN95\CAB_08.CAB
7/11/95	44,991	MDMUSRSP.INF	C:\WINDOWS\INF	INF	\WIN95\CAB_08.CAB
7/11/95	50,051	MDMUSRWP.INF	C:\WINDOWS\INF	INF	\WIN95\CAB_08.CAB
7/11/95	33,304	MDMVV.INF	C:\WINDOWS\INF	INF	\WIN95\CAB_17.CAB
7/11/95	16,156	MDMZOOM.INF	C:\WINDOWS\INF	INF	\WIN95\CAB_08.CAB
7/11/95	23,916	MDMZYP.INF	C:\WINDOWS\INF	INF	\WIN95\CAB_08.CAB
7/11/95	9,166	MDMZYXEL.INF	C:\WINDOWS\INF	INF	\WIN95\CAB_08.CAB
7/11/95	7,887	MF.INF	C:\WINDOWS\INF	INF	\WIN95\PRECOPY2.CAB
7/11/95	7,288	MFOSI.INF	C:\WINDOWS\INF	INF	\WIN95\PRECOPY2.CAB
7/11/95	5,315	MIDI.INF	C:\WINDOWS\INF	INF	\WIN95\PRECOPY2.CAB
7/11/95	37,061	MMOPT.INF	C:\WINDOWS\INF	INF	\WIN95\PRECOPY2.CAB
7/11/95	1,773	MODEMS.INF	C:\WINDOWS\INF	INF	\WIN95\PRECOPY2.CAB
7/11/95	37,649	MONITOR.INF	C:\WINDOWS\INF	INF	\WIN95\PRECOPY2.CAB
7/11/95	55,766	MONITOR2.INF	C:\WINDOWS\INF	INF	\WIN95\PRECOPY2.CAB
7/11/95	56,254	MONITOR3.INF	C:\WINDOWS\INF	INF	\WIN95\PRECOPY2.CAB
7/11/95	42,030	MONITOR4.INF	C:\WINDOWS\INF	INF	\WIN95\PRECOPY2.CAB
7/11/95	46,923	MOS.INF	C:\WINDOWS\INF	INF	\WIN95\PRECOPY2.CAB
7/11/95	47,846	MOTOWN.INF	C:\WINDOWS\INF	INF	\WIN95\PRECOPY2.CAB

Date of File	Size of File	Installed Name	Installed Location	Type of File	Location on CD
7/11/95	58,621	MSBASE.INF	C:\WINDOWS\INF	INF	\WIN95\PRECOPY2.CAB
7/11/95	951	MSCDROM.INF	C:\WINDOWS\INF	INF	\WIN95\PRECOPY2.CAB
7/11/95	21,472	MSDET.INF	C:\WINDOWS\INF	INF	\WIN95\PRECOPY2.CAB
7/11/95	40,877	MSDISP.INF	C:\WINDOWS\INF	INF	\WIN95\PRECOPY2.CAB
7/11/95	10,998	MSDOS.INF	C:\WINDOWS\INF	INF	\WIN95\PRECOPY2.CAB
7/11/95	3,657	MSFDC.INF	C:\WINDOWS\INF	INF	\WIN95\PRECOPY2.CAB
7/11/95	12,267	MSHDC.INF	C:\WINDOWS\INF	INF	\WIN95\PRECOPY2.CAB
7/11/95	36,068	MSMAIL.INF	C:\WINDOWS\INF	INF	\WIN95\PRECOPY2.CAB
7/11/95	13,322	MSMOUSE.INF	C:\WINDOWS\INF	INF	\WIN95\PRECOPY2.CAB
7/11/95	9,510	MSPORTS.INF	C:\WINDOWS\INF	INF	\WIN95\PRECOPY2.CAB
7/11/95	46,309	MSPRINT.INF	C:\WINDOWS\INF	INF	\WIN95\PRECOPY2.CAB
7/11/95	37,350	MSPRINT2.INF	C:\WINDOWS\INF	INF	\WIN95\PRECOPY2.CAB
7/11/95	1,891	MTD.INF	C:\WINDOWS\INF	INF	\WIN95\PRECOPY2.CAB
7/11/95	11,024	MULLANG.INF	C:\WINDOWS\INF	INF	\WIN95\CAB_13.CAB
7/11/95	25,665	MULTILNG.INF	C:\WINDOWS\INF	INF	\WIN95\PRECOPY2.CAB
7/11/95	21,393	NET.INF	C:\WINDOWS\INF	INF	\WIN95\PRECOPY2.CAB
7/11/95	31,895	NET3COM.INF	C:\WINDOWS\INF	INF	\WIN95\PRECOPY2.CAB
7/11/95	19,762	NETAMD.INF	C:\WINDOWS\INF	INF	\WIN95\PRECOPY2.CAB
7/11/95	153	NETAUXT.INF	C:\WINDOWS\INF	INF	\WIN95\PRECOPY2.CAB
7/11/95	4,152	NETBW.INF	C:\WINDOWS\INF	INF	\WIN95\PRECOPY2.CAB
7/11/95	25,234	NETCABLE.INF	C:\WINDOWS\INF	INF	\WIN95\PRECOPY2.CAB
7/11/95	30,838	NETCD.INF	C:\WINDOWS\INF	INF	\WIN95\PRECOPY2.CAB
7/11/95	2,810	NETCEM.INF	C:\WINDOWS\INF	INF	\WIN95\PRECOPY2.CAB
7/11/95	16,390	NETCLI.INF	C:\WINDOWS\INF	INF	\WIN95\PRECOPY2.CAB
7/11/95	28,011	NETCLI3.INF	C:\WINDOWS\INF	INF	\WIN95\PRECOPY2.CAB
7/11/95	6,816	NETCPQ.INF	C:\WINDOWS\INF	INF	\WIN95\PRECOPY2.CAB
7/11/95	16,782	NETDCA.INF	C:\WINDOWS\INF	INF	\WIN95\PRECOPY2.CAB
7/11/95	20,208	NETDEC.INF	C:\WINDOWS\INF	INF	\WIN95\PRECOPY2.CAB
7/11/95	10,275	NETDEF.INF	C:\WINDOWS\INF	INF	\WIN95\PRECOPY2.CAB
7/11/95	12,788	NETDLC.INF	C:\WINDOWS\INF	INF	\WIN95\PRECOPY2.CAB
7/11/95	22,103	NETEE16.INF	C:\WINDOWS\INF	INF	\WIN95\PRECOPY2.CAB
7/11/95	2,634	NETEVX.INF	C:\WINDOWS\INF	INF	\WIN95\PRECOPY2.CAB
7/11/95	7,168	NETFLEX.INF	C:\WINDOWS\INF	INF	\WIN95\PRECOPY2.CAB
7/11/95	4,125	NETFTP.INF	C:\WINDOWS\INF	INF	\WIN95\PRECOPY2.CAB
7/11/95	4,039	NETGEN.INF	C:\WINDOWS\INF	INF	\WIN95\PRECOPY2.CAB
7/11/95	10,111	NETHP.INF	C:\WINDOWS\INF	INF	\WIN95\PRECOPY2.CAB
7/11/95	17,817	NETIBM.INF	C:\WINDOWS\INF	INF	\WIN95\PRECOPY2.CAB
7/11/95	19,419	NETIBMCC.INF	C:\WINDOWS\INF	INF	\WIN95\PRECOPY2.CAB
7/11/95	25,842	NETMADGE.INF	C:\WINDOWS\INF	INF	\WIN95\PRECOPY2.CAB
7/11/95	16,525	NETNCR.INF	C:\WINDOWS\INF	INF	\WIN95\PRECOPY2.CAB
7/11/95	3,808	NETNICE.INF	C:\WINDOWS\INF	INF	\WIN95\PRECOPY2.CAB
7/11/95	22,774	NETNOVEL.INF	C:\WINDOWS\INF	INF	\WIN95\PRECOPY2.CAB
7/11/95	21,733	NETOLI.INF	C:\WINDOWS\INF	INF	\WIN95\PRECOPY2.CAB

App
G

continues

Date of File	Size of File	Installed Name	Installed Location	Type of File	Location on CD
7/11/95	3,811	NETOSI.INF	C:\WINDOWS\INF	INF	\WIN95\PRECOPY2.CAB
7/11/95	11,080	NETPCI.INF	C:\WINDOWS\INF	INF	\WIN95\PRECOPY2.CAB
7/11/95	2,883	NETPPP.INF	C:\WINDOWS\INF	INF	\WIN95\PRECOPY2.CAB
7/11/95	12,890	NETPROT.INF	C:\WINDOWS\INF	INF	\WIN95\PRECOPY2.CAB
7/11/95	8,055	NETRACAL.INF	C:\WINDOWS\INF	INF	\WIN95\PRECOPY2.CAB
7/11/95	12,223	NETSERVR.INF	C:\WINDOWS\INF	INF	\WIN95\PRECOPY2.CAB
7/11/95	7,524	NETSILC.INF	C:\WINDOWS\INF	INF	\WIN95\PRECOPY2.CAB
7/11/95	36,024	NETSMC.INF	C:\WINDOWS\INF	INF	\WIN95\PRECOPY2.CAB
7/11/95	2,593	NETSMC32.INF	C:\WINDOWS\INF	INF	\WIN95\PRECOPY2.CAB
7/11/95	4,543	NETSMCTR.INF	C:\WINDOWS\INF	INF	\WIN95\PRECOPY2.CAB
7/11/95	8,345	NETSNIP.INF	C:\WINDOWS\INF	INF	\WIN95\PRECOPY2.CAB
7/11/95	3,155	NETSOCK.INF	C:\WINDOWS\INF	INF	\WIN95\PRECOPY2.CAB
7/11/95	16,149	NETTCC.INF	C:\WINDOWS\INF	INF	\WIN95\PRECOPY2.CAB
7/11/95	4,828	NETTDKP.INF	C:\WINDOWS\INF	INF	\WIN95\PRECOPY2.CAB
7/11/95	37,248	NETTRANS.INF	C:\WINDOWS\INF	INF	\WIN95\PRECOPY2.CAB
7/11/95	1,980	NETTULIP.INF	C:\WINDOWS\INF	INF	\WIN95\PRECOPY2.CAB
7/11/95	13,101	NETUB.INF	C:\WINDOWS\INF	INF	\WIN95\PRECOPY2.CAB
7/11/95	24,805	NETXIR.INF	C:\WINDOWS\INF	INF	\WIN95\PRECOPY2.CAB
7/11/95	3,831	NETZNOTE.INF	C:\WINDOWS\INF	INF	\WIN95\PRECOPY2.CAB
7/11/95	2,572	NODRIVER.INF	C:\WINDOWS\INF	INF	\WIN95\PRECOPY2.CAB
7/11/95	25,550	OLE2.INF	C:\WINDOWS\INF	INF	\WIN95\PRECOPY2.CAB
7/11/95	10,079	PCMCIA.INF	C:\WINDOWS\INF	INF	\WIN95\PRECOPY2.CAB
7/11/95	2,538	PRECOPY.INF	C:\WINDOWS\INF	INF	\WIN95\PRECOPY2.CAB
7/11/95	20,851	PRTUPD.INF	C:\WINDOWS\INF	INF	\WIN95\PRECOPY2.CAB
7/11/95	7,703	REN.INF	C:\WINDOWS\INF	INF	\WIN95\PRECOPY2.CAB
7/11/95	10,611	RNA.INF	C:\WINDOWS\INF	INF	\WIN95\PRECOPY2.CAB
7/11/95	35,741	SCSI.INF	C:\WINDOWS\INF	INF	\WIN95\PRECOPY2.CAB
7/11/95	55,858	SETUPC.INF	C:\WINDOWS\INF	INF	\WIN95\PRECOPY2.CAB
7/11/95	4,242	SETUPPP.INF	C:\WINDOWS\INF	INF	\WIN95\PRECOPY2.CAB
7/11/95	48,580	SHELL.INF	C:\WINDOWS\INF	INF	\WIN95\PRECOPY2.CAB
7/11/95	46,936	SHELL2.INF	C:\WINDOWS\INF	INF	\WIN95\PRECOPY2.CAB
7/11/95	7,272	SHELL3.INF	C:\WINDOWS\INF	INF	\WIN95\PRECOPY2.CAB
7/11/95	1,046	TAPI.INF	C:\WINDOWS\INF	INF	\WIN95\PRECOPY2.CAB
7/11/95	46,060	TIMEZONE.INF	C:\WINDOWS\INF	INF	\WIN95\PRECOPY2.CAB
7/11/95	462	UNKNOWN.INF	C:\WINDOWS\INF	INF	\WIN95\PRECOPY2.CAB
7/11/95	2,158	VIDCAP.INF	C:\WINDOWS\INF	INF	\WIN95\PRECOPY2.CAB
7/11/95	62,619	WAVE.INF	C:\WINDOWS\INF	INF	\WIN95\PRECOPY2.CAB
7/11/95	1,932	WINPOPUP.INF	C:\WINDOWS\INF	INF	\WIN95\CAB_12.CAB
7/11/95	56,062	WINVER.INF	C:\WINDOWS	INF	\WIN95\PRECOPY2.CAB
7/11/95	10,491	WORDPAD.INF	C:\WINDOWS\INF	INF	\WIN95\PRECOPY2.CAB
7/11/95	8,622	AVWIN.INI	C:\WINDOWS	INI	\WIN95\CAB_13.CAB
7/11/95	52,899	CPQMODE.INI	C:\WINDOWS	INI	\WIN95\CAB_04.CAB
7/11/95	41,810	CPQMON.INI	C:\WINDOWS	INI	\WIN95\CAB_04.CAB

Date of File	Size of File	Installed Name	Installed Location	Type of File	Location on CD
7/11/95	67	DESKTOP.INI	C:\WINDOWS	INI	\WIN95\CAB_03.CAB
7/11/95	10,398	IOS.INI	C:\WINDOWS	INI	\WIN95\CAB_03.CAB
7/11/95	328	PSCRIPT.INI	C:\WINDOWS	INI	\WIN95\CAB_09.CAB
7/11/95	7,270	SCANDISK.INI	C:\WINDOWS\COMMAND	INI	\WIN95\CAB_02.CAB
7/11/95	358	SYSTEM.INI	C:\WINDOWS	INI	\WIN95\MINI.CAB
7/11/95	165	WIN.INI	C:\WINDOWS	INI	\WIN95\MINI.CAB
7/11/95	611	KBDBE.KBD	C:\WINDOWS\SYSTEM	KBD	\WIN95\CAB_06.CAB
7/11/95	403	KBDBLL.KBD	C:\WINDOWS\SYSTEM	KBD	\WIN95\CAB_13.CAB
7/11/95	403	KBDBLR.KBD	C:\WINDOWS\SYSTEM	KBD	\WIN95\CAB_13.CAB
7/11/95	613	KBDBR.KBD	C:\WINDOWS\SYSTEM	KBD	\WIN95\CAB_06.CAB
7/11/95	403	KBDBUL.KBD	C:\WINDOWS\SYSTEM	KBD	\WIN95\CAB_13.CAB
7/11/95	621	KBDCA.KBD	C:\WINDOWS\SYSTEM	KBD	\WIN95\CAB_06.CAB
7/11/95	804	KBDCZ.KBD	C:\WINDOWS\SYSTEM	KBD	\WIN95\CAB_13.CAB
7/11/95	796	KBDCZ1.KBD	C:\WINDOWS\SYSTEM	KBD	\WIN95\CAB_13.CAB
7/11/95	603	KBDDA.KBD	C:\WINDOWS\SYSTEM	KBD	\WIN95\CAB_06.CAB
7/11/95	398	KBDDV.KBD	C:\WINDOWS\SYSTEM	KBD	\WIN95\CAB_06.CAB
7/11/95	693	KBDFC.KBD	C:\WINDOWS\SYSTEM	KBD	\WIN95\CAB_06.CAB
7/11/95	610	KBDFI.KBD	C:\WINDOWS\SYSTEM	KBD	\WIN95\CAB_06.CAB
7/11/95	574	KBDFR.KBD	C:\WINDOWS\SYSTEM	KBD	\WIN95\CAB_06.CAB
7/11/95	520	KBDGK.KBD	C:\WINDOWS\SYSTEM	KBD	\WIN95\CAB_13.CAB
7/11/95	499	KBDGK220.KBD	C:\WINDOWS\SYSTEM	KBD	\WIN95\CAB_13.CAB
7/11/95	495	KBDGK319.KBD	C:\WINDOWS\SYSTEM	KBD	\WIN95\CAB_13.CAB
7/11/95	539	KBDGL220.KBD	C:\WINDOWS\SYSTEM	KBD	\WIN95\CAB_13.CAB
7/11/95	569	KBDGL319.KBD	C:\WINDOWS\SYSTEM	KBD	\WIN95\CAB_13.CAB
7/11/95	547	KBDGR.KBD	C:\WINDOWS\SYSTEM	KBD	\WIN95\CAB_06.CAB
7/11/95	547	KBDGR1.KBD	C:\WINDOWS\SYSTEM	KBD	\WIN95\CAB_06.CAB
7/11/95	786	KBDHU.KBD	C:\WINDOWS\SYSTEM	KBD	\WIN95\CAB_13.CAB
7/11/95	501	KBDHU1.KBD	C:\WINDOWS\SYSTEM	KBD	\WIN95\CAB_13.CAB
7/11/95	670	KBDIC.KBD	C:\WINDOWS\SYSTEM	KBD	\WIN95\CAB_06.CAB
7/11/95	509	KBDIR.KBD	C:\WINDOWS\SYSTEM	KBD	\WIN95\CAB_06.CAB
7/11/95	424	KBDIT.KBD	C:\WINDOWS\SYSTEM	KBD	\WIN95\CAB_06.CAB
7/11/95	518	KBDIT1.KBD	C:\WINDOWS\SYSTEM	KBD	\WIN95\CAB_06.CAB
7/11/95	575	KBDLA.KBD	C:\WINDOWS\SYSTEM	KBD	\WIN95\CAB_06.CAB
7/11/95	635	KBDNE.KBD	C:\WINDOWS\SYSTEM	KBD	\WIN95\CAB_06.CAB
7/11/95	610	KBDNO.KBD	C:\WINDOWS\SYSTEM	KBD	\WIN95\CAB_06.CAB
7/11/95	774	KBDPL.KBD	C:\WINDOWS\SYSTEM	KBD	\WIN95\CAB_13.CAB
7/11/95	528	KBDPL1.KBD	C:\WINDOWS\SYSTEM	KBD	\WIN95\CAB_13.CAB
7/11/95	593	KBDPO.KBD	C:\WINDOWS\SYSTEM	KBD	\WIN95\CAB_06.CAB
7/11/95	473	KBDRU.KBD	C:\WINDOWS\SYSTEM	KBD	\WIN95\CAB_13.CAB
7/11/95	403	KBDRU1.KBD	C:\WINDOWS\SYSTEM	KBD	\WIN95\CAB_13.CAB
7/11/95	615	KBDSF.KBD	C:\WINDOWS\SYSTEM	KBD	\WIN95\CAB_06.CAB
7/11/95	727	KBDSG.KBD	C:\WINDOWS\SYSTEM	KBD	\WIN95\CAB_06.CAB
7/11/95	592	KBDSP.KBD	C:\WINDOWS\SYSTEM	KBD	\WIN95\CAB_06.CAB

continues

App
G

Date of File	Size of File	Installed Name	Installed Location	Type of File	Location on CD
7/11/95	781	KBDSV.KBD	C:\WINDOWS\SYSTEM	KBD	\WIN95\CAB_13.CAB
7/11/95	610	KBDSW.KBD	C:\WINDOWS\SYSTEM	KBD	\WIN95\CAB_06.CAB
7/11/95	430	KBDUK.KBD	C:\WINDOWS\SYSTEM	KBD	\WIN95\CAB_06.CAB
7/11/95	398	KBDUS.KBD	C:\WINDOWS\SYSTEM	KBD	\WIN95\CAB_06.CAB
7/11/95	794	KBDUSX.KBD	C:\WINDOWS\SYSTEM	KBD	\WIN95\CAB_06.CAB
7/11/95	95,719	FONTS.MFM	C:\WINDOWS\SYSTEM	MFM	\WIN95\CAB_10.CAB
7/11/95	20,861	CANYON.MID	C:\WINDOWS\MEDIA	MID	\WIN95\CAB_13.CAB
7/11/95	23,165	PASSPORT.MID	C:\WINDOWS\MEDIA	MID	\WIN95\CAB_13.CAB
7/11/95	4,313	REDIRECT.MOD	C:\WINDOWS\SYSTEM	MOD	\WIN95\CAB_04.CAB
7/11/95	8,592	AHA154X.MPD	C:\WINDOWS\SYSTEM\ IOSUBSYS	MPD	\WIN95\CAB_04.CAB
7/11/95	5,040	AHA174X.MPD	C:\WINDOWS\SYSTEM\ IOSUBSYS	MPD	\WIN95\CAB_05.CAB
7/11/95	23,824	AIC78XX.MPD	C:\WINDOWS\SYSTEM\ IOSUBSYS	MPD	\WIN95\CAB_05.CAB
7/11/95	13,600	ALWAYS.MPD	C:\WINDOWS\SYSTEM\ IOSUBSYS	MPD	\WIN95\CAB_05.CAB
7/11/95	13,264	AMSINT.MPD	C:\WINDOWS\SYSTEM\ IOSUBSYS	MPD	\WIN95\CAB_05.CAB
7/11/95	34,848	ARROW.MPD	C:\WINDOWS\SYSTEM\ IOSUBSYS	MPD	\WIN95\CAB_03.CAB
7/11/95	8,144	BUSLOGIC.MPD	C:\WINDOWS\SYSTEM\ IOSUBSYS	MPD	\WIN95\CAB_05.CAB
7/11/95	12,000	DPTSCSI.MPD	C:\WINDOWS\SYSTEM\ IOSUBSYS	MPD	\WIN95\CAB_05.CAB
7/11/95	10,736	FD16_700.MPD	C:\WINDOWS\SYSTEM\ IOSUBSYS	MPD	\WIN95\CAB_05.CAB
7/11/95	8,352	FD8XX.MPD	C:\WINDOWS\SYSTEM\ IOSUBSYS	MPD	\WIN95\CAB_05.CAB
7/11/95	53,264	MKECR5XX.MPD	C:\WINDOWS\SYSTEM\ IOSUBSYS	MPD	\WIN95\CAB_05.CAB
7/11/95	21,968	MTMMINIP.MPD	C:\WINDOWS\SYSTEM\ IOSUBSYS	MPD	\WIN95\CAB_05.CAB
7/11/95	11,120	NCR53C9X.MPD	C:\WINDOWS\SYSTEM\ IOSUBSYS	MPD	\WIN95\CAB_05.CAB
7/11/95	9,920	NCRC700.MPD	C:\WINDOWS\SYSTEM\ IOSUBSYS	MPD	\WIN95\CAB_05.CAB
7/11/95	10,352	NCRC710.MPD	C:\WINDOWS\SYSTEM\ IOSUBSYS	MPD	\WIN95\CAB_05.CAB
7/11/95	10,848	NCRC810.MPD	C:\WINDOWS\SYSTEM\ IOSUBSYS	MPD	\WIN95\CAB_05.CAB
7/11/95	25,056	NCRSDMS.MPD	C:\WINDOWS\SYSTEM\ IOSUBSYS	MPD	\WIN95\CAB_05.CAB
7/11/95	4,304	PC2X.MPD	C:\WINDOWS\SYSTEM\ IOSUBSYS	MPD	\WIN95\CAB_05.CAB
7/11/95	31,632	SLCD32.MPD	C:\WINDOWS\SYSTEM\ IOSUBSYS	MPD	\WIN95\CAB_05.CAB
7/11/95	16,960	SPARROW.MPD	C:\WINDOWS\SYSTEM\	MPD	\WIN95\CAB_05.CAB

Date of File	Size of File	Installed Name	Installed Location	Type of File	Location on CD
			IOSUBSYS		
7/11/95	18,944	SPARROWX.MPD	C:\WINDOWS\SYSTEM\ IOSUBSYS	MPD	\WIN95\CAB_05.CAB
7/11/95	5,280	SPOCK.MPD	C:\WINDOWS\SYSTEM\ IOSUBSYS	MPD	\WIN95\CAB_05.CAB
7/11/95	11,104	T160.MPD	C:\WINDOWS\SYSTEM\ IOSUBSYS	MPD	\WIN95\CAB_05.CAB
7/11/95	11,584	T348.MPD	C:\WINDOWS\SYSTEM\ IOSUBSYS	MPD	\WIN95\CAB_05.CAB
7/11/95	13,984	T358.MPD	C:\WINDOWS\SYSTEM\ IOSUBSYS	MPD	\WIN95\CAB_05.CAB
7/11/95	12,048	TMV1.MPD	C:\WINDOWS\SYSTEM\ IOSUBSYS	MPD	\WIN95\CAB_05.CAB
7/11/95	4,912	ULTRA124.MPD	C:\WINDOWS\SYSTEM\ IOSUBSYS	MPD	\WIN95\CAB_05.CAB
7/11/95	4,624	ULTRA14F.MPD	C:\WINDOWS\SYSTEM\ IOSUBSYS	MPD	\WIN95\CAB_05.CAB
7/11/95	4,256	ULTRA24F.MPD	C:\WINDOWS\SYSTEM\ IOSUBSYS	MPD	\WIN95\CAB_05.CAB
7/11/95	4,448	WD7000EX.MPD	C:\WINDOWS\SYSTEM\ IOSUBSYS	MPD	\WIN95\CAB_05.CAB
7/11/95	1,632	NETWARE.MS	C:\WINDOWS\SYSTEM	MS	\WIN95\CAB_12.CAB
7/11/95	109,229	NET.MSG	C:\WINDOWS	MSG	\WIN95\CAB_12.CAB
7/11/95	73,275	NETH.MSG	C:\WINDOWS	MSG	\WIN95\CAB_12.CAB
7/11/95	4	THEMIC~1.MSN	C:\PROGRAM FILES\ THE MICROSOFT NETWORK	MSN	\WIN95\CAB_07.CAB
7/11/95	214,528	BBSNAV.NAV	C:\PROGRAM FILES\ THE MICROSOFT NETWORK	NAV	\WIN95\CAB_07.CAB
7/11/95	31,744	DSNAV.NAV	C:\PROGRAM FILES\ THE MICROSOFT NETWORK	NAV	\WIN95\CAB_07.CAB
7/11/95	40,960	GUIDENAV.NAV	C:\PROGRAM FILES\ THE MICROSOFT NETWORK	NAV	\WIN95\CAB_07.CAB
7/11/95	36,864	DSNED.NED	C:\PROGRAM FILES\ THE MICROSOFT NETWORK	NED	\WIN95\CAB_07.CAB
7/11/95	88,544	COMMDLG.NEW	C:\WINDOWS	NEW	\WIN95\CAB_11.CAB
7/11/95	14,757	DLLNDIS.NEW	C:\WINDOWS	NEW	\WIN95\CAB_17.CAB
7/11/95	16,588	DLLNDIST.NEW	C:\WINDOWS	NEW	\WIN95\CAB_17.CAB
7/11/95	116,144	SHELL.NEW	C:\WINDOWS	NEW	\WIN95\CAB_11.CAB
7/11/95	5,329	SRM.NEW	C:\WINDOWS	NEW	\WIN95\CAB_17.CAB
7/11/95	12,144	VER.NEW	C:\WINDOWS	NEW	\WIN95\CAB_10.CAB
7/11/95	61,680	WINOA386.NEW	C:\WINDOWS	NEW	\WIN95\CAB_03.CAB
7/11/95	9,124	CP_1250.NLS	C:\WINDOWS\SYSTEM	NLS	\WIN95\CAB_13.CAB
7/11/95	6,868	CP_1251.NLS	C:\WINDOWS\SYSTEM	NLS	\WIN95\CAB_13.CAB

continues

App

G

Date of File	Size of File	Installed Name	Installed Location	Type of File	Location on CD
7/11/95	9,194	CP_1252.NLS	C:\WINDOWS\SYSTEM	NLS	\WIN95\CAB_09.CAB
7/11/95	6,856	CP_1253.NLS	C:\WINDOWS\SYSTEM	NLS	\WIN95\CAB_13.CAB
7/11/95	9,522	CP_437.NLS	C:\WINDOWS\SYSTEM	NLS	\WIN95\CAB_09.CAB
7/11/95	6,600	CP_737.NLS	C:\WINDOWS\SYSTEM	NLS	\WIN95\CAB_13.CAB
7/11/95	9,826	CP_850.NLS	C:\WINDOWS\SYSTEM	NLS	\WIN95\CAB_09.CAB
7/11/95	9,618	CP_852.NLS	C:\WINDOWS\SYSTEM	NLS	\WIN95\CAB_13.CAB
7/11/95	7,316	CP_866.NLS	C:\WINDOWS\SYSTEM	NLS	\WIN95\CAB_13.CAB
7/11/95	7,240	CP_869.NLS	C:\WINDOWS\SYSTEM	NLS	\WIN95\CAB_13.CAB
7/11/95	127,912	LOCALE.NLS	C:\WINDOWS\SYSTEM	NLS	\WIN95\CAB_09.CAB
7/11/95	34,676	UNICODE.NLS	C:\WINDOWS\SYSTEM	NLS	\WIN95\CAB_09.CAB
7/11/95	7,188	MVIFM.PAT	C:\WINDOWS\SYSTEM	PAT	\WIN95\CAB_08.CAB
7/11/95	41,369	PHONE.PBK	C:\PROGRAM FILES\ THE MICROSOFT NETWORK	PBK	\WIN95\CAB_07.CAB
7/11/95	851	STATE.PBK	C:\PROGRAM FILES\ THE MICROSOFT NETWORK	PBK	\WIN95\CAB_07.CAB
7/11/95	23,758	ESDI_506.PDR	C:\WINDOWS\SYSTEM\ IOSUBSYS	PDR	\WIN95\CAB_05.CAB
7/11/95	18,998	HSFLOP.PDR	C:\WINDOWS\SYSTEM\ IOSUBSYS	PDR	\WIN95\CAB_05.CAB
7/11/95	13,229	RMM.PDR	C:\WINDOWS\SYSTEM\ IOSUBSYS	PDR	\WIN95\CAB_05.CAB
7/11/95	23,133	SCSIPORT.PDR	C:\WINDOWS\SYSTEM\ IOSUBSYS	PDR	\WIN95\CAB_05.CAB
7/11/95	545	DOSPRMPT.PIF	C:\WINDOWS	PIF	\WIN95\CAB_03.CAB
7/11/95	995	LMSCRIPT.PIF	C:\WINDOWS	PIF	\WIN95\CAB_12.CAB
7/11/95	12,288	POWERPNT.PPT	C:\WINDOWS	PPT	\WIN95\CAB_11.CAB
7/11/95	12,701	FREELANC.PRE	C:\WINDOWS	PRE	\WIN95\CAB_11.CAB
7/11/95	11,971	MAPIRPC.REG	C:\WINDOWS\SYSTEM	REG	\WIN95\CAB_07.CAB
7/11/95	144,902	BACHSB~1.RMI	C:\WINDOWS\MEDIA	RMI	\WIN95\CAB_13.CAB
7/11/95	92,466	BEETHO~2.RMI	C:\WINDOWS\MEDIA	RMI	\WIN95\CAB_13.CAB
7/11/95	27,940	CLAIRE~1.RMI	C:\WINDOWS\MEDIA	RMI	\WIN95\CAB_14.CAB
7/11/95	20,906	DANCEO~2.RMI	C:\WINDOWS\MEDIA	RMI	\WIN95\CAB_14.CAB
7/11/95	21,312	FURELI~1.RMI	C:\WINDOWS\MEDIA	RMI	\WIN95\CAB_14.CAB
7/11/95	38,444	HALLOF~2.RMI	C:\WINDOWS\MEDIA	RMI	\WIN95\CAB_14.CAB
7/11/95	18,130	MOZART~2.RMI	C:\WINDOWS\MEDIA	RMI	\WIN95\CAB_14.CAB
7/11/95	4,570	AMIPRO.SAM	C:\WINDOWS	SAM	\WIN95\CAB_11.CAB
7/11/95	728	HOSTS.SAM	C:\WINDOWS	SAM	\WIN95\CAB_12.CAB
7/11/95	3,691	LMHOSTS.SAM	C:\WINDOWS	SAM	\WIN95\CAB_12.CAB
7/11/95	34,832	SYNTHGM.SBK	C:\WINDOWS\SYSTEM	SBK	\WIN95\CAB_08.CAB
7/11/95	15,872	BEZIER.SCR	C:\WINDOWS\SYSTEM	SCR	\WIN95\CAB_11.CAB
7/11/95	9,728	SCRNSAVE.SCR	C:\WINDOWS\SYSTEM	SCR	\WIN95\CAB_11.CAB
7/11/95	14,336	SSFLYWIN.SCR	C:\WINDOWS\SYSTEM	SCR	\WIN95\CAB_11.CAB
7/11/95	18,944	SSMARQUE.SCR	C:\WINDOWS\SYSTEM	SCR	\WIN95\CAB_11.CAB
7/11/95	20,992	SSMYST.SCR	C:\WINDOWS\SYSTEM	SCR	\WIN95\CAB_11.CAB

Date of File	Size of File	Installed Name	Installed Location	Type of File	Location on CD
7/11/95	15,872	SSSTARS.SCR	C:\WINDOWS\SYSTEM	SCR	\WIN95\CAB_11.CAB
7/11/95	461	PRESENTA.SHW	C:\WINDOWS\SHELLNEW	SHW	\WIN95\CAB_11.CAB
7/11/95	7,098	A_PNT518.SPD	C:\WINDOWS\SPOOL	SPD	\WIN95\CAB_10.CAB
7/11/95	22,106	APLW8101.SPD	C:\WINDOWS\SPOOL	SPD	\WIN95\CAB_10.CAB
7/11/95	19,120	APLWIIF1.SPD	C:\WINDOWS\SPOOL	SPD	\WIN95\CAB_10.CAB
7/11/95	15,266	APLWIIG1.SPD	C:\WINDOWS\SPOOL	SPD	\WIN95\CAB_10.CAB
7/11/95	8,913	APLWNTR1.SPD	C:\WINDOWS\SPOOL	SPD	\WIN95\CAB_10.CAB
7/11/95	13,016	APLWSEL.SPD	C:\WINDOWS\SPOOL	SPD	\WIN95\CAB_10.CAB
7/11/95	5,681	APPLE230.SPD	C:\WINDOWS\SPOOL	SPD	\WIN95\CAB_10.CAB
7/11/95	6,046	APPLE380.SPD	C:\WINDOWS\SPOOL	SPD	\WIN95\CAB_10.CAB
7/11/95	15,105	APTOLLD1.SPD	C:\WINDOWS\SPOOL	SPD	\WIN95\CAB_10.CAB
7/11/95	14,580	APTOLLW1.SPD	C:\WINDOWS\SPOOL	SPD	\WIN95\CAB_10.CAB
7/11/95	4,436	AST__470.SPD	C:\WINDOWS\SPOOL	SPD	\WIN95\CAB_10.CAB
7/11/95	16,062	CP_PS241.SPD	C:\WINDOWS\SPOOL	SPD	\WIN95\CAB_10.CAB
7/11/95	16,432	CPPER241.SPD	C:\WINDOWS\SPOOL	SPD	\WIN95\CAB_10.CAB
7/11/95	17,878	CPPMQ151.SPD	C:\WINDOWS\SPOOL	SPD	\WIN95\CAB_10.CAB
7/11/95	19,463	CPPMQ201.SPD	C:\WINDOWS\SPOOL	SPD	\WIN95\CAB_10.CAB
7/11/95	5,794	CPPRO518.SPD	C:\WINDOWS\SPOOL	SPD	\WIN95\CAB_10.CAB
7/11/95	9,343	CPPSNB10.SPD	C:\WINDOWS\SPOOL	SPD	\WIN95\CAB_10.CAB
7/11/95	8,806	CPPSX241.SPD	C:\WINDOWS\SPOOL	SPD	\WIN95\CAB_10.CAB
7/11/95	94	D17_MS.SPD	C:\WINDOWS\SPOOL	SPD	\WIN95\CAB_16.CAB
7/11/95	99	D1712_MS.SPD	C:\WINDOWS\SPOOL	SPD	\WIN95\CAB_16.CAB
7/11/95	98	D176_MS.SPD	C:\WINDOWS\SPOOL	SPD	\WIN95\CAB_16.CAB
7/11/95	99	D20_MS.SPD	C:\WINDOWS\SPOOL	SPD	\WIN95\CAB_16.CAB
7/11/95	89	D2150_MS.SPD	C:\WINDOWS\SPOOL	SPD	\WIN95\CAB_10.CAB
7/11/95	89	D2250_MS.SPD	C:\WINDOWS\SPOOL	SPD	\WIN95\CAB_10.CAB
7/11/95	94	D32_MS.SPD	C:\WINDOWS\SPOOL	SPD	\WIN95\CAB_16.CAB
7/11/95	94	D40_MS.SPD	C:\WINDOWS\SPOOL	SPD	\WIN95\CAB_16.CAB
7/11/95	93	D5100_MS.SPD	C:\WINDOWS\SPOOL	SPD	\WIN95\CAB_16.CAB
7/11/95	5,593	DATAP462.SPD	C:\WINDOWS\SPOOL	SPD	\WIN95\CAB_10.CAB
7/11/95	9,476	DC1152_1.SPD	C:\WINDOWS\SPOOL	SPD	\WIN95\CAB_10.CAB
7/11/95	11,025	DC1152F1.SPD	C:\WINDOWS\SPOOL	SPD	\WIN95\CAB_10.CAB
7/11/95	9,072	DC2150P1.SPD	C:\WINDOWS\SPOOL	SPD	\WIN95\CAB_10.CAB
7/11/95	13,611	DC2250P1.SPD	C:\WINDOWS\SPOOL	SPD	\WIN95\CAB_10.CAB
7/11/95	29,406	DC5100_1.SPD	C:\WINDOWS\SPOOL	SPD	\WIN95\CAB_10.CAB
7/11/95	4,545	DCCOLOR1.SPD	C:\WINDOWS\SPOOL	SPD	\WIN95\CAB_10.CAB
7/11/95	9,656	DCD11501.SPD	C:\WINDOWS\SPOOL	SPD	\WIN95\CAB_10.CAB
7/11/95	9,552	DCLF02_1.SPD	C:\WINDOWS\SPOOL	SPD	\WIN95\CAB_10.CAB
7/11/95	10,914	DCLF02F1.SPD	C:\WINDOWS\SPOOL	SPD	\WIN95\CAB_10.CAB
7/11/95	3,851	DCLN03R1.SPD	C:\WINDOWS\SPOOL	SPD	\WIN95\CAB_10.CAB
7/11/95	10,167	DCLPS171.SPD	C:\WINDOWS\SPOOL	SPD	\WIN95\CAB_10.CAB
7/11/95	10,876	DCLPS321.SPD	C:\WINDOWS\SPOOL	SPD	\WIN95\CAB_10.CAB
7/11/95	6,908	DCLPS401.SPD	C:\WINDOWS\SPOOL	SPD	\WIN95\CAB_10.CAB

App
G

continues

Date of File	Size of File	Installed Name	Installed Location	Type of File	Location on CD
7/11/95	18,566	DCPS1721.SPD	C:\WINDOWS\SPOOL	SPD	\WIN95\CAB_10.CAB
7/11/95	18,213	DCPS1761.SPD	C:\WINDOWS\SPOOL	SPD	\WIN95\CAB_10.CAB
7/11/95	7,935	DCTPS201.SPD	C:\WINDOWS\SPOOL	SPD	\WIN95\CAB_10.CAB
7/11/95	11,669	DEC3250.SPD	C:\WINDOWS\SPOOL	SPD	\WIN95\CAB_10.CAB
7/11/95	7,376	EPL75523.SPD	C:\WINDOWS\SPOOL	SPD	\WIN95\CAB_10.CAB
7/11/95	5,476	F71RX503.SPD	C:\WINDOWS\SPOOL	SPD	\WIN95\CAB_10.CAB
7/11/95	9,435	HP_3D522.SPD	C:\WINDOWS\SPOOL	SPD	\WIN95\CAB_10.CAB
7/11/95	7,743	HP_3P522.SPD	C:\WINDOWS\SPOOL	SPD	\WIN95\CAB_10.CAB
7/11/95	12,334	HP1200C1.SPD	C:\WINDOWS\SPOOL	SPD	\WIN95\CAB_10.CAB
7/11/95	9,365	HP3SI523.SPD	C:\WINDOWS\SPOOL	SPD	\WIN95\CAB_10.CAB
7/11/95	14,273	HP4M_V4.SPD	C:\WINDOWS\SPOOL	SPD	\WIN95\CAB_10.CAB
7/11/95	12,236	HP4ML_V4.SPD	C:\WINDOWS\SPOOL	SPD	\WIN95\CAB_10.CAB
7/11/95	12,605	HP4MP_V4.SPD	C:\WINDOWS\SPOOL	SPD	\WIN95\CAB_10.CAB
7/11/95	18,906	HP4MV_V4.SPD	C:\WINDOWS\SPOOL	SPD	\WIN95\CAB_10.CAB
7/11/95	12,996	HP4PLUS4.SPD	C:\WINDOWS\SPOOL	SPD	\WIN95\CAB_10.CAB
7/11/95	14,880	HP4SI_V4.SPD	C:\WINDOWS\SPOOL	SPD	\WIN95\CAB_10.CAB
7/11/95	8,617	HPIID522.SPD	C:\WINDOWS\SPOOL	SPD	\WIN95\CAB_10.CAB
7/11/95	7,581	HPIII522.SPD	C:\WINDOWS\SPOOL	SPD	\WIN95\CAB_10.CAB
7/11/95	7,288	HPIIP522.SPD	C:\WINDOWS\SPOOL	SPD	\WIN95\CAB_10.CAB
7/11/95	9,632	HPLJ_31.SPD	C:\WINDOWS\SPOOL	SPD	\WIN95\CAB_10.CAB
7/11/95	14,102	HPLJ_3D1.SPD	C:\WINDOWS\SPOOL	SPD	\WIN95\CAB_10.CAB
7/11/95	11,136	HPLJ_3P1.SPD	C:\WINDOWS\SPOOL	SPD	\WIN95\CAB_10.CAB
7/11/95	14,100	HPLJP_V4.SPD	C:\WINDOWS\SPOOL	SPD	\WIN95\CAB_10.CAB
7/11/95	14,442	HPPJXL31.SPD	C:\WINDOWS\SPOOL	SPD	\WIN95\CAB_10.CAB
7/11/95	9,076	IB401917.SPD	C:\WINDOWS\SPOOL	SPD	\WIN95\CAB_10.CAB
7/11/95	10,431	IB401939.SPD	C:\WINDOWS\SPOOL	SPD	\WIN95\CAB_10.CAB
7/11/95	10,784	IB402917.SPD	C:\WINDOWS\SPOOL	SPD	\WIN95\CAB_10.CAB
7/11/95	12,152	IB402939.SPD	C:\WINDOWS\SPOOL	SPD	\WIN95\CAB_10.CAB
7/11/95	12,116	IBM20470.SPD	C:\WINDOWS\SPOOL	SPD	\WIN95\CAB_10.CAB
7/11/95	5,825	IBM30505.SPD	C:\WINDOWS\SPOOL	SPD	\WIN95\CAB_10.CAB
7/11/95	4,586	IBM31514.SPD	C:\WINDOWS\SPOOL	SPD	\WIN95\CAB_10.CAB
7/11/95	12,095	IBM4039.SPD	C:\WINDOWS\SPOOL	SPD	\WIN95\CAB_10.CAB
7/11/95	15,322	IBM4039P.SPD	C:\WINDOWS\SPOOL	SPD	\WIN95\CAB_10.CAB
7/11/95	6,451	IBM4079.SPD	C:\WINDOWS\SPOOL	SPD	\WIN95\CAB_10.CAB
7/11/95	5,725	KDCOLOR1.SPD	C:\WINDOWS\SPOOL	SPD	\WIN95\CAB_10.CAB
7/11/95	5,825	L100_425.SPD	C:\WINDOWS\SPOOL	SPD	\WIN95\CAB_10.CAB
7/11/95	7,838	L200_471.SPD	C:\WINDOWS\SPOOL	SPD	\WIN95\CAB_10.CAB
7/11/95	7,845	L300_471.SPD	C:\WINDOWS\SPOOL	SPD	\WIN95\CAB_10.CAB
7/11/95	7,843	L500_493.SPD	C:\WINDOWS\SPOOL	SPD	\WIN95\CAB_10.CAB
7/11/95	13,705	LH330__1.SPD	C:\WINDOWS\SPOOL	SPD	\WIN95\CAB_10.CAB
7/11/95	13,953	LH530__1.SPD	C:\WINDOWS\SPOOL	SPD	\WIN95\CAB_10.CAB
7/11/95	12,216	LH630__1.SPD	C:\WINDOWS\SPOOL	SPD	\WIN95\CAB_10.CAB
7/11/95	6,427	LWNT_470.SPD	C:\WINDOWS\SPOOL	SPD	\WIN95\CAB_10.CAB

Date of File	Size of File	Installed Name	Installed Location	Type of File	Location on CD
7/11/95	6,379	LWNTX470.SPD	C:\WINDOWS\SPOOL	SPD	\WIN95\CAB_10.CAB
7/11/95	3,853	MT_TI101.SPD	C:\WINDOWS\SPOOL	SPD	\WIN95\CAB_10.CAB
7/11/95	5,925	N2090522.SPD	C:\WINDOWS\SPOOL	SPD	\WIN95\CAB_10.CAB
7/11/95	5,227	N2290520.SPD	C:\WINDOWS\SPOOL	SPD	\WIN95\CAB_10.CAB
7/11/95	5,472	N890_470.SPD	C:\WINDOWS\SPOOL	SPD	\WIN95\CAB_10.CAB
7/11/95	5,483	N890X505.SPD	C:\WINDOWS\SPOOL	SPD	\WIN95\CAB_10.CAB
7/11/95	3,403	NCCPS401.SPD	C:\WINDOWS\SPOOL	SPD	\WIN95\CAB_10.CAB
7/11/95	4,658	NCCPS801.SPD	C:\WINDOWS\SPOOL	SPD	\WIN95\CAB_10.CAB
7/11/95	4,563	NCOL_519.SPD	C:\WINDOWS\SPOOL	SPD	\WIN95\CAB_10.CAB
7/11/95	6,713	NCS29901.SPD	C:\WINDOWS\SPOOL	SPD	\WIN95\CAB_10.CAB
7/11/95	8,307	NCSW_951.SPD	C:\WINDOWS\SPOOL	SPD	\WIN95\CAB_10.CAB
7/11/95	4,264	O5241503.SPD	C:\WINDOWS\SPOOL	SPD	\WIN95\CAB_10.CAB
7/11/95	5,136	O5242503.SPD	C:\WINDOWS\SPOOL	SPD	\WIN95\CAB_10.CAB
7/11/95	5,830	OKI830US.SPD	C:\WINDOWS\SPOOL	SPD	\WIN95\CAB_10.CAB
7/11/95	6,899	OKI840US.SPD	C:\WINDOWS\SPOOL	SPD	\WIN95\CAB_10.CAB
7/11/95	7,028	OKI850US.SPD	C:\WINDOWS\SPOOL	SPD	\WIN95\CAB_10.CAB
7/11/95	10,570	OKOL8701.SPD	C:\WINDOWS\SPOOL	SPD	\WIN95\CAB_10.CAB
7/11/95	5,551	OL830525.SPD	C:\WINDOWS\SPOOL	SPD	\WIN95\CAB_10.CAB
7/11/95	6,641	OL840518.SPD	C:\WINDOWS\SPOOL	SPD	\WIN95\CAB_10.CAB
7/11/95	6,651	OL850525.SPD	C:\WINDOWS\SPOOL	SPD	\WIN95\CAB_10.CAB
7/11/95	6,481	P4455514.SPD	C:\WINDOWS\SPOOL	SPD	\WIN95\CAB_10.CAB
7/11/95	4,128	PAP54001.SPD	C:\WINDOWS\SPOOL	SPD	\WIN95\CAB_10.CAB
7/11/95	7,607	PAP54101.SPD	C:\WINDOWS\SPOOL	SPD	\WIN95\CAB_10.CAB
7/11/95	3,458	PHIIPX.SPD	C:\WINDOWS\SPOOL	SPD	\WIN95\CAB_10.CAB
7/11/95	79	Q2200_MS.SPD	C:\WINDOWS\SPOOL	SPD	\WIN95\CAB_10.CAB
7/11/95	79	Q2210_MS.SPD	C:\WINDOWS\SPOOL	SPD	\WIN95\CAB_10.CAB
7/11/95	7,328	Q2220523.SPD	C:\WINDOWS\SPOOL	SPD	\WIN95\CAB_10.CAB
7/11/95	78	Q800_MS.SPD	C:\WINDOWS\SPOOL	SPD	\WIN95\CAB_10.CAB
7/11/95	78	Q810_MS.SPD	C:\WINDOWS\SPOOL	SPD	\WIN95\CAB_10.CAB
7/11/95	84	Q810T_MS.SPD	C:\WINDOWS\SPOOL	SPD	\WIN95\CAB_10.CAB
7/11/95	78	Q820_MS.SPD	C:\WINDOWS\SPOOL	SPD	\WIN95\CAB_10.CAB
7/11/95	5,699	Q820T517.SPD	C:\WINDOWS\SPOOL	SPD	\WIN95\CAB_10.CAB
7/11/95	11,333	Q860PLS2.SPD	C:\WINDOWS\SPOOL	SPD	\WIN95\CAB_10.CAB
7/11/95	10,440	QCS1000.SPD	C:\WINDOWS\SPOOL	SPD	\WIN95\CAB_10.CAB
7/11/95	4,763	QCS10503.SPD	C:\WINDOWS\SPOOL	SPD	\WIN95\CAB_10.CAB
7/11/95	4,786	QCS30503.SPD	C:\WINDOWS\SPOOL	SPD	\WIN95\CAB_10.CAB
7/11/95	8,236	QM1700_1.SPD	C:\WINDOWS\SPOOL	SPD	\WIN95\CAB_10.CAB
7/11/95	8,620	QM2000_1.SPD	C:\WINDOWS\SPOOL	SPD	\WIN95\CAB_10.CAB
7/11/95	8,006	QM825MR1.SPD	C:\WINDOWS\SPOOL	SPD	\WIN95\CAB_10.CAB
7/11/95	7,238	QMPS4101.SPD	C:\WINDOWS\SPOOL	SPD	\WIN95\CAB_10.CAB
7/11/95	9,083	QMS1725.SPD	C:\WINDOWS\SPOOL	SPD	\WIN95\CAB_10.CAB
7/11/95	9,873	QMS3225.SPD	C:\WINDOWS\SPOOL	SPD	\WIN95\CAB_10.CAB

App

G

continues

Date of File	Size of File	Installed Name	Installed Location	Type of File	Location on CD
7/11/95	8,507	QMS420.SPD	C:\WINDOWS\SPOOL	SPD	\WIN95\CAB_10.CAB
7/11/95	10,650	QMS45252.SPD	C:\WINDOWS\SPOOL	SPD	\WIN95\CAB_10.CAB
7/11/95	7,717	QMS860.SPD	C:\WINDOWS\SPOOL	SPD	\WIN95\CAB_10.CAB
7/11/95	5,395	QMS8P461.SPD	C:\WINDOWS\SPOOL	SPD	\WIN95\CAB_10.CAB
7/11/95	7,933	QMSCS210.SPD	C:\WINDOWS\SPOOL	SPD	\WIN95\CAB_10.CAB
7/11/95	8,673	QMSCS230.SPD	C:\WINDOWS\SPOOL	SPD	\WIN95\CAB_10.CAB
7/11/95	33,024	SKPSFA_1.SPD	C:\WINDOWS\SPOOL	SPD	\WIN95\CAB_10.CAB
7/11/95	4,779	STLS04SS.SPD	C:\WINDOWS\SPOOL	SPD	\WIN95\CAB_10.CAB
7/11/95	4,832	STLS08LP.SPD	C:\WINDOWS\SPOOL	SPD	\WIN95\CAB_10.CAB
7/11/95	4,938	STLS5TTU.SPD	C:\WINDOWS\SPOOL	SPD	\WIN95\CAB_10.CAB
7/11/95	7,063	TIM17521.SPD	C:\WINDOWS\SPOOL	SPD	\WIN95\CAB_10.CAB
7/11/95	8,179	TIM35521.SPD	C:\WINDOWS\SPOOL	SPD	\WIN95\CAB_10.CAB
7/11/95	17,135	TIMLP232.SPD	C:\WINDOWS\SPOOL	SPD	\WIN95\CAB_10.CAB
7/11/95	17,049	TK200172.SPD	C:\WINDOWS\SPOOL	SPD	\WIN95\CAB_10.CAB
7/11/95	9,742	TK220171.SPD	C:\WINDOWS\SPOOL	SPD	\WIN95\CAB_10.CAB
7/11/95	18,748	TKP200I2.SPD	C:\WINDOWS\SPOOL	SPD	\WIN95\CAB_10.CAB
7/11/95	11,782	TKP220I1.SPD	C:\WINDOWS\SPOOL	SPD	\WIN95\CAB_10.CAB
7/11/95	18,614	TKP2SDX1.SPD	C:\WINDOWS\SPOOL	SPD	\WIN95\CAB_10.CAB
7/11/95	21,941	TKP300I1.SPD	C:\WINDOWS\SPOOL	SPD	\WIN95\CAB_10.CAB
7/11/95	10,995	TKPH4801.SPD	C:\WINDOWS\SPOOL	SPD	\WIN95\CAB_10.CAB
7/11/95	19,639	TKPHZR22.SPD	C:\WINDOWS\SPOOL	SPD	\WIN95\CAB_10.CAB
7/11/95	27,202	TKPHZR32.SPD	C:\WINDOWS\SPOOL	SPD	\WIN95\CAB_10.CAB
7/11/95	2,185	TRIUMPH1.SPD	C:\WINDOWS\SPOOL	SPD	\WIN95\CAB_10.CAB
7/11/95	3,260	TRIUMPH2.SPD	C:\WINDOWS\SPOOL	SPD	\WIN95\CAB_10.CAB
7/11/95	4,900	U9415470.SPD	C:\WINDOWS\SPOOL	SPD	\WIN95\CAB_10.CAB
7/11/95	1,969	VT600480.SPD	C:\WINDOWS\SPOOL	SPD	\WIN95\CAB_10.CAB
7/11/95	9,719	ANSI.SYS	C:\WINDOWS\COMMAND	SYS	\WIN95\CAB_09.CAB
7/11/95	1,105	ASPI2HLP.SYS	C:\WINDOWS	SYS	\WIN95\CAB_03.CAB
7/11/95	24,626	CMD640X.SYS	C:\WINDOWS	SYS	\WIN95\CAB_03.CAB
7/11/95	20,901	CMD640X2.SYS	C:\WINDOWS	SYS	\WIN95\CAB_03.CAB
7/11/95	27,094	COUNTRY.SYS	C:\WINDOWS\COMMAND	SYS	\WIN95\CAB_09.CAB
7/11/95	13,390	CSMAPPER.SYS	C:\WINDOWS\COMMAND	SYS	\WIN95\CAB_09.CAB
7/11/95	2,100	DBLBUFF.SYS	C:\WINDOWS	SYS	\WIN95\CAB_09.CAB
7/11/95	35,328	DC21X4.SYS	C:\WINDOWS	SYS	\WIN95\CAB_12.CAB
7/11/95	17,175	DISPLAY.SYS	C:\WINDOWS\COMMAND	SYS	\WIN95\CAB_09.CAB
7/11/95	15,831	DRVSPACE.SYS	C:\WINDOWS\COMMAND	SYS	\WIN95\PRECOPY1.CAB
7/11/95	39,424	E100.SYS	C:\WINDOWS	SYS	\WIN95\CAB_12.CAB
7/11/95	14,256	E20N3.SYS	C:\WINDOWS	SYS	\WIN95\CAB_12.CAB
7/11/95	15,328	E21N3.SYS	C:\WINDOWS	SYS	\WIN95\CAB_12.CAB
7/11/95	31,744	E22N3.SYS	C:\WINDOWS	SYS	\WIN95\CAB_12.CAB
7/11/95	16,896	EE16.SYS	C:\WINDOWS	SYS	\WIN95\CAB_12.CAB
7/11/95	24,064	EWRK3.SYS	C:\WINDOWS	SYS	\WIN95\CAB_08.CAB
7/11/95	32,935	HIMEM.SYS	C:\WINDOWS	SYS	\WIN95\CAB_03.CAB

Date of File	Size of File	Installed Name	Installed Location	Type of File	Location on CD
7/11/95	3,708	IFSHLP.SYS	C:\WINDOWS	SYS	\WIN95\CAB_12.CAB
7/11/95	34,566	KEYBOARD.SYS	C:\WINDOWS\COMMAND	SYS	\WIN95\CAB_09.CAB
7/11/95	31,942	KEYBRD2.SYS	C:\WINDOWS\COMMAND	SYS	\WIN95\CAB_09.CAB
7/11/95	129,078	LOGOS.SYS	C:\WINDOWS	SYS	\WIN95\CAB_11.CAB
7/11/95	129,078	LOGOW.SYS	C:\WINDOWS	SYS	\WIN95\CAB_11.CAB
7/11/95	41,616	MDGMPORT.SYS	C:\WINDOWS	SYS	\WIN95\CAB_12.CAB
7/11/95	6,140	NDISHLP.SYS	C:\WINDOWS	SYS	\WIN95\CAB_13.CAB
7/11/95	18,432	NE1000.SYS	C:\WINDOWS\SYSTEM	SYS	\WIN95\CAB_12.CAB
7/11/95	18,256	NE2000.SYS	C:\WINDOWS\SYSTEM	SYS	\WIN95\CAB_12.CAB
7/11/95	19,152	NE3200.SYS	C:\WINDOWS\SYSTEM	SYS	\WIN95\CAB_12.CAB
7/11/95	30,992	NETFLX.SYS	C:\WINDOWS\SYSTEM	SYS	\WIN95\CAB_12.CAB
7/11/95	85,504	OCTK16.SYS	C:\WINDOWS	SYS	\WIN95\CAB_12.CAB
7/11/95	12,663	RAMDRIVE.SYS	C:\WINDOWS	SYS	\WIN95\CAB_09.CAB
7/11/95	1,536	RPLBOOT.SYS	C:\WINDOWS	SYS	\WIN95\CAB_17.CAB
7/11/95	129,078	SULOGO.SYS	C:\WINDOWS	SYS	\WIN95\CAB_10.CAB
7/11/95	24,224	TDKCD02.SYS	C:\WINDOWS	SYS	\WIN95\CAB_12.CAB
7/11/95	223,148	WINBOOT.SYS	C:\WINDOWS	SYS	\WIN95\PRECOPY1.CAB
7/11/95	5,532	STDOLE.TLB	C:\WINDOWS\SYSTEM	TLB	\WIN95\CAB_09.CAB
7/11/95	7,168	STDOLE32.TLB	C:\WINDOWS\SYSTEM	TLB	\WIN95\CAB_09.CAB
7/11/95	4,136	MAPIWM.TPL	C:\PROGRAM FILES\ MICROSOFT EXCHANGE	TPL	\WIN95\CAB_07.CAB
7/11/95	1,168	MMTASK.TSK	C:\WINDOWS\SYSTEM	TSK	\WIN95\CAB_08.CAB
7/11/95	28,896	UNIMDM.TSP	C:\WINDOWS\SYSTEM	TSP	\WIN95\CAB_03.CAB
7/11/95	65,412	ARIAL.TTF	C:\WINDOWS\SYSTEM	TTF	\WIN95\CAB_04.CAB
7/11/95	66,952	ARIALBD.TTF	C:\WINDOWS\SYSTEM	TTF	\WIN95\CAB_04.CAB
7/11/95	73,984	ARIALBI.TTF	C:\WINDOWS\SYSTEM	TTF	\WIN95\CAB_04.CAB
7/11/95	62,968	ARIALI.TTF	C:\WINDOWS\SYSTEM	TTF	\WIN95\CAB_04.CAB
7/11/95	98,872	COUR.TTF	C:\WINDOWS\SYSTEM	TTF	\WIN95\CAB_04.CAB
7/11/95	84,360	COURBD.TTF	C:\WINDOWS\SYSTEM	TTF	\WIN95\CAB_04.CAB
7/11/95	85,152	COURBI.TTF	C:\WINDOWS\SYSTEM	TTF	\WIN95\CAB_04.CAB
7/11/95	82,092	COURI.TTF	C:\WINDOWS\SYSTEM	TTF	\WIN95\CAB_04.CAB
7/11/95	138,332	LARIAL.TTF	C:\WINDOWS\SYSTEM	TTF	\WIN95\CAB_13.CAB
7/11/95	139,284	LARIALBD.TTF	C:\WINDOWS\SYSTEM	TTF	\WIN95\CAB_13.CAB
7/11/95	159,720	LARIALBI.TTF	C:\WINDOWS\SYSTEM	TTF	\WIN95\CAB_13.CAB
7/11/95	139,172	LARIALI.TTF	C:\WINDOWS\SYSTEM	TTF	\WIN95\CAB_13.CAB
7/11/95	168,792	LCOUR.TTF	C:\WINDOWS\SYSTEM	TTF	\WIN95\CAB_13.CAB
7/11/95	174,376	LCOURBD.TTF	C:\WINDOWS\SYSTEM	TTF	\WIN95\CAB_13.CAB
7/11/95	179,848	LCOURBI.TTF	C:\WINDOWS\SYSTEM	TTF	\WIN95\CAB_13.CAB
7/11/95	187,948	LCOURI.TTF	C:\WINDOWS\SYSTEM	TTF	\WIN95\CAB_13.CAB
7/11/95	184,328	LTIMES.TTF	C:\WINDOWS\SYSTEM	TTF	\WIN95\CAB_13.CAB
7/11/95	177,800	LTIMESBD.TTF	C:\WINDOWS\SYSTEM	TTF	\WIN95\CAB_13.CAB
7/11/95	166,456	LTIMESBI.TTF	C:\WINDOWS\SYSTEM	TTF	\WIN95\CAB_13.CAB
7/11/95	176,736	LTIMESI.TTF	C:\WINDOWS\SYSTEM	TTF	\WIN95\CAB_13.CAB

App

G

continues

Date of File	Size of File	Installed Name	Installed Location	Type of File	Location on CD
7/11/95	17,412	MARLETT.TTF	C:\WINDOWS\SYSTEM	TTF	\WIN95\CAB_05.CAB
7/11/95	60,096	SYMBOL.TTF	C:\WINDOWS\SYSTEM	TTF	\WIN95\CAB_05.CAB
7/11/95	85,240	TIMES.TTF	C:\WINDOWS\SYSTEM	TTF	\WIN95\CAB_04.CAB
7/11/95	83,228	TIMESBD.TTF	C:\WINDOWS\SYSTEM	TTF	\WIN95\CAB_04.CAB
7/11/95	77,080	TIMESBI.TTF	C:\WINDOWS\SYSTEM	TTF	\WIN95\CAB_04.CAB
7/11/95	79,672	TIMESI.TTF	C:\WINDOWS\SYSTEM	TTF	\WIN95\CAB_04.CAB
7/11/95	71,196	WINGDING.TTF	C:\WINDOWS\SYSTEM	TTF	\WIN95\CAB_04.CAB
7/11/95	17,752	CONFIG.TXT	C:\WINDOWS	TXT	\WIN95\CAB_03.CAB
7/11/95	15,954	DISPLAY.TXT	C:\WINDOWS	TXT	\WIN95\CAB_03.CAB
7/11/95	7,072	EXCHANGE.TXT	C:\WINDOWS	TXT	\WIN95\CAB_03.CAB
7/11/95	2,685	EXTRA.TXT	C:\WINDOWS	TXT	\WIN95\CAB_03.CAB
7/11/95	40,378	FAQ.TXT	C:\WINDOWS	TXT	\WIN95\CAB_03.CAB
7/11/95	17,965	GENERAL.TXT	C:\WINDOWS	TXT	\WIN95\CAB_03.CAB
7/11/95	21,548	HARDWARE.TXT	C:\WINDOWS	TXT	\WIN95\CAB_03.CAB
7/11/95	3,277	INTERNET.TXT	C:\WINDOWS	TXT	\WIN95\CAB_03.CAB
7/11/95	5,532	MOUSE.TXT	C:\WINDOWS	TXT	\WIN95\CAB_03.CAB
7/11/95	42,205	MSDOSDRV.TXT	C:\WINDOWS	TXT	\WIN95\CAB_03.CAB
7/11/95	4,111	MSN.TXT	C:\PROGRAM FILES\ THE MICROSOFT NETWORK	TXT	\WIN95\CAB_03.CAB
7/11/95	4	MSNVER.TXT	C:\PROGRAM FILES\ THE MICROSOFT NETWORK	TXT	\WIN95\CAB_07.CAB
7/11/95	18,538	NETWORK.TXT	C:\WINDOWS	TXT	\WIN95\CAB_03.CAB
7/11/95	16,199	PRINTERS.TXT	C:\WINDOWS	TXT	\WIN95\CAB_03.CAB
7/11/95	35,070	PROGRAMS.TXT	C:\WINDOWS	TXT	\WIN95\CAB_03.CAB
7/11/95	24,482	SUPPORT.TXT	C:\WINDOWS	TXT	\WIN95\CAB_03.CAB
7/11/95	2,640	TESTPS.TXT	C:\WINDOWS	TXT	\WIN95\CAB_09.CAB
7/11/95	28,617	TIPS.TXT	C:\WINDOWS	TXT	\WIN95\CAB_03.CAB
7/11/95	1,056	WINNEWS.TXT	C:\WINDOWS	TXT	\WIN95\CAB_06.CAB
7/11/95	64,432	THREED.VBX	C:\WINDOWS\SYSTEM	VBX	\WIN95\CAB_17.CAB
7/11/95	25,402	AFVXD.VXD	C:\WINDOWS\SYSTEM	VXD	\WIN95\CAB_12.CAB
7/11/95	22,631	AM1500T.VXD	C:\WINDOWS\SYSTEM	VXD	\WIN95\CAB_12.CAB
7/11/95	29,404	APIX.VXD	C:\WINDOWS\SYSTEM	VXD	\WIN95\CAB_03.CAB
7/11/95	25,737	ATI.VXD	C:\WINDOWS\SYSTEM	VXD	\WIN95\CAB_04.CAB
7/11/95	11,860	AVVXP500.VXD	C:\WINDOWS\SYSTEM	VXD	\WIN95\CAB_14.CAB
7/11/95	24,214	AZT16.VXD	C:\WINDOWS\SYSTEM	VXD	\WIN95\CAB_08.CAB
7/11/95	32,841	BIOS.VXD	C:\WINDOWS\SYSTEM	VXD	\WIN95\CAB_09.CAB
7/11/95	18,077	BIOSXLAT.VXD	C:\WINDOWS\SYSTEM	VXD	\WIN95\CAB_03.CAB
7/11/95	58,620	CDFS.VXD	C:\WINDOWS\SYSTEM\ IOSUBSYS	VXD	\WIN95\CAB_03.CAB
7/11/95	13,883	CDTSD.VXD	C:\WINDOWS\SYSTEM\ IOSUBSYS	VXD	\WIN95\CAB_03.CAB
7/11/95	14,962	CDVSD.VXD	C:\WINDOWS\SYSTEM\ IOSUBSYS	VXD	\WIN95\CAB_03.CAB
7/11/95	38,352	CE2NDIS3.VXD	C:\WINDOWS\SYSTEM	VXD	\WIN95\CAB_08.CAB

Date of File	Size of File	Installed Name	Installed Location	Type of File	Location on CD
7/11/95	22,617	CENDIS.VXD	C:\WINDOWS\SYSTEM	VXD	\WIN95\CAB_12.CAB
7/11/95	18,590	CHIPS.VXD	C:\WINDOWS\SYSTEM	VXD	\WIN95\CAB_04.CAB
7/11/95	16,950	CIRRUS.VXD	C:\WINDOWS\SYSTEM	VXD	\WIN95\CAB_04.CAB
7/11/95	22,109	CM2NDIS3.VXD	C:\WINDOWS\SYSTEM	VXD	\WIN95\CAB_08.CAB
7/11/95	10,401	COMBUFF.VXD	C:\WINDOWS\SYSTEM	VXD	\WIN95\CAB_03.CAB
7/11/95	17,913	COMPAQ.VXD	C:\WINDOWS\SYSTEM	VXD	\WIN95\CAB_04.CAB
7/11/95	85,613	CONFIGMG.VXD	C:\WINDOWS\SYSTEM\ IOSUBSYS	VXD	\WIN95\CAB_09.CAB
7/11/95	31,837	CPQNDIS3.VXD	C:\WINDOWS\SYSTEM	VXD	\WIN95\CAB_12.CAB
7/11/95	50,775	CTNDW.VXD	C:\WINDOWS\SYSTEM	VXD	\WIN95\CAB_08.CAB
7/11/95	18,639	DBKVSSD.VXD	C:\WINDOWS\SYSTEM	VXD	\WIN95\CAB_09.CAB
7/11/95	15,062	DECCORE.VXD	C:\WINDOWS\SYSTEM	VXD	\WIN95\CAB_17.CAB
7/11/95	27,213	DECLAN.VXD	C:\WINDOWS\SYSTEM	VXD	\WIN95\CAB_12.CAB
7/11/95	36,587	DECLICL.VXD	C:\WINDOWS\SYSTEM	VXD	\WIN95\CAB_17.CAB
7/11/95	16,478	DISKTSD.VXD	C:\WINDOWS\SYSTEM\ IOSUBSYS	VXD	\WIN95\CAB_03.CAB
7/11/95	10,094	DISKVSD.VXD	C:\WINDOWS\SYSTEM\ IOSUBSYS	VXD	\WIN95\CAB_03.CAB
7/11/95	106,862	DOSMGR.VXD	C:\WINDOWS\SYSTEM	VXD	\WIN95\CAB_03.CAB
7/11/95	13,912	DOSNET.VXD	C:\WINDOWS\SYSTEM	VXD	\WIN95\CAB_03.CAB
7/11/95	54,207	DRVSPACX.VXD	C:\WINDOWS\SYSTEM	VXD	\WIN95\CAB_09.CAB
7/11/95	26,982	DYNAPAGE.VXD	C:\WINDOWS\SYSTEM	VXD	\WIN95\CAB_03.CAB
7/11/95	31,636	E30N3.VXD	C:\WINDOWS\SYSTEM	VXD	\WIN95\CAB_12.CAB
7/11/95	31,636	E31N3.VXD	C:\WINDOWS\SYSTEM	VXD	\WIN95\CAB_12.CAB
7/11/95	17,993	EBIOS.VXD	C:\WINDOWS\SYSTEM	VXD	\WIN95\CAB_03.CAB
7/11/95	23,129	EE16.VXD	C:\WINDOWS\SYSTEM	VXD	\WIN95\CAB_12.CAB
7/11/95	13,669	EISA.VXD	C:\WINDOWS\SYSTEM	VXD	\WIN95\CAB_09.CAB
7/11/95	48,710	EL59X.VXD	C:\WINDOWS\SYSTEM	VXD	\WIN95\CAB_12.CAB
7/11/95	29,379	ELNK16.VXD	C:\WINDOWS\SYSTEM	VXD	\WIN95\CAB_12.CAB
7/11/95	30,773	ELNK3.VXD	C:\WINDOWS\SYSTEM	VXD	\WIN95\CAB_12.CAB
7/11/95	31,325	ELNKII.VXD	C:\WINDOWS\SYSTEM	VXD	\WIN95\CAB_12.CAB
7/11/95	28,787	ELNKMC.VXD	C:\WINDOWS\SYSTEM	VXD	\WIN95\CAB_12.CAB
7/11/95	29,785	ELPC3.VXD	C:\WINDOWS\SYSTEM	VXD	\WIN95\CAB_12.CAB
7/11/95	43,197	ENABLE.VXD	C:\WINDOWS\SYSTEM\ VMM31	VXD	\WIN95\CAB_02.CAB
7/11/95	25,154	ENABLE2.VXD	C:\WINDOWS\SYSTEM\ VMM32	VXD	\WIN95\CAB_02.CAB
7/11/95	21,629	ENABLE4.VXD	C:\WINDOWS\SYSTEM	VXD	\WIN95\CAB_02.CAB
7/11/95	25,152	EPRO.VXD	C:\WINDOWS\SYSTEM	VXD	\WIN95\CAB_12.CAB
7/11/95	18,072	ES1488.VXD	C:\WINDOWS\SYSTEM	VXD	\WIN95\CAB_08.CAB
7/11/95	22,168	ES1688.VXD	C:\WINDOWS\SYSTEM	VXD	\WIN95\CAB_08.CAB
7/11/95	18,071	ES488.VXD	C:\WINDOWS\SYSTEM	VXD	\WIN95\CAB_08.CAB
7/11/95	19,607	ES688.VXD	C:\WINDOWS\SYSTEM	VXD	\WIN95\CAB_08.CAB
7/11/95	23,025	FILESEC.VXD	C:\WINDOWS\SYSTEM	VXD	\WIN95\CAB_12.CAB

App
G

continues

Date of File	Size of File	Installed Name	Installed Location	Type of File	Location on CD
7/11/95	3,706	FLS1MTD.VXD	C:\WINDOWS\SYSTEM	VXD	\WIN95\CAB_09.CAB
7/11/95	3,810	FLS2MTD.VXD	C:\WINDOWS\SYSTEM	VXD	\WIN95\CAB_09.CAB
7/11/95	35,629	HPEISA.VXD	C:\WINDOWS\SYSTEM	VXD	\WIN95\CAB_12.CAB
7/11/95	39,494	HPFEND.VXD	C:\WINDOWS\SYSTEM	VXD	\WIN95\CAB_12.CAB
7/11/95	43,588	HPISA.VXD	C:\WINDOWS\SYSTEM	VXD	\WIN95\CAB_12.CAB
7/11/95	43,588	HPMCA.VXD	C:\WINDOWS\SYSTEM	VXD	\WIN95\CAB_12.CAB
7/11/95	39,250	IBMTOK.VXD	C:\WINDOWS\SYSTEM	VXD	\WIN95\CAB_12.CAB
7/11/95	35,086	IBMTOK4.VXD	C:\WINDOWS\SYSTEM	VXD	\WIN95\CAB_12.CAB
7/11/95	165,029	IFSMGR.VXD	C:\WINDOWS\SYSTEM	VXD	\WIN95\CAB_03.CAB
7/11/95	9,934	INT13.VXD	C:\WINDOWS\SYSTEM	VXD	\WIN95\CAB_03.CAB
7/11/95	68,289	IOS.VXD	C:\WINDOWS\SYSTEM	VXD	\WIN95\CAB_03.CAB
7/11/95	41,075	IRMATRAC.VXD	C:\WINDOWS\SYSTEM	VXD	\WIN95\CAB_12.CAB
7/11/95	18,817	ISAPNP.VXD	C:\WINDOWS\SYSTEM	VXD	\WIN95\CAB_09.CAB
7/11/95	69,231	LMOUSE.VXD	C:\WINDOWS\SYSTEM	VXD	\WIN95\CAB_08.CAB
7/11/95	11,637	LOGGER.VXD	C:\WINDOWS\SYSTEM	VXD	\WIN95\CAB_10.CAB
7/11/95	35,479	LPT.VXD	C:\WINDOWS\SYSTEM	VXD	\WIN95\CAB_03.CAB
7/11/95	17,179	LPTENUM.VXD	C:\WINDOWS\SYSTEM	VXD	\WIN95\CAB_09.CAB
7/11/95	9,818	MGA.VXD	C:\WINDOWS\SYSTEM	VXD	\WIN95\CAB_04.CAB
7/11/95	11,844	MMDEVLDR.VXD	C:\WINDOWS\SYSTEM	VXD	\WIN95\CAB_08.CAB
7/11/95	46,746	MRCI2.VXD	C:\WINDOWS\SYSTEM	VXD	\WIN95\CAB_09.CAB
7/11/95	15,804	MSMOUSE.VXD	C:\WINDOWS\SYSTEM	VXD	\WIN95\CAB_08.CAB
7/11/95	12,972	MSMPU401.VXD	C:\WINDOWS\SYSTEM	VXD	\WIN95\CAB_08.CAB
7/11/95	23,897	MSODISUP.VXD	C:\WINDOWS\SYSTEM	VXD	\WIN95\CAB_12.CAB
7/11/95	13,462	MSOPL.VXD	C:\WINDOWS\SYSTEM	VXD	\WIN95\CAB_08.CAB
7/11/95	17,562	MSSBLST.VXD	C:\WINDOWS\SYSTEM	VXD	\WIN95\CAB_08.CAB
7/11/95	28,400	MSSNDSYS.VXD	C:\WINDOWS\SYSTEM	VXD	\WIN95\CAB_08.CAB
7/11/95	21,657	MSSP.VXD	C:\WINDOWS\SYSTEM	VXD	\WIN95\CAB_12.CAB
7/11/95	8,898	MVPAS.VXD	C:\WINDOWS\SYSTEM	VXD	\WIN95\CAB_08.CAB
7/11/95	99,084	NDIS.VXD	C:\WINDOWS\SYSTEM	VXD	\WIN95\CAB_12.CAB
7/11/95	23,744	NDIS2SUP.VXD	C:\WINDOWS\SYSTEM	VXD	\WIN95\CAB_12.CAB
7/11/95	9,929	NECATAPI.VXD	C:\WINDOWS\SYSTEM	VXD	\WIN95\CAB_03.CAB
7/11/95	45,756	NETBEUI.VXD	C:\WINDOWS\SYSTEM	VXD	\WIN95\CAB_12.CAB
7/11/95	22,609	NICE.VXD	C:\WINDOWS\SYSTEM	VXD	\WIN95\CAB_12.CAB
7/11/95	23,606	NSCL.VXD	C:\WINDOWS\SYSTEM	VXD	\WIN95\CAB_12.CAB
7/11/95	51,001	NWLINK.VXD	C:\WINDOWS\SYSTEM	VXD	\WIN95\CAB_12.CAB
7/11/95	46,653	NWNBLINK.VXD	C:\WINDOWS\SYSTEM	VXD	\WIN95\CAB_12.CAB
7/11/95	123,963	NWREDIR.VXD	C:\WINDOWS\SYSTEM	VXD	\WIN95\CAB_12.CAB
7/11/95	130,636	NWSERVER.VXD	C:\WINDOWS\SYSTEM	VXD	\WIN95\CAB_12.CAB
7/11/95	14,438	NWSP.VXD	C:\WINDOWS\SYSTEM	VXD	\WIN95\CAB_12.CAB
7/11/95	14,476	OAK.VXD	C:\WINDOWS\SYSTEM	VXD	\WIN95\CAB_04.CAB
7/11/95	72,655	OCTK32.VXD	C:\WINDOWS\SYSTEM	VXD	\WIN95\CAB_12.CAB
7/11/95	39,827	OTCETH.VXD	C:\WINDOWS\SYSTEM	VXD	\WIN95\CAB_12.CAB
7/11/95	13,905	PAGESWAP.VXD	C:\WINDOWS\SYSTEM	VXD	\WIN95\CAB_03.CAB

Date of File	Size of File	Installed Name	Installed Location	Type of File	Location on CD
7/11/95	23,105	PARALINK.VXD	C:\WINDOWS\SYSTEM	VXD	\WIN95\CAB_10.CAB
7/11/95	9,801	PARITY.VXD	C:\WINDOWS\SYSTEM	VXD	\WIN95\CAB_03.CAB
7/11/95	77,661	PCCARD.VXD	C:\WINDOWS\SYSTEM	VXD	\WIN95\CAB_09.CAB
7/11/95	24,535	PCI.VXD	C:\WINDOWS\SYSTEM	VXD	\WIN95\CAB_09.CAB
7/11/95	35,461	PCNTN3.VXD	C:\WINDOWS\SYSTEM	VXD	\WIN95\CAB_12.CAB
7/11/95	30,811	PE3NDIS.VXD	C:\WINDOWS\SYSTEM	VXD	\WIN95\CAB_12.CAB
7/11/95	22,583	PERF.VXD	C:\WINDOWS\SYSTEM	VXD	\WIN95\CAB_12.CAB
7/11/95	18,458	PPM.VXD	C:\WINDOWS\SYSTEM	VXD	\WIN95\CAB_08.CAB
7/11/95	135,264	PPPMAC.VXD	C:\WINDOWS\SYSTEM	VXD	\WIN95\CAB_10.CAB
7/11/95	38,995	PROTEON.VXD	C:\WINDOWS\SYSTEM	VXD	\WIN95\CAB_12.CAB
7/11/95	9,787	QEMMFIX.VXD	C:\WINDOWS\SYSTEM\ VMM32	VXD	\WIN95\CAB_03.CAB
7/11/95	22,127	REBOOT.VXD	C:\WINDOWS\SYSTEM	VXD	\WIN95\CAB_03.CAB
7/11/95	17,087	S3.VXD	C:\WINDOWS\SYSTEM	VXD	\WIN95\CAB_04.CAB
7/11/95	54,363	SB16.VXD	C:\WINDOWS\SYSTEM	VXD	\WIN95\CAB_08.CAB
7/11/95	40,014	SBAWE.VXD	C:\WINDOWS\SYSTEM	VXD	\WIN95\CAB_08.CAB
7/11/95	19,189	SCSI1HLP.VXD	C:\WINDOWS\SYSTEM\ IOSUBSYS	VXD	\WIN95\CAB_05.CAB
7/11/95	19,899	SERENUM.VXD	C:\WINDOWS\SYSTEM	VXD	\WIN95\CAB_03.CAB
7/11/95	18,572	SERIAL.VXD	C:\WINDOWS\SYSTEM	VXD	\WIN95\CAB_03.CAB
7/11/95	31,838	SETP3.VXD	C:\WINDOWS\SYSTEM	VXD	\WIN95\CAB_12.CAB
7/11/95	78,964	SHELL.VXD	C:\WINDOWS\SYSTEM\ IOSUBSYS	VXD	\WIN95\CAB_11.CAB
7/11/95	36,959	SMC8000W.VXD	C:\WINDOWS\SYSTEM	VXD	\WIN95\CAB_12.CAB
7/11/95	28,765	SMC80PC.VXD	C:\WINDOWS\SYSTEM	VXD	\WIN95\CAB_12.CAB
7/11/95	71,773	SMC8100W.VXD	C:\WINDOWS\SYSTEM	VXD	\WIN95\CAB_12.CAB
7/11/95	28,767	SMC8232W.VXD	C:\WINDOWS\SYSTEM	VXD	\WIN95\CAB_12.CAB
7/11/95	29,433	SMC9000.VXD	C:\WINDOWS\SYSTEM	VXD	\WIN95\CAB_12.CAB
7/11/95	13,884	SNAPSHOT.VXD	C:\WINDOWS\SYSTEM	VXD	\WIN95\CAB_17.CAB
7/11/95	27,217	SNIP.VXD	C:\WINDOWS\SYSTEM	VXD	\WIN95\CAB_12.CAB
7/11/95	27,217	SOCKET.VXD	C:\WINDOWS\SYSTEM	VXD	\WIN95\CAB_12.CAB
7/11/95	9,806	SOCKETSV.VXD	C:\WINDOWS\SYSTEM	VXD	\WIN95\CAB_09.CAB
7/11/95	9,908	SPAP.VXD	C:\WINDOWS\SYSTEM	VXD	\WIN95\CAB_10.CAB
7/11/95	17,996	SPENDIS.VXD	C:\WINDOWS\SYSTEM	VXD	\WIN95\CAB_12.CAB
7/11/95	2,596	SPLITTER.VXD	C:\WINDOWS\SYSTEM	VXD	\WIN95\CAB_07.CAB
7/11/95	27,196	SPOOLER.VXD	C:\WINDOWS\SYSTEM	VXD	\WIN95\CAB_09.CAB
7/11/95	3,202	SRAMMTD.VXD	C:\WINDOWS\SYSTEM	VXD	\WIN95\CAB_09.CAB
7/11/95	63,935	T20N3.VXD	C:\WINDOWS\SYSTEM	VXD	\WIN95\CAB_12.CAB
7/11/95	64,027	T30N3.VXD	C:\WINDOWS\SYSTEM	VXD	\WIN95\CAB_12.CAB
7/11/95	37,616	TCTOKCH.VXD	C:\WINDOWS\SYSTEM	VXD	\WIN95\CAB_12.CAB
7/11/95	52,627	TLNK3.VXD	C:\WINDOWS\SYSTEM	VXD	\WIN95\CAB_12.CAB
7/11/95	14,531	TSENG.VXD	C:\WINDOWS\SYSTEM	VXD	\WIN95\CAB_04.CAB
7/11/95	31,311	UBNEI.VXD	C:\WINDOWS\SYSTEM	VXD	\WIN95\CAB_12.CAB
7/11/95	41,598	UNIMODEM.VXD	C:\WINDOWS\SYSTEM	VXD	\WIN95\CAB_03.CAB

continues

App

G

Date of File	Size of File	Installed Name	Installed Location	Type of File	Location on CD
7/11/95	95,387	V86MMGR.VXD	C:\WINDOWS\SYSTEM	VXD	\WIN95\CAB_03.CAB
7/11/95	19,566	VCACHE.VXD	C:\WINDOWS\SYSTEM	VXD	\WIN95\CAB_03.CAB
7/11/95	23,939	VCD.VXD	C:\WINDOWS\SYSTEM	VXD	\WIN95\CAB_03.CAB
7/11/95	22,408	VCDFSD.VXD	C:\WINDOWS\SYSTEM	VXD	\WIN95\CAB_03.CAB
7/11/95	32,638	VCOMM.VXD	C:\WINDOWS\SYSTEM	VXD	\WIN95\CAB_03.CAB
7/11/95	53,438	VCOND.VXD	C:\WINDOWS\SYSTEM	VXD	\WIN95\CAB_04.CAB
7/11/95	73,592	VDD.VXD	C:\WINDOWS\SYSTEM	VXD	\WIN95\CAB_04.CAB
7/11/95	9,768	VDEF.VXD	C:\WINDOWS\SYSTEM	VXD	\WIN95\CAB_03.CAB
7/11/95	41,844	VDMAD.VXD	C:\WINDOWS\SYSTEM	VXD	\WIN95\CAB_03.CAB
7/11/95	57,917	VFAT.VXD	C:\WINDOWS\SYSTEM	VXD	\WIN95\CAB_03.CAB
7/11/95	16,831	VFBACKUP.VXD	C:\WINDOWS\SYSTEM	VXD	\WIN95\CAB_03.CAB
7/11/95	5,857	VFD.VXD	C:\WINDOWS\SYSTEM	VXD	\WIN95\CAB_03.CAB
7/11/95	7,723	VFLATD.VXD	C:\WINDOWS\SYSTEM	VXD	\WIN95\CAB_04.CAB
7/11/95	14,624	VGAFULL.3GR	C:\WINDOWS\SYSTEM	VXD	\WIN95\CAB_04.CAB
7/11/95	42,749	VGATEWAY.VXD	C:\WINDOWS\SYSTEM	VXD	\WIN95\CAB_07.CAB
7/11/95	14,938	VIDEO7.VXD	C:\WINDOWS\SYSTEM	VXD	\WIN95\CAB_04.CAB
7/11/95	20,590	VJOYD.VXD	C:\WINDOWS\SYSTEM	VXD	\WIN95\CAB_08.CAB
7/11/95	45,371	VKD.VXD	C:\WINDOWS\SYSTEM	VXD	\WIN95\CAB_03.CAB
7/11/95	13,973	VMCPD.VXD	C:\WINDOWS\SYSTEM	VXD	\WIN95\CAB_03.CAB
7/11/95	9,815	VMD.VXD	C:\WINDOWS\SYSTEM	VXD	\WIN95\CAB_08.CAB
7/11/95	411,132	VMM32.VXD	C:\WINDOWS\SYSTEM	VXD	\WIN95\CAB_03.CAB
7/11/95	32,815	VMOUSE.VXD	C:\WINDOWS\SYSTEM	VXD	\WIN95\CAB_08.CAB
7/11/95	30,931	VMPOLL.VXD	C:\WINDOWS\SYSTEM	VXD	\WIN95\CAB_03.CAB
7/11/95	16,030	VMVID.VXD	C:\WINDOWS\SYSTEM	VXD	\WIN95\CAB_08.CAB
7/11/95	27,221	VNETBIOS.VXD	C:\WINDOWS\SYSTEM	VXD	\WIN95\CAB_12.CAB
7/11/95	19,129	VNETSUP.VXD	C:\WINDOWS\SYSTEM	VXD	\WIN95\CAB_12.CAB
7/11/95	18,494	VOLTRACK.VXD	C:\WINDOWS\SYSTEM\ IOSUBSYS	VXD	\WIN95\CAB_03.CAB
7/11/95	21,094	VPASD.VXD	C:\WINDOWS\SYSTEM	VXD	\WIN95\CAB_08.CAB
7/11/95	22,618	VPD.VXD	C:\WINDOWS\SYSTEM	VXD	\WIN95\CAB_03.CAB
7/11/95	46,543	VPICD.VXD	C:\WINDOWS\SYSTEM	VXD	\WIN95\CAB_03.CAB
7/11/95	19,669	VPOWERD.VXD	C:\WINDOWS\SYSTEM	VXD	\WIN95\CAB_07.CAB
7/11/95	140,343	VREDIR.VXD	C:\WINDOWS\SYSTEM	VXD	\WIN95\CAB_12.CAB
7/11/95	5,721	VSD.VXD	C:\WINDOWS\SYSTEM	VXD	\WIN95\CAB_03.CAB
7/11/95	108,264	VSERVER.VXD	C:\WINDOWS\SYSTEM	VXD	\WIN95\CAB_12.CAB
7/11/95	14,926	VSHARE.VXD	C:\WINDOWS\SYSTEM	VXD	\WIN95\CAB_05.CAB
7/11/95	31,684	VTD.VXD	C:\WINDOWS\SYSTEM	VXD	\WIN95\CAB_03.CAB
7/11/95	18,546	VTDAPI.VXD	C:\WINDOWS\SYSTEM	VXD	\WIN95\CAB_03.CAB
7/11/95	54,497	VWIN32.VXD	C:\WINDOWS\SYSTEM	VXD	\WIN95\CAB_04.CAB
7/11/95	35,112	VXDLDR.VXD	C:\WINDOWS\SYSTEM	VXD	\WIN95\CAB_03.CAB
7/11/95	18,328	WD.VXD	C:\WINDOWS\SYSTEM	VXD	\WIN95\CAB_04.CAB
7/11/95	5,816	WSHTCP.VXD	C:\WINDOWS\SYSTEM	VXD	\WIN95\CAB_12.CAB
7/11/95	14,521	WSIPX.VXD	C:\WINDOWS\SYSTEM	VXD	\WIN95\CAB_12.CAB
7/11/95	15,522	WSOCK.VXD	C:\WINDOWS\SYSTEM	VXD	\WIN95\CAB_12.CAB

Date of File	Size of File	Installed Name	Installed Location	Type of File	Location on CD
7/11/95	92,244	WSVV.VXD	C:\WINDOWS\SYSTEM	VXD	\WIN95\CAB_17.CAB
7/11/95	20,151	XGA.VXD	C:\WINDOWS\SYSTEM	VXD	\WIN95\CAB_04.CAB
7/11/95	135,876	MSSOUND.WAV	C:\WINDOWS\MEDIA	WAV	\WIN95\CAB_08.CAB
7/11/95	15,932	CHIMES.WAV	C:\WINDOWS\MEDIA	WAV	\WIN95\CAB_14.CAB
7/11/95	24,994	CHORD.WAV	C:\WINDOWS\MEDIA	WAV	\WIN95\CAB_14.CAB
7/11/95	11,586	DING.WAV	C:\WINDOWS\MEDIA	WAV	\WIN95\CAB_14.CAB
7/11/95	336,938	JUNGLE~1.WAV	C:\WINDOWS\MEDIA	WAV	\WIN95\CAB_14.CAB
7/11/95	142,888	JUNGLE~2.WAV	C:\WINDOWS\MEDIA	WAV	\WIN95\CAB_14.CAB
7/11/95	145,450	JUNGLE~3.WAV	C:\WINDOWS\MEDIA	WAV	\WIN95\CAB_14.CAB
7/11/95	184,872	JUNGLE~4.WAV	C:\WINDOWS\MEDIA	WAV	\WIN95\CAB_14.CAB
7/11/95	89,126	JUNGLEAS.WAV	C:\WINDOWS\MEDIA	WAV	\WIN95\CAB_14.CAB
7/11/95	143,914	JUNGLECL.WAV	C:\WINDOWS\MEDIA	WAV	\WIN95\CAB_14.CAB
7/11/95	175,146	JUNGLECR.WAV	C:\WINDOWS\MEDIA	WAV	\WIN95\CAB_14.CAB
7/11/95	140,330	JUNGLEDE.WAV	C:\WINDOWS\MEDIA	WAV	\WIN95\CAB_14.CAB
7/11/95	166,954	JUNGLEER.WAV	C:\WINDOWS\MEDIA	WAV	\WIN95\CAB_14.CAB
7/11/95	147,754	JUNGLEEX.WAV	C:\WINDOWS\MEDIA	WAV	\WIN95\CAB_14.CAB
7/11/95	169,010	JUNGLEMA.WAV	C:\WINDOWS\MEDIA	WAV	\WIN95\CAB_14.CAB
7/11/95	74,026	JUNGLEME.WAV	C:\WINDOWS\MEDIA	WAV	\WIN95\CAB_14.CAB
7/11/95	169,010	JUNGLEMI.WAV	C:\WINDOWS\MEDIA	WAV	\WIN95\CAB_14.CAB
7/11/95	129,578	JUNGLEOP.WAV	C:\WINDOWS\MEDIA	WAV	\WIN95\CAB_14.CAB
7/11/95	145,446	JUNGLEQU.WAV	C:\WINDOWS\MEDIA	WAV	\WIN95\CAB_14.CAB
7/11/95	159,782	JUNGLERE.WAV	C:\WINDOWS\MEDIA	WAV	\WIN95\CAB_14.CAB
7/11/95	474,238	JUNGLEWI.WAV	C:\WINDOWS\MEDIA	WAV	\WIN95\CAB_14.CAB
7/11/95	21,816	MUSICA~1.WAV	C:\WINDOWS\MEDIA	WAV	\WIN95\CAB_15.CAB
7/11/95	8,288	MUSICA~2.WAV	C:\WINDOWS\MEDIA	WAV	\WIN95\CAB_15.CAB
7/11/95	12,490	MUSICA~3.WAV	C:\WINDOWS\MEDIA	WAV	\WIN95\CAB_15.CAB
7/11/95	12,054	MUSICA~4.WAV	C:\WINDOWS\MEDIA	WAV	\WIN95\CAB_15.CAB
7/11/95	28,338	MUSICAAS.WAV	C:\WINDOWS\MEDIA	WAV	\WIN95\CAB_15.CAB
7/11/95	45,816	MUSICACL.WAV	C:\WINDOWS\MEDIA	WAV	\WIN95\CAB_15.CAB
7/11/95	10,272	MUSICACR.WAV	C:\WINDOWS\MEDIA	WAV	\WIN95\CAB_15.CAB
7/11/95	6,262	MUSICADE.WAV	C:\WINDOWS\MEDIA	WAV	\WIN95\CAB_15.CAB
7/11/95	20,344	MUSICAER.WAV	C:\WINDOWS\MEDIA	WAV	\WIN95\CAB_15.CAB
7/11/95	9,584	MUSICAEX.WAV	C:\WINDOWS\MEDIA	WAV	\WIN95\CAB_15.CAB
7/11/95	8,608	MUSICAMA.WAV	C:\WINDOWS\MEDIA	WAV	\WIN95\CAB_15.CAB
7/11/95	8,186	MUSICAME.WAV	C:\WINDOWS\MEDIA	WAV	\WIN95\CAB_15.CAB
7/11/95	7,800	MUSICAMI.WAV	C:\WINDOWS\MEDIA	WAV	\WIN95\CAB_15.CAB
7/11/95	43,096	MUSICAOP.WAV	C:\WINDOWS\MEDIA	WAV	\WIN95\CAB_15.CAB
7/11/95	11,932	MUSICAQU.WAV	C:\WINDOWS\MEDIA	WAV	\WIN95\CAB_15.CAB
7/11/95	20,596	MUSICARE.WAV	C:\WINDOWS\MEDIA	WAV	\WIN95\CAB_15.CAB
7/11/95	49,026	MUSICAWI.WAV	C:\WINDOWS\MEDIA	WAV	\WIN95\CAB_15.CAB
7/11/95	249,570	ROBOTZ~1.WAV	C:\WINDOWS\MEDIA	WAV	\WIN95\CAB_15.CAB
7/11/95	71,868	ROBOTZ~2.WAV	C:\WINDOWS\MEDIA	WAV	\WIN95\CAB_15.CAB
7/11/95	49,578	ROBOTZ~3.WAV	C:\WINDOWS\MEDIA	WAV	\WIN95\CAB_15.CAB

App
G

continues

Date of File	Size of File	Installed Name	Installed Location	Type of File	Location on CD
7/11/95	109,688	ROBOTZ~4.WAV	C:\WINDOWS\MEDIA	WAV	\WIN95\CAB_15.CAB
7/11/95	70,426	ROBOTZAS.WAV	C:\WINDOWS\MEDIA	WAV	\WIN95\CAB_15.CAB
7/11/95	94,818	ROBOTZCL.WAV	C:\WINDOWS\MEDIA	WAV	\WIN95\CAB_15.CAB
7/11/95	54,150	ROBOTZCR.WAV	C:\WINDOWS\MEDIA	WAV	\WIN95\CAB_15.CAB
7/11/95	44,546	ROBOTZDE.WAV	C:\WINDOWS\MEDIA	WAV	\WIN95\CAB_15.CAB
7/11/95	49,284	ROBOTZER.WAV	C:\WINDOWS\MEDIA	WAV	\WIN95\CAB_15.CAB
7/11/95	30,194	ROBOTZEX.WAV	C:\WINDOWS\MEDIA	WAV	\WIN95\CAB_15.CAB
7/11/95	74,722	ROBOTZMA.WAV	C:\WINDOWS\MEDIA	WAV	\WIN95\CAB_15.CAB
7/11/95	13,920	ROBOTZME.WAV	C:\WINDOWS\MEDIA	WAV	\WIN95\CAB_15.CAB
7/11/95	150,442	ROBOTZMI.WAV	C:\WINDOWS\MEDIA	WAV	\WIN95\CAB_15.CAB
7/11/95	81,390	ROBOTZOP.WAV	C:\WINDOWS\MEDIA	WAV	\WIN95\CAB_15.CAB
7/11/95	79,002	ROBOTZQU.WAV	C:\WINDOWS\MEDIA	WAV	\WIN95\CAB_15.CAB
7/11/95	119,134	ROBOTZRE.WAV	C:\WINDOWS\MEDIA	WAV	\WIN95\CAB_15.CAB
7/11/95	275,950	ROBOTZWI.WAV	C:\WINDOWS\MEDIA	WAV	\WIN95\CAB_15.CAB
7/11/95	27,516	TADA.WAV	C:\WINDOWS\MEDIA	WAV	\WIN95\CAB_15.CAB
7/11/95	86,798	UTOPIA~1.WAV	C:\WINDOWS\MEDIA	WAV	\WIN95\CAB_15.CAB
7/11/95	2,692	UTOPIA~2.WAV	C:\WINDOWS\MEDIA	WAV	\WIN95\CAB_15.CAB
7/11/95	5,120	UTOPIA~3.WAV	C:\WINDOWS\MEDIA	WAV	\WIN95\CAB_15.CAB
7/11/95	15,372	UTOPIA~4.WAV	C:\WINDOWS\MEDIA	WAV	\WIN95\CAB_15.CAB
7/11/95	95,708	UTOPIAAS.WAV	C:\WINDOWS\MEDIA	WAV	\WIN95\CAB_15.CAB
7/11/95	4,616	UTOPIACL.WAV	C:\WINDOWS\MEDIA	WAV	\WIN95\CAB_15.CAB
7/11/95	5,824	UTOPIACR.WAV	C:\WINDOWS\MEDIA	WAV	\WIN95\CAB_15.CAB
7/11/95	9,946	UTOPIADE.WAV	C:\WINDOWS\MEDIA	WAV	\WIN95\CAB_15.CAB
7/11/95	24,596	UTOPIAER.WAV	C:\WINDOWS\MEDIA	WAV	\WIN95\CAB_15.CAB
7/11/95	13,026	UTOPIAEX.WAV	C:\WINDOWS\MEDIA	WAV	\WIN95\CAB_15.CAB
7/11/95	14,922	UTOPIAMA.WAV	C:\WINDOWS\MEDIA	WAV	\WIN95\CAB_16.CAB
7/11/95	3,462	UTOPIAME.WAV	C:\WINDOWS\MEDIA	WAV	\WIN95\CAB_16.CAB
7/11/95	14,990	UTOPIAMI.WAV	C:\WINDOWS\MEDIA	WAV	\WIN95\CAB_16.CAB
7/11/95	10,760	UTOPIAOP.WAV	C:\WINDOWS\MEDIA	WAV	\WIN95\CAB_16.CAB
7/11/95	13,084	UTOPIAQU.WAV	C:\WINDOWS\MEDIA	WAV	\WIN95\CAB_16.CAB
7/11/95	98,330	UTOPIARE.WAV	C:\WINDOWS\MEDIA	WAV	\WIN95\CAB_16.CAB
7/11/95	156,760	UTOPIAWI.WAV	C:\WINDOWS\MEDIA	WAV	\WIN95\CAB_16.CAB
7/11/95	4,017	QUATTRO.WB2	C:\WINDOWS\SHELLNEW	WB2	\WIN95\CAB_11.CAB
7/11/95	2,448	LOTUS.WK4	C:\WINDOWS\SHELLNEW	WK4	\WIN95\CAB_11.CAB
7/11/95	22,679	WIN.CNF	C:\WINDOWS\SYSTEM	WPC	\WIN95\CAB_03.CAB
7/11/95	62,464	WRITE32.WPC	C:\PROGRAM FILES\ ACCESSORIES	WPC	\WIN95\CAB_02.CAB
7/11/95	30	WORDPFCT.WPD	C:\WINDOWS\SHELLNEW	WPD	\WIN95\CAB_11.CAB
7/11/95	2,274	INFORMS.WPF	C:\WINDOWS\SHELLNEW	WPF	\WIN95\CAB_11.CAB
7/11/95	57	WORDPFCT.WPG	C:\WINDOWS\SHELLNEW	WPG	\WIN95\CAB_11.CAB
7/11/95	1,371	WORDPFCT.WPW	C:\WINDOWS\SHELLNEW	WPW	\WIN95\CAB_11.CAB
7/11/95	5,632	EXCEL.XLS	C:\WINDOWS\SHELLNEW	XLS	\WIN95\CAB_11.CAB
7/11/95	1,518	EXCEL4.XLS	C:\WINDOWS\SHELLNEW	XLS	\WIN95\CAB_11.CAB

Internet Resources for Windows 95

Windows 95 is hot, and it's new. Thus, the amount of new information and programs that becomes available each day is staggering. If you don't want to wait for the next Windows 95 super book or next month's magazine, you have to go online to get it. You can get a lot of information through commercial online services such as CompuServe, America Online, or The Microsoft Network. You'll find more variety, and potentially more useful information, however, on the Internet.

That's where this appendix comes in. It points you to some of the best resources on the Internet for Windows 95 information and programs. Keep in mind that there are hundreds of other Internet sites for each Windows 95 site that you find in this appendix. I didn't include most of them because they contain links to the other sites. The result is a Web of Windows 95 pages, all linked together, that contains nothing but links.

http://www.mcp.com/que

This chapter teaches you about

+ *FTP Servers.* It's usually easier to find shareware programs on the World Wide Web, but this sample of FTP sites collects so many programs in a few areas that they're worth checking out.

+ *Mailing lists.* Sometimes it's easier to let the information you want come to you, instead of going out onto the Internet to look for it. Mailing lists deliver information directly to your mailbox.

+ *UseNet newsgroups.* Newsgroups are the place to look for quickly changing information. If you need help, you can find what you need here.

+ *World Wide Web.* There's little doubt that the Web is the hottest resource on the Internet. You find a variety of Web pages dedicated to Windows 95, including personal and corporate Web pages.

On the Web

You can find shortcuts to the Internet address described here at Que's Web site at
http://www.mcp.com.

FTP Servers

The FTP servers in this section contain large collections of Windows 95 shareware programs. They are all well organized, so you can quickly find the program you're looking for. Note that most of these sites are indexed by **Shareware.com**. See "Shareware.com," later in this chapter, for more information.

Tip

If you don't have an FTP client, you can use your Web browser to access FTP servers. Type **ftp://** followed by the FTP address in your Web browser's address bar.

Microsoft

FTP address: **ftp://ftp.microsoft.com**

This is the place to look for updated drivers, new files for Windows 95, and sometimes free programs. My favorite part of this FTP site is the Knowledge Base articles that answer common questions about most of Microsoft's programs. If you're having trouble finding your way around, look for a file called Dirmap.txt, which tells you what the different folders have in them. Here's what you will find under each of the folders on this site:

- **/BUSSYS.** Files for business systems, including networking, mail, SQL Server, and Windows NT.

- **/DESKAPPS.** Files for all of Microsoft's desktop applications, including Access, Excel, PowerPoint, Project, and Word. You can also find information for the Home series, including games and Works.

- **/DEVELPR.** The place to look if you're a developer. There are folders for Visual C++, Visual Basic, various utilities, the Microsoft Developer Network, and more. If you subscribe to the *Microsoft Systems Journal*, check here to find the source code for articles.

- **/KBHELP.** Microsoft's Knowledge Base folder. A *knowledge base*, in this context, is a help file that contains common questions and answers about Microsoft products. This folder contains one self-extracting, compressed file for each Microsoft product. The Windows 95 Knowledge Base files are under yet another folder called **WIN95**. If you're having difficulty with a Microsoft product, download the appropriate file, decompress it, and double-click it to load it in Help.

- **/SOFTLIB.** The folder to check out if you're looking for updated drivers, patches, or bug fixes. This folder contains more than 1,500 files, though, so you need to review Index.txt first to locate what you want.

- **/PEROPSYS.** For personal operating systems. If you're looking for back issues of WINNEWS, look in the **WIN_NEWS** folder. There are other folders relating to all versions of Windows, MS-DOS, and Microsoft hardware.
- **/SERVICES.** Contains information about TechNet, Microsoft educational services, sales information, and so on.

 Note Many of the folders on the Microsoft FTP site have two files that you should read: Readme.txt and Index.txt.

Readme.txt describes the type of files you find in the current folder and any subfolders. It also may describe recent additions and files that have been removed.

Index.txt describes each file in the folder. It's a good idea to search for the file you want in Index.txt before trying to pick it out of the listing. Note that Microsoft's site is constantly changing, so you'll want to check back here often.

The Oak Software Repository

FTP address: **ftp://oak.oakland.edu**

The Oak Software Repository is another large site of freeware and shareware programs sponsored by Oakland University in Rochester, MI. You can find all the Windows 95 files in /SIMTEL/WIN95. The following table shows the folders that you will find for Windows 95. If you're still looking for DOS and Windows 3.1 files, you can find those here, too. Take a look at Readme for more information about the files on this FTP site.

Folders Under /SIMTEL/WIN95

animate	graphics
archiver	info
cad	multimed
canon	pgmtools
commprog	pim
desktop	sysutil
editor	txtutil
filedocs	virus
fileutil	winword

Walnut Creek

FTP address: **ftp://ftp.cdrom.com**

I consider myself lucky to get on this FTP site. It's incredibly popular. Walnut Creek sells CD-ROMs that are packed with freeware and shareware programs. Files from these CD-ROMs are available from the Walnut Creek FTP site, too. The following table shows you the folders that you can find for Windows 95.

Interesting Folders Under /PUB/WIN95

cdextras	incoming
demos	inetapps
drivers	misc
patches	multimedia
graphics	utils

Tip

This site if usually very crowded. If you get onto this site, don't let yourself get disconnected by taking a coffee break—it could be awhile before you get on again.

WinSite (formerly known as CICA)

FTP address: **ftp://ftp.winsite.com**

This archive used to be managed by the Center for Innovative Computing Applications (CICA). It's created a new group called *WinSite* to manage the archive.

This could be the only FTP site that you need. It has the largest collection of freeware and shareware programs on the Internet. It's the Internet equivalent of CompuServe's WinShare forum (a forum on CompuServe that contains shareware Windows programs). The following table describes what you can find in each of the folders on the WinSite FTP server.

Folders Under /PUB/PC/WIN95

access	patches
demo	pdoxwin
desktop	pim
drivers	programr
dskutil	sounds
excel	sysutil
games	txtutil
icons	uploads
misc	winword
miscutil	wpwin
netutil	

Troubleshooting

I've tried over and over to log onto the WinSite FTP server. A very large number of Internet users look for files at this FTP site. So, you'll find it's very crowded most of the time. Keep trying. If you still can't get onto it, look at the log file that your FTP client program displays to find a *mirror site* (FTP servers containing the exact same files) near you.

Mailing Lists

Windows 95-related mailing lists keep your mailbox full of messages. I've received more than 100 messages a day from such mailing list. There's a lot of noise generated by these lists, but you can find a lot of gems, too.

Microsoft DevWire

This is for Windows programmers. You'll find news and product information, such as seminar schedules and visual tool release schedules. To subscribe, send an e-mail to **DevWire@microsoft.nwnet.com** with **subscribe DevWire** in the body of your message.

Microsoft WinNews

This weekly newsletter keeps you up-to-date on the latest happenings at Microsoft. You will also find product tips and press releases. To subscribe, send an e-mail to **enews99@microsoft.nwnet.com** and type **subscribe winnews** in the body of your message.

Micosoft Support Newsgroups

Microsoft has moved all online support for Windows 95 off of online services (such as CompuServe), and onto its own NNTP-compliant newsreader (you can download one from **http:www.microsoft.com** as your news server.

The official Microsoft Support Newsgroups include:

> Microsoft.public.win95.commtelephony
>
> Microsoft.public.win95.dialupnetworking
>
> Microsoft.public.win95.exchangefax
>
> Microsoft.public.win95.filediskmanagement
>
> Microsoft.public.win95.msdosapps
>
> Microsoft.public.win95.multimedia
>
> Microsoft.public.win95.networking
>
> Microsoft.public.win95.printingfontsvideo
>
> Microsoft.public.win95.setup
>
> Mimcrosoft.public.win95.shellui
>
> Microsoft.public.win95.wind95applets

UseNet Newsgroups

As of this writing, there aren't very many UseNet newsgroups dedicated to Windows 95, although the older Windows 3.1 groups are leaning in that direction. The following table lists the newsgroups that you may find useful. The only two that are dedicated to Windows 95, however, are **win95.misc** and **win95.setup**.

Newsgroups Under **comp.os.ms-windows**

advocacy	programmer.graphics
announce	programmer.memory

apps.comm	programmer.misc
apps.financial	programmer.multimedia
apps.misc	programmer.networks
apps.utilities	programmer.ole
apps.winsock.mail	programmer.tools
apps.winsock.misc	programmer.tools.mfc
apps.winsock.news	programmer.tools.misc
apps.word-proc	programmer.tools.owl
misc	programmer.tools.winsock
networking.misc	programmer.vxd
networking.ras	programmer.winhelp
networking.win95	programmer.win32
networking.tcp-ip	setup
networking.windows	video
programmer.controls	win95.misc
programmer.drivers	win95.setup

World Wide Web

The explosive growth of Windows 95 Web pages is evident if you search for the keyword **Windows 95** using Yahoo, WebCrawler, Excite, or Lycos. You can find thousands of Web pages dedicated to Windows 95, some from the corporate community such as Microsoft or Symantec. Many more exist from individuals who want to make their mark on the world by sharing what they know about Windows 95.

The Web pages in this section are only a start. Each one contains links to other Windows 95 sites. Before you know it, your Windows 95 hot list will grow by leaps and bounds.

Microsoft Corporation

URL address: **http://www.microsoft.com**

Microsoft's Web site contains an amazing amount of information about its products, services, plans, job opportunities, and more (see fig. H.1). You can find the two most useful Windows 95 Web pages by clicking

Search

FIG. H.1 ⇒
Click Search to
find exactly what
you're looking for
on the Microsoft
Web site.

the Products link or the Support link.

Here's what you find on each:

+ *Products link.* This Web page contains links for most Microsoft
  products, including Windows 95. You find links to Microsoft
  pages for Windows 95, Office, BackOffice, NT Workstation, and
  more. The bulletin board on this page also contains the latest
  information about Microsoft products.

+ *Support link.* The Support Desktop Web page provides access to
  the Microsoft Knowledge Base, which you can use to search for
  articles based on keywords that you specify. It also contains links
  to the Microsoft Software Library and Frequently Asked Questions (FAQ) Web pages.

On the Web

This site is best viewed with Microsoft's Internet Explorer. You can get your
own copy of Internet Explorer at
http://www.microsoft.com/windows/ie/ie.htm.

And it's free, too.

BugNet

URL address: **http://www.pacificrim.net/~bugnet/**

If you're not getting anywhere with that support line, try out this Web site. It documents all the latest bugs, and sometimes offers solutions or workarounds. You can report a bug to this site as well. This site is particularly useful to check out the stability of a product before you fork out your hard-earned cash.

Dylan Greene's Windows 95 Starting Page

URL address: **http://www.wam.umd.edu/~dylan/win95.html**

Here's an example of a good Web page. Not only is Dylan Greene's Web page packed with graphics (see fig. H.2), it's also packed with useful information about Windows 95. You will find links for FAQs, troubleshooting, setting up your dial-up connection, and shareware libraries at this site.

FIG. H.2 ⇒
To get the full benefit of the Windows 95-like menus, you need to use Netscape 2.0.

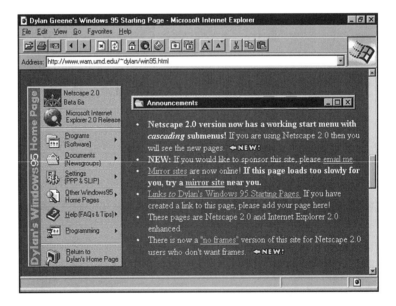

Frank Condron's Windows 95 Page

URL address: **http://www.rust.net/~frankc/**

This Web site was chosen as a ClubWin Web site. *ClubWin* is a collection of Web sites that have been recognized by Microsoft as providing outstanding Windows 95 support and information on the Web. This page fits the bill. It has updated drivers, software, hints, and links to other ClubWin sites.

Getting the Most from the Windows95 Registry

URL address: **http://www.usa.net/~rduffy/registry.htm**

This Web page contains a basic introduction to the Registry. It also has some tips that involve editing the Registry.

In Touch Win 95

URL address: **http://www.islandnet.com/~sword/win95.html**

This Web site tracks Windows 95 and its related products. You will find news about the latest shareware and commercial product releases for Windows 95. Most important, you can subscribe to a mailing list at this site, which keeps you informed about Windows 95.

Jerry Honeycutt

URL address: **http://rampages.onramp.net/~jerry**

My Web page. Besides the usual boasting that you might expect, you find useful tips for Windows 95 and the Internet.

Stroud's CWSApps List

URL address: **http://cwsapps.texas.net/**

This Web site contains every Windows Winsock program available on the Internet. You find World Wide Web, FTP, e-mail, IRC, and UseNet client programs. You also find HTML editors and communication suites.

In addition to the standard Winsock programs, this site contains all of the essential utilities that you need for Windows 95, such as WinZip 95 and ViruScan for Windows 95.

Figure H.3 shows the easy-to-use interface for this Web site. Click a category to see a list of shareware programs for that category.

FIG. H.3 ⟹

Click the Windows 95 Section link to see a list that is limited to Windows 95 programs.

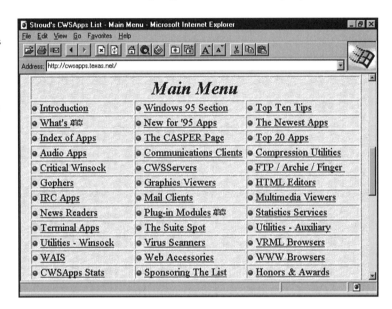

Windows 95 Annoyances

URL address: **http://www.creativelement.com/win95ann/**

Just like the name implies, this site is dedicated to all the annoying features in Windows 95. The authors of this site don't just gripe about it, however. They offer solutions. If you don't like the desktop icons, for example, you learn how to change them at this site. If you're having trouble with networking in Windows 95, you will find information here that just might help you.

FedCenter

URL address: **http://199.171.16.49/fedcenter/fw95.html**

This Web page is sponsored by The InterFed Group (an organization dedicated to helping government employees participate in the Internet). It contains information about Windows 95 events and shareware programs, as well as links to numerous other Windows 95 Web pages.

PC World's Windows 95

URL address: **http://www.pcworld.com/win95/**

Wow! This Web page has links to almost everything you need for Windows 95. It has articles about Windows 95 that you can search. *PC World* claims to have the largest collection of Windows 95 shareware on the Internet. It may be right.

Tip

Sign up at this Web page for a free subscription to the Windows 95 Tip-of-the-Day mailing list.

Que's Windows 95 Event Page

URL address: **http://www.mcp.com/que/win95/**

This appendix wouldn't be complete without at least one reference to Que's Web site. You will find troubleshooting information and tips at this particular page. It's not just a list of Que's books, either, as it contains excerpts from Windows 95 books, links to shareware programs, and access to Que's own Windows 95 "hypermail" forum (see fig. H.4).

FIG. H.4 ⟹
Click the Que logo to see all of Que's product offerings.

Que logo ⎯

Shareware.com

URL address: **http://www.shareware.com**

Shareware.com is a hot new Web site that indexes shareware and freeware products on the Internet. You can search for products by platform, category, and so on. You can also look up the top products based on the number of downloads or recent submissions. If you're looking for a shareware product, you don't need to log onto the online service anymore; you can find it here (see fig. H.5).

FIG. H.5 ⇒
Click Subscribe to join the Shareware Dispatch mailing list—a weekly mailing list that keeps you informed about the latest shareware programs.

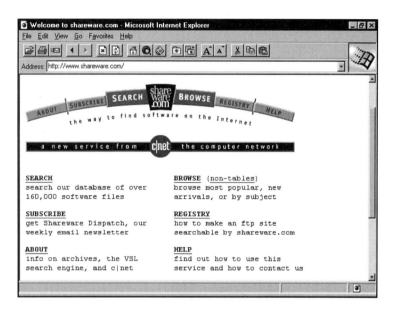

Windows95.com

URL address: **http://www.windows95.com/**

Windows95.com is another graphically intensive page. It contains lots of links to other Windows 95 sites, but you will also find that it has useful information in its own right, such as plenty of 32-bit shareware—particularly for new users.

Tip

Be sure to check out the Internet Hyperglossary, which defines some of the Internet terminology that escapes us all.

Windows 95 Tips

URL address: **http://www.process.com/win95/win95tip.htm**

This Web site contains tips for doing things faster in Windows 95. You will also find tips that involve customizing Windows 95 through the Registry.

Windows 95 Tips and Tricks

URL address: **http://www2.infowest.com/hyper95/get/tricks.html**

Figure H.6 shows why this innovative Web site is different from all the others. It's a Web-based discussion group that has real tips and tricks you can use while working in Windows 95.

FIG. H.6 ⇒

The icon next to each posting indicates what type of posting it is. A light bulb, for example, indicates an idea.

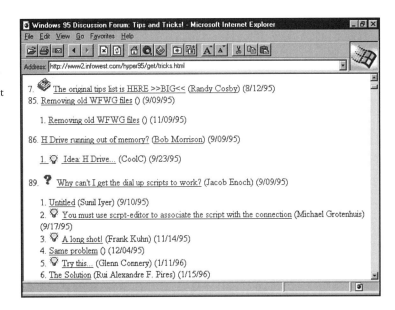

Tip

Tips and Tricks is a rather large Web page. Use your Web browser's search capability to find postings that interest you. In Internet Explorer, choose Edit, Find; type the text you're looking for; and press Enter.

Inside the Windows Registry

URL addresses:

http://www.zdnet.com/~pcmag/issues/1418/pcm00083.htm

http://www.zdnet.com/~pcmag/issues/1419/pcm00116.htm

http://www.zdnet.com/~pcmag/issues/1501/pcm00121.htm

These three Web pages represent a three-part series from *PC Magazine* about the Registry. If you're looking for concise information about the Registry, check these out.

ZD Net Windows 95 Shareware Collection

URL address: **http://www.zdnet.com/~zdi/software/win95/**

Ziff-Davis's site contains some of the best Windows 95 shareware on the Internet. You find applications, utilities, games, and communications programs. You also find some special utilities written by Ziff-Davis just for Windows 95 power users (see fig. H.7).

FIG. H.7

Click one of the categories at the top of the page to see programs in that category.

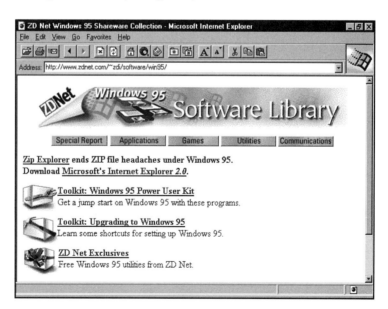

Using the CD-ROM

Using the Self-Test Software

The tests on this CD-ROM consist of performance-based questions. This means that instead of asking you what function an item would fulfill (knowledge-based question), you will be presented with a situation and asked for an answer that shows your ability to solve the problem.

The program consists of three main test structures:

- *Self-Assessment Test*. This would typically be the test you take first. This test is meant to give you a sense of where your strengths and weaknesses are on Windows 95. You will get immediate feedback on your answer. It will either be correct and you will be able to go to next question, or it will be incorrect and the system will recommend what part of the study guide to research and you will be prompted to try again.

+ *Chapter Tests.* After reading a chapter from the study guide, you will have the option to take a mini-test consisting of questions relevant only to the given chapter. You will get immediate feedback on your answer as well as an indication of what subsection to find the answer in should your response be incorrect.

+ *Mastery Test.* This is the big one. This test is different from the two others in the sense that feedback is not given on a question-by-question basis. It simulates the exam situation, so you will give answers to all questions and then get your overall score. In addition to the score, for all wrong answers, you will get pointers as to where in the study guide you need to study further. You will also be able to print a report card featuring your test results.

All test questions are multiple choice, offering three to five possible answers. The answers are labeled A, B, C, D, and E. There may be one, two, or three alternatives representing the right answer; thus, a right answer might be "A & D," or any other combination.

Equipment Requirements

To run the self-test software, you must have *at least* the following equipment:

+ IBM-compatible PC I386

+ Microsoft DOS 5.0

+ Microsoft Windows 3.x

+ 4M of RAM

+ 256-color display adapter

+ Double-speed CD-ROM drive

To take full advantage of the software and run it at a more acceptable speed, however, the following equipment is recommended:

- IBM-compatible I486 DX
- Microsoft Windows 3.1 or better
- 8M of RAM
- 256-color display adapter or better
- Quad-speed CD-ROM drive

Running the Self-Test Software

The self-test software runs directly from the CD-ROM, and does not require you to install any files to your hard drive. After you have followed these simple start-up steps, you will find the software very intuitive and self-explanatory.

If you are using Windows 3.x, Windows NT, or Windows for Workgroups:

1. Insert the disc in your CD drive.
2. Select Run from the File menu of your Windows Program Manager, click on Browse, and select the letter of your CD drive (typically D). Double-click on the file name welcome.exe and the self-test program will be activated.

If you are using Windows 95:

1. Insert the disc in your CD drive.
2. Click the Start button on the Windows 95 Taskbar, select Run, and click Browse. Select My Computer and double-click welcome.exe.

As soon as welcome executes, you will be in the program. Just follow the instructions or click your selections.

App

I

Sample Tests

Using the Self-Tests

The tests in this appendix are performance-based questions designed to test your problem-solving capabilities. The questions are divided into three main test structures:

+ *Self-Assessment Test.* This would typically be the test you take first. This test is meant to give you a sense of where your strengths and weaknesses are on Windows 95.

+ *Chapter Test.* After reading a chapter from the study guide, you will have the option to take a mini-test consisting of questions relevant only to the given chapter. These questions are listed in order of the chapters in this book.

+ *Mastery Test.* This test simulates the exam situation, so you will answer all the questions and then get your overall score.

All test questions are multiple choice, offering three to five possible answers. The answers are labeled A, B, C, D, and E. There may be one, two, or three alternatives representing the right answer; thus, a right answer might be "A & D," or any other combination.

Note These questions also are included on the CD-ROM that accompanies this book. See Appendix I, "Using the CD-ROM," for information on how to access these questions and run the software included with the CD.

Self-Assessment Test

Note The answers to these questions can be found in order at the end of this section. The resource line following each question number is the section in the book where information regarding that question is located. ▦

Question #1

Resource: Chapter 25, "Using Microsoft Exchange"

Microsoft Exchange can be used to send and receive e-mail messages over which online service?

    A. America Online

    B. CompuServe

    C. Prodigy

    D. The Source

App

J

Question #2

Resource: Chapter 13, "Real-Mode Configuration"

If there is not a Win.com command in the Autoexec.bat file, which program will be run directly?

    A. Win.exe

    B. Vmm32.vxd

    C. Vdef.exe

    D. Configure.com

Question #3

Resource: Chapter 24, "Phone Dialer"

When choosing to utilize the Telephone Dialer, which two of the following represent advantages available to you under Windows 95?

    A. The inherent Phone Call Logs the dialer keeps.

    B. As a TAPI application, the Telephone Dialer remembers location information.

C. The Telephone Dialer reminds you of the most economical calling rates.

D. The Telephone Dialer displays time and billing information after each call.

Question #4

Resource: Chapter 18, "NetWare Loadable Module (NLM)"

Netware Loadable Modules can be loaded and unloaded while the Netware 3.x server is running. These Modules are initialized utilizing the load command from the system console. Where in the NetWare 3.x directory structure are NLM files typically stored?

A. SYS:Public

B. SYS:Login

C. SYS:System

D. SYS:NLMs

Question #5

Resource: Chapter 3, "Intel 386DX or Better Processor"

A customer is concerned about the performance of his Windows applications under Windows 95. Upon inspection of his system, you find that the customer is running Windows 95 on an 80386SX processor. What information should the customer be informed of to improve his system performance?

A. Windows 95 will run on an 80386SX processor-based system but will require additional memory than an 80386DX processor-based system and he should upgrade his memory.

B. An 80386SX processor is built as a 32-bit processor on the inside but as a 16-bit processor externally requiring two read requests for each operation and slowing performance. He should upgrade his processor to a minimum of an 80386DX/20.

C. An Intel 80386SX processor is insufficient for running Windows 95 applications and the minimum system requirement is an 80486/33-based system. He should upgrade his processor.

D. An Intel 80386SX processor-based system is more than sufficient for running Windows 95 and performance is probably being affected by the speed of his hard disk drive.

Question #6

Resource: Chapter 10, "Display Resolutions and Color Depth"

When setting up display information under the Display Properties Dialog the Color Palette drop-down box allows you to choose among all of the available color-depth choices for the video card. Of the available options, which is typically the most popular and uses 8 BPP?

A. 16 color

B. 256 color

C. High color

D. True color

Question #7

Resource: Chapter 25, "Microsoft Fax Properties"

The Dialing Properties sheet you to configure how FAX numbers are dialed. What are the two options under this sheet?

A. I'm Dialing From...

B. Time to Send

C. Retries

D. Message Properties

Question #8

Resource: Chapter 7, "Using Disk Compression"

Disk compression in Windows 95 incorporates the use of a large file on the uncompressed drive which contains compressed files. What is this file called?

A. Compressed Volume File

B. Compression File

C. Main File

D. Open File

Question #9
Resource: Chapter 5, "General Protection Faults"

A General Protection Fault is generally caused by an improperly written application. What is the most likely result of this error if it occurs in a 16-bit application?

    A. The system will automatically reboot.

    B. The system will automatically recover.

    C. All applications are suspended until the system is rebooted.

    D. All other 16-bit applications stop running until the GPF dialog box is closed.

Question #10
Resource: Chapter 6, "Defining Plug and Play"

In describing the utilization of Plug and Play components to a customer, the main benefit of taking advantage of Plug and Play technology could be described as what?

    A. The installation process is faster and requires little or no user input.

    B. It allows "legacy drivers" to be integrated with little user input.

    C. It allows for the sharing of IRQs, so more devices may be added to the system.

    D. It allows for one driver to support many devices, thus freeing memory.

Question #11
Resource: Chapter 12, "Using ScanDisk"

The 32-bit version of ScanDisk fully supports long file names, checks for cross-linked files, checks for lost clusters, etc. and can be run in the background while other tasks are being performed. It has two distinct test types that may be selected by the user. From the list below, what are the two types of tests?

    A. Complete

    B. Thorough

C. Full

D. Standard

Question #12

Resource: Chapter 9, "3–4G Reserved System Arena"

The memory area between 0 and 4M is reserved for Real Mode Device Drivers, MS-DOS TSRs and 16-bit applications. What do we refer to this area as?

A. MS-DOS Compatibility Arena

B. Shared Arena

C. Private Arena

D. Reserved System Arena

Question #13

Resource: Chapter 22, "System Policy Editor"

The System Policy Editor is used to create and edit System Policies. The System Policy Editor operates in two modes. What are these modes called?

A. Network Mode

B. Registry Mode

C. File Mode

D. Default Mode

Question #14

Resource: Chapter 4, "Understanding the Registry"

Although the Windows 95 System Registry replaces many of the .ini files used in the previous versions of Windows, it does not replace all of them. Windows 95 still supports .ini files for backwards compatibility with 16-bit applications. Along with the System Registry, which .ini file is read for Windows 95 to determine which drivers to load for a given application?

A. Win.ini

B. Control.ini

C. System.ini

D. Config.ini

Question #15

Resource: Chapter 26, "Out of Directory Entries"

An "Out of Directory Entries" error can occur when many files with long file names exist on the Root Directory where the number of directory entries is fixed. How many directory entries are usually allowed at the Root Directory?

A. 64

B. 128

C. 256

D. 512

Question #16

Resource: Chapter 3, "Key Concept: Detection Log Files"

If the computer fails during Hardware Detection as part of the *normal* setup, Windows 95 creates a file called Detcrash.log that is only readable by Windows 95. This file details exactly what the detection module was running and what it was trying to do at the point of failure. In which equivalent file should you look for a text explanation of this information?

A. Setup.log

B. Detlog.log

C. Detcrash.txt

D. Detlog.txt

Question #17

Resource: Chapter 27, "Microsoft TechNet"

Microsoft TechNet is Microsoft's primary resource for technical professionals. TechNet contains the full Microsoft Knowledge base, training material, drivers, patches, and a host of other vital and changing information, programs, and utilities. The annual subscription entitles the subscriber to how many updates per year?

A. 6

B. 4

C. 1

D. 12

Question #18

Resource: Chapter 10, "Display Resolutions and Color Depth"

Color depth is dependent upon the number of bits used to display the color of each pixel in video memory. This is referred to as bits per pixel or BPP. How many BPP are required to display 256 colors?

A. 4

B. 15

C. 16

D. 8

Question #19

Resource: Chapter 2, "Comparing Windows 95 to Windows NT"

There are typically three questions which you should be able to answer yes to prior to deciding to install Windows NT Workstation instead of Window 95. Which of the following represent the questions that should be asked?

A. Are there drivers under Windows NT for my existing applications?

B. Will my current version of DOS support Windows NT Workstation?

C. Do I have enough resources?

D. Are my applications compatible with Windows NT Workstation?

Question #20

Resource: Chapter 16, "TCP/IP and Windows 95"

You are installing a TCP/IP connection using the Microsoft Installation Wizard provided in Microsoft Plus! for Windows 95. What should you

App

J

investigate as being the most likely reason for a local TCP/IP connection to stop working?

A. The Microsoft Installation Wizard is not using standard routing information.

B. The Microsoft Installation Wizard has replaced the default IP address with a custom IPX address.

C. The Microsoft Installation Wizard has replaced the local TCP/IP values with values for a dial-up provider.

D. The Microsoft Installation Wizard has attempted to store routing information in packets instead of a custom routing file.

Question #21

Resource: Chapter 21, "NetWare Connect (NRN)"

NetWare Connect is a proprietary connection protocol which can be used to dial into a Novell NetWare server. What is the only supported transport protocol that can be used?

A. NetBEUI

B. TCP/IP

C. IPX/SPX

D. SLIP

Question #22

Resource: Chapter 11, "Understanding Printer Drivers"

If printing to a color printer, the Windows 95 printer drivers do not use the monochrome DIB engine. Instead, which DLL file do they use?

A. DIBColor.DLL

B. ColPrint.DLL

C. NewColor.DLL

D. DMColor.DLL

Question #23

Resource: Chapter 16, "Resolving IP Addresses to NetBIOS Names"

You can use either of three existing methods in Windows 95 to resolve NETBIOS names to IP addresses. Of the three, which is preferred because it generates the least amount of network traffic and is dynamic?

    A. WINS

    B. WINNT

    C. Broadcasts

    D. LMHOSTS

Question #24

Resource: Chapter 26, "Examining the Windows 95 Log Files"

Windows 95 is capable of generating a number of log files to help you troubleshoot problems. What information is contained in the Ios.log file found in the Windows folder?

    A. Video driver error information

    B. Startup operating system errors

    C. Error messages from SCSI devices

    D. Registry messages

Question #25

Resource: Chapter 20, "Microsoft Networks"

Whether the installable file system or network redirector is used depends on the type of print function being called. If it is a printing function (i.e., Open Print Job, Write to Print Job, etc.), the call is submitted to which program?

    A. VReDir.vxd

    B. NWReDir.vxd

    C. IFSMGR

    D. Nwpp32.dll

Question #26
Resource: Chapter 3, "Installing over Windows 3.x"

You can set up a Windows 95 installation to Dual Boot between Windows 95 and your previous version of MS-DOS and Windows. Dual Booting in this environment will only work in which of the following situations?

    A. Your previous version of MS-DOS was at least version 5.0 or later.

    B. Your previous version of Windows was at least version 3.10 or later.

    C. You have installed Windows 95 over your existing copy of Windows 3.X.

    D. Your computer is at least an 80486-based system and capable of preemptive multitasking.

Question #27
Resource: Chapter 16, "Default Gateway"

A key advantage of TCP/IP is that it is a routable protocol; that is, it is a protocol which allows the use of routers to interconnect different subnets. TCP/IP packets contain no routing information, only source and destination addresses. TCP/IP can eliminate the need for every computer to maintain a routing table with the routes to every other computer or network on the Internet through the use of which of the following entities?

    A. Default Routers

    B. Default Gateways

    C. Backbone Routers

    D. Backbone Gateway

Question #28
Resource: Chapter 23, "Creating a Shared Installation"

When configuring a shared Windows 95 shared installation and after running the server-based setup, a setup script must be created. Which format must this setup script be created in?

A. Msbatch.inf

B. Msbatch.bin

C. TXT format

D. Registry format

Question #29

Resource: Chapter 21, "Connecting with Dial-Up Networking"

Dial-Up Networking allows your computer to act as a network node while connected to a Dial-Up connection such as an ordinary modem. Which Windows 3.x utility did it replace?

A. Remote Control

B. DialNet

C. WinNet

D. Remote Access Services

App

J

Question #30

Resource: Chapter 13, "Real-Mode Configuration"

To maintain backwards compatibility, the Real Mode Configuration Phase allows the loading of applications and utilities from which two files?

A. The System Registry and System.ini

B. System.dat and System.da0

C. Autoexec.95 and Win.ini

D. Config.sys and Autoexec.bat

Question #31

Resource: Chapter 22, "System Policy Editor"

There are three possible states for each checkbox in the System Policy Editor. What are they?

A. Checked

B. Cleared

C. Checked and grayed

D. Blackened

E. Grayed

Question #32

Resource: Chapter 23, "Running Server-Based Setup"

In addition to having a computer set up and attached to a network server, server-based setup is only available if what other requirement is met?

    A. Microsoft Plus! is installed.

    B. You are running the CD-ROM version.

    C. You are running the floppy version.

    D. You have at least 16 megabytes of memory.

Question #33

Resource: Chapter 24, "Windows 95 Communications Architecture"

VComm provides protected mode services between the Unimodem and Port drives. In addition to allowing Windows applications to access modem and port services, with which Windows driver file does VComm interface to provide communications support to 16-bit Windows applications?

    A. Win.ini

    B. Modem.drv

    C. Comm.drv

    D. Port.drv

Question #34

Resource: Chapter 17, "Browsing the Network"

Windows 95, like other Microsoft networking systems, provides a method of locating shared resources on the network. The method used by Windows 95 is based on the one used by Windows for Workgroups and Windows NT. What is this method called?

    A. Searching

    B. Browsing

    C. Seeking

    D. Identifying

Question #35

Resource: Chapter 10, "Display Drivers"

Through the use of mini-driver technology and Windows 95 Plug and Play capabilities, Windows 95 eases the configuration of display equipment by allowing what to take place?

    A. The limiting of the number of adapters to choose from

    B. Windows 95 automatically detects the display adapter and loads the proper driver.

    C. Windows 95 sets all display adapters to monochrome mode until after installation is complete.

    D. Windows 95 invokes a software graphics accelerator that functions with all supported monitors

Question #36

Resource: Chapter 6, "Hardware Tree and the Registry"

When booting, a Plug and Play BIOS accesses _____ to determine which Plug and Play cards should be enabled; where their option ROMs should be mapped; and what I/O, DMA, and other assignments are to be given to the cards.

    A. nonvolatile RAM

    B. system BIOS

    C. the Plug and Play configuration file

    D. the Registry

Question #37

Resource: Chapter 20, "Installing Network Printers"

Since Windows NT and Windows 95 use different printer drivers, printers attached to an NT server cannot support Point and Print directly. The user will therefore not be prompted for the printer model name if which two conditions exist?

    A. Windows 95 and Windows NT use the same driver name.

    B. Windows 95 and Windows NT use the same inf files.

App

J

C. Windows 95 and Windows NT use different driver names.

D. Windows 95 and Windows NT use different inf files.

Question #38
Resource: Chapter 19, "Device Driver Interface"

Windows 95 supports both ODI and NDIS network device drivers. Although ODI was defined by Novell, why does Windows 95 prefer NDIS 3 drivers instead?

A. They are 32-bit protected mode drivers.

B. They were designed by Microsoft.

C. They are Windows 95-exclusive.

D. They are supported under NT while ODI is not.

Question #39
Resource: Chapter 5, "General Protection Faults"

A General Protection Fault occurs in an MS-DOS application. Since MS-DOS applications all run in separate Virtual Machines, what will happen when the user closes the GPF Dialog?

A. Only the MS-DOS application and its associated Virtual Machine will terminate.

B. All MS-DOS and Windows 16-bit applications will terminate when the GPF Dialog is closed.

C. All applications will terminate and the user will be returned to the startup screen.

D. Only the offending MS-DOS application will terminate. Its associated Virtual Machine will need to be manually reset.

Question #40
Resource: Chapter 9, "Understanding Memory Configuration"

When discussing PC memory, which of the following terms best describes the memory space from above the HMA through the end of Physical Memory?

A. Extended Memory

B. Expanded Memory

C. Conventional Memory

D. Virtual Memory

Question #41

Resource: Chapter 26, "Out of Directory Entries"

Although long file names can be as much as 256 characters, it is recommended that long file names be kept under 50 characters in length. This will prevent the file name from being too long to fit into the complete path statement. What is the total number of characters a complete path statement can be?

A. 1,024

B. 512

C. 260

D. 256

Question #42

Resource: Chapter 11, "Image Color Matching"

Utilizing Image Color Matching, each device's color properties are stored in a profile whose format was determined by a group of hardware vendors and industry standards-setting bodies. Together, this consortium is known as what?

A. ColorSpec

B. KMASS

C. InterColor 3.0

D. Colorgraph 1.0

Question #43

Resource: Chapter 19, "Transport Protocols"

In connecting a Windows 95 computer to a Novell network using the Microsoft Client for NetWare, which compatible transport protocol is required to communicate with a Novell server?

A. IPX/SPX

B. TCP/IP

App

J

C. TCNX

D. NetBEUI

Question #44

Resource: Chapter 17, "Understanding Protocol Support"

What protocol do both the Microsoft Client for Microsoft Networks and File and Printer Sharing for Microsoft Networks support for file sharing?

A. Server Message Block Protocol

B. IPX/SPX

C. Microsoft User Share Protocol

D. Microsoft File Share Protocol

Question #45

Resource: Chapter 12, "Using Disk Defragmenter"

One of the two options under disk defragmenter is "Check Drive For Errors." If this checkbox is checked, what utility will be automatically run?

A. CHKDSK

B. MS Virus Scan

C. ScanDisk

D. MSD

Question #46

Resource: Chapter 7, "SCSI"

Windows 95 includes 32-bit disk drivers for most of the popular SCSI controllers, including those from Adaptec and Future Domain. What are the names of the programs from Adaptec and Future Domain that support SCSI devices?

A. ASPI

B. ADAP

C. FutDom

D. CAM

Question #47

Resource: Chapter 18, "Novell NetWare Basics"

NetWare controls file actions through its File Attributes. These attributes determine whether or not a file may be written to, shared, compressed, deleted, etc. What is another NetWare term for these attributes?

- A. Rights
- B. Privileges
- C. Contexts
- D. Flags

Question #48

Resource: Chapter 14, "Token Ring"

Token Ring is configured as a physical star but is a logical ring, running either 4 MBPS or 16 MBPS network interface cards. In this physical star topology, a central wiring hub is used. By what name do we refer to this Token Ring central wiring hub?

- A. Multi-Station Access Unit (MAU)
- B. Multiple Drop Interface (MDI)
- C. Multiple Connection Unit (MCU)
- D. Multiple Computer Connector (MCC)

Question #49

Resource: Chapter 8, "Preemptive"

Windows 95 utilizes Preemptive Multitasking for 32-bit applications, which means that the operating system controls the Time Slicing function and allocates slices of processor time equally among running applications. The operating system can actually interrupt a running application when its time slice is up. About how long is each time slice?

- A. 20 Milliseconds
- B. 10 Milliseconds
- C. 40 Milliseconds
- D. 60 Milliseconds

App
J

Question #50

Resource: Chapter 15, "Understanding Integrated Networking"

Because Apple Macintosh computers handle files differently than other computer systems, if part of your attached network handles Apple Macintosh computers, which two options do you have to enable sharing files between a Mac and a Windows 95 computer?

    A. Install a Windows NT server.

    B. Configure your Windows 95 workstation for Local Talk.

    C. Run the Mac.exe utility.

    D. Install a Netware server.

Question #51

Resource: Chapter 14, "Thicket (10base5)"

You are designing the cable plant for your 10base5 network. To ensure that segment cable distances are kept within specification, how are the drop cable lengths calculated into the total maximum segment length?

    A. Add the total number of workstations times 2.5 ft. and add to the existing segment length.

    B. Add 50 meters to the total existing segment length to ensure a margin of safety.

    C. Measure each drop cable length and add that total to the existing segment length.

    D. Drop cable lengths are not calculated into the maximum cable length equation.

Question #52

Resource: Chapter 20, "Digital Print Server Support"

The Digital Print Server support under Windows 95 is implemented as a Print Monitor and is streamed to the print server with TCP/IP by the Digital Print Server Port Monitor dll file. What is the name of the Port Monitor dll?

    A. Decpsw4.dll

    B. Decprint.dll

C. Printdec.dll

D. Digportw.dll

Question #53

Resource: Chapter 14, "NDIS"

The initial communications channel between the protocol driver and the MAC driver is established through a process called _____.

A. Loading

B. Linking

C. Binding

D. Attaching

Question #54

Resource: Chapter 23, "Running Server-Based Setup"

When running Server-Based Setup, clicking on Install will open the Source Path dialog box, which contains three options. Under the Install Policy option, if you do not want users to be able to set up their computers as shared installations of Windows 95, what sub-option must you select?

A. Local Hard Drives

B. Server

C. Path to Install Files

D. User's Choice

Question #55

Resource: Chapter 18, "Security"

Netware security is comprised of six categories of security features. They include Login Security, Trustees, Rights, Attributes, Inheritance, and Effective rights. Of these, which feature controls what users have access to files, directories, and other objects?

A. Rights

B. Attributes

C. Trustees

D. Inheritance

Question #56
Resource: Chapter 11, "Location of Printer Components"

Windows 95 stores its printer drivers and spooled print jobs on the hard disk. Where does it store its other printing components?

A. System.ini

B. In Non-Volatile RAM

C. In the Registry

D. Printer.ncf

Question #57
Resource: Chapter 15, "WinNet 16"

Windows 95 supports a single 16-bit WinNet driver for support of a network product not offering 32-bit network support, as well as support for how many 32-bit network providers?

A. 8

B. 6

C. 16

D. 10

Question #58
Resource: Chapter 12, "Using ScanDisk"

One of the options of the Thorough Test under the Windows 95 version of ScanDisk is to Not Repair Sectors in Hidden and System Files. When is it important to utilize this option?

A. If virus protection software has not been run for some time

B. If old software is installed

C. If Microsoft Plus! has been installed

D. If you have selected the Do Not Perform Write Testing option

Question #59
Resource: Chapter 24, "TAPI Services"

When you are installing a modem in Windows 95, the use of TAPI frees applications from each having to know any of the modem settings or command string specifics. Which two of the following represent additional levels of support that are provided under Windows 95 automatically?

A. Call Routing

B. ISDN

C. Selective Answer

D. PBX

Question #60

Resource: Chapter 5, "Drivers"

Real mode Windows drivers are usually loaded from the System.ini file and have a .drv extension. These drivers are 16-bit and intended for earlier versions of Windows. In which folder should you look for these files?

A. C:\Windows

B. C:\Windows\Temp

C. C:\

D. C:\Windows\System

Question #61

Resource: Chapter 2, "Comparing Windows 95 to Windows NT"

When discussing data integrity between Windows 95 and Windows NT Workstation, it is important to explain to a potential customer the inherent ability of Windows NT Workstation to protect against the loss of system data from malicious or naive users by the use of a secure file system. What is this file system called?

A. NTFS

B. Super FAT

C. HTML

D. NTNX

App

J

Question #62

Resource: Chapter 17, "User-Level Security"

When setting up a shared network folder, you may choose from three access types to control user access. What are these three access types called?

A. Read–Only

B. Full

C. Private

D. Partial

E. Depends on Password

Question #63

Resource: Chapter 8, "Thread Scheduling"

Each thread in a Windows 95 environment can be in one of several states. From the list below, select the three most important states that a thread can be in.

A. Waiting

B. Stopped

C. Ready

D. Running

E. Terminated

Question #64

Resource: Chapter 8, "Thread Scheduling"

The Thread Priority Range is divided into 2 ranges: 0–15 and 16–31. Which type of threads are designated in the 0–15 priority range?

A. Real Time

B. Variable Priority

C. High Priority

D. Single Priority

Question #65

Resource: Chapter 7, "Understanding Long File Name Support"

Windows 95 support of long file names allows file names to include spaces, periods, and text strings up to how many characters long?

A. 16

B. 8

C. 256

D. 255

Question #66

Resource: Chapter 4, "Using the Registry Editor"

Because of the potential for damage, Windows 95 does not add the Registry Editor into the Programs folder. If Setup is run from the Windows 95 CD, the Registry Editor is copied into the Windows folder. What file would you look for to start the Registry Editor?

A. Registry.exe

B. Editor.exe

C. EditReg.exe

D. Regedit.exe

Question #67

Resource: Chapter 22, "Registry Editor"

You can use the Registry Editor to edit the Registry on remote computers if both computers are using the same security providers and what other requirement has been met by both computers?

A. Share-Level Security is being used.

B. User-Level Security is being used.

C. Common Profiles exist.

D. User Policies exist.

App

J

Question #68
Resource: Chapter 6, "Plug and Play"

Docking refers to the process by which a mobile computer reestablishes its link to a docking station. Docking typically involves the connecting of additional hardware resources. Windows 95 supports three types of docking. What are they?

  A. Reentrant, removable, portable

  B. Fast, quick, slow

  C. Hot, warm, cold

  D. Connect, attached, functional

Question #69
Resource: Chapter 21, "Mobile Computing"

When configuring a Dial-Up Networking server, there are some security issues you should consider. If running the Dial-Up Networking Server, how should you control who accesses your server?

  A. By using User-Level Security

  B. By using Share-Level Security

  C. By using Connection Dial Back

  D. By limiting telephone number distribution

Question #70
Resource: Chapter 4, "Using the Registry Editor"

The Registry contains six top-level subtrees. Of these subtrees, which of the following contains the configuration settings for all of the hardware devices ever installed on this computer?

  A. HKEY_DYN_DATA

  B. HKEY_CURRENT_CONFIG

  C. HKEY_LOCAL_MACHINE

  D. HKEY_CLASSES_ROOT

Question #71

Resource: Chapter 15, "Windows NP/PP"

Besides allowing access to Novell resources, the Windows 95 NetWare Network Provider and Print Provider provide which two additional functions?

    A. Provide Internet access

    B. Manage security levels

    C. Logging on and off NetWare servers

    D. Queuing print jobs

Answer Key

App

J

Question	Answer	Question	Answer	Question	Answer
1	B	18	D	35	B
2	B	19	A, C, D	36	A
3	A, B	20	C	37	A, B
4	C	21	C	38	A
5	B	22	D	39	A
6	B	23	A	40	A
7	A, C	24	C	41	C
8	A	25	C	42	C
9	D	26	A	43	A
10	A	27	B	44	A
11	B, D	28	A	45	C
12	A	29	D	46	A, D
13	B, C	30	D	47	D
14	C	31	A, B, E	48	A
15	D	32	B	49	A
16	D	33	C	50	A, D
17	D	34	B	51	D

Question	Answer	Question	Answer	Question	Answer
52	A	59	B, D	66	D
53	C	60	D	67	B
54	A	61	A	68	C
55	C	62	A, B, E	69	A
56	C	63	A, C, D	70	C
57	D	64	B	71	C, D
58	B	65	D		

Chapter Tests

Note   The answers to these questions can be found in order at the end of this section. The resource line following each question number is the section or chapter in the book where information regarding that question is located.

Chapter 2

Question #02-01

Resource: Chapter 2, "Exploring Features New to Windows 95"

You should recommend Windows 95 over Windows NT Workstation to a customer who is a heavy traveler for reasons that include which two of the following?

App
J

   A. Plug and Play Support

   B. Remote Networking

   C. NTFS Support

   D. Automatic system failure recovery

Question #02-02

Resource: Chapter 2, "Exploring Features New to Windows 95"

You can more easily identify saved files under Windows 95 than you can under previous versions of DOS and Windows due to what inherent capability?

   A. 8.3 naming conventions

   B. Its ability to handle text files

   C. The new Registry information

   D. Long file name support

Question #02-03

Resource: Chapter 2, "Comparing Windows 95 to Windows NT"

Windows NT is a good solution to suggest for engineering professionals who usually maintain multiple computers on their desks to utilize a

PC for business applications and a UNIX-based computer for technical applications. Why is Windows NT a better solution for this type of user than Windows 95?

A. Windows NT requires a more minimal configuration than Windows 95 and is therefore more cost effective when needing to allow for the expense of a UNIX-based computer.

B. Windows NT for UNIX provides full support of 16-bit Windows device drivers.

C. Windows NT users can combine both types of applications on a single Windows NT workstation, receiving the same performance at a fraction of the cost.

D. Windows NT and UNIX applications are both written as 16-bit applications and are easily interchangeable.

Question #02-04

Resource: Chapter 2, "Comparing Windows 95 to Windows NT"

There are typically three questions that you should be able to answer yes to prior to deciding to install Windows NT Workstation instead of Window 95. Which of the following represent the questions that should be asked?

A. Are there drivers under Windows NT for my existing applications?

B. Will my current version of DOS support Windows NT Workstation?

C. Do I have enough resources?

D. Are my applications compatible with Windows NT Workstation?

Question #02-05

Resource: Chapter 2, "Comparing Windows 95 to Windows NT"

When discussing data integrity between Windows 95 and Windows NT Workstation, it is important to explain to a potential customer the inherent ability of Windows NT Workstation to protect against the loss of system data from malicious or naive users by the use of a secure file system. What is this file system called?

A. NTFS

B. Super FAT

C. HTML

D. NTNX

Question #02-06

Resource: Chapter 2, "Exploring Features New to Windows 95"

In discussing 32-bit application support with a customer, it should be pointed out that both Windows 95 and Windows NT Workstation support 32-bit applications through the use of a common application programming interface. What is this interface called?

A. The Windows programming interface

B. Win32 API

C. Win 16/32 interface

D. Users.dat

Question #02-07

Resource: Chapter 2, "Exploring Features New to Windows 95"

Windows 95 is the first version of Windows to be specifically designed for use on large networks. As such, it offers support for which two of the following?

A. Multiple network clients

B. Multiple stack arrays

C. Multiple processors

D. Multiple network transports

Chapter 3

Question #03-01

Resource: Chapter 3, "Intel 386X or Better Processor"

A customer is concerned about the performance of his Windows applications under Windows 95. Upon inspection of his system you find that the customer is running Windows 95 on an 80386SX processor. What

App

J

information should the customer be informed of to improve his system performance?

A. Windows 95 will run on an 80386SX processor based system but will require more memory than an 80386DX processor based system and he should upgrade his memory.

B. An 80386SX processor is built as a 32-bit processor on the inside but as a 16-bit processor externally requiring 2 read requests for each operation and slowing performance. He should upgrade his processor to a minimum of an 80386DX/20.

C. An Intel 80386SX processor is insufficient for running Windows 95 applications and the minimum system requirement is an 80486/33 based system. He should upgrade his processor.

D. An Intel 80386SX processor-based system is more than sufficient for running Windows 95 and performance is probably being affected by the speed of his hard disk drive.

Question #03-02

Resource: Chapter 3, "Key Concept: How Much RAM did You Say?"

You are installing Windows 95 on an 80386DX system with 4M of RAM and a 9600 baud modem. The system boots fine, but you are unable to access the Microsoft Network. In order to achieve access to the Microsoft Network, you must perform which of the following upgrade procedures?

A. Upgrade the system RAM to a minimum of 8M.

B. Upgrade the system processor to a minimum of an 80486/33 processor.

C. The system configuration is fine and you should investigate the phone line.

D. Upgrade the modem to a minimum of a Hayes Compatible 14400 baud modem.

Question #03-03

Resource: Chapter 3, "The Hardware Compatibility List"

You are upgrading your system hardware to run Windows 95. You want to ensure the highest level of compatibility and performance following your upgrade. You should specifically shop for which of the following hardware designations?

    A. The Double Sigma stamp

    B. Designed for Windows 95

    C. Yes, It Runs Microsoft Windows

    D. Microsoft Windows 95 Compatible

Question #03-04

Resource: Chapter 3, "Installing over Windows 3.x"

App

J

You are installing Windows 95 over a previous version of Windows. Although you will not be able to run your previous version of Windows, which of the following actions will be necessary to run your existing Windows applications?

    A. You will need to upgrade your applications to 32 bit programs but your user preferences will remain unchanged.

    B. Nothing. All of your program groups and most of your user preferences will be migrated automatically.

    C. All of your programs should function normally, but you will need to reconfigure your program groups and user preferences.

    D. Installing over a previous version of Windows will work, but is not recommended since none of your programs or user preferences will function properly.

Question #03-05

Resource: Chapter 3, "Key Concept: Setup Options"

You need to determine which setup option will be adequate for your needs. You have several areas of critical data and require periodic data backups. Either two of the following setup options will provide you with this capability.

A. Compact

B. Custom

C. Portable

D. Typical

Question #03-06

Resource: Chapter 3, "Windows 95 Setup from the User's Perspective"

Using the Setup Wizard, you wish to maintain and migrate your application and group settings from your previous version of Windows. To accomplish this, you must perform which of the following steps?

A. You must install Windows 95 into a separate directory from your previous version of Windows 3.x or Windows for Workgroups and run the Migrate utility.

B. You must install Windows 95 into the same directory as your previous version of Windows 3.x or Windows for Workgroups to migrate your .ini files automatically.

C. You must install Windows 95 into a separate directory from your previous version of Windows 3.x or Windows for Workgroups and manually copy your .grp and .ini files to the new installation.

D. The Setup Wizard will only migrate your group settings. Your application settings will need to be reconfigured manually.

Question #03-07

Resource: Chapter 3, "Invasive Hardware Detection"

After a successful Safe Hardware Detection, Setup begins an Invasive Hardware Detection. The progress indicator in the Analyzing Your Computer dialog box is an indicator of both progress and setup failure. During this operation the Analyzing Your Computer dialog box indicates that the process may take A Long Time. How long should you wait with no movement on the progress indicator before assuming a setup failure?

A. 1 minute

B. 3 minutes

C. 5 minutes

D. 10 minutes or more

Question #03-08

Resource: Chapter 3, "Dual Booting with Windows 3.x"

You can set up a Windows 95 installation to Dual Boot between Windows 95 and your previous version of MS-DOS and Windows. Dual booting in this environment will only work in which of the following situations.

A. Your previous version of MS-DOS was at least version 5.0 or later.

B. Your previous version of Windows was at least version 3.10 or later.

C. You have installed Windows 95 over your existing copy of Windows 3.x.

D. Your computer is at least an 80486-based system and capable of preemptive multitasking.

Question #03-09

Resource: Chapter 3, "Deciding Which Components Get Installed"

When you configure your system for Dual Boot capabilities after installing Windows 95, what does Windows 95 rename Io.sys and Msdos.sys prior to copying them to the root directory of the boot drive?

A. Io.001 and Msdos.001

B. Io.bin and Msdos.bin

C. Io.dos and Msdos.dos

D. Io.old and Msdos.old

Question #03-10

Resource: Chapter 3, "Key Concept: Detection Log Files"

If the computer fails during Hardware Detection as part of the *normal* setup, Windows 95 creates a file called Detcrash.log, which is only readable by Windows 95. This file details exactly what the detection module

App

J

was running and what it was trying to do at the point of failure. In which equivalent file should you look for a text explanation of this information?

    A. Setup.log

    B. Detlog.log

    C. Detcrash.txt

    D. Setuplog.txt

Chapter 4

Question #04-01
Resource: Chapter 4, "Understanding the Registry"

Although the Windows 95 System Registry replaces many of the .ini files used in the previous versions of Windows, it does not replace all of them. Windows 95 still supports .ini files for backwards compatibility with 16-bit applications. Along with the System Registry, which .ini file is read for Windows 95 to determine which drivers to load for a given application?

    A. Win.ini

    B. Control.ini

    C. System.ini

    D. Config.ini

Question #04-02
Resource: Chapter 4, "Understanding the Registry"

Physically, the Registry is divided into two files—one containing settings specific to the computer and one containing settings specific to the user. Of the following, which two file names represent the names of these files?

    A. System.dat

    B. User.dat

    C. Computer.dat

    D. Network.dat

Question #04-03

Resource: Chapter 4, "Understanding the Registry"

The Registry contains six top-level subtrees. Of these subtrees, which of the following contains the configuration settings for all of the hardware devices ever installed on this computer?

A. HKEY_DYN_DATA

B. HKEY_CURRENT_CONFIG

C. HKEY_LOCAL_MACHINE

D. HKEY_CLASSES_ROOT

Question #04-04

Resource: Chapter 4, "Understanding the Registry"

The three properties of registry values are name, data type, and value. In which of the following values would you expect to find a value that is limited to a maximum of 4 bytes in size?

A. Binary

B. String

C. Entry

D. Dword

App

J

Question #04-05

Resource: Chapter 4, "Using the Registry Editor"

Because of the potential for damage, Windows 95 does not add the Registry Editor into the Programs Folder. If setup is run from the Windows 95 CD, the Registry Editor is copied into the Windows folder. What file would you look for to start the Registry Editor?

A. Registry.exe

B. Editor.exe

C. EditReg.exe

D. Regedit.exe

Question #04-06

Resource: Chapter 4, "Working with the Control Panel"

With the desktop themes option of the Windows 95 Control Panel you can select various themes, which include wallpaper, sounds, cursors, etc. This option is only available if you have met which of the following criteria?

A. Themes.com has been installed.

B. Microsoft Plus! has been installed.

C. Sound for Windows 95 has been installed.

D. The Multimedia extension has been installed.

Question #04-07

Resource: Chapter 4, "Working with the Control Panel"

The International option under Windows 3.x controlled locally defined settings such as currency symbols and the date display format. Which Windows 95 Control Panel option would you now use to control these functions?

A. Display

B. Regional Settings

C. ODBC

D. Accessibility Options

Question #04-08

Resource: Chapter 4, "Working with the Control Panel"

If you have installed the Microsoft Internet Jump-start Kit, there is a Windows 95 Control Panel option which allows you to choose how you want to connect to the Internet. Which of the following options would you utilize to configure these settings?

A. Internet

B. Mail and Fax

C. Microsoft Mail Post Office

D. Network

Question #04-09

Resource: Chapter 4, "Working with the Control Panel"

When you are viewing the status of installed components under the Windows Setup tab, the check boxes next to each available component have three states: a check mark in the check box, a check mark in a filled-in check box, and an empty check box. How would you interpret a check mark in a filled-in check box?

    A. All of a component's sub-components are installed.

    B. Only some of a component's sub-components are installed.

    C. None of a component's sub-components is installed.

    D. The component is not available for installation.

Question #04-10

Resource: Chapter 4, "Adding and Removing Windows 95 Components and Applications"

The final tab in the Add/Remove Software option is the Setup Disk tab, which allows you to create a startup disk. Which two of the following files would you expect to be included on the startup disk?

    A. Command.com

    B. EBD.sys

    C. Config.sys

    D. Autoexec.bat

Chapter 5

Question #05-01

Resource: Chapter 5, "Virtual Machines in Windows 95"

Which of the following represents the best way to visualize a Virtual Machine?

    A. A Virtual Machine is a function of Windows 95 used for accessing 32-bit DLL files.

    B. A Virtual Machine is a protected mode function that is reserved for running only Windows 95 32-bit applications.

App

J

C. A Virtual Machine is an unaddressed computer on the network which handles network printing and routing functions.

D. A Virtual Machine is an environment set up in memory by the operating system, which appears as a complete computer with all necessary resources.

Question #05-02

Resource: Chapter 5, "Hung 16-Bit Windows Applications"

A 16-bit application hangs and eventually all other 16-bit applications hang. What is the best way to recover from this event?

A. Reboot the system and restart Windows 95.

B. Perform a local reset and terminate the application.

C. Wait until Windows 95 releases the hung application automatically.

D. Perform a series of local resets and terminate all 16-bit applications.

Question #05-03

Resource: Chapter 5, "General Protection Faults"

A General Protection Fault is generally caused by an improperly written application. What is the most likely result of this error if it occurs in a 16-bit application?

A. The system will automatically reboot.

B. The system will automatically recover.

C. All applications are suspended until the system is rebooted.

D. All other 16-bit applications stop running until the GPF dialog box is closed.

Question #05-04

Resource: Chapter 5, "General Protection Faults"

A General Protection Fault occurs in an MS-DOS application. Since MS-DOS Applications all run in separate Virtual Machines, what will happen when the user closes the GPF dialog box?

A. Only the MS-DOS application and its associated Virtual Machine will terminate.

B. All MS-DOS and Windows 16-bit applications will terminate when the GPF dialog box is closed.

C. All applications will terminate and the user will be returned to the startup screen.

D. Only the offending MS-DOS application will terminate. Its associated Virtual Machine will need to be manually reset.

Question #05-05

Resource: Chapter 5, "Ring '0' and Ring '3' "

The architecture of the Intel 80386 Microprocessor defines four privilege levels, which are designed to protect data and code from being damaged by less privileged code. Of these four levels, 0 through 3, in which two does Microsoft Windows 95 function?

App

J

A. 0

B. 1

C. 2

D. 3

Question #05-06

Resource: Chapter 5, "Kernel Functions"

In troubleshooting a Windows installation, it is important to know the underlying core system functions. Windows 95, like Windows 3.X, contains three core components. These components are Kernel, GDI, and User. The Windows 95 Kernel is responsible for which three of the following basic operating system functions?

A. Managing Virtual Memory

B. File security

C. Task scheduling

D. File I/O services

E. Video addressing

Question #05-07

Resource: Chapter 5, "Windows 95 Core Components"

Each of the Core Components contains both 16-bit and 32-bit DLL (Dynamic Link Libraries) files. 16-bit applications require 16-bit DLLs; however, the Kernel is entirely 32-bit. What is the process called by which a 16-bit DLL calls the 32-bit DLL to implement a desired function?

   A. Thinking

   B. Thunking

   C. Rectifying

   D. Rotating

Question #05-08

Resource: Chapter 5, "Other System DLLs"

Microsoft Windows 95 utilizes an array of Dynamic Link Libraries and Device Drivers to perform its various inherent functions. Other than the 16- and 32-bit DLLs associated with the Core Components, which of the following represent other important system DLLs?

   A. VXD

   B. OLE

   C. Multimedia

   D. WinSum

Question #05-09

Resource: Chapter 5, "Drivers"

Real mode Windows drivers are usually loaded from the System.ini file and have a .drv extension. These drivers are 16-bit and intended for earlier versions of Windows. In which directory should you look for these files?

   A. C:\Windows

   B. C:\Windows\Temp

   C. C:\

   D. C:\Windows\System

Question #05-10

Resource: Chapter 5, "Drivers"

Windows uses a minidriver approach to most of the common device drivers. In this approach, a portion of the device driver is common code written by Microsoft. How would you describe the minidriver portion of the device driver?

    A. A universal, device-independent piece of code designed to work with a family of products.

    B. A device-specific portion of code written by the hardware device's manufacturer.

    C. A common piece of code written by a group of manufacturers to address common interfacing problems.

    D. A piece of code developed by Microsoft with the device manufacturer's input.

App
J

Chapter 6

Question #06-01

Resource: Chapter 6, "Defining Plug and Play"

In describing the utilization of Plug and Play components to a customer the main benefit of Plug and Play technology could be described as what?

    A. The installation process is faster and requires little or no user input.

    B. It allows legacy drivers to be integrated with little user input.

    C. It allows for the sharing of IRQs, so more devices may be added to the system.

    D. It allows for one driver to support many devices, thus freeing memory.

Question #06-02

Resource: Chapter 6, "Hardware Tree and the Registry"

When booting, a Plug and Play BIOS accesses _____ to determine which Plug and Play cards should be enabled, where their option ROMs should be mapped, and what I/O, DMA, and other assignments are to be given to the cards.

    A. nonvolatile RAM

    B. System BIOS

    C. the Plug and Play configuration file

    D. the Registry

Question #06-03

Resource: Chapter 6, "Understanding the Plug and Play Process"

To configure an adapter for Plug and Play, Windows automatically configures _____ for Plug and Play-compliant adapters.

    A. IRQ, DMA, and I/O Port

    B. IRQ, BIOS, and DMA

    C. DMA, BIOS, and NVRAM

    D. SRAM, IRQ, DMA, and I/O Port

Question #06-04

Resource: Chapter 6, "Understanding the Plug and Play Process"

During the hardware detection phase, Windows 95 analyzes the system and builds a database of the information that it finds and stores it in the

_____.

    A. Registry

    B. Plug and Play

    C. System.ini

    D. BIOS

Question #06-05

Resource: Chapter 6, "Hot Docking"

Plug and Play allows "hot docking." What represents three benefits of this feature?

    A. The operating system allows for pre-boot configuration for different configurations.

B. The operating system recognizes the new device automatically.

C. Applications are notified about dynamic events.

D. Changing configuration files and restarting the computer is not needed.

E. It is necessary to run Setup each time new hardware is added.

Question #06-06

Resource: Chapter 6, "Defining Plug and Play"

When discussing the available hardware devices for Windows 95, "Legacy" equipment describes what?

A. A pre-Plug and Play Device

B. A device designed to enable for hot docking

C. A device designed for advanced disk space management

D. A device that can be shared between Windows 95 and Windows NT

Question #06-07

Resource: Chapter 6, "Understanding Docking"

Docking refers to the process by which a mobile computer reestablishes its link to a docking station. Docking typically involves the connecting of additional hardware resources. Windows 95 supports three types of docking. What are they?

A. Reentrant, removable, portable

B. Fast, quick, slow

C. Hot, warm, cold

D. Connect, attached, functional

Question #06-08

Resource: Chapter 6, "Configuration Mode"

During configuration, the Plug and Play software uses three 8 bit I/O ports to send commands to any present Plug and Play adapters. What do we call the series of commands that causes the adapters to activate their Plug and Play logic circuits?

App

J

    A. The Activation Key

    B. The Initiation Key

    C. The Startup Key

    D. The Ramp-Up Key

Question #06-09

Resource: Chapter 6, "Operating System"

In order for a Computer System to be considered as a Plug and Play system it must have three major components. Identify these from the list below.

    A. Plug and Play BIOS

    B. Plug and Play hardware

    C. Manual setup capabilities

    D. Plug and Play operating system

    E. Third-party Plug and Play configuration utilities

Question #06-10

Resource: Chapter 6, "Device Manager"

The Device Manager is the primary tool used to modify configurations. It is accessed from the System option in the Control Panel. What are the two available views for viewing devices under the Device Manager?

    A. Type

    B. Response

    C. Alternate

    D. Connection

    E. Primary

Chapter 7

Question #07-01

Resource: Chapter 7, "Exploring the Installable File System Manager (IFSMGR)"

Multiple file systems can coexist on a Windows 95 computer because of which of its architectural features?

    A. Multitasking capabilities

    B. Installable File System

    C. DiskTSD driver support

    D. Virtual Machine Emulation

Question #07-02

Resource: Chapter 7, "Virtual Fat (VFAT)"

Windows 95's primary file system is a virtualized MS-DOS file system, which is implemented entirely in 32-bit code and cannot be disabled. What is this file system called?

App

J

    A. Vcache

    B. NDIS

    C. VFAT

    D. NDFS

Question #07-03

Resource: Chapter 7, "Volume Tracker"

Windows 95 tracks removable media to make sure that the correct media is in the drive. How does Windows 95 accomplish this with write-protected media?

    A. It caches the disk's label, serial number, and BIOS parameter block.

    B. It adds a unique ID in the disk's FAT header.

    C. It builds a database table to track the media's volume serial number.

    D. It asks the user to supply information on all write-protected media used.

Question #07-04

Resource: Chapter 7, "Port Drivers"

Port Drivers are 32 bit protected mode drivers that communicate with a specific disk device. Which Windows 3.1 driver are they similar to?

A. Vcache

B. FastDisk

C. EMM386

D. Vdisk

Question #07-05

Resource: Chapter 7, "SCSI"

Windows 95 includes 32-bit disk drivers for most of the popular SCSI controllers, including those from Adaptec and Future Domain. What are the names of the programs from Adaptec and Future Domain that support SCSI devices?

A. ASPI

B. ADAP

C. FutDom

D. CAM

Question #07-06

Resource: Chapter 7, "Key Concept: Long File Names"

Windows 95 support of long file names allows file names to include spaces, periods, and text strings up to how many characters long?

A. 16

B. 8

C. 256

D. 255

Question #07-07

Resource: Chapter 7, "Understanding Long File Name Support"

To maintain compatability with applications that expect eight-character names with three-character extensions, Windows 95 automatically generates 8.3 names for each long file name created. What are these names known as?

A. 8.3 names

B. Shortnames

C. Standard names

D. Normal names

Question #07-08

Resource: Chapter 7, "Backup Tools"

To facilitate the use of a backup tool that does not preserve long file names, Windows 95 provides a utility on the Windows 95 CD, which copies the long file names to a file. What is this file called?

A. Lfnbk.exe

B. Lfn283.exe

C. 8_3.exe

D. LongBack.exe

Question #07-09

Resource: Chapter 7, "Using Disk Compression"

Which type of disk compression does Windows 95 utilize in its inherent DriveSpace utility?

A. Real Time

B. Cache Compressed

C. Delayed

D. Token Sector

Question #07-10

Resource: Chapter 7, "Using Disk Compression"

Disk compression in Windows 95 incorporates the use of a large file on the uncompressed drive, which contains compressed files. What is this file called?

A. Compressed Volume File

B. Compression File

C. Main File

D. Open File

App

J

Chapter 8

Question #08-01

Resource: Chapter 8, "Understanding Process versus Thread"

A Process is one or more operating system resources such as code, data, pipes, files, etc., that make up an executing application. What is the name of the base entity that executes Process code?

A. Executor

B. Thread

C. Implementor

D. Initializer

Question #08-02

Resource: Chapter 8, "Multitasking"

Windows 95 is referred to as a multitasking operating system, which creates the illusion of multiple applications executing at once. How does Windows 95 accomplish this?

A. By splitting the CPU and allocating equal portions of the processor to each running application

B. Through its ability to use multiple processors

C. By rapidly switching processor control between all running applications

D. By executing threads two at a time

Question #08-03

Resource: Chapter 8, "Preemptive"

Windows 95 utilizes Preemptive Multitasking for 32 bit applications, which means that the operating system controls the time slicing function and allocates slices of processor time equally among running applications. The operating system can actually interrupt a running application when its time slice is up. About how long is each time slice?

A. 20 Milliseconds

B. 10 Milliseconds

   C. 40 Milliseconds

   D. 60 Milliseconds

Question #08-04

Resource: Chapter 8, "Cooperative"

Previous versions of Windows utilized Cooperative Multitasking, in which each application is required to relinquish control to the operating system either explicitly or when the application checks the message queue. What is an inherent application problem in this environment?

   A. The operating system loses track of running applications.

   B. Only two applications can run at the same time.

   C. A process priority must be set for each application.

   D. The application can "hog" the processor.

Question #08-05

Resource: Chapter 8, "Thread Priorities"

Every thread in a Windows 95 system has an associated priority, which the scheduler uses to determine which thread to allow to run next. Thread priorities can range from 0 on the low end to what value on the high end?

   A. 20

   B. 42

   C. 31

   D. 56

Question #08-06

Resource: Chapter 8, "Thread Scheduling"

Each thread in a Windows 95 environment can be in one of several states. From the list below, select the three most important states that a thread can be in.

   A. Waiting

   B. Stopped

App

J

    C. Ready

    D. Running

    E. Terminated

Question #08-07

Resource: Chapter 8, "Thread Scheduling"

The VMM schedules threads based on a 32-level priority mechanism. This is done to maintain compatibility with which other operating system?

    A. Windows 3.X

    B. MS-DOS

    C. OS/2

    D. Windows NT

Question #08-08

Resource: Chapter 8, "Thread Scheduling"

The Thread Priority Range is divided into two ranges: 0-15 and 16-31. Which type of threads are designated in the 0-15 priority range?

    A. Real Time

    B. Variable Priority

    C. High Priority

    D. Single Priority

Question #08-09

Resource: Chapter 8, "Secondary Scheduler"

The VMM is divided into two schedulers: the Primary Scheduler and the Secondary Scheduler. Which scheduling function is associated with the Secondary Scheduler?

    A. Ensuring that the highest-priority thread runs first

    B. Ensuring that no thread "hogs" the scheduler

    C. Determining which thread runs first if two share the same priority

    D. Ensuring that no two threads run at the same time

Question #08-10

Resource: Chapter 8, "Synchronization"

Windows 95 uses Synchronization Objects to synchronize operations between multiple threads. Which two additional functions are Synchronization Objects used for?

    A. Protecting a resource from being used by more than one thread at a time

    B. Ensuring that an object can only be used by the threads of a single process

    C. Signaling another thread that an event has occurred

    D. Providing exclusive access to a shared resource

Chapter 9

Question #09-01

Resource: Chapter 9, "Understanding Memory Configuration"

When discussing PC Memory, which of the following terms best describes the memory space from above the HMA through the end of Physical Memory?

    A. Extended Memory

    B. Expanded Memory

    C. Conventional Memory

    D. Virtual Memory

Question #09-02

Resource: Chapter 9, "Understanding Memory Configuration"

Unused regions within the Upper Memory Area are called UMBs (Upper Memory Blocks). These can be used to store MS-DOS device, drivers, thus freeing up additional conventional memory. Which two of the following processors would you require to take advantage of this function?

    A. 8086

    B. 80286

C. 80386

D. 80486

Question #09-03

Resource: Chapter 9, "Understanding Memory Configuration"

Bank Switching makes EMS possible by switching memory in and out of a page frame one piece of memory at a time. How big is the piece of memory that is used for Bank Switching?

A. 32K

B. 64K

C. 16K

D. 256K

Question #09-04

Resource: Chapter 9, "Memory Drivers"

In a Demand Paged Virtual Memory System, an application's code and data can be larger than the system's physical memory. This is accomplished by swapping out data which is not being utilized with data that is immediately required. Where is this data swapped out and stored to?

A. A temporary file on disk

B. The HMA

C. Extended Memory

D. Conventional Memory

Question #09-05

Resource: Chapter 9, "Virtual Address Spaces"

Each Windows 95 process is allocated a unique virtual address space of 4G. Of this 4G of virtual address space, how much is set aside for the process' storage requirements?

A. 1G

B. 2G

C. 3G

D. 4G

Question #09-06

Resource: Chapter 9, "Swap Files"

The Windows 95 swap file provides the best features and functionality of both the temporary and permanent swap files under Windows 3.x. Which two of the following best explain why?

    A. It is dynamic.

    B. Is a contiguous memory block.

    C. It is static.

    D. It can exist on a compressed volume.

Question #09-07

Resource: Chapter 9, "Pages versus Segments"

In addition to the memory support provided by the Windows 95 Linear Addressing Model, how much private, addressable memory space can each 32-bit windows application access?

    A. 4G

    B. 1G

    C. 2G

    D. 3G

Question #09-08

Resource: Chapter 9, "Virtual Memory Manager"

The Windows 95 Virtual Memory Driver is a Ring 0 Service provided by the Windows 95 Kernel. The VMM provides which of the following two functions?

    A. Memory Allocation

    B. Video Memory Swapping

    C. Paging

    D. Virtual Caching

Question #09-09

Resource: Chapter 9, "2–3G DLLs and Shared Objects (Shared Arena)"

App

J

In the memory space between 2G and 3G, Windows 95 maps core system components, shared DLLs, and 16 bit Widows applications. Which of the following represent file names of two of the 32-bit shared DLLs mapped to this area?

A. User32.dll

B. Kernel.dll

C. Memory.dll

D. Cache32.dll

Question #09-10

Resource: Chapter 9, "3–4G reserved system arena"

The memory area between 0 and 4M is reserved for real mode device drivers, MS-DOS TSRs, and 16-bit applications. What do we refer to this area as?

A. MS-DOS Compatibility Arena

B. Shared Arena

C. Private Arena

D. Reserved System Arena

Chapter 10

Question #10-01

Resource: Chapter 10, "Display Drivers"

Through the use of minidriver technology and Windows 95 Plug and Play capabilities, Windows 95 eases the configuration of display equipment by allowing what to take place?

A. The limiting of the number of adapters to choose from.

B. Windows 95 automatically detects the display adapter and loads the proper driver.

C. Windows 95 sets all display adapters to monochrome mode until after installation is complete.

D. Windows 95 invokes a software graphics accelerator that functions with all supported monitors.

Question #10-02

Resource: Chapter 10, "Display Drivers"

The DIB engine (Device Independent Bitmap), is responsible for all in-memory graphics operations and on-screen operations that are not handled by accelerator hardware on the adapter. The engine allows for fast drawing on what two types of display adapters?

A. High-resolution adapters

B. Non-interlaced adapters

C. Frame buffer-based adapters

D. Frame-interlaced adapters

Question #10-03

Resource: Chapter 10, "Display Drivers"

When a Windows 95 display driver fails to load or initialize, the system employs a mechanism which uses a generic VGA driver to allow access to the system. What is this mechanism referred to?

A. Generic VGA

B. VGA Always

C. VGA Fallback

D. Generic Viewing

Question #10-04

Resource: Chapter 10, "Display Resolutions and Color Depth"

Color depth is dependent upon the number of bits that are used to display the color of each pixel in video memory. This is referred to as bits per pixel or BPP. How many BPP are required to display 256 colors?

A. 4

B. 15

C. 16

D. 8

App

J

Question #10-05

Resource: Chapter 10, "Display Resolutions and Color Depth"

When setting up display information under the Display Properties dialog, the Color Palette drop-down box allows you to choose among all of the available color depth choices for the video card. Of the available options, which is typically the most popular and uses 8 BPP?

A. 16 color

B. 256 color

C. High color

D. True color

Question #10-06

Resource: Chapter 10, "Display Resolutions and Color Depth"

The desktop slidebar allows you to select the resolution used for the display. The selections are dynamic unless a change of driver or color depth is required. In that case what will it be necessary to do?

A. Restart the computer.

B. Reload the Windows display drivers.

C. Reload Windows.

D. Close and reopen the desktop.

Question #10-07

Resource: Chapter 10, "Monitor Type"

In addition to setting the display type, Windows 95 recognizes a monitor type. You should manually set the monitor type to match your monitor. What does Windows 95 use this information for?

A. Prompting you for a proper disk to use to install the correct driver

B. Determining which display resolution to make available to you

C. Automatically determining the color depth

D. Recommending the optimum palette settings

Question #10-08

Resource: Chapter 10, "Monitor Type"

The display monitor is typically the largest consumer of electrical power in a computer system. Windows 95 can assist in the limiting of power consumption through the use of energy-management functionality if your monitor conforms to what specification?

A. U.S. Energy Specification

B. Universal Energy Control Specification (UECS)

C. Energy Star Specification

D. Microsoft Energy Control Specification (MECS)

Question #10-09

Resource: Chapter 10, "Monitor Type"

Plug and Play monitors conform to the VESA Display Data Channel Specification or DDC. A combination of a DDC monitor and adapter allows the display drivers to automatically set display information including which two of the following?

A. Refresh Rate

B. Image Color Matching

C. True Color Synchronization

D. Absolute Color Processing

Question #10-10

Resource: Chapter 10, "Display Resolutions and Color Depth"

The Color Palette drop-down box allows you to choose among all of the color depth choices for the video card regardless of resolution. What is the highest color depth level?

A. 16 color

B. 256 color

C. High Color

D. True Color

App

J

Chapter 11

Question #11-01

Resource: Chapter 11, "Bidirectional Communications"

Which two of the following represent mandatory requirements for using Bidirectional Communications with your printer?

    A. Use an IEEE 1284-compliant printer cable.

    B. Install a third-party bidirectional communications utility.

    C. Run Bidirect.exe.

    D. Have a bidirectional printer.

Question #11-02

Resource: Chapter 11, "Plug and Play Support"

Of the following, select two times at which Windows 95 will check for a Plug and Play printer.

    A. Every 10 minutes

    B. During Setup

    C. During Post

    D. During Windows 95 Boot Sequence

Question #11-03

Resource: Chapter 11, "Image Color Matching"

The Image Color Matching technology Microsoft utilizes in Windows 95 increases the consistency of displayed and printed colors. Who owns this technology?

    A. IBM

    B. Kodak

    C. Sony

    D. Mitsubishi

Question #11-04

Resource: Chapter 11, "Image Color Matching"

Utilizing Image Color Matching, each device's color properties are stored in a profile whose format was determined by a group of hardware vendors and industry standards setting bodies. Together, this consortium is known as what?

A. ColorSpec

B. KMASS

C. InterColor 3.0

D. Colorgraph 1.0

Question #11-05

Resource: Chapter 11, "Printing Devices"

If printing to a color printer, the Windows 95 printer drivers do not use the monochrome DIB engine. Instead, which DLL file do they use?

A. DIBColor.dll

B. ColPrint.dll

C. NewColor.dll

D. DMColor.dll

Question #11-06

Resource: Chapter 11, "Windows 95 Printer driver Enhancements"

Windows 95 printer drivers allow you to use up to 32 characters to describe your printer in human, sensible terms. What is the feature referred to as?

A. Friendly Names

B. Printer ID

C. Printer Direct

D. Happy Names

Question #11-07

Resource: Chapter 11, "Location of Printing Components"

Windows 95 stores its printer drivers and spooled print jobs on the hard disk. Where does it store its other printing components?

A. System.ini

B. In Non-Volatile RAM

C. In the Registry

D. Printer.ncf

App

J

Question #11-08

Resource: Chapter 11, "Image Color Matching"

There are three color rendering intents which control how Image Color Matching matches colors. Identify them from the list below.

   A. Brightness

   B. Colorimetric

   C. Contrast

   D. Saturation

   E. Sparcity

Question #11-09

Resource: Chapter 11, "Working with the Printers Folder"

In the Printers folder, every printer is shown along with a visual status que. What does an image of a disk represent?

   A. A local printer

   B. A printer printing to a file

   C. A network printer

   D. An offline printer

Question #11-10

Resource: Chapter 11, "Installing and Managing Printers"

There are two ways in which a printer is installed under Windows 95. One is for the users to explicitly choose it. What is the other way?

   A. By default in Setup

   B. By using the generic printer option

   C. By Plug and Play

   D. By converting from Windows 3.x

Chapter 12

Question #12-01

Resource: Chapter 12, "Using Windows 95's Disk Utilities"

Windows 95 contains several disk utilities for managing disk data storage and recovery. Disk utilities provided with previous versions of

MS–DOS or Windows should never be used because of what Windows 95 feature?

    A. Long file name support

    B. Preemptive Multitasking

    C. The new System Registry

    D. The new directory structure

Question #12-02

Resource: Chapter 12, "Using ScanDisk"

The 32 bit version of ScanDisk fully supports long file names, checks for cross-linked files, checks for lot clusters, etc., and can be run in the background while other tasks are being performed. It has two distinct test types, which may be selected by the user. From the list below, what are the two types of tests?

    A. Complete

    B. Thorough

    C. Full

    D. Standard

Question #12-03

Resource: Chapter 12, "Using ScanDisk"

The choosing of the Thorough test enables several options such as which part of the disk you would like to scan along with two additional options. From the list below, what are these two additional options?

    A. Do not perform write testing.

    B. Write corrections to a disk file.

    C. Do not repair bad sectors in hidden and system files.

    D. Confirm all corrections.

Question #12-04

Resource: Chapter 12, "Using ScanDisk"

One of the options of the Thorough Test under the Windows 95 version of ScanDisk is to Not Repair Sectors in Hidden and System Files. When is it important to utilize this option?

App

J

A. If virus–protection software has not been run for some time

B. If old software is installed

C. If Microsoft Plus! has been installed

D. If you have selected the Do Not Perform Write Testing option

Question #12-05

Resource: Chapter 12, "Using ScanDisk"

One of the available options under Advanced Options is to determine how to handle cross-linked files. This sub-option determines whether to delete both files which are cross-linked, copy the contents of both files to a new file, or ignore the whole process. Of these options, which provides the highest possibility of data recovery?

A. Delete

B. Copy to

C. Ignore

D. None of the above

Question #12-06

Resource: Chapter 12, "Using ScanDisk"

The Check Files For option under Advanced Options in the Windows 95 version of ScanDisk checks files for invalid names and/or invalid dates and times. What might be the effect of a file with an invalid date and time?

A. It cannot be saved correctly.

B. It cannot be opened properly.

C. It will not sort correctly.

D. It cannot be backed up.

Question #12-07

Resource: Chapter 12, "Using Backup"

To guard against a data disaster the first time you run Microsoft Backup from the System Tools folder, the Windows 95 Backup utility performs a scan of your system hardware and creates an appropriate primary backup set. What is this backup set named?

A. Backup Disk

B. Full System Backup

C. First Backup

D. Win95 Backup

Question #12-08
Resource: Chapter 12, "Using Backup"

Under the Backup Settings of Microsoft Backup there are three sets of settings that you may configure by choosing the Settings option from the menu bar. What are two of these settings?

A. File Sorting

B. File Filtering

C. Drop and Drag

D. File Grooming

App
J

Question #12-09
Resource: Chapter 12, "Using Disk Defragmenter"

One of the two options under the Disk Defragmenter is "Check Drive For Errors." If this check box is checked, what utility will be automatically run?

A. CHKDSK

B. MS Virus Scan

C. ScanDisk

D. MSD

Question #12-10
Resource: Chapter 12, "Using Disk Defragmenter"

Over time, a disk can become fragmented; that is, the disk data is written over a wide area of the disk. What is a primary effect of disk fragmentation?

A. Data corruption

B. Disk performance will deteriorate

C. Backup will be difficult to verify

D. Directory will not be sorted

Chapter 13

Question #13-01

Resource: Chapter 13, "Real Mode Operating System Compatibility Phase"

The booting of Windows 95 Protected Mode Operating System is broken down into four distinct phases. During which phase does the loading of MS-DOS drivers occur?

A. Bootstrapping Phase

B. Real Mode Compatibility Phase

C. Static VXD Loading Phase

D. Protected Mode Operating System Loading Phase

Question #13-02

Resource: Chapter 13, "Bootstrap Phase"

Following the running of the Power On Self Test by the bootstrap code, computers with a Plug and Play BIOS perform some steps prior to looking for a boot device. The first step of the Plug and Play configuration process looks for Plug and Play configuration information. Where does the Plug and Play BIOS look for these configuration settings?

A. In Non-Volatile RAM

B. In a disk-based configuration file

C. In the System BIOS

D. In the System Registry

Question #13-03

Resource: Chapter 13, "Real Mode Operating System Compatibility Phase"

As part of the Real Mode Compatibility Phase, the disk boot program reads Io.sys from the root directory into memory. Io.sys then loads a minimal program which, aside from loading the opening graphic logo information, is capable of only reading which file?

A. Command.com

B. The System Registry

C. Msdos.sys

D. Autoexec.bat

Question #13-04

Resource: Chapter 13, "Real Mode Configuration"

To maintain backwards compatibility, the Real Mode Configuration Phase allows the loading of applications and utilities from which two files?

A. The System Registry and System.ini

B. System.dat and System.dao

C. Autoexec.95 and Win.ini

D. Config.sys and Autoexec.bat

App

J

Question #13-05

Resource: Chapter 13, "Real Mode Configuration"

If there is not a Win.Com command in the Autoexec.Bat file, which program will be run directly?

A. Win.exe

B. VMM32.VxD

C. VDEF.exe

D. Configure.com

Chapter 14

Question #14-01

Resource: Chapter 14, "Examining the ISO OSI Model"

In 1983, the ISO defined a networking model referred to as the OSI (Open Systems Interconnect). This model is divided into layers and describes the flow of information between the physical network and applications. How many layers make up the OSI Reference Model?

A. 4

B. 5

C. 7

D. 8

Question #14-02

Resource: Chapter 14, "Examining the ISO OSI Model"

Each layer of the OSI Model provides a specific function in the passing of data through the network. Of these layers the actual communications and flow of data from one computer to another occurs at the Physical Layer. What specifically does the Physical Layer define?

A. Packet protocols

B. Cable interfaces

C. Node addresses

D. Error correction

Question #14-03

Resource: Chapter 14, "IEEE 802 Model"

According to the IEEE, the Data Link Layer establishes the logical link between the network nodes and handles frame sequencing and frame traffic control. Because of its complexity, the Data Link Layer is divided into two Sub-Layers. Which two of the following represent the Sub-Layers of the Data Link Layer?

A. Media Access Control

B. Logical Access Control

C. Logical Link Control

D. Media Link Access

Question #14-04

Resource: Chapter 14, "IEEE 802 Model"

The IEEE developed another network model in 1980 to address the rapid development of LAN products. This IEEE project was named 802.

Which of the following represents the key difference between the IEEE and the ISO models?

  A. The division of the Data Link Layer.

  B. The 802 model is divided into 11 layers.

  C. The 802 model only addresses Ethernet communications.

  D. The ISO model is obsolete.

Question #14-05

Resource: Chapter 14, "Understanding Network Topologies"

You are planning your LAN installation, which will encompass several floors of a building. Which topology would provide the greatest assurance against multiple system downtime due to a network cable failure?

  A. Physical Ring

  B. Physical Star

  C. Logical Ring

  D. Linear Bus

Question #14-06

Resource: Chapter 14, "Understanding Architectures"

The IEEE defines several substandards for various networking archetectures, such as the Ethernet definition known as 802.3. Which of the following represents the designation for a Token Ring architecture?

  A. 802.1

  B. 802.2

  C. 802.5

  D. 802.7

Question #14-07

Resource: Chapter 14, "Token Ring"

Token Ring is configured as a physical star but is a logical ring, running either 4 MBPS or 16 MBPS network interface cards. In this physical star topology, a central wiring hub is used. By what name do we refer to this Token Ring central wiring hub?

A. Multi-Station Access Unit (MAU)

B. Multiple Drop Interface (MDI)

C. Multiple Connection Unit (MCU)

D. Multiple Computer Connector (MCC)

Question #14-08

Resource: Chapter 14, "Token Ring"

You are designing an 802.5 network. Network speed is a known critical issue. You know that to ensure optimum performance, the network will run at 16 MBPS if which of the following conditions is met?

A. All network NICs are capable of running at 16 MBPS.

B. A combination of 4 and 16 MBPS cards is used, but the server NIC must be a 16 MBPS version.

C. There are no more than 240 computers on the network

D. There are at least 3 MAUs on the ring.

Question #14-09

Resource: Chapter 14, "Thicknet (10Base5)"

You are designing the cable plant for your 10base5 network. To ensure that segment cable distances are kept within specification, how are the drop cable lengths calculated into the total maximum segment length?

A. Add the total number of workstations times 2.5 ft. and add to the existing segment length.

B. Add 50 meters to the total existing segment length to ensure a margin of safety.

C. Measure each drop cable length and add that total to the existing segment length.

D. Drop cable lengths are not calculated into the maximum cable length equation.

Question #14-10

Resource: Chapter 14, "Thinnet (10Base2)"

You have a particularly long cable run to make in the design of a 10base2 (Thinnet) network. How many 185-meter cable segments can be joined together with the use of repeaters to form a single logical cable segment?

    A. 5

    B. 3

    C. 7

    D. 2

Question #14-11

Resource: Chapter 14, "NDIS"

The initial communications channel between the protocol driver and the MAC driver is established through a process called _____.

    A. Loading

    B. Linking

    C. Binding

    D. Attaching

App

J

Chapter 15

Question #15-01

Resource: Chapter 15, "Understanding Integrated Networking"

Windows 95 can support up to ten 32-bit protected mode clients through its Network Provider Interface. Besides running clients for NetWare, Banyan Vines, and NT, a single Windows 95 computer can also simultaneously run clients for which two additional network operating systems?

    A. Sun NFS

    B. Digital PathWorks

    C. Promise LAN

    D. AT&T StarLan

Question #15-02

Resource: Chapter 15, "Understanding Integrated Networking"

Because Apple Macintosh computers handle files differently than other computer systems, if part of your attached network handles Apple

Macintosh computers, which two options do you have to enable sharing files between a Mac and a Windows 95 computer?

A. Install a Windows NT server

B. Configure your Windows 95 workstation for Local Talk

C. Run the Mac. exe utility

D. Install a NetWare Server

Question #15-03

Resource: Chapter 15, "Windows Sockets (WinSock)"

Windows Sockets is a protocol-independent networking API that is supported in Windows 95 over which two transport protocol stacks?

A. LocalTalk

B. IPX/SPX

C. TCP/IP

D. NFS

Question #15-04

Resource: Chapter 15, "Client-Side Named Pipes"

Windows 95 client-side named pipe support provides compatibility with applications written for Microsoft LAN Manager. Windows 95 named pipe support is limited to the client applications for which network operating system?

A. VINES

B. NetWare

C. Microsoft

D. Pathworks

Question #15-05

Resource: Chapter 15, "Understanding the Universal Naming Convention"

Which part of the following UNC name represents the network share name?

\\MyServer\MyDisk\Myfiles\Mine.Doc

A. MyServer

B. MyDisk

C. Myfiles

D. Mine.Doc

Question #15-06

Resource: Chapter 15, "Examining Network Architecture"

Windows 95 network components are implemented as 32-bit virtual device drivers and are dynamically loaded and unloaded as needed. How much conventional memory do they use?

A. 0K

B. 32K

C. 64K

D. 256K

Question #15-07

Resource: Chapter 15, "WinNet 16"

Windows 95 supports a single 16-bit WinNet driver for support of a network product not offering 32-bit network support, as well as support for how many 32-bit network providers?

A. 8

B. 6

C. 16

D. 10

Question #15-08

Resource: Chapter 15, "Windows NP/PP"

Besides allowing access to Novell Resources, the Windows 95 NetWare Network Provider and Print Provider provide which two additional functions?

A. Provide Internet access

B. Manage security levels

C. Logging on and off NetWare servers

D. Queuing print jobs

Question #15-09

Resource: Chapter 15, "Transport Protocols"

Windows 95 provides three transport protocols. Identify them from the list below.

    A. NetBEUI

    B. ODI

    C. NDIS

    D. IPX/SPX

    E. TCP/IP

Question #15-10

Resource: Chapter 15, "NDIS"

Windows 95 supports NDIS-2 and NDIS-3 Drives but prefers NDIS 3.1 drivers, which have been enhanced to support which Windows 95 feature?

    A. Preemptive Multitasking

    B. Plug and Play

    C. Multiple Network Client Support

    D. IFS

Chapter 16

Question #16-01

Resource: Chapter 16, "TCP/IP and Windows 95"

You are installing a new version of Windows 95, which must be connected to the Internet. In order to accomplish this connection, you must perform which of the following steps?

    A. Install DHCP

    B. Install TCP/IP

    C. Install the MSN software

    D. Configure a MAC address

Question #16-02

Resource: Chapter 16, "TCP/IP and Windows 95"

You are installing a TCP/IP connection using the Microsoft Installation Wizard provided in Microsoft Plus! for Windows 95. What should you investigate as being the most likely reason for a local TCP/IP connection to stop working?

 A. The Microsoft Installation Wizard is not using standard routing information.

 B. The Microsoft Installation Wizard has replaced the default IP address with a custom IPX address.

 C. The Microsoft Installation Wizard has replaced the local TCP/IP values with values for a dial-up provider.

 D. The Microsoft Installation Wizard has attempted to store routing information in packets instead of a custom routing file.

App

J

Question #16-03

Resource: Chapter 16, "IP Addresses"

As a network administrator, you must assign valid and unique IP addresses to each newly installed TCP/IP connection. The following condition must exist for the Dynamic Host Configuration Protocol to automate this process.

 A. A dial-up connection must be established to a remote network.

 B. Two or more Windows 95 computers must exist on the network.

 C. A Windows NT server running version 3.51 must be installed on the network.

 D. A Windows NT server running version 3.51 must not be installed as part of the network.

Question #16-04

Resource: Chapter 16, "How the IP Address and Subnet Mask Interact"

In order to determine a TCP/IP network address, an AND'ING function between which of the following parameters must be performed?

A. The first and second "octet"

B. The IP address and the subnet mask

C. The IP address and the primary port address

D. The server node address and the internal IPX number

Question #16-05

Resource: Chapter 16, "IP Addresses"

If you must manually configure an IP address using the Network configuration dialog, you must be careful to ensure which of the following?

A. The Dynamic Host Configuration Protocol is running.

B. You have selected a single 8-bit number between 0 and 255 Hex.

C. You have selected distinctively separate host and network addresses.

D. The TCP/IP protocol is bound to the network card you are configuring.

Question #16-06

Resource: Chapter 16, "Default Gateway"

A key advantage of TCP/IP is that it is a routable protocol; that is, a protocol which allows the use of routers to interconnect different subnets. TCP/IP packets contain no routing information, only source and destination addresses. TCP/IP can eliminate the need for every computer to maintain a routing table with the routes to every other computer or network on the Internet through the use of which of the following entities?

A. Default routers

B. Default gateways

C. Backbone routers

D. Backbone gateway

Question #16-07

Resource: Chapter 16, "Resolving IP Addresses to NetBIOS Names"

You can use either of three existing methods in Windows 95 to resolve NETBIOS names to IP addresses. Of the three, which is preferred because it generates the least amount of network traffic and is dynamic?

    A. WINS

    B. WINNT

    C. Broadcasts

    D. LMHOSTS

Question #16-08

Resource: Chapter 16, "Resolving IP Addresses to NetBIOS Names"

If you are utilizing DHCP to assign IP addresses to Windows 95 computers, and the computers are sharing resources with remote computers, the LMHOSTS method of resolving NetBIOS names to IP addresses is unusable. The solution is to include a WINS server, which, like a DHCP server, is a computer operating as which of the following?

    A. A Windows 95 workstation running 1.x

    B. A Windows NT server running version 3.5 or higher

    C. An MS-DOS workstation running version 6.2x or higher

    D. A Windows for Workgroups server running version 3.11 or higher

Question #16-09

Resource: Chapter 16, "Using TCP/IP Utilities"

You are setting up a connection to the Internet utilizing Windows 95. Which two TCP/IP connectivity utilities are available to you as part of the Windows 95 software?

    A. CICS

    B. TelNet

    C. FTP clients

    D. Win Connect

App

J

Question #16-10
Resource: Chapter 16, "Terminal Emulation: TelNet"

You are experiencing communications problems using the Windows 95 terminal emulation utility (TelNet). Which two TelNet ports are you able to attach to, to assist in diagnosing a potential problem?

    A. Echo

    B. Gotd

    C. Daytime

    D. Chargen

Chapter 17

Question #17-01
Resource: Chapter 17, "Understanding Domains and Workgroups"

Microsoft uses two different methods for grouping users for administrative ease. What are these methods called?

    A. Communities

    B. Domains

    C. Entities

    D. Workgroups

Question #17-02
Resource: Chapter 17, "Comparing User-Level and Share-Level Security"

Windows 95 allows you to control the security access to your network resources by two methods. One controls access by password-protecting resources. The other allows you to assign individual permissions to a resource. What are these two security levels?

    A. Share-Level

    B. User-Level

    C. Network-Level

    D. Workstation-Level

Question #17-03

Resource: Chapter 17, "User-Level Security"

When setting up a shared network folder, you may choose from three access types to control user access. What are these three access types called?

    A. Read-Only

    B. Full

    C. Private

    D. Partial

    E. Depends on Password

Question #17-04

Resource: Chapter 17, "Comparing User-Level and Share-Level Security"

When setting up security, open the Network option in Control Panel and select the Access Control Panel tab. By default, which level of security is chosen?

    A. Share-Level

    B. User-Level

    C. Network-Level

    D. Workstation-Level

Question #17-05

Resource: Chapter 17, "Domains"

What type of computer is required to act as a controller of a domain?

    A. Windows 95

    B. Netware server

    C. Windows 3.x

    D. Windows NT Server

App

J

Question #17-06
Resource: Chapter 17, "Browse Master"

Windows 95, like other Microsoft Networking Systems, provides a method of locating shared resources on the network. The method used by Windows 95 is based on those used by Windows for Workgroups and Windows NT. What is this method called?

   A. Searching

   B. Browsing

   C. Seeking

   D. Identifying

Question #17-07
Resource: Chapter 17, "Browse Master"

There are three possible options you may choose from when controlling whether a given computer can become a Browse server. Besides enabled and disabled, what is your third option?

   A. Automatic

   B. Dependent

   C. Scheduled

   D. Fall Back

Question #17-08
Resource: Chapter 17, "Building the Browser List"

On a TCP/IP internetwork, what must you add to LMHOSTS in order for browsing to work across the network?

   A. Browse

   B. WINS

   C. #DOM

   D. Find

Question #17-09

Resource: Chapter 17, "Comparing User-Level and Share-Level Security"

What protocol do both the Microsoft Client for Microsoft Networks, and File and Printer Sharing for Microsoft Networks support for file sharing?

    A. Server Message Block Protocol

    B. IPX/SPX

    C. Microsoft User Share Protocol

    D. Microsoft File Share Protocol

Question #17-10

Resource: Chapter 17, "Using Group Accounts"

Windows NT has two types of groups: Local Groups and Global Groups. The distinction between the two focuses on where they can be used. Windows 95 User-Level Security however is only aware of which group type?

    A. Local

    B. Global

    C. Regional

    D. Virtual

App

J

Chapter 18

Question #18-01

Resource: Chapter 18, "NetWare DOS Requester"

The NetWare DOS Requester replaced the NetWare Shell with a number of modules instead of a single monolithic file. What are these modules called collectively?

    A. Netware Loadable Modules

    B. Virtual Loadable Modules

    C. Internetwork Packet Exchanges

    D. Internet Protocol Transports

Question #18-02
Resource: Chapter 18, "Servers"

In NetWare 3.X, the establishment of an internal network number, along with the loading of disk drivers, NIC drivers, and other NLMs are configurable and loaded in which two NetWare files?

    A. Autoexec.ncf

    B. Control.ncf

    C. Drivers.ncf

    D. Startup.ncf

Question #18-03
Resource: Chapter 18, "NetWare Loadable Module (NLM)"

NetWare Loadable Modules can be loaded and unloaded while the NetWare 3.x server is running. These modules are initialized utilizing the load command from the system console. Where in the NetWare 3.x directory structure are NLM files typically stored?

    A. SYS:Public

    B. SYS:Login

    C. SYS:System

    D. SYS:NLMs

Question #18-04
Resource: Chapter 18, "Name Spaces"

To add name space support for supporting non–8.3 naming conventions to a particular disk volume under NetWare 3.X, you must first load the name space NLM. What command must you then run from the system console to configure the volume?

    A. Expand Name Space

    B. Extend Names

    C. Extend 8.3

    D. Add Name Space

App

J

Question #18-05

Resource: Chapter 18, "IPX"

Each network cable segment used with IPX must have an arbitrary but unique external network number. You assign this network number utilizing what command in the Autoexec.ncf file?

A. Attach

B. Bind

C. Configure

D. Cable Number Equals

Question #18-06

Resource: Chapter 18, "TCP/IP"

Through which TCP/IP function does NetWare TCP/IP support communications between NetWare networks across an IP Internet that does not support IPX directly?

A. TCP/IP Expansion

B. SPX/IP Interchange

C. IPX/IP Tunneling

D. NetWare Core Protocol

Question #18-07

Resource: Chapter 18, "Browsing Protocols"

The Get Nearest Server and Give Nearest Server requests to and from a server are an example of which protocol?

A. NCP

B. SAP

C. NDS

D. SPX

Question #18-08

Resource: Chapter 18, "Security"

NetWare Security is comprised of six categories of security features. They include Login Security, Trustees, Rights, Attributes, Inheritance, and Effective rights. Of these, which feature controls what users have access to files, directories, and other objects?

  A. Rights

  B. Attributes

  C. Trustees

  D. Inheritance

Question #18-09
Resource: Chapter 18, "Login Security"

Under NetWare 4.X, user names and passwords are established by the Network Supervisor by creating a user object in the NetWare Directory Services (NDS). What system utility in NetWare 2.X and 3.X is used for configuring this information?

  A. Syscon

  B. Session

  C. Security

  D. Filer

Question #18-10
Resource: Chapter 18, "Attributes (flags)"

NetWare controls file actions through its file attributes. These attributes include whether or not a file may be written to, shared, compressed, deleted, etc. What is another NetWare term for these attributes?

  A. Rights

  B. Privileges

  C. Contexts

  D. Flags

Chapter 19

Question #19-01
Resource: Chapter 19, "Redirector"

The Microsoft Client for NetWare uses the NetWare core protocol, which is NetWare's native protocol for file sharing. Which compatible transport protocol does the NCP redirector use to communicate with the NetWare server?

A. TCP/IP

B. IPX/SPX

C. NDIS

D. TCNX

Question #19-02

Resource: Chapter 19, "Services"

In addition to acting as a client on a NetWare network, Windows 95 also can provide network file and print services to other client computers on the network running which client software?

A. DECNet client

B. Microsoft Network client

C. TCP/IP client

D. NetWare client

Question #19-03

Resource: Chapter 19, "Transport Protocols"

In connecting a Windows 95 computer to a Novell network using the Microsoft Client for NetWare, which compatible transport protocol is required to communicate with a Novell server?

A. IPX/SPX

B. TCP/IP

C. TCNX

D. NetBEUI

Question #19-04

Resource: Chapter 19, "Transport Protocols"

For historical reasons, NetWare networks support three basic types of frames: the IEEE 802.3, IEEE 802.2, and Ethernet II standards. While both NetWare and Windows NT can configure to use multiple frame types on the same computer, in order for two computers to communicate using IPX/SPX, what must they use?

A. One must use IPX and the other SPX.

B. They both must use Ethernet II.

C. They must use a common frame type.

D. Any NetWare-supported frame type will do.

Question #19-05

Resource: Chapter 19, "Device Driver Interface"

Windows 95 supports both ODI and NDIS network device drivers. Although ODI was defined by Novell, why does Windows 95 prefer NDIS 3 drivers instead?

A. They are 32-bit protected mode drivers.

B. They were designed by Microsoft.

C. They are Windows 95 exclusive.

D. They are supported under NT while ODI is not.

Question #19-06

Resource: Chapter 19, "Using Real Mode Netware Clients"

Although the use of real mode NetWare clients imposes a severe performance penalty, they may be necessary to maintain compatibility with some older, undocumented functionality of older shells. Which two real-mode clients are available to you in this event?

A. NETX

B. IPX/SPX

C. VLM

D. MSNet

Question #19-07

Resource: Chapter 19, "Configuring File and Printers Sharing Services for Netware"

What effect will you achieve by using File and Printer Sharing Services for NetWare instead of the File and Printer Sharing Services for Microsoft networks?

A. Resources on your computer will be available for use by NetWare clients.

B. Windows 95 users will be able to use NetWare Printer Services.

C. NT systems will be able to communicate with the Novell print servers.

D. The two services are basically identical.

Chapter 20

Question #20-01

Resource: Chapter 20, "Print Providers"

The Print Provider Interface is used by the Print Router to communicate with the Print Provider. The PPI is modular and allows how many 32-bit print providers to be installed automatically?

A. 6

B. 16

C. Any number

D. 32

Question #20-02

Resource: Chapter 20, "Print Providers"

A Print Provider is a 32 bit DLL responsible for providing functions such as opening and closing a printer, queuing print jobs, and print queue management. What are the three types of print providers?

A. Regional

B. Local

C. Network

D. Global

E. Win16Net

Question #20-03

Resource: Chapter 20, "Print Providers"

The WinNet16 Print Provider provides compatability with WinNet16 network drivers for which operating system?

App

J

    A. Windows NT

    B. Windows 3.x

    C. Windows 95

    D. MS-DOS

Question #20-04

Resource: Chapter 20, "Microsoft Networks"

Whether the installable file system or network redirector is used depends on the type of print function being called. If it is a printing function, (i.e., Open Print Job, Write to Print Job, etc.), the call is submitted to which program?

    A. VReDir.vxd

    B. NWReDir.vxd

    C. IFSMGR

    D. Nwpp32.dll

Question #20-05

Resource: Chapter 20, "NetWare Networks"

The NetWare Print Provider handles calls made by the Print Router through the Print Provider Interface (PPI). The NetWare Print Provider is implemented in which two DLL files?

    A. Nwpp32.dll

    B. Nwnet32.dll

    C. Ppnw32.dll

    D. Pp32.dll

Question #20-06

Resource: Chapter 20, "Installing Network Printers"

Installing a network printer involves the driver for the printer telling Windows 95 where the printer is. What are the two different ways to accomplish these tasks?

    A. Arbitrary

    B. Manually

C. Automatically

D. Point and Print

Question #20-07

Resource: Chapter 20, "Point and Print"

Point and Print makes installation of network printers much easier because it automates virtually all of the process. In order for Point and Print to function, what must the printer be?

A. An HP-compatible laser printer

B. Point and Print-enabled

C. Attached to an NT server

D. Attached to a NetWare server

Question #20-08

Resource: Chapter 20, "Point and Print"

Since Windows NT and Windows 95 use different printer drivers, printers attached to an NT server cannot support Point and Print directly. The user will therefore not be prompted for the printer model name if which two conditions exist?

A. Windows 95 and Windows NT use the same driver name.

B. Windows 95 and Windows NT use the same INF files.

C. Windows 95 and Windows NT use different driver names.

D. Windows 95 and Windows NT use different INF files.

Question #20-09

Resource: Chapter 20, "Point and Print"

In setting up a Point and Print Printer there are two selectable options under Point and Print setup: "Set Printer Model" and "Set Driver Path." What dialog does selecting "Set Print Model" open up?

A. A dialog to confirm that everyone has Read and File Scan rights

B. A dialog to confirm Automatic Setup

C. The standard print setup for changing the Print Model Name

D. A dialog to choose the location of the UNC pathname

App

J

Question #20-10

Resource: Chapter 20, "Supporting Digital PrintServer"

The Digital Print Server support under Windows 95 is implemented as a Print Monitor and is streamed to the print server with TCP/IP by the Digital Print Server Port Monitor DLL file. What is the name of the Port Monitor DLL?

A. Decpsw4.dll

B. Decprint.dll

C. Printdec.dll

D. Digportw.dll

Chapter 21

Question #21-01

Resource: Chapter 21, "Mobile Computing"

Windows 95 contains a mobile computing file-synchronization tool whose primary function is to ensure that files stored in two places remain identical. What is this tool called?

A. FileSync

B. Briefcase

C. Syncup

D. Transport

Question #21-02

Resource: Chapter 21, "Using Dial-Up Networking"

Dial-Up Networking allows your computer to act as a network node while connected to a dial-up connection, such as an ordinary modem. Which Windows 3.x utility did it replace?

A. Remote Control

B. DialNet

C. WinNet

D. Remote Access Services

Question #21-03

Resource: Chapter 21, "Using Dial-Up Networking"

Under Windows 95 there are two types of protocols that you can configure for a Dial-Up Networking connection. Identify them from the list below.

    A. Physical Protocols

    B. Transport Protocols

    C. Line Protocols

    D. Network Protocols

Question #21-04

Resource: Chapter 21, "Using Dial-Up Networking"

Windows 95 Dial-Up Networking supports all of the transport protocols supported by Windows 95 for communicating with other Windows 95 computers including NetBEUI, IPX/SPX, and TCP/IP. What is the common requirement for obtaining connection?

    A. The computer must be running a protected mode network client.

    B. The computer must be configured as a remote server.

    C. The computer must have an IP address.

    D. The computer must be running Microsoft Plus!.

Question #21-05

Resource: Chapter 21, "NetWare Connect (NRN)"

NetWare Connect is a proprietary connection protocol that can be used to dial into a Novell NetWare server. What is the only supported transport protocol that can be used?

    A. NetBEUI

    B. TCP/IP

    C. IPX/SPX

    D. SLIP

App

J

Question #21-06

Resource: Chapter 21, "Using Dial-Up Networking"

To install Dial-Up Networking after Windows 95 is installed, what must you do?

    A. Select Add/Remove Software from the Control Panel.

    B. Install NetBios Support.

    C. Install Microsoft Plus!.

    D. Ensure that you have enough RAM.

Question #21-07

Resource: Chapter 21, "Security"

When configuring a Dial-Up Networking server, there are some security issues you should consider. If running the Dial-Up Networking server, how should you control who accesses your server?

    A. By using User-Level Security

    B. By using Share-Level Security

    C. By using Connection Dial Back

    D. By limiting telephone number distribution

Question #21-08

Resource: Chapter 21, "Security"

Along with other security measures, you can restrict certain users from accessing Dial-Up Networking. How is this accomplished?

    A. Through the use of a firewall

    B. Through Password Protection

    C. Through User Policies

    D. Through Share-Level Security

Question #21-09

Resource: Chapter 21, "Direct Cable Connection"

When using Direct Cable Connection, which two types of cables can be used?

A. Parallel

B. RG-59

C. Null Modem

D. AUI

Chapter 22

Question #22-01

Resource: Chapter 22, "Understanding User Profiles"

Windows 95 allows users to use any computer on a network and still receive their own desktop settings and preferences through which feature?

A. Remote Access

B. Follow-Me Preferencing

C. Roving Users

D. Remote Control

Question #22-02

Resource: Chapter 22, "Using User Profiles"

Which three of the following options can you set to be different for each user, by using User Profiles?

A. Long File Name Support

B. Network Assignments

C. Programs Menu

D. Start Menu

E. User Desktop

Question #22-03

Resource: Chapter 22, "Using Policies"

Policies give a network administrator control over what a user can do on the computer. In order to implement Policies, what else must you create?

App

J

A. User Profiles

B. Access Control

C. Dial-Up Networking

D. Roving Users

Question #22-04

Resource: Chapter 22, "System Policy Editor"

The System Policy Editor is used to create and edit System Policies. The System Policy Editor operates in two modes. What are these modes called?

A. Network Mode

B. Registry Mode

C. File Mode

D. Default Mode

Question #22-05

Resource: Chapter 22, "System Policy Editor"

When using the System Policy Editor in Registry Mode, changes on the local or remote computer are written immediately to which two files?

A. System.dat

B. Edit.dat

C. Policy.dat

D. User.dat

Question #22-06

Resource: Chapter 22, "System Policy Editor"

When using the System Policy Editor in File Mode, which files must be distributed to the appropriate network location prior to any users being affected?

A. .pol files

B. .use files

C. .pro files

D. .edt files

Question #22-07

Resource: Chapter 22, "System Policy Editor"

There are three possible states for each check box in the System Policy Editor. What are they?

A. Checked

B. Cleared

C. Checked and grayed

D. Blackened

E. Grayed

Question #22-08

Resource: Chapter 22, "Server-Based Policies"

In order for Load Balancing to occur on a Windows NT network, what must be enabled on the Windows NT servers?

A. Replication

B. Auto Logon

C. Net Watcher

D. Balance Net

Question #22-09

Resource: Chapter 22, "Net Watcher"

Under the Net Watcher View by Connection view, what does the right-hand panel show?

A. The computer's folders available for sharing

B. A list of all shared folders on the monitored computer

C. Computers connected to the highlighted share

D. Computer connected to the network

Question #22-10

Resource: Chapter 22, "Registry Editor"

You can use the Registry Editor to edit the Registry on remote computers if both computers are using the same security providers and what other requirement has been met by both computers?

    A. Share-Level Security is being used.

    B. User-Level Security is being used.

    C. Common Profiles exist.

    D. User Policies exist.

Chapter 23

Question #23-01

Resource: Chapter 23, "Server-Based Setup of Windows 95"

Although Windows 3.X provided various network setup options for configuring Windows interact or run from a network installation, Windows 95 represents a significant improvement in the setup of Windows over a network. What is the program called that gives the system administrator complete control over all aspects of the server-based setup process?

    A. SetNet.exe

    B. NetSetup.exe

    C. NetConfig.exe

    D. NetTool.exe

Question #23-02

Resource: Chapter 23, "Creating a Shared Installation"

When configuring a shared Windows 95 shared installation and after running the server-based setup, a setup script must be created. Which format must this setup script be created in?

    A. MSbatch.inf

    B. MSbatch.bin

C. .txt format

D. Registry format

Question #23-03

Resource: Chapter 23, "Understanding Server-Based Setup Issues"

If RIPL is supported, a workstation can boot up and log into a shared Windows 95 installation without the use of which of the following?

A. A network connection

B. A keyboard

C. A password

D. A disk drive

Question #23-04

Resource: Chapter 23, "Machine Directories"

On a Windows 95 shared installation using diskless workstations with Machine Directories, where is it best to locate the Machine Directory to assist in Load Balancing?

A. On the same computer as the shared installation directory

B. On a different computer than the shared installation directory

C. In a subdirectory under the shared installation directory

D. Directly off the root directory of the computer hosting the shared Windows installation

Question #23-05

Resource: Chapter 23, "Shared Installation Files"

A Windows 95 shared installation stores system files in three locations—on the startup disk, in the machine directory, and where else?

A. In the root directory

B. On the hard disk drive of the local computer

C. In the Nettools directory

D. In the Shared Installation directory

App

J

Question #23-06
Resource: Chapter 23, "Running Server-Based Setup"

When running Server-Based Setup, clicking on Install will open up the Source Path dialog box which contains three options. Under the Install Policy option, if you do not want users to be able to set up their computers as shared installations of Windows 95, what sub-option must you select?

    A. Local Hard Drives

    B. ServerV

    C. Path to Install Files

    D. User's Choice

Question # 23-07
Resource: Chapter 23, "Running Server-Based Setup"

After choosing your install policies and clicking OK, if you choose the Don't Create Default button, which file will not be created?

    A. Install.ini

    B. MSbatch.inf

    C. Policy.inf

    D. Config.inf

Question # 23-08
Resource: Chapter 23, "Running Server-Based Setup"

After the installation options you want, the next dialog asks you for the Product Information Number which is located on the yellow sticker on your Windows 95 CD case. What is this number called?

    A. The Verification Key

    B. The Validation Key

    C. The License Key

    D. The CD KEY

Question #23-09

Resource: Chapter 23, "Running Server-Based Setup"

In addition to having a computer set up and attached to a network server, Server-Based Setup is only available if what other requirement is met?

    A. Microsoft Plus! is installed.

    B. You are running the CD-ROM version.

    C. You are running the floppy version.

    D. You have at least 16 megabytes of memory.

Chapter 24

Question #24-01

Resource: Chapter 24, "Working with Modems"

Prior to the introduction of the Telephony API, all modems used a different interpretation of which common modem instruction set?

    A. AT commands

    B. Modem commands

    C. TA commands

    D. TAPI commands

Question #24-02

Resource: Chapter 24, "Installing and Configuring a Modem"

You have several applications running under Windows 95 that require the use of a modem. Previously, this would have presented a series of installation and configuration issues. Why does Windows 95 represent a significant improvement over previous operating systems?

    A. Only minor configuration changes need to be made for each application.

    B. A single modem installation under Windows 95 makes the modem available for all applications.

App

J

C. Windows 95 supports multiple modems for ease of application installation.

D. Thirty-two applications use multiplexed modem support for multitasking.

Question #24-03

Resource: Chapter 24, "TAPI Services"

When you are installing a modem in Windows 95, the use of TAPI frees applications from each having to know any of the modem setting or command string specifics. Which two of the following represents additional levels of support that are provided under Windows 95 automatically?

A. Call Routing

B. ISDN

C. Selective Answer

D. PBX

Question #24-04

Resource: Chapter 24, "Locations"

One of the most annoying drawbacks to portable computing is often the requirement that dialing information must be changed as you travel from one location to another location in a new city or country.

Windows 95 addresses this problem through the use of dialing Locations. Which three of the following represent information contained in a Locations setting?

A. Area code

B. Credit card information

C. Dialing type

D. Long distance rate information

Question #24-05

Resource: Chapter 24, "Phone Dialer"

When choosing to utilize the Telephone Dialer, which two of the following represent advantages available to you under Windows 95?

A. The inherent Phone Call Logs the dialer keeps.

B. As a TAPI application, the Telephone Dialer remembers location information.

C. The Telephone Dialer reminds you of the most economical calling rates.

D. The Telephone Dialer displays time and billing information after each call.

Question #24-06

Resource: Chapter 24, "Windows 95 Communications Architecture"

If you have an older version of the Unimodem driver, you should upgrade it to Unimodem V. Unimodem V supports which of the following?

A. Codex and multiplexer support

B. Multiple communication sessions

C. Voice/data/fax modems

D. Fax/data modems

Question #24-07

Resource: Chapter 24, "Windoes 95 Communications Architecture"

VComm provides protected mode services between the Unimodem and Port drives. In addition to allowing Windows applications to access modem and port services, with which Windows driver file does VComm interface to provide communications support to 16-bit Windows applications?

A. Win.ini

B. Modem.drv

C. Comm.drv

D. Port.drv

Question #24-08

Resource: Chapter 24, "Windows 95 Communication Architecture"

Of the available communication port options, port drivers are responsible for accessing hardware connected to which two of the following port options?

A. IDE

B. SCSI

C. Parallel

D. Serial

Chapter 25

Question #25-01

Resource: Chapter 25, "Sharing a Fax Modem"

Sharing a fax over a Microsoft Network can be accomplished _____ .

A. by selecting the Tools menu from the Inbox icon

B. only if you have User-Level Security

C. only if you have Share-Level Security

D. only if you have Dial-Up Network capabilities

Question #25-02

Resource: Chapter 25, "Configuring Personal Address Book and Folders"

The two information services that are included in every profile are the Personal Address Book and the Personal Folder services. Where is the Personal Address Book information stored on the system?

A. C:\exchange\Address.pab

B. C:\exchange\Mailbox.pab

C. C:\exchange\Mailbox.pst

D. C:\exchange\Personal.pab

Question #25-03

Resource: Chapter 25, "Connecting to the Internet"

If you have Microsoft Plus! installed, Microsoft Exchange can connect to an Internet Mail Service running which protocol?

A. IPX/SPX Emulation

B. TelNet

C. TCP/IP

D. Post Office Protocol 3

Question #25-04

Resource: Chapter 25, "Connecting to CompuServe"

Microsoft Exchange can be used to send and receive e-mail messages over which online service?

A. America Online

B. CompuServe

C. Prodigy

D. The Source

Question #25-05

Resource: Chapter 25, "MicroSoft Fax Properties"

The Dialing Properties sheet allows you to configure how FAX numbers are dialed. What are the two options under this sheet?

A. I'm Dialing From…

B. Time to Send

C. Retries

D. Message Properties

Question #25-06

Resource: Chapter 25, "Configuring Personal Address Book and Folders"

When you are using Personal Folders and multiple users are using the computer, which file should you change the name of to match the user's login name?

A. Mailbox.pst

B. Mailbox.pab

C. Folders.pab

D. User.pab

Chapter 26

Question #26-01
Resource: Chapter 26, "Troubleshooting Windows 95"

When troubleshooting a Windows 95 computer which contains critical data, a troubleshooting switch may be selected that will continuously flush all data to the hard disk drive to ensure data loss is prevented. What is this switch called?

    A. Disable 32-bit Disk Drivers

    B. Disable Synchronous Buffer Commits

    C. Disable Write-behind Caching for all drives

    D. Disable Protect-mode hard disk interrupt handing

Question #26-02
Resource: Chapter 26, "Debugging Switches"

The "Disable new file sharing and locking semantics" troubleshooting switch can be used as a temporary file for older programs that require which MS-DOS program to run?

    A. Himem.sys

    B. Share.exe

    C. EMM386.exe

    D. Mem.com

Question #26-03
Resource: Chapter 26, "Out of Directory Entries"

Long file names are stored as extra directory entries with a special format. How many directory entries does each file with a long file name take up?

    A. 2

    B. 3

    C. 1

    D. 4

Question #26-04

Resource: Chapter 26, "Out of Directory Entries"

An "Out of Directory Entries" error can occur when many files exist on the Root Directory, where the number of directory entries is fixed. How many directory entries are usually allowed on the Root Directory?

    A. 64

    B. 128

    C. 256

    D. 512

Question #26-05

Resource: Chapter 26, "Troubleshooting the File System"

Since File Manager under 3.x is a 16-bit program, using File Manager under Windows 95 is not recommended due to file problems it can cause. What is a key file problem that may result from its use under Windows 95?

    A. All files will be corrupted.

    B. All directory entries will be lost.

    C. Long file names will be lost.

    D. All file attributes will change.

Question #26-06

Resource: Chapter 26, "Other Long File Name Problems"

Although long file names can be as much as 256 characters, it is recommended that long file names be kept under 50 characters in length. This will prevent the file name from being too long to fit into the complete path statement. What is the total number of characters a complete path statement can be?

    A. 1,024

    B. 512

    C. 260

    D. 256

App

J

Question #26-07

Resource: Chapter 26, "VGA Fall Back"

If for any reason Windows 95 cannot find a video driver for the video card installed or cannot set it up correctly, Windows 95 will automatically load the generic VGA driver. What is the name of this Windows 95 function?

    A. VGA Fall Back

    B. Video Assurance

    C. VGA Auto

    D. Video Write

Question #26-08

Resource: Chapter 26, "Troubleshooting Startup"

When troubleshooting Startup Errors, you may press F8 at the logo to open the Windows 95 Startup Menu. If you select the logged option, a list of components which load or fail to load will be created. What file name will this log be written to?

    A. BootEror.txt

    B. Bootlog.txt

    C. Bootlist.txt

    D. Error.log

Question #26-09

Resource: Chapter 26, "Startup Switches"

Several switches exist for compatibility purposes that can be used with Win.com. What effect does running Win.com with the /D:F switch have?

    A. Disables 32-bit disk access

    B. Enables Safe Mode

    C. Enables Safe Mode with Networking

    D. Prevents Windows from using upper memory

Question #26-10

Resource: Chapter 26, "Examining the Windows 95 Log Files"

Windows 95 is capable of generating a number of log files to help you troubleshoot problems. What information is contained in the IOS.LOG file found in the Windows folder?

    A. Video driver error information

    B. Startup operating system errors

    C. Error messages from SCSI devices

    D. Registry messages

Chapter 27

Question #27-01

Resource: Chapter 27, "Windows 95 Resource Kit"

All technical documentation for Windows 95 is included in what Microsoft calls the Windows 95 Resource Kit. The Resource Kit is provided as a Help File. Where can you find the Microsoft Resource Kit?

    A. On the disk labeled "Resource"

    B. On the CD-ROM version

    C. On the Microsoft Home Page

    D. All of the above

Question #27-02

Resource: Chapter 27, "Windows 95 Resource Kit"

There are three help files that make up the Windows 95 Resource Kit. In which of these help files would you look to find information on System Administration?

    A. Win95rk

    B. Tour4ADM

    C. Macusers

    D. WinAdmin

App

J

Question #27-03

Resource: Chapter 27, "Microsoft TechNet"

Microsoft TechNet is Microsoft's primary resource for technical professionals. TechNet contains the full Microsoft Knowledge base, training material, drivers, patches, and a host of other vital and changing information, programs, and utilities. The annual subscription entitles the subscriber to how many updates per year?

    A. 6

    B. 4

    C. 1

    D. 12

Question #27-04

Resource: Chapter 27, "Windows 95 Resource Kit"

The Windows 95 Resource Kit contains a valuable tool for administrators to use to learn how to implement the various features of Windows 95, as well as enabling them to justify enterprise deployment projects. In what file would you find this information?

    A. Win95rk

    B. Tour4ADM

    C. Featur95

    D. Beneft95

Question #27-05

Resource: Chapter 27, "Windows 95 Resource Kit"

In which Microsoft material would you find strategic information on technologies to keep you up to date on the direction Microsoft and its products are taking?

    A. TechNet

    B. Windows 95 Resource Kit

    C. Developers Network

    D. WinNews

    E. Tour4ADM

Answer Key

Chapter Tests

Chapter 2

Question	Answer
02-01	A, B
02-02	D
02-03	C
02-04	A, C, D
02-05	A
02-06	B
02-07	A, D

Chapter 3

Question	Answer
03-01	B
03-02	A
03-03	B
03-04	B
03-05	B, D
03-06	B
03-07	D
03-08	A
03-09	C
03-10	D

Chapter 4

Question	Answer
04-01	C
04-02	A, B
04-03	C
04-04	D
04-05	D
04-06	B
04-07	B
04-08	A
04-09	B
04-10	A, B

Chapter 5

Question	Answer
05-01	D
05-02	B
05-03	D
05-04	A
05-05	A, D
05-06	A, C, D
05-07	B
05-08	B, C
05-09	D
05-10	B

Chapter 6

Question	Answer
06-01	A
06-02	A
06-03	A
06-04	A
06-05	B, C, D
06-06	A
06-07	C
06-08	B
06-09	A, B, D
06-10	A, D

Chapter 7

Question	Answer
07-01	B
07-02	C
07-03	A
07-04	B
07-05	A, D
07-06	D
07-07	B
07-08	A
07-09	A
07-10	A

Chapter 8

Question	Answer
08-01	B
08-02	C
08-03	A
08-04	D
08-05	C
08-06	A, C, D
08-07	D
08-08	B

App
J

Question	Answer
08-09	B
08-10	A, C

Chapter 9

Question	Answer
09-01	A
09-02	C, D
09-03	B
09-04	A
09-05	B
09-06	A, D
09-07	C
09-08	A, C
09-09	A, B
09-10	A

Chapter 10

Question	Answer
10-01	B
10-02	A, C
10-03	C
10-04	D
10-05	B
10-06	A
10-07	B
10-08	C
10-09	A, B
10-10	D

Chapter 11

Question	Answer
11-01	A, D
11-02	B, D
11-03	B
11-04	C
11-05	D
11-06	A
11-07	C
11-08	B, C, D
11-09	B
11-10	C

Chapter 12

Question	Answer
12-01	A
12-02	B, D
12-03	A, C
12-04	B
12-05	B
12-06	C
12-07	B
12-08	B, C
12-09	C
12-10	B

Chapter 13

Question	Answer
13-01	B
13-02	A
13-03	C
13-04	D
13-05	B

Chapter 14

Question	Answer
14-01	C
14-02	B
14-03	A, C
14-04	A
14-05	B
14-06	C
14-07	A
14-08	A
14-09	D
14-10	A
14-11	C

Chapter 15

Question	Answer
15-01	A, B
15-02	A, D
15-03	B, C
15-04	C
15-05	B
15-06	A
15-07	D
15-08	C, D
15-09	A, D, E
15-10	B

Chapter 16

Question	Answer
16-01	B
16-02	C
16-03	C

Question	Answer
16-04	B
16-05	D
16-06	B
16-07	A
16-08	B
16-09	B, C
16-10	A, D

Chapter 17

Question	Answer
17-01	B, D
17-02	A, B
17-03	A, B, E
17-04	A
17-05	D
17-06	B
17-07	A
17-08	C
17-09	A
17-10	B

Chapter 18

Question	Answer
18-01	B
18-02	A, D
18-03	C
18-04	D
18-05	B
18-06	C
18-07	B
18-08	C

Question	Answer
18-09	A
18-10	D

Chapter 19

Question	Answer
19-01	B
19-02	D
19-03	A
19-04	C
19-05	A
19-06	A, C
19-07	A

Chapter 20

Question	Answer
20-01	C
20-02	B, C, E
20-03	B
20-04	C
20-05	A, B
20-06	B, D
20-07	B
20-08	A, B
20-09	C
20-10	A

Chapter 21

Question	Answer
21-01	B
21-02	D
21-03	B, C
21-04	A

Question	Answer
21-05	C
21-06	A
21-07	A
21-08	C
21-09	A, C

Chapter 22

Question	Answer
22-01	C
22-02	C, D, E
22-03	A
22-04	B, C
22-05	A, D
22-06	A
22-07	A, B, C
22-08	A
22-09	C
22-10	B

Chapter 23

Question	Answer
23-01	B
23-02	A
23-03	D
23-04	A, B
23-05	D
23-06	A
23-07	B
23-08	D
23-09	B

App
J

Chapter 24

Question	Answer
24-01	A
24-02	B
24-03	B, D
24-04	A, B, C
24-05	A, B
24-06	C
24-07	C
24-08	C, D

Chapter 25

Question	Answer
25-01	A
25-02	B
25-03	D
25-04	B
25-05	A, C
25-06	A

Chapter 26

Question	Answer
26-01	C
26-02	B
26-03	A
26-04	D
26-05	C
26-06	C
26-07	A
26-08	B
26-09	A
26-10	C

Chapter 27

Question	Answer
27-01	B, C
27-02	A
27-03	D
27-04	B
27-05	A, C, D

Mastery Test

Note The answers to these questions can be found in order at the end of this section. The resource line following each question number refers to the chapter where information regarding that question is located. ▦

Question #1
Resource: Chapter 14

Token Ring is configured as a physical star but is a logical ring, running either 4 MBPS or 16 MBPS network interface cards. In this physical star topology, a central wiring hub is used. By what name do we refer to this Token Ring central wiring hub?

A. Multi-Station Access Unit (MAU)

B. Multiple Drop Interface (MDI)

C. Multiple Connection Unit (MCU)

D. Multiple Computer Connector (MCC)

Question # 2
Resource: Chapter 23

After choosing your install policies and clicking OK, if you choose the Don't Create Default button, which file will not be created?

A. Install.ini

B. MSbatch.inf

C. Policy.inf

D. Config.inf

Question #3
Resource: Chapter 25

The two information services that are included in every profile are the Personal Address Book and the Personal Folder Services. Where is the Personal Address Book information stored on the system?

A. C:\exchange\Address.pab

B. C:\exchange\Mailbox.pab

App

J

    C. C:\exchange\Mailbox.pst

    D. C:\exchange\Personal.pab

Question #4

Resource: Chapter 4

When you are viewing the status of installed components under the Windows Setup tab, the checkboxes next to each available component have three states: a checkmark in the checkbox, a checkmark in a filled-in checkbox, and an empty checkbox. How would you interpret a checkmark in a filled-in checkbox?

    A. All of a component's sub-components are installed.

    B. Only some of a component's sub-components are installed.

    C. None of a components' sub-components is installed.

    D. The component is not available for installation.

Question #5

Resource: Chapter 16

If you are utilizing DHCP to assign IP addresses to Windows 95 computers, and the computers are sharing resources with remote computers, the LMHOSTS method of resolving NetBIOS names to IP addresses is unusable. The solution is to include a WINS server, which, like a DHCP server, is a computer operating as which of the following?

    A. A Windows 95 workstation running 1.x

    B. A Windows NT server running version 3.5 or higher

    C. An MS-DOS workstation running version 6.2x or higher

    D. A Windows for Workgroups server running version 3.11 or higher

Question #6

Resource: Chapter 3

If the computer fails during Hardware Detection as part of the *normal* setup, Windows 95 creates a file called Detcrash.log, which is only readable by Windows 95. This file details exactly what the detection module was running and what it was trying to do at the point of failure. In which equivalent file should you look for a text explanation of this information?

   A. Setup.log

   B. Detlog.log

   C. Detcrash.txt

   D. Setuplog.txt

Question #7
Resource: Chapter 9

In addition to the memory support provided by the Windows 95 Linear Addressing Model, how much private, addressable memory space can each 32-bit Windows application access?

   A. 4G

   B. 1G

   C. 2G

   D. 3G

Question #8
Resource: Chapter 7

Windows 95 tracks removable media to make sure that the correct media is in the drive. How does Windows 95 accomplish this with write-protected media?

   A. It caches the disk's label, serial number, and BIOS parameter block.

   B. It adds a unique ID in the disk's FAT header.

   C. It builds a database table to track the media's volume serial number.

   D. It asks the user to supply information on all write-protected media used.

App

J

Question #9

Resource: Chapter 15

Besides allowing access to Novell resources, the Windows 95 NetWare Network Provider and Print Provider provide which two additional functions?

    A. Provide Internet access

    B. Manage security levels

    C. Log on and off NetWare servers

    D. Queue print jobs

Question #10

Resource: Chapter 7

Windows 95's primary file system is a virtualized MS-DOS file system, which is implemented entirely in 32-bit code and cannot be disabled. What is this file system called?

    A. Vcache

    B. NDIS

    C. VFAT

    D. NDFS

Question #11

Resource: Chapter 2

You should recommend Windows 95 over Windows NT Workstation to a customer who is a heavy traveler for reasons that include which two of the following?

    A. Plug and Play support

    B. Remote networking

    C. NTFS support

    D. Automatic system failure recovery

Question #12

Resource: Chapter 16

If you must manually configure an IP address using the Network configuration dialog, you must be careful to ensure which of the following?

A. The Dynamic Host Configuration Protocol is running.

B. You have selected a single 8-bit number between 0 and 255 Hex.

C. You have selected distinctively separate host and network addresses.

D. The TCP/IP protocol is bound to the network card you are configuring.

Question #13

Resource: Chapter 26

When troubleshooting a Windows 95 computer that contains critical data, a troubleshooting switch may be selected that will continuously flush all data to the hard disk drive to ensure that data loss is prevented. What is this switch called?

A. Disable 32-bit Disk Drivers

B. Disable Synchronous Buffer Commits

C. Disable Write-behind Caching for all drives

D. Disable Protect-mode hard disk interrupt handing

Question #14

Resource: Chapter 15

Windows 95 provides three transport protocols. Identify them from the list below.

A. NetBEUI

B. ODI

C. NDIS

D. IPX/SPX

E. TCP/IP

App

J

Question #15
Resource: Chapter 16

You are installing a new version of Windows 95, which must be connected to the Internet. In order to accomplish this connection, you must perform which of the following steps?

    A. Install DHCP.

    B. Install TCP/IP.

    C. Install the MSN software.

    D. Configure a MAC address.

Question #16
Resource: Chapter 21

To install Dial-Up Networking after Windows 95 is installed, what must you do?

    A. Select Add/Remove Software from the Control Panel.

    B. Install NetBIOS support.

    C. Install Microsoft Plus!.

    D. Ensure you have enough RAM.

Question #17
Resource: Chapter 7

Port Drivers are 32-bit protected mode drivers that communicate with a specific disk device. Which Windows 3.1 driver are they similar to?

    A. Vcache

    B. FastDisk

    C. EMM386

    D. Vdisk

Question #18
Resource: Chapter 6

Plug and Play allows "hot docking." What are three benefits of this feature?

A. The operating system allows for pre-boot configuration for different configurations.

B. The operating system recognizes the new device automatically.

C. Applications are notified about dynamic events.

D. Changing configuration files and restarting the computer are not needed.

E. It is neccessary to run Setup each time new hardware is added.

Question #19
Resource: Chapter 3

You can set up a Windows 95 installation to Dual Boot between Windows 95 and your previous version of MS-DOS and Windows. Dual Booting in this environment will only work in which of the following situations?

A. Your previous version of MS-DOS was at least version 5.0 or later.

B. Your previous version of Windows was at least version 3.10 or later.

C. You have installed Windows 95 over your existing copy of Windows 3.x.

D. Your computer is at least an 80486-based system and capable of preemptive multitasking.

Question #20
Resource: Chapter 12

One of the two options under the options the Disk Defragmenter is Check Drive For Errors. If this checkbox is checked, what utility will be automatically run?

A. CHKDSK

B. MS Virus Scan

C. ScanDisk

D. MSD

App
J

Question #21
Resource: Chapter 24

Prior to the introduction of the Telephony API, all modems used a different interpretation of which common modem instruction set?

A. AT commands

B. Modem commands

C. TA commands

D. TAPI commands

Question #22
Resource: Chapter 5

The architecture of the Intel 80386 Microprocessor defines four privilege levels, which are designed to protect data and code from being damaged by less privileged code. Of these four levels, 0 through 3, in which two does Microsoft Windows 95 function?

A. 0

B. 1

C. 2

D. 3

Question #23
Resource: Chapter 6

To configure an adapter for Plug and Play, Windows automatically configures _____ for Plug and Play-compliant adapters.

A. IRQ, DMA, and I/O Port

B. IRQ, BIOS, and DMA

C. DMA, BIOS, and NVRAM

D. SRAM, IRQ, DMA, and I/O Port

Question #24
Resource: Chapter 10

Plug and Play monitors conform to the VESA Display Data Channel specification or DDC. A combination of a DDC monitor and adapter allows the display drivers to automatically set display information, including which two of the following?

    A. Refresh rate

    B. Image Color Matching

    C. True Color synchronization

    D. Absolute Color processing

Question #25
Resource: Chapter 26

Windows 95 is capable of generating a number of log files to help you troubleshoot problems. What information is contained in the Ios.log file found in the Windows folder?

    A. Video driver error information

    B. Startup operating system errors

    C. Error messages from SCSI devices

    D. Registry messages

Question #26
Resource: Chapter 15

Because Apple Macintosh computers handle files differently than other computer systems, if part of your attached network handles Apple Macintosh computers, which two options do you have to enable sharing files between a Mac and a Windows 95 computer?

    A. Install a Windows NT server.

    B. Configure your Windows 95 workstation for Local Talk.

    C. Run the MAC.EXE utility.

    D. Install a Netware server.

Question #27
Resource: Chapter 10

When setting up display information under the Display Properties dialog, the Color Palette drop-down box allows you to choose among all of the available color depth choices for the video card. Of the available options, which is typically the most popular and uses 8 BPP?

App

J

A. 16 color

B. 256 color

C. High color

D. True color

Question #28
Resource: Chapter 22

Windows 95 allows users to use any computer on a network and still receive their own desktop settings and preferences through which feature?

A. Remote Access

B. Follow-Me Preferencing

C. Roving Users

D. Remote Control

Question #29
Resource: Chapter 17

Microsoft uses two different methods for grouping users for administrative ease. What are these methods called?

A. Communities

B. Domains

C. Entities

D. Workgroups

Question #30
Resource: Chapter 20

The Print Provider Interface is used by the Print Router to communicate with the Print Provider. The PPI is modular and allows how many 32-bit Print Providers to be installed automatically?

A. 6

B. 16

C. Any number

D. 32

Question #31

Resource: Chapter 8

Previous versions of Windows utilized cooperative multitasking, in which each application is required to relinquish control to the operating system either explicitly or when the application checks the message queue. What is an inherent application problem in this environment?

    A. The operating system loses track of running applications.

    B. Only two applications can run at the same time.

    C. A process priority must be set for each application.

    D. The application can "hog" the processor.

Question #32

Resource: Chapter 11

In the Printers folder, every printer is shown along with a visual status que. What does an image of a disk represent?

    A. A local printer

    B. A printer printing to a file

    C. A network printer

    D. An offline printer

Question #33

Resource: Chapter 7

Which type of disk compression does Windows 95 utilize in its inherent DriveSpace utility?

    A. Real Time

    B. Cache Compressed

    C. Delayed

    D. Token Sector

Question #34

Resource: Chapter 3

You need to determine which setup option will be adequate for your needs. You have several areas of critical data and require periodic data

App

J

backups. Either two of the following setup options will provide you with this capability.

A. Compact

B. Custom

C. Portable

D. Typical

Question #35
Resource: Chapter 3

Using the Setup Wizard, you wish to maintain and migrate your application and group settings from your previous version of Windows. To accomplish this, you must perform which of the following steps?

A. Install Windows 95 into a separate directory from your previous version of Windows 3.x or Windows for Workgroups and run the Migrate utility.

B. Install Windows 95 into the same directory as your previous version of Windows 3.x or Windows for Workgroups to migrate your .ini files automatically.

C. Install Windows 95 into a separate directory from your previous version of Windows 3.x or Windows for Workgroups and manually copy your .grp and .ini files to the new installation.

D. The Setup Wizard will only migrate your group settings. Your application setting will need to be reconfigured manually.

Question #36
Resource: Chapter 25

Microsoft Exchange can be used to send and receive e-mail messages over which online service?

A. America Online

B. CompuServe

C. Prodigy

D. The Source

Question #37

Resource: Chapter 17

Windows 95 allows you to control the security access to your network resources by two methods. One controls access by password-protecting resources. The other allows you to assign individual permissions to a resource. What are these two security levels?

    A. Share-Level

    B. User-Level

    C. Network-Level

    D. Workstation-Level

Question #38

Resource: Chapter 14

App

J

You have a particularly long cable run to make in the design of a 10base2 (Thinnet) network. How many 185-meter cable segments can be joined together with the use of repeaters to form a single logical cable segment?

    A. 5

    B. 3

    C. 7

    D. 2

Question #39

Resource: Chapter 21

Dial-Up Networking allows your computer to act as a network node while connected to a dial-up connection, such as an ordinary modem. Which Windows 3.x utility did it replace?

    A. Remote Control

    B. DialNet

    C. WinNet

    D. Remote Access Services

Question #40
Resource: Chapter 4

Because of the potential for damage, Windows 95 does not add the Registry Editor into the Programs folder. If Setup is run from the Windows 95 CD, the Registry Editor is copied into the Windows folder. What file would you look for to start the Registry Editor?

   A. Registry.exe

   B. Editor.exe

   C. EditReg.exe

   D. Regedit.exe

Question #41
Resource: Chapter 23

When configuring a shared Windows 95 shared installation and after running the Server-Based Setup, a setup script must be created. Which format must this setup script be created in?

   A. MSbatch.inf

   B. MSbatch.bin

   C. .txt format

   D. Registry Format

Question #42
Resource: Chapter 9

Unused regions within the Upper Memory Area are called UMBs (Upper Memory Blocks). These can be used to store MS-DOS device drivers, thus freeing up additional conventional memory. Which of the following processors would you require to take advantage of this function?

   A. 8086

   B. 80286

   C. 80386

   D. 80486

Question #43

Resource: Chapter 26

Since File Manager under 3.x is a 16-bit program, using File Manager under Windows 95 is not recommended due to file problems it can cause. What is a key file problem that may result from its use under Windows 95?

    A. All files will be corrupted.

    B. All directory entries will be lost.

    C. Long file names will be lost.

    D. All file attributes will change.

Question #44

Resource: Chapter 23

On a Windows 95 shared installation using diskless workstations with Machine Directories, where is it best to locate the Machine Directory to assist in Load Balancing?

    A. On the same computer as the shared installation directory

    B. On a different computer than the shared installation directory

    C. In a subdirectory under the shared installation directory

    D. Directly off the root directory of the computer hosting the shared Windows installation

Question #45

Resource: Chapter 4

Physically, the Registry is divided into two files: one containing settings specific to the computer and one containing settings specific to the user. Of the following, which two file names represent the names of these files?

    A. System.dat

    B. User.dat

    C. Computer.dat

    D. Network.dat

App
J

Question #46
Resource: Chapter 13

The booting of Windows 95 Protected Mode Operating System is broken down into four distinct phases. During which phase does the loading of MS-DOS drivers occur?

A. Bootstrapping Phase

B. Real-Mode Compatibility Phase

C. Static VXD Loading Phase

D. Protected-Mode Operating System Loading Phase

Question #47
Resource: Chapter 14

Each layer of the OSI model provides a specific function in the passing of data through the network. Of these layers the actual communications and flow of data from one computer to another occurs at the Physical Layer. What specifically does the Physical Layer define?

A. Packet protocols

B. Cable interfaces

C. Node addresses

D. Error correction

Question #48
Resource: Chapter 21

When configuring a Dial-Up Networking server, there are some security issues you should consider. If running the Dial-Up Networking Server, how should you control who accesses your server?

A. By using User-Level Security

B. By using Share-Level Security

C. By using Connection Dial Back

D. By limiting telephone number distribution

Question #49
Resource: Chapter 15

Windows 95 client-side named pipe support provides compatibility with applications written for Microsoft LAN Manager. Windows 95 named pipe support is limited to the client applications for which network operating system?

    A. VINES

    B. NetWare

    C. Microsoft

    D. Pathworks

Question #50
Resource: Chapter 6

During the hardware detection phase, Windows 95 analyzes the system and builds a database of the information that it finds and stores it in the

_____.

    A. Registry

    B. Plug and Play

    C. System.ini

    D. BIOS

Question #51
Resource: Chapter 10

The DIB (Device Independent Bitmap) engine is responsible for all in-memory graphics operations and on-screen operations that are not handled by accelerator hardware on the adapter. The engine allows for fast drawing on what two types of display adapters?

    A. High-resolution adapters

    B. Non-interlaced adapters

    C. Frame buffer-based adapters

    D. Frame-interlaced adapters

App

J

Question #52
Resource: Chapter 3

You are installing Windows 95 over a previous version of Windows. Although you will not be able to run your previous version of Windows, which of the following actions will be necessary to run your existing Windows applications?

    A. You will need to upgrade your applications to 32-bit programs, but your user preferences will remain unchanged.

    B. Nothing. All of your program groups and most of your user preferences will be migrated automatically.

    C. All of your programs should function normally, but you will need to reconfigure your program groups and user preferences.

    D. Installing over a previous version of Windows will work but is not recommended since none of your programs or user preferences will function properly.

Question #53
Resource: Chapter 15

Windows 95 network components are implemented as 32-bit virtual device drivers and are dynamically loaded and unloaded as needed. How much conventional memory do they use?

    A. 0K

    B. 32K

    C. 64K

    D. 256K

Question #54
Resource: Chapter 24

VComm provides protected mode services between the Unimodem and Port drives. In addition to allowing Windows applications to access modem and port services, with which Windows driver file does VComm interface to provide communications support to 16-bit Windows applications?

A. Win.ini

B. Modem.drv

C. Comm.drv

D. Port.drv

Question #55

Resource: Chapter 9

In a demand paged virtual memory system, an application's code and data can be larger than the system's physical memory. This is accomplished by swapping out data which is not being utilized with data that is immediately required. Where is this data swapped out and stored to?

A. A temporary file on disk

B. The HMA

C. Extended Memory

D. Conventional Memory

Question #56

Resource: Chapter 5

Windows uses a minidriver approach to most of the common device drivers. In this approach, a portion of the device driver is common code written by Microsoft. How would you describe the minidriver portion of the device driver?

A. A universal, device-independent piece of code designed to work with a family of products

B. A device-specific portion of code written by the hardware device's manufacturer

C. A common piece of code written by a group of manufacturers to address common interfacing problems

D. A piece of code developed by Microsoft with the device manufacturer's input

App

J

Question #57
Resource: Chapter 4

With the desktop themes option of the Windows 95 Control Panel, you can select various themes which include wallpaper, sounds, cursors, etc. This option is only available if you have met which of the following criteria?

- A. Themes.com has been installed.
- B. Microsoft Plus! has been installed.
- C. Sound for Windows 95 has been installed.
- D. The Multimedia extension has been installed.

Question #58
Resource: Chapter 2

In discussing 32-bit application support with a customer, it should be pointed out that both Windows 95 and Windows NT Workstation support 32-bit applications through the use of a common application programming interface. What is this interface called?

- A. The Windows programming interface
- B. Win32 API
- C. Win 16/32 interface
- D. Users.dat

Question #59
Resource: Chapter 22

The System Policy Editor is used to create and edit system policies. The System Policy Editor operates in two modes. What are these modes called?

- A. Network Mode
- B. Registry Mode
- C. File Mode
- D. Default Mode

Question #60
Resource: Chapter 20

In setting up a Point and Print printer, there are two selectable options under Point and Print setup: Set Printer Model and Set Driver Path. What dialog does selecting Set Print Model open up?

A. A dialog to confirm that everyone has Read and File Scan rights

B. A dialog to confirm Automatic Setup

C. The standard print setup for changing the Print Model Name

D. A dialog to choose the location of the UNC pathname

Question #61
Resource: Chapter 27

There are three help files that make up the Windows 95 Resource Kit. In which of these help files would you look to find information on system administration?

A. Win95rk

B. Tour4ADM

C. Macusers

D. WinAdmin

Question #62
Resource: Chapter 11

From the following, select two times at which Windows 95 will check for a Plug and Play printer.

A. Every 10 minutes

B. During Setup

C. During Post

D. During Windows 95 Boot Sequence

App

J

Question #63
Resource: Chapter 17

What protocol do both the Microsoft Client for Microsoft networks, and File and Printer Sharing for Microsoft networks support for file sharing?

    A. Server Message Block Protocol

    B. IPX/SPX

    C. Microsoft User Share Protocol

    D. Microsoft File Share Protocol

Question #64
Resource: Chapter 9

The Windows 95 Virtual Memory Driver is a Ring 0 Service provided by the Windows 95 Kernel. The VMM provides which of the following functions?

    A. Memory Allocation

    B. Video Memory Swapping

    C. Paging

    D. Virtual Caching

Question #65
Resource: Chapter 8

A process is one or more operating system resources such as code, data, pipes, files etc., that make up an executing application. What is the name of the base entity that executes process code?

    A. Executor

    B. Thread

    C. Implementor

    D. Initializer

Question #66

Resource: Chapter 18

Through which TCP/IP function does NetWare TCP/IP support communications between NetWare networks across an IP Internet that does not support IPX directly?

A. TCP/IP Expansion

B. SPX/IP Interchange

C. IPX/IP Tunneling

D. NetWare Core Protocol

Question #67

Resource: Chapter 12

The Check Files For option under Advanced Options in the Windows 95 version of ScanDisk checks files for invalid names and/or invalid dates and times. What might be the effect of a file with an invalid date and time?

A. It cannot be saved correctly.

B. It cannot be opened properly.

C. It cannot be sort correctly.

D. It cannot be backed up.

Question #68

Resource: Chapter 19

For historical reasons, NetWare networks support three basic types of frames, the IEEE 802.3, IEEE 802.2, and Ethernet II standards. While both NetWare and Windows NT can configure to use multiple frame types on the same computer, in order for two computers to communicate using IPX/SPX, what must they use?

A. One must use IPX and the other SPX.

B. They both must use Ethernet II.

C. They must use a common frame type.

D. Any NetWare-supported frame type will do.

App

J

Question #69
Resource: Chapter 22

There are three options under User Profiles to control which items will be different for each user. Which items do these options control?

A. Long File Name Support

B. Network assignments

C. Programs Menu

D. Start Menu

E. User Desktop

Question #70
Resource: Chapter 13

As part of the Real Mode Compatibility Phase, the disk boot program reads Io.sys from the root directory into memory. Io.sys then loads a minimal program which, besides from the loading of the opening graphic logo information, is capable of only reading which file?

A. Command.com

B. The System Registry

C. Msdos.sys

D. Autoexec.bat

Question #71
Resource: Chapter 21

Windows 95 Dial-Up Networking supports all of the transport protocols supported by Windows 95 for communicating with other Windows 95 computers, including NetBEUI, IPX/SPX, and TCP/IP. What is the common requirement for obtaining connection?

A. The computer must be running a protected mode network client.

B. The computer must be configured as a remote server.

C. The computer must have an IP address.

D. The computer must be running Microsoft Plus!.

Question #72

Resource: Chapter 26

The "Disable new file sharing and locking semantics" troubleshooting switch can be used as a temporary file for older programs that require which MS-DOS program to run?

A. Himem.sys

B. Share.exe

C. EMM386.exe

D. Mem.com

Question #73

Resource: Chapter 25

The Dialing Properties sheet allows you to configure how FAX numbers are dialed. What are the two options under this properties sheet?

A. I'm Dialing From...

B. Time to Send

C. Retries

D. Message Properties

Question #74

Resource: Chapter 5

Which of the following represents the best way to visualize a virtual machine?

A. A virtual machine is a function of Windows 95 used for accessing 32-bit DLL files.

B. A virtual machine is a protected mode function which is reserved for running only Windows 95 32-bit applications.

C. A virtual machine is an unaddressed computer on the network which handles network printing and routing functions.

D. A virtual machine is an environment set up in memory by the operating system, which appears as a complete computer, with all necessary resources.

App

J

Question #75
Resource: Chapter 10

In addition to setting the display type, Windows 95 recognizes a monitor type. You should manually set the monitor type to match your monitor. What does Windows 95 use this information for?

   A. Prompting you for a proper disk to use to install the correct driver

   B. Determining which display resolution to make available to you

   C. Automatically determining the color depth

   D. Recommending the optimum Palette Settings

Question #76
Resource: Chapter 5

A 16-bit application hangs and eventually all other 16-bit applications hang. What is the best way to recover from this event?

   A. Reboot the system and restart Windows 95.

   B. Perform a local reset and terminate the application.

   C. Wait until Windows 95 releases the hung application automatically.

   D. Perform a series of local resets and terminate all 16 bit applications.

Question #77
Resource: Chapter 2

When discussing data integrity between Windows 95 and Windows NT Workstation, it is important to explain to a potential customer the inherent ability of Windows NT Workstation to protect against the loss of system data from malicious or naive users by the use of a secure file system. What is this file system called?

   A. NTFS

   B. Super FAT

   C. HTML

   D. NTNX

Question #78
Resource: Chapter 23

In addition to having a computer set up and attached to a network server, Server-Based Setup is only available if what other requirement is met?

   A. Microsoft Plus! is installed.

   B. You are running the CD-ROM version.

   C. You are running the floppy version.

   D. You have at least 16 megabytes of memory.

Question #79
Resource: Chapter 19

Windows 95 supports both ODI and NDIS network device drivers. Although ODI was defined by Novell, why does Windows 95 prefer NDIS 3 drivers instead?

   A. They are 32 bit protected mode drivers.

   B. They were designed by Microsoft.

   C. They are Windows 95-exclusive.

   D. They are supported under NT while ODI is not.

Question #80
Resource: Chapter 6

In describing the utilization of Plug and Play components to a customer, the main benefit of taking advantage of Plug and Play technology could be described as what?

   A. The installation process is faster and requires little or no user input.

   B. It allows legacy drivers to be integrated with little user input.

   C. It allows for the sharing of IRQs, so more devices may be added to the system.

   D. It allows for one driver to support many devices, thus freeing memory.

App

J

Question #81
Resource: Chapter 10

When a Windows 95 display driver fails to load or initialize, the system employs a mechanism that uses a generic VGA driver to allow access to the system. What is this mechanism referred to?

   A. Generic VGA

   B. VGA Always

   C. VGA Fallback

   D. Generic Viewing

Question #82
Resource: Chapter 17

On a TCP/IP internetwork, what must you add to LMHOSTS in order for browsing to work across the network?

   A. Browse

   B. WINS

   C. #DOM

   D. Find

Question #83
Resource: Chapter 12

Over time, a disk can become fragmented; that is, the disk data is written over a wide area of the disk. What is a primary effect of disk fragmentation?

   A. Data corruption.

   B. Disk performance will deteriorate.

   C. Backup will be difficult to verify.

   D. Directories will not be sorted.

Question #84
Resource: Chapter 11

The Image Color Matching technology Microsoft utilizes in Windows 95 increases the consistency of displayed and printed colors. Who owns this technology?

A. IBM

B. Kodak

C. Sony

D. Mitsubishi

Question #85
Resource: Chapter 22

You can use the Registry Editor to edit the Registry on remote computers if both computers are using the same security providers and what other requirement has been met by both computers?

A. Share-Level Security is being used.

B. User-Level Security is being used.

C. Common Profiles exist.

D. User Policies exist.

Question #86
Resource: Chapter 8

Each thread in a Windows 95 environment can be in one of several states. From the list below, select the three most important states that a thread can be in.

A. Waiting

B. Stopped

C. Ready

D. Running

E. Terminated

Question #87
Resource: Chapter 17

When setting up a shared network folder, you may choose from three access types to control user access. What are these three access types called?

A. Read-Only

B. Full

C. Private

D. Partial

E. Depends on Password

Question #88

Resource: Chapter 16

You are installing a TCP/IP connection using the Microsoft Installation Wizard provided in Microsoft Plus! for Windows 95. What should you investigate as being the most likely reason for a local TCP/IP connection to stop working?

A. The Microsoft Installation Wizard is not using standard routing information.

B. The Microsoft Installation Wizard has replaced the default IP address with a custom IPX address.

C. The Microsoft Installation Wizard has replaced the local TCP/IP values with values for a dial-up provider.

D. The Microsoft Installation Wizard has attempted to store routing information in packets instead of a custom routing file.

Question #89

Resource: Chapter 23

If RIPL is supported, a workstation can boot up and log into a shared Windows 95 installation without the use of which of the following?

A. A network connection

B. A keyboard

C. A password

D. A disk drive

Question #90

Resource: Chapter 21

Along with other security measures, you can restrict certain users from accessing Dial-Up Networking. How is this accomplished?

A. Through the use of a firewall

B. Through password protection

C. Through user policies

D. Through share-level security

Question #91

Resource: Chapter 14

According to the IEEE, the Data Link Layer establishes the logical link between the network nodes and handles frame sequencing and frame traffic control. Because of its complexity the Data Link Layer is divided into 2 Sub-Layers. Which two of the following represents the Sub-Layers of the Data Link Layer?

A. Media Access Control

B. Logical Access Control

C. Logical Link Control

D. Media Link Access

Question #92

Resource: Chapter 15

Which part of the following UNC name represents the network share name?

\\MyServer\MyDisk\Myfiles\Mine.Doc

A. MyServer

B. MyDisk

C. Myfiles

D. Mine.Doc

Question #93

Resource: Chapter 26

When troubleshooting startup errors, you may press F8 at the logo to open the Windows 95 Startup menu. If you select the logged option, a list of components which load or fail to load will be created. What file will this log be written to?

App

J

A. BootEror.txt

B. Bootlog.txt

C. Bootlist.txt

D. Error.log

Question #94
Resource: Chapter 9

The Windows 95 swap file provides the best features and functionality of both the temporary and permanent swap files under Windows 3.x. Which two of the following best explain why?

A. It is dynamic.

B. Is a contiguous memory block.

C. It is static.

D. It can exist on a compressed volume.

Question #95
Resource: Chapter 26

Several switches exist for compatibility purposes which can be used with Win.com. What effect does running Win.com with the /D:F switch have?

A. Disables 32-bit disk access

B. Enables Safe Mode

C. Enables Safe Mode with Networking

D. Prevents Windows from using upper memory

Question #96
Resource: Chapter 12

One of the options of the Thorough Test under the Windows 95 version of ScanDisk is to Not Repair Sectors in Hidden and System Files. When is it important to utilize this option?

A. If virus protection software has not been run for some time

B. If old software is installed

C. If Microsoft Plus! has been installed

D. If you have selected the Do Not Perform Write Testing option

Question #97

Resource: Chapter 20

Point and Print makes installation of a network printer much easier because it automates virtually all of the process. In order for Point and Print to function, what must the printer be?

A. An HP-compatible laser printer

B. Point and Print-enabled

C. Attached to an NT server

D. Attached to a NetWare server

Question #98

Resource: Chapter 18

NetWare controls file actions through its file attributes. These attributes include whether or not a file may be written to, shared, compressed, deleted, etc. What is another NetWare term for these attributes?

A. Rights

B. Privileges

C. Contexts

D. Flags

Question #99

Resource: Chapter 7

Windows 95 support of long file names allows file names to include spaces, periods, and text strings up to how many characters long?

A. 16

B. 8

C. 256

D. 255

App
J

Question #100
Resource: Chapter 21

Windows 95 contains a mobile computing file synchronization tool whose primary function is to ensure that files stored in two places remain identical. What is this tool called?

- A. FileSync
- B. Briefcase
- C. Syncup
- D. Transport

Question #101
Resource: Chapter 24

When choosing to utilize the Telephone Dialer, which two of the following are advantages available to you under Windows 95?

- A. The inherent Phone Call Logs the dialer keeps.
- B. As a TAPI application, the Telephone Dialer remembers location information.
- C. The Telephone Dialer reminds you of the most economical calling rates.
- D. The Telephone Dialer displays time and billing information after each call.

Question #102
Resource: Chapter 19

In addition to acting as a client on a NetWare network, Windows 95 also can provide network file and print services to other client computers on the network running which client software?

- A. DECNet Client
- B. Microsoft Networks Client
- C. TCP/IP Client
- D. NetWare Client

Question #103
Resource: Chapter 8

The VMM is divided into two schedulers, the Primary Scheduler and the Secondary Scheduler. Which scheduling function is associated with the Secondary Scheduler?

    A. Ensuring that the highest-priority thread runs first

    B. Ensuring that no thread "hogs" the scheduler

    C. Determining which thread runs first if two share the same priority

    D. Ensuring that no two threads run at the same time

Question #104
Resource: Chapter 8

Windows 95 utilizes Preemptive Multitasking for 32-bit applications, which means that the operating system controls the Time Slicing function and allocates slices of processor time equally among running applications. The operating system can actually interrupt a running application when its time slice is up. About how long is each time slice?

    A. 20 Milliseconds

    B. 10 Milliseconds

    C. 40 Milliseconds

    D. 60 Milliseconds

Question #105
Resource: Chapter 18

In NetWare 3.x, the establishment of an internal network number along with the loading of disk drivers, NIC drivers, and other NLMs are configurable and loaded in which two NetWare files?

    A. Autoexec.ncf

    B. Control.ncf

    C. Drivers.ncf

    D. Startup.ncf

App
J

Question #106

Resource: Chapter 5

Each of the core components contain both 16-bit and 32-bit DLL (Dynamic Link Libraries) files. 16-bit applications require 16-bit DLLs; however, the kernel is entirely 32-bit. What is the process called by which a 16-bit DLL calls the 32-bit DLL to implement a desired function?

   A. Thinking

   B. Thunking

   C. Rectifying

   D. Rotating

Question #107

Resource: Chapter 20

Since Windows NT and Windows 95 use different printer drivers, printers attached to an NT server cannot support Point and Print directly. The user will therefore not be prompted for the printer model name if which two conditions exist?

   A. Windows 95 and Windows NT use the same driver name.

   B. Windows 95 and Windows NT use the same inf files.

   C. Windows 95 and Windows NT use different driver names.

   D. Windows 95 and Windows NT use different inf files.

Question #108

Resource: Chapter 16

You are setting up a connection to the Internet utilizing Windows 95. Which two TCP/IP connectivity utilities are available to you as part of the Windows 95 software?

   A. CICS

   B. TelNet

   C. FTP Clients

   D. Win Connect

Question #109
Resource: Chapter 19

The Microsoft Client for NetWare uses the NetWare core protocol, which is NetWare's native protocol for file sharing. Which compatible transport protocol does the NCP redirector use to communicate with the NetWare server?

   A. TCP/IP

   B. IPX/SPX

   C. NDIS

   D. TCNX

Question #110
Resource: Chapter 13

Following the running of the Power On Self Test by the bootstrap code, computers with a Plug and Play BIOS perform some steps prior to looking for a boot device. The first step of the Plug and Play configuration process looks for Plug and Play configuration information. Where does the Plug and Play BIOS look for these configuration settings?

   A. In Non-Volatile RAM

   B. In a Disk-Based Configuration file

   C. In the System BIOS

   D. In the System Registry

Question #111
Resource: Chapter 6

During configuration, the Plug and Play software uses three 8-bit I/O ports to send commands to any present Plug and Play adapters. What do we call the series of commands that causes the adapters to activate their Plug and Play logic circuits?

   A. The Activation Key

   B. The Initiation Key

   C. The Startup Key

   D. The Ramp-Up Key

App

J

Question #112
Resource: Chapter 10

The Color Palette drop-down box allows you to choose among all of the color depth choices for the video card, regardless of resolution. What is the highest color depth level?

    A. 16 color

    B. 256 color

    C. High Color

    D. True Color

Question #113
Resource: Chapter 11

There are three color rendering intents that control how Image Color Matching matches colors. Identify them from the list below.

    A. Brightness

    B. Colorimetric

    C. Contrast

    D. Saturation

    E. Sparcity

Question #114
Resource: Chapter 24

Of the available communication port options, port drivers are responsible for accessing hardware connected to which of the following port options?

    A. IDE

    B. SCSI

    C. Parallel

    D. Serial

Question #115

Resource: Chapter 11

There are two ways in which a printer is installed under Windows 95. One is for the users to explicitly choose it. What is the other way?

A. By default in Setup

B. By using the generic printer option

C. By Plug and Play

D. By converting from Windows 3.x

Question #116

Resource: Chapter 8

Every thread in a Windows 95 system has an associated priority, which the scheduler uses to determine which thread to allow to run next. Thread priorities can range from 0 on the low end to what value on the high end?

A. 20

B. 42

C. 31

D. 56

Question #117

Resource: Chapter 4

The International Option under Windows 3.x controlled locally defined settings such as currency symbols and the date display format. Which Windows 95 Control Panel option would you now use to control these functions?

A. Display

B. Regional Settings

C. ODBC

D. Accessibility Options

App

J

Question #118

Resource: Chapter 27

All technical documentation for Windows 95 is included in what Microsoft calls the Windows 95 Resource Kit. The Resource Kit is provided as a Help File. Where can you find the Microsoft Resource Kit?

A. On the disk labeled "Resource"

B. On the CD–ROM version

C. On the Microsoft Home Page

D. All of the above

Question #119

Resource: Chapter 17

When setting up security, open the Network option in Control Paneland select the Access Control Panel tab. By default, which level of security is chosen?

A. Share-Level

B. User-Level

C. Network-Level

D. Workstation-Level

Question #120

Resource: Chapter 6

In order for a computer system to be considered as a Plug and Play system it must have three major components. Identify these from the list below.

A. Plug and Play BIOS

B. Plug and Play hardware

C. Manual setup capabilities

D. Plug and Play operating system

E. Third-party Plug and Play configuration utilities

Question #121

Resource: Chapter 22

Policies gives a network administrator control over what a user can do on the computer. In order to implement policies, what else must you create?

    A. User Profiles

    B. Access Control

    C. Dial-Up Networking

    D. Roving Users

Question #122

Resource: Chapter 18

Under NetWare 4.x, user names and passwords are established by the Network Supervisor by creating a user object in the NetWare Directory Services (NDS). What system utility in NetWare 2.x and 3.x is used for configuring this information?

    A. Syscon

    B. Session

    C. Security

    D. Filer

App
J

Question #123

Resource: Chapter 18

NetWare security is comprised of six categories of security features. They include Login Security, Trustees, Rights, Attributes, Inheritance, and Effective rights. Of these, which feature controls what users have access to files, directories, and other objects?

    A. Rights

    B. Attributes

    C. Trustees

    D. Inheritance

Question #124
Resource: Chapter 2

There are typically three questions which you should be able to answer yes to prior to deciding to install Windows NT Workstation instead of Windows 95. Which of the following represent the questions that should be asked?

    A. Are there drivers under Windows NT for my existing applications?

    B. Will my current version of DOS support Windows NT Workstation?

    C. Do I have enough resources?

    D. Are my applications compatible with Windows NT Workstation?

Question #125
Resource: Chapter 9

The memory area between 0 and 4M is reserved for real mode device drivers, MS-DOS TSRs, and 16-bit applications. What do we refer to this area as?

    A. MS-DOS Compatibility Arena

    B. Shared Arena

    C. Private Arena

    D. Reserved System Arena

Question #126
Resource: Chapter 14

You are designing an 802.5 network. Network speed is a known critical issue. You know that to ensure optimum performance, the network will run at 16 MBPS if which of the following conditions is met?

    A. All network NICs are capable of running at 16 MBPS.

    B. A combination of 4 and 16 MBPS cards are used, but the server NIC must be a 16 MBPS version.

C. There are no more than 240 computers on the network.

D. There are at least three MAUs on the ring.

Question #127
Resource: Chapter 5

In troubleshooting a Windows installation it is important to know the underlying core system functions. Windows 95, like Windows 3.x, contains three core components. These components are Kernel, GDI, and User. The Windows 95 Kernel is responsible for which three of the following basic operating system functions?

A. Managing Virtual Memory

B. File Security

C. Task Scheduling

D. File I/O Services

E. Video Addressing

Question #128
Resource: Chapter 11

Utilizing Image Color Matching, each device's color properties are stored in a profile whose format was determined by a group of hardware vendors and industry standards setting bodies. Together, this consortium is known as what?

A. ColorSpec

B. KMASS

C. InterColor 3.0

D. Colorgraph 1.0

Question #129
Resource: Chapter 2

You can more easily identify saved files under Windows 95 than you can under previous versions of DOS and Windows due to what inherent capability?

A. 8.3 naming conventions

B. Its ability to handle text files

C. The new registry information

D. Long file name support

Question #130
Resource: Chapter 14

You are planning your LAN installation, which will encompass several floors of a building. Which Topology would provide the greatest assurance against multiple system downtime due to a network cable failure?

A. Physical Ring

B. Physical Star

C. Logical Ring

D. Linear Bus

Question #131
Resource: Chapter 7

Windows 95 includes 32-bit disk drivers for most of the popular SCSI controllers, including those from Adaptec and Future Domain. What are the names of the programs from Adaptec and Future Domain that support SCSI devices?

A. ASPI

B. ADAP

C. FutDom

D. CAM

Question #132
Resource: Chapter 20

The WinNet16 Print Provider provides compatability with WinNet16 network drivers for which operating system?

A. Windows NT

B. Windows 3.x

C. Windows 95

D. MS-DOS

Question #133

Resource: Chapter 16

A key advantage of TCP/IP is that it is a routable protocol; that is, a protocol that allows the use of routers to interconnect different subnets. TCP/IP packets contain no routing information, only source and destination addresses. TCP/IP can eliminate the need for every computer to maintain a routing table with the routes to every other computer or network on the Internet through the use of which of the following entities?

A. Default routers

B. Default gateways

C. Backbone routers

D. Backbone gateway

Question #134

Resource: Chapter 12

To guard against a data disaster the first time you run Microsoft Backup from the System Tools Folder, the Windows 95 Backup utility performs a scan of your system hardware and creates an appropriate primary backup set. What is this backup set named?

A. Backup Disk

B. Full System Backup

C. First Backup

D. Win95 Backup

Question #135

Resource: Chapter 27

Microsoft TechNet is Microsoft's primary resource for technical professionals. TechNet contains the full Microsoft Knowledge base, training material, drivers, patches, and a host of other vital and changing

App

J

information, programs, and utilities. The annual subscription entitles the subscriber to how many updates per year?

A. 6

B. 4

C. 1

D. 12

Question #136
Resource: Chapter 24

You have several applications running under Windows 95 that require the use of a modem. Previously, this would have presented a series of installation and configuration issues. Why does Windows 95 represent a significant improvement over previous operating systems?

A. Only minor configuration changes need to be made for each application.

B. A single modem installation under Windows 95 makes the modem available for all applications.

C. Windows 95 supports multiple modems for ease of application installation.

D. Thirty-two applications use multiplexed modem support for multitasking.

Question #137
Resource: Chapter 14

According to the IEEE, the Data Link Layer establishes the logical link between the network nodes and handles frame sequencing and frame traffic control. Because of its complexity, the Data Link layer is divided into two Sub-Layers. Which two of the following represents the Sub-Layers of the Data Link layer?

A. Media Access Control

B. Logical Access Control

C. Logical Link Control

D. Media Link Access

E. Add Name Space

Questions #138
Resource: Chapter 18

Each network cable segment used with IPX must have an arbitrary but unique external network number. You assign this network number utilizing what command in the Autoexec.ncf file?

A. Attach

B. Bind

C. Configure

D. Cable Number Equals

Question #139
Resource: Chapter 4

The three properties of registry values are name, data type, and value. In which of the following values would you expect to find a value which is limited to a maximum of 4 bytes in size?

A. Binary

B. String

C. Entry

D. Dword

Question #140
Resource: Chapter 22

Under the Net Watcher View by Connection view, what does the right-hand panel show?

A. The computer's folders available for sharing

B. A list of all shared folders on the monitored computer

C. Computers connected to the highlighted share

D. Computer connected to the network

App

J

Question #141
Resource: Chapter 12

The 32 bit version of ScanDisk fully supports long file names, checks for cross-linked files, checks for lost clusters, etc., and can be run in the background while other tasks are being performed. It has two distinct test types which may be selected by the user. From the list below, what are the two types of tests?

   A. Complete

   B. Thorough

   C. Full

   D. Standard

Question #142
Resource: Chapter 20

The Digital Print Server support under Windows 95 is implemented as a Print Monitor and is streamed to the print server with TCP/IP by the Digital Print Server Port Monitor DLL file. What is the name of the Port Monitor DLL?

   A. Decpsw4.dll

   B. Decprint.dll

   C. Printdec.dll

   D. Digportw.dll

Question #143
Resource: Chapter 3

You are installing Windows 95 on an 80386DX system with 4M of RAM and a 9600 baud modem. The system boots fine but you are unable to access The Microsoft Network. In order to achieve access to The Microsoft Network, you must perform which of the following upgrade procedures?

   A. Upgrade the system RAM to a minimum of 8M.

   B. Upgrade the system processor to a minimum of an 80486/33 processor.

C. The system configuration is fine and you should investigate the phone line.

D. Upgrade the modem to a minimum of a Hayes Compatible 14400 baud modem.

Question #144

Resource: Chapter 25

When you are using Personal folders and multiple users are using the computer, which file should you change the name of to match the user's login name?

A. Mailbox.pst

B. Mailbox.pab

C. Folders.pab

D. User.pab

App

J

Answer Key

Question	Answer	Question	Answer	Question	Answer
1	A	14	A, D, E	27	B
2	B	15	B	28	C
3	B	16	A	29	B, D
4	B	17	B	30	C
5	B	18	B, C, D	31	D
6	D	19	A	32	B
7	C	20	C	33	A
8	A	21	A	34	B, D
9	C, D	22	A, D	35	B
10	C	23	A	36	B
11	A, B	24	A, B	37	A, B
12	D	25	C	38	A
13	C	26	A, D	39	D

Question	Answer	Question	Answer	Question	Answer
40	D	68	C	96	B
41	A	69	C, D, E	97	B
42	C, D	70	C	98	D
43	C	71	A	99	D
44	B	72	B	100	B
45	A, B	73	B	101	A, B
46	B	74	D	102	D
47	B	75	B	103	B
48	A	76	B	104	A
49	C	77	A	105	A, D
50	A	78	B	106	B
51	A, C	79	A	107	A, B
52	B	80	A	108	B, C
53	A	81	C	109	B
54	C	82	C	110	A
55	A	83	B	111	B
56	B	84	B	112	D
57	B	85	B	113	A, C, E
58	B	86	A, C, D	114	C, D
59	B, C	87	A, B, E	115	C
60	C	88	C	116	C
61	A	89	D	117	B
62	B, D	90	C	118	B, C
63	A	91	A, C	119	A
64	A, C	92	B	120	A, B, D
65	B	93	B	121	A
66	C	94	A, D	122	A
67	C	95	A	123	C

Question	Answer	Question	Answer	Question	Answer
124	A, C, D	131	A, D	138	B
125	A	132	B	139	D
126	A	133	B	140	C
127	A, C, D	134	B	141	B, D
128	C	135	D	142	A
129	D	136	B	143	A
130	B	137	A, C	144	A

App

J

Index

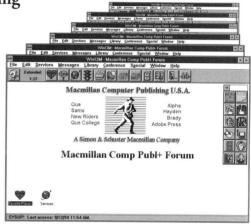

Check out Que® Books on the World Wide Web
http://www.mcp.com/que

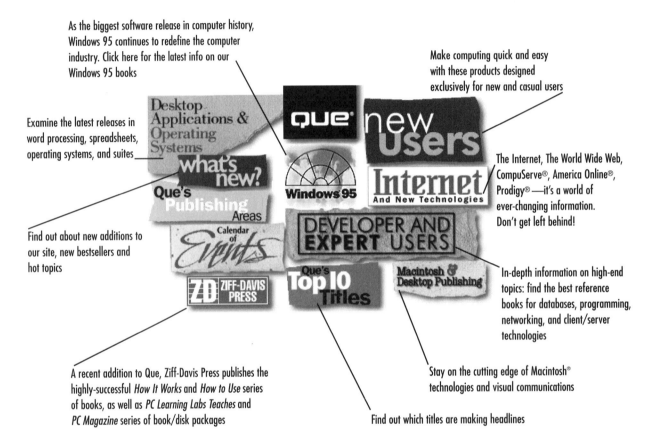

As the biggest software release in computer history, Windows 95 continues to redefine the computer industry. Click here for the latest info on our Windows 95 books

Make computing quick and easy with these products designed exclusively for new and casual users

Examine the latest releases in word processing, spreadsheets, operating systems, and suites

The Internet, The World Wide Web, CompuServe®, America Online®, Prodigy®—it's a world of ever-changing information. Don't get left behind!

Find out about new additions to our site, new bestsellers and hot topics

In-depth information on high-end topics: find the best reference books for databases, programming, networking, and client/server technologies

A recent addition to Que, Ziff-Davis Press publishes the highly-successful *How It Works* and *How to Use* series of books, as well as *PC Learning Labs Teaches* and *PC Magazine* series of book/disk packages

Stay on the cutting edge of Macintosh® technologies and visual communications

Find out which titles are making headlines

With 6 separate publishing groups, Que develops products for many specific market segments and areas of computer technology. Explore our Web Site and you'll find information on best-selling titles, newly published titles, upcoming products, authors, and much more.

- Stay informed on the latest industry trends and products available
- Visit our online bookstore for the latest information and editions
- Download software from Que's library of the best shareware and freeware

Complete and Return this Card
for a *FREE* Computer Book Catalog

Thank you for purchasing this book! You have purchased a superior computer book written expressly for your needs. To continue to provide the kind of up-to-date, pertinent coverage you've come to expect from us, we need to hear from you. Please take a minute to complete and return this self-addressed, postage-paid form. In return, we'll send you a free catalog of all our computer books on topics ranging from word processing to programming and the internet.

Mr. ☐   Mrs. ☐   Ms. ☐   Dr. ☐

Name (first) ☐☐☐☐☐☐☐☐☐☐☐ (M.I.) ☐ (last) ☐☐☐☐☐☐☐☐☐☐☐☐☐☐☐☐☐

Address ☐☐☐☐☐☐☐☐☐☐☐☐☐☐☐☐☐☐☐☐☐☐☐☐☐☐☐☐☐☐☐☐

☐☐☐☐☐☐☐☐☐☐☐☐☐☐☐☐☐☐☐☐☐☐☐☐☐☐☐☐☐☐☐☐

City ☐☐☐☐☐☐☐☐☐☐☐☐☐☐☐☐☐☐ State ☐☐ Zip ☐☐☐☐☐ ☐☐☐☐

Phone ☐☐☐ ☐☐☐ ☐☐☐☐ Fax ☐☐☐ ☐☐☐ ☐☐☐☐

Company Name ☐☐☐☐☐☐☐☐☐☐☐☐☐☐☐☐☐☐☐☐☐☐☐☐☐☐☐☐☐☐

E-mail address ☐☐☐☐☐☐☐☐☐☐☐☐☐☐☐☐☐☐☐☐☐☐☐☐☐☐☐☐☐☐

1. Please check at least (3) influencing factors for purchasing this book.

Front or back cover information on book .... ☐
Special approach to the content .... ☐
Completeness of content...................................... ☐
Author's reputation .... ☐
Publisher's reputation .... ☐
Book cover design or layout .... ☐
Index or table of contents of book .... ☐
Price of book.. ☐
Special effects, graphics, illustrations .... ☐
Other (Please specify): _____ ☐

2. How did you first learn about this book?

Saw in Macmillan Computer Publishing catalog .... ☐
Recommended by store personnel .... ☐
Saw the book on bookshelf at store .... ☐
Recommended by a friend .... ☐
Received advertisement in the mail .... ☐
Saw an advertisement in: _____ ☐
Read book review in: _____ ☐
Other (Please specify): _____ ☐

3. How many computer books have you purchased in the last six months?

This book only .... ☐   3 to 5 books..................... ☐
2 books.................. ☐   More than 5..................... ☐

4. Where did you purchase this book?

Bookstore .... ☐
Computer Store .... ☐
Consumer Electronics Store .... ☐
Department Store .... ☐
Office Club .... ☐
Warehouse Club .... ☐
Mail Order .... ☐
Direct from Publisher .... ☐
Internet site .... ☐
Other (Please specify): _____ ☐

5. How long have you been using a computer?

☐ Less than 6 months   ☐ 6 months to a year
☐ 1 to 3 years   ☐ More than 3 years

6. What is your level of experience with personal computers and with the subject of this book?

	With PCs	With subject of book
New	☐	☐
Casual	☐	☐
Accomplished	☐	☐
Expert	☐	☐

Source Code ISBN: 0-7897-0744-6

7. Which of the following best describes your job title?

Administrative Assistant ☐
Coordinator ☐
Manager/Supervisor ☐
Director ☐
Vice President ☐
President/CEO/COO ☐
Lawyer/Doctor/Medical Professional ☐
Teacher/Educator/Trainer ☐
Engineer/Technician ☐
Consultant ☐
Not employed/Student/Retired ☐
Other (Please specify): _____ ☐

8. Which of the following best describes the area of the company your job title falls under?

Accounting ☐
Engineering ☐
Manufacturing ☐
Operations ☐
Marketing ☐
Sales ☐
Other (Please specify): _____ ☐

9. What is your age?

Under 20 ☐
21-29 ☐
30-39 ☐
40-49 ☐
50-59 ☐
60-over ☐

10. Are you:

Male ☐
Female ☐

11. Which computer publications do you read regularly? (Please list)

_____
_____
_____
_____
_____
_____
_____
_____
_____

Comments: _____
_____
_____

Fold here and scotch-tape to mail.

Instructor-Led Training on Windows 95

Productivity Point International *is pleased to present the purchaser of this QUE book with a 10% discount on Microsoft Official Curriculum 540:* **Supporting Windows 95** *instructor-led training. Call 1-800-367-9372 to register at your nearest location. Use reference number Q95.*

- Payment due upon registration.

- Cancellations or reschedules for all classes listed under the general heading of Client/Server and IS Professional Seminars may be made up to ten full business days prior to the first day of the seminar. After this date, the entire invoice amount is due.

- PPI accepts corporate checks, Visa, Mastercard, and American Express for payment of classes.*

* Certain state restrictions apply to personal payment.

Productivity
P I N T
I N T E R N A T I O N A L
COMPUTER TRAINING SERVICES

The Point Is Time.

Microsoft®
Windows 95

Before using any of the software on this disc, you need to install the software you plan to use. See Appendix I, "Using the CD-ROM," for information on installing this software correctly. If you have problems with this disk, please contact Macmillan Technical Support at (317) 581-3833. We can be reached by e-mail at **support@mcp.com** or on CompuServe at **GO QUEBOOKS**.

License Agreement

This package contains a CD-ROM that includes software described in this book. See applicable chapters for a description of these programs and instructions for their use.

By opening this package you are agreeing to be bound by the following:

This software is copyrighted and all rights are reserved by the publisher and its licensers. You are licensed to use this software on a single computer. You may copy the software for backup or archival purposes only. Making copies of the software for any other purpose is a violation of United States copyright laws. THIS SOFTWARE IS SOLD AS IS, WITHOUT WARRANTY OF ANY KIND, EITHER EXPRESSED OR IMPLIED, INCLUDING BUT NOT LIMITED TO THE IMPLIED WARRANTIES OF MERCHANTABILITY AND FITNESS FOR A PARTICULAR PURPOSE. Neither the publisher nor its licensers, dealers, or distributors assumes any liability for any alleged or actual damages arising from the use of this software. (Some states do not allow exclusion of implied warranties, so the exclusion may not apply to you.)

The entire contents of this disc and the compilation of the software are copyrighted and protected by United States copyright laws. The individual programs on this disc are copyrighted by the authors or owners of each program. Each program has its own use permissions and limitations. To use each program, you must follow the individual requirements and restrictions detailed for each. Do not use a program if you do not agree to follow its licensing agreement.